C000185559

SQL SERVER 2000

SQL Server 2000 Backup & Recovery

ANIL DESAI

Osborne/**McGraw-Hill**

Berkeley New York St. Louis San Francisco
Auckland Bogotá Hamburg London Madrid
Mexico City Milan Montreal New Delhi Panama City
Paris São Paulo Singapore Sydney
Tokyo Toronto

Osborne/**McGraw-Hill**
2600 Tenth Street
Berkeley, California 94710
U.S.A.

For information on translations or book distributors outside the U.S.A., or to arrange bulk purchase discounts for sales promotions, premiums, or fund-raisers, please contact Osborne/**McGraw-Hill** at the above address.

SQL Server 2000 Backup & Recovery

1234567890 CUS CUS 01987654321

Publisher
  Brandon A. Nordin
Vice President & Associate Publisher
  Scott Rogers
Acquisitions Editor
  Ann Sellers
Project Editor
  Madhu Prasher
Acquisitions Coordinator
  Tim Madrid
Technical Editor
  David Garner
Copy Editor
  Judith Brown

Proofreader
  Paul Tyler
Indexer
  Valerie Robbins
Computer Designers
  Jean Butterfield
  Lauren McCarthy
  Tara Davis
Illustrator
  Michael Mueller
Series Design
  Peter F. Hancik
Cover Design
  Will Voss

This book was composed with Corel VENTURA™ Publisher.

To Monica

ABOUT THE AUTHOR

Anil Desai, MCSE, MCSD, MCDBA, is a Technical Architect for QuickArrow, Inc., in Austin, Texas. He has consulted for several companies, ranging from small startups to multinational organizations. Anil has given many conference presentations on Windows-based technologies. He is the author of *MCSE: Windows 2000 Directory Services Implementation Exam Guide, SQL Server 7 Backup and Recovery, Windows NT Network Management: Reducing Total Cost of Ownership,* and co-author of *MCSE Fast Track: SQL Server 2000 Administration.*

ACKNOWLEDGMENTS

This is the first revision of a book that I have ever written, but it was still a lot of work! I really enjoyed having the opportunity to take an existing work and improve it—there was a lot of information that I wasn't able to squeeze into the previous edition. I hope you'll find that the end result is an indispensable resource for information related to data protection in SQL Server 2000. This book didn't magically appear, however. I owe thanks to many individuals who have helped in one way or another.

First and foremost, I'd like to thank my wife, Monica, for her patience and assistance in writing this book. She has survived many nights falling asleep to the clicking of a laptop keyboard and has never complained (well, almost never). Although she's not a true techie, she has been able to live with and support one quite well.

Next, I'd like to thank the staff at QuickArrow and, especially, my manager Jennie Hoff, for all of their support. For a while, it seemed as if we added employees to the company faster than I could add pages to this book! I've never before had the pleasure of working with so many dedicated, hard-working, and focused individuals. QuickArrow may have, once, seemed like a startup. I think it's safe to say that we're a "real company" now.

Finally, I'd like to thank the staff at Osborne/McGraw-Hill. Many individuals worked hard to put together the book you're reading. All of their names are already listed in the front of this book, but I'd like to take the time to especially thank Ann Sellers, Madhu Prasher, Judith Brown, and Tim Madrid for working closely with me on this project. Also, you can thank David Garner for performing a technical edit of the content and for verifying the numerous scripts and procedures you'll find within this book.

There's never enough space in the acknowledgments to thank all the people who should be recognized for assisting me in writing this book. I hope this covers most of them. And, for the rest, I'll continue to write books so that I can add them in the future!

CONTENTS

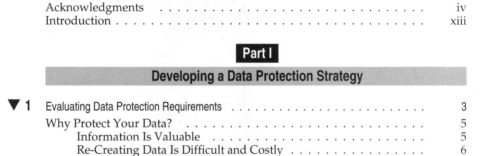

Part I

Developing a Data Protection Strategy

Part II

Understanding Data Protection Technology

Part III

Backup Procedures and Methods

Part IV

Advanced Data Protection Methods

INTRODUCTION

It's a thankless job, and if you do it well, no one will ever know. Maybe that sounds a little cynical (it is), but there's a point. Some may think I'm referring to IT in general. Although that may be true for some of you, I'm specifically talking about backup and recovery. In many environments, performing backup and recovery operations is a necessary evil—a sort of insurance policy for which you pay huge premiums and hope you'll never need to use the policy. If you perform the job well, it's unlikely that anyone will ever know. Your critical systems will continue to hum along while the rest of your organization goes about its daily tasks.

The fact that you're reading this book demonstrates that you understand the importance of protecting your organization's valuable data. That's a great first step! When it comes to working with computers, the really important stuff—your data—is often neglected. And, there are often many reasons for this. Day-to-day tasks like supporting end-user applications and managing resources on servers can account for full-time jobs themselves. Unfortunately, there's a side effect, which is that other more important (but less visible) tasks are overlooked.

Business and technical professionals alike seem to overlook the importance of performing and testing backups. There's usually a strong reason for this. In many environments, business leaders don't fully understand the mortality of computing hardware and software. IT professionals are often working overtime just to deal with PC and application rollouts. There's hardly enough time to handle the immediate and urgent tasks, let alone routine maintenance. And, unless you have occasion to save the day, there's little chance that you'll be rewarded for performing adequate backup of data. What is visible, however, is that performing backup and recovery tasks takes time, effort, and money. That might seem like a high premium for an insurance policy. But compared to the potential consequences, it's a small drop in a very large bucket.

So that brings us to the subject at hand: SQL Server 2000 data protection. One of the most important features of SQL Server 2000 is its simplified administration. Anyone who has worked with other relational database management systems is likely to praise the simplified administration and maintenance features of Microsoft's relational database platform. But performing actual backup operations is only a small part of a much bigger picture. As I began to write this book, a lot of the details involved in the implementation of an actual backup plan began to surface. In addition to describing the backup and recovery operations themselves, I felt it was important to cover such related issues as server architecture, security, and business policies.

The true challenge for IT professionals is not in technical implementation, but in determining your specific business challenges and finding the best solutions. The responsibilities for achieving this goal extend far outside the realm of the IT organization and must involve everyone in the organization. From clerical workers to executives, staff should make data protection a foremost concern. True company-wide data protection is not something that you can implement only within the restricted environment of the data center or server room. Neither is it the responsibility of the network manager or systems administrator alone. Instead, a solid data protection plan involves people from all levels of the organization. Throughout this book, I'll explain how almost everyone in your organization can contribute to ensuring that your information is safe.

If you've forgotten the syntax of the BACKUP command and just need a quick refresher, this book probably provides much more information than you need. However, if you're interested in designing and implementing a full data protection plan for *your* business, you've come to the right place!

HOW TO THINK ABOUT BACKUP AND RECOVERY

The data protection process can be approached from many different angles. Almost all explanation, however, seems to focus on technical solutions. Such detail may meet part of your needs, but, as I mentioned earlier, there's much more to the big picture. Properly configured server hardware and software will make little difference if your users don't understand the importance of saving their files to the file server. Most literature that focuses on backup, restoration, and data protection topics tends to describe methods from an idealized view. Of course, it would be great if all hardware were designed to be redundant, and if restoration operations were tested regularly and frequently; in the real world, however, things don't always run so smoothly. Your company's budget, for example, is one potential roadblock (or, at the very least, a speed bump). Few real-life IT departments have all the time and expertise needed to properly implement all of the tools and tactics available. It may be easy—and even fun—to focus on what a systems administrator might do if given unlimited time, money, and other resources, but most actual business scenarios call for a more pragmatic approach.

This book will emphasize the value of good backup and restoration techniques from a practical business point of view. Along the way I will present a number of broader issues, such as the importance of establishing workable policies and procedures. Although the primary goal here is to provide you with in-depth technical knowledge about SQL Server 2000 backup and recovery, you will find that the writing style is casual and that the text is easy to read from start to finish. And that's my recommendation—that you start with Chapter 1 and progress sequentially through the rest of the text. The time you spend will pay off greatly in the long run.

The chapters here are organized for maximum accessibility. (I've tried to ensure that *this* is the book you'll grab from the shelf to help you plan for and implement your own backup and recovery solution.) For example, the issues related to designing a backup plan, implementing the plan, and choosing appropriate hardware, respectively, are covered in separate areas of the text. Though all of these processes are necessary, it is best that you consider them one at a time as you develop your overall solution. Finally, advanced technologies, such as clustering, replication, and using standby servers, are presented for those who are interested in these topics.

The Importance of Data Protection

In a highly competitive and technical business marketplace, the lifeblood of an organization is its information. Data is its single most important asset and resource. Many organizations are coming to this realization and are investing accordingly in their IT departments. And, for Internet-based companies such as Application Service Providers (ASPs) and dot-com businesses, often the computing resources *are* the product.

One of the most important functions of IT professionals is ensuring that the company's data is reasonably protected, while simultaneously making sure that it is accessible. This raises the topics of security and data protection. Unfortunately, however, backing up and restoring data is an area that is often neglected by many database and systems administrators. Time and resource constraints force this extremely vital function to the back burner, after more "immediate" topics, such as monitoring performance and daily systems administration. It is often not until after significant data loss occurs that systems administrators and managers realize that they have inadequate backup processes. It is estimated that a large percentage of businesses that experience significant data loss never reopen. And, although it is difficult to measure and quantify, almost all business leaders will find that costs associated with investing in a data protection plan are minor compared with the potentially major impacts of data loss.

Today, the majority of data in many organizations is stored in relational database systems. Although there are many different types of data repositories in use in most companies, the choice is usually one that is made after considerable evaluation. Microsoft's latest entry into this quickly evolving marketplace is SQL Server 2000. The SQL Server platform, thanks largely to the dramatic improvements in SQL Server 7, has made great inroads into environments that support systems ranging from laptop computers to large data centers. It is with good reason that SQL Server has received so much praise from industry analysts. New features in the product make common operations such as systems administration, data file management, and the actual database backup and restoration extremely simple. And, new performance benchmarks indicate that SQL Server delivers the level of performance required by the world's largest organizations at a cost that is dramatically lower than that of competing platforms.

One of Microsoft's main design goals was to improve the scalability, performance, and reliability of the SQL Server platform. We'll cover the details within the technical chapters of this book. For now, here is a quick overview of new data protection features in SQL Server 2000:

▼ Improvements to administrative tools allow for simplified management. Building on the usefulness of the many wizards and tools available in Enterprise Manager, SQL Server 2000 allows database administrators to perform fairly complicated tasks (such as managing replication and implementing log-shipping) with just a few mouse clicks.

■ A flexible data storage architecture allows for simplified file and database storage management and the ability to back up and restore individual files and filegroups.

■ Support has been added for features that increase performance and uptime, including clustering (fail-over support) and standby servers.

▲ Performance-enhancing features, such as support for federated server configurations, materialized views, and a new database recovery model that balances performance with the possibility of data loss, have been added.

Some IT functions are reactive—that is, systems and database administrators often respond to problems after they occur. A common example is troubleshooting performance issues or accommodating a rapidly growing database. Planning and implementing backup and restoration procedures, however, require that IT planners think ahead to ensure that their information is sufficiently protected *before* problems occur. One major reason for backing up data is to protect against data loss due to hardware failures. A crashed hard disk or a damaged power supply can affect hundreds of users throughout an organization. It certainly is scary to think that your organization's livelihood could depend on the proper functioning of a $45 part! Although hardware failures do occur, they are not the only reason for backing up data. Contrary to what is often portrayed in popular technical media, one of the threats to data loss that is most likely to happen comes from within an organization. In most environments, it's much more likely that a user or developer will mistakenly (or purposely) delete or corrupt information. Finally, you must also protect your proprietary data from outsiders who may attempt to gain access to it.

Although they realize the importance of backing up data, many IT professionals neglect to perform the tasks related to protecting data. Two of the most common reasons for this are lack of time and lack of knowledge.

▼ **Lack of time** Systems and database administrators face many other challenges that are often more "visible" than running backups, such as managing performance and carrying out routine system administration tasks. The tendency is to give those higher-visibility tasks priority when time is limited. In an ideal world, no one would ever know whether backups were performed, because data loss would never occur; but in reality, people and machines often cause errors or fail.

▲ **Lack of knowledge** Many resources—including books and documentation—outline how backups can be performed. Though they often provide a wealth of technical information, they leave out the most important part: planning for, evaluating, and implementing the right technologies. This book will fill that gap by providing the information that real-world database administrators, constrained by budgets and limited resources, can use to develop, manage, plan, and implement a data protection solution in their own environment.

Focusing on Your Specific Environment

I don't expect every reader of this book to follow all the practices set forth here. Even if there were enough hours in the day to follow all the tips and techniques presented within the chapters, the effort might not be worthwhile in your particular environment. And, therein lies the challenge—selecting the technical solutions that will work best for you and your business.

Like any techie, you've probably thumbed through various sections of this book already (and, hopefully, you decided to buy it). Yes, there are a lot of pages! Chances are good that you won't have time to perform all the data protection practices mentioned here. You'll be pulled away by different responsibilities that may be as important. It would be easy for me to write a book that focused on specifically what you *must* do to ensure data protection without taking into account the real-world challenges most of us face. However, these are the facts:

▼ Most business environments don't have dedicated data protection specialists.

■ IT professionals are constrained by time and budget resources that prevent them from getting the hardware, software, and networking equipment necessary to set up an "ideal" solution.

■ Prioritizing data protection can be difficult. Data backup and recovery are issues usually considered subservient to production, sales, and all the other challenges in the business environment.

▲ There are very few real-world rewards for implementing data protection methodologies, unless the unlikely event of large-scale data loss occurs.

This book is not about just getting the job done. Performing backup and recovery operations in SQL Server 2000 has been reduced to extremely simple tasks that can be performed by even the least-experienced database administrators. Instead, the book focuses on doing the job *correctly*. That's why you'll find a lot of information related to planning for data protection.

THE "BIG" PICTURE

So, why is this book so big? Well, as I mentioned earlier, performing actual backup and restoration operations is a very small portion of the overall data protection process. The main challenges lie in deciding *how* your business should protect its information, which is why the first two chapters in this book focus on those issues alone. You won't find much technical information regarding backup and recovery procedures in those areas. Even if you're dealing with only one or a few servers in a small business environment, it's important to set forth clear data protection guidelines. Managers and users should know, for example, whether or not their laptops and workstations are being backed up. And, is it really worthwhile to back up all the data on your servers? Certainly, network shares that contain the entire contents of the Microsoft Office 2000 CD-ROMs can be left out if time and capacity constraints prevent backing this up.

In looking at other books dedicated to covering the topics of backup and recovery, I noticed that they had a *lot* of detailed information on backups. One, for example, took great pains to note the pinouts of SCSI cables and the acceptable voltages carried on these wires. Although this makes for a complete reference, it's difficult to see how that information would be useful to a systems administrator who has to perform 12 tasks each morning—all before her coffee gets cold. Other backup and recovery books seem to focus on the actual operations required to protect data—definitely an important point and one that most readers of this book will expect.

Although becoming familiar with the actual operations is important, I've found that the hardest part of purchasing a tape backup solution is deciding exactly what you need. Sure, if you're backing up a single NT box that performs file/print services, you can get a local tape drive that can manage its total capacity. But, what happens when you outgrow this? I, for one, wouldn't like to go to management every quarter to request more hardware. But, at the same time, it would be difficult to justify $16 million to make *everything* fully redundant. It gets even more complicated if you have multiple servers and also want to back up clients. Centralized storage has always seemed like a good idea, but planning for it can be as challenging as implementation.

Before any of those questions can be answered, you must look at the business requirements of your company as a whole. If you have thumbed through the book already, you probably noticed that the first two chapters don't have many screenshots. Nor do they give more than a brief mention of SQL Server. Determining business requirements before implementing technical solutions is very important to the success of your backup and recovery plan.

Before beginning any project (IT related or otherwise), you should clearly define your goals. With this in mind, you'll always know in which direction you're heading and why. With this book, I wanted to accomplish the following:

▼   Create a resource that will be used as a primary source of reference when implementing SQL Server 2000 backup and recovery procedures

■   Provide an in-depth discussion of the issues that must be answered before an organization-wide data protection plan can be developed

■ Present information in a clear and easy-to-read way without sacrificing technical depth

■ Place emphasis on real-world challenges, constraints, and practical applications and ensure that all information presented is relevant

■ Provide best practices for implementing data protection regardless of operating system or database server versions

▲ Do all of the preceding in a clear, practical, and easy-to-read book that provides planning and business information in addition to technical details for backing up data on SQL Server 2000

One of the toughest steps in writing a technical book is establishing its boundaries—deciding exactly what information should be covered. Although the focus of this book will be on protecting information that resides on your database servers, almost everything you learn can be applied to working with other types of backups in your environment. For example, we'll briefly discuss the issues associated with backing up client workstations and file/print servers. And, we'll cover issues related to protecting Windows NT 4.0 and Windows 2000 servers. This information is applicable to almost any type of machines on your network, from Macintosh- to UNIX- to Windows-based platforms. Each chapter begins with an introduction explaining *why* the information it contains is important and relevant. And remember: the knowledge you gain will benefit many different individuals in your environment, whether or not their business roles are technical in nature.

WHO SHOULD READ THIS BOOK

To cover complex technical information related to backup and recovery of database servers, some level of knowledge on these types of issues is required. However, I've tried to include information that will appeal to both nontechnical business planners and those who actually set up the backup and recovery processes. Many IT professionals wind up working with database servers out of sheer necessity. A common statement might be "Oh, and John, as long as you're backing up the file/print servers, make sure you back up Database Server 1, as well."

I already mentioned how IT professionals at all levels and areas of expertise within an organization are responsible for protecting data and ensuring its availability. The topics covered in this book will appeal to a wide range of information technology professionals. Specifically, here are some benefits for people, based on their roles:

▼ **Database administrators**   It's likely that if you purchased this book, you're filling the role of a database administrator (DBA). DBAs plan for, implement, and manage SQL Server 2000 installations. However, even those who work with SQL Server regularly may neglect to learn about all the data protection features offered by the current version of the product. Dedicated and "part-time" DBAs will find the business focus and detailed coverage of advanced topics in this book to be relevant and useful in implementing solutions for their own environment. The technical processes and details provided in Part III will also serve as a useful reference for some lesser-known functionality available within the product.

- ■ **Systems/network administrators** Increasingly, more network and systems administrators are moving into the role of managing basic database operations, including backup and recovery. Although protecting information is one of their foremost responsibilities, the area of database administration is one that is often left to the "experts." However, Microsoft has taken great pains to make the functionality of SQL Server 2000 accessible to anyone with a technical background. IT professionals who are not necessarily familiar with SQL Server will especially benefit from the discussion of backup methodologies and the overview of the architecture of the product itself. Both topics are often seen as mysterious and are poorly understood by nondatabase professionals. With the information in this book, network and systems administrators should be well prepared to protect their database information as part of an overall backup and recovery plan.

- ▲ **IT managers** Though they are seldom responsible for actually performing the details of implementing a solution, IT managers will find information about the pros and cons of backup and restoration options. This information will be useful for determining the level of data protection their business requires. If you're filling a management and planning role, you'll most likely be interested in the issues covered in Part I of the book. There, we'll focus on business challenges and how they can be met with a well-thought-out data protection plan. Furthermore, when you need to dive into technical details, all the steps required to understand database and operating system security and architecture are at your fingertips.

MAKING THE MOST OF THIS BOOK

So far, I've probably answered many of your questions regarding the purpose of this book. For example, I mentioned who will benefit from this book and provided an overview of how the information would be covered.

I highly recommend that you read through the book in sequence. Although the topic of each chapter can stand on its own, the content of each chapter is designed to rely upon information presented in earlier ones. The short amount of time that you spend reading through information about planning will be well spent, considering the time you'll save trying to make these decisions later in the process. For example, if you want to implement a backup plan for your servers, you'll first need to decide what your business requirements really are. Jumping ahead to Part III might show you *how* to implement specific operations, but this won't help you in the overall, bigger picture—determining what level of data protection you need throughout the organization.

With that said, there might be valid reasons for skipping to certain sections of the book. If, for example, you want to implement a backup solution for one or a few servers, then you might start with Chapter 6. Similarly, if you need to recover information, you can move directly to Chapter 7. How you use the book is up to you, but, again, you'll get the most out of it (and out of your own data protection plan) by starting at the beginning.

What's New?

I remember writing the initial manuscript of *SQL Server 7 Backup and Recovery*. It was a little over a year ago (although it seems like ages since I was writing the technical material for that book). At the time, SQL Server 7 had been on the market for a while and had established a solid foothold in the market. Still, there were many improvements to be made. Fortunately, Microsoft did not rest on its successes and has continued to add new features and technologies to the SQL Server platform. And, instead of writing about Windows 2000 in the future tense, I can assume that most of you have worked with (or at least are aware of) the Windows 2000 operating system.

So what exactly is new in this revision? First and foremost, as you might expect, the technical content has been updated to cover the changes and new features in SQL Server 2000. Several other things have changed, as well. We're beginning to see increasing focus on two very important measurements of manageability and value: Total Cost of Ownership (TCO) and Return on Investment (ROI). Even more importantly, we're seeing all areas of organizations understand that information technology (IT) should be a means to an end. And, it can be a very powerful method for helping a business. All IT staffers—from executives to help desk staffers—should understand that the core responsibility of IT is to help the company achieve its goals. Given that idea, it's up to the technical people to find the best solutions for some very challenging problems. You'll find a new chapter with case studies that can be applied to environments of various sizes. And, you'll find more in-depth technical details related to the backup and recovery procedures, tools, and best practices.

THE BEGINNING...

Before you picked up this book, you probably understood many of the challenges associated with protecting information. That's a great first step, and probably the most important one. In this introduction, I provided an overview of how I plan to tackle the many considerations that must be addressed when planning to protect information in your organization. With all of this in mind, let's move on to the actual business and technical solutions you can implement in your own environment. Good luck!

PART I

Developing a Data Protection Strategy

CHAPTER 1

Evaluating Data Protection Requirements

One of the foremost concerns of IT professionals should be ensuring that their organizations' interests are being served through technical solutions. This is as true for e-commerce web sites as it is for data protection. There will always be trade-offs—good solutions aren't cheap, and ideal ones are even more expensive. The best way to ensure that you meet your company's goals is to ensure that you *know* those goals and fully understand them. That's the purpose of this chapter. Here, we'll discuss several ways to determine the real data protection requirements in your organization.

At first, it might seem very easy to determine business requirements. For example, if you were to ask an executive at any organization which data is important, you'd likely hear something similar to "All of it!" Perhaps that's true. But, do you really have the resources available to back up all of the information in your environment? Unless you work for a large data storage company, chances are, you don't. Tell the same executive what it would cost to back up every hard drive in the entire organization, and you'll probably get more realistic answers. For example, perhaps it doesn't make sense to back up everyone's WINNT and Program Files directories since the operating system and applications can be reinstalled should the need arise.

As we'll see, the decisions related to protection of important information stored in databases are no exception to this give-and-take. Ideally, we'd like to ensure that there will be zero downtime and that no information would ever be lost. In some cases, this might actually be a necessity. However, in keeping the business goals in mind, it just may not be financially feasible to do this. Again, it comes to a question of trade-offs and determining what level of data protection you *really* need.

Before you begin to implement any data protection strategy, you'll need to evaluate the purpose of backing up your information. Most people will probably say that the primary reason to back up data is to protect against its loss. This is a good reason, as it encompasses all of the various scenarios that can cause a loss of data. These situations range from the accidental loss of some information due to user error to the failure of mission-critical server hardware. Regardless of the reason for protecting data, the question still remains: *What* should be backed up, and *how often* should it be protected?

In this chapter, we'll start looking at the real issues involved with developing a data protection policy. First, we'll discuss the reasons for protecting information—a few of which you may not have considered. This information will be useful to keep in mind when creating any type of data protection policy. Next, we'll look at what you can do to protect information in an ideal world. Because we don't live in an ideal world, however, we'll also review the types of constraints we normally work within. Based on this information, we'll look at the detailed considerations you will need to make when determining how your data should be protected.

The most important step in creating a data protection plan is to evaluate your organization's current environment. After all, without knowing what you currently support (and *why*), you have little chance of addressing all of your business concerns. Having gathered all this information, we'll be ready to form a business requirements document. I'll provide information on how you can apply this document to the task at hand: developing a data protection strategy for your business.

If you have a very technical background and are expecting to hit the technical issues right away, you'll have to wait a bit, because Part I of this book doesn't include code or many commands and screenshots that are specific to SQL Server. Even if you are a techie at heart, however, I highly recommend that you read the contents of this chapter and the next since they will set the context for the types of business and technical challenges we'll be trying to solve. In many cases, the solution is quite easy—perhaps a few mouse clicks through the Database Maintenance Plan Wizard. But don't let that fool you—the real task is to determine the business requirements.

On the other hand, if you are responsible for managing business processes and making data protection decisions, you should feel right at home discussing the details of planning for the implementation of data protection. Regardless of your background or your position within your organization, I urge you not to skip this chapter. It presents some important points that you'll need to understand thoroughly before you can get the most out of this book and your data protection strategy.

WHY PROTECT YOUR DATA?

The fact that you've made it to the second section of Chapter 1 probably means that you have an idea of the importance of protecting your organization's information. A cynic might say that you're protecting data so that you can save your job in case anything goes wrong with your organization's system. That's not a bad reason (especially if you like your job), but it doesn't really explain the business purposes for protecting that data. Although many of the reasons for protecting data might be obvious, taking some time to review these reasons is worthwhile, before we dive into the details of evaluating your business requirements. In this part of the chapter, we'll look at some good reasons for protecting information.

Information Is Valuable

It's no secret that companies are increasingly relying on computing resources. Think about it: How many employees in your organization are able to do their jobs without the use of computers (and the information they store)? And, what would be the impact if all of the information became unavailable (or, worse yet, was lost entirely)? It's easy to lose sight of the fact that information is valuable since we have come to rely heavily on its availability.

Employees may come and go, but traditional businesses survive based on the powers of their products. For example, a company that makes, packages, and sells soft drinks might undergo many changes, but its basic knowledge must remain a part of the company if it plans to survive. A less obvious example might be a consulting organization. Although the people *are* the product, the success of the company depends on many other factors. In this case, the infrastructure of the company, along with lessons learned from past projects, can be of immense value.

Several studies have been done to estimate the costs of data loss caused by various factors. One such study is the Computer Security Institute's "1999 CSI/FBI Computer Crime & Security Survey" (**www.gocsi.com/losses.htm**), which provides the following conclusions:

▼ Financial losses due to computer security breaches amounted to over $100,000,000 for the third straight year. One hundred sixty-three out of 521 respondents in the 1999 CSI/FBI survey reported a total of $123,779,000 in losses.

▲ The most serious financial losses occurred through theft of proprietary information. Twenty-three out of 521 respondents reported a total of $42,496,000 (an increase from $33,545,000) in the '98 survey and $20,048,000 in the '97 survey, a rise of over 100 percent in only three years. Theft of proprietary information is perhaps the greatest threat to U.S. economic competitiveness in the global marketplace.

It's not difficult to find more examples and statistics similar to those above. In fact, we often read about data loss and corruption in technical trade journals. Statements like these really bring home the point of how important our data is to the well-being of our businesses.

Re-Creating Data Is Difficult and Costly

A company's data not only is important, but it's also very difficult to replace if lost. As anyone who has suffered the pain of re-creating data files after a hard disk crash or power outage can attest, it's much easier to make the effort to protect the information up front. Although this alone is a compelling enough reason to perform adequate backups, many other reasons exist.

The conclusion is simple: restoring data from backups is much easier than re-creating it manually. Statistics show that over 80 percent of businesses that experience significant data loss never reopen their doors. Why is data loss such a potentially disastrous event? We already gave examples of why information is important. I cringe at the thought of losing my grocery list. Imagine losing a day's worth of sales information from 20 stores! Not only would that information be lost, but any reports that depend on it would be inaccurate. Imagine the footnotes on weekly, monthly, and annual reports: "Information for September 7, 2000 is only an estimate."

In some cases, the data can't be re-created, while in other cases, it can. Even when it can be re-created, however, the process takes time and a lot of patience. The time itself is costly, because we all have more productive tasks to do than to redo something we have already completed. The difficulty and cost associated with re-creating information should provide strong motivation for protecting it.

Downtime Is Expensive

Businesses and consumers alike have become extremely dependent on computers. Even ordering a meal at a restaurant depends on computer technology. The proliferation of new "dot com" companies and application service providers demonstrates this point. For these businesses, the machines *are* the product or the service. The Dell Corporation web site (**www.dell.com**) reports online sales of many millions of dollars per day. You can imagine what the downtime would cost if this system were unavailable for even a few *minutes.* Orders may not be placed (or might be lost), thereby causing lost revenue. Although that may be bad enough, also consider secondary damages that could result due to customer frustration and a tarnished business reputation.

Public Perception Can Make or Break Your Business

Although public relations might not be the primary reason for why you want to protect your information, it should be considered an important factor. Your customers expect some assurances that they are safe doing business with you. The reasons for why they expect such assurances are obvious with respect to institutions such as banks and online trading services, but these expectations affect all companies to some degree. For example, how many times would you have to reregister your information on a company's web site before you would give up and go to one of its competitor's sites? If you're like me, the answer is not many. Often, companies that allow online retail sales come into the limelight when they have technical failures that prevent their customers from placing orders. This is especially true during times of high activity or when data loss prevents consumers from receiving the products they have purchased. Clearly, this is a situation that no company wants to be associated with.

Finally, looking at all the potential problems related to the recent Y2K panic underscores the importance of computers in everything we do. People and businesses now rely more than ever on computers and the information they store. If they're unavailable, people will know about it and complain.

THREATS TO YOUR DATA

So far we've looked at some reasons why your data is important. Now, let's look at why your organization's information might not be as safe as it should be. Some concepts related to data protection are quite obvious, but others may be less evident. For example, we're all very well aware of the effects of hardware failures. Whether it's a hard disk or a power supply, the failure of these parts can cause a lot of headaches. In most cases, users will instantly notice that data has been lost, corrupted, or is unavailable. However, your information can be compromised in other, less obvious ways, and although you may not think of these breaches as readily as other failures, they are, in some cases, much more likely to occur.

As an example, consider the chapter that I am now writing in Microsoft Word. I could easily lose all the information in this document simply by pressing CTRL-A (to select all the text), hitting the DELETE key (to delete it all), and then saving and closing the document. In this case, none of the standard recovery methods (the Windows Recycle Bin or the Microsoft Word Undo feature) would bring the information back. And, I'd be stuck trying to rewrite this entire chapter from scratch!

On a database server, it's even easier to wreak havoc. I could enter a SQL DELETE query (covered later in this book) and forget to enter a WHERE clause. This would delete all the information in one of my database tables, and it would be time to start digging out my backup tapes. From personal experience, I can attest to the fact that these scenarios are much more likely to occur than a hard disk crash. So, let's look at the *real* threats to your information to determine what you're actually protecting *against*.

Hardware and Software Failures

Most systems or network administrators have experienced the true mortality of computer hardware. Regardless of the precautions you might take, computer equipment will fail. When talking about data protection, I often hear comments about protecting against hardware and software failures as the main reason for performing backups. These problems are very real, and a few of us have stories about systems administrators who have lost their jobs when data protection wasn't properly performed.

I can add my own story to that pool: I once worked in an environment in which a systems administrator was trying to replace a failed drive in a redundant array but pulled the wrong drive. We'll cover the technical details of Redundant Array of Independent Disks (RAID) technology in later chapters, but if you're unfamiliar with RAID, you should know that, generally, a single RAID array is designed to withstand the failure of a single disk within an array. In this case, two failures occurred: First, the original disk that had failed was no longer usable. Second, the drive that was incorrectly removed from the array was unusable. The end result was a total loss of all of the data in the array. This is a good example of how a technical failure, combined with human error, contributed to a catastrophic loss of data.

The general method of protecting against a hardware failure is to implement *redundancy*. Redundant systems often have one or more backup (redundant) parts that can be used in the event that the primary part fails. This is commonly done with power supplies and hard disks. Although the concept of redundancy has some negative connotations in conventional language, it is very important in data protection situations. Later in this book, we'll look at examples of how redundant components can improve network performance. When you're designing a redundant system, manual intervention may be required to prevent downtime and to replace failed parts. Redundancy also applies to software and data; we maintain copies of this information on other forms of media so that it can be replaced if lost. However, it's important to understand that redundancy can be handled at many levels and that *complete redundancy* is a difficult goal to achieve.

Even within the area of hardware and software failures, many misconceptions and oversights exist. For example, assume that you implement hard disk redundancy to protect against disk failures. This doesn't protect against a power supply failure, so you choose to upgrade to a server that has redundant power supplies. You also place an uninterruptible power supply (UPS) on the circuit to prevent power problems external to the machine. Now, you have reasonably protected this machine against disk and power failures. But, what if a critical motherboard component or a disk controller fails? Or, suppose that your entire data center suffers from a natural disaster or prolonged loss of power. As you can see, the list of things you need to protect against is a long one, and not all types of protection are practical. We'll cover all of these topics later in the book. Although hardware and software failures are very real possibilities that shouldn't be ignored, there are several other events you must protect against.

People with Good Intentions

Problems may occur by sheer accident. I gave an example earlier about how easy it might be to lose information in this Microsoft Word chapter file (and yes, I have made several backups since then). In many environments, user error is by far the most common cause of data loss or corruption. Users and systems administrators, even with the best of intentions, sometimes make minor syntactical and procedural mistakes, although software and operating system developers go to reasonable lengths to ensure that we don't make common mistakes (like deleting critical system files in order to free disk space). Thankfully, features such as the Windows Recycle Bin can save us from some errors. Those annoying dialog boxes that constantly ask whether you're sure you want to perform an operation can save you a lot of time in the long run. But, for the most part, you operate without a safety net when you work in a networked environment.

Can accidents involving the loss of data be prevented? In some cases, the answer is "No." Accidents will occur due to lack of communication, inadequate training, and even physical mistakes. (Ever dropped coffee on a keyboard or accidentally rebooted a server?) However, you can take many measures to diminish the likelihood of these problems occurring. Best practices, such as managing security permissions and educating users, easily qualify as the ounce of prevention that may prevent the need for a pound of cure. In later chapters, we'll look at several ways to protect against good people who make bad mistakes.

People with Bad Intentions

Let's face it—some people are out to get you and your data. They may try to bring down your mission-critical servers or steal information. Measuring this as a real threat is difficult, because organizations that have been victims of such foul play often try to cover it up. It's embarrassing that users can hack into some of the world's best-protected networks. In a few well-publicized cases, teenage intruders have infiltrated bank systems and proprietary company databases.

Systems administrators and technical staff often place much of their attention on protecting sensitive information from unauthorized access, especially unauthorized access via the Internet. The reason why this must be done is obvious in some cases. For example, human resources departments must keep salary information confidential, and health care organizations must maintain the privacy of patients' health records. However, almost all information can cause problems if it falls into the hands of the wrong people. This makes it much more important to understand the real threats. Much purposeful data loss or corruption likely will occur from within an organization. After all, who has better methods, means, and motives to access your information than a disgruntled employee?

The threat of external intrusion, of course, is a possibility and should still be protected against.

Common examples of high-tech vandalism are those that occur when popular web sites are defaced. Hackers will circumvent the security of a popular web server and then change the content (usually to some meaningless and poorly written message to the world). Although the actual effects of the "data loss" may not have been extreme (that is, the web site could be rebuilt from a development server very quickly), the impact on public opinion could be severe.

The potential problem is even more pronounced for those companies that offer their applications on the Internet in the form of a service. These companies, called Application Service Providers (ASPs), can provide mission-critical data to hundreds of customers. These customers, in turn, depend on the ASP in order to please their customers. It's easy to see how a single failure or loss of data in this interdependent chain could cascade into a catastrophe for the affected businesses.

In most cases, systems and network administrators already have several measures that discourage users from breaking company policies. The threat of legal prosecution is probably the most effective (at least as a deterrent). The most common technical counter-measures used include authentication and encryption safeguards. Even these measures are not fail-safe, however. In some cases, the motivation to perform restricted actions on data can be high. Corporate espionage is a real threat and should be considered. The problem can be compounded by the fact that companies are often reluctant to prosecute violators of policies, out of fear of negative publicity. Bringing instances of security violations to light may be embarrassing to an organization, but it can help justify the costs associated with protecting information (or *not* protecting it, as the case may be). Combine all this with a highly mobile workforce and the ease of transferring large quantities of data, and you have some very realistic potential problems. Later in this book, we'll cover the ways you can use technology and policies to prevent data loss to unauthorized users.

Natural Disasters

We just can't control some things, no matter how hard we try. One of those is the occurrence of a natural disaster. Of course, certain areas of the world are at more risk than others, but you don't have to read many newspapers to realize that natural disasters are a risk everywhere. In many ways, we always protect against natural disasters. For example, buildings are designed to resist fire and, in some cases, earthquakes and tornadoes. When we need help, we usually call an emergency line that is staffed by waiting people whose sole purpose is to help us.

Although we can't prevent natural disasters from happening, there are ways to protect against the *effects* of a natural disaster. When it comes to information systems, well-planned networks provide for a secondary site that can be used to host critical servers, if necessary. Although this type of redundancy can be quite costly, many organizations have found that the costs are justified when compared to the possibility of unplanned downtime. It's important to remember that you're trying to protect against what *could* happen, not just what is likely to happen.

Other Potential Problems

If I haven't painted a bleak enough picture already, wait—there are more threats to your data! It's important to understand that your business can't exist in a vacuum—you are in many ways dependent on tens or even hundreds of other organizations performing their jobs. Unfortunately, many businesses may be unable to manage issues related to their business partners. For example, if your electric utility department is not operating properly, you won't be able to keep your business running. You would have had to go to extreme measures to ensure that your computer systems would be available even in the event of an extended power outage.

Or, if a vendor or third-party supplier of widgets is unable to match demand, your business may not be able to get the parts it needs to send to its customers. Such was the basis of many fears regarding the Y2K problem: people thought, I can ensure that I've done my part, but I have to take it on faith that others have done theirs. For large retail companies, this meant coordinating efforts with thousands of suppliers.

OK, I'll bet that by now I've illustrated two important points: data is important, and there are many good reasons to protect it. Now, let's shift gears and look at what you can do to protect your critical information systems against these threats, given all of the resources you could possibly need.

IN AN IDEAL WORLD

IT professionals are usually well aware of many of the constraints under which they work. For example, if you asked a help desk analyst why everyone isn't using the latest technology in desktop computers, you'd probably hear explanations about the time it takes to roll out machines or budgetary constraints.

In an ideal world, your IT department would have unlimited resources for protecting information. Before we start looking at the complicated issues of the real world, let's see what you might do without those real-world constraints. The goal in this section is to determine the types of data protection we would *like* to have. The following are the features of an ideal world, in which data protection is not necessary:

▼ **Redundancy is complete.**   Not a single piece of data is ever the only copy of that information. Every piece of information is stored in at least two places. In fact, this world would be so redundant that even backups have backups and all hardware components would contain identical duplicate devices just standing by to spring into action.

■ **People never make mistakes.**   All people in the ideal world are so well trained that they rarely, if ever, make a mistake. Even if someone does make a mistake, another person can easily correct it. In the rare instance that someone inadvertently affects data, the changes can easily be rolled back.

■ **Computers never make mistakes.**   Okay, so maybe the computers aren't at fault for most errors. But, this is not an issue in an ideal world, because mistakes don't ever occur—no calculation problems, no incorrect results, no database corruption, no erroneous information at all. Better yet, users rarely have to wait for these perfect results, because response times are almost instant.

■ **The laws of physics have been mastered.**   Engineers are no longer bound by limitations that affect the rate of data transfer or the limits of data storage. Gone are concerns related to finishing long-running tasks on time or deciding how to archive information. Instead, everyone can focus on the quality of the information itself.

■ **People have good intentions.**   No one in this ideal world would even think of stealing or improperly modifying any of your information. Because no competition exists (only cooperation), everyone's best interest is to make sure that these types of problems don't occur for their own organizations and for those with which they do business.

■ **People plan appropriately.**   Information is as important in the ideal world as it is in the real world. Fortunately, everyone realizes this and takes the necessary steps and precautions to make sure that their assets are safe. Not only are good backup procedures implemented, but they are tested regularly. Furthermore, employees designated as "Data Protection Optimizers" (a highly coveted position that requires intense training and comes with a huge salary) are constantly looking for better ways of doing things.

■ **Machines don't fail.**   Hardware devices never fail; they simply last forever (or until they are retired). Nor do machines incur any downtime for routine maintenance, upgrades, or configuration changes.

■ **Money grows on trees.**   Better yet, money is completely unnecessary. All of the world's technology is available for solving your problems. It is a rare case, indeed, when you are not able to get something you need (including people, hardware, software, or networking devices). So, you can choose from the best solutions people and technology can offer.

▲ **Qualified people are everywhere.**   There's no shortage of qualified information technology professionals. Any time a problem or business challenge arises, one or more of these ever-present individuals can quickly jump into action based on a thoroughly tested data recovery plan. No decisions are made in haste or without the approval of at least 10 others to ensure that the right steps are being taken.

Indeed, if we actually lived and operated in an ideal world, this book would be considerably shorter! However, we are bound by many constraints that make solutions designed for the ideal world impractical. Let's get back to reality.

CHALLENGES IN THE REAL WORLD

In the real world of information technology, you will be working within many constraints. These constraints are what make our jobs challenging. Some are obvious, but others will require further examination. If you're a critical reader, you've probably already started thinking about the reasons why 100 percent protection against all potential problems is almost impossible. That's true. However, to find out what the major speed bumps are, we need to look at the reasons why many organizations don't take even the most basic steps to ensure their information is protected. The goal here is to assess the business and technical considerations that *prevent* ideal data protection.

Financial Constraints

You probably aren't surprised to know that one of the limiting factors regarding technology adoption has to do with costs. Although technology is available for performing adequate backup and restore operations, the necessary hardware and software may be priced too far out of reach to be practical for your business. This makes it important to consider what level of protection you absolutely *need* and to plan resource purchases more accurately. If you're in the position of making recommendations in these areas, be sure that you document your opinion and the fact that upper management has decided not to follow it, if applicable. This information might become very important in the event of data loss. If you could see into the future, you would know exactly which problems would occur and plan for those. Instead, you have to make a best guess at what is likely to occur, and base your data protection strategies on those eventualities. However, you should always be aware of the trade-offs you're making.

The central debate involves the costs associated with *protecting* data versus the potential costs of *losing* it. Somehow, the decision makers in your organization need to find a happy middle ground between these two factors. Nevertheless, the systems administrators likely will be blamed for data loss resulting from anything along the entire spectrum of possibilities—from user error to hardware failures. Keep this in mind when trying to justify the safeguards your company needs. Later in this chapter, we'll look at what's needed to develop a preliminary budget.

Staffing Constraints

People can be a costly but irreplaceable resource. In fact, they're probably one of your business's greatest strengths. In recent years, finding and retaining qualified information technology professionals has been a topic of great concern in many organizations. When it comes to protecting information, you'll need people to make sure that your systems are configured properly and to plan, test, and manage the solutions upon which you rely. Thus, the lack of qualified people is another constraint that your data protection policy needs to take into account.

One of the most common excuses for not performing backups (and even more so for not testing them) is that "There's just not enough time to do it all." It always seems that other tasks take a higher priority. To make the case worse for performing backups, the job itself is almost invisible—if things are going well, people see only that you're not performing other jobs during the time spent implementing and managing data security measures. This is in sharp contrast to other IT functions, such as implementing new systems, supporting users, and optimizing performance—all of which are the kinds of things you're likely to be rewarded for doing. The attitude that "I've got better things to do than manage a stack of tapes" might *never* cause any problems in your environment. That's very unlikely, though. As already mentioned, data loss is a very real risk. So, the challenge becomes having the time and expertise to implement and maintain a suitable data protection plan.

Technical Constraints

Even if all of these constraints don't affect you (which is highly unlikely), you are still bound by the laws of physics and our understanding of them. For example, it is very difficult to fully protect against natural disasters in a single location. Being able to predict all natural disasters within the amount of time required to avoid them is not something humans will be able to do in the foreseeable future.

Technical constraints apply to our information systems, as well. For example, at the hardware level, media has a finite capacity, and hardware has real performance limitations. Although new technologies try to keep pace with requirements, the increasing demands that are placed on computing systems make it difficult. The most common issue is that, even with some of the most advanced solutions on the market (which are quite costly), simply too much information exists to manage it all practically. So, compromises must be made. Instead of making sure that data is backed up every second, we choose to back up data every day. And, instead of protecting all the information on all of your business systems, you must concede that some information can be replaced the hard way.

Again, if you make compromises, be sure that you document *why* and *how* they were determined. Enumerating the drawbacks beforehand can go a long way in protecting technical staff from taking the blame for poor business decisions. However, keep in mind that trade-offs are necessary, due to technological limitations.

Lack of Understanding

IT professionals often joke that users know a systems administrator is doing his or her job when they don't realize it is being done at all. Everything works as expected, so users may not even know that someone had to work hard to get their systems in that position. With data protection, the same applies. In the best-case scenario, your organization never loses important information and no one ever knows that backups were being performed. No one, that is, except those who have to pay the costs for these functions. Ironically, the fact that no significant data loss has occurred can make it *more* difficult to justify increased spending for data protection.

If you are a systems or network administrator, one of your major challenges will be to get buy-in from upper management on backup and recovery solutions. This often is a tough sell, because you can't really offer any tangible benefit. The act of performing back-ups won't reduce operating costs, and may not present a low total cost of ownership (TCO). However, these functions *are* good investments. The benefits will be realized only if data loss (due to another problem) occurs. So, part of the challenge in putting together a data protection plan is to educate decision makers on the real benefits of protecting data, and the potential *consequences* if you don't. As with many good ideas, this might seem like an uphill battle, but the results can pay off in the event of significant data loss or hardware failures.

The Speed of E-Business

Recently, the rapid rise in popularity and availability of the Internet brought with it new demands. It is no longer acceptable, for example, to be unable to receive technical support for a product outside of business hours. If I'm at home, working on my PC, I would ex-pect hardware vendors to make drivers and technical information available on the Internet. Furthermore, if I want to order some books from an online bookstore, being "down for maintenance" is not an acceptable excuse.

Of course, the new demands from users have placed many pressures on businesses to deliver their Internet-based products (whether they are web portals, application services, or retail shopping) quickly, reliably, and accurately. These goals have quickly gone from being luxuries to being prerequisites for staying in business. Therefore, there is much em-phasis within e-businesses on developing new products and dealing with performance and reliability of a computing infrastructure. However, all of this comes at a price. Unfor-tunately, for many, data protection is an afterthought—usually something considered in hindsight after catastrophic data loss occurs. Ironically, it is for these Internet-based com-panies that data protection is of the utmost importance!

Political Issues

In addition to the preceding issues, you'll have to worry about the opinions of others when designing a workable data protection plan. One example is the common plague of many businesses—politics. It's very difficult to implement security measures without running into a quagmire of differing views and power struggles. Users might want com-plete freedom (whether or not they actually use it), but don't realize that it comes at a price of potentially serious problems. Others may see no harm in having the ability to modify information stored in large databases. However, with decreased security comes an increase in the likelihood of accidental data loss.

Lack of understanding, as mentioned earlier, is one of the main problems. And, orga-nizations compound the problem by placing the emphasis of technical resources on im-proving performance or implementing new systems. For some individuals, data protection is, at best, a necessary evil. These attitudes can stand in the way of implement-ing and maintaining an adequate backup and recovery plan. Again, the solution is to edu-cate users and decision makers on the need for trade-offs between security and capabilities.

Summing It All Up

By now, you have probably realized that all of these challenges apply to your organization. Few companies are not bound by financial constraints or technology. Furthermore, all of these constraints are interdependent. Limitations of money may cause human resources limitations. Finally, political issues can cause great constraints even if none of the others apply.

I hope I haven't made things look too dismal! Rest assured, your organization is not the only one that is facing these challenges. And, many companies have found very good solutions for them. Now that we have a clear description of the problems and the challenges, let's look at how you can evaluate data protection in your own environment. First, we need to look at how you can evaluate the systems and information on which your company depends.

EVALUATING YOUR ENVIRONMENT

In most organizations, computing technology is used to fulfill some business need. For example, an executive might decide that a sales-tracking database would be a valuable asset. So, a database developer builds a back-end data repository, and a client-server programmer writes a client-side application that fulfills the business requirements. Systems and network administrators configure servers and clients to support these systems. Hopefully, the application will meet the needs of the company's salespeople. Seeing how useful this system is, the company might next decide to implement a system for tracking all transactions that occur at its stores. Again, a back-end database and a client application are developed, along with the infrastructure to support them. Now, the company has two systems to manage. This raises some important questions:

▼ Should the two functions be combined at the database level?

■ How can the overall administration requirements be reduced for this solution?

■ Three years from now, will both systems even be needed?

▲ Who is responsible for protecting the information stored on these systems?

As these questions indicate, combining these systems creates a quite complicated network. Add issues such as developers coming and going from the organization, and you have a bunch of puzzle pieces but no clear picture of where they fit. Before you develop a complete data protection plan, you must take the time to evaluate the business requirements of your IT infrastructure. This includes looking at all the hardware and software you currently support and finding out why (or whether) users require them.

Why Evaluate?

In all but the best-managed network environments, determining what you are supporting and why you are supporting it takes considerable time and effort. The results can sometimes be surprising. Stories of users whose daily struggles include converting spreadsheet files among three different formats might paint pictures of hidden inefficiencies. All too often, IT managers try to solve problems in a very simplistic manner. For example, if users complain that a server is too slow, the IT department might upgrade the server. Although there might be some increase in performance, it won't be worth the acquisition and implementation costs if the application was poorly designed to begin with. And, what if the real problem was a client-side issue or a network bandwidth bottleneck?

The benefits of evaluating your business systems will likely go much further than just data protection itself. If you have a good idea of what all of your systems are doing, you'll be able to make much more intelligent choices about how to best manage them. Consolidating functions onto fewer servers and retiring old systems that are rarely used can reduce many hassles for systems administrators and can lead to some very attractive and tangible benefits. First, the costs associated with managing many different systems can be greatly reduced. Along with reduced complexity come the benefits of better service to end users, who want to focus on doing their jobs—not trying to remember on which server the file they need resides. Finally, you're likely to find cost savings in licenses that are unnecessary (or can be reallocated more efficiently).

Generally, information technology resources fall into one of several categories. The following sections look at the roles of these devices and applications and how they can help you meet your business requirements.

Business Applications

All the servers and workstations in your environment would be useless without the software that they run. It is these applications that users interact with directly. Typical applications include the following:

- ▼ **Productivity ("front-office") applications**   These are the common programs (such as those included in the Microsoft Office suite) that allow users to perform everyday functions, such as creating word processor documents and simple spreadsheets.

- ■ **Messaging applications**   Enabling employees to communicate with each other is an important part of any company's infrastructure. Accordingly, messaging applications (such as Microsoft Outlook) are designed to do everything from transferring messages to tracking information, such as calendar data. When combined with *group workflow* applications, messaging applications enable users to easily share information, such as commonly used documents and messages in discussions forums.

- ■ **Internet applications**   Due to the popularity of the Internet, a desktop computer without a web browser is rare. Most company users have access to browsing the web and using other Internet-enabled tools for information access. In addition to browsing the web, users may rely on access to USENET newsgroups, instant messaging, and real-time collaboration applications.

■ **Line-of-business (LOB) applications**   LOB applications typically are custom developed or purchased to meet some specific business need. For example, an organization's accounting department might purchase a financials package.

▲ **Outsourced applications**   Outsourcing is becoming increasingly common as businesses realize the full costs of implementing and managing applications in-house. A new group of companies—the Application Service Providers, mentioned earlier—are filling the market with full-featured business applications that have few client-side requirements. The ASPs themselves are often responsible for managing data protection, security, and availability. Nevertheless, IT staff must be ultimately responsible for ensuring that acceptable service is being provided.

When combined, all of these applications make up the interface between your employees' minds and your information technology infrastructure.

The Network Infrastructure

The tie that binds together all of these information technology systems is your organization's network. If asked to point to a network a few years ago, a systems administrator would likely point to the wires that connect into a network's hubs and routers. Basically, anything connected to those wires was considered part of the network, and everything else was outside the network. Now, however, networks are much more complex. The Internet is a vital part of most business infrastructures, and wide area networks (WANs) are common. Add to that remote users, virtual private networks (VPNs), and branch offices, and you have a much larger environment to support.

Workstations (Clients)

The main purpose for client systems is to serve as individuals' workstations. These systems normally are used to run productivity applications, such as Microsoft Office applications, web browsers, and other programs. Based on a company's policy, users may or may not store their data on their local machines. Smaller organizations might find it easier to back up selected directories and file types on each user's machine. When dealing with many desktop computers, however, this can become impractical. Therefore, larger organizations often force their users to store information only on file servers. Only the information on the servers is backed up, and users are aware that they could lose any information stored on their local machines.

Servers

Small companies often use one or a few servers that are responsible for the majority of the company's processing, file and print services, and data storage. In larger business environments, multiple servers perform various tasks. These functions may be similar (in the case of a web server farm) or very different (as in specialized database or application servers). In any case, you have to consider the roles of these machines when you are deciding how to best protect them. We'll spend time determining the different data protection requirements for these machines in later chapters. For now, concentrate on the various roles that database servers might assume in your environment; the key for this discussion is to recognize why you have database servers, instead of focusing on the specific implications of managing each.

Directory Services Servers

Almost all networks have at least one type of directory service that is used for managing security permissions. For example, in the Windows NT world, domains could be used to centrally manage users and computers. The goal was to ease administration and improve security through the use of features such as a single sign-on (so users must remember only one password to access various resources on the network). Traditionally, network operating systems were designed to manage information related to network resources and security.

The domain system used in Windows NT was fairly limited in many ways, including scalability, ease of administration (especially for large environments), and customizability. With Windows 2000 and the Active Directory, Microsoft has expanded upon the ideas related to traditional network directory services. The Active Directory uses an extensible schema and is designed to track more than just network-related information (see Figure 1-1). We'll cover the details of working with the Active Directory in Chapter 3.

Servers that participate in directory services (*domain controllers*, in Windows terminology) may have special data protection requirements. First and foremost, it's important that the security information they contain is not lost. It would be difficult, time consuming, and risky to attempt to re-create all of the users and accounts that are required for proper network access. To that end, however, Windows NT and Active Directory domains have a built-in method for fault tolerance and data protection. They work through a system of multiple domain controllers, each of which stores at least a portion of the overall directory information. However, this level of data protection may not be enough. Although having multiple domain controllers will reduce the chances of downtime or inaccessibility of resources due to a server failure, it will not help you recover from an accidental deletion of many user accounts. If you rely heavily upon directory services in your environment (and there's a good chance that you do), be sure to understand any special data protection requirements.

File/Print Servers

File and print servers, which typically are run by one or more network operating systems (such as Windows NT/2000, Novell NetWare, or UNIX-based platforms), are responsible for storing user files and for providing access to printers managed by the organization.

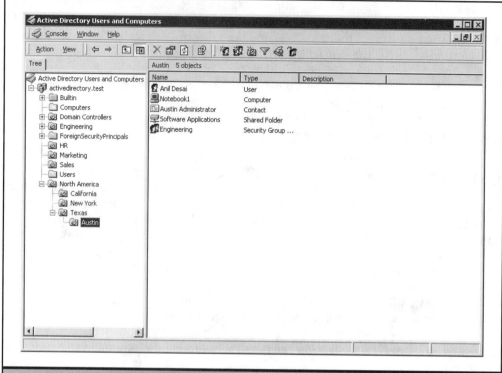

Figure 1-1. Organizing information about users, computers, groups, and other objects in the Active Directory

Additionally, these servers store user accounts and manage security for the types of information they store. File and print servers are critical for normal day-to-day operations for most users. If these servers are unavailable, many employees may be unable to access important spreadsheets or documents.

Application Servers and Multitier Architecture

Multitier (also called *n*-tier) applications are designed to take true advantage of distributed computing by allowing servers to "specialize" in performing certain tasks. Figure 1-2 provides a high-level overview of a multitier solution based on Microsoft technologies.

In this type of application architecture, the various functions that are required to provide information to users are distributed to different machines. For example, all data is located on a database server (sometimes called the *back end* or the *storage tier*). The middle-tier server is responsible for containing all the business logic and for processing information. Data access components—portions of the application that retrieve data from database servers—may be located with the middle tier or as a separate tier of their own.

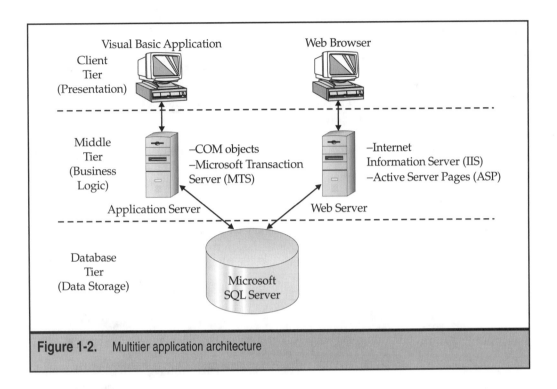

Figure 1-2.   Multitier application architecture

The code at the middle layer translates user requests into database requests, obtains the data, processes it, and sends the information back to the user. The front-end process might be a client application (for example, a Visual Basic program) or a web browser that is used by the client to work with the application.

Obviously, developing such an application can take more planning and time than writing a single, monolithic piece of code that resides on one server. So, why would anyone go through all this trouble? Using a multitier server architecture offers many benefits, including its modular architecture (which provides for functional specialization), scalability (more servers can be added at tiers where bottlenecks occur), and performance (each server can be tuned to specialize on one function).

Regarding data protection, it's important to assess the types of information stored on each of the servers in a multitier application. In some cases, data protection might not be important at all. Consider, for example, an architecture that uses multiple redundant middle-tier servers. If all of the code is safely stored elsewhere on the network, it might be easier to simply rebuild a server from scratch than to restore data from tape. It is also likely that no user data is ever stored on these machines, at all. For back-end data storage servers, however, data protection might be of the utmost importance—it is here that valuable user and application information is stored. Although the servers themselves could be rebuilt in the event of a failure or accidental data corruption, there may be no way to retrieve the data they store without adequate backups.

Web Servers

It's rare nowadays for a company not to have some form of web server for a web-based intranet or an Internet site. At the most basic level, web servers work like file servers in that they are responsible for sending static Hypertext Markup Language (HTML) files to clients. However, modern web servers, such as Microsoft Internet Information Server (IIS), are far more versatile. Specifically, server-side processing can be implemented using a variety of languages, including Common Gateway Interface (CGI), Java and JavaScript, and Active Server Pages (ASPs). These dynamic tools allow developers to create entire applications that are accessible via web browsers and require no client installations. Examples of this type of site can be found almost anywhere on the web that provides dynamic content (such as online retailers). Figure 1-3 provides an example of a site with dynamic content.

When protecting data stored on web servers, it's important to assess the value of data protection and to determine the real requirements. For many types of web-based applications, the content stored on the servers is fairly static (that is, the web page content files do

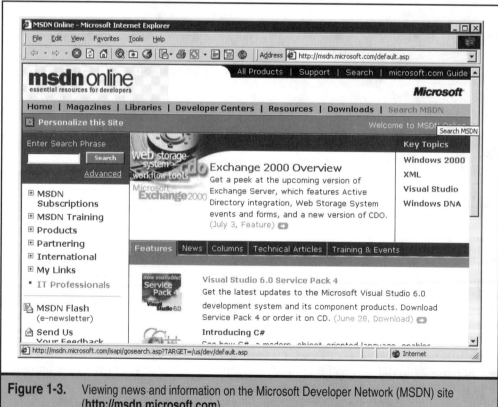

Figure 1-3.   Viewing news and information on the Microsoft Developer Network (MSDN) site (**http://msdn.microsoft.com**)

not directly change as the result of end-user interaction). It is also likely that the code that runs on these machines is already available elsewhere (for example, on a development or staging server). In the event of a server failure, web servers can often be easily rebuilt with minimal configuration. If, on the other hand, the web server configuration and application are sufficiently complex, it might make more sense to simply back up the entire server.

Specialized Servers

In addition to the types of servers mentioned already, there are other applications that depend on server-based computing resources. Most small organizations don't have special-function servers; rather, they consolidate applications and services on the same machines to reduce costs and administrative overhead. But medium- to large-sized organizations usually invest in building servers that are specialized for certain tasks. A few of these types of applications include

▼   **Messaging servers**   For example, Microsoft's Exchange Server platform is responsible for routing e-mail messages between users using industry-standard protocols. It also offers support and integration for Internet mail protocols and connectivity to other messaging systems. Messaging servers are increasingly being used for productivity applications. New features allow users to share schedule information and work together on files. There are also options for real-time collaboration and streaming media. Finally, the popularity of the Internet and web-based applications hasn't gone unnoticed by messaging server vendors. For example, Microsoft's Outlook Web Access (part of Exchange Server 5.5) allows users to access their e-mail and other information using a standard web browser (see Figure 1-4).

▲   **Terminal servers**   Technologies such as Citrix WinFrame, Microsoft's Windows NT Server, Terminal Server Edition, and all editions of Windows 2000 Server allow users to log on to a central host server. This centralized machine is responsible for providing all the computing power and data storage required by users. The clients, in turn, are reduced to simple input/output devices. The major benefits of terminal servers are centralized management and reduced client requirements. There are drawbacks, however, including price barriers, increased network bandwidth requirements, and application performance. Figure 1-5 provides an overview of terminal server architecture vs. traditional client-server computing. Data protection for terminal servers can be extremely important. In many environments, users will store all of their important data on these machines. Therefore, it is often unacceptable to suffer any data loss on these machines. Even more important, however, is uptime and availability. By their very nature, terminal servers are important machines. If they are unavailable, *many* users could be unable to perform even their most simple computing-related job functions. Therefore, high-availability solutions are often implemented for terminal servers.

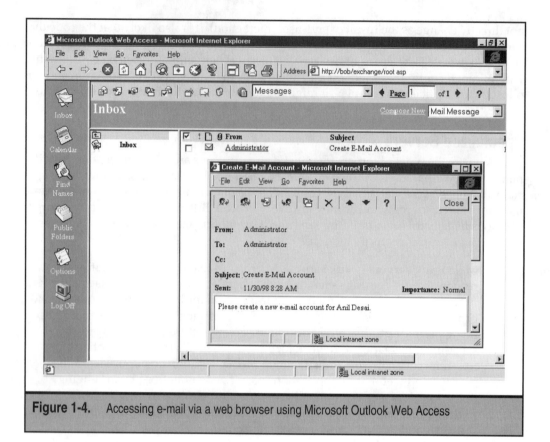

Figure 1-4. Accessing e-mail via a web browser using Microsoft Outlook Web Access

Relational Database Servers

Thus far, we have examined the roles of several different types of machines in typical network environments. Now it's time to discuss one of the most important types of server. Relational database management systems (RDBMSs) are used to store relatively large volumes of information that is accessed by many users throughout the organization. Indeed, the very reason for the existence of much of your computing infrastructure is to provide support for these critical applications. For example, the network infrastructure is used to connect database servers with the users who need the data housed on the servers. Clients are used for processing information and for managing input and output for the user. Other types of servers, such as web servers or middle-tier application servers, might specialize in making the data stored in RDBMSs more easily accessible to users.

Your database servers might partake in one or more roles within your environment. It's important to have a basic understanding of the function of database servers in your

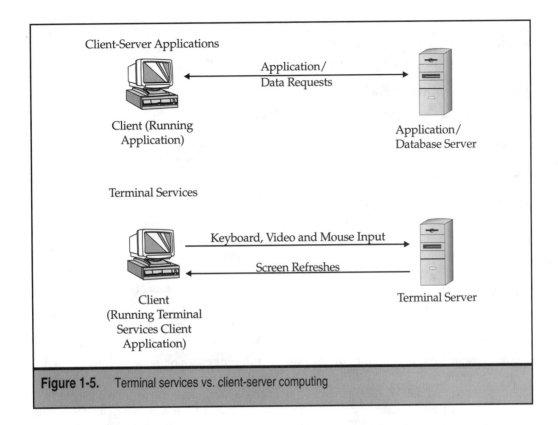

Figure 1-5.   Terminal services vs. client-server computing

environment. Ideally, each server has a function that can't easily be combined on another server (for political or technical reasons). It's possible that you have database servers that really aren't needed at all and can be either eliminated or combined with other servers. This section looks at how RDBMSs are typically used to fulfill business requirements.

Online Transaction Processing (OLTP)

Online transaction processing (OLTP) services are often the most common functions of database servers in many organizations. These systems are responsible for receiving and storing information that is accessed by client applications and other servers. OLTP databases are characterized by having a high level of data modification (inserting, updating, and deleting rows). Therefore, they are optimized to support dynamically changing data. Generally, they store large volumes of information that can balloon very quickly if not managed properly.

Backing up data on OLTP systems is extremely important since any loss of transactional information can lead to inconsistencies in reports and projections. Unfortunately, performing backups on OLTP systems can be problematic. This is because performance and availability of database servers are very important in OLTP systems, and backup operations can often decrease performance. There are, however, many creative solutions for backing up OLTP data. We'll cover the details in later chapters.

Data Warehousing

Many companies go to great lengths to collect and store as much information as possible. But what good is this information if it can't easily be analyzed? The primary business reason for storing many types of information is to use this data eventually to help make business decisions. Although reports can be generated against OLTP database servers, there are several potential problems:

▼ OLTP servers are not optimized for the types of queries used in reporting, thus making the problem worse. Traditionally, OLTP servers will host a "normalized" database schema—one that is optimized for reducing redundancy in information and that is designed for performing rapid data modifications. Reporting requirements are very different—in these types of systems, the main type of transaction is in performing data analysis.

■ OLTP systems get bogged down when the amount of data in the databases gets very large. Therefore, production OLTP data must often be archived to other media or stored in another data repository.

▲ Organizations are likely to have many different types of database servers that operate on different platforms. The data stored in these databases might not be stored in a consistent format. For example, a sales-tracking application might store a client's state as a two-letter code (such as TX), whereas a manufacturing database might store the same information spelled out (such as Texas).

All of these factors make obtaining decision-support information difficult on OLTP systems. That's where the idea of data warehousing steps in. *Data warehousing* is the practice of taking information from multiple sources and consolidating it in a single repository. Information may be obtained from a variety of sources, such as Oracle servers, Microsoft SQL Server, and Microsoft Access. All the information is then processed so that the data is consistent, and then it is stored in a single database. This single central database can then be used to generate reports from all types of data stored within the company's database servers. Data warehouses are characterized by having very large data stores that are primarily treated as read-only. Periodic updates to the information are made to keep the information current.

Although data warehouses solve one challenge—making data available for reporting—another problem exists: analyzing large quantities of data in meaningful ways is very difficult. Furthermore, reports that are run across all of this information can take a long time to process. Fortunately, there are several good solutions to these challenges.

OLAP Services

As their name might suggest, data warehouses can often become very large. Although all of the information stored in these systems is useful in one way or another, the most significant use for business decision makers is in generating and running meaningful reports. In a traditional relational database, you could use simple SQL queries to obtain the information you're seeking. Although this is possible for data warehouses, the amount of time it takes to process and return the desired data can make it impractical. For example, suppose a manager wants to obtain a report showing the total sales for all departments within a large organization for a given year. Although the query to generate this information might be relatively simple, the time it takes to process potentially millions of rows could be prohibitive. And, what happens if the manager decides that she would like to drill down on information for only a specific department? Another report would need to be generated, and the database server would be required to redo some significant amount of number crunching. Clearly, a better solution is needed.

Online analytical processing (OLAP) services are used to analyze the types of information stored in data warehouses. Using the analogy of multidimensional data structures called *cubes,* OLAP services provide for complex analysis of database information. To improve performance, the OLAP server precalculates many data combinations (called *aggregations*) to speed analyses. These aggregate values are then stored in multidimensional structures. In the earlier example about the manager who wanted a report on sales information, these queries might run hundreds of times faster since the total values are already stored in the database. Instead of adding up all of the sales information each time such a report is requested, an OLAP cube would already contain the required sums.

Of course, no technology is truly useful unless it can make users' jobs easier. Fortunately, there are now many tools on the market that can be used for performing ad hoc queries against a multidimensional cube. On the client side, users can use OLAP-enabled tools to easily generate meaningful reports. Furthermore, these reports can be interactive; that is, users can perform drill-downs and roll-ups of information with just a few mouse clicks. A good example of such a tool is Microsoft Excel 2000's PivotTable feature (shown in Figure 1-6).

The result of creating an OLAP system is a server that is well tuned to provide meaningful analyses of complex data relationships. The details of implementing OLAP services are beyond the scope of this book, but many good references are available via the Microsoft SQL Server web site (**www.Microsoft.com/sql**).

Data warehouses and OLAP-based systems might have data protection requirements that are quite different from those of other database servers. First of all, they may not need to be backed up as frequently. Depending on the design of the data warehouse, in the event of a complete loss of specific information, the data could be recovered from production servers. Secondly, infrequent backups might be adequate since the data within these systems is not expected to change much.

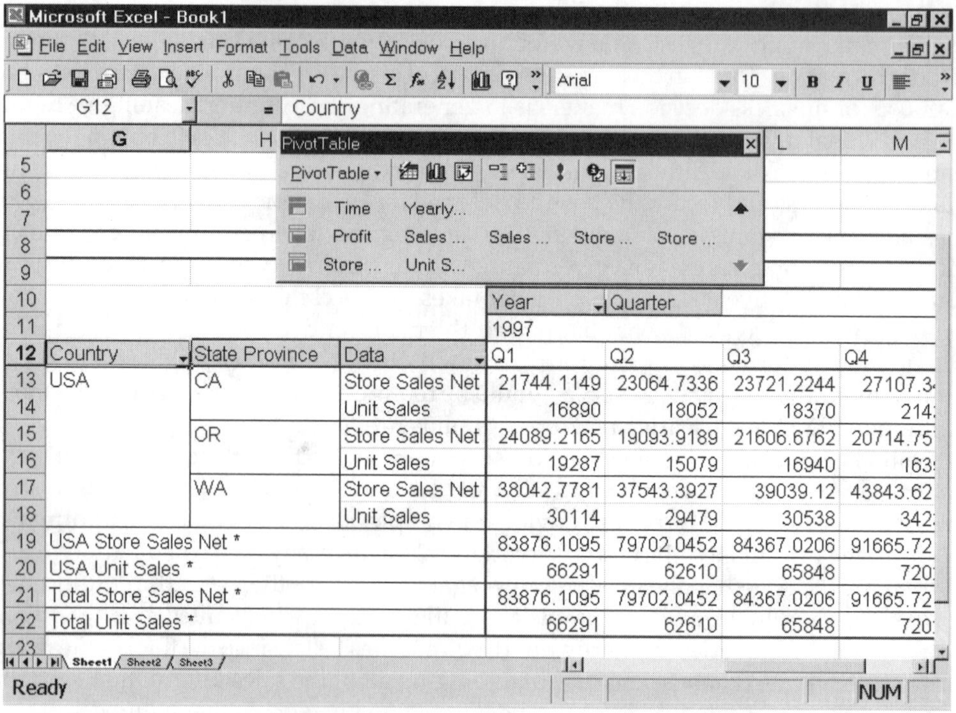

Figure 1-6.   Using OLAP services to analyze data

Human Resources

Thus far, we have looked at how you can assess the various types of computing resources that are present in your network environment. None of this would be possible, however, without one resource—people. It's important to make sure you have enough people to maintain any type of backup solution you implement. The world's safest and most efficient data protection solution might turn out to be worthless if there's no one around to implement, monitor, and manage it!

When you're determining your business requirements, be sure to measure how much time your IT staff has to implement and manage a backup solution. Before you develop your data protection plan (which we'll cover in the next chapter), there's no easy way to determine who will have time to take care of these tasks or even how much time and effort your backup solution will take. For now, take a good inventory of how many people are available in the IT department and how many might have time to perform the necessary tasks. If you find that everyone is already overloaded, it might be necessary to hire more people to share the anticipated workload. Or, a reprioritization of job responsibilities might be in order—after all, what's more important than ensuring that information is not lost in the event of server failures?

Additionally, working with any new technologies that you choose to implement will require new skills. The backup hardware and software you choose will undoubtedly require some expertise. Hopefully, much of the training can be obtained from manuals and support forums. For more extensive tasks, such as disaster recovery planning, you'll probably need to send individuals to training classes where they can learn from experts.

Finally, when you evaluate the labor costs, you'll need to look at the *opportunity* costs of performing data protection tasks. That is, while individuals are managing backup and recovery options, they're *not* spending time doing other tasks, such as systems administration or new machine rollouts. These indirect costs may be hard to measure, so most organizations figure the employee's "cost" (based on his or her salary and benefits) when trying to calculate hard numbers.

EVALUATING YOUR BUSINESS REQUIREMENTS

So far, we've talked about the best-case scenarios (essentially, creating a bubble) and looked at real-world constraints (bursting it). In all likelihood, none of this information was shocking to you. The real challenge is in determining what backup strategies apply to your own environment. You'll need to find out what your working limitations are. This won't be an easy task, even in the best-managed organizations. It involves finding information from all types of individuals and departments within the company. You'll have to work hard to find existing data, and make best guesses and estimates for areas in which data isn't available.

Let's start collecting some of this information by determining the types of protection your business requires. After we have a rough estimate of this information, we'll put it together into a sample business requirements worksheet. Rest assured that all of this data will be extremely important when discussing data protection strategies in future chapters.

Deciding What to Protect

Before you can start developing a data protection plan, you'll need to consider what information you want to protect. We've already discussed why it's not feasible to protect everything (remember the real-world constraints?). Certain types of information are more important than other types, and your data protection plan must treat them accordingly. The best plan will be based on the specific details of your business environment. For example, if a group of users is primarily responsible for entering data into a centralized database system, it might not be necessary to back up each of the client machines. In this case, a good strategy might be to back up a typical configuration once and use it to rebuild machines in the event of a failure or loss of data. In a very different computing environment, however, the goals may be quite different. Suppose you have engineers who store large drawings and schematics locally on their workstations. In this case, you need to back up information on their machines. None of these types of decisions can be made without first having a solid understanding of how users access these systems.

Many different types of information are stored on your network, and all are important. For example, an e-mail message to a coworker regarding lunch plans is important to the sender, even if it is not mission critical to the organization as a whole. Therefore, you may have to make some trade-offs. For example, the most important piece of information in the world to an individual might be the Microsoft Word document he or she was working on immediately before a disk crash. This, in itself, might not sound catastrophic. But, if this individual was your CEO drafting a message to shareholders, the disk crash would be quite costly (especially to the system administrator's career!).

So, how do you decide what to protect? One method is to classify the importance of your various pieces of information. For example, your sales databases might be of "Mission Critical" importance, whereas daily spreadsheets generated from this data might rank "Low Priority" on the scale. If you think you know this information, you can provide a baseline estimate of what's required and then present it to those who are affected. In all cases, however, make sure you talk to these people. Managers may have a very different idea of the importance of data when compared to other users (who actually deal with this information frequently). Keep in mind that determining how to protect information must be a *team* effort if it is to be accurate and successful. This information will be very important in determining a backup plan. An example is shown in Table 1-1.

Estimating Your Data Storage Requirements

After you look at the types of information you're likely to have in your computing environment and rank the importance of each type, you need to estimate *how much* information will be stored on your network's machines. In general, this is not an easy task; even so, you have several options for assessing your storage needs before you choose a backup solution. On servers, for example, you can determine how much data is currently being stored and get a good impression of how often the information changes. The same is true for database servers: you can view the current size of a database, along with other vital information, by using administrative tools.

When estimating your data storage requirements, be sure to plan for the future. Users have an uncanny skill for filling up any amount of storage you give them. Obtain information on server upgrades and configuration information. Also, if you're currently performing backups, look at the amount of data that has been collected over time. To plan for the future, consider how quickly your organization is growing, and make estimates on future requirements. You'll use this information when you develop your business requirements document.

Resource	Importance	Notes
OLTP server	Critical	Information can't be easily re-created, and data loss will lead to inaccurate or misleading reports.
File/print server	High	All important user data is stored on file servers.
E-mail server	High	Recovering lost messages and user mailboxes is very difficult.
Decision-support server (data warehouse)	Medium	Information can be regenerated from other sources.
Intranet web server	Medium	Content is important, but it is replicated between multiple machines as part of development processes.
User workstation	Low	Documents should be stored on file servers; machines can be easily reconstructed from automated install scripts. In special cases, user workstations may be backed up regularly.

Table 1-1.   Sample Categorization of Data Based on Importance

Availability of Crucial Information

Have you ever tried to find sales information from 1992 on your database server? Having this information readily available might have been useful to your company at one point in time, but it's much more likely that last year's numbers are much more relevant now. If you had unlimited resources, you'd make sure that all of your information would be available at all times. However, large amounts of data can become unmanageable on a technical level. For example, database searches slow down significantly as more information is stored on a server. Likewise, searching through a file server that contains every file you've ever created can be quite a chore. So, it's important to determine which information must be readily available and what you can do without (or at least do without having immediately available to you).

To avoid some of the problems related to managing large volumes of information with limited storage resources, organizations routinely archive older information. *Archiving* is the process of moving certain data to other types of media from which they are usually not as easy to access. For example, user files that have not been accessed for over three months on a Windows NT file server might be archived to tape. Similarly, database records that represent transactions in the previous fiscal year might be moved to offline storage. Depending on the solution chosen, the information may still be available automatically, but it might take longer. Table 1-2 lists some typical requirements for accessibility of information. Since we're in the planning stages now, it's important to find out what time limits are *tolerable*—not ideal.

There are many reasons for storing historical information. Your organization is required to keep certain records (such as tax and payroll information) for several years, in

Type of Information	Archiving Interval	Access Time	Notes
Engineering drawings	One year	15 minutes	Files are made available automatically by data archival software.
Intranet web content	N/A (managed by the web administrator)	N/A	Content is unavailable once retired.
OLTP database records	One year	Instant	Old transactions are stored on other database servers that are online.
User files	120 days	One business day	Data requires manual restoration from backup tapes.

Table 1-2. Information Accessibility Requirements

case it's needed. Also, for decision-support systems, reviewing information from previous years can be quite useful. For this reason, you should plan to protect archived information as closely as you protect online data.

Backup Requirements

For some mission-critical applications, uptime and availability are of the utmost concern. It's important to determine the information associated with how long a backup operation may take. This period is often called the *backup window*. In calculating the time available for performing backups, you'll need to consider the nature of the system and details about your business operations. For example, if your organization is multinational and requires OLTP systems to be available 24 hours per day, your backup requirements must be scheduled for times that are least busy, to avoid adversely affecting users. If the majority of employees work in a single time zone from 8:00 A.M. to 5:00 P.M., however, you will be able to find much larger windows of time for these operations. Note that it's possible that what you *think* are the busiest hours may not be. Different types of users might perform operations (such as scheduled jobs) at times that you would not have otherwise expected. Be sure to monitor database activity before jumping to conclusions. In later chapters, we'll use the information about the backup window to decide what type of hardware to implement.

Recovery Requirements

When planners are evaluating business needs, they may forget to factor in the potential time for recovering information. The question they should ask is the following: "If we lose data due to failure or corruption, how long will it take to get it back?" In some cases, the answer will be based on the technical limitations of the hardware you select. For example, if you back up 13GB of data to tape media and then lose it all, the recovery time might be two hours. But what if that's not fast enough? Suppose your systems must be available within half that time—one hour. In that case, you'll need to make some important decisions. An obvious choice is to find suitable backup hardware to meet these constraints. If budgetary considerations don't allow that, however, you'll need to find another way. In later chapters, we'll look at several technical solutions. For now, consider how long your business can *realistically* tolerate having certain information unavailable.

Budgeting for Data Protection

When you are developing the real business constraints for your backup plan, higher-level managers often ask the question "What is this solution going to cost?" Information technology professionals, on the other hand, ask "What is the budget for this solution?" Both questions are valid, but neither can be answered without first determining how expensive the alternative is: losing information. Indeed, the types of solutions you choose will depend on your actual budget constraints.

Nobody likes to experience data loss. It's frustrating and can undermine productivity. Unfortunately, similar complaints are often heard about backup operations—that they take up time and other resources. Somewhere in the middle is an optimal solution that provides adequate (though not perfect) data protection methodologies. When presenting a data protection strategy to upper management, you'll likely be asked why certain types of failures should be protected against *at all*. Though the answer may seem obvious at first, we need to quantify our preconceptions of the impact of data loss. Thus, we'll now look at how to prioritize the value of your data, based on some simple questions.

Estimating the Cost of Downtime

Let's start by trying to weigh the costs of losing information. This can be quite difficult in most situations, because exact values often aren't known, and you may have to do your homework before you can calculate what your data is worth. In many cases, however, it's not important to have exact values; approximations are enough. Using these ideas, let's look at how we might calculate the costs of downtime for an e-mail server.

First, you might start by figuring out how many users depend on the server. However, this information alone doesn't give you everything you need. It's a simple fact of business that not all e-mail being sent is mission critical. Plus, the company might be impacted more if an executive can't send messages than if administrative assistants can't send messages. In any case, you can attempt to get more information (such as the average number of e-mail messages that are sent to and from the server per hour) and assemble a best guess on the value of the machine. Also, the longer a server is down, the greater the cost of the downtime. If the accounting department is down for only 15 minutes, clerks might be able to catch up with their workload by the end of the day without missing any deadlines. However, if the server is down for a whole day, many business processes might be disrupted. It is these ripple effects that are most difficult to calculate.

Table 1-3 offers some guesses as to what downtime for various machines might cost an example organization.

Remembering our goal—to find the value of data protection—we could further complicate matters by factoring in the probability that these machines will be unavailable. If your company has kept good historical logs of downtime, this might be possible. However, it's probably more likely that you'll assume that the probability for downtime is a constant. Of course, the costs associated with downtime are only part of the picture. The preceding example assumes that information will not be lost. But what about situations when it is?

Estimating the Cost of Data Loss

How valuable is your information? This probably is a question that you don't often have to answer, since you just *assume* that protecting your data is important (regardless of whether you actually do protect it). But, when it comes to devoting time and financial resources to protecting against data loss, you must have some idea about the value of your

Machine	Number of Users	Downtime Cost (per hour)	Downtime Cost (per day)	Notes
Accounting server	23	$3,000	$40,000	May disrupt other business processes.
Accounting workstation	1	$25	$500	Individual users may be able to use other machines.
E-mail server	430	$16,500	$250,000	Estimates assume that data is not lost.
File/print server	100 (average)	$20,000	$175,000	Costs will vary by department and by the functions of individuals.
Warehouse inventory database	100	$12,000	$125,000	Customers and suppliers will also be affected.

Table 1-3.   Sample Estimates of the Costs of Downtime per Resource

information. As when developing downtime cost estimates, you must consider the number of users that might be affected and the types of information involved. Instead of going through the thorough analysis we've performed in this chapter, you may wish to simply consider some examples of these costs.

First of all, in most cases, data loss is probably not complete. That is, some level of backups will be available. The question regards how much data loss you can afford. Therefore, based on how important you feel the information is, you can determine the financial effects. For example, if a file/print server for the marketing department loses a week's worth of data, it would take significant time and expense to recover the information. On the other hand, if your data warehouse loses information from the last periodic update, the data can be regenerated from the source systems (assuming time allows for the operation).

Developing a Budget

You now have an idea of what your information systems are worth to the organization. However, even with this information, developing a budget won't be easy. In many cases, a systems or network administrator will be asked to evaluate various backup solutions and provide the results to a manager for approval. For example, the cost of 12 tape drives, an autoloader, and enough media for a month might offer one level of protection and have a certain cost. Another solution might provide better protection, but the costs will be much higher. We'll examine all the parameters involved in choosing the right technology in Chapter 5. For now, keep in mind the tentative numbers you've calculated.

A Sample Business Requirements Worksheet

So far, we've gone over a lot of information related to determining business requirements. As mentioned at the beginning of this chapter, it is of critical importance that you define your business requirements before you look at the technical requirements of your solution. The purpose of this chapter is to help you think about what your data protection needs really are. Now it's time to bring a lot of this information together. Table 1-4 serves as a business requirements worksheet to help you summarize what you think your organization's data protection needs are.

Machine	Amount of Data	Backup Window	Acceptable Downtime	Acceptable Data Loss	Other Requirements
Server 1 (file/print services)	6.5GB	12 hours	1 day	1 day	General file/print server
Server 2 (file services)	17GB	6 hours	3 hours	4 hours	Engineering file server
SQL Server 1 (Sales OLTP)	6.0GB	12 hours	30 minutes	1 hour	Sales order entry
Shipping server	17.5GB	2 hours	5 minutes	None	Must remain online at all times; transactions cannot be lost

Table 1-4. Sample Data Protection Requirements Worksheet Based on Business Requirements

In addition to these requirements, you might also have a preliminary budget limit that can serve as a guideline for evaluating solutions. You should also begin thinking about personnel and the types of expertise you'll need available to implement a solution.

SUMMARY

In this chapter, we focused on how a business uses—and depends upon—its information. First, we considered the numerous reasons for protecting crucial data. Then, after speculating on how data protection might work in an ideal world, we identified reasons why our world isn't ideal. Specifically, time, technology, and other constraints prevent you from storing every piece of data on your systems forever. We examined the threats that lurk in the ever-changing world of computing—threats that are just waiting to annihilate your data. Recognizing these hazards, we began exploring how business systems are used to meet data protection goals in a less-than-ideal world. Then we addressed the real challenge: using all of this information to determine what data should be protected, how often it should be protected, and how it can best be recovered when necessary. This groundwork will be extremely useful for developing a data protection plan and choosing the appropriate equipment and solutions—tasks that we'll tackle in the following chapters.

CHAPTER 2

Developing the Data Protection Plan

In Chapter 1, we examined the business issues that you need to consider before you dive into implementing a data protection policy. These included the problems, challenges, and requirements associated with determining the business requirements for data protection. Now it's time to see how we can address those problems in a data protection plan. For the purpose of this discussion, we'll define a data protection plan as a culmination of the business requirements for your organization and an overview of the technical solutions you plan to implement.

This chapter provides a brief overview of the types of solutions we're going to discuss later in the book. The details aren't important for now; just pay attention to the best practices for implementing backup and recovery policies and procedures in your environment. The goal is to become familiar with the major tools and concepts related to backup and recovery. By the end of this chapter, you should have a good idea of exactly *how* you plan to protect your essential information. With these decisions in mind, it will be much easier to evaluate and implement the various methods that are available for performing backup and recovery operations.

Before we start looking at business and technical concerns, it's important first to establish a methodology for designing a plan that will provide adequate protection for your organization's data. Developing a suitable data protection plan involves the following steps. Figure 2-1 provides an illustration of the process.

1. Determine the business requirements.
2. Develop a data protection plan.
3. Evaluate technology solutions.
4. Implement and test the plan.
5. Refine the plan as necessary.

Note that planning for data protection is not a one-time operation but rather a constant process. That is, as business needs change and your environment grows, you'll need to revisit and update the data protection plan you create. Rest assured, though, that the process is not as tedious as it may at first sound. And, there's a good chance that you're doing a lot of this planning in your environment already.

We'll cover all of the steps in the development process in this book. Note that it's important to plan for backup and recovery operations together. Business requirements will place constraints on both operations. Furthermore, the details related to recovery requirements will affect backup requirements, and vice versa. We'll begin by looking at the various backup methodologies that are available. Then, we'll move on to an overview of the types of hardware and software solutions available. Next, we'll examine various policies and best practices that apply to data protection. Notice that many of these policies and practices are *not* technical. The old saying that an "ounce of prevention is worth a pound of cure" applies here, and taking the proper management steps to reduce the chances of data loss will definitely pay off in the long run. Finally, the last section of this chapter will bring all of these best practices together into a single example of a data pro-

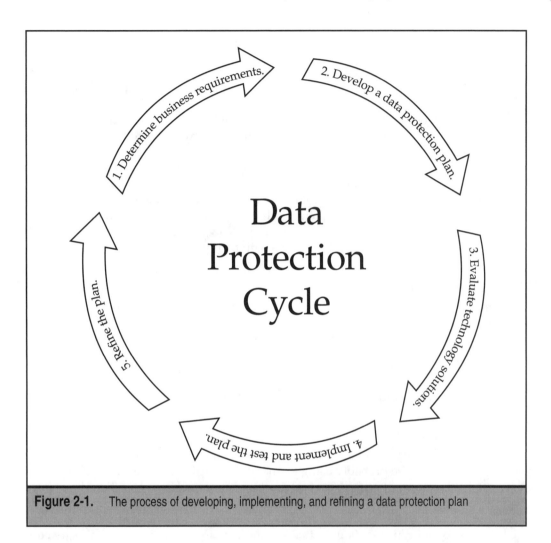

Figure 2-1. The process of developing, implementing, and refining a data protection plan

tection plan. This is something that I hope you can use as a starting point for implementing a data protection plan in your own environment. Now that we know the task ahead of us, let's get started!

DATA PROTECTION METHODOLOGIES

Before you dive into choosing the required hardware, software, and network devices required for protecting your information, you must decide *how* you plan to protect your information. There are various backup methodologies you can choose from when making these decisions. Let's start by looking at several techniques you might use to protect your information, along with the pros and cons of each.

In many cases, we'd like business requirements to lead to technical solutions. For example, if I need to be able to back up 40GB by the end of next year for a specific server, I will choose the hardware that allows this capacity of data. However, in some cases, the opposite will be required. For example, if the most cost-efficient tape backup device stores 20GB of data, and all I have is 10GB of information on the "Critical" backup list, I can now start choosing which items I'd like to protect from the less-critical list. This makes efficient use of the resources. On the other hand, if my budget only allows for purchasing half of the hardware and software I need, I will have to make compromises elsewhere.

Each type of backup solution is best for protecting specific types of information, but there's a good chance that you'll need to implement many of them in your environment. In Chapter 1, we looked at the different roles your servers and systems may play within your computing environment. We then classified them into groups based on how often (if at all) your information should be backed up. Now, it's time to look at the various methodologies you can use to achieve the backup plan you have selected.

Backup Scenarios

The first step in determining a good data protection plan is to decide how you are going to perform backups. There are several different ways to configure your systems to protect information. Here, we'll look at the most common methods—local and remote backups—and some less common methods that might give you some ideas for your own environment. Keep in mind that you can use several different backup scenarios in a single data protection plan and that you should always keep your business requirements in mind as you evaluate each of the following options.

Local Backups

Let's start with a simple backup scenario—local backups. If you back up files on your home computer, you're probably using a tape backup drive (or other removable media devices) that is physically attached to that machine. The idea is that you should regularly copy data from your "live" system (your hard disks) to a safer medium for storage. This is as efficient as you can get when only one or a few machines are available and you have to make copies of your information. In this situation, a tape backup drive is directly connected to the local machine via a parallel port, IDE, SCSI, or other interface:

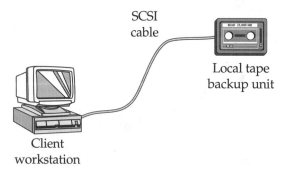

Users install tape backup software and then either perform backup operations on demand or schedule the operations to occur at regular intervals. Generally, backups occur relatively quickly since there is no network to pose a bottleneck. Additionally, backup devices can be purchased inexpensively based on the amount of information that must be protected. There are many different tools available to help in performing single-machine backups. If you're using any current version of Windows (Windows 95/98/ME, Windows NT 4.0, or Windows 2000), you already have a basic backup tool included in the operating system. Figure 2-2 shows the interface of the Windows 2000 Backup utility.

Performing local backups becomes less efficient when you have to manage several machines. First of all, purchasing separate tape backup devices for each of the computers can be expensive. Installing the devices can be a real exercise in patience. Other major problems are related to administering the solution. Each backup drive and software program must be configured and managed separately. Also, the usage of tape capacity may not be efficient—that is, some machines may have only a small amount of data to back up, while others might require several pieces of media to complete a single backup operation. Still, in a networked environment, you might want to choose a local backup system if you

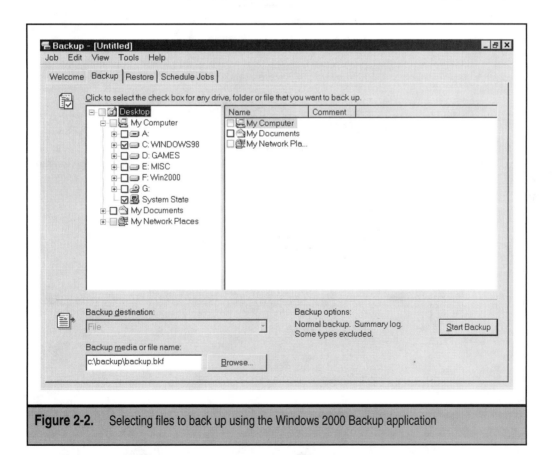

Figure 2-2.   Selecting files to back up using the Windows 2000 Backup application

have only a single server or a few servers and cannot afford to invest in larger, centralized storage systems.

Remote Backups

Perhaps the most common scenario for data protection in networked environments is that of performing data backups over the network. Remote backups are those in which information on one machine is protected by a backup solution on another machine. The other machine might be a dedicated backup server, or it could be a standard file/print server that is also responsible for backup functions (see Figure 2-3). Generally, data is transferred over the network. Based on your requirements, you might choose to back up client workstations or multiple servers from a single centralized backup server.

Here are some of the major benefits of remote backups:

▼ **Ease of administration** Since all management can be done on one or a few machines, systems administrators need only log on to one console to monitor

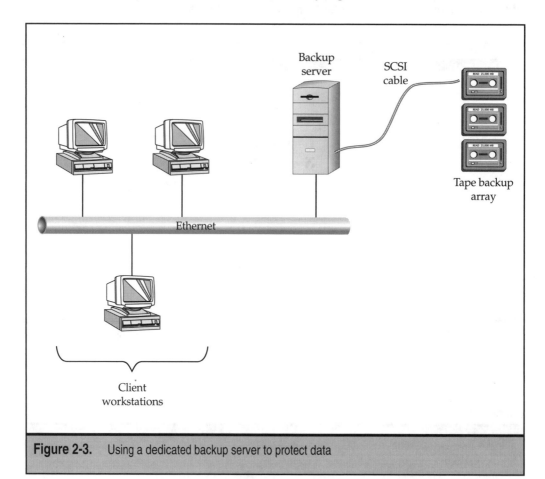

Figure 2-3. Using a dedicated backup server to protect data

operations. From this centralized management interface, administrators can specify which data should be backed up and when these backup operations should run. Additionally, backup media must be managed on only a few dedicated backup hardware devices. These are clearly huge advantages over the manageability of local backup solutions.

■ **Lower costs**   Having a few larger backup solutions can be less costly to purchase and implement than the many independent units required for local backups. By using a single common backup solution for several machines, administrators can ensure more efficient use of the full capacity of backup drives and media. When the time to upgrade arrives, new hardware can work alongside older devices to lower overall costs.

▲ **Transparent to users**   An important feature of performing remote backups is that end users are removed from the tedium of having to monitor their own backup operations. Cataloging and managing media is simplified and can be handled by trained IT staff instead of end users.

Disadvantages of performing remote backups include the load that is placed on the network. When backup operations are being performed, other users on the network may experience reduced performance. Perhaps more significant is the load that is placed on the backup server itself. Saving information to tape drives increases the disk I/O system processing load. Using a separate server that is dedicated to performing backups can alleviate some of these effects. However, backups are generally performed during off-peak hours. Furthermore, for fast backup solutions, the network can be a bottleneck. Overall, however, most organizations find that the benefits of centrally managing backups outweigh the potential performance impact.

When developing a backup plan, it's important to consider factors that relate to the manageability of your solution. Specifically, you'll want to know how much time and effort it will take to back up essential information for your organization. There are several important considerations, the most crucial being how best to administer the solutions and where the information should reside. Let's look at two major issues: administration and storage.

Centralized vs. Distributed Administration

The administration of a backup solution is, perhaps, one of the most important factors contributing to the success of a data protection plan. Making the plan too dependent on human intervention will likely cause problems in the long run. On the other hand, relying too much on automated processes can cause systems administrators to pay less attention than they should to these important operations. Additionally, the costs and tedium of managing such a solution will be quite high. When discussing the administration of backup solutions, there are two basic methodologies that might be employed:

▼ **Centralized administration**   In a centrally administered system, specific individuals (usually IT staff) are assigned the task of implementing, managing, and monitoring data protection solutions. Users may be responsible for storing information in specific directories or servers, but dedicated staff handles the majority of administration. From a technical standpoint, all of the data is stored on backup devices that reside in one area of the network.

▲ **Distributed administration**   Often, the data that needs to be protected falls outside the realm of a single network or building. In this scenario, an IT organization might choose to distribute data protection responsibilities to multiple individuals. For example, if a company has a branch office in New York and another in Boston, personnel might be assigned at each site to perform the backups. Additionally, each site would have its own backup hardware and software resources.

In many cases, centralizing the administration and management of data protection makes sense. In this way, all actions can be coordinated among the individuals and computers involved. However, this might not work well in other situations. If you have several branch offices that have systems support personnel and slow WAN links, it's probably better to perform backups at each site. Other business models lend themselves to decentralized (or distributed) administration. This is the case, for example, in companies where each business unit has its own IT department. The rationale behind this setup is that employees of those departments will better manage the specialized needs of each of those departments.

By now, you can probably see that there is no single "best choice" for all backup scenarios. The choices you make will largely be based on your company's business requirements. Let's look at another similar issue: data storage.

Centralized vs. Distributed Data Storage

When deciding where to store data, organizations must evaluate the relative costs of keeping data in a single location versus distributing it throughout the organization. The case for centralized data storage can easily be made for all of the resources that are stored within a single site connected by a high-speed network. This information can be accessed, managed, and backed up within a single central repository. Again, the benefits include reduced time and effort for administration.

Distributed data storage, on the other hand, is much more appropriate for environments where information resides on servers that are connected by slow network connections placed in branch offices. In this case, it is not practical to transfer user files and database information from remote sites, due to bandwidth restrictions. Larger companies will combine both strategies. For example, data will be stored centrally for all machines within the corporate office, whereas remote locations will be responsible for their own data protection.

Storage Area Networks

A newer concept in the realm of data management is the Storage Area Network (SAN). SAN technology segregates all data storage resources into a single area on the network. Information is managed within large data storage arrays, which are then accessed by all the servers in the environment. A SAN network generally consists of servers that are connected together through the use of Fibre Channel architecture, which can greatly increase performance. Figure 2-4 provides a graphic overview of a SAN topology.

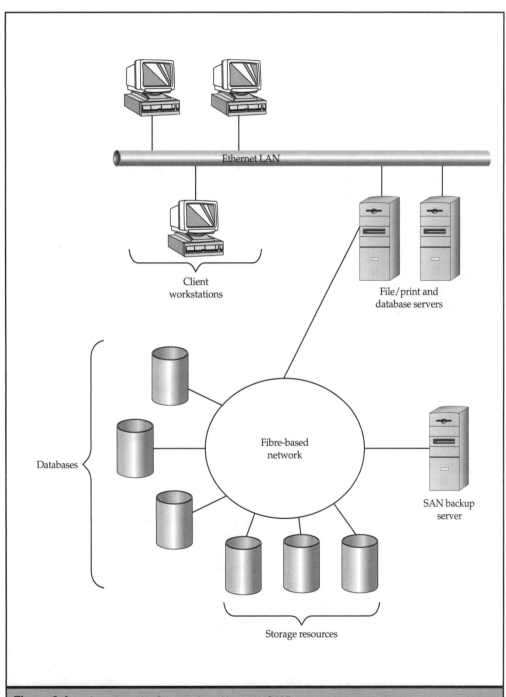

Figure 2-4.   Overview of a Storage Area Network (SAN)

The key difference between a SAN backup and standard server-based backups is that centralized servers are responsible for backing up all the information stored within the SAN. In this way, a SAN provides for easier management and for performance that can keep up with today's fastest backup hardware. This methodology also enables servers to focus on the tasks that they're designed to perform instead of on the storage of information.

The SAN methodology also avoids several problems related to resource usage. First, in a typical remote backup scenario, network bandwidth requirements for backups can be quite high. Backup servers compete for network resources with users of the system, thus causing potential bottlenecks and reduced performance. Establishing a baseline of network performance can be helpful in determining the relative requirements. The problem is even worse over slow WAN links. Second, SANs provide for centralized storage and administration. Instead of having to work with hundreds of servers located throughout an enterprise network, systems administrators can focus on controlling resources that are isolated from the rest of the environment. Finally, SANs bring the advantage of modularity and efficient disk space utilization. Any number of servers may be able to attach to a given storage resource. This can improve performance by allowing multiple database servers to access the same disk resources, for example—and disk space can be more efficiently utilized, because free space can be reallocated as business needs change.

SAN technology also has its drawbacks, however. Since the idea of SANs is relatively new in the marketplace, vendors must still do some work to make sure that products integrate properly and that standards are developed and upheld. Some questions regarding the actual performance benefits of using a SAN have also been raised. Is it really cost efficient to invest in implementing a SAN architecture when existing network resources are so cheap? Also, are Fibre Channel and other technical solutions mature enough to be practical today? For some organizations, the time, money, and effort will be justified. For others, however, more traditional data storage methods will persist, at least for the next several years, because it is too costly to upgrade a working infrastructure.

Outsourced Backups

Several third-party vendors offer backup services. Many of these operate over the Internet or a WAN connection. There are several benefits to this type of service. First, all backups are performed from a remote location. This fact alone means that your data is protected off-site. Second, the costs associated with implementing and managing your backups is offloaded to a company that specializes in such services. Finally, the hardware, software, and storage requirement costs are offloaded to another organization. Generally, if you need to restore information, you can send a request through the remote backup service provider's web site, and transfers are automatic.

The limitations of outsourcing include restrictions caused by the amount of available network bandwidth for performing backups. While backing up data over a modem might be fine for small numbers of data files, backing up a medium-sized server over the same link might take a prohibitively long time. Add in multiple servers and workstations, and you'll probably be pushing the limits of your Internet bandwidth. Even with much faster Internet links, performance can be unacceptable. For this reason, outsourced backups are currently recommended only to protect very important data files for home or business users who do not have other means of protecting their information.

Backup Operations

There are several different ways in which you can perform backups. Here, we'll provide an introduction to these ideas. In later chapters, we'll apply these concepts to working with a real data protection plan. Figure 2-5 compares the types of data stored in the various backup types. The major types of data backups include

▼   **Full backups**   All data on a machine is backed up and marked as backed up with this operation. Full backups are done periodically to make sure that all data resides on a single piece or set of media. These backups are the basis for

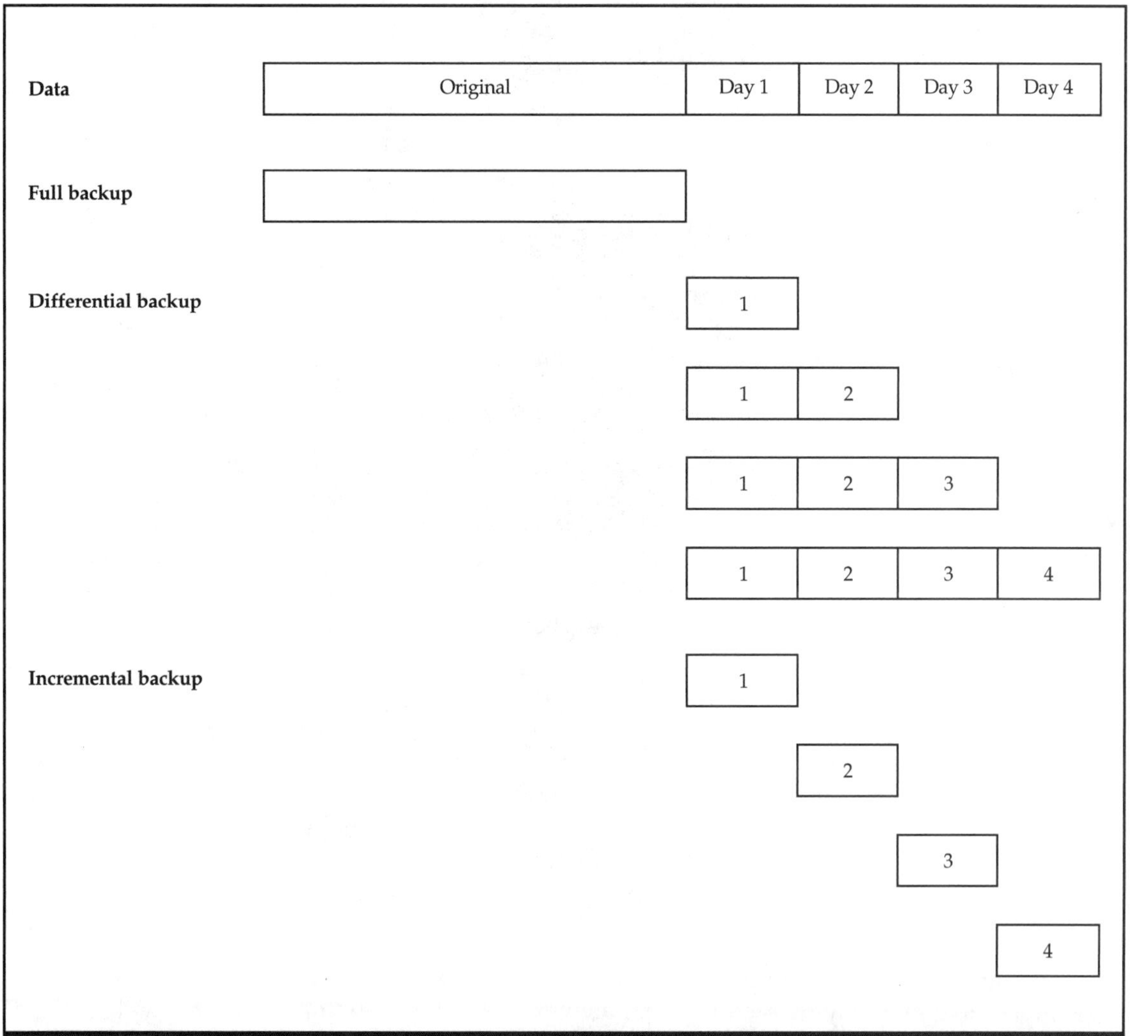

Data		Original	Day 1	Day 2	Day 3	Day 4
Full backup						
Differential backup			1			
			1	2		
			1	2	3	
			1	2	3	4
Incremental backup			1			
				2		
					3	
						4

Figure 2-5.   Comparing the data stored with full, differential, and incremental backup types

other types of backups (differential and incremental). If only full backups are implemented, only the full backup media is required to restore data.

- **Incremental backups**   An incremental backup stores all files that have changed since the last backup and marks them as backed up. The result is that incremental backups will store only information that has changed since the last full *or* incremental backup. When restoring with incremental backups, the last full backup and *all* incremental backup sets are required.

- **Differential backups**   A differential backup stores all files that have changed since the last backup, but it does not mark the data as having been backed up. The effect is that differential backups will store all information that has changed since the last full backup. When restoring differential backups, the full backup media and the latest differential media are needed.

NOTE: If you plan to include both differential and incremental backups in your data protection plan, be sure that you understand the various scenarios that exist for backup and restoration procedures. If the process is not well documented, it can cause confusion about the types of information stored, and can create unnecessary complexity during restoration.

- **Archive or copy backups**   Archival copies (or simply "copy" backups) back up all files on a system *without* marking them as backed up. This might be important if your data protection plan calls for a full backup to be taken off-site, independent of other backup operations. During recovery, only the archive or copy backup media is needed.

- **Daily backups**   Some backup systems allow administrators to generate a backup of only the files that have been changed on a certain day. This might be useful, for example, if backups do not occur on a fixed schedule and files should be archived by day. A daily backup does not need to rely on whether the files have been marked as backed up or not; instead it uses the date/timestamp of when the file was last modified to determine whether the file should be stored.

- **Database backups**   When you are dealing with database backups, several other factors must be considered. Relational database management systems (RDBMSs), such as SQL Server, have transaction logs and typically use large files that must remain internally consistent. The overall concepts are the same—backups can store either all information or just changes. However, the details are quite different—databases require many different mechanisms to ensure that data is consistent to a specific point in time. We'll look at the details in later chapters.

In choosing the types of backup operations to use, you must have a good understanding of the nature of the data you are protecting. For example, how much information changes per day? Based on the capacity of the backup solution, how often will tape changes be required? We'll put these items into perspective later in this chapter when we evaluate our information systems.

Choosing the Right Method

So far, we've looked at several different methods of performing backups. Chances are good that more than one will apply to your environment. For example, developers' workstations that contain large amounts of information might need to be backed up using local backup solutions, whereas a server farm would be a better scenario for a centralized solution. In many cases, the pros and cons of the potential solutions will make the decision obvious. In other cases, however, the scenario you choose will be based on time, administration, and technical constraints. With this in mind, let's move on to look at an overview of the technology available for accomplishing these tasks.

BACKUP AND RECOVERY TECHNOLOGY

Thus far, we've looked at some of the different ways data can be protected at a management level. Now, it's time to discuss the issues associated with real-world hardware and software options. Evaluating data protection hardware and software solutions can be quite confusing. We won't be going into much technical detail in this chapter, though. We'll limit ourselves to the depth of information that is necessary to form a good data protection plan and leave the details to Chapter 5.

Hardware Solutions

The central concept behind performing backups is to move information into less expensive, removable forms of storage. Economy and efficiency are the objectives behind this idea. Backup hardware comes in many shapes and forms. Traditionally, when systems administrators heard the phrase "backup and recovery," they thought "tape drives." Tape-based media has many advantages and can meet business requirements. Several years ago, when hard drives were relatively expensive, tape backup units offered large storage capacities and good performance. Of course, there are trade-offs: tape media usually is not randomly accessible. Thus, if you need to access a piece of data in the middle of a tape, you may spend a large percentage of your time simply finding the data. Consequently, running applications or accessing data files regularly from tape is prohibitively slow.

Nowadays, hard disk space is cheap, and buying an additional drive can often provide the level of data redundancy needed as an adequate (though very cumbersome) solution for client machines. The large amounts of data normally stored on the server side, however, still create the requirement for tape devices (which have evolved significantly in the last few years). These days, it's likely that more than one solution will fit an organization's data protection needs. The challenge has been reduced to making the best choice, instead of trying to find just *anything* that meets the goals. The details of the solutions will be based on the business's constraints and on technology.

So, how can you choose the *best* hardware solution for backups? We'll cover the specifics of various hardware solutions in Chapter 5. For now, know that the following issues will affect your data protection plan:

▼ **Backup capacity**   When shopping for backup hardware devices, you'll probably first look at the capacities of a potential solution. If you have about 20GB to back up, a very convenient choice will be a solution that can record this much information on a single piece of media. That way, you won't be stuck in the server room on a Friday evening, waiting to change tapes. Backup hardware vendors often assume that your data will compress to half its normal size (a 2:1 ratio). This might occur for some types of data, but in general it is an idealistic value, and you should use better estimates. We'll look at some recommendations in later chapters. For now, keep in mind that a major factor in your decision will be how much data can be stored on a single piece of media.

■ **Backup speed**   Removable media drives can only transfer data up to a maximum rate. Factors that affect performance include the data transfer bus (such as SCSI buses) and the physical characteristics of the drive and the media. Depending on the volume of data to be backed up and the amount of time available for doing it, backup speed will play a role in finding the right solution.

■ **Hardware reliability**   The investment you make in backup hardware can be significant—tape and other removable media solutions are not cheap! Almost all physical devices (especially those with moving parts) will fail at some point. It's important to consider how long the solution you have selected will last. Having tape devices fail can be quite costly, since you will need to obtain a replacement immediately, and backups may be skipped. Vendors often cite statistics based on mean time between failures (MTBF). Use this as a guideline to determine the longevity and reliability of your solution.

▲ **Shelf life of media**   The media used in removable storage drives has a finite life span. That is, tapes and other forms of media will eventually degrade to the point where data recovery is no longer possible. Although this might not be an issue for weekly backups, it's important when organizations attempt to store archived information for years. Generally, backup media is expected to last decades, but shelf life is affected by usage and environmental storage conditions. This is usually long enough for allowing systems administrators to find another solution—such as transferring all historical information to newer backup devices with larger capacities and more reliable media.

Again, we'll cover the details of these solutions in later chapters. The goal here is to give you an idea of the technical constraints that will affect your data protection plan.

Software Solutions

The real interface between systems administrators and their backup hardware is the software solution used. Within the backup tools and utilities, users can set up what should be backed up, to which media, and how often. A good example is the Backup utility included in all current versions of Windows operating systems. Additionally, more complex operations, such as performing backups of remote servers and workstations, can be managed. Backup software must also be able to handle special types of operations. In later chapters, we'll see how third-party programs include options for backing up items such as Microsoft SQL Server databases while they are in use. Overall, these tools help you manage the complexities of dealing with security and distributed data stored on heterogeneous client and server types.

Disaster Recovery

Part of the purpose of planning for data protection is to shield your data against the worst-case scenario. What situation might this be? For the sake of our discussion, let's assume that a comet speeds through millions of miles of space and lands right in the middle of your data center, thereby wiping out your entire site. This might sound like the plot for a popular (though not necessarily original) movie, but it helps to illustrate the point. All of your hardware, software, and data would be completely eliminated.

When planning for disasters, you can take nothing for granted. Assumptions about the availability of adequate backups, power supplies, or even building infrastructure will not apply. One way to prepare for such an occurrence is to have a secondary site available. This is most important if your business must continue operations even in the face of a natural disaster. Such is the case for public utilities, certain government agencies, and other companies whose proper operations are very important to the public at large. Creating a Disaster Recovery Plan (DRP) or Business Continuity Plan (BCP) can be a time-consuming task. Fortunately, help is available from several resources and organizations:

- ▼ **Binomial**   www.binomial.com
- ■ **Disaster Recovery Journal**   www.drj.com
- ■ **Federal Emergency Management Agency**   www.fema.gov
- ■ **Rothstein Catalog on Disaster Recovery**   www.rothstein.com
- ▲ **Survive**   www.survive.com

It is beyond the scope of this book to cover the details associated with planning for disaster recovery, but be aware that this should not be overlooked in a complete data protection plan. In order to successfully implement a disaster recovery plan—a potentially expensive undertaking—you must first have complete buy-in from your organization's upper management. Note that disaster recovery planning goes far beyond the realm of the IT department.

BUSINESS AND MANAGEMENT SOLUTIONS

If you ask systems or network administrators what is required to solve data protection problems in their own environments, you'll likely get answers that mention redundancy, fault tolerance for hardware and software, and backup hardware and software. These are good answers, but they focus only on the technical side of things. Often, the real challenge of creating a data protection plan is coordinating this effort with all areas of your company. In Chapter 1, we covered the importance of defining why we are protecting information. A complete data protection plan takes into account both the management and people side and the technical issues involved with performing backups. In this part of the chapter, we'll look at some best practices for performing data protection on the management side.

Management Solutions

Technology has its limits. Hardware, software, and networks can only go so far in changing people's minds. That's where human intervention is required. Sometimes, good planning and procedures are all it takes to prevent data loss. Here are some procedures that will help you implement a successful data protection program:

▼ **End-user education** If users understand your information system, including its limitations, they'll be able to help protect that information. For example, if they know that your backup policies don't include backing up their local machines (and they understand the differences), they'll be much more likely to store their information on designated server shares.

■ **Proactive management** It's often *much* easier to protect against data loss than it is to replace information that is lost. All too often, we wait until an accident happens before we do anything to take care of it. I have seen many backup solutions become priorities *after* data has been lost, whereas addressing this potential issue earlier would have saved a lot of time and headaches. Management and users must realize the importance of a proactive program.

■ **Management buy-in** In many businesses, IT is seen as a *cost center*. By this, people usually mean that their IT organizations don't generate revenue. However, IT is critical in supporting those users who do generate revenue and, if used properly, can be a great investment for businesses of any size. Every user in your organization needs to understand the importance of data protection. Many companies are now realizing that their IT departments can give them a competitive advantage and can help in making strategic business decisions. This realization can help enhance both the perception of IT and the value of data protection within the company.

- ■ **The right tools**   Having the right tools can really help in making sure that bad things don't happen to your resources. For example, the prefailure notification components available in newer server hardware solutions can help you detect a problem before something goes wrong (and takes your precious data with it). I'm hoping that the ideas included in this book will also help. Keep in mind that your tools don't have to be technical by nature; however, knowing what's available will help you make informed decisions as you design your own data protection plan.

- ▲ **The right people**   Regardless of the tools and technologies you use, you'll need people who can make sure the tools are used properly. Sometimes, all it takes is a single individual who truly understands the business and technical issues associated with developing a data protection plan. A discussion of how to find and keep dedicated and competent personnel would take more space than is available in this book, but keep in mind that realizing the value of people in forming a data protection plan is key to its success.

Getting Help: Outsourcing

If you are short any of the resources mentioned earlier, chances are good that you'll need to get more help. Fortunately, many organizations specialize in providing this type of help. For example, if you need assistance in developing best practices for implementing your data protection plan, you can hire a consultant to evaluate your current environment and make recommendations. Or, if you just need people to handle the day-to-day operations of maintaining backup media, you can hire contractors. Earlier, we also mentioned the availability of Internet backups. These organizations can assume the responsibility for all of the tedious work—managing media, scalability, and uptime.

When used properly, outsourcing can help a business focus on what it does best and leave other jobs to the experts. However, in the short term, outsourcing fees might seem very high. Nevertheless, with third parties as ever-present options, "not having enough time" is not a good excuse for not protecting information. In such a case, more time and personnel resources may be required, or the standards and requirements for data protection must be lowered (and documented). Note also that outsourcing will not automatically solve your problems. In order for an outsourced arrangement to be successful, managers and technical staff must take the time to ensure that operations are being carried out properly and that these actions are in line with business requirements.

Organizing Backups and Media

It is important to have an organized cataloging system for specifying the information stored on tapes. Be sure to keep log files regarding backup failures or any files that are not backed up. Cataloging and organizing backup media may seem fairly simple at first, but there are many reasons to come up with a good system initially. First, if only a date is used on backup tapes, you may be unsure whether the media contains full backups or only incremental backups. Also, to perform a restoration, you'll need to find all necessary tapes. If a set of tape numbers is used, the contents must be described in detail elsewhere. Here is an example of a tape-labeling scheme:

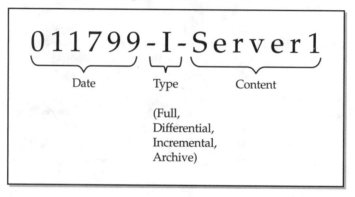

A good cataloging system will do the following:

▼ Allow for tapes to be reused (if this is in accordance with the backup policy)

■ Specify when tapes will be transferred off-site

■ Describe the type of backup (full, incremental, differential, or archive)

▲ Clearly indicate the contents of all backup media

Alternatively, you may choose to use a sequential logging scheme, in which all tapes are numbered (or otherwise uniquely identified) and a separate log is kept describing their contents. Either way, it's important that you keep operations organized. Regular testing of your backup and restoration procedures will help you refine your media organization scheme.

Developing IT Policies

A clearly defined set of policies for information technology resource usage can go a long way toward telling users what to expect. This works in both directions. First, it is very important to communicate to users what is expected from them. Information outlining disk quotas, server storage areas, and Internet usage policies should be provided. However, the second part of this equation—the part that is often overlooked—is to notify users regarding what to expect from IT staff. No one likes to be told what to do, so it is important to involve users and managers from other departments, as well as systems, database, and network administrators. Good policies will answer the following questions:

▼ What is the best way to report a problem to or request a change from IT?

■ How/when will IT inform me if network services will be unavailable for a specific amount of time?

- How will IT deal with unplanned downtime?

- Is my server-based data being backed up regularly? May I request that my local workstation be backed up?

- What is the expected turnaround of a help desk ticket on an issue I call in? How are calls prioritized?

- How can I check the status of an overdue request?

- What are the support boundaries for the IT department? In addition to troubleshooting and systems management, decide whether help desk staff should be responsible for teaching users how to use applications.

- How long will typical calls take to address?

- Which types of issues take priority over others? It's good to have a set priority for expected events, such as moves, additions, and changes, and a separate plan for troubleshooting problems that prevent multiple users from working.

- ▲ How can a user check on the status of a help request? If the request is not fulfilled on time, with whom can the user talk?

Addressing these issues in advance not only states the service level attempted by IT, but also sets concrete goals for IT personnel. Many organizations have found that providing help desk personnel with daily and weekly statistics helps keep the group focused, motivated, and goal oriented. It also offers management the feedback required to judge performance of IT staffers during regular reviews.

Publicizing Your Policies

There are many ways to make your corporate policies known. Some organizations include this information with the typical human resources paperwork that employees must complete before joining a company. It is important that users are aware of the very real dangers of losing data. Remind users periodically that losing all the information on their hard drives could cause a lot of unnecessary work.

Once you come up with your backup strategy, it's important to make sure that all who are affected by it are aware of the limitations. Users should know, for example, whether their local workstations are being backed up. If so, they should know how often this might occur. If not, they should be given proper procedures. Users should be made aware that protecting information is everyone's responsibility. Just as they would lock filing cabinets containing sensitive information, they should be aware of several other policies:

- ▼ **Passwords should be memorized.** Users should not write their passwords on sticky notes and store them on their monitors or under their keyboards.

- **Passwords should not be easy to guess.** By far, the most common method of security in current networked environments involves usernames and passwords. If not properly instructed otherwise, users will often choose passwords that are easy to guess. If I were trying to guess a password, I would start by using personal names—the names of family members or pets. Password-cracking utilities do the same thing, using dictionary-based algorithms.

▲ **Proprietary data belongs to the company.**   Users should be made aware that information stored on company resources is the property of the organization, not the individual who created it. Based on this, IT departments have the right to manage the information as they see fit.

There are many ways to publicize policies. Perhaps the most traditional (and potentially inefficient) is the standard method of handing out procedure handbooks to employees. There are probably better ways, though. Posting information on the company's intranet and sending occasional reminders to users can also be very helpful, as long as the information is maintained and revised as necessary. Better yet, if time permits, hands-on classes that end with users signing acknowledgment sheets can ensure that the information is conveyed effectively.

Keeping Users Informed

For many users, the functions and responsibilities of IT are enigmatic. Typical workstation users are not interested in the routers and servers that must be working in order for them to do their jobs. That's one reason IT-related problems can be so frustrating. By keeping users informed, you can avoid surprises and prevent many calls to the help desk. You will also give those who are affected by IT's actions time to make alternate plans. These simple practices can improve your users' customer service experiences and thus help improve their perception of your IT department. When problems occur, our reflex is to correct it. Often, we hope that nobody is adversely affected, and handle any issues through the help desk. While this is certainly one approach, it is much better to notify users of unplanned downtime after it occurs and to keep them informed of any issues related to incomplete backups. By doing this, you can avoid having to make excuses later.

The People Factor

Managing security and user permissions can often be a touchy subject for all involved. Employees may feel that they are not trusted if you limit their user access permissions. Explaining the real reasons for limiting permissions—protecting accidental or malicious data loss—can sometimes be the cure. However, there will still be political barriers. Creating new user accounts and changing passwords are permissions given to administrators by default, and administrators will undoubtedly create test accounts that may have weak passwords. Restricting permissions to only those who are needed to complete job functions can help prevent sloppy security implementations.

Educating the End Users

In many network environments, the knowledge of a simple password can circumvent any level of security. Perhaps one of the most important security measures an administrator can take is to educate users about potential security risks. Tell users never to share their passwords with other users, and inform them that IT staff will never ask them for this information, because an administrator can always change their password, if needed. A good way to enforce this policy is to recommend that they choose an embarrassing or very personal password. Finally, to keep users from sticking scraps of paper to the bottoms of their keyboards, notify them that they will be held responsible if another user accesses their account without permission, unless adequate security measures are taken. Also, make sure that users have a basic understanding of the Windows NT File System (NTFS) permissions—file and directory permissions may change if these objects are moved or copied to different locations. (For technical details, see Chapter 3.)

In many ways, maintaining a secure environment depends more on personnel and policy issues than on technology. Suppose an administrative assistant or other user accidentally deletes a file, or makes unwelcome changes to it. Compare that possibility with the risk that an outsider will attack your system and attempt to corrupt or destroy your data. Although everyday data crises don't get as much media attention as hacker attacks, the potential for mishaps during routine business use is an important reason for establishing a good security and data protection policy. Data entry clerks, for example, should generally not have the permissions needed to drop a table into a database, regardless of whether or not they know how to do it.

Users should be aware of the following recommendations:

▼   **Lock workstations when they're unattended.**   This will prevent anyone from walking up to a user's computer and casually viewing onscreen information (or using the user's permissions). To lock a Windows NT/2000 computer, a user can press CTRL-ALT-DELETE and click Lock Workstation. Unfortunately, Windows 95/98 offers very little security for the local machine. Under these systems, users should not store sensitive information on their hard drives; instead, they should save it on secure server shares, where it will be far more difficult to access.

■   **Comply with password policies.**   Users should understand that they will never be asked for password information from *anyone*. This includes their direct managers, IT staff, and other personnel. In the event that someone legitimately needs access to another user's information, IT administrators can reset passwords or change permissions as necessary. Furthermore, users should not share passwords under any circumstance. If two or more people routinely access the same user account, you won't know for certain which user is performing which actions. Users should be strongly discouraged from ever revealing their passwords to others. Finally, for additional security, passwords should be changed regularly to prevent hacked passwords from being used without detection.

▲   **Manage saved passwords.**   Cached passwords can present several potential security problems. Passwords can be cached for many different functions that require them. For example, when mapping to a network share, users can choose to save their password. Additionally, some web browsers (such as Internet Explorer 5) can save username and password information used to access web sites. All of this information will be readily accessible to any user who has physical access to a client machine.

These simple, practical security measures make it much easier for IT to focus on its own tasks—performing backup and recovery operations and implementing new technology for business purposes.

It's important that users understand their responsibilities in the backup process. For example, if someone accidentally overwrites a Microsoft Word document and does not realize it until 30 days later, should this be considered an IT issue? Some would say that the user is responsible for properly protecting his or her data, and that calling in IT to restore the file would be more costly than re-creating the document from scratch. In a case like this, you could place the burden of the decision on the user (or the user's manager).

In an upcoming section, we'll cover the use of *chargebacks*: in a chargeback system, IT organizations pass costs back to the departments that use their services. In many organizations, managers are responsible for requesting and processing all recovery operations. With this level of approval, IT does not have to worry about political and management issues, and can focus on the real technical tasks at hand.

Managing Costs

If you're pitching a data protection plan to company management, you should try to look at things from management's perspective. It's important to be able to justify the costs that will be incurred in this process and their potential paybacks. In the case of a data protection plan, this can be a hard sell. Protecting data, in itself, will not increase revenues or improve business processes. In fact, it will *cost* money and expend time. Essentially, what you are selling is an insurance policy to your upper-level managers, and anyone who has ever sold insurance can tell you how challenging it is to convince the customer of its value and necessity. Evaluating costs for a backup solution can be quite challenging due to the nature of the operations. Guessing how much the loss of data might cost is no easier. Essentially, you're protecting against something that might *never* happen. When it comes to looking at a return on investment (ROI), the only way a backup solution can pay for itself is if significant data loss actually does occur.

However, there are ways to justify the costs of implementing a sound data protection plan. Managing costs will likely involve working with others in the organization and distributing expenses to those who are really "purchasing" the insurance policy. Let's look at some ways in which you might do this.

Sharing the Burden

The costs related to protecting information can be very high in some cases. Some organizations will show that all of these costs are associated with IT. However, IT departments themselves are, for the most part, protecting information for others. By making IT the focal point of these expensive procedures, it might seem that the IT department is a bigger cost center than it really is. When you must ask management for further funding to implement backup and recovery procedures, the expenses can be difficult to justify.

It's important to distribute the costs of performing backups across the departments for which they are performed. This makes it much easier for department managers to choose what information really must be backed up. When asked about which information is most important, a typical response is likely to be "It's all important and must be backed up." However, after realizing the costs associated with the backups, expectations and "requirements" become much more realistic. To cover the costs associated with performing backups and recovering data as needed, IT departments may choose to implement a chargeback scheme. In this method, departments are billed for the IT resources they use. For example, an IT department might develop costs based on the use of resources that are typically shared throughout the organization. This system is shown in Table 2-1.

Service/Resource	Cost	Notes
Move/add/change request	$45.00/hour	Includes cost of setting up a new user (hardware, software, and network).
Memory upgrade	$25.00/machine	Does not include price of memory.
End-user training	$35.00/hour	Covers training of users on operating system and basic application usage.
Disk space	$.05/MB/day	Based on storage used by department members.
Database servers	Various rates based on application	The total annual cost of maintaining a database server will be divided among the users of the system and will be based on the level of data protection that is required.

Table 2-1.   Sample Data Protection Chargebacks

Though at first it might seem a little strange to treat your own users as customers of a service, these charges can help all users and departments realize the value of your services. It can also help reduce costs, because this will be in everyone's best interest. For example, if one-on-one end-user training from the help desk is considerably more expensive than sending a group of users to a class, departments will choose the latter as the better solution (unless other business reasons prevent it).

Some companies have taken this even further by requiring their internal support and services departments to compete with outside hardware, software, and service vendors. It's an important concept, since it forces internal departments to stay focused and competitive. If they are unable to perform as good a service as outside organizations, perhaps they should not be in "business" at all.

Overall, these creative ways of distributing the costs associated with IT departments can help better conserve, manage, and distribute these resources within the company. They also show how the costs and tasks related to data protection affect the entire company, not just the IT department.

Service Level Agreements

A fundamental rule of good customer service is to "under-promise and over-deliver." A similar rule in business is "If you can't measure it, you can't manage it." Combining these words of wisdom, we can see the value of creating service level agreements (SLAs) that establish policies and performance levels that IT will attempt to deliver. An SLA provides a goal for the level of support end users will receive from their IT organization. An example might be that typical "move/add/change" requests are taken care of within 24 hours. The idea behind the SLA is that users should be given accurate expectations on problem resolutions. SLAs can help enforce compliance with other IT policies. For example, all assistance with tested and supported applications may receive priority and a four-hour response time. Help with unsupported applications will be provided as quickly as possible, but with no guarantee on a turnaround time.

SLAs also give IT management an easier way to discuss issues with other departments. For example, if accounting managers feel that a three-hour problem resolution time is unacceptable, they may be willing to pay for additional staff to reduce the time. Even if they choose not to do this, the support level will be seen as a cooperative choice made between the departments, not as one arbitrarily defined by IT. Although the very nature of some types of IT support is to solve problems after they occur, users can have a very positive experience when they know what to expect.

GENERAL IT BEST PRACTICES

In the previous sections, we covered ways in which you can use business and management strategies to improve your data protection measures. There are several best practices you can employ in IT departments that can result in a more secure environment and protect sensitive company information. Many of the best practices will seem obvious.

Who would argue that taping passwords to your monitor is not a security problem? However, the real challenge is in developing, documenting, and enforcing policies that prevent this frivolous but potentially serious security breach. In this section, we'll look at some best practices for managing IT issues related to data protection.

Determining Security Requirements

Implementing security will use time and resources. As with any investment, you should first consider your goal. For example, if a group of users is to perform basic data entry of customer information, it may be appropriate to simply set default permissions for all users. Since their job functions do not require further access, the biggest problem to worry about is incorrect data entry. However, if sensitive financial information is being stored, it is important that each user be given appropriate access only to the files he or she requires in order to perform the job. It is also a good idea to enforce some level of accountability for all users. Finally, assess the impact on convenience this policy will have. If the security policy makes it difficult for employees to perform their jobs, it may not be worth it.

In many ways, security risks are overstated. Often, popular technical media will "expose" some shortcoming in a networking protocol and thus give the impression that no computer is safe. A common example is a legitimate warning about a virus that will affect very few (if any) systems. It's important not to underestimate what people may do. For this reason, it's best to consider what is possible instead of what is probable. Many organizations keep controls in human resources departments for handling salary information. However, they overlook the fact that a junior database administrator may have unrestricted access to this information. Clearly, both a management and a technical solution are required to prevent problems.

Security vs. Usability

If you really wanted to secure your server, you'd probably bury it in six feet of concrete and make sure that a network cable gets nowhere near it. Then, even the best hackers won't be able to get to it (unless, perhaps, they do part-time masonry work). However, this causes another problem: no one who *should* be able to get information from the machine can do so. On the other end of the spectrum, you could forget security entirely. The most usable system design is probably one in which all data resides in an organized collection that is accessible to all users.

Preventing unauthorized access to data will always include a trade-off between security and convenience. If policies are too strict, legitimate users (the majority of people in your company) will find it difficult to get their jobs done. With this in mind, the main goal of security should be to give users only the appropriate permissions for performing business-related tasks.

So, what is the problem with having a very secure system? Well, if policies are considered too restrictive, users will find a way to circumvent them. For example, an administrative assistant may choose never to log out of his machine at night so that all of the login information is stored. This causes other security problems, however, since any user could simply walk up to the machine and gain the same access. In some cases, technology might be the cure. Several products are available for synchronizing passwords between disparate systems. A major design goal for the Windows NT and Windows 2000 operating systems was to support the use of a single sign-on. However, in working with other systems, it's not quite that easy. Decreasing productivity and encouraging users to find security holes are real problems that must be faced. Keep in mind that these are authorized users who are trying to do their jobs.

I once did some consulting work for an organization whose IT support was almost nonexistent. In talking with users, however, I found that their systems were configured quite well for what they were doing, and I asked who was responsible for managing the systems. When they responded that they all took care of their own machines, I checked the security permissions and found that all of the users were members of the Administrators group and that any user (including the Guest account) had permissions on all files. Certainly, this is a very usable system, but that is also its problem. In this case, large amounts of engineering data were stored on each of the machines. Unauthorized users will also find this type of setup quite usable, but for their own purposes.

Make Rules and Enforce Them

IT professionals often view security as a technical problem that has a technical solution. We provide firewalls, implement complex authentication mechanisms, and keep security databases updated. The best of these practices, however, will not protect your network from someone who finds a password taped to the side of a monitor or under a keyboard. Many security analysts agree that managing security is at least as dependent on policy as it is on technology. Let's look at some general policies.

▼ **Educate users.** The importance of securing network resources can hardly be overstated. Make sure your users realize that a password can give any network user access to their e-mail, applications, and locally stored data. The best data protection plans are useless if people aren't aware of them. Make users understand *why* they need to protect information. Just as human resources departments in larger organizations go to great lengths to teach employees about the importance of cultural diversity and intellectual property, IT departments need to teach employees that protecting the company's most valuable asset—information—should be placed high on the priority list.

■ **Hold end users responsible.** The ultimate responsibility for protecting passwords and other company resources lies in the hands of the users themselves. Be sure that employees are aware of this and know that it is up to them to protect company data.

■ **Give users only necessary permissions.** Just as you wouldn't grant Administrator access to a novice user, be sure that all personnel have permissions to view and modify only the information they require.

- **Review security permissions.**   It's easy for systems administrators to make slight mistakes that may give users inappropriate permissions. Be sure to review access to particularly sensitive information frequently, and make changes as necessary.

- **Assign only one user per account.**   Often, network environments use one Administrator account, and several people know the password. Even as a consultant, I am often greeted at the door with the Administrator password for a server.

- **Perform external security audits.**   External consultants can be called on to perform a security evaluation. This can help ensure that security settings are appropriate and that no single user has too much control over the system.

- ▲ **Enable auditing.**   Modern network operating systems allow you to make a note of every instance that specific resources are accessed. You can extend this to physical resources: take note of when servers and other computers are physically accessed and what changes are made. Reviewing the data collected is as important as recording the information.

Support Only What's Necessary

By default, network operating systems offer a wide range of features. Though these features are the reason for the success of the network OS platform, they can also cause security problems when you enable features you're not using. For example, if you don't need to use the FTP service, you should make sure that it is turned off. In the case that you do need to use it, however, you can still make configuration changes that will increase the security overall. On a network level, for example, you can disable protocols that are not being used. This can improve security by shutting down avenues of entry into your system. Generally, all that is required is knowledge of the specific systems in question. Some decisions will be obvious. For example, if you're not allowing Internet access to certain user workstations, they do not require use of TCP/IP. We already mentioned policies that might be implemented to prevent the sharing of passwords or other information.

Standardization

Systems administrators who work in heterogeneous environments can attest to the fact that it's much easier to manage several similar servers than it is to work with very different platforms. One of the basic steps in reducing environment complexity is the creation of standards. Standards are so important that we often take them for granted. In searching for a common item, such as a music CD, we can be sure that the same media will work in all of our CD players. Imagine how much more complex (and costly) this would be if there were several different sizes of compact discs!

Consistency is also important when you're considering your client hardware and software. IT departments should work toward creating approved hardware, software, and network buying lists. The enforcement policy could state that any items not on the list or specifically approved otherwise will not be supported by the IT department or will receive a lower priority. A policy might specify several choices for desktop systems, a standard notebook configuration, and a list of supported applications. Here are some of the benefits of standardization:

▼ **Providing better support to end users**   When IT and help desk staff can focus on working with similar applications and troubleshooting, they will quickly develop a knowledge base for handling specific problems. This information can be used to troubleshoot user problems quickly and efficiently.

■ **Reducing costs**   By having standardized platforms, you'll be able to swap parts and/or perform upgrades more efficiently. It may even be worthwhile to have a spare machine available to minimize downtime. Larger companies will be able to obtain preferred customer discounts from vendors. Support contracts may be better negotiated, and a technology refresh cycle might be easier to implement.

▲ **Making good purchasing decisions**   IT personnel are often more qualified than management to make decisions regarding which hardware and software will fit best into the environments they support. To verify claims made by zealous product vendors, you can compare different products and test their actual features for compatibility, performance, and value.

Regarding software, an approved application list should be developed and distributed. If users require additional software, they should contact IT first regarding an evaluation of the product. This allows an organization to keep track of licenses and list all the applications installed on users' systems. Problems such as software incompatibilities can be detected in a test lab environment without impacting critical business functions. If users do not go through this process, they should know that they will receive limited or no support from IT other than reinstalling their systems. Here are some recommendations:

▼ **Choose supported hardware.**   Although purchasing generic computers from a local store might be cheaper in the short run, the money you save might be spent several times over in management and support-related costs. Generally, larger manufacturers offer better support contracts and can be helpful in troubleshooting problems that may occur.

▲ **Manage client applications.**   Too many organizations allow their users to install any software whenever they want it. Tangible material is easy to track—if I sell you a car, it's yours and you can do whatever you want with it. Software, however, is a lot trickier. A single installation media can be used to install the software on thousands of computers. It's also important to manage software to ensure that your organization is in compliance with licensing restrictions. Adding to the confusion are complex licensing agreements and issues about whether software is licensed to an individual (a named user), a workstation, or a concurrent connection.

There are, of course, some trade-offs in adhering to standards. For example, computer CPUs could be made much faster than current Intel processors and clones if they were redesigned from the ground up. However, a major factor in the success of current and future Intel-based chips is that they must support previous CPU instructions. Intel's Pentium III processor, for example, allows you to run programs that were designed to run on the Intel 386 or later processors. Determining the proper items to standardize and making sound choices on which standards to support can help to drastically increase supportability and reduce the complexity of creating a working data protection plan.

Change and Configuration Management

With today's pace of business expansions, the only constant is change. Few networking environments are free from the problems associated with users installing applications at will on any machines. This not only causes license management and support headaches, but can also be counterproductive and costly. If your organization is not continually evolving, chances are good that it will fall behind its competitors. The main difference is how quickly and efficiently you can adapt to changes.

IT software, hardware, and network devices change frequently throughout the days and years of a company's operations. When people move out of a specific job function, they may take with them valuable information about a system. All of a sudden, "Jane's Server" has become "the web server," and no one has any idea how to administer it. Also, it is quite easy to forget any changes that were made on a specific piece of equipment, until problems crop up. To avoid these potential problems, it is extremely important that any and all changes be documented completely.

It may seem difficult to take the time to develop a change management procedure, but a simple sheet like the one shown in Table 2-2 may be sufficient.

Date	Action Performed	IT Staff
01/11/2001	Installed Windows 2000 Server with all default options plus Terminal Services in Remote Administration mode.	John Smith, Systems Administrator (ext. 1234)
01/15/2001	Implemented daily incremental and weekly full backups using Windows 2000 Backup.	Jane Doe, Network Operations Specialist (ext. 555)
03/17/2001	Installed network version of Microsoft Office 2000 for Developers group.	John Smith, Systems Administrator (ext. 1234)

Table 2-2.   A Basic Change Management Sheet

If you can get in the habit of doing this regularly, you'll realize that you have plenty of time to document most changes while waiting for application installations and server reboots. The information can be invaluable in troubleshooting problems and in keeping an accurate hardware and software inventory.

Knowledge Management

One of the most important assets your company has is its knowledge. Though employees may come and go, it is the responsibility of all business units to ensure that information is kept within the company and transferred onward. The IT organization can be instrumental in this procedure. Consider some of the information stored in very large databases managed throughout the company. Look for ways that this information could be better used. Could data from a sales-related database be useful to marketing department users for demographic information? The goal should be to make the information easily accessible and useful. Although a data protection plan might not include provisions for making data access easier for users, it should not increase complexity.

Controlling Resource Usage

Server and network resources can be very costly to purchase and maintain. Earlier in this chapter, we discussed the possibility of implementing departmental chargebacks. This mechanism allows those who use resources to pay for what they need. End users should be made aware that storing large downloaded files in their home directories is inappropriate and wastes space on servers. Ideally, IT could prepare a report of disk space usage by user account. In many cases, users may be unaware of the size of their e-mail files or download directories stored on the server. On the other hand, modern computers come with plenty of local storage space, and noncritical data can be stored on cheap desktop hard drives. If appropriate, make sure users understand that this information will not be regularly backed up.

Consolidating multiple servers into fewer, more powerful machines can help lower costs. Managing multiple machines that serve similar purposes can be quite demanding for IT personnel. Resources required include labor costs, backup and data management costs, and the hardware cost itself. Also, centralized management can increase efficiency and reduce the likelihood of configuration errors. The technical chapters of this book are devoted to solving such problems in detail.

CREATING THE DATA PROTECTION PLAN

So far, we've looked at a lot of best practices related to data protection in an environment. Again, we've stayed away from the technical part of the picture and focused on policies, procedures, and business methodologies. Once you have made decisions in those areas, it's time to bring them together into a coherent document. Creating a data protection plan will probably prove to be at least as challenging as implementing it. With that in mind, let's look at some good ways to go about assembling the necessary information. At the end of this chapter, we'll consider what a typical data protection plan might look like.

Studying Your Environment

It's important to understand what parameters will affect your backups. In Chapter 1, we examined the business requirements you need to consider. Here, we'll look at other factors:

▼ **User requirements**   Users throughout your environment will require various types of data to complete their tasks. Managers, for example, need to be able to generate up-to-date reports, while data entry personnel must have access to their database. These types of users will have different performance and usage requirements. It's important to recognize the reasons these systems are used to determine what level of data protection is required.

■ **Network issues**   In all but the smallest environments, chances are good that you'll be backing up systems remotely over the network. Having a good idea of when network utilization is highest will help you to determine *when* to perform bandwidth-intensive tasks, and having a good idea of the WAN topology will help you determine *how* to best protect information.

▲ **Performance and perception**   Do employees notice network access is slow during peak periods (such as in the morning, when many users are logging on to the system)? It's likely that your business systems will have uneven loads throughout the day. When are certain systems most active? Which systems must be available at all times? By determining the answers to these questions, you'll be able to form a data protection plan that provides for minimal impact to end users.

Based on your answers to the preceding questions, you'll have a good idea of what needs to be protected and how it should be done. Now, let's use this information in the development of policies and practices.

Defining Backup Policies

Before you implement a backup solution designed to protect an entire network, it is important to establish a set of policies and procedures. Unfortunately, it's often impractical to back up all the data on all the machines on your network. Fortunately, it is also often unnecessary. Unlike user data, you can easily restore operating system and program files by reinstalling from the original media. Here are some important questions to answer before you implement a backup solution:

▼ For how long after a file is modified will a user be able to request that the original be retrieved?

■ Which storage areas will be backed up? If only files stored on servers will be backed up, then users must be notified. If workstation files will be backed up, then users must be told exactly what data will be saved (all directories, or specific data directories only).

■ Do certain types of systems require special backup procedures? For example, mission-critical online transaction processing (OLTP) databases might require transaction log backups as often as several times per hour. Large databases might require the use of partial database backups due to the amount of data that must be stored.

▲ Can backups be done during normal business hours, or must they be performed when there is a reduced load on the network resources?

Based on your answers to the preceding questions, you can form an estimate of the amount of data you expect to back up. It's important to consider how long a typical backup and/or data restoration might take. A tape backup unit may meet your other requirements, but if a full backup takes ten hours, this might not be practical on a busy server. Recovery times are important, as well. Finally, and most importantly, this solution must fit into your IT budget. We'll find solutions that meet these criteria in Chapter 5. For now, though, keep these considerations in mind.

Using the Iterative Approach and Setting Milestones

If you're managing more than a few servers in your environment, you'll find it difficult to implement a new data protection plan for all of them. When dealing with a large task, it's often a good idea to break it into more manageable pieces. A series of smaller tasks has several benefits. First, small successes are psychologically encouraging. If you're not trying to fix all of your problems at once, you can focus on a few tasks and devote your full attention to them. Second, in prioritizing the milestones, be sure to get management input not only from the IT department, but also from the affected department heads.

In developing a data protection plan, the *iterative* approach involves establishing a baseline plan and then refining it over time. Table 2-3 shows an example of how a complex task—protecting data throughout a large organization—can be made more manageable. Notice that we start with a baseline (a minimal level of data protection) and then refine the process to make sure that systems are protected appropriately. Then, we focus on improving performance in areas where this can improve the users' experience. Finally, we choose to improve upon the data protection plan itself by measuring the effects of changes and feeding them back into the overall strategy.

If your environment has any level of data protection, you have probably already met some of the requirements. If that's the case, be sure to document which areas are already taken care of, so that this information is known. Based on this rollout plan, you can tell others what to expect.

Getting Others Involved

In many organizations, the IT department seems to be responsible for creating, implementing, and revising the data protection plan. On the surface, this makes sense. After all, who would better understand the technical issues associated with performing backups

Milestone	Task	Target Date	Percentage Complete
0	Analyze departmental requirements and form a data protection plan.	03/01/2001	100%
1	Verify that all business systems are receiving a minimal level of data protection.	03/17/2001	100%
2	Fully protect all marketing servers.	04/01/2001	100%
3	Fully protect all engineering servers.	05/15/2001	75%
4	Optimize OLTP backup performance for point-of-sale applications.	05/25/2001	25%
5	Evaluate effects of changes and refine the data protection plan based on user feedback.	06/15/2001	0%

Table 2-3.   Tasks and Milestones for the Implementation of a Data Protection Plan

than IT staff? However, as we saw in Chapter 1, the real challenge is in determining business requirements. Department heads and users are likely to understand their real requirements better than anyone else. Combined with the technical expertise of IT, they can come up with a good plan for data protection.

Once the basic requirements have been established, it's important to have the users who are affected review the basics of a plan. Surprising insight might be gained from this step. For example, a backup strategy based on full and differential backups might apply perfectly to the sales group. However, the engineering department might do full builds of all software on Wednesday nights (thus making a full backup more appropriate). Such information is rarely found in information from the IT department alone.

Archiving

Though we'd all like to keep our data online forever, this is often impractical. As mentioned earlier, large amounts of data can be unmanageable. The larger the haystack we have to search through, the less likely it is that we'll find that needle! Also, more online data will slow down business applications and servers, thus affecting the more common operations using current data. Again, when developing a data retention plan, IT and department managers must find the best solution based on costs and resources. A typical archival plan will include provisions for periodically taking data offline and placing it in another repository. It will also include processes for restoring and accessing this information as the need arises.

Documenting the Plan

The best data protection plan in the world is useless if no one knows or understands it. We have already talked about the benefits of educating end users on recommended data protection and security practices. The same is required for the IT staff who will be required to perform the types of operations required in your data protection plan. Documentation can include flowcharts for backup and recovery and should include schedules that clearly designate who should do what when. We'll see examples of this type of documentation in the section "A Sample Data Protection Plan," later in this chapter.

IMPLEMENTING THE DATA PROTECTION PLAN

Once you have a working plan developed, it's time to put it to use. In many cases, the execution will be at least as important as appropriate planning. In this section, we'll look at best practices for implementing the data protection plan that you've created. Factors to consider include who will be responsible for performing the necessary tasks and when and how they should be performed.

Training the Right People

It's important that individuals who are responsible for data protection understand their duties. In most organizations, *every* employee will fit this description. For example, clerical workers are probably responsible for locking filing cabinets that hold sensitive paper-based records. On the other end of the spectrum, executive officers must keep certain business strategies secret from competitors. When it comes to the technical aspects of performing the tasks associated with backup procedures, you should make sure that network, systems, and database administrators know their roles. In some cases, this will require additional training. Keep in mind that even minor miscommunications can cause major problems in the long run, potentially weakening your data protection plan.

Developing a Schedule

A schedule for performing certain tasks can be quite useful, because it clearly sets forth the tasks that must be performed. Table 2-4 shows a schedule that might be used in a typical IT department.

The use of workgroup and workflow applications can be very helpful in this area. For example, Microsoft Outlook forms can be used for notifying users of certain issues. Or, jobs can be created in SQL Server 7 to automatically notify operators of seldom-performed tasks (such as a quarterly backup log review).

Delegating Responsibility

When the time to recover lost information arrives, no one wants to hear "I thought *you* were supposed to be doing that!" To avoid a lack of communication, you should delegate specific roles and responsibilities to various individuals. For example, a specific systems administrator should be responsible for changing tapes in the autoloader, while another's duty is to make sure that tapes are taken off-site. A third person, the auditor,

Task	Frequency	Dates	Notes	IT Staff
Perform a test restoration.	Monthly	First Tuesday of each month	Every server backup should be tested at least once per quarter.	Jane Admin
Check media logs.	Weekly	Every Friday	Verify that no tapes are missing and that the appropriate tapes are available.	John Admin
Perform backup verifications.	Biweekly	First and third Monday of each month	Not needed where verification operations are automated.	John Admin

Table 2-4.   A Backup Operations Assignment Schedule

should verify that the tasks have been performed—and serve as a backup when special needs arise. Finally, everyone should record these actions in a log that is periodically reviewed by managers.

At first it might sound like a hassle to set up such a detailed system, but in practice, it's quite easy. The key is to make administrators realize that they're carrying out an important function, even if it is mundane and lacks glamour. To add some variety to the routine, you can also rotate roles among individuals. This provides the added benefit of cross-training people on others' jobs. I wish I could say I've worked in environments where people enjoyed performing backup duties, but most well-managed environments have people that don't mind it.

REVIEWING AND MAINTAINING THE PLAN

A good data protection plan will include provisions for performing a "checkup" on its own status. The plan is never really finalized, as we described when discussing the iterative approach. As the needs of the organization change and grow, so too should the plan itself. Few plans are ever perfect, and if you do reach that status with yours, chances are good that before you can celebrate for too long, the business requirements will change. There are several ways to ensure that your data protection plan is not outdated by the time you implement it. Keep these in mind as you review and maintain your data protection plan.

Ensuring That the Plan Is Flexible

When designing the plan, make sure it is flexible. Wherever possible, avoid posting hard numbers, because they are moving targets. For example, a backup plan from just a few years ago might have categorized machines supporting 400MB databases as "large database servers." That number has changed dramatically with the need for more information and greater reliance on data support systems. Additionally, network infrastructure changes regularly. Plans to protect Windows NT 4 servers will also need to change as upgrades are made to Windows 2000 Servers. Flexible plans use percentages and approximations to remain relevant even when changes to business requirements occur. Changing the data protection plan itself, of course, is not out of the question. But, it's much easier to make addendums and slight modifications to forward-looking policies.

Ensuring Physical Security

All the configuration options in the world cannot prevent someone from carrying your server out of the building if it's not physically secured. Also, most common functions on a Windows NT/2000 computer can be performed from a remote workstation. It's important that you control who has access to the different computers on your network. There are several ways to physically secure your servers. First, many organizations have security guards who control access to certain areas of their buildings. It is very important that these individuals know the company policy, for instance, on carrying large, expensive computer equipment in and out of the door. Second, physical access to the server room should be restricted. Pass-card security systems have become quite affordable, and they are easy to manage. Consider how these and similar measures might enhance your data protection plan.

What Would an Intruder Do?

Ancient wisdom tells us that it is wise to know the ways of one's enemies. A routine practice in some companies is to run the Windows NT security accounts database through a password-cracking utility. Any password that can be cracked using this brute-force method should be retired and the user instructed to choose a stronger one. Another tactic is to try accessing certain files and systems by impersonating a user who should not be able to do so. If your data protection plan fails any of these simple tests, it's probably time to make revisions.

CAUTION: Before you undertake any aggressive password-testing measures, be sure to seek permission from upper management—preferably in writing. Although walking through unlocked doors might seem harmless enough, you may be breaking company regulations by tinkering with people's passwords.

Establishing External Security Audits

Sometimes, the people who implement security and data protection are not the best people to test it. Usually, implementers will test only for the problems they have protected against and will not solve the potentially more dangerous problems that they are not aware of. The use of consultants or other outside individuals can be very useful here. Generally, external network security auditors will try to penetrate your network and operating system defenses (after obtaining your written permission). They will then document the security issues and, optionally, describe ways in which these hacks can be prevented. Regularly performing such audits can ensure that you have protected against at least the most common intrusion attempts.

A SAMPLE DATA PROTECTION PLAN

So far, we've covered business management best practices, IT recommendations, and the steps involved in creating a data protection plan. Many people like to learn by example; just ask developers how they feel about sample code! If you're one of these people, then this section is for you. The following is a sample data protection plan for a medium-sized business (although most of the policy information you see here will apply to businesses of any size). As you read through the sample plan, think about which elements may or may not apply in your own environment.

Data Protection Policy

The IT department is dedicated to protecting the company's intellectual property and vital business information, using the resources available for these tasks. This document will outline the Data Protection Policy, including details of the level of data protection that will be provided. All users and managers are encouraged to provide input regarding the details of this plan. Furthermore, this document will continually evolve as business needs change. The most recent copy of this document will always be available via the IT intranet. If you have any questions regarding the data protection plan, please call the IT help desk at extensions 0937. Note: It is the responsibility of all IT personnel to fully understand all of the procedures listed in this document.

To ensure the continued protection of crucial company data, and to accommodate the security needs of the organization, the following policies have been put in place:

▼ **Backup limitations**   Current backup plans are designed to protect only information that is stored on servers. Client workstations will not be backed up, as a general rule, unless otherwise arranged. All network users are encouraged to store information on their home drives (H for most users). This information is actually copied to a network server that will be backed up regularly.

■ **Backup frequency**   Backups of all information will be performed nightly, unless otherwise arranged. It is expected that all backup operations will begin at 12:00 midnight and will be complete by 5:00 A.M. Nightly backups will ensure that the maximum amount of data that may be lost is one day's worth.

▲ **Data retention**   Backups will be archived monthly, and monthly tapes will be retained for a period of five years, unless otherwise arranged.

IT Responsibilities

IT will be responsible for maintaining the security of various types of corporate information, as agreed upon by upper management at the December 12 Executive Meeting. Following are the staff members whose roles are designed to meet these goals, along with descriptions of their respective responsibilities:

▼ **Data Protection Implementer**   Add new workstations and servers to the existing backup solution as they are added to the network, and update the data protection plan as needed.

■ **Backup Operations Manager**   Make configuration changes to accommodate changing business requirements, verify that backups are being performed on schedule, and update the data protection plan as needed.

- ■ **Media Manager**   Switch media in devices when appropriate; label, catalog, and organize media.

- ■ **End-User Support Technician**   Assist users with general questions about backup and recovery issues and perform basic support.

- ■ **Backup Verification Engineer**   Periodically perform test recovery operations based on the schedule set forth in the data protection plan.

- ▲ **Data Recovery Engineer**   Perform recovery of information that is lost due to hardware failure, user error, or other problems, and record this information in the IT Chargeback Log.

Staff Assignments   The following individuals will be responsible for fulfilling the roles enumerated in the preceding section for January 2001. In the event that someone is unable to complete these tasks, he or she should notify the "Fall-Back Team Member," whose duty it will then become to finish the assigned tasks for that role.

Role	Staff Assignment	Fall-Back Team Member
Data Protection Implementer	Jason R.	Jane D.
Backup Operations Manager	Robert D.	Jason R.
Media Manager	Pedro M.	James K.
End-User Support Technician	James K.	Pedro M.
Backup Verification Engineer	Monica D.	Robert D.
Data Recovery Engineer	Jane D.	Monica D.

In order to provide all IT staff with the experience of working on all tasks, individual responsibilities will rotate on a predefined schedule.

The Request Process   The following flowchart documents the basic flow of a data protection request from when it is first called into the Help Desk through to resolution. All technicians should follow the appropriate procedures, based on the severity of the call and the individuals involved. The help desk staffer who receives the call will be responsible for "owning" the issue. Even if the call is to be resolved by another IT staffer, the individual who receives the call must ensure that the issue has been closed out. Please direct questions on this policy to any IT manager.

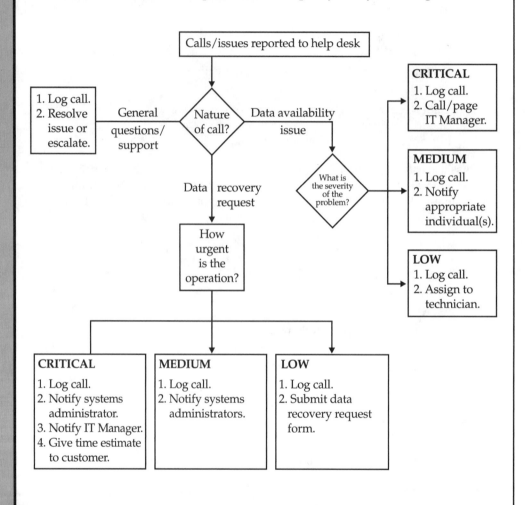

Management and User Responsibilities

Department managers are responsible for notifying the IT department of any moves, additions, or changes that might require changes to the data protection plan.

This includes the addition or removal of any workstation and additions or modifications to any servers not performed by IT department staff.

Data Recovery Requests   IT will make backed-up data available for a period of 30 days. The major purpose for performing data protection is to prevent against system failures (such as the malfunctioning of a hard disk) or natural disasters. IT realizes that there are many cases in which users will lose data that is not business critical, but still very important. Unfortunately, all of these restorations cannot be performed, due to limitations on time and resources.

To request a data restoration, end users should contact their managers. Managers should call the Help Desk at extension 5937 and explain the issue. If you have lost information due to reasons other than a hardware failure, you must obtain your manager's permission before requesting a recovery operation. Based on the importance of the information, your manager will assign one of the following priority levels to the recovery time:

▼   **Critical**   Restorations that affect more than five users and prevent them from working. These restorations will begin as soon as possible upon reporting of the problem and are expected to be complete within one hour.

■   **High Priority**   Restorations will be completed within four hours of the report of the problem.

■   **Medium Priority**   Restorations will be completed before the close of business on the same day if reported before 2:00 P.M. Otherwise, the restoration will be done before noon on the following day.

▲   **Low Priority**   All efforts will be made to recover lost information within 24 hours from the report of loss, but no guarantee is provided. It is recommended that all user files that are not business critical be submitted as Low Priority.

The chargeback costs associated with this operation will be based on how quickly the data must be restored. (See "Costs.") With this approval, please call the Help Desk at extension 5937 for more information on the turnaround time of your request.

General Support   For general questions and comments, or for support on issues not related to data protection, contact the Help Desk at extension 5937.

Data Protection Service Costs

Based on last year's information and statistics, the following costs are expected for service:

Maximum Backup Storage	Cost per MB per Month	Monthly Chargeback	Annual Chargeback
< 200MB	None	None	None
1GB	6¢	$60	$720
4GB	8¢	$320	$3,840
7GB	10¢	$700	$8,400
15GB	12¢	$1,800	$21,600
50GB	20¢	$10,000	$120,000
100GB	22¢	$22,000	$264,000
500GB	26¢	$130,000	$1,560,000

These are only estimates. As the costs of storage devices decrease, it is expected that the overall costs will remain the same or decrease slightly for this year. Incremental cost "steps" cover costs associated with autoloaders and specialized hardware for larger backup requirements.

Data Recovery Charges   The following charges will be incurred for data recovery operations that are not due to a systems failure:

Recovery Priority	Turnaround	Cost per Request
Critical	< 1 hour; $400	$400
High	2–4 hours	$125
Medium	Usually 6–12 hours	$75
Low	Usually < 24 hours	$25

Recovery requests must be submitted with a manager's approval and may be made by calling the Help Desk or by completing a form on the Help Desk intranet page.

Logs, Records, and Billing   IT will maintain on a chart a log of all the services performed for departments. The following is an example of the type of billing report that department managers will receive on the last day of each month:

Date	Action Performed	Cost Center	Cost
01/17/2001–02/17/2001	Backup: 7GB	ACC003	$700
06/05/2001	Recovery for Jane Doe (per Joe Manager): Medium Priority	MKT115	$75
08/01/2001	Restoration of Server1 Home Directories (hardware failure)	ENG001	no charge

Questions regarding billing may be directed to the IT Manager at ext. 1173.

SUMMARY

The goal of this chapter was to provide the knowledge base you'll need in order to put together a successful data protection plan. You should definitely consider the ideas presented here as you decide what features to include in the plan you devise for your own organization.

We started by looking at various backup scenarios and methodologies; chances are good that you're already using some of these ideas in one way or another. We then briefly surveyed the hardware and software available for performing backup and recovery operations. Next, we presented some practical considerations crucial to a sound data protection policy, and some management tools that can help you ensure your policy's success.

With all the business requirements and fundamental decisions now out of the way, we can focus on the more technical aspects of data protection. In the next chapter, we'll discuss how you can secure your Windows NT and Windows 2000 operating systems.

PART II

Understanding Data
Protection Technology

CHAPTER 3

Windows NT/2000 Security and Data Protection

A database server is only as secure as the operating system (OS) on which it is run. Even the strongest security measures for an installation of SQL Server can be compromised by sloppy network policies and settings. In this chapter, we'll look at some general best practices for securing the Windows NT and Windows 2000 machines in your environment and for implementing a solid data protection plan that takes advantage of various tools and techniques that you probably already have available.

Before we get into the technical details of dealing with security on the Windows NT/2000 operating systems, it's important to consider some basic concepts. Far too often, systems administrators start implementing security measures without considering exactly what it is they are protecting *against*. Before making any policy or setting changes, it's important that you answer a few questions regarding needs that are specific to your environment. In many cases, it's much too easy to create security policies without paying attention to what the policies really mean and how they'll affect your business environment. In this chapter, we'll look at some questions to answer before implementing a policy.

I strongly recommend that you read the "General IT Best Practices" section presented in Chapter 2, if you haven't done so already. That section outlines the security requirements and general steps that are vital to protecting your information. There are many ways in which technology can help protect information. Network operating systems, such as Windows NT and the Windows 2000 platform, provide many features that, when employed properly, can help prevent potential problems. In this chapter, we'll focus on the technical aspects of *how* you can implement some of these best practices. For example, we'll cover the ways you can use Windows NT and Windows 2000's security features in your environment.

However, covering all the features of Windows NT 4 and Windows 2000 operating systems is far beyond the scope of this book. For details, you may be referred to other resources. Always keep in mind that the online help resources included with these products are great places to start. Let's get started by looking at some best practices for managing security and data protection, and then we'll move on to the specifics of working in Windows-based network environments.

SECURITY AND DATA PROTECTION BEST PRACTICES

There are two major issues to consider when you're trying to increase security. The first is authentication, and the other is encryption. Authentication is designed to determine whether a user is who he or she claims to be. Encryption, on the other hand, prevents the usability of data in case the wrong people intercept it. Most forms of security measures use these two concepts to prevent the unauthorized use of information.

The Windows NT/2000 line of operating systems was designed with security as a major concern. For example, Windows NT Domain security allows for the creation of network accounts on secure servers. These are the only accounts that may be granted network access. To log on to resources located on any computer within a Windows NT Domain, the user must first have a domain account. And, with Windows 2000 and the Active Directory, the ability to control specific permissions and accessibility to data has become easier to manage.

Remember that users in the Administrators group have a great deal of power and flexibility. For example, they can add other users to the Administrators group and change the password of any existing account (and thus be able to use it for login purposes). In this part of the chapter, we'll cover some best practices that can be used in networked environments. Although most of this information will pertain to all network operating systems, our focus will be on Windows NT and Windows 2000.

> **NOTE:**   This chapter focuses on technical ways to protect information on Windows NT and Windows 2000 OS platforms. We won't cover Windows 95/98/ME security in depth, because these platforms have not been designed for security. As we'll see later in this chapter, the lack of a secure file system makes it difficult to protect information on Windows 95/98/ME.

Know the Ways of Your Enemies

Experienced network security analysts understand that it's wise to know how individuals may invade networks or perform unauthorized actions. When designing security policies, you should always think about where the gaps are. Also, it's tempting to implement "security through obscurity." For example, you might set up a server with an IP address that is unlisted in DNS and other name resolution services. The administrator may think that this server is fairly secure, because few people will know that the machine is there. However, there are several tools and tactics that hackers can use to find it:

▼   **Network analyzers**   Also called *sniffers*, these devices can monitor and intercept raw data packets that are traveling on your network. The contents of these packets may include password information (hopefully encrypted) and all data that is transferred between computers on the network.

■   **Password-breaking tools**   Tools that test files against a dictionary of common passwords can be used to attempt to break into accounts. As a systems administrator, it's a good idea to routinely use these tools on your own accounts database to identify user accounts with weak passwords. You can then notify users of these potential security problems and instruct them to choose better passwords. Password-breaking tests should be performed regularly to ensure that there are no "open doors" to your network.

■   **Impersonation**   Perhaps the best way to get a user's password is to call him or her and say that you're calling from the IT department and need their password to make changes to their e-mail account. Many users, without thinking twice, will simply provide the information, thinking that they're giving it to a credible person.

▲   **Exploiting known bugs**   Many hacks are performed after information on bugs or security flaws is discovered and publicized. Usually, there are patches or configuration work-arounds that can reduce the risk of these attacks. It's important for systems administrators to find out about the latest security breaches as soon as possible. Later in this chapter, we'll look at some good resources for keeping on top of security issues.

Physical Security

An often-overlooked area of security is that of protecting your critical business systems *physically*. Very little can be done if someone simply walks away with one of your servers or even a laptop that has sensitive business information stored on it. Of course, most businesses have security guards and locked rooms to protect against these actions. It is worth noting, however, that just as with any other security technique, you should maintain the maximum amount of security available without hindering usability. Usually, systems and network administrators will have access to server rooms and wiring closets. If possible, access to these areas should be logged, and pass codes should be changed frequently. IT staff should also understand that it is their responsibility to make sure that these areas remain secure and that pass codes or other secret information is not given out. With adequate physical security in place, you can move on to protecting your data from those that try to get to it from your network.

Managing User Security

To properly manage your network, it is necessary to give all users (including Administrators) sufficient permissions to carry out their tasks. It is also important to restrict access to tools that they do not use or should not have access to. Here, we'll look at some of the features for restricting access that are included with Windows NT. User rights can be used to restrict the functions that can be performed by users with above-normal user permissions.

For example, in Windows NT User Manager, an Administrator can restrict the workstations that a user may log on to:

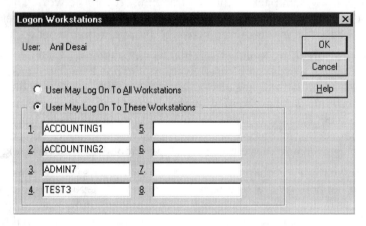

This feature may be useful if you have a set group of users who share machines, but you do not want these people to log on to other computers.

To prevent the loss of data, all network operating systems feature a user account or a group from which all rights are inherited. In Windows NT, this is the Administrators group. Managing permissions for Administrator accounts is particularly important.

Many organizations set up a single user account as the Administrator and give several people the Administrator password. However, this poses several major security problems. First of all, if more than one user can log on to the system as the Administrator, the possibility of accountability provided by auditing is made very difficult. For this reason, it is recommended that all users be given separate accounts.

Managing User Accounts

The 32-bit Windows client OSs (Windows 95/98/ME, Windows 2000, and Windows NT) allow for the implementation of certain policies and profiles that, when used properly, give users enough freedom to do their jobs without allowing them to delete files to which they should not have access. Users who are network/systems administrators should be given two user accounts. The first should be the main user account under which they will log in for all normal tasks. A second Administrator account should be used only when necessary. For example, a network administrator named Jane Doe would have two user accounts: Jdoe and Jdoe-Admin.

Account Policies

The default account policies used by Windows NT/2000 are created for convenience. For example, a user may use a blank password and may choose a password of any length. In the real world, such account policies increase the likelihood of hack attempts, and should be changed in all but the least secure environments. Figure 3-1 shows the various options available; to access them, select Account | Policy within User Manager. The Account Policy features are described in Table 3-1.

Account lockout is an automatic process. Accounts cannot be manually locked by an Administrator (though they can be disabled). An Administrator can, however, unlock an account that has been locked (by a specific number of bad logon attempts, for example). Note that the built-in Administrator account itself cannot be locked out, regardless of policy settings. This prevents individuals from accidentally being locked out of their servers entirely. Therefore, the Administrator password should be made especially difficult to guess.

Password Policies

In several ways, the idea of network security goes hand-in-hand with the ideas discussed in earlier chapters. No matter how strong your router security or how restrictive your Internet firewall, the weakest point in your defenses is in the password policy. An easy way for anyone to gain access to a system is to call a user and simply ask for his or her password information by claiming to be "from the IT department." Instruct users *never* to give out their passwords. Even if network administrators require this information, they have specific methods of gaining access to a resource that do not require asking users for their passwords. One good way to enforce strong password policies is to instruct users to choose personal or secret information about themselves—this will make them think twice before divulging the password to others.

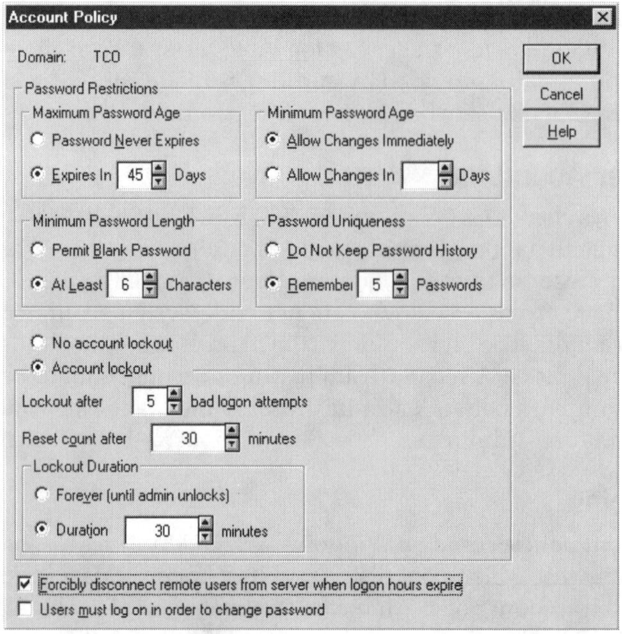

Figure 3-1.   Viewing Windows NT Account Policy settings

Feature	Recommended Setting	Function
Minimum Password Age	3 days. (Allow changes immediately if Password Uniqueness is enforced.)	Prevents users from immediately changing their passwords back to the original settings. Also, prevents someone from logging on with a generic password (for example, after a password has been reset) and then changing it immediately.

Table 3-1.   Recommended Windows NT Account Policy Settings

Feature	Recommended Setting	Function
Maximum Password Age	45 days	Forces users to periodically change passwords to prevent the usability of a compromised password for long periods of time.
Minimum Password Length	6 to 8 characters	Makes passwords more difficult to guess.
Password Uniqueness	5 passwords	Prevents users from reusing the same passwords.
Account Lockout	After 5 attempts; reset count after 30 minutes	Prevents password-guessing hack attempts.
Lockout Duration	30 minutes	Prevents password-guessing hack attempts by forcing users to wait before retrying.
Forcible disconnection of remote users when logon hours expire	Enabled if using logon hour restrictions	Prevents violation of shift-work or no-overtime policies.
Specifying that users must log on in order to change passwords	Disabled (to prevent Administrative work)	Prevents users from renewing passwords that have expired.

Table 3-1. Recommended Windows NT Account Policy Settings *(continued)*

NOTE: In Windows NT and Windows 95/98/ME, usernames are case insensitive. However, Windows NT passwords are case sensitive. Windows 95/98/ME does not support case-sensitive passwords, but the authenticating server retains the case information. This is important if the user will also use a Windows NT computer because case sensitivity will then be enforced.

Using the Password Filter DLL file, you can force the use of stronger passwords. Passwords will be required to have at least one character from among three of the following categories:

▼ Lowercase characters

■ Uppercase characters

■ Numbers

▲ Symbols (such as ! @ # $ % ^ & *)

How does this increase security? A typical hack method for cracking passwords is to use a dictionary of common passwords. The common passwords include first and last names, common English words, and so forth. It is important that IT find a way to hold users responsible for hacks under their accounts. If an employee absentmindedly left a key near the company safe, he or she would be accountable for anyone's entry into that area. Though the passfilt.dll file is included with Windows NT Service Packs, it is not enabled by default.

Protecting Against Viruses and Malicious Code

Although the overwhelming majority of virus scares are bogus, viruses do present a real threat to your network. These simple pieces of code are designed to quickly replicate throughout your network and can cause problems ranging from mild annoyances to systemwide data loss. Unlike the stories that are common in science fiction and tabloid media, viruses rarely render machines unbootable or cause widespread disk corruption. The more common viruses are those that are included in macros (in Microsoft Word or Excel documents, for example) and those that simply do nothing other than replicate between machines.

An example of a damaging virus that is probably close to the hearts of many IT professionals is the so-called "ILOVEYOU" virus. This extremely simple piece of Visual Basic Script (VBS) code was transmitted as an e-mail attachment. When the attachment was launched, the script file performed many actions. The most destructive were those that replaced certain file types (for example, GIFs and JPEGs) with the contents of the script file itself. This made any form of recovering that information (other than from backups) impossible. And it prevented many critical applications from working properly. In most cases, IT staffs would choose to rebuild the computer from scratch or to perform a complete recovery of all of the data. As if this wasn't enough, the virus then sent copies of itself to all of the users within the user's address book. This quickly amounted to millions of e-mails for even medium-sized companies and brought mail servers to a crawl.

There are many tools that can be installed for protecting against viruses on clients and servers. They offer varying levels of protection that are configurable by the end user. Network-aware versions of these types of software allow systems administrators to centrally define virus-scanning policies. For example, some utilities allow you to automatically scan your machines during a network login. This is useful, as it ensures that machines are scanned regularly.

Keep in mind, however, that some forms of virus protection can be much more trouble than they're worth. For example, performing a virus scan at every login can be a waste of time and resources and can lower productivity. On the client side, certain virus-scanning utilities automatically scan all files whenever they're accessed. Again, this can significantly reduce performance by requiring additional disk I/O and CPU time. Overall, antivirus utilities should be used judiciously; otherwise, the cure might be worse than the "disease"! For more information on virus protection tools and technologies, see Chapter 5.

Defining a Backup Schedule

In many cases, doing a single full backup and then backing up selective files will be adequate for meeting the requirements. For example, if you have 10GB of data to back up, but only a small portion of this changes, it would be most efficient to have a full backup and then subsequent backups of only the files that change. As we discussed in Chapter 2, there are three main types of backups:

▼ **Full backup**   Stores all files on the selected partitions

■ **Differential backup**   Stores all files since the last full backup

▲ **Incremental backup**   Stores all files since the last full or incremental backup

Differential and incremental backups use the archive bit, which is stored for every file in the file system (whether NTFS or FAT). Full and incremental jobs always reset the archive bits for any files that they back up. Differential backups do not reset the archive bit. You should not mix full and incremental backups. Incremental backups are often faster than differential backups, but restoring incrementally takes longer, because all tapes in the series must be loaded sequentially. Differential backups will store more data on each backup, but restorations will only require the full backup and the last differential backup.

We covered the topics of determining business requirements and establishing policies in previous chapters. At the very least, you should have answers to the following questions before implementing any data protection operations:

▼ How much data will you need to back up?

■ How much tape or other storage space is available?

■ Should operating systems and applications be backed up, or should only user data be stored?

■ Will any data on users' local machines be backed up, or must they store all data on the servers?

■ How much data changes daily? Weekly? Monthly?

▲ What are the business requirements regarding time for a complete restoration?

Using this information, you can define an appropriate schedule for backing up files. Figure 3-2 shows a method that includes reusing tapes and storing information off-site.

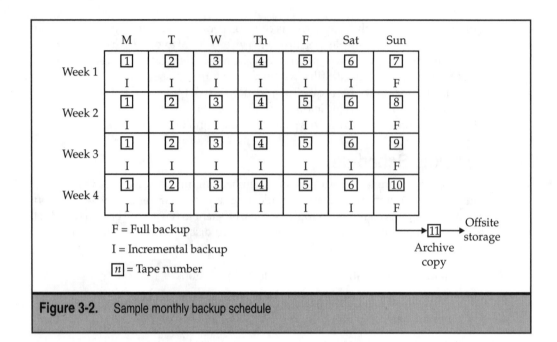

Figure 3-2. Sample monthly backup schedule

Security Management Tools

The United States National Security Agency (NSA) has defined various levels of security certifications for network OSs. Described within these guidelines are issues regarding the ownership of files, auditing, and sharing of resources. One specification is known as C2-level security. By default, many of the security options are configured for usability. Because a given installation of Windows NT/2000 will be secure only if certain options are implemented and others are disabled, systems administrators must determine whether they need this level of security. Again, the trade-off is usability. For those who wish to meet some of the stringent guidelines set forth in the C2 documentation, Microsoft has made available the C2 Configuration Manager program, shown in Figure 3-3. This program queries the status of the current configuration and can fix options to increase security. The utility can be obtained as part of Windows NT/2000 Resource Kit.

In addition, Windows NT Service Pack 4 (and later) includes a tool called Security Configuration Manager (SCM). The purpose of SCM is to provide a single point of centralized administration for NT's security features. Systems administrators can specify various security configurations and enforce them on a per-machine basis. SCM allows systems administrators and users to quickly determine which security options are enabled within the OSs. If changes are needed, they can be implemented directly through the use of this tool. SCM is shown in Figure 3-4; for more information, see **www.microsoft.com/security** and read the release notes that accompany Windows NT Service Packs. More information on obtaining and installing Service Packs will be covered later in this chapter.

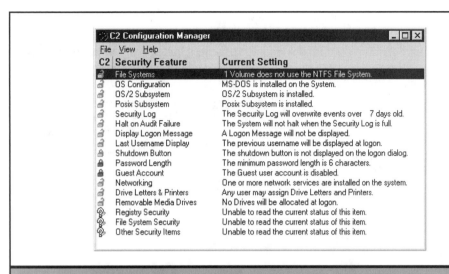

Figure 3-3.   Checking security settings with the C2 Configuration Manager

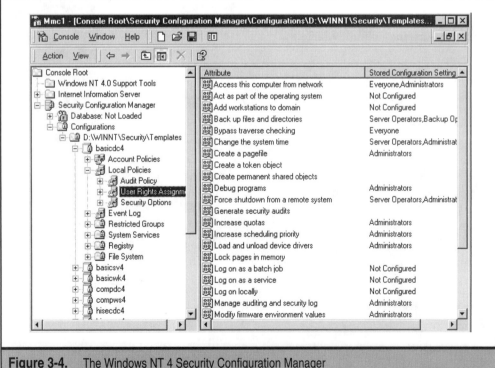

Figure 3-4.   The Windows NT 4 Security Configuration Manager

WINDOWS NT 4 DATA PROTECTION

In the previous sections, we examined some best practices for securing your network environment. Now it's time we put those ideas into practice by implementing security and data protection features. In this part of the chapter, we'll examine several ways in which you can use the features of Windows NT 4 to better protect your information. The focus will be on providing an overview of tools and technologies. If you need further information on implementing them, be sure to check out the Windows NT 4 Resource Kits. (See Appendix B.)

Windows NT Backup

Windows NT Backup, shown in Figure 3-5, was created to be a very simple disk-to-tape storage utility. It provides all the functions necessary to back up and restore data on your

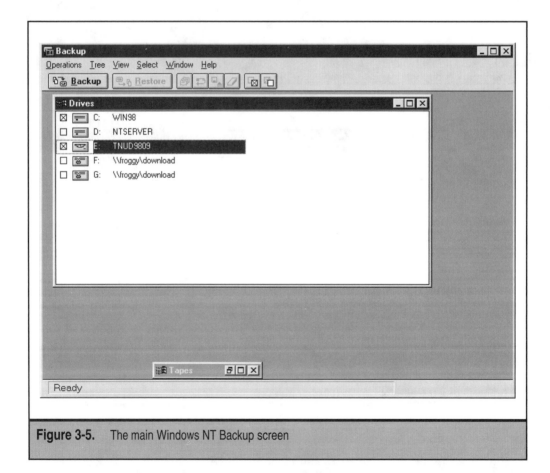

Figure 3-5.   The main Windows NT Backup screen

server. To use Windows NT Backup, you must first install and configure any tape devices you have available. Then, click NTBackup in the Administrative Tools program group.

Windows NT Backup can copy all local files to tape, including the Windows Registry. The user running the backup operation must have Read access to the files or must have the user right to bypass file system security. You can optionally back up remote network drives through drive mappings. Note that Windows NT Backup cannot back up the Registry of a remote machine.

Windows NT Backup jobs can be run from the command line and can be included in batch files. Figure 3-6 shows the Help file describing basic options that can be used from the command line. For a complete listing of the various options available, see the Windows NT Backup Help file.

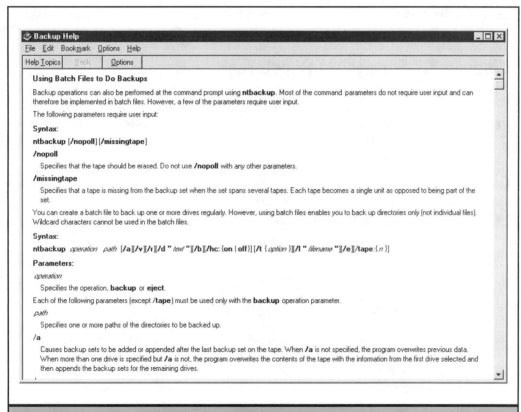

Figure 3-6.   Viewing the Windows NT Backup Help file

The following is an example of running NT Backup from the command line:

```
Ntbackup backup c: /t normal /b /d "Full backup of Server1"
/v /l "c:\NTBackup.log"
```

This command tells NT Backup to do the following:

▼   Back up all files on the C drive (c:).

■   Add a description to the backup set (/d "Full backup of Server1").

■   Back up the Windows NT Registry (/b).

■   Verify the backup (/v).

▲   Write a backup log to a text file on the C drive (/l "c:\NTBackup.log").

The command can be called from a batch file when, for example, you wish to map network drives before running the backup command. This also makes it easy to schedule the backup program to run via the AT or WinAT command.

The Windows NT Emergency Repair Disk

Although complete backups will protect your Windows NT installations even in a worst-case scenario, it is often unnecessary to resort to formatting the hard drive, reinstalling the operating system, and then restoring from tape. The problem may be a corrupt Registry or some other minor problem, such as a corrupt boot file. Windows NT includes the ability to back up the essentials of your system configuration to an Emergency Repair Disk (ERD) and use it to restore the system if there is some future problem. On a Windows NT computer, this information includes portions of the Registry, the Security database (including all user accounts and groups), and hard disk information. The Repair Disk Utility (RDISK) can be used to back up this data to a floppy:

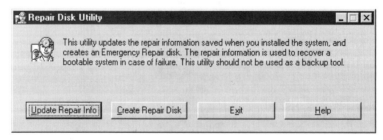

To use RDISK, choose Start | Run, and type **RDISK**.

The data copied to the floppy is taken from the operating system root folder on your hard drive. The files in this directory are automatically refreshed every time you click the Update Repair Info button. Note that this does not back up to your floppy disk—you will be prompted to do this after the update is finished. It is very important to maintain regular updates of the data stored on the ERD. Also, as the program will warn you, it is important that you store these disks in a secure location, since they include security and account information. Just like backups, the ERD is only current up to the point of the last successful update. Also, note that restoring these files will reset your system to its configuration at the time of the backup. This is especially important when you have changed your disk configuration via the Disk Administrator or have added Service Packs or other OS updates. The data stored on ERDs is specific to each computer, and you should never use an ERD created from a different machine. Later in the chapter, we'll talk about recovery and how you can solve simple problems by using the ERD that you've created.

NOTE: By default, the RDISK utility does not back up the Security Accounts Manager Database. This is by design, because this database can be very large for environments with many users. However, you can use the rdisk /s command to update this information in the Windows NT system root directory and then back up to a floppy.

Implementing Strong Password Policies

One of the main challenges faced by organizations is enforcing the use of secure passwords. No level of configuration will protect against users (and sometimes even systems administrators) who use, for example, their first name for a password. Windows NT 4 Service Pack 3 and later includes a new DLL file (passfilt.dll) that lets you enforce stronger password requirements for users. Passfilt.dll provides enhanced security against password guessing, or "dictionary attacks," by outside intruders. Passfilt.dll implements the following password policies:

▼   Passwords must be at least six characters long.

■   Passwords must contain characters from at least three of the following four classes: English uppercase letters (A through Z); English lowercase letters (a through z); Westernized Arabic numerals (0, 1, 2, and so on); nonalphanumeric ("special") characters, such as punctuation symbols.

▲   Passwords cannot contain your username or any part of your full name.

These requirements are hard-coded in the passfilt.dll file and cannot be changed through the user interface or the Registry. To enable strong passwords, you can make the changes described in the steps below on your Windows NT systems.

STEP-BY-STEP

Enabling Strong Password Requirements

1. Use Registry Editor (regedt32.exe) and open HKEY_LOCAL_MACHINESYSTEM.

2. If it does not already exist, add the value **Notification Packages**, of type REG_MULTI_SZ, under the LSA key.

3. Double-click the Notification Packages key and add the following value: **PASSFILT**. If the value FPNWCLNT is already present, place the PASSFILT entry beneath the FPNWCLNT entry.

4. Click OK, and then exit Registry Editor.

5. Restart the computer.

Another useful feature is the ability to set password protection and wait time for the Windows NT screensaver. A password and short wait time, such as 15 minutes, will en-sure that if users leave their machines unattended, the workstation will be locked, thereby preventing others from accessing information.

Auditing

There are many reasons for implementing auditing on an NT Server. First, it is impor-tant to verify that only authorized people can access the information on your network. One of the best ways to track this information is to audit logon and logoff attempts. A large number of failed logon attempts will alert you to the fact that a user may be trying to guess a password.

One of the best security measures is the audit log. Though it technically won't *prevent* unauthorized access, auditing a system can be used to determine how an illegal activity occurred, and can also serve as a deterrent. In the following sections, we'll look at how to generate an audit trail for specific objects and how to manage the audit information once it's available.

Enabling Auditing

On a Windows NT Workstation or Server, there are two major steps to activate auditing. First, the auditing feature must be enabled for the object type you wish to examine. This makes the second step—actually setting specifics on which actions to audit—possible. To enable the auditing function, you must have the Access the Audit Information user permission. (Permissions will be described in detail later in this chapter.)

STEP-BY-STEP

Enabling Windows NT Auditing

To turn on auditing, follow these steps:

1. Select Start | Programs | Administrative Tools | User Manager for Domains.

2. Select Policies | Auditing and turn on the various available auditing options. You'll see the following dialog box:

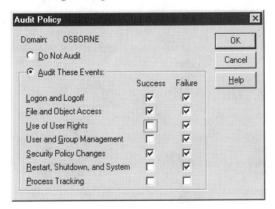

3. When you have selected the appropriate options, click OK to activate your selections.

Choosing What to Audit

You can enable some types of auditing simply by placing a check mark in the appropriate box. For example, to store logon information, nothing more must be done. For each type of event, you can choose to audit successes, failures, or both. You should always record any changes to the audit log itself to prevent users from turning off the audit log, performing some actions, and then restarting the log. Additionally, a good general guideline is to always audit at least logon failures.

Other auditing options require you to specify which objects and actions are recorded in the log. One example is the File and Object Access option. Assuming that this feature is enabled in User Manager, you can right-click any file or folder that resides on an NTFS volume and click Auditing in the Security tab. You can then set your auditing permissions on the screen that appears:

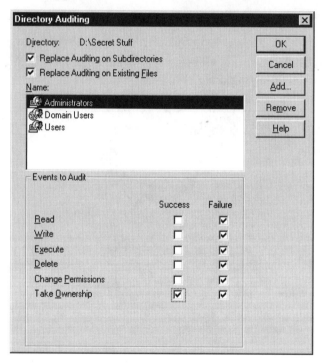

Viewing the Audit Log

Now that you've told your NT machine to capture the information you're interested in, you can use Event Viewer to view the data.

STEP-BY-STEP

Viewing the Audit Log

1. Open Event Viewer in the Administrative Tools program group.

2. To view the Security log, click Log and select Security.

3. To view further information on a specific item, simply double-click it on the list. This will show you details about the specific action, as shown in this example:

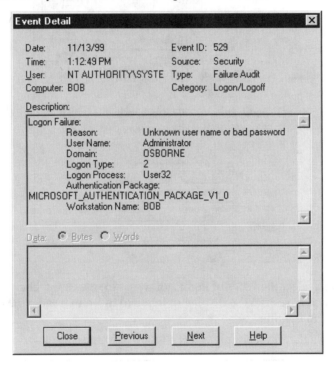

Often, you may be searching for only specific information in a very large event log. Manually looking through the list for items of interest can be quite tedious. Fortunately, there's a better way. If you're searching for specific information, such as failed logon attempts from a single machine, you can apply a filter. The filter affects only the display of data in Event Viewer—it does not delete any data. In the following example, we'll search for failed logon attempts on the local server. This example assumes that you have enabled the Logon and Logoff attempts option in the Audit Policy dialog box. (Refer back to the "Step-by-Step: Enabling Windows NT Auditing" section.)

STEP-BY-STEP

Searching for Specific Auditing Events

1. Open Event Viewer from the Administrative Tools program group.

2. Select View | Filter Events. You'll see the following dialog box:

3. After you select the types of items you want to search for, click OK. This will automatically restrict the display of items to those that meet the criteria you specified in the filter.

4. To remove the filter, simply select View | All Items.

It is a good idea to change the default options for Windows NT Event Log. The default is for the log files to be set to 512K and for events to be overwritten only after a certain number of days. On highly active systems, the logs may become full very quickly. Therefore, it is a good idea to increase the log files and choose the Overwrite Events As Needed option.

It is important to audit only information that you feel will be useful. If you audit all successful accesses to a specific share, for example, you'll find your event log growing out of control. Also, auditing will decrease system performance. Remember, enabling any security option will require some trade-off.

Using Windows NT Diagnostics

It's difficult to find all the information you need about a workstation or server in one place. However, when troubleshooting and managing machines on your network, you must know what you're dealing with. In Windows NT 4, a good first place to look is the Windows NT Diagnostics utility, which can be run using the shortcut in the Administrative Tools program group. Figure 3-7 shows the types of information you can easily view.

Windows NT Diagnostics also allows you to view information about remote machines. To do this, choose File | Select Computer. Note that you won't be able to access all of the same information, but if you're wondering about general configuration of a machine, Windows NT Diagnostics is a quick way to get what you need.

Windows System Policies

In certain situations, you'll have little control over the circumstances that lead to data loss. However, in other cases—such as preventing mistakes made by users—there are steps you can take to ward off trouble. We have already talked about the benefits of restricting network functions on the server side. Now let's look at it from the client's point of view. The potential problem is the same: the Windows NT OS offers a lot of power, but most users don't need it all. Fortunately, there's a way to lock down certain functions—and thus prevent users from inadvertently making errors.

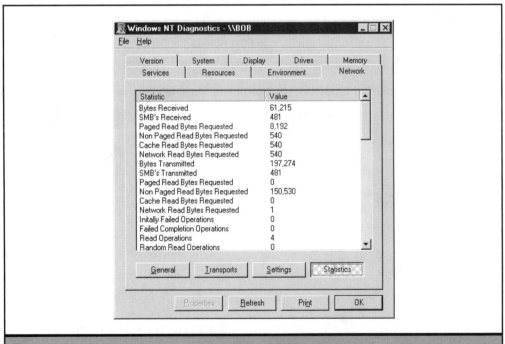

Figure 3-7.   Viewing network statistics in Windows NT Diagnostics

In general, planning for and implementing Windows NT system policies can take considerable time. Additionally, political issues often are involved in the decisions made. In some cases, the costs of unauthorized users accessing information may be as little as an employee playing unauthorized games on the network. However, it could be much more serious—a malicious employee could obtain confidential information, such as salary records. System policies are especially useful in preventing accidental problems that occur when users inadvertently change system settings, or delete files to which they should not have access. Taking the time to restrict the actions a user can perform is a great way to avoid problems in the future and can significantly protect your total cost of ownership.

System policies are based on Windows 95/98/ME and Windows NT Registry settings and restrict the functions that users can perform on specific machines. Although all of these changes can be made with the Registry Editor tool, it is often very difficult, among the thousands of keys available, to find the keys that you wish to modify. Furthermore, having to make these changes on individual systems in your environment is not practical. The System Policy Editor tool included with Windows NT was created to make this process easier and more manageable. In the following sections, we'll see how you can create policies based on templates and then assign them to user accounts.

The Windows Registry

Windows 95/98/ME and Windows NT computers store information in a single location called the Registry. These files contain information on hardware devices and drivers, application-specific settings, and user settings. The Registry itself consists of files that serve as a central repository of this data. Table 3-2 lists the default Registry filenames and tells

Filename(s)	Default Location	Contents
system.dat	Windows Root	Windows 95/98/ME System Settings
user.dat	Windows Root	Windows 95/98/ME User Settings
Classes.dat	Windows Root	Windows ME software class information (resides within the other two Registry files on Windows 95/98 machines)
Various LOG files	Winnt	Windows NT System Settings
Ntuser.dat	Winnt	Windows NT User Settings

Table 3-2.   Windows Registry Filenames and Locations

you where they're located. The OS automatically makes modifications to the Registry whenever user or system changes are made. This might include changing service startup options or installing new programs.

> **NOTE:** As a safety precaution, the Registry files have the Hidden attribute enabled. To see them from the file system, you need to make sure you're viewing hidden files. In DOS, you can use the dir /a command, and in Windows Explorer, you can select View | Options.

For editing the Registry, Windows 95/98/ME/NT users can use the RegEdit program. This tool provides an Explorer-style interface; to use it, select Start | Run, and then type **RegEdit** or **RegEdt32**. Windows NT supports RegEdit and also includes the RegEdt32 program (shown in Figure 3-8) that enables you to set security on Registry keys. You cannot use this utility, however, to view or modify remote Windows 95/98/ME Registry settings.

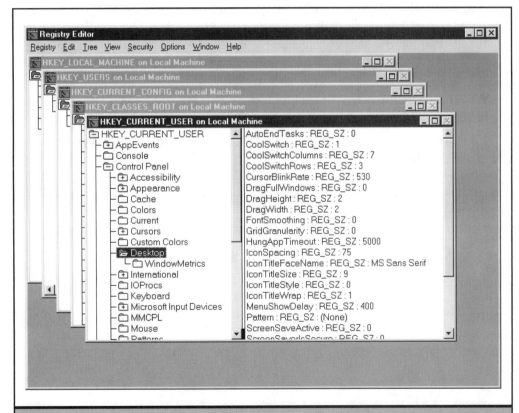

Figure 3-8. The Windows NT RegEdt32 application

> **CAUTION:** Incorrectly modifying the Registry can prevent system bootup and force you to reinstall your OS. Most modifications to the Registry and system settings can be performed through the Windows user interface. If you must make Registry modifications, be sure to back up the appropriate files. To easily back up the Windows NT Registry, use the Emergency Repair Disk Utility. In Windows 95/98, you can manually copy the Registry files to another directory. Windows 98/ME also include a handy utility called ScanReg for backing up and troubleshooting the Registry automatically.

Although no single authoritative source exists for all possible Registry keys and settings, documentation is available from multiple sources. If you're looking for Registry settings specific to a certain application, you need to contact the program's vendor.

System Policy Templates

The System Policy Editor tool provides a graphical interface for setting various Registry options. Policy templates are special text files that specify the options that can be set. Figure 3-9 illustrates how these pieces fit together. A policy template lists Registry settings, along with options for that setting. This information is used by System Policy Editor to provide a much more user-friendly prompt that describes its effects.

The Registry models of Windows 95/98/ME and Windows NT vary, so performing the same function on these OSs may require the modification of different Registry keys. By default, Windows NT includes the following templates:

▼ **Windows.adm**   Options for Windows 95/98/ME computers

■ **Winnt.adm**   Options for Windows NT computers

▲ **Common.adm**   Options that are common to both Windows 95/98/ME and Windows NT

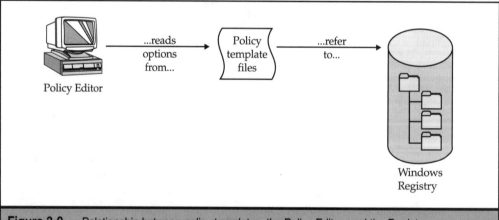

Figure 3-9.   Relationship between policy templates, the Policy Editor, and the Registry

By default, the system policy files are installed in the Windows NT system root directory. Here is a portion of the common.adm file:

```
CLASS MACHINE

CATEGORY !!Network
CATEGORY !!Update
POLICY !!RemoteUpdate
KEYNAME System
ACTIONLISTOFF
VALUENAME "UpdateMode" VALUE NUMERIC 0
END ACTIONLISTOFF
PART !!UpdateModeDROPDOWNLIST REQUIRED
VALUENAME "UpdateMode"
ITEMLIST
NAME !!UM_Automatic VALUE NUMERIC 1
NAME !!UM_Manual    VALUE NUMERIC 2
END ITEMLIST
END PART

PART !!UM_Manual_Path EDITTEXT
VALUENAME "NetworkPath"
END PART

PART !!DisplayErrorsCHECKBOX
VALUENAME "Verbose"
END PART

PART !!LoadBalanceCHECKBOX
VALUENAME "LoadBalance"
END PART
END POLICY
END CATEGORY; Update

END CATEGORY; Network
```

Custom System Policy template items can be created for any Registry settings you wish to change. This may be helpful if you want to set options for specific company applications or would like to change Registry settings not specified in the default ADM files. Various applications, especially those from Microsoft, also include their own ADM files. For example, ADM files are available for users of Microsoft Office products.

Defining System Policies with System Policy Editor

System Policy Editor provides a graphical interface for creating and assigning policies:

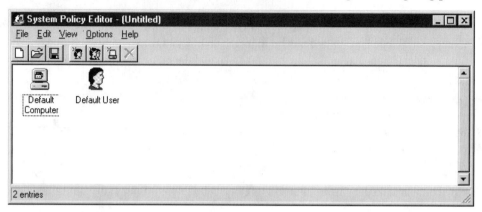

It uses the information stored in policy templates to provide the list of options that may be set for a specific value.

In this example, we'll create a system policy that does the following:

▼ Runs the WordPad application on startup

■ Specifies a directory that will hold all desktop icons

▲ Enables a logon banner warning users that the system is for authorized use only

> **CAUTION:** It is possible (and potentially embarrassing!) to lock yourself out of the system by setting policies that are too restrictive. Be careful when you make changes, especially to the Administrator account, and always be sure to leave a user account available as a safety net to make changes. If such an account is not available, you will need to circumvent the policies by either deleting or disabling them through the use of another user account.

STEP-BY-STEP

Setting Up System Policies

1. Start System Policy Editor from the Administrative Tools program group.

2. Select File | New Policy to create a new policy file. The basic default policy template files are already loaded.

3. Select Default Computer | Run and place a check mark next to the Run command. The values in this section are selected (check mark), not selected (unchecked), or unspecified (a grayed-out box):

4. For the program name, type **WordPad.exe**. The illustration provides examples of other options.

5. Select Windows NT Shell | Custom Shared Folders and place a check mark next to Custom Shared Desktop Icons. This will allow you to specify a path to use for shared icons. In the example below, I'm using the path %SystemRoot%\Profiles\ All Users\Start Menu\Startup.

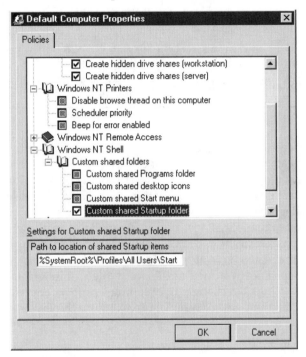

6. Select Windows NT System | Logon | Logon Banner and enable the selection.

7. Click OK to accept these settings. Now, you simply need to save the settings (File | Save). For this example, name the file **ntconfig.pol** and make a note of where you saved it.

Now that we've defined the system policies, it's time to apply them to clients.

Applying System Policies

Thus far, we've created a System Policy, but we haven't yet assigned it to any machine or users.

STEP-BY-STEP

Assigning System Policies to Machines and Users

1. Select File | Open in System Policy Editor and select the ntconfig.pol file we created in the preceding section.
2. Click Add Computer, and then select the computer to which you want to apply the machine settings.
3. Click Add User, and then select the user account to which you want to apply the user settings.
4. Save the updated policy file by selecting File | Save.

Both the User Account and Computer will inherit the default settings that you have already defined. You can, however, override or change any of these settings by double-clicking the User or Computer icon you wish to affect. System Policy Editor can also be used to directly modify the settings in a local or remote Registry. To do this, select File | Open Registry (for the local Registry), or File | Connect (to access remote computers).

Finally, we need to make this new policy file available to all network users. Simply copy the ntconfig.pol file to the NETLOGON share on the primary domain controller (PDC). Make sure that users have at least Read permissions to this directory. Any computers that are not specifically added to the policy file will inherit the Default User and Default Computer settings. To change these settings, simply reopen the ntconfig.pol file in System Policy Editor and add or remove users and machines.

Creating Policy Groups

To ease administration of environments with many workstations, you can place users and computers in policy groups. To create a policy group using System Policy Editor, select Edit | Add Group. Specific user profiles take precedence over group profiles if both exist. If users or computers belong to more than one group, you need to set a preference order in which policies will be applied. In this case, the highest-preference settings that are enabled are chosen. An "enabled" setting is one that is either checked or blank. The unspecified setting is represented by a grayed-out box, which indicates that the setting should not be affected by this policy.

STEP-BY-STEP

Modifying System Policy Group Settings

1. Create the group by selecting Edit | Add Group and entering a name.
2. Make any settings that you want members of this group to use.

3. Select Options | Group Priority. You'll see the following screen:

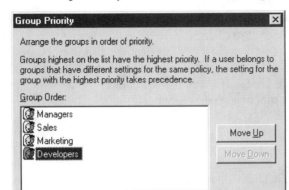

4. From here, you can move groups up and down in the list to assign their order of precedence.

More Policy Information

By default, the ntconfig.pol file is downloaded from a domain controller (DC) of the domain in which the machine is a member. However, if a user of the client computer chooses to log on to another domain, he or she will receive the user policy from the domain controller instead. Additionally, you can specify a Manual Update path for users to obtain policy information from a hard-coded path (for example, \server1). For more information on changing the update mode, see the topic "To change the system policy file path for manual update" in System Policy Editor Help.

Windows 95/98/ME policies must specifically be created with System Policy Editor on computers running the Windows 95/98/ME OS. These policy files will not be compatible with Windows NT computers (or vice versa). Windows 95/98/ME policy files are named config.pol and must be stored in the user's home directory on a server or in the NETLOGON share. Also, to enable support for Group Policies, you'll need to add Group Policy support. To do this, select Control Panel | Add/Remove Programs | Windows Setup | System Tools. If it's not already checked, install the Group Policies option. Windows 98/ME additionally include special policy template files that can be used to customize the settings of Internet Explorer, Outlook Express, and other applications. More information is available in Windows 95/98/ME documentation.

Even though a policy file can be used to restrict a user from performing specific functions, policies are enforced only when a user logs in to a domain. It's important to understand that system policies, by themselves, may not be sufficient. For example, preventing a user from accessing the Control Panel will not directly prevent him or her from deleting system files or making Registry modifications manually. Therefore, system policies must be used in conjunction with well-managed file system permissions and user rights.

Securing the File System

The Windows NT File System (NTFS) has been created to be a secure method for storing data on fixed and removable disks. Before users can access files on NTFS, they must authenticate with a trusted Windows NT computer and then be granted specified usage permissions for those files. File system permissions are cumulative, with the exception of the No Access option. That is, if a user is a member of a group that has Read-Only permissions and of a group that has Write-Only permissions, the user will effectively be able to read and write to files.

For networked environments, Windows NT enables you to set share-level and file system–level permissions. Though you can implement both, many administrators choose to leave the share-level permissions set to Full Control for the Everyone group, and then enforce restrictions via NTFS. This makes managing permissions easier and more efficient.

The file allocation table (FAT) file system was not designed to be secure and therefore can only use share-level permissions. Though this may be okay for network users, any user who can log on locally will be able to access all files on a FAT partition. Finally, FAT partitions have a larger cluster size and will waste more space on large drives (especially if the drive contains many small files).

NTFS was created to allow for security and recoverability in the Windows NT OS. Both of these features are unavailable in FAT (the file system used by MS-DOS and Windows 95/98/ME machines) or any other version of Windows. NTFS uses a transaction logging function for all disk functions. Basically, this means that before any disk operation is attempted, a log of that action is created. The transaction is then attempted. If, for any reason, the command cannot be completed, it is rolled back and no data is written to the disk. The operation can then be retried. Relational databases operate in much the same way to protect the integrity of their data—you would never want half of an operation to complete. Imagine the fun you'd have if a customer's street address was updated but her zip code remained the same.

On a side note, you might be wondering how a backup program can access all files on your hard drives without having the permissions of all users on your network. Windows NT handles this by allowing you to assign a special user right, Bypass File Security for Backing Up Files. With this granted, the account is allowed to back up any files on a system. In Windows 2000, special database management roles can be enabled to allow backup permissions as needed. Security is still maintained, since only an Administrator or users who have appropriate permissions can restore and access these files.

Fault Tolerance: RAID

Apart from storing data files on tapes, you can replicate the data on multiple hard disks to protect against a disk failure. The Redundant Array of Independent Disks (RAID) specification was developed to allow several devices to function as a single logical device. One of the least reliable (yet, most relied upon) components in modern computers is the hard disk drive. Ironically, it is the information stored on these devices that is most difficult to retrieve in the case of a failure. Even with exemplary system backups, retrieving data can be time consuming. For many businesses, this time is worth money. To protect against hard drive failures, it is possible to configure drives to automatically back up each other while they are in use.

We'll look at the details of evaluating and implementing RAID in Chapter 5 and in Chapter 6. Here, we'll cover the basics of RAID as it pertains to the Windows NT OS.

Using Windows NT Disk Administrator

The key to managing your hardware storage devices is understanding the Disk Administrator program. To run this application, click the Disk Administrator icon in the Administrative Tools program group. The default screen looks like the one shown in Figure 3-10.

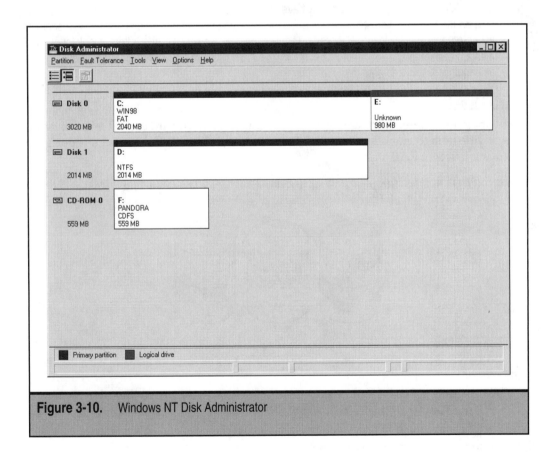

Figure 3-10.   Windows NT Disk Administrator

NOTE: The first time you use Disk Administrator, you will be told that the program needs to add information to the drive. This is a safe process and is used by Windows NT to uniquely identify each disk in your system (since drive labels, locations, and boot status can all be changed).

The graphical display of Disk Administrator shows you the relationship between the physical drives and logical partitions on your system. Figure 3-10 shows a configuration of three logical disk partitions located on two physical drives and one CD-ROM drive. A many-to-many correspondence exists between disks and partitions in NT. For example, you could have several disks make up a single partition (as is the case with disk striping, described later), or you may have one physical disk with multiple partitions. Additionally, in Windows NT, you can assign specific drive letters to each partition: simply right-click the desired partition and choose Change Drive Letter.

CAUTION: Changing drive letters may have effects outside of Windows NT. If you are running other OSs on the machine, you should not change the drive letters from their defaults; otherwise some of your programs may fail to run. Also, certain applications will use specific drive letters to look for needed media. For example, if you change the letter of your CD-ROM drive, your favorite game may not be able to access required data from the CD.

RAID Levels

RAID specifies different arrangements of physical and logical hard disks. Levels of RAID can provide fault tolerance, improve performance, or do both. Windows NT supports the following levels of RAID:

▼ **RAID 0: Disk Striping**   Optimizes performance by spreading data across several physical drives:

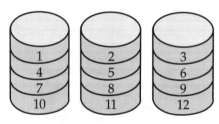

Data: 1 2 3 4 5 6 7 8 ...

Disk Striping offers no fault tolerance, but it enhances manageability by creating one large volume from at least two smaller disks.

■ **RAID 1: Disk Mirroring**   Stores all data on two physical drives, which are always kept synchronized:

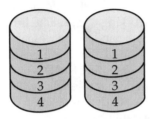

Disk Mirroring provides fault tolerance and a slight performance increase, but reduces usable storage space by 50 percent.

▲ **RAID 5: Disk Striping with Parity**   Uses one disk in an array as a "parity" drive:

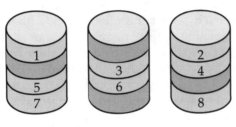

▨ = Parity information

Disk Striping with Parity can survive a failure in any disk without data loss or interruption of service (although performance will decrease).

Table 3-3 compares the general effects on performance and disk space when these RAID levels are implemented. One limitation is that Windows NT Boot and System Partitions

RAID Level	Performance Effect	Loss of Disk Space	Fault Tolerant?
0	Increase	0%	No
1	Increase (slight)	50%	Yes
5	Faster reads, slower writes	Up to 33% (equal to the size of one of the drives in the array)	Yes

Table 3-3.   Effects of Various RAID Levels

can only use RAID Level 1 (Disk Mirroring) for protection. Implementing RAID Level 5 (Disk Striping with Parity) does come at a price: server processing and memory will be used for calculating, reading, and writing the additional information required. However, having multiple physical disks working at the same time will decrease data access times, and performance degradation with modern processors will be negligible. In Chapter 5, we'll examine the benefits of choosing a hardware-based RAID solution.

It is important to note that implementing RAID is not a substitute for maintaining regular backups. Although RAID-based fault tolerance will protect against physical disk failures, it will not protect against the accidental deletion of files or a natural disaster. As we saw in previous chapters, loss of data is often more likely due to user error and other unwanted changes than to hardware failures. Nevertheless, on the server side, systems administrators find investing in RAID solutions to be an excellent data protection solution.

Windows NT Network Security

Making sure that a network operating system is secure on the network is a part of NOS security that is often neglected by systems administrators. Although this security measure is very important to maintaining security permissions and network accounts, it may not protect against someone who exploits a security flaw in the protocol stack. A Windows NT skeptic once commented to me that the only way to make Windows NT secure is to "unplug it from the network and bury it in six feet of concrete." Although that solution would deter many security hacks (at least those performed without a jackhammer), it wouldn't make for a very useful server. A much better solution is to protect your server from unwanted network access attempts by removing unnecessary protocols or services.

In the following sections, we'll look at the steps you can take to protect your system against network hacks. In most cases, all that is necessary are a few minor changes within the OS. Keep in mind, however, that new hacks and exploitations are found very frequently, so you should regularly monitor web sites such as Microsoft's Security Advisor (**www. microsoft.com/security**) to find out the latest information on new hacking methods and security holes.

TCP/IP Security

The TCP/IP protocol has been the target of many hacking attempts, mainly due to its ubiquity on the worldwide Internet and its widespread support for different applications. However, several ways exist to reduce the likelihood of successful attacks. First and foremost, it is important for network administrators to pay attention to security alerts and apply the appropriate security measures to prevent these problems from occurring in their environments. For example, a large number of failed logon attempts should be investigated. Most commonly, this will involve calling a user to resolve the problem. However, in the rare case that a user is unaware of or not responsible for the password entry attempts, it will be worth the extra effort.

Windows NT Server does not provide a firewall, but it does feature several ways in which the server can be made more secure. First, packet filtering for TCP/IP data can be enabled. This feature is available on a per-adapter basis and is set as part of the advanced settings for the TCP/IP protocol (see Figure 3-11). Therefore, if you have a server with an

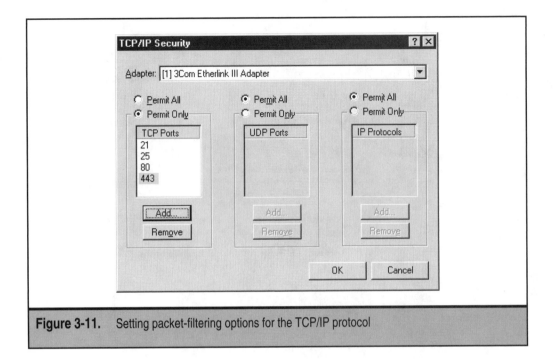

Figure 3-11. Setting packet-filtering options for the TCP/IP protocol

ISDN connection to the Internet and network access to a LAN, you can choose to allow only certain types of Internet packets to be recognized by the server while allowing all data to be transmitted to and from the LAN.

Internet Information Server

Microsoft's Internet Information Server (IIS) was designed to make Windows NT Server computers more accessible via intranets and the global Internet. In other chapters, we'll see how IIS can be used to help in remote administration, in FTP services, and in publishing web-based information. Although this service may prove indispensable in some environments, it can also cause many different problems for systems administrators. There are several ways to secure an IIS installation. Each involves the correct combination of IIS permissions, web application permissions, and NTFS permissions. Figure 3-12 shows the various security options.

Firewalls

The purpose of networking computers is to share data. For this reason, networked environments greatly increase the risks of illegal access and unauthorized access of a system. However, security restrictions should be put in place so that only certain users can access certain resources. One method for protecting information on a network—especially a network connected to a public network, such as the Internet—is through the use of a firewall.

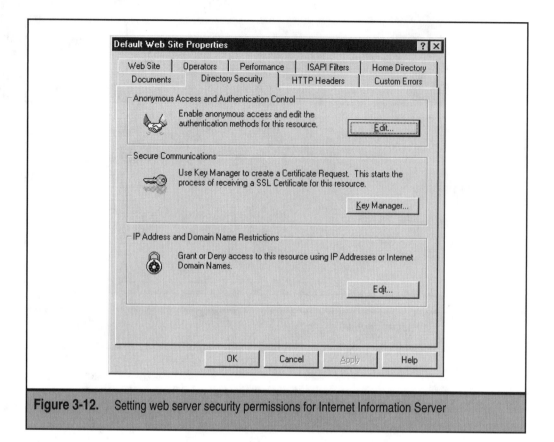

Figure 3-12.   Setting web server security permissions for Internet Information Server

An exact description of a firewall is difficult to find. At best, the term is used to describe a collection of technologies. The purpose of firewall technology, however, is obvious: to prevent unauthorized access to system resources. On its most basic level, a firewall provides packet-filtering capabilities. Instead of allowing any and all packets to traverse the network, the packet filter performs some type of check to make sure that this data should be allowed to pass. This is especially important to network security, because many networks have recently been opened up to the Internet, which essentially enables any user in the world to attempt access.

Though firewalls are most commonly used to filter Internet traffic, they may also be used to enforce security between networks. The check may be based on the source address of the sending computer, or it may restrict traffic to certain packet types (FTP data in the case of an FTP server, for example). Figure 3-13 shows a firewall that accepts all TCP/IP packets originating from a remote branch office, and rejects all packets from all other users (including those from the Internet). In this example, Internet users access a web server located outside the firewall.

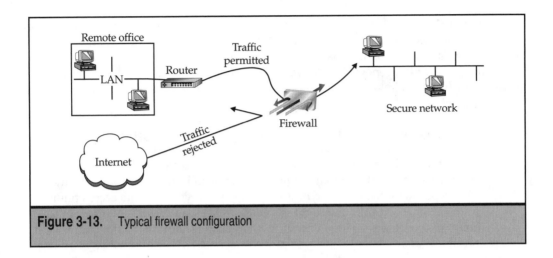

Figure 3-13. Typical firewall configuration

Network Address Translation (NAT) is the second mode of protection provided by a firewall. NAT allows users to have Internet access without giving out the internal addressing scheme. NAT tables hold information that tracks the relationships between legal Internet IP addresses and those on your own network.

Finally, authentication services can be implemented in firewalls. These techniques range from simple password-based logons to more complex methods utilizing digital cipher cards.

When considering firewalls, we again see the trade-off between security and performance. Firewalls are generally implemented with one of two methodologies: accept all packets (for maximum application compatibility) or deny all packets (for maximum security). In either case, only the exceptions to the rule are specified. It's important to note that specific applications will require certain TCP/IP ports to be open for communications. (One example is Windows NT trust relationships that require certain types of NetBIOS traffic.) For this reason, you need to test your firewall policies with actual business applications before deploying technology that may impede your system. Physically, a firewall may be a piece of software, a router with specialized features, or a stand-alone server optimized to look at packets. Each solution varies in security, price, and performance. Microsoft's Proxy Server product has been designed to provide basic firewall protection. More information can be found from Microsoft and from various company web sites.

Remote Access Security

The use of remote access is becoming much more common in many businesses today. Users are increasingly depending on the ability to access information stored on a corporate network from remote locations, whether they are traveling and dialing in from a hotel room or connecting over VPN from home. For over a decade, the most common method of connecting to a remote network was through the use of an analog phone line and a modem. Windows NT Remote Access Service (RAS) has been designed to support this type of connectivity. In Windows NT 4 and Windows 2000, however, even more functionality is supported, such as virtual private networks (VPNs).

Although all of the general Windows NT best practices for managing security apply to using RAS, the following are additional considerations you must make to secure remote access:

▼ **Managing dial-in permissions** Using either User Manager or the Remote Access Administrator tools, you can specify which users can— and cannot—dial in to your Windows NT system from remote locations. It is important to ensure that only users who need remote access are granted dial-in permissions, since anyone who is aware of your remote access phone number can attempt to guess these values. Additionally, you might want to enforce restrictions on logon hours so that users cannot dial in, for example, on weekends.

■ **Auditing** We discussed the auditing of logons and logoffs earlier in this chapter, but it's worth mentioning again here since you should be particularly interested in which individuals are logging on to your network.

▲ **Setting call-back security** For dial-up point-to-point connections, such as ISDN lines or analog modems using telephone lines, you can set up call-back security. In User Manager, you can specify one of the three Call Back options shown here:

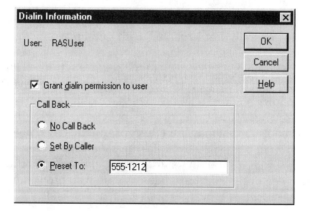

Call-backs can help you ensure that people are calling from expected locations. For example, if a user should only have permissions to dial in to the corporate network from home, he or she should not be able to dial in using the same username and password from a different phone number. Call-backs are also useful in helping to control remote access costs. By having a user dial in to the remote access server and specify a number, the costs associated with toll-free numbers or borne by the client can be eliminated.

For more information on using RAS and VPN features in Windows NT 4 or Windows 2000, start at the Microsoft Communications page: **www.microsoft.com/communications**. There, you'll find links to white papers and to more information on configuring, managing, and securing remote access for your organization.

Client-Side Security

One of the most often neglected security measures is protecting clients. Systems administrators seem to understand the implications of managing security on the server side, since that is what they directly control. However, potential unauthorized users usually start their hack attempts from the client side. There are several steps that you can take to make sure that information stored on clients is relatively safe.

The Windows 95/98/ME operating systems were not designed to meet strict security standards and thus offer only limited security capabilities. Because they are targeted toward home users, they lack many of the security features available in Windows NT. However, many organizations have still deployed Windows 95/98/ME computers in their environments for all types of users. Many applications that run on Windows NT can run with little or no modifications on the Windows 95/98/ME platform.

The major source of concern regarding security of client systems is the file system. Windows 95/98/ME support the FAT file system (or, in Windows 95 OSR2 and later, FAT32, which allows for larger partition sizes and more efficient use of space). The FAT/FAT32 file systems do not support the use of security settings. Simply booting the system from a DOS floppy disk and accessing data files can easily defeat any level of control exerted at the OS. Because of this, network users who work on Windows 95/98/ME OSs need to store their files on a secure server share. Usually, systems administrators set up a home directory to which all data files are stored, and change users' default save paths to this location. This gives the added benefit of being able to back up data from a central location.

WINDOWS 2000 DATA PROTECTION

You would have to be living in a cold, dark server room (without Internet access) not to have heard about Microsoft's Windows 2000 operating system platform. This platform represents a significant evolution in Windows-based operating systems. There are many new and improved features in Windows 2000—so many, in fact, that there's not enough room in this book to cover all of them. Therefore, we'll focus on new tools and techniques related to the topic at hand: data protection. I'll also point you to several resources for more information so you can learn about these topics in depth.

Among the many design goals for Windows 2000, Microsoft identified areas related to reliability, scalability, manageability, security, and performance. Although Windows NT did a reasonable job of meeting these goals (at least for small- to medium-sized organizations), many improvements were required in order to move the operating system into larger environments.

Particularly relevant to our discussion is the fact that Windows 2000 includes many features that can increase the level of security and data protection in your environment. Regardless of all of the marketing hype surrounding the new release, Windows 2000 is based on the same Windows NT features and technologies covered in previous sections. The concepts of auditing, setting file and object permissions, and security have not changed significantly. However, the way these tasks are performed has changed. Therefore, in this section, we'll focus on the differences between Windows NT 4 Workstation and Server and the Windows 2000 platform.

NOTE: It is well beyond the scope of this chapter to discuss details of Windows 2000 in depth. Here, we'll focus on the major new features and how they can best be used. For further information, see **www.microsoft.com/windows2000** and the additional resources mentioned in Appendix B.

Microsoft has created four different versions of the Windows 2000 platform, to meet the needs of everyone from desktop users to large-enterprise-level users. Table 3-4 lists the various versions of Windows 2000 and the major differences between them.

Edition	Target Use	Maximum CPUs	Major Features
Professional	Client-side computers and workstations in businesses and other secure environments	2	Client-side support for Active Directory and other major improvements in the Windows 2000 platform
Server	Mainstream business server for file/print, web, and application services	4	Support for Active Directory and Terminal Services

Table 3-4.   Comparing Editions of Windows 2000

Edition	Target Use	Maximum CPUs	Major Features
Advanced Server	Midrange servers (large departments, corporate offices)	8	All features of Server Edition, plus fail-over clustering, network load balancing, component load balancing, and support for up to 8GB of memory
DataCenter Server	Enterprise-level servers	Up to 32	Advanced clustering options and support for more CPUs; primarily available from third-party hardware vendors that sell Windows 2000 DataCenter Server solutions

Table 3-4.   Comparing Editions of Windows 2000 (*continued*)

Let's start with an overview of the new features in Windows 2000 and how they can help you secure and protect your data.

Active Directory

If someone asked you to describe the major network differences between Windows NT 4 and Windows 2000, there's a good chance that you'd mention the Active Directory. This feature alone will provide the most compelling reason for users in a Windows-based environment to upgrade (at least on the server side).

Active Directory has been designed to allow for the management of user resources in a single scalable and extensible schema. It is a complete replacement for the essentially flat domain model supported in Windows NT 4. For communications, Active Directory uses the industry-standard Lightweight Directory Access Protocol (LDAP). This ensures its compatibility with other directory services, such as Novell Directory Services (NDS), as well as third-party tools and utilities through the Active Directory Services Interface (ADSI). The Active Directory schema is extensible, and knowledgeable administrators and developers can add their own information to it. Figure 3-14 shows some of the administration tools used to manage the Active Directory.

NOTE: In Windows NT 4, you could get by without much planning of domains in all but the largest organizations. The situation is quite different with Windows 2000's Active Directory. If you are planning to deploy Active Directory in your environment, be sure to take the necessary time to plan an effective configuration that matches your business and network environment.

Microsoft's Active Directory technology helps to solve many of the problems related to managing users and groups in Windows NT 4. Whereas the Windows NT 4 account database is logically flat, Active Directory is hierarchical in nature. Through the use of

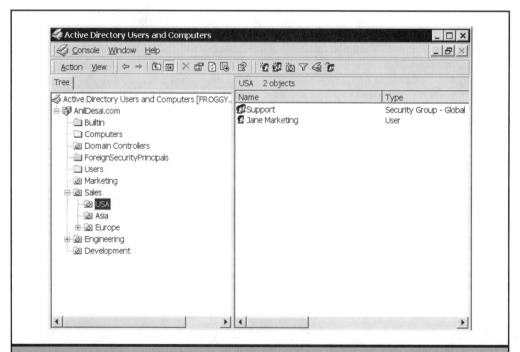

Figure 3-14. Viewing information about the Windows 2000 Active Directory

objects called Organizational Units (OUs), companies can mirror their own organizational structure within the Active Directory. These features allow flexibility and manageability of even the largest environments. They also allow companies to place all of their user information into logically grouped categories—a great benefit for security administrators. Designing an Active Directory that maps well to business requirements can be challenging, but the effort can pay for itself very quickly in management and administration savings.

NOTE: If you're looking for further information related to implementing the Active Directory, or if you're planning to pursue the Microsoft Certified Systems Engineer (MCSE) certification, I trust that you will find *MCSE: Windows 2000 Directory Services Administration Study* (Sybex, 2000) to be useful. I wrote the book to serve as an excellent resource for knowledgeable systems administrators who are planning to take full advantage of features of Windows 2000 and the Active Directory.

Pertaining to data protection and security, Active Directory allows for much more flexibility in several areas. The Active Directory database is designed to be a fault-tolerant, distributed repository that is stored on all of the domain controllers of an organization. This enables you to make the information available on systems that are on the same network or on those that are connected by slow WAN links. Microsoft has included the concept of Sites that allow systems administrators to control the replication behavior of the Active Directory. Furthermore, Windows 2000 Server computers can be easily promoted to domain controllers without a reinstallation of the operating system! I can sense a huge sigh of relief from those of you who had to deal with reinstalling Windows NT computers.

From a systems administrator's view, Active Directory allows for the use of many new features. Built-in server roles make it easy to delegate specific user permissions and rights accordingly. In Windows NT 4, some administrative functions took an all-or-nothing approach—that is, a user either was in the Administrators group (and could perform all server administration tasks) or wasn't (and had limited capabilities).

Active Directory provides for scalability to millions of objects. Its replication architecture is designed to allow for management of even the largest and most distributed enterprises. From a systems administration standpoint, this allows for centralized administration of resources, whether they are located on the LAN or across the world. At the same time, it allows for the delegation of permissions to, for example, remote support personnel. From a security standpoint, the use of Active Directory allows administrators to place permissions on all types of objects. When combined with file system security, this allows for greater control over permissions and network security. Whenever necessary, a "delegation of control" operation can be used to allow one or more administrators to control portions of the directory. This feature is very helpful in distributed environments, where security and control are vital.

NOTE: In distributed environments, backup and recovery of Active Directory can be much more complicated. Be sure you understand these issues and incorporate this information in your company-wide data protection plan. For more information, see the online help included with Windows 2000.

Again, it is beyond the scope of this section to describe the Active Directory features in detail. Instead, I'll give you an overview of the benefits of Active Directory and how it can help in your environment.

Group Policies

Common criticisms of system policies in Windows NT 4 include difficult configuration and the lack of administrative methods to cover the entire enterprise. Although policies can still be placed on local machines, Windows 2000 includes the Group Policies feature to allow the restriction of client-side activities to be controlled across sites and various levels of organizational units (OUs). Figure 3-15 shows some of the options you can choose from when configuring Group Policies. The interface is also extensible, so systems administrators can configure additional options to meet business requirements.

The administration of policies has been made much easier through the use of Group Policy Objects (GPOs). These objects are created once and then applied to any users or groups within an Active Directory environment by linking them to Organizational Units. If changes to Group Policies must be made (in response to changing business needs or to accommodate new applications), only the GPO must be modified. This modular method can greatly decrease the time spent in administering policies.

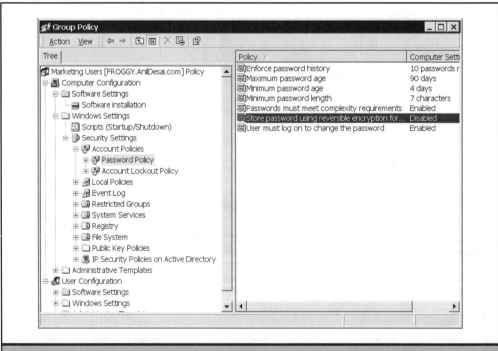

Figure 3-15.   Configuring Group Policies for use with the Active Directory

When configuring Windows 2000's Group Policies, be sure to do the following:

▼ **Disable unused GPOs.**   The use of GPOs involves some overhead in processing and network resources. If you're not using some of the GPOs that are configured, be sure to disable them so that they are not processed each time a client logs in.

■ **Pay attention to policy inheritance.**   Although being able to set permissions in a hierarchical manner can greatly reduce administration, it can make pinpointing security problems and configuration errors difficult. Be sure you plan for the inheritance features of GPOs before you apply them to specific objects in Active Directory.

▲ **Consolidate common GPOs.**   It will take longer for users with multiple GPOs to log in, since each of these items must be processed. As long as it is practical, be sure to consolidate commonly used policies and apply them directly to the appropriate groups.

Group Policies can also be used to cure some of the sore points of managing software and configuration options. For example, software management features allow for the automatic installation or update of applications on demand and from a central location. Also, user directories can be specified with greater granularity, and systems administrators can ensure that important information is stored securely on servers. This is a vital part of any organization-wide data protection plan that does not include complete backups of information stored on laptops and client workstations. Additional information on implementing, managing, and using Group Policies is available in the online help that is installed with Windows 2000 Server.

Distributed File System

Another welcome addition in Windows 2000 is Distributed File System (DFS) technology. Although this option was available for Windows NT 4 as an add-on, it was rarely deployed because of the OS updates required on client and server computers. DFS allows systems administrators to abstract the underlying location and organization of shared folders and to greatly simplify accessing data. It does this by setting up a DFS root on one machine and creating one or more share points. Now, instead of remembering that a resource is available via a share on Server 12, users can access a single server and browse the share tree to find what they need.

The benefits go much farther than that, however. The share points that are configured within DFS can be easily changed on the server side without requiring any reconfiguration on clients. Additionally, load balancing is supported. This is useful for busy shares that store files that are generally used as read-only (for example, a distribution point for Microsoft Office 2000). If configured with multiple share points for this resource, DFS will automatically distribute requests between the available servers. Better yet, if one of the share points is unavailable, users will automatically be redirected when they try to connect. The end result is a better end-user experience and the ability to easily distribute information on various file servers with minimal reconfiguration. Note, however, that it is up to systems administrators to ensure that the files in these directories stay synchronized. Figure 3-16 shows how the DFS Administrator utility can be used to configure and maintain DFS.

Finally, users of UNIX-based operating systems will be happy to hear that Windows 2000 supports the use of remote "mount points" within the file system. This allows a logical path (for example, "c:\Data\Software") to be mapped to a remote file system (for example, "\\Server5\Software"). This greatly increases the manageability of servers and allows systems administrators to take advantage of storage resources through their environments.

To ease administration, DFS roots can be configured as stand-alone or they can be integrated with Active Directory. If configured to use Active Directory, automatic file replication is available. This feature allows administrators to automatically keep all changes between multiple share points synchronized. For more information on using and configuring DFS, see the online help included with the DFS Administrator utility.

Backup and Recovery Tools

Windows 2000 offers a much-improved version of the basic Backup utility included in earlier versions of Windows NT. Although the tool does not provide all the advanced features present in many commercial backup applications, it does provide for automatically scheduling operations, storing to fixed and removable media types, and saving predefined backup job selections. Figure 3-17 shows the main screen of the Windows 2000 Backup program.

The new Backup utility allows systems administrators to configure and schedule new jobs by using wizards. Three main operations are supported: Backup, Restore, and the

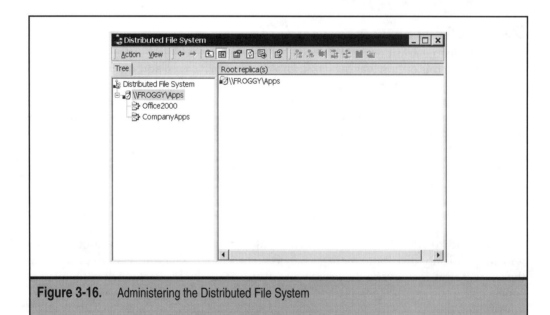

Figure 3-16.   Administering the Distributed File System

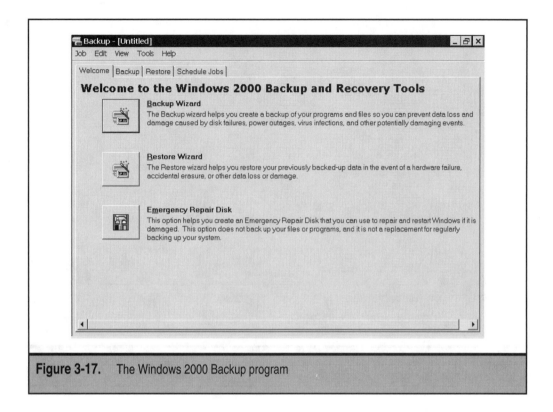

Figure 3-17.   The Windows 2000 Backup program

Emergency Repair Disk (ERD). The ERD option is similar to the Windows NT 4 RDISK utility and is used for storing critical information on floppies. This data can be used to repair and boot the OS if a failure occurs. Note that the critical information in the Windows 2000 Registry is usually far too large to store on floppies (especially if Active Directory is being used). Therefore, the ERD should be used only in troubleshooting, and not as an alternative for other backup methods.

Another useful option is the Windows 2000 System State. This option allows systems administrators to back up the Registry, Component Object Model (COM) registration information, and any other system-specific information that might be required to rebuild the computer. The general process for using System State information after a failure is, first, to reinstall the operating system. Then, Windows 2000 Backup (or any other compatible utility) can be used to restore as much data as is available. As part of the process, the System State can be restored so that all application, user, and operating system settings are restored to their initial state.

The Backup and Restore Wizards automate the most common tasks and allow administrators to choose which information should be protected. For those who are more familiar with backup operations, the interface also allows you to perform the same tasks with more configuration options. Figure 3-18 shows how you can easily select files for backup using the Backup Wizard.

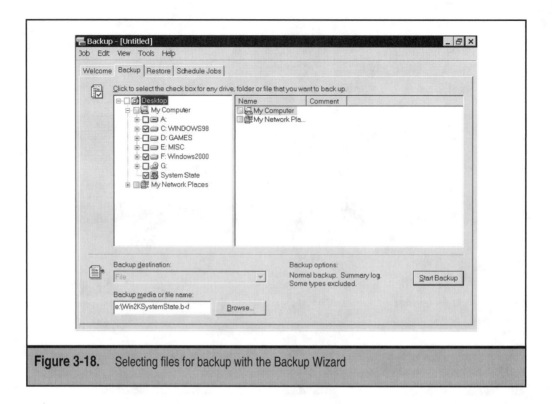

Figure 3-18. Selecting files for backup with the Backup Wizard

In addition to the basic functions, the Backup utility allows you to schedule jobs. This is very useful in ensuring that your data protection plan is properly and automatically followed. Be sure to take the time to schedule full, differential, incremental, and other backup jobs appropriately. Figure 3-19 shows the Backup utility's scheduling interface.

Overall, the Backup utility is an excellent tool for providing the most common backup operations required in many environments. It includes many features in an easy-to-use interface and is a significant upgrade to the utilities provided in earlier versions of Windows NT. In Chapter 5, we'll take a look at some of the advanced features available in third-party backup software products.

File System Changes

New features in NTFS 5 give administrators additional levels of configuration flexibility. Major improvements include support for encryption, compression, enforcement of disk quotas, and the ability to configure distributed file systems.

Encryption protects information even if a hard disk is removed from the OS and put into another machine. It also protects against third-party utilities that might attempt to circumvent the security settings configured at the file system level. The major benefit of NTFS 5 encryption is that it works in conjunction with the Windows 2000 user accounts

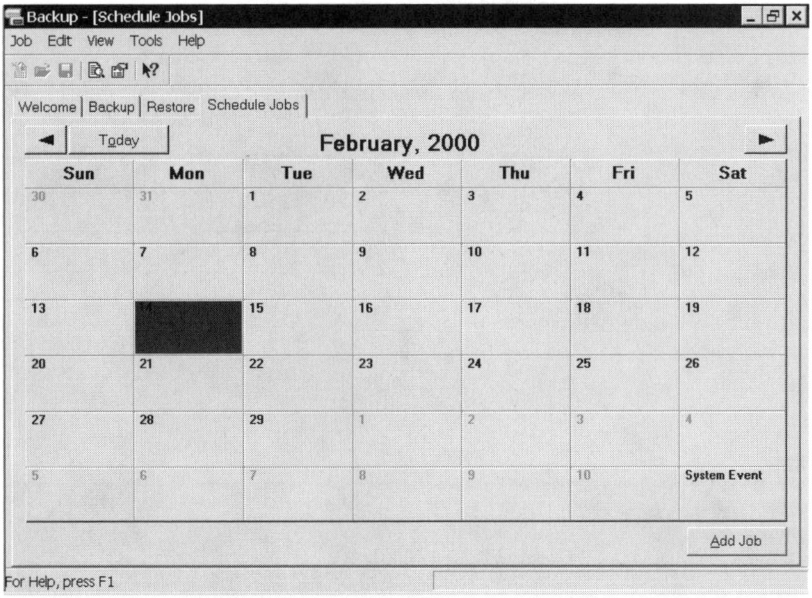

Figure 3-19.   Scheduling backup jobs

database. Therefore, it is much easier to administer than other solutions that require the use of separate accounts or authentication mechanisms. To enable encryption for specific files or folders, simply right-click the file system object and select Properties. Click Advanced to view the Advanced Attributes page (see Figure 3-20). Using these settings, you can specify whether or not these objects will be encrypted. There are drawbacks to encryption, however. Specifically, some CPU overhead is involved in encrypting and decrypting files as they are accessed. On very busy file servers, this can significantly reduce overall performance. Therefore, it is recommended that you encrypt data only if doing so is absolutely required.

NTFS 5, like previous versions of NTFS, allows for compression of partitions, files, and directories. The process is very similar to setting encryption values. Windows 2000 will automatically compress files when they are written to folders that have the compression attribute set, and will automatically decompress them when they are requested for use. Because less disk space is used, some performance gains can be realized since fewer disk I/O operations are required to access information. As with encryption, however, compression methods can utilize CPU resources and thus reduce overall performance. Again, I recommend using NTFS compression only when necessary. Also, note that you cannot enable NTFS compression and encryption for the same files or folders.

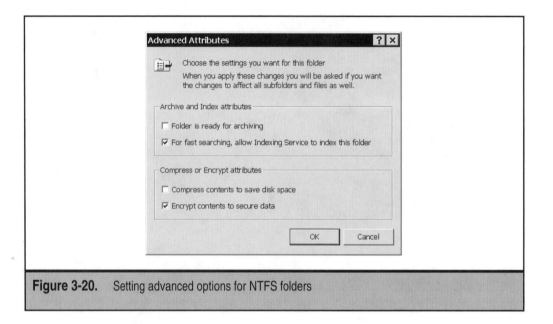

Figure 3-20. Setting advanced options for NTFS folders

Windows NT 4 did not include any built-in disk-quota software, which made it difficult for systems administrators to put reigns on the amount of space users could occupy. Often, users have little concept of the limited storage on file servers and rarely take the time to remove or archive unused information. Without using manual procedures or third-party tools, there was no way to force users to clear out their home directories. In NTFS 5, you can easily create and enforce quotas at the file system level by right-clicking a partition and selecting Properties. Figure 3-21 shows the Quota tab and the various features available. Disk quotas are an excellent way to enforce service level agreements and ensure that all users are sharing the available resources.

However, one major limitation of disk quota support in Windows 2000 is that it applies only at the partition level. A systems administrator cannot control disk usage at finer levels of granularity, such as at the folder level. Nevertheless, having the ability to limit disk usage for volumes is a great improvement and one that will help limit the amounts of user data that must be regularly backed up. By properly planning for and implementing these new features of NTFS 5, you can better administer your storage resources.

Disk Management and Dynamic Volumes

Configuring and managing hard disk storage resources can be quite a challenge because business needs increase very rapidly. The new Disk Management administrative interface lets you view physical and logical configurations on both local and remote servers. This tool can be accessed through the Computer Management tool. Figure 3-22 shows an example of the information you can see. Using this interface, you can initialize, format, and reconfigure storage resources. To make some of the more complex tasks much more intuitive, a wizard can be used for operations such as creating partitions.

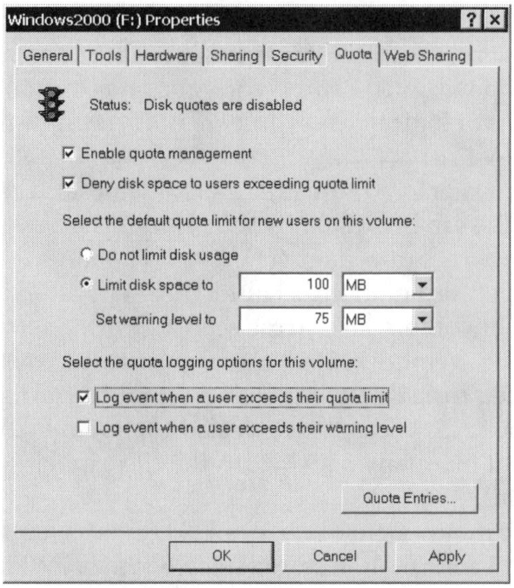

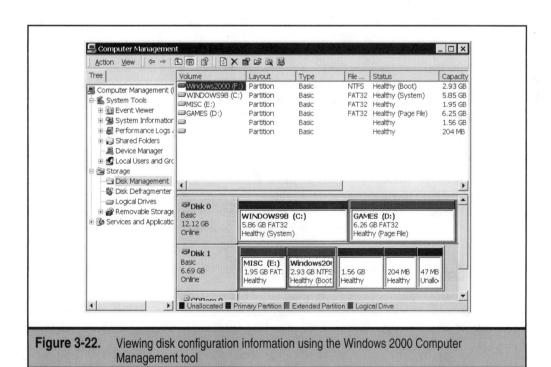

Figure 3-21. Establishing disk quota settings on an NTFS volume

Figure 3-22. Viewing disk configuration information using the Windows 2000 Computer Management tool

One of the challenges in working with software disk configurations is that many changes require a reboot of the server. Although this is acceptable in smaller environments, mission-critical servers cannot afford the amount of downtime. To address this issue, hard disks in Windows 2000 can be configured as *dynamic disks*. Dynamic disks cannot contain partitions or logical drives and are not accessible from earlier OSs (such as DOS, Windows 95/98/ME, or NT 4).

Using this feature, systems administrators can choose to perform RAID reconfigurations and add new disks to the system without requiring a restart of the OS. Of course, the hardware must support "hot-plugging" drives. The same RAID levels supported in Windows NT 4 (described earlier in this chapter) are supported in Windows 2000. However, the configuration of volume sets, stripe sets, and stripe sets with parity is only supported for dynamic disks. Windows 2000 also supports the use of the FAT, FAT32, and NTFS file systems (called *basic disks*), but changes to disk configurations may require a reboot of the server. Basic disks can be converted to dynamic disks, but they cannot be converted back (without manually backing up the files, making configuration changes, and then restoring them).

You can also specify mount points within an NTFS partition so that users and administrators can easily access information stored deep within a folder hierarchy. This feature is very helpful, especially when large disks or disk arrays are being used. For more information, see the online help included with Windows 2000.

Network-Level Security

Windows 2000 provides many additions to the network-level security measures included in Windows NT 4. First and foremost, the primary communications protocol used by Windows 2000 is TCP/IP. Instead of relying on Microsoft-based name resolution (such as the Windows Internet Naming Service, or WINS), Windows 2000 and Active Directory are both based on the Internet standard Domain Name System (DNS). Reliance on DNS allows Windows 2000 to integrate well with UNIX operating systems and allows for much greater scalability. To further aid in the administration of networks, information from the Dynamic Host Configuration Protocol (DHCP) service is automatically integrated with the DNS database. DHCP automatically assigns IP addresses to machines that support TCP/IP on the network (as long as this option is enabled). The DNS integration automates the formerly tedious process of managing machine name-to-IP address mappings and helps ensure that address databases are always up-to-date. For backward compatibility, previous name-resolution systems are also supported.

In addition to better network management tools and technologies, Windows 2000 provides several new features. Let's examine the major ones.

Routing and Connection Sharing

The Routing and Remote Access Service (RRAS) features of Windows 2000 allow the OS to perform many tasks that were previously left to costly dedicated hardware devices. Windows 2000 supports the use of the Routing Information Protocol (RIP) version 2 and Open Shortest Path First (OSPF) technologies. Both of these standards allow routers to communicate information to each other automatically, and reduce the need for manual administration of complex route tables. RRAS can also be configured to create *demand-dial connections*—connections between servers that are established only when needed, and are taken down during periods of inactivity. This feature can greatly reduce costs for many businesses that rely on leased lines. Finally, authentication mechanisms are extensible so that newer technologies can be integrated. One example is in the area of *biometrics*—the use of fingerprint, retina, or other scans to identify users. As these methods become more affordable, they will move from the pages of science fiction novels into corporate networks. Figure 3-23 shows the user interface of the Routing and Remote Access Service.

A fundamental requirement for most business networks nowadays is Internet access for all LAN users. New networking features include the ability to perform Internet Connection Sharing (ICS) and Network Address Translation (NAT). Both technologies enable you to provide access to remote networks (such as the Internet) for an entire LAN by using a single Windows 2000 Server machine. From a security standpoint, these technologies can reduce the chances of network intrusion; you can use them to hide the internal TCP/IP addresses of computers on the network while still allowing authorized users to request information from outside the LAN.

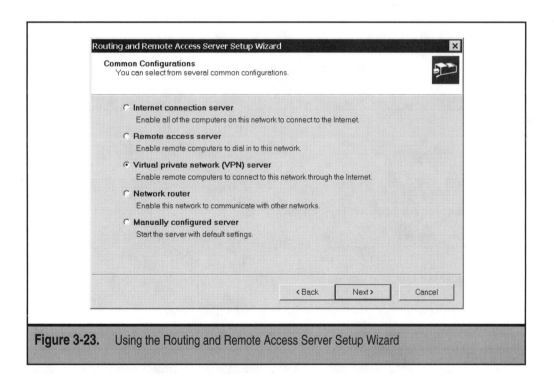

Figure 3-23.   Using the Routing and Remote Access Server Setup Wizard

Virtual Private Networking

A major challenge for organizations of any size is keeping people connected with their home networks. Traditional remote access solutions (generally using modems and leased lines) leave a lot to be desired. First, they are expensive to purchase and implement. For example, if I wanted to set up a remote dial-in solution, I'd have to purchase and install proprietary hardware. If scalability were a requirement, I would need to purchase and add ports to the configuration. Worse yet, when new modem technologies came around, I'd have to upgrade the ports. Finally, if I wanted to support newer remote access technologies, such as cable modems and an Asynchronous Digital Subscriber Loop (ADSL), a completely different solution would be necessary. All of these communications also work over costly leased lines that incur charges for data transport and connection times. Long-distance telephone charges alone can account for a significant portion of an IT department's budget.

One of the most significant advances in the area of remote access is the virtual private network (VPN). VPNs allow companies to use the infrastructure of a public network (such as the Internet) to transfer information securely. A VPN provides this security by managing authentication and by encrypting all information traveling between the client and the server. Figure 3-24 diagrams the setup of a basic VPN. The steps are logically very simple. First, clients connect to the Internet using any of a variety of mechanisms. Then, they connect to a remote VPN server using protocols that provide for authentication and data encryption. Once they are authenticated, users can use this "tunnel" to transfer data between clients and servers.

VPNs are not limited to connecting users for the purpose of remote access, however. Many hardware and software implementations support secure connections between

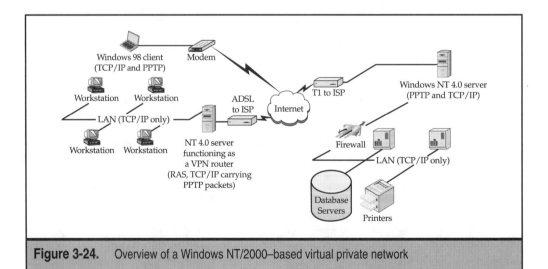

Figure 3-24.   Overview of a Windows NT/2000–based virtual private network

servers and machines in remote offices. For implementing a VPN, Windows 2000 supports the use of the Layer 2 Tunneling Protocol (L2TP) and Internet Protocol Security (IPSec). Both standards provide for the encryption of data as it travels over a public network and allow remote users to securely connect to their company servers. More information on Windows 2000 VPNs is available from SQL Server Books Online and from **www.microsoft.com/communications**.

Improved Authentication

For authentication, Windows 2000 has replaced the methods used by previous versions of Windows NT. Windows 2000 uses the industry-standard Kerberos version 5 protocol. Although the underlying mechanisms for this type of authentication are considerably more complicated, Kerberos provides additional security by requiring both the client and the server to securely identify themselves. The goal is to provide for a single sign-on to access all network resources. Apart from being convenient for end users, it relieves systems administrators from having to implement and maintain multiple security databases.

For securing other resources, Certificate Services can be used. The goal is for environments to be able to set up their own public-key-based security infrastructures. These methods will allow you to protect data by using Secure Sockets Layer (SSL) and *smart cards* (devices that present authentication information), as well as other methods of digital signatures for e-mail and other resources. Again, the technology is significantly more complex by nature, but in environments where authentication is of vital importance, it is invaluable.

For more information on using these advanced security features, see the online documentation installed with Windows 2000 and **www.microsoft.com/security**.

Remote Storage

One difficulty in working with various types of disk-storage and management options is making data available to users regardless of where it's stored on your network. Unfortunately, this is often a tedious and manual procedure. When files are being archived in larger environments, it is not uncommon for users to have to fill out a form to request files that have been taken offline or otherwise archived. The information is still "available"—just not convenient to access. They would then have to wait at least several hours while the information was retrieved from the selected media and placed back on the network. Windows 2000 automates many of these features through the use of a feature known as Remote Storage.

Remote Storage can be configured to automatically move files from disk devices to tape devices. The main benefit is in cost savings—tape storage is much cheaper than disk storage. Remote Storage works on a system of storage "levels." The two defined levels include local storage (for data stored on hard disks) and remote storage (for data off-loaded to tape). A systems administrator can specify the amount of free space that should remain available on a specific volume. When it is set up, Remote Storage automatically copies specific files to a tape device but also maintains the local copy. When the drive begins to fill past the preset value, Remote Storage automatically deletes files located on the volume and replaces them with pointers. Data can be automatically copied based on a preset schedule. The other benefit of using Remote Storage is that files can be automatically retrieved when needed. The process automatically copies the requested information back to local storage. In fact, other than the delay in accessing the files, users may not even notice that seldom-used data has been off-loaded to tape devices.

To set up Remote Storage, you must first have a compatible tape device installed in Windows 2000. Next, you can specify one or more NTFS volumes as "managed" volumes. This setting enables Remote Storage. Since it is not installed by default, you can install Remote Storage to your Windows 2000 installation by using the Add/Remove icon in the Control Panel. Once Remote Storage is installed, you can configure its settings by using the MMC snap-in component. For each managed volume, you can specify settings for how much free space should remain and which files can be off-loaded, as shown in Figure 3-25. For more information on using Remote Storage, see Windows 2000 Books Online. (This is the online help file installed by default with all versions of Windows 2000.)

WINDOWS NT/2000 DATA RECOVERY

So far, we have discussed several ways to protect information on the Windows NT 4 and Windows 2000 operating systems. Many of these techniques ensure that your data is protected, but how exactly do you recover from a situation in which data loss or corruption has occurred? In this part of the chapter, we'll look at the various ways in which you can

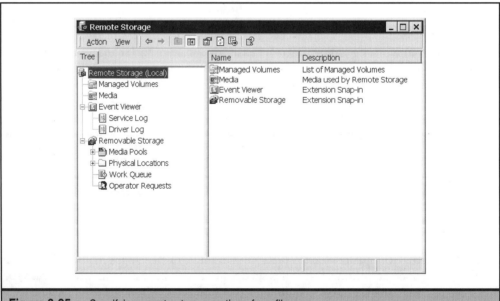

Figure 3-25.   Specifying remote storage options for a file

recover data at the OS level. In some cases, the solutions will be quite obvious. For example, if you need to recover a file that was previously backed up to tape, you can simply use your backup application to perform the necessary operations. But what if your OS won't boot, due to a corruption in system files or misconfiguration? In this case, the best answer might be to fix the corrupt files instead of recovering all the data on the server manually. Let's look at ways in which you can recover from various scenarios.

> **NOTE:**   The information in this section focuses on an overview of the methods for recovering from data loss scenarios. If you need further information on performing these tasks, please see the online help that is provided with Microsoft Windows NT and Windows 2000. It is important to take the time to ensure that you understand the actual processes completely, before a data loss situation occurs.

Recovering Data

The simplest situation for data recovery is that in which the OS is working fine, but certain data files have been lost. If you have a working backup of your information, you should be able to use your tape-backup software to restore the necessary information. In the case of a failed volume, for example, you can replace the hardware and then restore all the files contained on this device. The backup utilities included with Windows NT and Windows 2000 enable you to easily select specific files from a backup set.

Although this technique works well for data files (such as users' home directories), other applications might require specific recovery techniques. A good example is SQL Server—if files were in use during the backup process, they may not have been stored to tape. Similarly, Microsoft Exchange Server's message store might not be consistent, depending on when the backup was performed and which tools were used. We'll discuss the issues related to backing up SQL Server databases and files in Chapter 6. For more information on other such applications, see the documentation that accompanies them. Let's move on to looking at other data recovery scenarios.

Fixing Corrupt Boot Files

You may be faced with a situation in which you receive errors on startup that prevent you from entering Windows NT or Windows 2000. In the case of corrupt boot files (that is, the data appears to be available on the drive, but Windows will not start), you may be able to verify the Windows installation. To do this, boot the system from the three boot floppy disks (which you can create from another computer by using the WINNT /ox command) or if your system supports it, boot from the Windows NT/2000 CD-ROM. At the initial prompt, choose the option to repair an existing installation. You'll then be given the following options:

▼   **Inspect Registry Files**   Enables you to restore specific portions of the Registry. Note that this will overwrite your current Registry with the one stored on your ERD. Depending on the age of your ERD and the system changes that have occurred since you first set it up, you may lose configuration information.

■ **Inspect Startup Environment** Verifies that the files needed to start Windows NT are available on the hard disk. If they are not, it will copy those files from the installation media.

■ **Verify Windows NT System Files** Enables you to replace essential files, if you're receiving error messages such as "Missing NTLDR" or "Can't Find NTOSKRNL.exe" on bootup.

▲ **Inspect Boot Sector** Makes sure that the system is set up to boot into Windows NT, and will rewrite the boot sector, if necessary. Use this option when you are receiving a "Missing Operating System" or an "Invalid System Disk" error.

If only the boot or system files have been corrupted, the preceding options will help you recover your system. This strategy is preferable by far to a time-consuming reinstallation of the server and potential loss of data. Windows 2000 includes additional features that allow systems administrators to boot to a Recovery Console. This command-line interface provides the ability to use various troubleshooting tools and access information stored on NTFS partitions (provided the user has the Administrator password).

Performing a Complete System Restoration

If you've lost all the data on a disk (such as in the case of a failed, non-fault-tolerant drive), you'll need to start from scratch. The general steps required are time consuming, but you may have no alternative. The first step is to replace any hardware that has failed. For example, you might need to replace a hard disk or network card that is no longer functioning. This step could be very difficult if you are unable to determine which component has failed. If uptime is important, it is a good idea to keep a "spare server" available. As long as the failure is not related to disk devices, you can remove the hard disks from the failed machine and plug them into another one with a similar configuration. A less costly alternative might be to enter into a service agreement with your hardware vendor or a third party who can guarantee replacement hardware within a few hours.

Once the hardware has been repaired or replaced, it's time to start recovering information. In Chapter 5, we'll look at various software and hardware devices that can be used to protect information. If you are using a third-party backup tool, you should follow the instructions included with that software. For example, certain types of backup software provide "disaster recovery" options. These features allow you to boot a minimal OS (using a CD-ROM or floppy disks) and begin a recovery operation immediately.

If your software does not support this, you should start by reinstalling the OS. Although a complete reconfiguration is not necessary, you'll need to install the bare minimum to boot the system. This might include any special drivers required by your hardware. Next, you'll need to reinstall the drivers for your backup device, along with any third-party backup tools or utilities used. Following these steps, you'll be able to start a full restoration from the media using your backup software. Be sure to specify that all files should be replaced, including the existing Windows NT/2000 system Registry. Assuming that the restoration is successful, you will be able to reboot the computer and be back in business!

NOTE: Backing up and recovering Windows 2000 Active Directory requires special consider-ations based on your configuration. The process is fairly simple in environments that have only a few domain controllers, but it can be considerably more complex for larger or more distributed organiza-tions. Be sure to plan adequately for restoring Active Directory to ensure that information is not lost due to system failures.

MONITORING AND OPTIMIZING PERFORMANCE

The task of monitoring and optimizing performance is especially important when per-forming backups. Fortunately, the tools for performance monitoring have changed rela-tively little and are consistent between Windows NT 4 and Windows 2000. Based on your server configuration and business environment, optimization can enable you to perform tasks more quickly without having to purchase and manage additional servers and workstations. Windows NT includes several tools that can aid in the evaluation of perfor-mance. In the next few sections, we'll cover the following:

▼   The Windows NT/2000 performance tools

■   Task Manager

▲   Network Monitor

Performance Monitoring Methodology

Often, systems administrators will use the trial-and-error approach to performance opti-mization. For example, if something is not running as fast as an administrator thinks it should, the administrator will make one or more changes. If performance "seems" faster after a change, the setting is retained. Otherwise, it's back to square one. Although this method might work occasionally, the configuration changes may or may not have had a positive effect. For example, the changes could have a negative performance impact on other subsystems. Or, worse yet, the change could have no real effect, because the per-ceived improvement was due to a change in conditions. Holistic performance monitoring is based on carefully using a consistent methodology.

To monitor performance, it is important that you first have a baseline of information. This baseline should be compiled over time and should be used for measuring any signif-icant changes to your system. Keep in mind that it is always a good practice to make only one change at a time. This way, you'll be able to measure the effects of modifying a single parameter. Also, if performance decreases or other problems come up, you'll know what must be changed to return to the original configuration. Documenting performance val-ues is just as important as making changes.

A nagging question that may have occurred to you is "By measuring performance, am I not actually decreasing it?" The short answer is "sometimes." In some cases, perfor-mance monitoring may present a significant drain on resources. For example, the Win-dows NT Performance Monitor application itself uses CPU time, memory, and display resources. On modern systems, however, the drain is often negligible. In other cases, it's worth the performance decrease to collect important information. Whether you are running Performance Monitor or not, Windows NT and Windows 2000 automatically keep track of performance data for tuning themselves. Therefore, it does not matter if you measure 100 different parameters or only 1. The impact of running Performance Monitor will also remain constant for most types of monitoring, so you need not worry about it as long as you're using the same tool to measure performance each time.

NOTE: The performance monitoring tools available in Windows NT and Windows 2000 allow you to monitor remote machines. As collecting and displaying performance information can generate a load on a system, a good idea is to use a nonproduction server for remotely monitoring and recording performance statistics. As we'll see in later chapters, this same technique applies to SQL Server 2000's performance monitoring tools.

Windows NT/2000 Performance Tools

Windows NT Performance Monitor is installed by default with all Windows NT and Windows 2000 installations. Clicking the Performance Monitor icon in the Administrative Tools program group will start the program. By default, you'll be presented with a blank Chart view, which includes no specific information. Performance Monitor includes many counters and objects with which you can monitor certain aspects of system performance. *Counters* are general aspects of the system that can be monitored (for example, memory or a processor). *Objects* are the actual details you wish to track for the selected object (such as bytes committed or processor utilization).

To add a counter to the default view, click the Add button and view the various options:

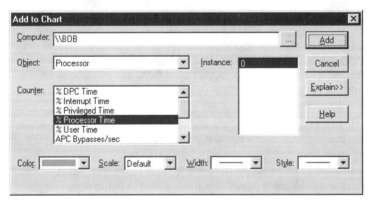

In the Add to Chart dialog box, you can click the Explain button to see more information about each of the available options. Depending on the types of counters you select, you may have an option for choosing one or more instances. For example, on a dual-processor server, you can choose to monitor data for one or both processors. Table 3-5 lists and describes some of the most useful measurements.

Counter	Object	Item Monitored	Usefulness*
Memory	Pages/sec	Number of times per second that the memory subsystem had to get information from the hard disk	If sustained greater than 5 pages/sec, you may want to consider a RAM upgrade.
Logical Disk	% Free Space	Percentage of free space per volume or per all volumes	A value of less than 10% indicates additional storage space is needed.
Physical Disk	Avg. Disk Queue Length	Number of tasks that had to wait for disk-based data	If high, disk performance may not be sufficient.
Server	Bytes Total/sec	Amount of data transferred by this server	High values indicate many and/or large file transfers to and from the server.
Server	Server Sessions	Number of active processes on this server	Indicates current activity; used to compare loads on different machines.
Network Segment	% Network Utilization	Percentage of the total network bandwidth in use	If sustained greater than 40%, performance may be decreasing.
Redirector	Reads/Writes denied/sec	Rejected requests for data transfer	Large file transfers may be occurring to/from this server.

Table 3-5.   Useful Performance Monitor Counters

Counter	Object	Item Monitored	Usefulness*
System	% Total Processor Time	Avg. processor utilization	High number indicates that the CPU may be overloaded.
System	Processor Queue Length	Threads waiting to be worked	Indicates the number of processes that are awaiting CPU time. (A high number indicates that the CPU is likely to be a bottleneck.)

*These guidelines should be taken as generalizations for sustained levels. It is common for pages/second, for example, to go above the recommended value for short periods of time.

Table 3-5. Useful Performance Monitor Counters (*continued*)

Specifically, relating to data protection, you'll want to look at the Windows NT Performance Monitor Logical and Physical Disk objects. The objects and counters that are available are based on the services and applications installed on the local machine. For example, if you have RAS installed, you will see the RAS Port and RAS Total counters. These counters help you determine the current situation of your remote access users. Microsoft ships Windows NT with basic performance counters enabled. For most systems administrators, these defaults are all they need. If you require more specific information, however, you can also enable other counters and objects. For example, to measure disk performance, you need to specifically turn on disk performance logging. To do this, you must go to a command prompt and type **diskperf -ye**. (The y flag activates disk performance monitoring, and the e flag specifies performance monitoring for stripe set volumes.) This change will take effect the next time you reboot the system. This option isn't enabled by default, because keeping track of disk performance information creates a slight decrease in performance. (Microsoft estimates less than five percent in most cases.) Whether or not this slowdown is worth the additional information depends on your environment and the use of the server. To monitor various network performance values, you also need to add the SNMP service and Network Monitor Agent in the Network Control Panel applet.

Chart view is only one way of viewing the information you are interested in monitoring. Performance Monitor offers four different views from which you can choose, depending on the type of data you want to collect and how you want to analyze and display this information:

▼ **Chart**   Graphs real-time system parameters over time.

■ **Alert**   Provides notification when certain criteria are met or exceeded.

■ **Log**   Records performance information for detecting trends over time.

▲ **Report**   Displays real-time data in column format.

Chart View

Chart view shows performance information in a graphical format. Figure 3-26 shows a typical chart generated by Windows NT's Performance Monitor. The X axis (horizontal) of the graph represents time. The Y axis (vertical) represents the measured performance values. To add information to a chart, select Edit | Add to Chart. You can then choose an object, a counter, and an instance to monitor. Additionally, you can select a color, scale, width, and style for the chart item.

The scale is a multiplier that can alter the range of values displayed on the Y axis of the graph. For most scenarios, the default values will be appropriate, but you can

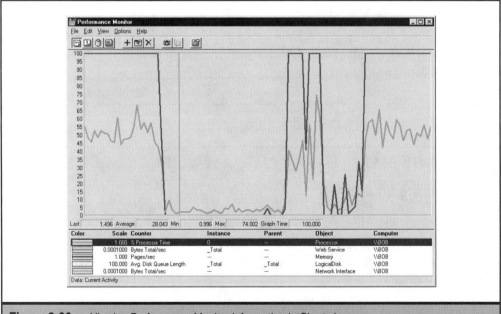

Figure 3-26.   Viewing Performance Monitor information in Chart view

change the multiplier based on what you are monitoring. For example, the default for the Number of Interrupts/sec counter (part of the processor object) uses a multiplier of 0.01, giving the Y axis a range of 0 to 10,000. If you rarely have a high Number of Interrupts/sec value, you can change the multiplier to 0.1 to more accurately view the information collected. Finally, you can configure more options by selecting Options | Chart. From there, you can modify display settings and set the update interval (which is set to 1.000 seconds by default).

CAUTION: Decreasing the measurement interval will increase the load on your system, and may decrease overall performance.

Alert View

Performance Monitor can be set up in Alert view to warn a user or systems administrator whenever a specific threshold is exceeded. This may be in the form of a maximum or minimum value for a counter or may be based on a percentage. In the following example, Performance Monitor is configured to warn the systems administrator when disk space falls below 10 percent free (a very common occurrence on my laptop!):

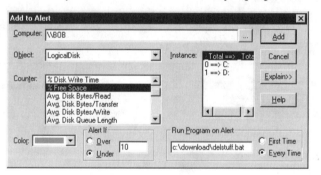

STEP-BY-STEP
Configuring an Alert

1. Select View | Alert.
2. Click Add to set up a new alert.
3. Choose the % Free Space counter of the LogicalDisk object and specify the Total Instance.

4. To set a threshold value, in the Alert If area, select the Under radio button and enter **10** as the list box value. (If you have more than 10 percent disk space available on your system, choose a higher percentage, such as 75 percent.)

5. Because we haven't created a specific batch file in this example, we'll leave the Run Program on Alert section blank. We could have created a batch file that clears out typical temporary files, however. Click Done to add this alert.

With these settings in place, if the combined free space on all of your drives is less than 10 percent of your total disk space, you'll see alerts start to appear in the Performance Monitor window. By default, an alert generates an entry in Performance Monitor Alert view only. You can configure other Alert methods by selecting Options | Alert. Using the Alert dialog box, you can choose to send a network message (making a dialog box appear on the user's screen) and/or add alert information to the Windows NT Event Log (to view events using Event Viewer).

Log View

You can choose to save performance-logging information to a disk file for later analysis or for keeping historical records. You can then use Performance Monitor or a third-party reporting program to report on this information.

STEP-BY-STEP
Logging Information in Performance Monitor

1. Open Performance Monitor and select View | Log.

2. Click the Add button and choose the following items: Processor, Physical Disk, and Server. Click Done to accept these choices.

3. To activate the logging, select Options | Log to specify a file to which to save information. For the filename, choose any valid name (for example, perfmon.log). Verify that the update interval is set to a reasonable time. Finally, click the Start Log button.

4. The screen shows that logging has been started and shows the current size of the log file (in bytes). While data is being collected, you can add a comment to the log by clicking the Place a Commented Bookmark into the Output Log button. This may be useful if you're performing specific operations on your system.

5. To stop the recording, select Options | Log | Stop Log.

Now that you've saved the information you're interested in, you can use the Report and Chart views to see the results. From either view, choose Options | Data From and specify the log file from which you want to obtain data. Then, add counters and objects just as you would if this were "live" information. Alternatively, you can prepare the data you are viewing to be examined outside Performance Monitor by selecting File | Export and choosing either TSV (tab-separated values) or CSV (comma-separated values) as the file type. These text file formats allow the data to be easily imported into reporting programs, such as Microsoft Excel.

It is important to note that logging with Performance Monitor logs every counter for the object selected. For example, if you select the Memory object, statistics for all of the counters within the Memory object will be measured and recorded. Because of this, log files can grow to become very large and can consume significant amounts of disk space. To prevent problems caused by reduced disk space, you should set the log on a nonsystem partition and ensure that space is available for generating a large log file. To reduce the amount of information recorded, you can limit logging to a high interval, thereby reducing the amount of statistical information that will be collected. Logging can also have negative impacts on CPU and memory utilization, so monitoring performance from a remote server can reduce the overall burden.

Report View

So far, we've seen that Performance Monitor's Chart view displays data in a visual format that is great for viewing trends over time. If you only want to see data values at specific intervals, Report view is for you.

STEP-BY-STEP

Using the Performance Monitor Report View

1. Select View | Report.
2. Modify the sampling rate by selecting Options | Report.
3. Click Add and add counters as you did in Chart view.

Figure 3-27 shows an example of the information provided by Report view.

Windows NT/2000 Task Manager

Sometimes, the information collected by Performance Monitor is more than you want to know. If you only want a snapshot of your system's current performance, you can use Windows NT Task Manager. You access Task Manager by pressing CTRL-SHIFT-ESC. Alternatively, you can right-click the taskbar and choose Task Manager, or press CTRL-ALT-DE-LETE and click Task Manager. There are three tabs on the Task Manager interface:

▼   **Applications**   Displays programs running on your system

■   **Processes**   Displays current tasks executing on your system

▲   **Performance**   Displays a snapshot of vital CPU and memory statistics

Windows NT Task Manager can be configured to your own preferences. On the View menu, you can choose to change the update frequency of Task Manager. Of course, the more frequently you update the display, the greater the performance load you will be exerting on your system (notice that the taskmgr.exe task uses CPU time, as well). Now that we've looked at some of the settings that can be made for Task Manager, let's look at the different tabs available within the application. Experiment with this utility—it will easily become your best friend when you're trying to figure out just what NT is up to!

The Applications Tab

The Applications tab shows a list of programs currently running on the system. These programs are referred to as *applications* or *tasks*. This list will only include programs that run as tasks and will exclude items such as services and other background tasks. Figure 3-28 shows several tasks running on the machine. Each name is a specific instance of a program. From this screen, you can choose to end a specific task (which shuts down a program or process) or switch to the highlighted task. You can also click the New Task button, which simply allows you to run an executable program.

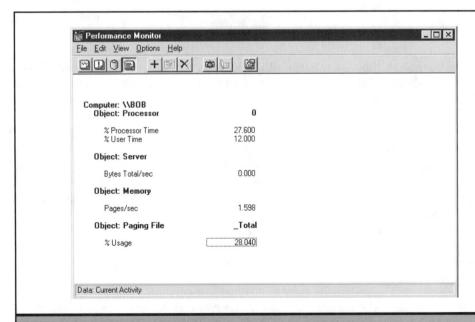

Figure 3-27.   Viewing Performance Monitor information using the Report view

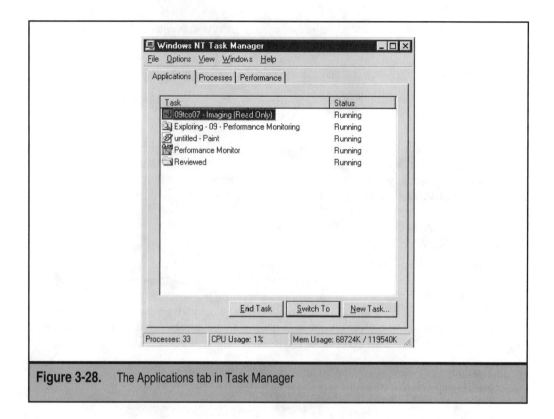

Figure 3-28.   The Applications tab in Task Manager

A menu on this tab allows you to tile all applications horizontally or vertically. This is a useful way of seeing what all of your applications are up to at any given time. If the Status column shows [Not Responding], the program likely is either waiting for you to input some information or has crashed.

The Processes Tab

The Processes tab, shown in Figure 3-29, displays the active processes currently running on your system. Are you surprised to see so many there? Even on a Windows NT system that is not running any programs that you can see, many background operations are running to keep the OS cranking.

These background operations include threads that execute as part of applications, system services, and other background tasks.

One item you'll recognize is the taskmgr.exe itself. In Figure 3-29, you can see the following column headings:

▼ **Image Name**   The name of the task that is running. In some cases, the task will have a friendly name (such as System or System Idle Process). Others have *.exe extension filenames that tell you what application is running.

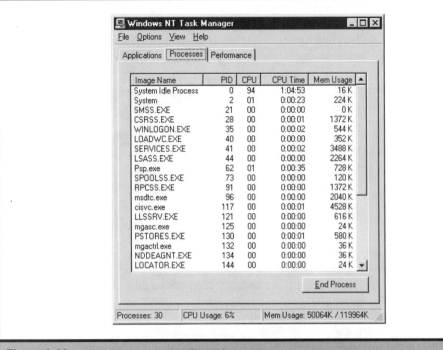

Figure 3-29. The Processes tab in Task Manager

- **PID**   The process ID. Windows NT assigns a unique PID to all tasks that run on the system. Note that these numbers may change when you run the same program several times.

- **CPU**   The percentage of the current CPU time allocated to the specific process. If the OS is not running a specific task, it will be running the System Idle Process.

- **CPU Time**   The amount of CPU time that has been used by this process. Windows NT automatically gives each process a certain amount of time to run its operations and then checks the next program in line. The format is in hh:mm:ss (hours:minutes:seconds). This is a great way to find out which applications are slowing down your system the most.

- ▲ **Mem Usage**   The amount of memory currently in use by the process. It is important to note that all of this memory may not be RAM alone—some of it may be paged to disk as virtual memory. When the application needs it, these pages of memory can be loaded into RAM for quicker execution.

You can click a column heading to sort by that value. For example, to sort programs by their usage of memory, click the Mem Usage column heading. If you'd like to reverse the sort order, click that heading again. You can also choose many additional parameters to view in this display by selecting View | Select Columns. The Select Columns dialog box will appear:

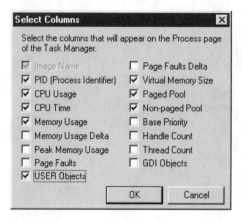

Here you can add and remove optional statistics from the display.

The following example describes how to check the amount of memory allocated by the OS when running Internet Explorer 5.

STEP-BY-STEP

Using Task Manager to Measure Memory Allocation

1. Make sure all programs are closed except Task Manager.

2. Go to the Processes tab and click the Mem Usage column to sort by this value. Make a mental note of the amount of total memory committed.

3. Launch the Internet Explorer application and wait until it is open.

4. Switch to the Performance tab and notice how much more memory is used when the Internet Explorer program is active. Also, click the Processes tab and then click the Mem Usage column to sort by this value to show exactly how much memory is currently in use.

You may not have realized it, but in performing this task, you have carried out the first two steps of performance monitoring: establishing a baseline (the amount of free memory before opening Internet Explorer) and making a single system change (opening Internet Explorer).

The Performance Tab

The Performance tab in Task Manager (see Figure 3-30) provides a readily available view of the current status of your system. It displays a snapshot of your CPU usage and memory statistics. Important information in the Performance tab includes the following values:

▼ **Totals**   The number of individual tasks running on the system

■ **Physical Memory**   The amount of RAM present in the system and its allocation

■ **Commit Charge**   The portion of memory currently being used by the system

▲ **Kernel Memory**   The amount of memory being used by the operating system

Each of these counters can provide valuable information when you're determining the exact load on your system. If things are running slowly, be sure to check them out.

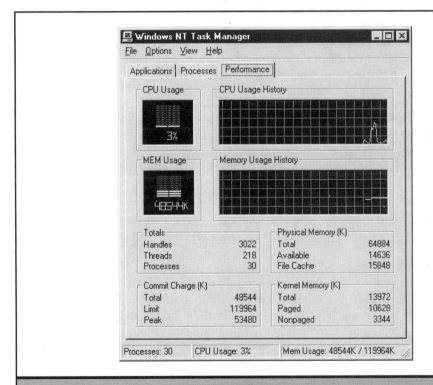

Figure 3-30.   The Performance tab in Task Manager

Windows NT/2000 Network Monitor

Windows NT Server includes a tool called Network Monitor. This useful application serves as a basic packet-level analyzer (sometimes referred to as a sniffer). Networking professionals often use dedicated devices to find information contained in packets traveling over the network. Network Monitor works in a similar way—it captures and examines all packets that are transferred over the network segment, and saves them to a buffer. To install Network Monitor, simply add the Network Monitoring Tools and Agent option in the Services tab. You then need to reboot the computer.

NOTE: The versions of Network Monitor included with Windows NT Server 4 and Windows 2000 Server are limited insofar as they can only monitor packets transmitted to and from the local machine. A full version of Network Monitor is included with Microsoft's Systems Management Server (SMS), which is also part of the BackOffice collection.

Network Monitor information can be especially useful for troubleshooting specific LAN connectivity problems. For example, suppose network clients have trouble receiving DHCP information. Network Monitor can be used to determine whether the client is sending out the appropriate broadcast request and whether the server is sending out a valid response. Figure 3-31 shows Network Monitor's main interface.

Note that collecting this type of data can affect the server's performance. One way to limit this is to restrict the buffer size. To do this, select Capture | Buffer Settings and specify the size of the buffer in megabytes. For most applications, a 2MB to 3MB buffer will be sufficient. If the server is unable to keep up with the flow of data packets, packets may be dropped. To increase performance, the Dedicated Capture mode can be used. With this setting, display statistics are not updated while packets are being detected; this reduces the load on the machine.

By using the filters available in the program, the potentially huge collection of data can be made manageable.

Network Monitor Example: Isolating PING Problems

Suppose a network administrator suspects that a user is running an application that is generating excessive PING traffic. However, the administrator is unsure where this data is originating.

The PING utility transmits and receives all data using Internet Control Messaging Protocol (ICMP) packets. The administrator begins a network capture and waits until the buffer (configured to be 2MB) is entirely full. The administrator then enables a filter that restricts the captured frames to only ICMP data. (The PING command sends ICMP packets only.) The exact process is described in the following steps.

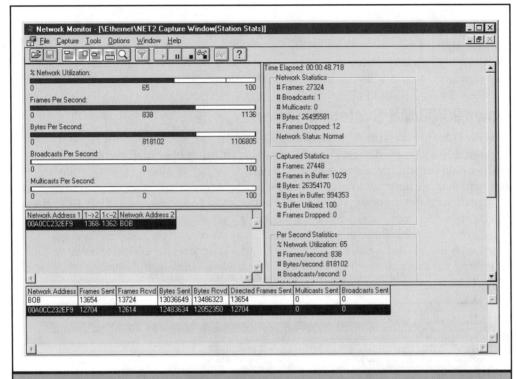

Figure 3-31.   Capturing network traffic statistics using Network Monitor

STEP-BY-STEP

Using Network Monitor to Measure PING Traffic

1. Select Capture | Buffer Settings and set the buffer size to 2MB.

2. Select Capture | Start.

3. Wait until the buffer is full, and then select Capture | Stop | View.

4. Click the Edit Display Filter button. Highlight the item that shows Protocol == Any, and click Expression in the edit frame.

5. In the Protocols tab, click Disable All. Then, highlight ICMP and click the Enable button. Click OK to accept these settings.

6. Click OK again to accept the new filter settings. The list of information should be restricted to only ICMP requests.

Figure 3-32 shows a filtered capture displaying only ICMP data. By examining these packets, the administrator knows that the PING commands are originating from IP address 10.1.1.1.

With Network Monitor, you can also save on your hard drive the information that you captured in a file. This information can then be recalled later for analysis, if required.

Windows 95/98/ME System Monitor

You don't have to be running Windows NT to do performance monitoring. Windows 95 and Windows 98 were designed to be consumer/end-user operating systems, but they can still provide valuable performance information. Although the tools are somewhat different (and much more limited), Windows 95/98/ME System Monitor can be used to find basic information on the status of your system. To run System Monitor, select Start | Programs | Accessories | System Tools | System Monitor. If the program is not installed, you can add it by using the Add/Remove Control Panel item. The interface for these tools is as user friendly as their Windows NT counterparts, and a Help file is available to assist you in determining the usefulness of information. Table 3-6 lists some useful items to monitor.

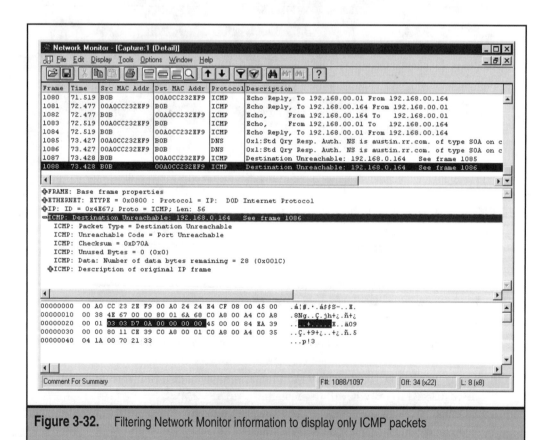

Figure 3-32.   Filtering Network Monitor information to display only ICMP packets

Counter	Item	Information Returned
Kernel	Processor Usage (%)	CPU workload
Memory Manager	Allocated memory	Memory in use
Memory Manager	Swapfile size	Data paged to disk
Dial-Up Adapter	Bytes Received/sec	Modem speed
Dial-Up Adapter	CRC Errors	Number of corrupted data packets (possibly indicative of phone line noise)
File System	Bytes Read/sec, Bytes Written/sec	Number of bytes read/written per second

Table 3-6.   Useful Windows 95/98/ME System Monitor Counters

Figure 3-33 shows Windows 98 System Monitor displaying basic statistics. This information can be useful to determine, for example, whether your system is overloaded or whether a dial-up adapter is performing poorly due to line noise or a low connection speed.

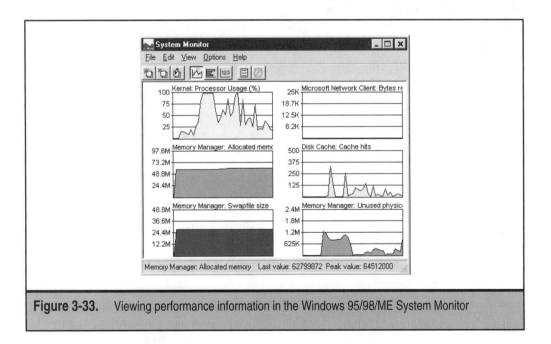

Figure 3-33.   Viewing performance information in the Windows 95/98/ME System Monitor

STAYING CURRENT

It's extremely important to stay current on operating systems. Anyone who has ever heard of a Service Pack or "hot fix" is aware that operating systems are imperfect and require regular updates. Microsoft and other vendors make updates available in several ways. Let's take a look at how you can find, install, and make the best of these updates.

To support the users of its products better, Microsoft often releases patches, updates, and free options for its OSs and applications. In most cases, these updates include important fixes and enhancements related to security and performance. Occasionally, they will also include additional functionality. In general, unless you have a compelling reason not to upgrade, you should ensure that all of your critical machines are running the latest available patches and fixes. Let's look into the types of updates that are available.

Windows NT Service Packs

Microsoft has been releasing OS patches in collections called Service Packs. The setup utilities for these files simply back up some of your existing system files (optional) and replace them if older versions are found. In general, it is a good idea to make sure you have the latest Service Pack installed on all of your Windows NT computers. Note also that Service Packs must be reapplied any time you install any software from the original Windows NT CD-ROM or from any other source. This includes situations in which you recover Windows NT data using an Emergency Repair Disk (described earlier in this chapter).

The Windows NT Option Pack

Microsoft releases other new OS features in its Option Packs. Option Packs include new programs and applets, and additional features not included in the "stock" operating system. The first Windows NT 4 Option Pack has been released, and is primarily aimed at users who are running Internet web and/or FTP services and those who are developing web-based applications. Among the major additions and upgrades in this package are the following:

▼ **Internet Information Server 4**   Includes versions 4.0 of the web and FTP services, including support for Active Server Pages, file uploading, and database connections.

■ **Microsoft Transaction Server 2**   Allows developers to easily create advanced code that shares data between applications.

■ **Microsoft Message Queue Server 1**   Allows web developers to queue data to be sent to remote computers in batches.

▲ **Internet Connection Services for Microsoft RAS**   Simplifies the management of dial-up connections.

The NT 4 Option Pack also includes numerous other OS extensions, many of which will greatly aid web developers, including:

▼ **Certificate Server**   Used for creating authentication certificates.

■ **Microsoft Index Server**   A search engine that can be used by visitors to your web site.

■ **FrontPage 98 Server Extensions**   Web server extensions used by Microsoft's FrontPage 98 web authoring tool.

■ **Microsoft Data Access Components**   New ODBC drivers and support for OLEDB and RDO.

■ **Microsoft Management Console**   A new interface for administering the IIS components.

■ **Microsoft Script Debugger**   A small tool that can be used by developers to debug Active Server Pages.

■ **Microsoft Site Server Express 2**   A scaled-down version of the full product that enables administrators to view web site usage information and verify sites for broken links.

■ **Visual Interdev Rapid Application Deployment Components**   Support for remotely debugging Active Server Pages and for managing server-side components.

▲ **Windows Scripting Host**   A scripting engine that allows users and systems administrators to quickly create and execute simple JScript and VBScript commands.

The Option Pack may be installed on Windows NT and Windows 95/98/ME computers. The specific components available will vary based on the OS you're using. Figure 3-34 shows a list of some of the items that are available for installation on a Windows NT 4.0 Server installation. Details are available in the Option Pack documentation. In general, it is a good idea to install only the components you require. However, many of the components previously described have dependencies on each other. If you are unsure what to install, choose the Typical option—it may take up a little more disk space, but it will prevent compatibility problems in the future. For details on components included with the Option Pack, see **www.microsoft.com/ntserver**.

Windows 2000 Updates

Recognizing that keeping up with technology updates can be a tedious and painful process, Microsoft has added functionality that allows Windows 2000 users to automatically connect to a single Internet site that can suggest and recommend updates to the operating system. This site can be accessed by clicking on Start and selecting Windows Update. The

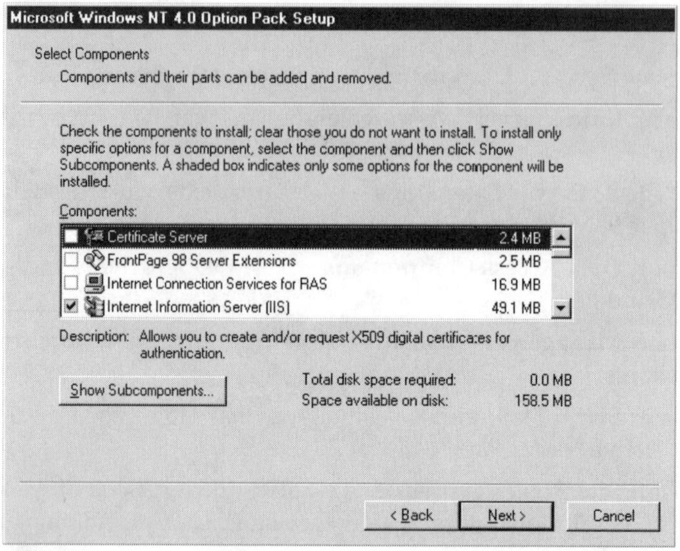

Figure 3-34. Choosing installation options for the Windows NT Option Pack

site will automatically check for installed software and make recommendations regarding available updates (see Figure 3-35). This is extremely helpful to systems administrators who are now able to ensure that their machines are running the latest code.

More information regarding updates to Windows 2000 is available at **www.microsoft.com/windows2000**.

Security-Related Hot Fixes, Patches, and Bulletins

Every once in a while, a press release regarding a security hole, problem, or work-around will surface through the media. Those who find the problem often claim that it's the end of the world or that Windows NT is no longer a useful OS. Others claim that the problem is negligible or has already been addressed. Of course, the truth is somewhere in between these two extremes. Nevertheless, because security is important, it requires constant monitoring of responsible sources of information. Microsoft's Security Advisor Program at **www.microsoft.com/security** provides one such source. An e-mail list is also available, to get your attention when new security patches are found.

Hot fixes are patches to fix a specific problem or add a specific feature to a portion of the operating system. These files typically are fairly small and are available for download. The fixes represent new code that should be implemented only by users who are experiencing a specific problem. In most cases, the fix will be released in the next Service Pack or operating system upgrade.

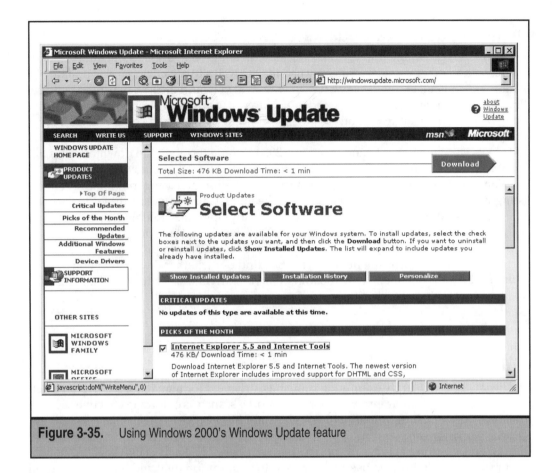

Figure 3-35.   Using Windows 2000's Windows Update feature

NOTE: As a product matures and is tested in real-world environments, problems will be found. However, as more and more people use Windows NT, it will continue to become more secure and stable. It isn't likely that the program has the kinds of flaws that would cause you serious security problems.

Windows 95/98/ME Updates

Many systems and network administrators do not realize that many different versions of Windows 95/98/ME are available. As of the time of this writing, there are at least four different versions of Windows 95. Most are only available through Original Equipment Manufacturer (OEM) releases, which are only available on new systems purchased from vendors. These "versions" are named Operating System Release (OSR) 2.*x*. For example, versions of Windows 95 labeled OSR 2.1 and above support the FAT32 file system, whereas other versions do not. Microsoft has also released Service Release 1 (SR1) for Windows 95, which is freely available for download. It is important to determine whether you need this set of patches and enhancements before you roll them out to a large number of machines, because it may not be worth the trouble.

Downloading Software Updates

I've avoided providing direct links for downloading the updates mentioned here. Microsoft and other vendors frequently change the web site organization and update filenames and content. Finding the patches and files that you need can most easily be done online. To start searching for product updates, go to **www.microsoft.com/windows**. Choose your OS from the main page and find the appropriate downloads. You can also find updates from the Microsoft.com Downloads Center at **www.microsoft.com/downloads/**. Windows 98, Windows ME, and Windows 2000 include the ability to download updates automatically from the OS. To get started, simply select Start | Windows Update.

You can't beat free software patches and upgrades for increasing the value of your existing systems. Upgrading your software and keeping it current will increase the life cycle of your applications and OS—and even delay costly upgrades. Keeping current on new technologies has always been a struggle for IT. Often, however, some additional driver support or a few enhanced software features can dramatically improve your system performance. If such improvements are available, find out whether they'll help you or your users, and if so, apply them. Downloading patches, drivers, and additional software can keep your machines consistent, up-to-date, and bug free—usually at a price you can't beat: free!

SUMMARY

We began this chapter by examining some best practices for managing security in a networked computing environment. A lot of these ideas, such as enforcing effective security policies and controlling system settings, are common practice in many business settings. Others, however, are less intuitive. Based on these goals and recommendations, we moved on to looking at ways of configuring Windows NT 4 and Windows 2000 to help ensure that only authorized users have access to your information and that the data itself is protected against willful or accidental loss. Finally, we looked at ways to monitor and optimize performance on Windows-based systems.

Savvy systems administrators are probably aware of many of the features and topics covered in this chapter. Knowledge is only half the battle, however. Equally important is ensuring that security policies and data protection methods are well implemented in your own environment. Now that we've discussed the basic platform for SQL Server 2000, let's move on to look at its features in more detail.

CHAPTER 4

SQL Server 2000 Architecture

It's increasingly common for network and systems administrators to be in charge of backing up a SQL Server database as part of their job responsibilities. Realizing this, Microsoft has gone to great lengths to ensure that SQL Server 2000 is easy to administer, even for novice users. By using the simple interface of Enterprise Manager, the most common tasks are just a few clicks away. But, if you're new to working with relational databases, don't let the simple interface fool you—there are several very important considerations that you should take into account before you work with a platform like SQL Server 2000.

Relational database systems deal with some issues that are very different from those affecting operating systems. The fundamental purpose of these machines is to store and provide data to many users quickly. They must do this while maintaining the integrity of the data they contain.

In this chapter, we'll cover the major features of SQL Server 2000 *except* those pertaining specifically to backup and restoration procedures (which we'll cover in later chapters). The purpose of this chapter is to give you a solid understanding of the architecture of SQL Server 2000. This includes details about the organization of relational information, how the data is stored, and how data is accessed. The goal of this chapter is not to teach procedures; instead, it is to familiarize you with working with SQL Server.

This chapter is designed to be useful for many different types of readers. Whether or not you're familiar with SQL Server, I urge you to read this chapter before continuing on to the portions of the book that are related to backup and recovery. Although you may not need to know all of the intricacies of SQL Server 2000 in order to perform backup and recovery options, there's a good chance that you'll learn something new about the product that will help you perform your job functions more quickly and easily. Needless to say, if you're new to SQL Server, you'll probably find this chapter filled with much new information. In any case, I hope that it will serve as a useful overview. Finally, if you're a database developer and you want more information on SQL query syntax and operations, see the *SQL Server 2000 Developer's Guide* (by Michael Otey and Paul Conte, Berkeley: Osborne/McGraw-Hill, 2000).

If you're interested in further details, you should be aware of other resources to which you can refer. Before we begin looking at technical information, I should familiarize you with something that will serve as a useful reference: SQL Server Books Online. Microsoft has provided an immense catalog of useful information in the online help included with SQL Server 2000. As I already mentioned, there is not nearly enough room in this chapter to cover all of the features of the product in detail. To access SQL Server Books Online, simply click Start | Programs | Microsoft SQL Server | Books Online. (See Figure 4-1.)

In this chapter, we'll start with some of the basic concepts related to database servers. You'll first read about the types of objects that make up a typical database. This is vital to understanding the content that follows. Specifically, you'll find details on how to implement and manage the features related to SQL Server's security architecture and how to measure and monitor performance. We'll also briefly cover other topics, such as the overall network and database architecture and information from a developer's point of view. Let's begin by looking at what makes up a relational database server.

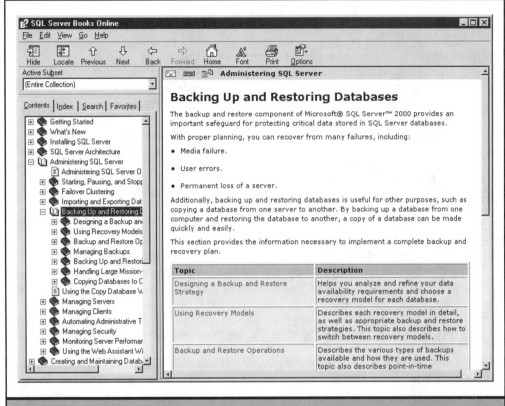

Figure 4-1. Viewing information in SQL Server 2000 Books Online

NOTE: Throughout this chapter, I will be referring to the various operating systems on which SQL Server 2000 can be run. These include Windows 95, Windows 98, Windows Millennium Edition (ME), Windows NT 4.0, and Windows 2000. In almost all cases, SQL Server 2000 functions the same way in Windows 2000 as in Windows NT—so when I refer to Windows NT/2000, I am referring to both operating system platforms. (Wherever differences do exist, I will state them explicitly.)

RELATIONAL DATABASES

All too often, technical people focus on finding the solution to a problem, sometimes forgetting to look at the big picture. When it comes to databases, it's important to first understand the reasons for having a database server. And, no, it's not just to keep you on your toes! Before moving into the specifics of SQL Server, it's worth taking some time to examine the fundamental concepts underlying database design.

Whether or not you've had experience with database management, this discussion should prove useful. For those who are new to the field, it will answer some questions about why database servers seem to be so complicated, and will provide a sound introduction to important data management issues. For old-timers, it may serve as a reminder of why we deal with such things as security and managing user access. And even if you've been around the database block (no pun intended), you'll probably still find it useful to review some basic issues that you may take for granted.

At its most basic level, a database is simply a repository for information. This data storage space is responsible for maintaining data in an organized fashion and then making this data available to users and applications that need it. Managing issues such as security, concurrency, and transactions is the responsibility of the database server engine. We'll get to these topics later in this chapter. First, though, we should examine the objects and relationships that make up a database.

NOTE: There are many different database platforms in the market today, and each uses slightly different terminology. For example, a "database instance" in the Oracle world is quite different from a "database" on SQL Server. Although the underlying concepts are the same, keep in mind that differences exist. I'll make notes where relevant, but the terminology I'll use throughout this book pertains mainly to the Microsoft SQL Server world.

Database Objects

Before diving too far into the technical guts of a relational database management system (RDBMS), let's look at the common types of database *objects* the system supports. These are the structures related to data with which users interact. The purpose of a database server is to store and manage data in an organized fashion. The goal is to be able to store and retrieve data easily. Database objects supported in SQL Server 2000 are described next.

Tables

The fundamental unit of data storage in a relational database is the table. Tables store information in rows. Each row, in turn, contains values for one or more columns that specify related information about a single data item. Tables are the structures in which actual information resides. Tables generally refer to a single logical entity. For example, I might create a table called "Employees." Within the Employees table, I might have rows that include information related to each employee (for example, "First Name," "Last Name," and so on). Of course, I can have many rows, each of which represents one instance of the entity that the table describes (in this case an employee). Table 4-1 provides an example of the structure of a simple database table.

In SQL Server, tables are built within a database (which, in turn, resides on a data file). We'll look at the actual storage concepts related to table data later in this chapter. For now, know that the majority of user-related database functions will involve the use of information stored in tables in one way or another. These are also the fundamental objects that you will be responsible for protecting in your backup and recovery plans.

Employee Number	First Name	Middle Initial	Last Name	Department	Phone Extension
1	Anil	K	Desai	Engineering	0937
2	Jane		User	Marketing	1554

Table 4-1.   Sample Table Containing Information About Employees

Views

A *view* is a database object that actually *refers* to data stored in one or more tables. Views are database objects that are defined by SQL queries (which we'll cover later). They specify which information is to be returned to a user. Users interact with views in the same way that they interact with tables. However, views do not actually store data; instead, they retrieve relational information from tables, as illustrated in Figure 4-2.

Views are used in several types of scenarios and can be very helpful in managing information. One benefit is in regard to security. You can create a view of a table that allows users to see only a subset of the information stored in one or more tables. This is useful, for example, if you have an employees table that contains sensitive information. You might create a view that allows users to query against all information except salary information. Furthermore, you might choose to restrict permissions on the underlying database itself and assign permissions to the view only. Additionally, views are useful for encapsulating business logic. By storing commonly used queries as views, you can reduce the chance that a developer will make an error in retrieving data. Views can even refer to other views, although this practice can sometimes make it difficult to debug any problems that crop up. Overall, though, views enable you to simplify administration, increase manageability, and improve security.

Indexes

Indexes are database objects that store a subset of a table's columns. They are used to speed data searches by minimizing the amount of information that must be searched by SQL Server. This works in much the same way as you might use the index of this book. Instead of flipping through all of the pages, you would look for simple keywords in the index. When you find what you're looking for, you're referred to a page number that contains the detailed information. Clearly, searching through the index is much quicker than searching through the entire book, page by page.

Indexes are used to reduce the amount of time it takes SQL Server to find the information a user requests. For example, suppose you often run queries that search for employees based on their last names. However, your database table for employee information actually contains much more information (for example, address, manager's name, and

	ID	Name	Quantity	Price
Table	1	Unit 1	1	$1.53
	2	Unit 2	12	$12.01
	3	Unit A7	5	$9.37
	4	Item 05	12	$0.73
	5	Item 12	18	$0.22
	6	Misc 01	37	$17.01

	Name	Total Amount
View	Unit 1	$1.53
	Unit 2	$144.12
	Unit A7	$46.85
	Misc 01	$629.37

Figure 4-2.   Logical overview of database views

job title). If an index is placed on the First Name and Last Name columns of this table, SQL Server will not have to search through all the information in the table to gain this information. Instead, it will search the index (in this case, a list of all of the last names) and then go to the pertinent rows for the remainder of the data. A query that refers only to indexed columns is often called a *covered query*. If details on those rows are required, the index will point to the appropriate data storage areas.

SQL Server 2000 supports two types of indexes—clustered and nonclustered. Clustered indexes involve the physical ordering of items in a database. This means that related information is physically stored together on the hard disk. By default, SQL Server automatically creates a clustered index on the primary key (described later) when a table is created. Since this type determines the actual order in which pages are stored on the disk, a table can have only one clustered index. Clustered indexes increase performance most when you will be returning an ordered subset of information. For example, if I frequently perform queries that require a range of part numbers (for example, Part #150055 – Part #15116), access will be much quicker with a clustered index, since these values are physically stored near each other on the disk and thus will require fewer I/O operations to retrieve. However, in databases that are used mainly for transaction information (such as a sales order entry system), clustered indexes can actually decrease performance.

Nonclustered indexes, in contrast, are separate structures that store a subset of the information in a table but do not affect the physical storage of data on the disk. A table may have many nonclustered indexes. These indexes actually store *links* to the information in the covered columns, to speed searches. We'll look more closely at indexes and their effects on performance later in this chapter. For now, however, understand that the proper use of indexes can dramatically improve SQL Server performance, especially for very large or very active databases.

Stored Procedures

Stored procedures are named Transact-SQL statements or transactions that are stored within a database as an object. They contain procedural code that can be executed on demand. There are several benefits to using stored procedures versus performing the same queries manually. Perhaps the most important benefit is the dramatic speed increase that stored procedures can cause. Stored procedures execute much more quickly than the same statements that execute on an ad hoc basis. The main reason for this performance increase is that the SQL Server 2000 database engine stores a predetermined optimal data recovery plan in cache memory. This is also one reason that you will get a much quicker response time from a query the second time you run it (provided that the data pages haven't yet expired from the cache due to other activities).

There are also security benefits to using stored procedures. Like views, stored procedures can be used to hide from users the underlying database objects that are being affected. This helps you restrict the actions that users can perform directly on database objects, and provides an alternative to relying on (and managing) complicated permissions structures. It also allows for better management of underlying table structures. For example, if you want to change an employee's address information in several tables at once, you can create a single stored procedure that will make sure that all the necessary operations are carried out. Additionally, stored procedures can call other stored procedures, allowing the development of modularly coded business rules and SQL statements.

Triggers

In some cases, you'll want to take some action every time data in a table is accessed or modified. *Triggers* allow you to automatically fire a SQL statement whenever users execute commands that access a table. The statement can then execute one or more SQL statements that modify data or perform validity checks on the operation. For example, a trigger may be used to automatically delete all employee time sheet data whenever an employee is deleted from the database. The trigger can access both "before" and "after" images of the data when it is executed. Optionally, SQL Server 2000 triggers can call other triggers to form a cascading effect (although care must be taken to avoid recursive loops).

Functions

Database administrators and designers are familiar with using functions that are built into SQL Server. For example, the GetDate( ) function can be used to retrieve the current date and time on the server. And, aggregate functions such as SUM, AVG, and COUNT can be used to calculate meaningful values from data. In SQL Server 2000, database administrators also have the ability to create their own custom functions. These functions might perform common tasks based on business logic. For example, a certain financial application might often perform some calculations on a customer's salary to determine the amount of a potential loan. A database administrator could create a custom function that performs this task. The following query shows how a function called CalcCustomerLoanAmount( ) can be used.

```
SELECT Salary, CalcCustomerLoanAmount(Salary) as MaximumLoan
FROM   Customers
WHERE LastName = 'Smith' and FirstName = 'Bob'
```

The result would include the desired information using the custom function. Note that the use of custom functions can sometimes dramatically decrease performance. If designed correctly and used sparingly, however, functions are a great way to expand the tools in a database developer's bag of tricks.

Defaults, Rules, and Constraints

Although triggers are a good solution for executing tasks based on user actions, it's often simpler to place restrictions on the types of information that are acceptable in a column of data. SQL Server provides several different types of *constraints*:

▼ **NOT NULL**   A value must be specific for this column.

■ **CHECK**   The values supplied must meet the criteria specified in the constraint. A database developer can define a CHECK constraint to ensure that an entered integer is an even, positive value.

■ **UNIQUE**   No values in this column may be duplicates of another. This might be used, for example, in an employee information table to prevent duplicate employee numbers from being entered.

■ **PRIMARY KEY**   Defines which column or columns uniquely identify each row in the database. No two rows can have the same values for the primary key.

▲ **FOREIGN KEY**   Enforces data integrity between tables by creating a reference for specific types of information.

We'll discuss the PRIMARY KEY and FOREIGN KEY constraints in later sections. CHECK constraints are place limitations on the types of information that can be stored in a specific column of data. For example, I might want to restrict the value in a phone number column to a 10-digit format (with no dashes or other characters). A constraint can ensure that information is entered in numeric format. If the information does not meet the criteria, an error is returned to the user. Constraints can be placed on one or more columns and can be quite complex.

Defaults are settings placed on a table that specify which values should be used if none is specified. This is commonly used in situations where the database assumes that values are set to False unless otherwise specified.

Rules function similarly to constraints but have the added benefit of existing as database objects. In contrast to constraints—which are defined as part of a column's definition—rules can be "bound" or "unbound" to columns. This allows the flexibility of disabling a rule without losing its definition. However, only one rule may apply to a column's definition. Rules are provided mainly for backward compatibility with SQL Server applications. Microsoft recommends that, wherever possible, CHECK constraints be used instead of rules.

Domain, Entity, and Referential Integrity

It is possible to create a database in which all the information stored in tables is completely unstructured and unrelated. This would lead to many problems, however, as is often learned by those who do not take the time to adequately plan the structure of their databases. Generally, different pieces of information stored in your database objects relate to each other in some way. A commonly used example is that of a sales database. Each sale might be tied to a customer, but the actual information about the customer (including shipping address and purchase history) might be stored in other tables. In this case, there is a clear relationship between the two tables that must be kept intact. Additionally, business rules might require that each customer have a unique customer number that should never be reused.

Integrity constraints are created to ensure that these relationships are maintained in a consistent manner. There are three major types of integrity that database designers must keep in mind, as illustrated in Figure 4-3.

▼ **Domain integrity**   Ensures that values stored within a column are consistent and in accordance with business rules. Domain integrity can be based on constraints such as UNIQUE and CHECK constraints that specify what values are acceptable for each column.

■ **Entity integrity**   Refers to information stored in rows. (Remember that each row in a table stores information about one entity of the type that the table describes.) This type of constraint makes sure that the information stored in rows within a table is consistent and follows the rules specified. For example, each row must contain the same number of columns (although some values may be left blank).

▲ **Referential integrity**   Applies across tables and ensures that information between these objects is consistent. Referential integrity includes relationships between tables. The actual columns that match between the tables are known as foreign keys and primary keys. Referential integrity ensures that related information remains consistent. It solves, for example, the problem we mentioned initially—ensuring that only valid customers are used for all orders placed in the database and avoiding the problem of "orphan rows." Orphans might occur, for example, when a customer row is deleted from the database, but the customer still has orders. In this case, the orders are orphans since their parent row (the customer information) no longer exists. When it comes time to fulfill the orders, users will find that they do not have enough information.

Structured Query Language

So far, we have talked about how data is stored in relational databases. We have not, however, discussed the important details related to retrieving and modifying data. The

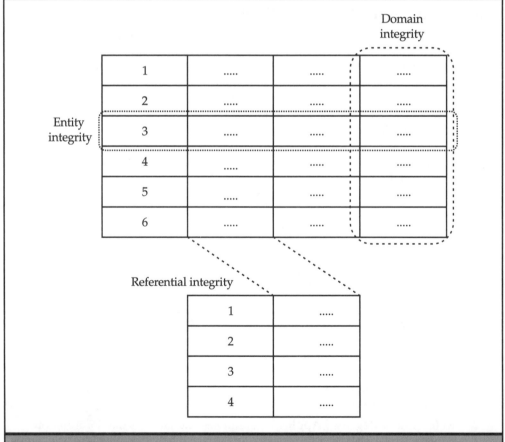

Figure 4-3. Comparing various types of database integrity

Structured Query Language (SQL, often pronounced "sequel") is the primary method used for obtaining information from an RDBMS. It is defined by the American National Standards Institute (ANSI) under several versions (often named after the year in which the standard was defined). For example, a commonly supported standard is called ANSI SQL-92. There are four main SQL Data Manipulation Language (DML) commands:

▼ **SELECT**   Returns information from one or more database tables

■ **INSERT**   Adds a new row to a table

■ **UPDATE**   Modifies information in an existing row

▲ **DELETE**   Removes one or more rows from a table

Figure 4-4 shows the results of a basic SQL SELECT statement executed in SQL Query Analyzer. It is beyond the scope of this book to examine SQL query syntax in depth. For that, please see other references, such as SQL Server 2000 Books Online or Otey and Conte's *SQL Server 2000 Developer's Guide*. However, in Chapter 6, we will examine the commands that are used specifically for data protection.

Batches and Transactions

SQL commands are often executed in groups of related commands called a *batch*. When you run queries in SQL Query Analyzer (a process that we'll cover in a later section), the commands are implicitly sent as batch statements. Certain types of statements are not permitted within the same batch, so you can use the GO command to separate them.

Transactions are SQL commands that are not necessarily related but must execute in an all-or-nothing fashion. Let's look at a common real-world example of a transaction. Assume that you want to carry out a financial transaction between two different banks. The basic operation should subtract money from User A's account and add the money to User B's account. For obvious reasons, you wouldn't want one of those transactions to occur without the other (or you will have made someone either very happy or very upset). To avoid this potential problem, you could combine both operations into a single transaction. In case an error occurred during the transaction (for example, one of the two servers was unavailable), neither of the two transactions would be performed.

Another example in applications is when you're updating information such as a customer's address. You wouldn't want an operation to update information regarding her street address without also updating her zip code. Again, this is a perfect place for a transaction.

Transactions must pass the "ACID" test, having all four of the following properties:

▼ **Atomicity**   Each transaction is represented by a single all-or-nothing operation: either all steps are carried out or the entire process is aborted.

■ **Consistency**   No data changes should violate the structure and design of the database.

■ **Independence**   Transactions are not aware that other transactions are being run at the same time.

▲ **Durability**   If an error occurs during the processing of a transaction, partial transactions should be reversed.

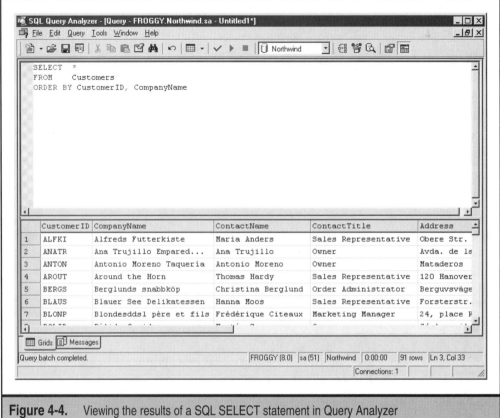

Figure 4-4.   Viewing the results of a SQL SELECT statement in Query Analyzer

Distributed Transactions

In most environments, data is stored in more than one data repository. It is often necessary to run transactions across multiple databases and platforms. The other data repositories you are trying to access might be as unique as a Microsoft Access database or an Excel spreadsheet, but could also be another RDBMS, such as an Oracle or Sybase server. SQL Server 2000 supports the use of *linked servers,* which allow users to enter queries that refer to objects stored on other machines. DBAs can also specify whether the statements will execute on the SQL Server or on the remote data repository. In this way, users can access information stored in various locations transparently.

SQL SERVER ARCHITECTURE

With the release of SQL Server 2000, Microsoft continued the usability and architectural enhancements it introduced with SQL Server 7.0. Users of previous versions of SQL

Server noticed significant improvements in scalability, performance, reliability, and ease of administration. SQL Server 2000 continues these enhancements by including even more new features.

One of Microsoft's foremost goals for the SQL Server platform is for it to be accepted into higher-end businesses and into enterprise-level data centers. Microsoft has made many inroads in these areas against several other well-known competitors (including Oracle and IBM's DB2). Recently, Microsoft demonstrated record-breaking cost versus performance results in the industry-standard Transaction Processing Council (TPC)-D Benchmark suite. (For more information about the TPC benchmarks, see **www.tpc.org**.) These results help prove the scalability and performance that SQL Server is able to provide.

SQL Server has many other advantages over competing platforms. Veteran DBAs and casual database users alike will appreciate the ease of management offered in SQL Server 2000. The updated visual tools (such as Enterprise Manager and Query Analyzer) make managing complex operations very simple for the end user. They also provide an intuitive method for performing common tasks that would otherwise require cracking open user guides (something that we know many users never consider!).

Now that you have a solid understanding of basic relational database concepts, it's time to look at how SQL Server 2000 is designed "under the hood." If you're new to Microsoft's premier database server platform, you'll likely find that it offers many new features that greatly help in the areas of administration, security, scalability, reliability, and performance. That's a tall order, however! Users of previous versions of SQL Server will see a marked improvement in performance and in the ease of management of the product. This allows developers and DBAs to focus on more important tasks, such as managing applications. Let's start by looking at the various editions of SQL Server 2000, and then move on to examine the architecture of the product itself.

Different Editions of SQL Server 2000

The SQL Server 2000 platform has been designed to run in many different environments. Microsoft has gone to great lengths to ensure that the same code base is used, regardless, in all versions of the product, from the desktop platform to enterprise-level servers. There are seven versions of SQL Server 2000, as listed in Table 4-2.

In most environments, servers will be installed with the Standard Server product. Desktop users (such as sales staff) who require their data "to go" will likely benefit from installing the Desktop Edition. On the other end of the spectrum, large installations of SQL Server will benefit from the enhanced scalability and reliability features of the Enterprise Edition. Fortunately, all three are installed, administered, and managed similarly, thus providing end users, developers, and high-end database administrators a similar console with which to work.

SQL Server Services

There are several different ways in which SQL Server can be run. On the Windows 95/98/ME platform, SQL Server runs as an application. That is, it is launched and managed

Edition	Operating Systems Supported	Licensing Options	Notes
Desktop	Windows 95/98/ME Windows NT 4 Workstation Windows 2000 Professional	Can be installed for no additional charge if users have named SQL Server Client Access Licenses	Has limited replication and DTS capabilities; decreased memory requirements
Standard Server	Windows NT 4 Server Windows 2000 Server Microsoft Small Business Server (10GB database size limit) Microsoft BackOffice Server	Per seat or per user	Includes Microsoft English Query and OLAP Services
Enterprise	Windows NT Server, Enterprise Edition Windows 2000 Advanced Server Windows 2000 Datacenter Server	Per seat or per user	Supports clustering and very large memory and additional Analysis Services features
64-bit Edition	64-bit versions of Windows 2000	Extremely high performance due to support for newer processor and server architectures	
Windows CE Edition	Windows Consumer Edition (CE) 2.11 or later PocketPC Other embedded systems (based on OEM support)	Designed as a storage engine for use with handheld and portable devices	Optimized for working in low-memory situations

Table 4-2.   Various Editions of SQL Server 2000 and Their Features

Edition	Operating Systems Supported	Licensing Options	Notes
Developer Edition	All 32-bit Windows-based operating systems	Version of SQL Server Enterprise Edition designed for development and testing purposes	
Desktop Engine	All 32-bit Windows-based operating systems	Designed for use by only a few users and can be embedded in applications	Replaces Microsoft Data Engine (MSDE); no licensing fees for small applications

Table 4-2. Various Editions of SQL Server 2000 and Their Features *(continued)*

under a specific user process. If necessary, you can use SQL Server the same way in Windows NT/2000; however, it's far more likely that you'll want the program to run as a service independent of user context. This allows SQL Server to continue running whether or not there is a user logged on to the system. In Windows NT/2000, SQL Server 2000 is generally run as a set of services. These system processes remain running and able to respond to requests on the operating system regardless of whether or not a user is logged on. The specific services that are available in SQL Server 2000 are listed in Table 4-3.

You may not need to install, or routinely use, all of the services listed in Table 4-3. In addition to being run as a service, SQL Server can be run as an application from the command line for special situations. The sqlservr command can be followed by a –m switch to start the database in single-user mode, or an –f switch to start with a minimum fail-safe configuration. Both options can be helpful in database maintenance and/or troubleshooting. Keep in mind that you cannot start, stop, or pause SQL Server by using the Services Control Panel applet if you started it from the command line, because this process is not running as a service. For more details related to starting SQL Server 2000 from the command line, see the SQL Server Books Online.

With SQL Server 2000, Microsoft has introduced the ability to run multiple independent instances of the database server on the same machine. This is useful for improving security, for performing testing, and for working in development environments. Figure 4-5 shows an example of the dialog box that allows you to install additional instances of SQL Server 2000. This is accessed by simply rerunning the SQL Server 2000 Setup process.

Service	Executable Name	Service Name	Function	Notes
SQL Server Service	Sqlservr.exe	MSSQLServer	The main database server engine	Can be started either as a service or from the command line. This is the main instance of Microsoft SQL Server 2000 on a machine.
SQL Server Service – Named Instances	Sqlservr.exe	MSSQL$InstanceName	Additional instances of SQL Server that reside on the same machine	Can be accessed by referring to the machine name and the instance name (for example, "Server1/ Instance1")
SQL Server Agent	SQLAgent.exe	SQLSERVERAGENT	Used for executing scheduled jobs	Account must have access to other machines to perform remote jobs
SQL Server Agent for named instances	SQLAgent.exe	SQLAgent$InstanceName	Used for executing jobs for named instances	Account must have access to other machines to perform remote jobs
MS Distributed Transaction Coordinator (MSDTC)	Msdtc.exe		Allows for processing and monitoring real-time transactions involving remote servers	
Full-Text Search	Mssearch.exe		Allows users to perform searches of TEXT column types	
Microsoft English Query	Mseq.exe		Allows end users to perform SQL queries in plain English	Installed separately after SQL Server is installed

Table 4-3. Various Services That Are Part of SQL Server 2000

Service	Executable Name	Service Name	Function	Notes
Microsoft OLAP Services	Msmdsrv.exe	MSSQLServerOlapService	Allows for complex data analysis using data cubes	Installed separately after SQL Server is installed
Microsoft SQL Server Active Directory Helper	sqladhlp.exe	MSSQLServerADHelper	Lists SQL Server resources within the Active Directory database	Designed for use in environments that use the Windows 2000 Active Directory

Table 4-3.   Various Services That Are Part of SQL Server 2000 *(continued)*

Furthermore, the default instance of SQL Server on any machine may be either a SQL Server 2000 installation or SQL Server 7.0. This provides excellent flexibility for environments in which you are attempting to upgrade but must run both versions during the transition.

Microsoft supports upgrading SQL Server 6.5 or later databases to SQL Server 2000. This procedure is easily performed using the SQL Server Upgrade Wizard, which can be accessed by clicking Start | Microsoft SQL Server – Switch | SQL Server Upgrade Wizard. (See Figure 4-6.)

Data Storage Architecture

When it comes to designing a database server platform, there are several main concerns:

▼ **Reliability**   Features of the database server platform that protect against data loss or corruption and allow for dependable access from clients.

■ **Availability (uptime)**   A measure of the stability of a database server based on the amount of time its services are available to end users. Availability is often measured in a percentage of uptime (for example, 99.999%, sometimes called "five-nines"). We'll discuss availability further in Chapter 10.

■ **Scalability**   The ability of a database server platform to take advantage of faster hardware and other resources.

▲ **Performance**   The overall efficiency of the database server at fulfilling data modification and retrieval based on business requirements.

The demands on data storage have risen exponentially in recent years. Therefore, a robust system for storing tables containing potentially billions of rows is necessary. SQL

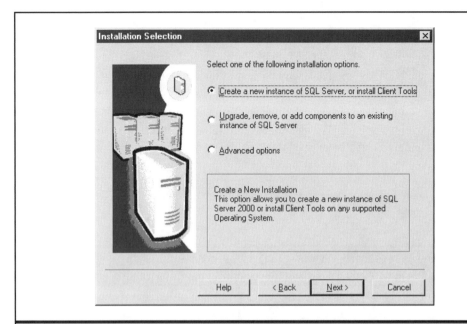

Figure 4-5. Installing a new instance of SQL Server 2000

Figure 4-6. Using the SQL Server Upgrade Wizard

Server stores information in standard operating system files that have a special format optimized for storing relational information. At the most basic level, these files are made up of *pages*. Pages store the actual data that makes up the rows of tables and indexes. A database page is exactly 8,192 bytes in length (including 96 bytes that are used for the header). Rows cannot span pages, and therefore the 8K limit is the maximum size a row may have (with the exception of text and image data types, which are stored on special page types apart from the rest of the row's data). There are various types of pages for the different types of data they can contain (for example, there are different page types for tables and for indexes).

To make disk access more efficient, SQL Server allocates space in *extents*. An extent is made up of eight pages and therefore is 64K in length. Extents may contain different types of pages, if necessary. (We'll revisit these numbers when we estimate data storage requirements in Chapter 5.)

SQL Server data files can be stored on File Allocation Table (FAT) and Windows NT File System (NTFS) partition types. The only requirement is that file system compression cannot be enabled for the data files.

The good news is that you won't have to worry about much of this when you're working with SQL Server 2000. The architecture of the product makes the creation, maintenance, and administration of data files easier by allowing dynamic file allocation. Database files can be set to grow and shrink automatically as needed.

Files and Filegroups

In SQL Server 2000, the term *database* refers to a logical structure containing a set of related objects. Unlike other RDBMSs, SQL Server allows objects within a database to be owned by different users, and allows the existence of many databases on the same server. In the simplest configuration, a database has one file for data and one file for a transaction log (as described in the next section).

A SQL Server database is made up of at least one data file (called the *primary data file*, with a default extension of .mdf) and exactly one transaction log file (which has an extension of .ldf). However, much more complex configurations are available. To spread data across multiple devices, you can choose to add one or more *secondary data files*. These data files can then contain specific database objects. This is a very powerful feature that allows you to specify exactly where information is stored. Spreading information across different drives can increase performance. For example, if you have two very active tables on your system, you may choose to place each on a different drive (by creating separate data files). Administering files can become complicated if you have multiple files. Also, the amount of data that must be backed up can become quite large. For this reason, you can group files into logical structures called *filegroups*.

SQL Server hides much of the complexity of managing data files, because they can be dynamically resized as needed. We'll talk more about files and filegroups as they pertain to implementing a backup and recovery plan in Chapter 6. As we'll see, files and filegroups allow for backing up portions of a database at a time when data volumes and performance constraints prevent full backups.

The Transaction Log

When a user executes a SQL query that modifies information on the database server, the actual changes are first written to a file called the *transaction log*. Pages that have been written to the transaction log but have not yet been committed to the physical file are known as *dirty pages*. The information is temporarily held in this file until a *checkpoint* occurs. At this time, the data is actually recorded in the database files themselves. The transaction log provides many benefits to database users:

▼ **Increasing performance by acting as a caching device** Instead of writing each transaction to the database individually, the server can wait until several items are ready to be written and then combine the changes into fewer operations.

■ **Ensuring data consistency** If an operation begins and then later aborts (due to a hardware failure or when it reaches a ROLLBACK TRANSACTION statement), all of the operations associated with this transaction can be rolled back.

▲ **Providing a "snapshot" of the database at a specific point in time** When it comes to working with many transactions that may be running at the same time, it's important for the queries to be working on a fixed set of data. For example, consider the case of a query that begins modifying 100 rows of data in separate steps. If another user attempts to make a change to some of the information at the same time, it might interfere with the logic of the query. In a case like this, the transaction log can provide a snapshot of the database at a specific point in time.

Figure 4-7 shows how the transaction log is used.

The transaction log cannot be disabled in SQL Server 2000, although you can choose to make it effectively useless by checking the Truncate Log on Checkpoint option for a database. This option deletes portions of the transaction log as soon as they are committed to disk. As we'll see in Chapter 6, safeguarding the transaction log is an important goal of a good data protection plan and can ensure that such features as recovering the database to a specific point in time will work properly when you need them.

Backup and Recovery Architecture

As you have probably guessed, Microsoft has made several major improvements to backup and recovery features in SQL Server 2000. We'll cover the details of these new features in Chapter 6. For now, however, here is a brief overview:

▼ **Recovery models** New in SQL Server 2000 is the ability to define a recovery model for each database. There are three main options: Simple (No Logging); Normal (Restore to point-in-time; largest log size); Bulk Logged (some operations are not logged). Each offers a unique balance between recoverability of database information and performance. We'll cover the details of the various recovery models in Chapter 6.

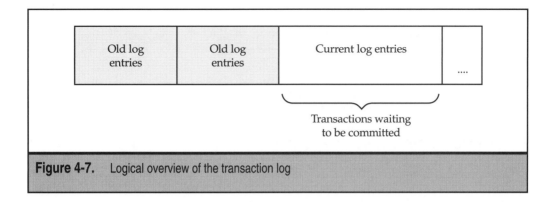

Figure 4-7. Logical overview of the transaction log

- **Fast differential backup** Differential backups store only the data pages that have been modified since the last full database backup. In SQL Server 7.0, differential backups used up less disk space, but they still required a scan of the entire database during a backup operation (thereby reducing performance). In SQL Server 2000, this entire scan of the database is no longer required.

- **Copy Database Wizard** SQL Server 2000 includes a new wizard called the Copy Database Wizard. The purpose of this tool is to copy databases between instances of SQL Server 2000, including all of the objects within a database. You can also use the wizard to upgrade SQL Server 7.0 databases to SQL Server 2000. We'll cover the Copy Database Wizard in greater detail in Chapter 6.

- **Snapshot backups** For mission-critical applications, keeping data synchronized between servers is extremely important. SQL Server 2000 supports the redundancy of data (for fault tolerance and performance reasons) through the use of snapshot backups. This feature is primarily designed for used by Original Equipment Manufacturers (OEM) on systems that are designed to make use of this functionality.

- **Standby server support** Log-shipping (copying the transaction log to another server) is a common technique that can be used in most relational database server platforms. Before SQL Server 2000, this method was supported, but it was generally a painstaking process to implement and administer. In the latest version of SQL Server, the graphical administration tools can be used to implement a standby server through the use of log-shipping. We'll cover the details of this process in Chapter 9.

- ▲ **Logical log marks (vs. point in time)** The ability to restore to a point in time using transaction log backups is extremely useful, if you know the time when the failure occurred. In SQL Server 2000, database users and applications can create a logical log mark that uses a specific identifier before beginning transactions. Should the need to perform a point-in-time recovery arise, the database can be restored up to one of these logical log marks.

There are many more enhancements and new features in the backup and recovery architecture of SQL Server 2000. There are so many, in fact, that we'll be devoting several chapters of this book to discussing them in detail. You'll find details on these new features in Chapters 6 through 9.

New Features in SQL Server 2000

With SQL Server 2000, Microsoft has included many new enhancements that affect the functionality of the product. Some of the features will be useful to all users of SQL Server (for example, the enhanced Enterprise Manager and Query Analyzer applications), while others are less evident. Let's take a quick look at some of the changes to SQL Server "under the hood."

Support for Extended Markup Language (XML)

XML is one of those technologies that is often cited by industry analysts and technical professionals as a revolutionary change. The idea underlying XML is to provide a standard, flexible mechanism for data interchange between applications, servers, and companies. The standard offers developers and users many advantages, including the ability to simply define and use a standard XML-based schema. Web developers, for example, can take advantage of XML technology to perform communications between different web servers, some of which may be operated by other companies.

Although it will take time for the industry to take full advantage of the features and capabilities of XML, many vendors and products are embracing it as a standard for data interchange. Microsoft is no exception, and SQL Server 2000 was designed to provide rich XML functionality. There are two main areas in which SQL Server 2000 supports XML. The first is through the use of the FOR XML clause in standard SQL queries. Now, database users can simply execute a query with this clause to return data in an XML format. For example, the following query (run against the default Northwind sample database),

```
SELECT     CustomerID, CompanyName, ContactName, ContactTitle, Country
FROM       Customers
WHERE      CustomerID = 'WILMK'
FOR XML AUTO
```

produces the following output:

```
XML_F52E2B61-18A1-11d1-B105-00805F49916B-----------------------------------------
<Customers CustomerID="WILMK" CompanyName="Wilman Kala" ContactName="Matti
Karttunen" ContactTitle="Owner/Marketing Assistant" Country="Finland"/>
```

Materialized Views

When interviewing technical professionals who claim they have database experience, I usually start with a simple question: "What is a view?" If they get that right, I move on to something slightly more difficult: "Where is the data for a view stored?" Those who really understand how a view works will answer that the data is stored in the underlying tables that are queried. The question that often makes people think, however, is "Can a view be indexed?" In previous versions of SQL Server, views could not be indexed because they did not store any data. (The purpose of indexing is to speed the retrieval of information from disk.) However, that has changed in SQL Server 2000.

A standard view is essentially a data retrieval query (usually a simple SELECT statement that may join several tables together to obtain useful information). A *materialized view* has the same purpose, but it is a database object that physically stores the results of a query to disk. Now, when queries require the specific information in the view, the query optimizer can quickly obtain the results from the materialized view instead of from the tables it references. Furthermore, the view can be indexed to further improve the performance of certain queries without reducing the performance of others ("over-indexing"). Although this could have been done through the creation of tables (for example, through "denormalization" of the schema), it would be up to database designers to create triggers and stored procedures to keep the data in these extra tables up-to-date. Materialized views handle this tedious and error-prone task automatically.

The use of materialized views can produce a dramatic improvement in the speed of certain types of queries. Of course, the trade-off is the additional disk space that is required to store the data that makes up the views.

Partitioned Views

A simple fact for most databases is that they will grow over time—sometimes at an exponential rate. Data has a tenacious tendency to accumulate as businesses grow! Although all of the data is important, not all of it will need to be immediately available. For example, consider a company that has stored 15 years of sales order data. Clearly, all of the information is useful (for historical reporting and comparisons). However, the most important data is probably that generated within the last five years. Assuming all of the data is stored within one database table, the existence of all of this excess data can greatly decrease performance by bogging down queries.

One potential solution is to partition the data horizontally. In this method, certain subsets of data are moved to other tables, databases, and/or servers (see Figure 4-8). This group of servers is often referred to as a "federation" of servers since they all work together to share the load for a single data repository. To simplify the process of accessing data across these partitions (for example, when a manager requests information that spans 10 years), partitioned views can be used. The query can be executed against the view, and the query optimizer will automatically access the required tables for information.

SQL Server 2000 also supports vertical partitioning. In this situation, a portion of a table—for example, a commonly used column—might be broken out into another table. (See Figure 4-9.) Again, partitioned views can be used to simplify access to the data. Overall, partitioned views can increase performance and decrease administration for medium- to large-sized databases.

Address Windowing Extensions (AWE)

Just a few short years ago, it seemed to be a distant dream that database servers would support many gigabytes of memory. Database administrators knew that adding memory to servers could provide dramatic improvements in performance. Now, however, larger amounts of RAM are often used to fulfill performance requirements. Coupled with the

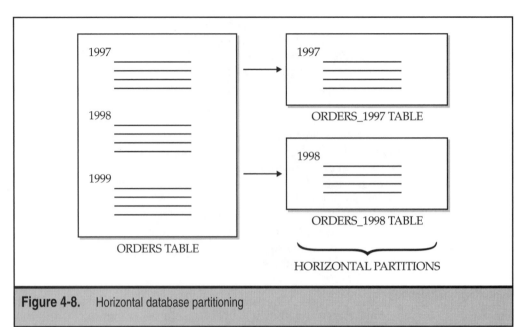

Figure 4-8. Horizontal database partitioning

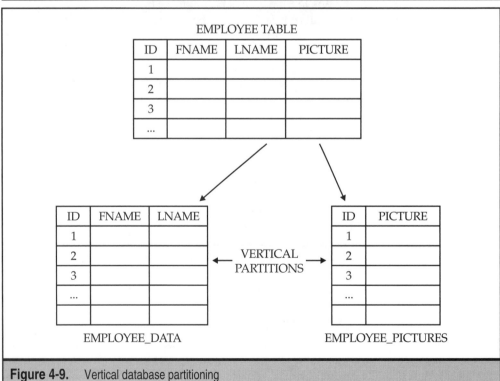

Figure 4-9. Vertical database partitioning

dramatic overall decrease in price of memory modules (and improvements in manufac-turing technology), systems with many gigabytes of RAM are not uncommon.

By default, the Windows NT/2000 operating systems support a memory address space of up to 4GB. Of this amount, up to 3GB can be physical RAM. (The rest must be vir-tual memory provided in a swap file.) With SQL Server 2000, however, a new technology called Address Windowing Extensions (AWE) allows a database server platform to ac-cess up to 64GB of usable memory. This architecture is optimized for large database serv-ers with many CPUs and can dramatically improve performance in high-performance systems. AWE is available with the Enterprise Edition of SQL Server 2000, running on Windows 2000 Advanced Server or Windows 2000 DataCenter Server.

Integration with the Active Directory

Microsoft designed the Active Directory to serve as a single repository for managing in-formation about a network environment. Commonly stored objects include users, groups, computers, and Organizational Units (OUs). By using the Active Directory, users and systems administrators can quickly and easily search for specific types of resources throughout the entire environment (for example, a color printer located in a specific building). So why not extend this functionality to apply to database servers as well?

Installations of SQL Server 2000 can be made available as objects within the Active Di-rectory. The SQL Server 2000 object can include information about the databases stored on a specific server and other information about its configuration. With this information stored within the Active Directory, users easily search for specific information. For exam-ple, I might want to find all of the SQL Server 2000 machines that host a copy of the Cus-tomers database. Using the Active Directory search functionality, this can be easily accomplished. (See Figure 4-10.)

Support for Multiple Database Versions

In an ideal world, all of our database servers would be magically upgraded to the latest version of database platform as soon as it was released (assuming this is what we wanted to do). In the real world, however, it can take months or even years of testing before a mi-gration to a new version is possible. To ease the migration to newer versions of SQL Server, SQL Server 2000 allows for backward compatibility. Each database can use one of the compatibility levels shown in Table 4-4.

These options are extremely helpful when testing the migration of SQL-based code between versions of SQL Server. Better yet, the compatibility modes can be changed sev-eral times, even while the database is running. Note, however, that if a database is run-ning in a backward-compatible mode, users will not be able to take full advantage of all the features of SQL Server 2000.

To change the database compatibility level using Enterprise Manager, simply right-click on the name of a database and select Properties. In the Options tab (shown in Figure 4-11), you'll be able to specify a compatibility level for this database.

The Transact-SQL Language

As mentioned previously, the standard language used for RDBMS communication is SQL. Microsoft's implementation of the SQL language is based on the ANSI-SQL92 standard

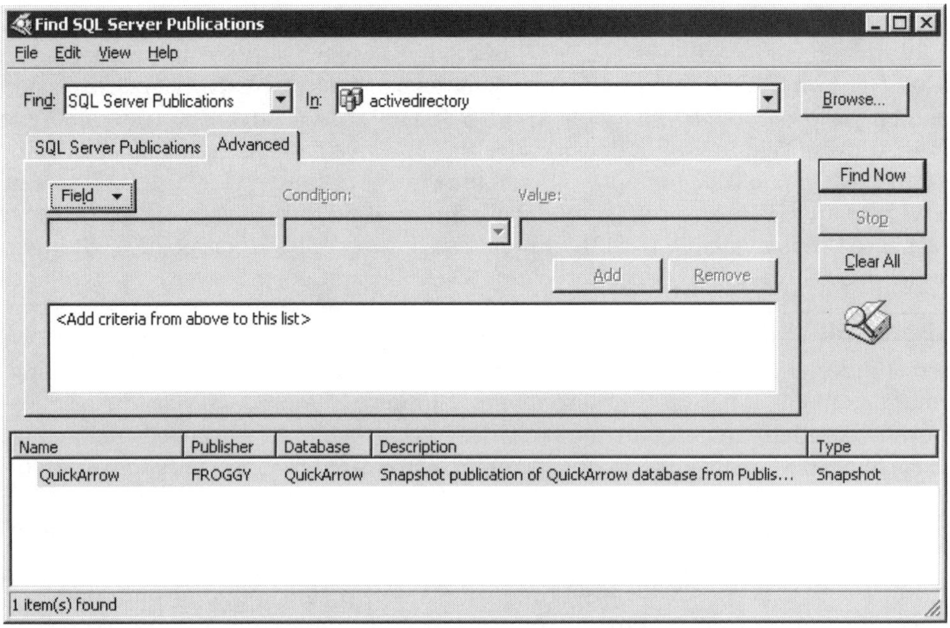

Figure 4-10. Searching the Active Directory for SQL Server replication information

and is called Transact-SQL (unofficially abbreviated TSQL). This includes the standard syntax for SELECT, UPDATE, INSERT, and DELETE statements (which we covered earlier in this chapter). In addition, Transact-SQL contains many additional commands and functions that are not provided for in the ANSI specifications. In later chapters, we'll cover the application of these commands as they pertain to backup and recovery operations.

SQL Server Version	Backward-Compatibility Setting
Microsoft SQL Server 2000	Database compatibility level 80
Microsoft SQL Server 7.0	Database compatibility level 70
Microsoft SQL Server 6.5	Database compatibility level 65
Microsoft SQL Server 6.0	Database compatibility level 60

Table 4-4. Database Compatibility Levels Supported by SQL Server 2000

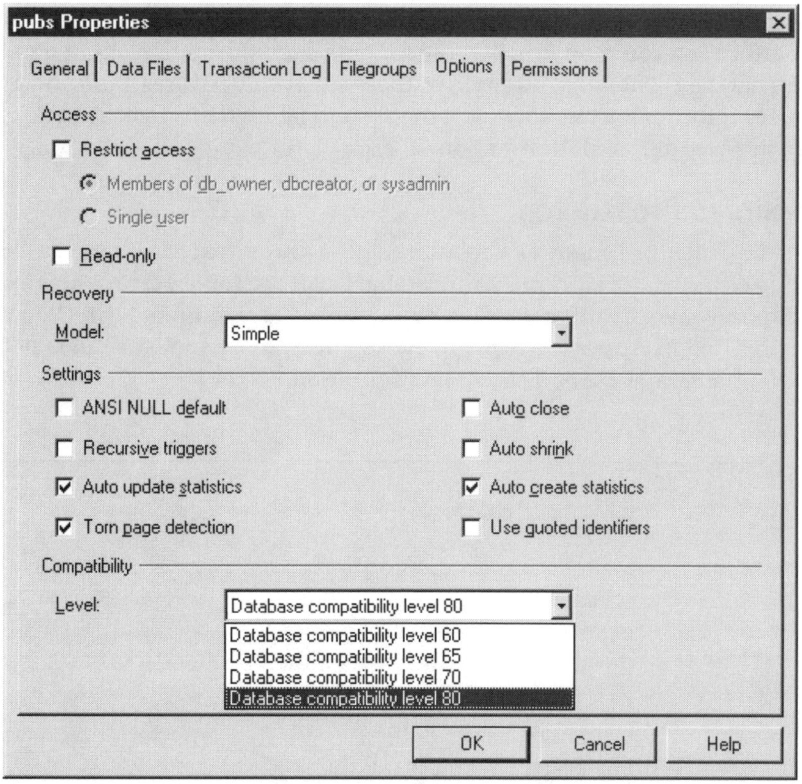

Figure 4-11.   Changing the database compatibility level

It is important to note that although ANSI-SQL92 is a "standard," support for various types of commands is not necessarily consistent between platforms. For example, the supported syntax for specific JOIN statements in Oracle is not compatible with the syntax used in SQL Server.

Although users can use any standard query application that can connect to SQL Server, it is increasingly common for database developers to write programs that encapsulate the queries and process information for users. Increasingly common are web-based applications in which a web server or "middleware" is responsible for performing the actual database queries that obtain information as needed. Connectivity between applications and SQL Server can use various standards, such as Open Database Connectivity (ODBC), ActiveX Data Objects (ADO), and Object Linking and Embedding for Databases (OLEDB). Information about using the Transact-SQL language and the various data access components is available from SQL Server Books Online.

Dealing with database objects can be quite challenging due to the complexity of some of the commands involved. SQL Server 2000 provides built-in procedures that can be used for performing common functions and compiling information about databases and the objects that they contain. In addition to these stored procedures, built-in views can be used to query information stored within the system tables. Let's look at some commonly used stored procedures and information schema views.

System-Stored Procedures

SQL Server 2000 includes many system-stored procedures that can be used for tasks such as managing security and working with database objects. Table 4-5 provides examples of a few commonly used commands. This by no means is a complete list. (You can find a more complete list in Appendix A.) However, it does show some useful ways to obtain information about database and server configuration.

Procedure	Information Returned	Example
sp_configure	Server configuration options, which can be modified with this procedure. (Certain changes to these options require use of the RECONFIGURE command.)	`sp_configure 'user connections', 35`
sp_depends	Dependencies of database objects (for example, all the tables to which a view refers)	`sp_depends myview`
sp_help	Information about a database object	`sp_help mydatabase`
sp_helpdb	The size and options used for a database	`sp_helpdb mydatabase`
sp_helptext	Help information regarding database objects such as triggers, views, and stored procedures	`sp_helptext trigger1`
sp_lock	Current locks on database objects	`sp_lock`
sp_monitor	Current database statistics	`sp_monitor`
sp_spaceused	Space used by a database table or the database itself	`sp_spaceused mytable`
sp_who	Current database connections	`sp_who`

Table 4-5.   Examples of Commonly Used SQL Server 2000 Stored Procedures

Figure 4-12 provides examples of the types of information you can obtain using a system-stored procedure.

In later chapters, we'll cover stored procedures and other commands related to data protection. And, for a more complete listing of stored procedures, see Appendix A.

Information Schema Views

Information schema views are built-in database objects that can be queried against. Unlike stored procedures, these views return relational output that can be processed in the same way as other query results. You can execute a SELECT statement against these values. Here's an example that returns the names of all the tables stored in a database:

```
Select * from information_schema.tables
```

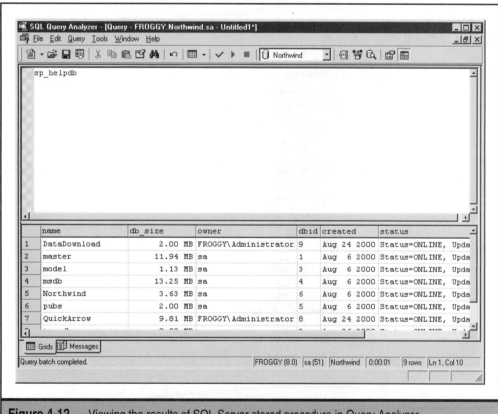

Figure 4-12.   Viewing the results of SQL Server stored procedure in Query Analyzer

Table 4-6 lists common information schema views and the typical purpose of each. For a complete list of all of the information schema views, see Appendix A.

It is important to note that the information schema views are security dependent. That is, users will only be able to see information about objects to which they have been granted the appropriate permissions.

Locking and Concurrency

To ensure that resources are available to multiple users at a time, individual sessions must lock data before users attempt to modify it. While certain information is locked, no other users can modify the same information. A major performance enhancement in SQL Server 2000 is the ability to perform row-level locking. This allows users to lock only a specific row within a table—instead of the table itself—while making changes. Row-level locking, therefore, allows multiple users to modify the same table at the same time. SQL Server also supports row locks (partial or complete), indexes, tables, and databases. Covering all of the issues related to locking can be quite complex and is beyond the scope of this book.

Network Communications

The real purpose of your database is to communicate with clients, whether they are end users who query your application directly, client/server applications, or other database servers. In order for clients and the database server to communicate, a common method of data transfer must be determined. The default selections for Network Libraries (shown in Figure 4-13) will be appropriate for most TCP/IP-based environments. SQL Server can

Information Schema View	Information Returned
Columns	A list of all columns in all accessible tables and views
Referential_Constraints	Information about primary key and foreign key relationships
Schemata	Information about all the databases on the current server
Table_Privileges	Security permissions on the tables within a database
Tables	A list of all tables and views in the database
Views	Information about the specified view

Table 4-6. Commonly Used SQL Server Information Schema Views

use any number of Network Libraries to communicate, but each must be enabled separately on both the client and the server.

Table 4-7 lists the available protocol types and the typical users of each.

If you're having trouble connecting to a SQL Server installation, the protocols likely are misconfigured. It has become increasingly common to connect to database servers over the Internet. Although this is supported using the TCP/IP protocol, you must also make sure that no firewalls block the appropriate communications ports. These options can be modified after SQL Server installation by using the Client Network Utility and Server Network Utility programs in the Microsoft SQL Server 2000 program group.

Note that encryption can be a very useful option for increasing the security of connections to SQL Server that occur over the Internet.

WORKING WITH SQL SERVER 2000

So far, we have been talking about SQL Server architecture. This topic is somewhat theoretical, but it is extremely helpful in understanding how SQL Server works "under the hood." Now, it's time to look at what you—the database administrator or implementer—work with daily. One of the most welcome enhancements to SQL Server 2000 is

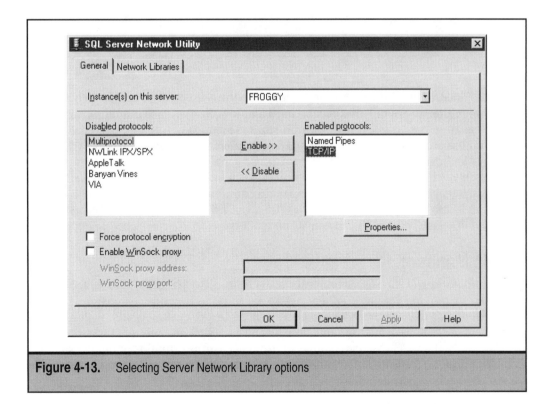

Figure 4-13. Selecting Server Network Library options

Protocol	Suggested Type of Client	Notes
AppleTalk	Macintosh clients	Uses local AppleTalk zone for communications
Banyan VINES	VINES clients	Supports SPP communications; only available on Intel platform
Multiprotocol	All	Uses any protocol type; data and authentication encryption are possible
Named pipes	Windows 95/98/ME and Windows NT/2000 only	Works on TCP/IP, NetBEUI, or IPX/SPX networks
NWLink IPX/SPX	Novell NetWare clients and servers	Can connect to NetWare Bindery
TCP/IP	All (requires TCP/IP connectivity)	Uses TCP port 1433 by default and can work over the Internet; also supports MS Proxy Server

Table 4-7.   SQL Server 2000 Network Libraries

easier administration. Database servers used to be the domain of specialists who understood the architecture of the product and used archaic commands to interact with the machine. Realizing that not all systems administrators are also DBAs, Microsoft has greatly simplified the processes involved in designing, implementing, and managing a database solution. We have already talked about features such as dynamic file management, but that's just scratching the surface. SQL Server 2000 includes many enhancements that improve manageability and decrease time spent in administration. Those who have worked with other RDBMSs will find the tools in SQL Server 2000 to be intuitive and easier to use. Let's start with the heart of the administrative interface.

Enterprise Manager

The central portion of the SQL Server interface is Enterprise Manager. Microsoft has standardized on moving its various heterogeneous tools to a single, extensible interface called Microsoft Management Console (MMC). Enterprise Manager is a plug-in that works within MMC to provide a uniform look and feel between different types of administration tools. It uses HTML capabilities to provide clear information about the status of databases and the various options available. Figure 4-14 shows the sort of information you might see in Enterprise Manager.

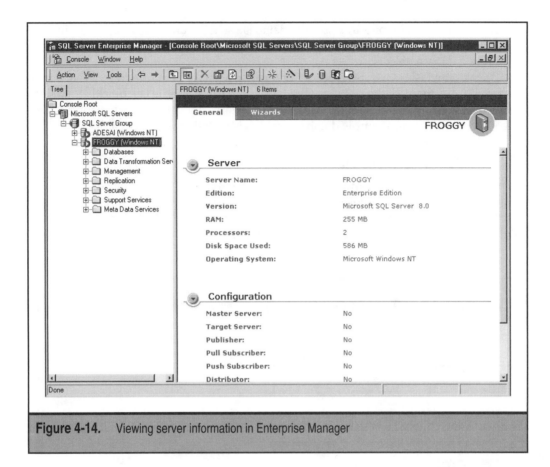

Figure 4-14. Viewing server information in Enterprise Manager

Almost all of the functions you will regularly have to perform on an installation of SQL Server can be performed from this interface. Enterprise Manager supports accessing remote servers from a single interface. A list of all the tasks available would be impossible, but Microsoft has taken the time to make some of the most complex operations accessible using wizards. A good example is the Database Maintenance Plan Wizard, which can automatically create and schedule jobs for performing database backup operations. (We'll revisit the example in Chapter 6.)

Database Schemas

A *database schema*, defined simply, is a statement of the relationships between database objects. Specifically, this means the relationships between tables using primary keys and foreign keys (discussed earlier). A great deal of time can (and should!) be spent in designing a database schema that meets business requirements. Usually, a database schema is represented in an Entity Relationship Diagram (ERD). These diagrams should display information about the tables in a specific database schema and document their interactions. Developers and database administrators can use ERDs when programming or managing database objects.

To make the task easier, SQL Server Enterprise Manager includes a tool that can be used to simplify many of the tasks involved. By using this tool, you can quickly and easily create, manage, and maintain database tables and definitions. Figure 4-15 shows a database schema for the *pubs* sample database (which is installed with SQL Server).

Data Transformation Services

On many different data platforms and RDBMSs, transferring data between systems can be quite a headache. Different database servers store information using various data types and in proprietary structures. Often, transferring information requires exporting information to a standard comma-separated values (CSV) file and then manually import-

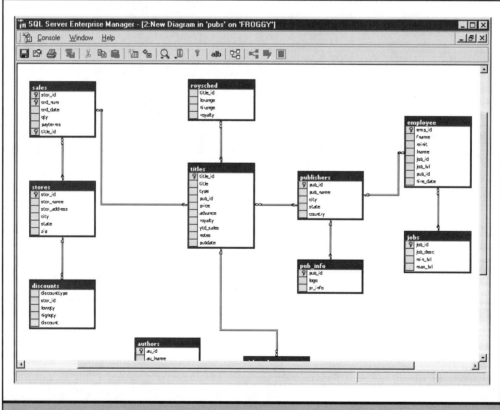

Figure 4-15.   Viewing database schema information in Enterprise Manager

ing the information. Microsoft has made the entire process much easier by providing Data Transformation Services (DTS) with SQL Server 2000. This architecture allows database designers and administrators to easily transfer information between supported information types. Through various interfaces, DTS supports moving information to and from nonrelational structures, such as Microsoft Excel and Access files, or from other database servers, such as Oracle. The easiest way to transfer information is to use the DTS Export Wizard (see Figure 4-16), which is included with SQL Server. The wizard walks you through the creation of basic packages that transfer data.

In addition to performing the important tasks of transferring information between heterogeneous sources, DTS goes one step further in letting you modify data as it is transferred. This is extremely important because various systems might use different formats for the same information. For example, one database might store the information about a customer's status as Active or Inactive, whereas another might have a true/false setting for a column entitled Active. This can be used for data warehousing (as described later in this chapter) or for moving heterogeneous data into a single, uniform repository. Figure 4-17 shows a sample DTS package that copies data from several sources into a single database server.

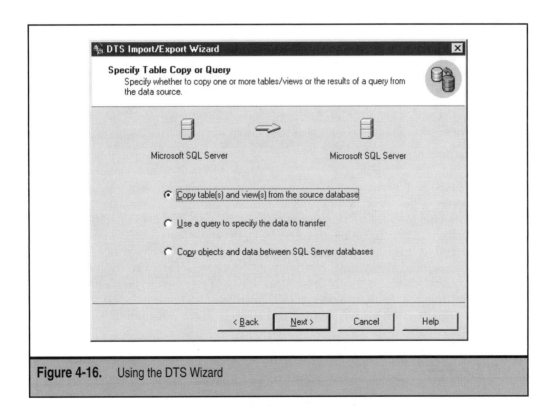

Figure 4-16.   Using the DTS Wizard

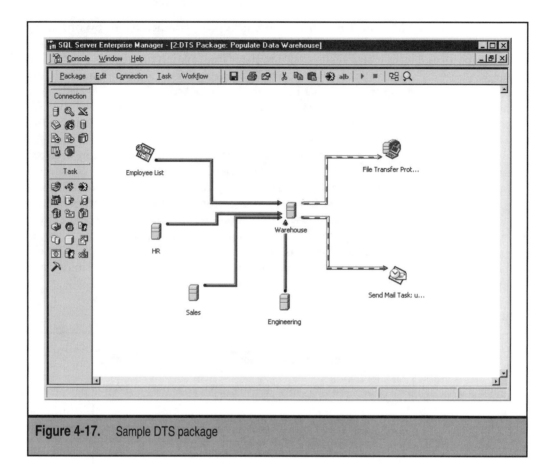

Figure 4-17. Sample DTS package

In some cases, you might want to run an operation just once (to copy a database, for example). In others, however, you might want to periodically coalesce data from multiple sources or perform exports to another server. To support this, DTS operations can be saved as "packages," which can be stored on SQL Server for later use. The packages can also be modified as business requirements change. Finally, you can easily schedule a package to be executed at any time. For database developers, DTS also supports the export of packages to Microsoft Visual Basic files. This code can then be used as a reference for creating custom applications based on DTS functionality. The end result is a lowered learning curve and a great savings in time and effort to move data among applications, databases, and servers.

SQL Query Analyzer

Although many of the operations you'll regularly perform on a SQL Server installation can be performed through Enterprise Manager, certain operations are easier to perform from a command-based environment. SQL Query Analyzer is an excellent tool for performing ad hoc queries against a database and for performing administrative functions using Transact-SQL. By using SQL Query Analyzer for executing database commands, you'll be able to see the output of your query either in standard text form or within a grid. Figure 4-18 shows the results of a query in text mode.

Developers can create some large and complicated queries, so the color-coding features of the SQL code can make managing long statements much easier. SQL Query Analyzer's usefulness doesn't stop there, however. In addition to being able to execute ad hoc queries, you can choose to view graphical statistics on the operations of a query (see Figure 4-19). Later in this chapter, we'll see how this function can be useful for finding performance problems.

One of the most difficult parts of using Transact-SQL is remembering command syntax. This is especially true if you're not used to development. With SQL Server 2000, Microsoft updated Query Analyzer to include several automated features. First is the

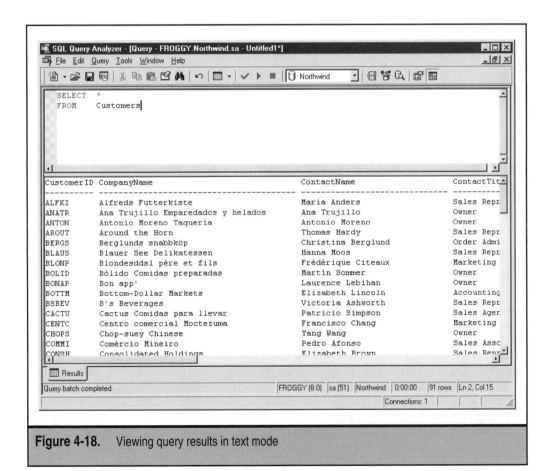

Figure 4-18. Viewing query results in text mode

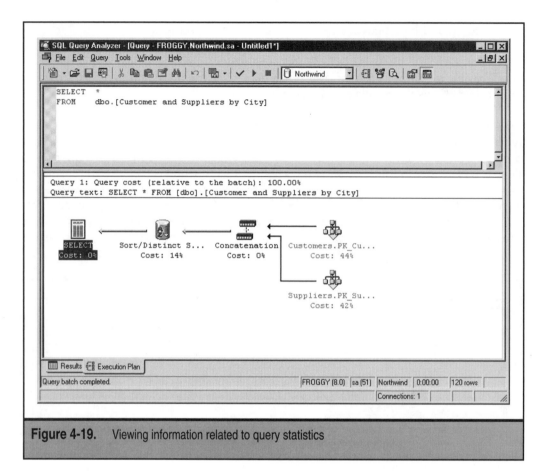

Figure 4-19.   Viewing information related to query statistics

option to view lists of database objects within the Query Analyzer Objects window (as shown in Figure 4-20).

By simply right-clicking on a database object, you can quickly and easily generate scripts related to working with the object. Additionally, these scripts might include replaceable parameters that allow you to replace options through the use of a dialog box. Figure 4-21 shows how a specific table can be scripted.

In the Common Objects section, you'll also be able to view lists of functions and other information that you can use when working with Transact-SQL. Overall, Query Analyzer is a flexible and powerful tool for Transact-SQL development. If you're a database developer, it is likely to be your best friend when it comes to working with SQL Server 2000!

SQL SERVER SECURITY

Database server security is something that is often ignored. Perhaps one reason is that it is not clearly understood. As emphasized in Chapter 3, it is imperative that you secure your

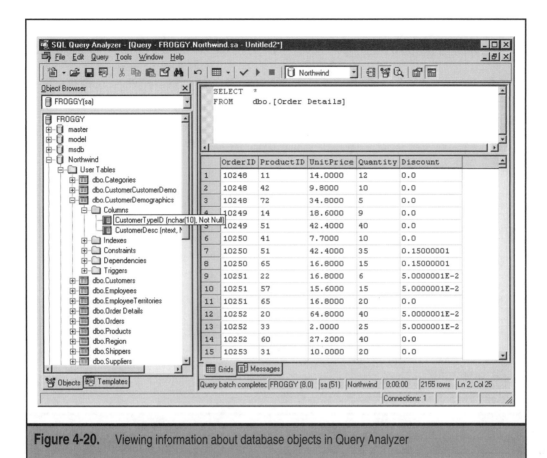

Figure 4-20.   Viewing information about database objects in Query Analyzer

operating system resources. Securing your database server platform is equally important. What is the exact relationship between operating system security and database server security? The security model of SQL Server 2000 includes many features that allow for integrating the two into a common database. Here, we'll examine the various levels of security settings and explore how they all interact. The main levels that must be considered are as follows:

▼ Operating system security

■ Database logins

■ Database user permissions

▲ Object permissions

To access your most trusted information, users will have to be able to jump all four of these hurdles. As a DBA, your job is to ensure that the hurdles are of the proper

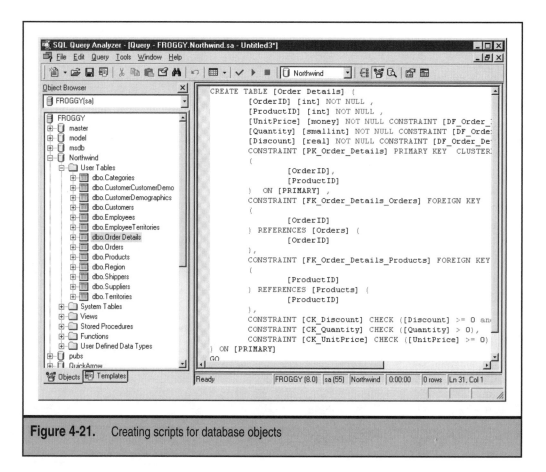

```
CREATE TABLE [Order Details] {
        [OrderID] [int] NOT NULL ,
        [ProductID] [int] NOT NULL ,
        [UnitPrice] [money] NOT NULL CONSTRAINT [DF_Order_
        [Quantity] [smallint] NOT NULL CONSTRAINT [DF_Orde
        [Discount] [real] NOT NULL CONSTRAINT [DF_Order_De
        CONSTRAINT [PK_Order_Details] PRIMARY KEY  CLUSTER
        (
                [OrderID],
                [ProductID]
        )  ON [PRIMARY] ,
        CONSTRAINT [FK_Order_Details_Orders] FOREIGN KEY
        (
                [OrderID]
        ) REFERENCES [Orders] (
                [OrderID]
        ),
        CONSTRAINT [FK_Order_Details_Products] FOREIGN KEY
        (
                [ProductID]
        ) REFERENCES [Products] (
                [ProductID]
        ),
        CONSTRAINT [CK_Discount] CHECK ([Discount] >= 0 an
        CONSTRAINT [CK_Quantity] CHECK ([Quantity] > 0),
        CONSTRAINT [CK_UnitPrice] CHECK ([UnitPrice] >= 0)
} ON [PRIMARY]
GO
```

Figure 4-21. Creating scripts for database objects

height—that is, your security model takes into account both security and usability. Since they're so important, let's take an in-depth look at each level of permissions. In Chapter 3, we looked at some of the measures you can take to secure your network operating system. Here, let's look at the other levels and how they relate to each other.

Server Logins

Microsoft has made providing for a single sign-on experience a major design goal in all of its products. Users and systems administrators alike benefit from being able to maintain and use a single account for all operations within the network. To accommodate this, the security architecture of SQL Server 2000 supports two security models:

▼ **Windows NT/2000 only**   This method uses built-in Windows NT/2000 user accounts that map to database server logins for permissions. In this mode, server logins are created from existing Windows NT/2000 group and user accounts. Users who have already been authenticated by an NT/2000 Server machine need not enter any more information before connecting to SQL Server.

▲ **SQL Server and Windows NT/2000** Supported mainly for backward compatibility, this security mode allows for the use of both integrated security and standard username/password combinations. Standard logins require the creation of new database server logins, including usernames and passwords within SQL Server itself. Application users can use this information to make a connection with your server. The disadvantages of this security model are the fact that you might have to support two different sets of user databases (one at the operating system level and another within SQL Server). Additionally, users might be forced to enter login information more than once to access the resources they require. However, non-Windows client types may not support Windows NT/2000 authentication and must use the standard username/ password method. You can set the SQL Server Security mode within Enterprise Manager (see Figure 4-22) by right-clicking on the name of a server, selecting Properties, and then clicking on the Security tab.

Auditing logon information is useful in holding users responsible for their actions and for managing performance (which we'll explore in more detail later in this chapter).

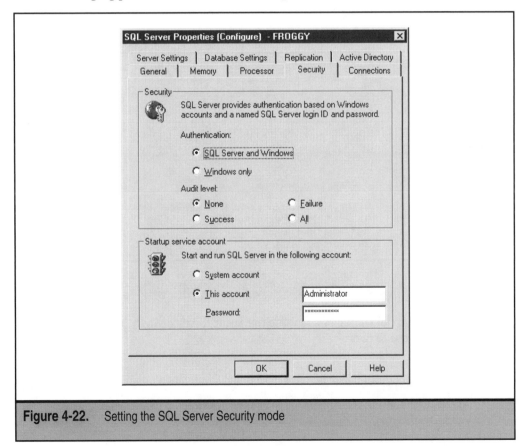

Figure 4-22. Setting the SQL Server Security mode

If SQL Server is running on a Windows 95/98/ME machine, users will not be able to use trusted connections. Therefore, Windows NT/2000–only authentication is not an available option, and all users who connect to that server will be required to provide a valid login and password.

Creating SQL Server Logins

After you set the appropriate authentication mode for your installation of SQL Server, you need to create logins. A login is used to authenticate a user before he or she connects to the database server. To create a SQL Server login based on a Windows NT/2000 user or group in Enterprise Manager, use the following procedure.

STEP-BY-STEP

Creating a Standard SQL Server Login

1. Select the server for which you want to create a login. Expand the Security folder. Right-click Logins and select New Login. You will see this dialog box:

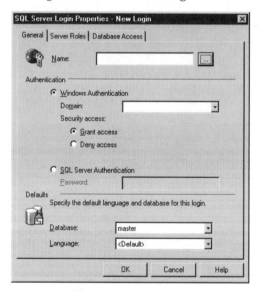

2. In the Name field, specify a unique name for the new login. This is the name a user must use to connect to the database server.

3. For Authentication, select SQL Server Authentication and enter a password to be used by a user or application to log in to the database.

4. Specify a default database to which the user will connect. Note that you may need to grant database permissions (described later) separately.

5. Click OK, and then verify the password to create the new login.

You can optionally specify server roles and database roles using the other tabs in this dialog box (described later). SQL Server login information is stored in the syslogins system table (located in the master database). Password information stored in this table is encrypted. When a user attempts to authenticate, SQL Server verifies whether a login and password are present in this table and if so, allows the login.

Mapping Windows NT/2000 Accounts

When administering user permissions in a network environment, maintaining logins at both the network operating system level and at the database level can be tedious, time consuming, and error prone. Windows NT/2000 accounts (groups and users) can be directly granted permissions to access a Microsoft SQL Server database if you're using Windows NT/2000 security or SQL Server and Windows NT/2000 security. In most cases, it is preferable to grant access to an entire group, to make administration easier. Consider placing all SQL Server users in one or more new Windows NT/2000 groups. If you're working in a domain-based environment, you can assign logon permissions to either global or local groups. Windows NT/2000 Authentication is supported by both Windows 95/98/ME and Windows NT/2000 clients, provided the users have accounts. Other client types (such as MS-DOS, Macintosh, and UNIX users) can only use SQL Server Authentication.

NOTE: By default, members of the Windows NT/2000 Administrators and Domain Administrators groups are granted system administrator (sa) access to the database. Although there is an option to set the password to blank, you should always set a strong password for the *sa* account during the installation of SQL Server 2000.

To create a SQL Server login based on a Windows NT/2000 user or group in Enterprise Manager, use the following procedure.

STEP-BY-STEP

Creating a SQL Server Login Based on Windows NT/2000 Security

1. Select the server to which you want to create a login. Expand the Security folder. Right-click Logins and select New Login. You'll see this dialog box:

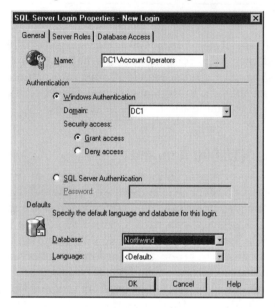

2. In the Name field, specify the name of a Windows NT/2000 user or group to which you want to grant login permissions. If you're working in a multidomain environment, you also need to specify the complete name, including the domain (such as Engineering).

3. Leave the Authentication setting as Windows NT/2000 Authentication. Users will not need to enter a username or password to gain access. For Security Access, choose whether this group should be granted or denied access.

4. Specify a default database to which the user will connect. Click OK to create the new login.

You can optionally specify server roles and database roles using the other tabs in this dialog box (described later). When a user attempts to log in to a database using Windows NT/2000 Authentication, SQL Server attempts to find a matching login in the syslogins table. If a Windows NT/2000 user attempts to log in from a nontrusted domain, he or she will be required to enter a username and password for the domain in which the SQL Server resides. The same will occur if the user is not a member of any Windows NT/2000 group or user account that has permissions to log in. In either case, if a login exists, the user is allowed to connect; otherwise, an error message is returned and the user is given a chance to provide a SQL Server login (as long as SQL Server and Windows NT/2000 security is enabled). To keep track of accounts when SQL Server and Windows NT/2000 security is used, database administrators should not create SQL Server login names that have the same names as Windows NT/2000 user accounts.

Database User Permissions

Although having access to a database server lets users log in, that alone does not give them the right to access information. The next step is to set permissions on logins to access one or more databases. A user must be added to a database before he or she can access any information in that database. There are two ways to add these permissions: you can add them when you create the login or you can add existing database logins.

To add database permissions when creating a login, use the following procedure.

STEP-BY-STEP

Setting Database Permissions When Creating a Login

1. In the New Login dialog box, click the Database Access tab:

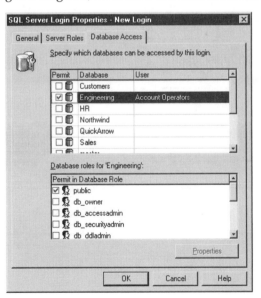

2. Place a check mark next to the database(s) the user should be able to access.

3. Optionally, you can assign database roles (described later) for these users.

Alternatively, you can add existing database logins to a database using the following procedure.

STEP-BY-STEP

Setting Database Permissions When Creating a Database User

1. Expand the database for which you want to add users.
2. Right-click the Database Users folder and select New Database User.
3. Select a Login Name. You can use the login name as the username within the database, or you can assign a unique name.

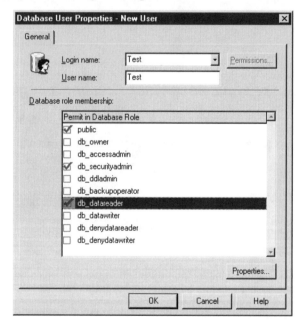

4. Add the users to any existing database roles (described later).

Roles

It's easier to assign permissions to groups of users who have similar functions than it is to manage individual accounts. The security architecture of SQL Server 2000 includes *roles* to make assigning permissions easier. Roles work much like groups in Windows NT/2000 but are defined based on the specific function of an individual. For example, if you have several users who should be able to view but not modify employee records, you may want to create a role called Employee Record Viewers. Roles can also contain other roles. The overall process is to define roles, assign users to roles, and then grant permissions to these roles, as shown in Figure 4-23. SQL Server logins are mapped to database user accounts. The user accounts are then added to one or more roles, and the roles themselves are granted specific object permissions.

Types of Roles

SQL Server supports several different types of roles. Table 4-8 lists the different types of roles and describes the purpose of each.

Server Roles

At the server level, you'll need to delegate specific tasks. Many functions are required to keep a SQL Server database operational. Managing backups, logins, and security accounts are important concerns. For small installations, it is likely that a single individual will be responsible for all of these tasks. In larger environments, however, it is more desirable to assign specific tasks to specific users. For example, one database administrator may be in charge of creating and modifying user accounts for multiple servers, while another may be responsible for managing backups on all servers. SQL Server provides

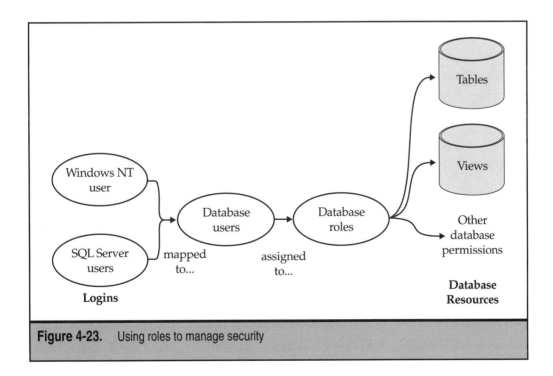

Figure 4-23.   Using roles to manage security

Type of Role	Function	Application
Fixed Server	Manages SQL Server configuration, including objects, alerts, tasks, and devices	Configuration and maintenance of the database server
Fixed Database	Allows specific database functions	Configuration and maintenance of databases
Public	Includes all users with permissions to access a database	Providing default access permissions to any user who can access the database
User-Defined Database	Provides group-based database-level permissions	Granting specific permissions to groups of users
Application	Used by a single application	Supporting applications that perform their own security control; requires a separate password

Table 4-8.   Types of SQL Server Roles

fixed, built-in server roles that have been created for making this process much easier. Table 4-9 lists the different server roles and their functions.

You can easily view the detailed permissions for server roles in Enterprise Manager by right-clicking on the server role name, selecting Properties, and then choosing the Permissions tab (see Figure 4-24).

By default, only the System Administrators role contains accounts. The members of this role include the Windows NT/2000 Administrators group and the SQL Server SA account. Also, note that members of each of the roles are allowed to assign the permissions of their role to another user account. For example, a user who is a member of the Setup Administrators role can add another user to this role. You can add user accounts to logins when they are created by accessing the Server Roles tab of the SQL Server Login Properties dialog box.

Role	Username	Function
Bulk Insert Administrators	Bulkadmin	Can perform BULK INSERT operations
Database Creators	Dbcreator	Creates, alters, and resizes databases
Disk Administrators	Diskadmin	Manages database storage files
Process Administrators	processadmin	Kills (stops) processes running on the server
Security Administrators	securityadmin	Creates and manages server logins and auditing
Server Administrators	serveradmin	Changes server configuration parameters and shuts down server
Setup Administrators	setupadmin	Manages replication and extended procedures
System Administrators	Sysadmin	Completes control over all database functions

Table 4-9. SQL Server 2000 Server Roles and Their Functions

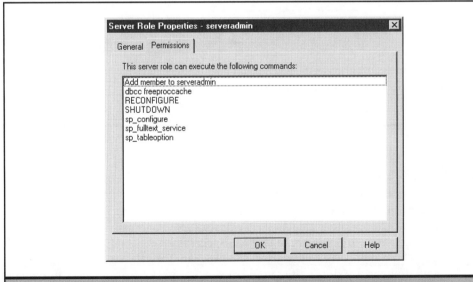

Figure 4-24. Viewing permissions for the Server Administrators role

To add existing logins to server roles, use the following steps.

STEP-BY-STEP

Adding Logins to Server Roles

1. In Enterprise Manager, expand the Security folder for the server you want to modify.
2. Click on Server Roles, and then double-click the name of a Server Role in the right panel and click Add. Highlight users to assign them to this role.

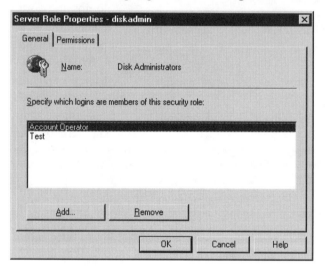

NOTE: You won't be able to change the options for built-in server roles.

Application Roles

Large and complex database applications often enforce their own security based on business rules. For example, an accounting package might enforce security permissions that allow a specific user to update a database only during specific hours. The application itself will use a single login and password that have access permissions to obtain and modify any data within a database. In this case, the program can use an application role to access the data it needs. By doing this, you can prevent DBAs from having to manage multiple accounts on the database level, and allow more complex security management within the application logic. Regardless of the authentication mode selected for server logins, application roles require the use of a login name, username, and password to access database information.

Database Roles

Within databases, users will be required to carry out specific functions. For small databases, a single individual might be responsible for all maintenance and administration. Large databases, on the other hand, will require multiple users to manage specific aspects of the configuration. To make managing permissions easier, SQL Server includes built-in database roles that allow administrators to easily assign only the permissions necessary for completing specific tasks. Table 4-10 lists the built-in roles generated for new databases.

Role	Permissions
db_owner	Has full control of the database and its objects, as well as other maintenance and configuration activities
db_accessadmin	Can add or remove Windows NT/2000 groups, Windows NT/2000 users, and SQL Server users in the database
db_datareader	Can see any data from all user tables in the database
db_datawriter	Can add, change, or delete data from all user tables in the database
db_ddladmin	Can perform Data Definition Language (DDL) operations to add, modify, or drop objects in the database
db_securityadmin	Can manage roles and members of SQL Server database roles, and can manage statement and object permissions in the database
db_backupoperator	Can back up the database
db_denydatareader	Cannot see any data in the database, but can make schema changes
db_denydatawriter	Cannot change any data in the database
Public	All users will automatically be members of the public role, and membership cannot be changed. Default permissions on database objects are often placed on the public role.

Table 4-10.   SQL Server 2000 Database Roles and Their Permissions

Users can be assigned to any of these roles based on the requirements of their job functions. By default, whenever a user creates a database object, he or she is defined as the owner of that object. Other users with appropriate permissions may change database ownership. To remove a database owner, you must first either drop any objects owned by the user or transfer ownership to another user or role.

User-Defined Database Roles

It's likely that the built-in database roles will cover many of your requirements. You can, however, create custom roles for common tasks that are performed within a database. With user-defined database roles, you can group users who have access to perform specific functions on tables, views, and other objects.

To create a new user-defined database role, follow the steps given next.

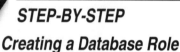

STEP-BY-STEP

Creating a Database Role

1. In Enterprise Manager, expand the database for which you want to create a role.

2. Right-click Roles and select New Database Role. You'll see this dialog box:

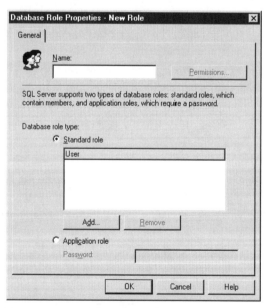

3. For the Database Role Type, select Standard Role. Click Add to assign existing database users to this role. If you choose to make this an Application Role, it must be assigned a password.

Once a role is created, you can assign users to it. A user can be assigned to multiple roles, according to the needed permissions. To add users to an existing role, expand the Database Roles folder within a database. Double-click an existing role and use the Add and Remove buttons to change assigned users. All users who are members of a role will inherit any permissions assigned to the role itself. Keep in mind that permissions are cumulative, with one exception: if a user is denied permissions at the user level or in any role, he or she will not have this permission regardless of other role permissions.

Object Permissions

So far, we've covered the steps that are necessary for creating server logins and databases. We also covered how you can use roles to simplify the administration of security. The final level of security—and the most granular—is at the actual level of SQL Server objects, such as tables, views, and stored procedures.

For managing security on database objects and actions, SQL Server supports three types of permissions; these are listed in Table 4-11.

Statement Permissions

Before user accounts and roles can be useful, you must assign them permissions on specific database objects. These permissions are called *statement permissions* because they control the types of commands that can be executed against database objects. The permissions possible for database objects are listed in Table 4-12.

For more detailed security, you can also place Select and Update permissions on specific columns within a database object. All database users will be members of the Public role by default, and this membership cannot be changed. This role permits them to perform functions that do not require specific permissions and to access any database via the Guest account (unless it is removed). You can define permissions by viewing either user

Type of Permission	Associated Functions
Statement permissions	Creating and modifying databases
Object permissions	Executing queries that display and modify database objects
Predefined (role-based) permissions	Tasks specific to fixed roles and object owners

Table 4-11.   Types of Permissions in SQL Server

Statement	Types of Object	Function
SELECT	Tables and views	Reads data from an existing database row
UPDATE	Tables and views	Modifies data in an existing database row
INSERT	Tables and views	Creates a new database row
DELETE	Tables and views	Removes an existing row from a database
Declarative Referential Integrity (DRI)	Tables	Allows users of other tables to refer to a key in the active table without having explicit permissions to view or modify that key directly
Execute Stored Procedures	Stored procedures	Causes statements to execute with the permissions of the stored procedure's owner, not the executing user's account

Table 4-12.   Database Object Permissions

information or database object information. To add or modify permissions for a specific database object, use the following procedure.

STEP-BY-STEP

Setting Object Permissions in Enterprise Manager

1. Expand the database for which you want to modify permissions.
2. Expand the folder for the type of object you want to assign permissions (such as Views).
3. Right-click the name of an object and select Properties.
4. Click Permissions. You'll see this dialog box:

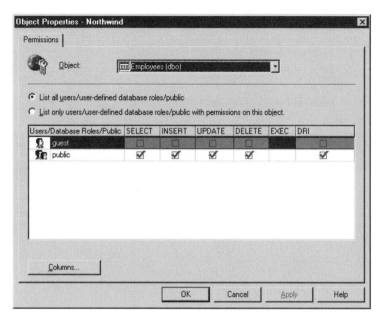

Here you can choose to list all users and roles, or just those who currently have access to the database. Note that you can further restrict permissions by clicking the Columns button. This will allow you to place permissions on specific database columns.

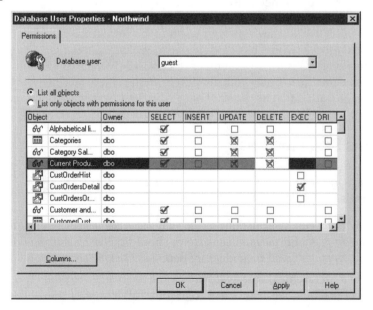

5. Place a check mark next to the permissions you want to grant to these database users. The meanings of the possible settings are listed here:

Setting	Symbol	Meaning
Grant	Check mark	The user has permissions.
Deny	Red X	The user does not have permissions.
Revoke	Blank	Unspecified. (The user can inherit permissions.)

To modify permissions on a per-user basis, double-click a username in the Database Users folder within a database. Click Permissions to view the security settings for this user. In general, permissions are *additive*. That is, if a user is a member of one group that is allowed SELECT permissions and another that is allowed INSERT and DELETE permissions, he or she will effectively have all three of these rights. However, if a user is a member of any group that is explicitly denied permissions to a resource, this setting overrides any other permissions. In this case, the user will not be able to perform the action until he or she is removed from the group that is denied access.

Permissions can also be set with the GRANT, REVOKE, and DENY statements using a SQL query tool. By default, the sysadmin, db_securityadmin, and db_owner roles have permissions to perform these functions. All permissions information is stored in the sysprotects system table. When a user executes a query or transaction, SQL Server checks for appropriate permissions in this table. Permissions are cumulative, unless they are specifically denied. For example, if John is a member of Group 1 (which has Select permissions) and Group 2 (which has Update permissions), he will be able to perform both functions. However, if he is also a member of Group 3 (which has Denied Select permissions), he will be unable to query information from the object. In this case, he will receive an error message stating that he does not have sufficient permissions to execute the query or transaction.

Permissions Best Practices

Setting permissions on database objects can be quite complicated if you don't fully understand the implications of the settings. In general, there are several good ways to manage permissions in databases of any size:

▼ **Use roles to grant permissions.**   Managing roles is much easier than granting permissions to individual users. Roles should be designed based on specific job functions and should provide only necessary permissions.

■ **Create a hierarchical role system.**   Some users may require basic read access to specific tables, while others will require full access to some tables and only read access to others. Since roles can be contained in other roles, it might be worthwhile to create groups such as DB – Basic Access, DB – Intermediate Access, and DB – Full Access. The intermediate role could contain Basic Access permissions plus additional permissions.

■ **Use stored procedures.** Apart from security management benefits, stored procedures execute much faster than the same SQL statements executed manually, and can thus cut down on network traffic. They also make interactions with database objects easier for developers and end users. We'll talk about the performance benefits of stored procedures later in this chapter.

▲ **Assign permissions on views and stored procedures.** If your database contains an employee information table that includes basic information (such as employee names and employee numbers) and sensitive information (such as salary figures), you may choose to create a view or stored procedure that does not return sensitive data. As long as the view owner has access to the table, the user of the view will be able to access all of the data in the table. You can deny everyone access to the table except the owner of the view or stored procedure. You can then grant users access to the view or stored procedure without worrying that they will query sensitive information.

Auditing

Though it won't necessarily prevent users from modifying information, auditing can be a very powerful security tool. SQL Server 2000 lets you automatically log actions performed by users on specific database objects. Although technically it won't prevent wrongdoing or protect data directly, auditing is a vital function of any secure database server implementation. To view auditing information, use the following procedure.

STEP-BY-STEP

Viewing Auditing Information in Enterprise Manager

1. Expand the Management folder for the server on which you want to view the audit logs.

2. In the SQL Server Logs folder, click the Current log to view the most recent information, or click an Archive log to view older data.

3. You can modify the view by clicking the log name and selecting View. You can also click a column heading to sort by that value.

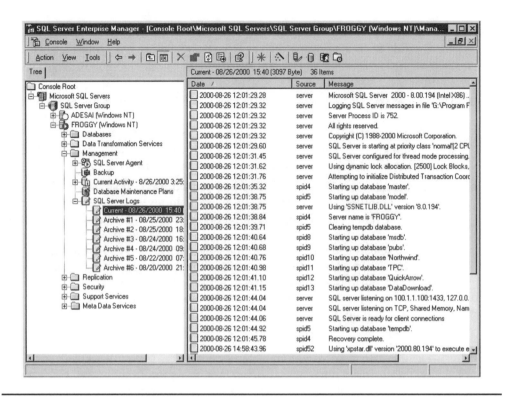

The information displayed includes the date and time of the logged item, the process ID that generated the event, and the text of the logged message. One of the most difficult parts of regularly reviewing audit logs is that there is a lot of information that is not necessarily important. To find what you're really looking for, be sure to use the filtering features in Enterprise Manager.

Specifying Auditing Settings with Alerts

In addition to the default alerts, you can track other actions of interest. You can log specific information by configuring SQL Server alerts in the SQL Server Agent Alerts option. To set an alert, use the following procedure.

STEP-BY-STEP

Specifying Auditing Settings Using Alerts

1. Expand the Management folder. Expand the SQL Server Agent folder, right-click Alerts, and select New Alert. You'll see this dialog box:

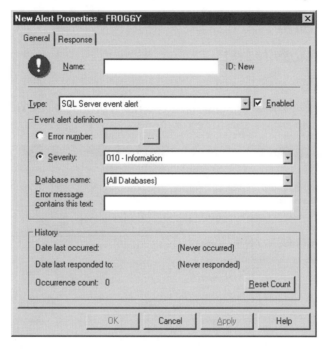

2. Name the alert and choose SQL Server Event Alert for the Type. Check the Enabled box.

3. To define the alert condition, choose to report on an error message number (which may be user defined) or on all events that have a specific severity. You can also assign the alert to a specific database. Finally, enter the text for the error message.

4. Optionally, you can use the settings on the Response tab to notify database administrators of problems. Click OK to accept the settings.

Viewing the Activity Log

Setting auditing is important, but it is useless if the audit logs are not regularly reviewed for suspicious activity. The activity logs can contain a lot of information, making it difficult to find exactly what you're looking for. To find a specific event, use the following procedure.

STEP-BY-STEP

Viewing the Activity Log

1. Select Tools | Manage SQL Server Messages.

2. In the Message Text Contains box, you can type in text you're searching for. You can also enter a specific error number and/or specify a certain severity.

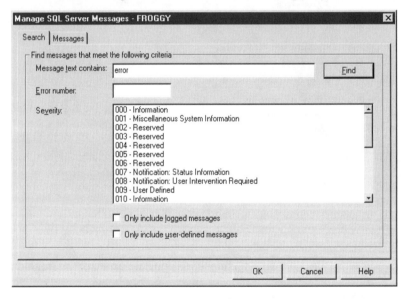

3. Click Find to start the search.

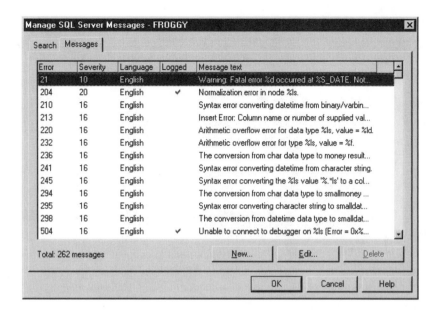

Server messages are also written to the Windows NT/2000 Application Log and can be viewed using the Event Viewer application.

Sometimes, you just want to get a quick snapshot of who's using the server and for what purpose. You can view current database activity by selecting Management | Current Activity | Process Info in Enterprise Manager. From this view, shown in Figure 4-25, you can find out which users are logged in to the database server, what operations are being performed, and which objects are currently locked. There are options to send a message to a connected user and to kill a specific process (if you have permissions).

SQL Server Security Best Practices

When dealing with database security, fitting the settings to your business requirements should be of the utmost concern. In dealing with SQL Server 2000 settings, the following measures are recommended:

▼   You should always choose to assign a strong password for the sa account during installation. Also, remember that members of the Windows NT/2000

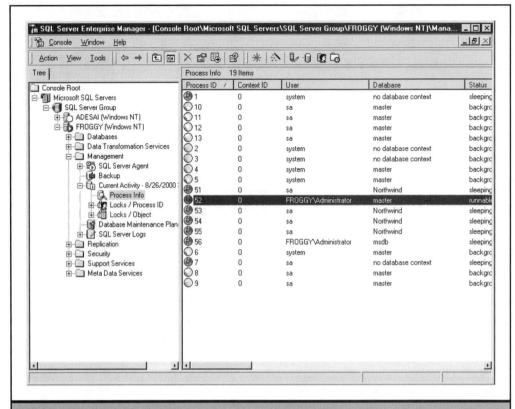

Figure 4-25. Viewing current database activity using Enterprise Manager

Administrators group are automatically given the same permissions as the sa account.

■ The default TCP/IP port used by SQL Server is 1433. Potential hackers will often scan for this port to find out which SQL Servers are running in your environment. Though this isn't a security breach in itself, finding the SQL Server installations in your environment may be the first step toward a hack attempt (especially on the Internet).

▲ You should make the password for the SQL Server service accounts very difficult to guess. You'll rarely need to use this account to log in, and if you do, any administrator can always change the password.

PERFORMANCE MONITORING AND OPTIMIZATION

Performance can be monitored and optimized at multiple levels. The goal is to provide low *response times* (how long it takes to receive the first records from a query) and high *throughput* (how quickly an entire result set can be returned). When discussing performance monitoring as related to database applications, it's important to make a distinction between these terms. Furthermore, optimization steps can often cause the balance between throughput and response times to tip in favor of one or the other. To find the optimal settings, you must understand business requirements. For example, if a user wants to scroll through a list of items, it is a good idea to return the first few items as quickly as possible. However, if a manager is creating a report on a desktop computer, it's likely that none of the calculations will be completed until all data is retrieved.

Overall database performance is based on the relationship between many different factors. You can optimize performance at one or more of several levels:

▼ **Server level**   Managing performance issues related to running multiple applications on the same machine

■ **Database level**   Managing database objects to offer the best response times and throughput

▲ **Query level**   Finding and optimizing long-running database queries

In this part of the chapter, we'll look at the tools and features available for monitoring and optimizing performance.

The Server Level

The first step in optimizing performance is to look at the overall configuration of the SQL Server. Included at this level will be considerations regarding other roles of this machine and the implementation of important resources. The three most important hardware-level parameters that affect a database server are the CPU, memory, and physical disk decisions. Let's look at how you can monitor and optimize these settings.

Using Windows NT/2000 Performance Monitor

It's often necessary to view overall system performance in relation to server resources. Windows NT/2000 Performance Monitor is the best tool for viewing and recording all of this information in a single place. When SQL Server 2000 is installed, several performance counters are added to the list of items available through Performance Monitor. One of the main challenges with using Performance Monitor is deciding *what* to monitor. To make this easier, Microsoft has included some preset counters that will be of interest to SQL Server DBAs. To access these counters, click the Performance Monitor icon in the SQL

Server 2000 program group. From there, you'll see the basic SQL Server performance statistics and will be able to add other information as necessary. (See Figure 4-26.) For example, if you're also running Internet Information Server (IIS) on the same machine, you might want to compare the number of web users to the number of database users currently on the system.

NOTE: As we mentioned in Chapter 3, the exact counters that are available for monitoring will be based on the software you have installed and various operating system settings. For example, in order to enable monitoring of physical hard disk activity, you must execute the diskperf –ye command and then reboot the computer. Or, to view certain network characteristics, you must have the appropriate services installed (for example, the Simple Network Management Protocol, or SNMP).

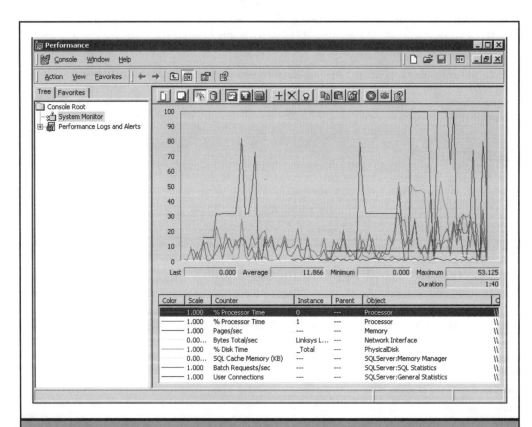

Figure 4-26.   Using the Windows 2000 Performance tool

Managing CPU and Memory Settings

The two most important resources in dealing with overall server performance are the CPU speed and memory. SQL Server is installed with default memory and CPU usage options that are appropriate for working in most environments. If you need to make changes, however, you have options. To set SQL Server memory and CPU settings, use the following procedure.

STEP-BY-STEP

Setting SQL Server Memory and CPU Settings in Enterprise Manager

1. In Enterprise Manager, right-click the name of the server you want to modify and select Properties.

2. In the Memory tab, you can modify the amount of memory the SQL Server will use:

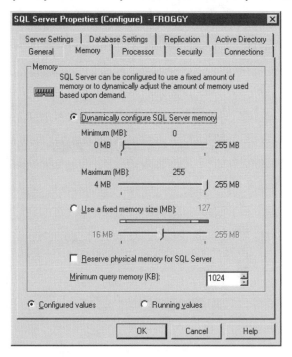

3. The default option—to dynamically configure memory usage—will be appropriate for most situations. If you have a large amount of RAM on the system, you might want to increase the minimum memory size. Alternatively, if your server will be running many other important applications, you might want to lower the maximum setting. If you have an accurate idea of how much

memory SQL Server will typically use, you can put the value at a fixed setting. This precaution will minimize the performance overhead caused by excessive paging of information to and from the hard disk.

4. You can check the Reserve Physical Memory for SQL Server option if you want Windows NT/2000 to set aside physical RAM for the service. This prevents the operating system from swapping this information to disk and can increase performance. The Minimum Query Memory and Maximum Query Memory options specify the limits of RAM that can be allocated to any single user transaction.

5. In the Processor tab, you can specify which CPU(s) in a multiprocessor system can be used by SQL Server. This is often useful if you want to dedicate one or more CPUs to operating system functions and other applications. The Maximum Worker Threads setting specifies how many operations SQL Server can perform simultaneously. A higher number allows more users and processes to occur, but performance might decrease as SQL Server switches between threads. If the value is exceeded, users will receive an error message when trying to execute a command.

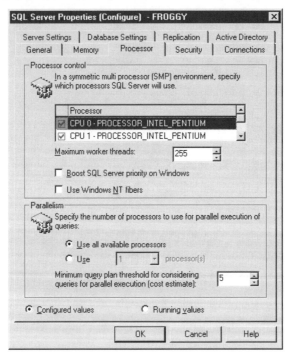

6. The Boost SQL Server Priority option is designed to give the SQL Server service more CPU time when multiple tasks are competing for resources. However, you should thoroughly test the effects of this setting, as it may provide only a

marginal improvement in performance and can cause problems with other applications.

7. Finally, in the Parallelism section, you can specify whether you want SQL Server to distribute query processing between multiple processors. Multiprocessing generally incurs overhead, and the default setting for the minimum query plan threshold will determine whether it is efficient to use multiple CPUs for this task. "Costs" are based on the time required to process a transaction. Legal values are between 0 and 32,767.

8. To accept all changes, click OK. Dynamic memory changes will take place immediately, but others might require a restart of the SQL Server.

Now that we've looked at two relatively easy ways to monitor and optimize overall server performance, let's move down a level and look at database settings.

The Database Level

Tuning performance options at the database level involves examining all the operations that are being performed on that database over time. Normally, if you're an applications developer, you can get a pretty good idea of how the system will perform overall based on this information. Fortunately, SQL Server includes the SQL Server Profiler tool for measuring database server performance at several levels. In this section, we'll walk through using SQL Server Profiler and then look at how this information can be used to optimize performance.

Using SQL Server Profiler

SQL Server Profiler can be used to monitor the performance of queries as they occur. It can display information about user logins, connections to the server, and starting and completion times for database transactions.

SQL Server Profiler works by using *traces*. These are files containing data about the events that you choose to monitor. Information obtained from running a trace file can be stored in a text file or in a SQL Server database table. You can launch SQL Server Profiler directly from the SQL Server 2000 program group or from Enterprise Manager by using the Tools menu.

STEP-BY-STEP

Creating a New Trace in SQL Server Profiler

1. Open Profiler from the Microsoft SQL Server program group.

2. Select File | New | Trace. Enter a trace name and select the server you want to monitor.

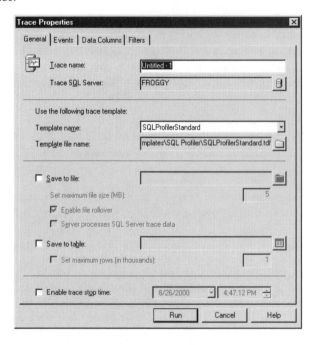

3. Choose to save the collected information to a text file or to a SQL Server database.

4. In the Events tab, add the events you want to monitor:

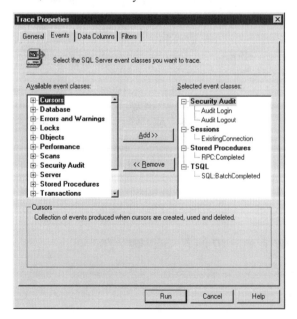

5. The lower portion of the dialog box will give you a brief description of each item.

6. In the Data Columns tab, choose the type of information you want to view for each event. Again, a brief description of each column type is provided.

7. Finally, on the Filters tab, you can select specific criteria to include and exclude in events for this trace.

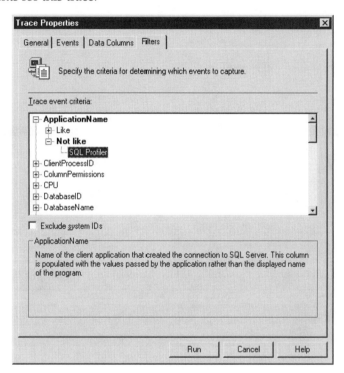

8. Click OK to save the trace file you've created.

To execute the trace, select File | Run Traces and select either a sample trace or one that you've created. A screen will appear showing information related to monitored events, as shown in Figure 4-27. You can run multiple traces at once to record different kinds of information (for example, query performance and overall server statistics). To simulate the recorded information at a later time, you can replay a trace by using the Replay menu. Finally, to view captured information, you can select File | Open and then select Trace File (if you've saved to a file) or Trace Table (if you've saved to a SQL Server table). Trace files can also be used with data analysis tools, such as Microsoft Access and Microsoft Excel.

Using the Index Tuning Wizard

Once you've captured the information you need, it's time to apply it. If you're really a hard-core DBA, you might start examining query statistics and optimizing indexes

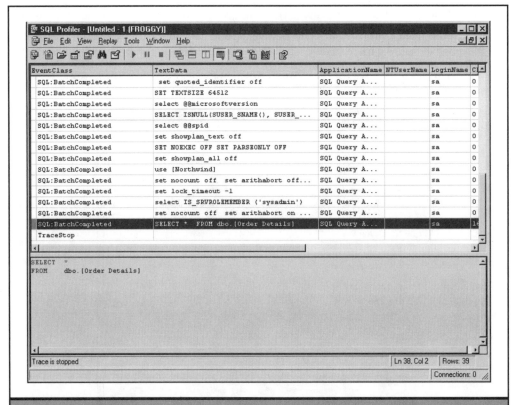

Figure 4-27. Viewing trace file information in SQL Server Profiler

manually. However, if you're like me (averse to long, complicated, boring tasks), you'll probably want the SQL Server Index Tuning Wizard to generate your reports automatically. The wizard can be launched from within SQL Server Enterprise Manager, and it can use the "workload" that you've generated with Profiler for analysis. The recommendations will look similar to the ones shown in Figure 4-28. You can choose to have the wizard automatically execute the recommendations or save them as a SQL script for later analysis.

The Query Level

At the level of the individual query, you can use features of SQL Query Analyzer to provide you with statistics and performance recommendations. These features are excellent for applications developers who want to test the effects that minor syntax changes have on performance, or optimize performance of a particularly slow-running query.

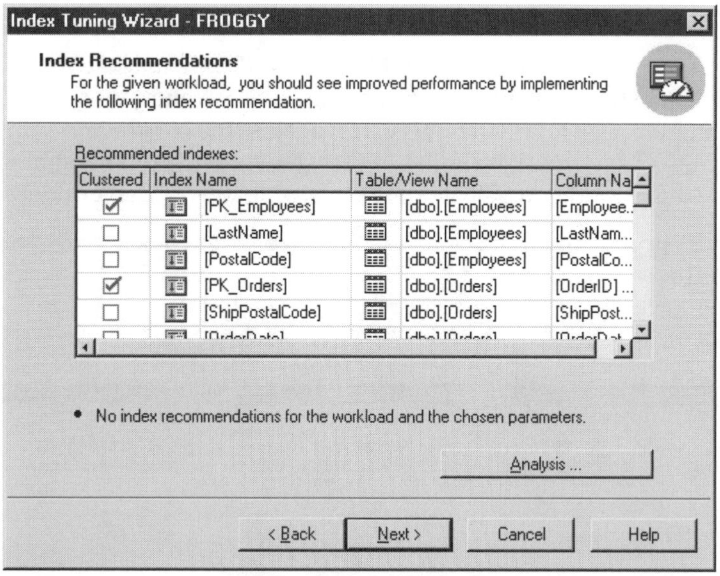

Figure 4-28. Viewing index recommendations in the Index Tuning Wizard

SQL Query Analyzer

SQL Query Analyzer is a powerful new tool included with SQL Server 2000. On a basic level, it provides a Transact-SQL command environment for executing SQL queries. However, it goes much further by color-coding queries and allowing users to display results in a grid format. For measuring the performance of specific queries, it can show the exact statistics for fulfilling a request. Finally, it can analyze queries and make recommendations as to which columns to place indexes in.

STEP-BY-STEP

Creating and Testing a SQL Query in Query Analyzer

1. Open SQL Query Analyzer either from the Microsoft SQL Server 2000 program group or by selecting Tools | Query Analyzer in Enterprise Manager.

2. If prompted, log on to a SQL Server database.

3. Type a standard SQL query in the main window. In general, the more complex the query, the more useful information you'll receive in the next step.

4. Select Query | Display Estimated Execution Plan to execute the query and record statistics. You might have to maximize the query window to see all the information. The following query, run against the Northwind sample database, will present information similar to that shown in the following illustration. (More information on SQL syntax is available in SQL Server Books Online.)

```
SELECT productname, SUM(od.unitprice * od.quantity) AS total
FROM [order details] od inner join products p
ON od.productid = p.productid
GROUP BY productname
```

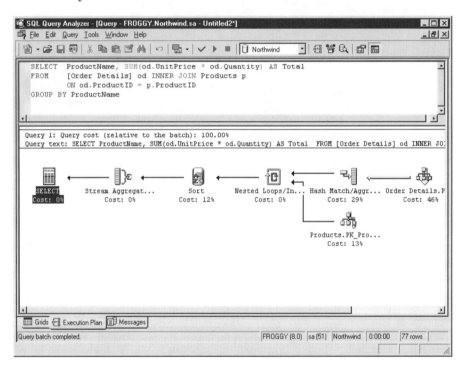

5. Hover the mouse over a specific step or arrow in the execution plan for the SQL query. A window will pop up providing detailed information about the steps required to complete the query.

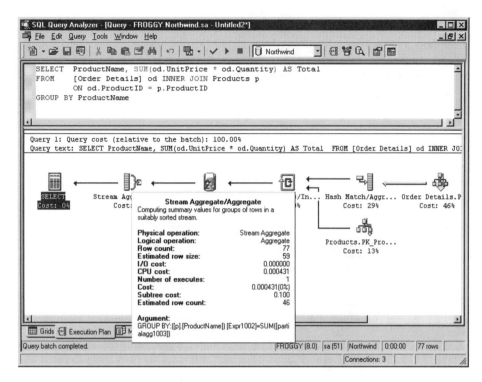

```
SELECT   ProductName, SUM(od.UnitPrice * od.Quantity) AS Total
FROM     [Order Details] od INNER JOIN Products p
         ON od.ProductID = p.ProductID
GROUP BY ProductName
```

Query 1: Query cost (relative to the batch): 100.00%
Query text: SELECT ProductName, SUM(od.UnitPrice * od.Quantity) AS Total FROM [Order Details] od INNER JO

Stream Aggregate/Aggregate
Computing summary values for groups of rows in a
suitably sorted stream.

Physical operation:	Stream Aggregate
Logical operation:	Aggregate
Row count:	77
Estimated row size:	59
I/O cost:	0.000000
CPU cost:	0.000431
Number of executes:	1
Cost:	0.000431(0%)
Subtree cost:	0.100
Estimated row count:	46

Argument:
GROUP BY:([p].[ProductName]) [Expr1002]=SUM([parti
alagg1003])

Hash Match/Aggr...   Order Details.P
Cost: 29%   Cost: 46%

Products.PK_Pro...
Cost: 13%

6. Optionally, select Query | Perform Index Analysis to rerun the same query and to make recommendations on index implementation. This option works only for certain types of queries that can be analyzed by SQL Query Analyzer.

Using Query Governor

It is often useful to be able to limit the resources used by a single query or transaction in SQL Server. For example, executing a query that asks for the sum of all values in a 3GB table would be quite costly to perform. Other users would suffer from slow response times, and the database server itself might be significantly slowed. In many cases, such a transaction might be executed by mistake. If the transaction must be carried out, it is a good idea to schedule it to occur at a later time.

SQL Server 2000 includes a server configuration parameter that can allow an administrator to limit the resources that can be used by a single operation. This option, the query governor cost limit, sets the longest time (in seconds) that a query may run. You can set this option in Enterprise Manager by right-clicking a server, selecting Properties, and then selecting the Server Settings tab. You can then enable or disable the "Use query governor to prevent queries exceeding specified cost" setting. (See Figure 4-29.)

To set these options for all databases on a server, you can use the sp_configure stored procedure, as follows:

```
USE master
EXEC sp_configure 'query governor cost limit', '1'
RECONFIGURE
EXEC sp_configure
```

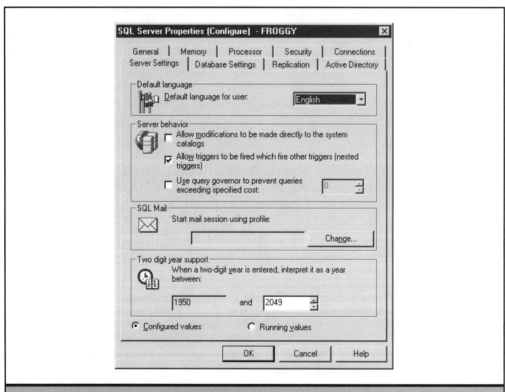

Figure 4-29. Setting query cost governor settings in Enterprise Manager

Before this setting will take effect, you need to stop and restart SQL Server. Finally, the query governor cost limit can be set on a per-transaction basis by using the following statement as part of a transaction:

```
SET QUERY_GOVERNOR_COST_LIMIT
```

A value of 0 will set no limit on the maximum query execution time. Any values greater than 0 will specify the number of seconds that a query may run. Note that the same query might take differing amounts of time to complete, based on server hardware configurations.

Using Stored Procedures

We discussed stored procedures at the beginning of this chapter. As promised, here's a discussion of how they can be used to optimize performance. SQL Server stored procedures use cached optimization plans to greatly speed the processing of queries. *Stored procedures* are precompiled collections of SQL statements that remain cached in memory and execute up to 20 times faster than the same statement run manually. They also have the following advantages:

▼ **Reduced network traffic**   Instead of sending large queries with hundreds of lines, a single command can be executed on the server.

■ **Modular and flexible code**   Stored procedures can call each other, and common procedures can be written only once and shared throughout a database.

▲ **Streamlined security**   Stored procedures can provide embedded security permissions logic. Since a stored procedure executes with the permission of its owner, security implementation is simplified. Furthermore, the definitions of stored procedures can be stored in an encrypted form within the database, thereby protecting business logic.

You can create a stored procedure in one of two ways. First, you can enter a query into SQL Query Analyzer. The CREATE PROC statement is used to create a new stored procedure, as in the following example (taken from the example Northwind database):

```
CREATE PROCEDURE CustOrderHist @CustomerID nchar(5)
AS
SELECT ProductName, Total=SUM(Quantity)
FROM Products P, [Order Details] OD, Orders O, Customers C
WHERE C.CustomerID = @CustomerID
AND C.CustomerID = O.CustomerID AND O.OrderID = OD.OrderID AND OD.ProductID =
P.ProductID
GROUP BY ProductName
```

To run the stored procedure, you can use the following command:

```
EXEC dbo.CustOrderHist 'ANATR'
```

This example will find all of the orders placed by the customer whose customer ID is "ANATR." Stored procedures can accept command-line arguments and can process complicated statements. Overall, the use of stored procedures improves performance, reduces chances of errors, and eliminates the tedium of rewriting complex queries.

Alternatively, you can use Enterprise Manager to create a new stored procedure. Right-click the Store Procedures object in a database and select New Store Procedure. In the window, type the SQL query to execute when the stored procedure is run.

Scalability and Benchmarks

People often refer to scalability when talking about the features of a database platform. However, the term itself—let alone the actual measurements—is open to interpretation. In general, we can define *scalability* as the ability of database server software to take advantage of upgraded hardware. The law of diminishing returns applies, though. The performance increase of adding a second CPU to a server might not be the 100 percent you would expect, due to the overhead involved with splitting operations between processors. Many efforts have been made to ensure that the architecture of SQL Server allows for scaling to large databases and making use of advanced options, such as multiple gigabytes of physical memory and parallel processing.

When measuring performance between different systems on different platforms, it's important to have a standard test. This test should not be written to prefer any database platform over another and should put a database through some real-world tests that can provide relevant and pertinent information. A real-world attempt at just such a test has been made by the TPC. You can get more information at **www.tpc.org**. There, you'll find the actual benchmarks posted for specific database servers. One important aspect of these benchmarks is that they take the factor of cost into account. Many vendors advertise about the levels of performance that they have been able to attain using the TPM benchmarks. However, this can be largely irrelevant to most businesses, because the costs of such systems are often far out of reach for business users. What is of more interest is how much "bang for the buck" you can get from a specific platform.

Scheduling Jobs with SQL Server Agent

One way to squeeze the maximum possible performance out of your machines is to use them when they're least busy. This is an important concept in relation to database backups. The properties of SQL Server Agent allow you to schedule tasks so that they occur when there is little or no activity on the database. Although it's often better to schedule jobs for times of the day or night when you know activity will be low, this isn't always possible.

STEP-BY-STEP

Configuring SQL Server Agent

1. Expand the Management folder, right-click SQL Server Agent, and select Properties. You'll see this dialog box:

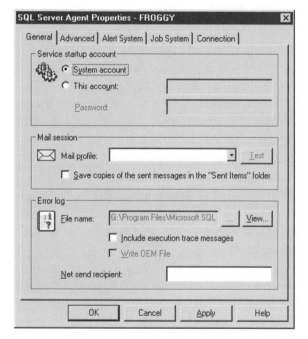

2. On the General tab, you can specify the account to be used by SQL Server Agent, the mail profile to be used for sending messages, and the name of the file to save error information to. Optionally, if you want a user to see a pop-up dialog box when errors occur, enter the name of the user who should be alerted.

3. On the Advanced tab, you can set the options under Idle CPU Condition as desired. The percentage threshold specifies the maximum CPU usage, and the number of seconds specifies the minimum duration of this level of activity before

tasks are run. You can also configure whether you want SQL Server Agent to restart when an unexpected stop occurs. Finally, you can choose to forward events to remote servers so that all information can be managed in a single location.

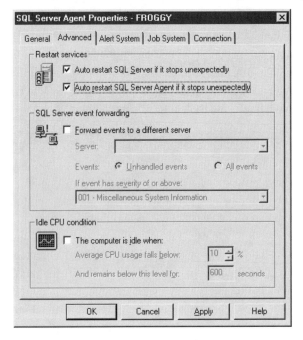

4. The Alert System tab allows you to send e-mail to a compatible pager. A fail-safe operator can also be set up as an alternative recipient when an error occurs.

5. The Job System tab allows you to configure settings for the maximum log size. Here, you can also restrict access for executing operating system commands to system administrators. This option prevents users from running jobs under elevated privileges using the CmdExec procedure.

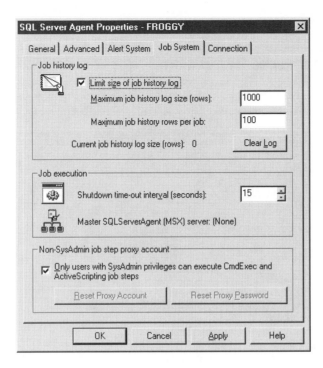

6. Finally, on the Connection tab, you can specify the account that SQL Server Agent will use to log on to SQL Server. When you're done with the configuration, click OK to accept the changes.

Scheduling jobs allows certain operations to occur when the staff is in a meeting, for example, or during lunchtime.

Setting Alerts

SQL Server Agent can be used to send alerts based on performance data. For example, if the number of user connections exceeds a certain value, a server administrator can be notified.

STEP-BY-STEP

Setting Performance-Based Alerts

1. Expand the Management folder, and then expand the SQL Server Agent item. Right-click Alerts and select New Alert.

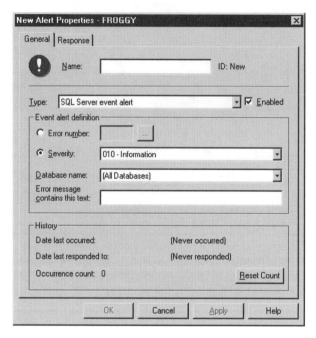

2. Name the alert and set the type to SQL Server Performance Condition Alert. Check the Enabled box.

3. To define the alert condition, choose an object and a counter. These are the same values that can be monitored by Performance Monitor (described earlier). Finally, set the alert to fire when a value is lower than, higher than, or equal to a certain number.

4. Optionally, you can use the settings in the Response tab to notify database administrators of problems.

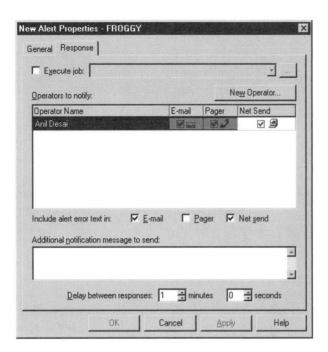

5. Click OK to accept the settings.

The alert must also be defined in SQL Server Performance Monitor. In order for the alerts to function, SQL Server Agent and SQL Server Performance Monitor must be running.

Choosing the Right Tool

SQL Server 2000 comes with so many different tools for monitoring and optimizing performance that the challenge has become choosing the best tool for the job. Table 4-13 lists the tools we've discussed thus far and provides recommendations for their use.

In general, it is recommended that you use all of the various tools. After all, highly optimized queries alone won't give you the performance you want if the server settings are not configured properly. It's a constant juggling act to optimally manage resources, but it's one that can easily pay for itself in reduced equipment costs and happier end users!

Tool	Best Use	Example
Performance Monitor	Measuring overall system performance; measuring overall database server performance over a given period of time	Troubleshooting sluggish system performance that occurs when a server is being used for multiple purposes
SQL Profiler	Logging performance and object access information for later analysis; monitoring multiple queries occurring on a server over a given period of time	Tracking exceptionally slow database performance that occurs when many users run a specific application
SQL Query Analyzer	Analyzing the performance of a specific query	Determining why a specific SELECT statement seems to be running slowly
SQL Server Alerts	Responding to a specific event of interest and notifying the appropriate personnel	Notifying a system administrator when a transaction log becomes full

Table 4-13.   SQL Server Performance Monitoring Tools and Their Functions

DEVELOPING SQL SERVER APPLICATIONS

The database server by itself can be useful, but before your end users will be able to take advantage of the information stored in it, you'll need to develop appropriate applications. We've already discussed some of the various roles that database servers might assume within your environment. Here, we'll look at just a few of the programming concepts related to working with SQL Server 2000. Unfortunately, we don't have the space to cover all the details. Books could be written on just a few of these technologies. In fact, they have! For more details, be sure to check out Otey and Conte's *SQL Server 2000 Developer's Guide* (Osborne/McGraw-Hill, 2000). Let's start by looking at typical application architecture, and then we'll look at data access methods.

n-Tier Client/Server Architecture

In many database applications, client software connects directly with a database server to obtain data for processing. For example, an order entry terminal at a store might use TCP/IP to communicate with a central inventory database server located in the "back office." This is the simplest client/server format, and it works well in some situations. The main benefit is that these types of applications are easy to develop initially. However, there are several drawbacks. First of all, much of the business logic needed to process data is stored on the client. Whenever this information changes or business rules are updated, client software must be upgraded. In most cases, this involves visiting each of the client machines and installing updates. Another potential drawback is in the area of scalability: if the database server or the client is overloaded with work, the user will experience slow response times and throughput. Overall system performance is based on that of the clients and servers.

Database servers are commonly used as part of a multitier client/server architecture. Here, a front-end client program (either a Visual Basic application or an Active Server Page (ASP)–based web application) connects to a middle-tier server that contains the business rules. These data objects are then responsible for obtaining and processing the information requested from the clients. How is it more efficient to have multiple machines perform the work of just one? There are two main benefits.

First, the middle-tier server can be optimized for performing business rules operations only. It can pool multiple requests for information and share these connections with the database server. The benefit for the database server is that it has to communicate directly with only one machine—the middle-tier server. Because database connections can use many resources to establish and destroy connections, this can represent a significant performance increase. An effective network design will optimize the bandwidth between these two machines, further increasing overall information throughput.

I promised two benefits of multitier solutions. We've already covered performance. The second is scalability. If, for example, it is found that the performance of middle-tier components is inadequate, an additional middle-tier server might be implemented to share the workload. Similarly, multiple database servers could provide the data required for the middle-tier components to continue to work at peak performance. Using this modular approach, code and hardware resources can be optimized independently at multiple levels. Additionally, it can be much easier to manage code and security settings when all the components are not located within one single piece of code.

Accessing Data from Applications

Many different methods can be used to access data from a SQL Server installation. Many are supported for backward compatibility, while others optimize performance and ease of use. The three main methods for accessing data from applications include Open Database Connectivity (ODBC), ActiveX Data Objects (ADO), and OLEDB. Which option you choose will be based on the requirements of your application and the development environment in which you work. For example, for web-based applications, the ease of use of ADO makes it a good choice. ADO is also well supported in such development tools as Microsoft Visual Basic and Microsoft Visual Interdev.

For further information on data access methods, see SQL Server Books Online and the Microsoft Developer Network (MSDN) Online web site at **http://msdn.microsoft.com**.

Programming Options

Microsoft has allowed external developers to access various portions of the SQL Server 2000 API. Table 4-14 lists the various APIs available. Although most users will not need to use these features in order to use the product, some businesses will want to create custom tools for their own use or to market commercially. Again, for more information, see SQL Server Books Online or **http://msdn.microsoft.com**.

API	Application	Notes
Data Transformation Services API	Providing highly customized DTS tasks	Can be used for creating customized packages that modify, import, and export data
Open Data Services API	Creating SQL Server extended stored procedures	Adds the benefits of working with languages such as Visual C++
Replication Component Programming API	Setting up and managing SQL Server replication	Provides greater control over the replication process for use in custom applications
SQL Control Manager (SCM)	Controlling SQL Server services	Can be used to start, stop, and pause SQL Server services
SQL Data Manipulation Objects (SQL-DMO)	Managing and modifying SQL Server configuration and settings	Useful for creating custom SQL Server administration and management tools

Table 4-14.   APIs Supported by SQL Server 2000

SQL SERVER 2000 ANALYSIS SERVICES

In addition to its ability to serve as a powerful and flexible "back-end" RDBMS, SQL Server offers many useful features for storing and managing large amounts of data. Additionally, it includes new features for analyzing your data. As mentioned before, there is a fundamental difference between the roles of an OLTP database and those of an OLAP server. In the following sections, we'll look at how decision-support services are supported in SQL Server 2000.

In SQL Server 2000, Microsoft has renamed and enhanced SQL Server 2000's Online Analytical Processing (OLAP) functionality. There are now two main components to what is called SQL Server 2000 Analysis Services. First, there is an improved and enhanced OLAP Services engine. Internally, this is referred to as OLAP 8.0. Second, there is a new data mining engine. Let's look at these features in greater detail.

Data Warehousing

Data warehousing is the act of taking information from various heterogeneous sources and storing it in a common location for data analysis. There are several challenges that systems and database administrators might face when creating a data warehouse:

▼ **Design of the data warehouse schema** The creation of denormalized database schema facilitates the types of reporting that will be common for users in the organization. It is absolutely critical that this phase include input from business leaders throughout an organization. Often, multiple schemas will need to be created to accommodate various requirements. The design of the schema itself will play a large part in the overall success and usefulness of the data warehouse.

■ **Population of the data warehouse** Information from several heterogeneous sources will need to be copied to the data warehouse. Data may come from a variety of platforms (such as relational and nonrelational databases), and may require "scrubbing" to iron out differences in data structure. In many cases, automated processes will be required to routinely refresh the information stored in the data warehouse.

■ **Management of the data warehouse** By their very nature, data warehouses tend to be large databases. Systems and database administrators must find ways to address performance and data storage concerns for the database.

▲ **Analysis** The end goal of most data warehouse projects is the extraction of useful information. Reporting is extremely important for business decision makers and other "data consumers."

Since analysis is a big part of this type of information, *decision support* is the term often used to describe the purpose of data warehouses. Various tools in SQL Server 2000 can be used to help in this goal. Earlier, we discussed how the Data Transformation Services

(DTS) can be used to merge data from many different sources into a single repository. Also, we covered the storage architecture of SQL Server. I mentioned how the limits on the database engine and storage have been greatly expanded—SQL Server 2000 can support databases that are multiple *terabytes* in size. These features and capabilities make SQL Server 2000 a good choice for developing a data warehouse. Of course, the data warehouse itself is not very useful if you don't analyze the information in meaningful ways.

Analysis Services and Online Analytical Processing (OLAP)

Many organizations go to great lengths to collect information, but fall short of the goal when it comes to analyzing the information to obtain useful results. For example, designing a system that collects all the information reported by store cash registers at the point of sale is much easier than combining this information with data from other stores and then forming reports that provide meaningful strategies. It is well beyond the scope of

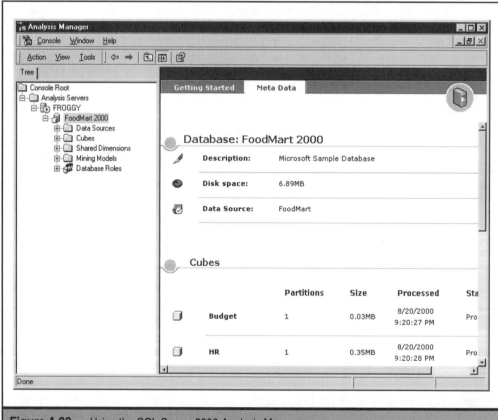

Figure 4-30.   Using the SQL Server 2000 Analysis Manager

this book to explain the intricacies of developing a well-designed OLAP solution. Suffice it to say that it takes a lot of careful planning and solid understanding of the information that you plan to analyze. Figure 4-30 shows the SQL Server 2000 OLAP Manager interface. Using this application, you can easily design and customize data cubes for later analysis.

On the client side, you'll need to have a tool that is easy enough for end users to access. Microsoft Excel 2000 provides many features for accessing OLAP information. The most obvious is the PivotTables feature, shown in Figure 4-31. PivotTables provide interactive data analysis, based on a graphical system. Instead of rephrasing SQL query syntax, the user only needs to drag and drop various columns into place to change views. When connected to an OLAP server, however, the PivotTables feature is greatly enhanced. The user can now form complex data relationships on two or more axes of the "cube." Furthermore, Microsoft has provided for storing *offline cubes*—data structures that store the information that is likely to be used in your OLAP analysis, except that it is stored on your local machine until needed. With this feature, queries can be run much

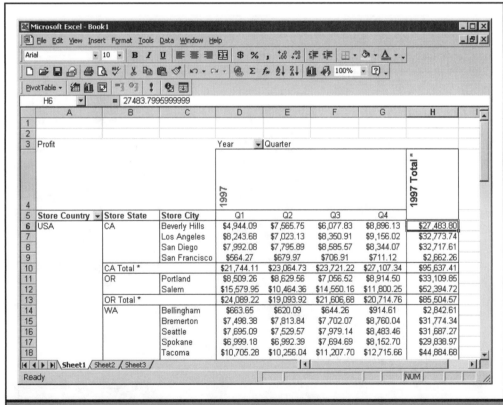

Figure 4-31. Using PivotTables to view and analyze OLAP-based data

more quickly (since they minimize data transfers on the network) and can even be run when not connected to a network at all.

Data Mining

New in SQL Server 2000 is a data mining engine. The concept behind *data mining* is to allow users to find patterns of information in their data. The results from performing well-designed data mining approaches can be very helpful in making business decisions. For example, suppose your database tracks sales that occur in stores throughout the country. In addition to tracking the sales of specific items, you also track information about the buyers (such as their location, income, and gender). You can use data mining techniques to find repeating patterns in the data. You might find, for example, that customers with high incomes located in the Northeast United States are much more likely to buy more of Product A, while the product is not very well received in other markets.

Figure 4-32 provides an example of the SQL Server 2000 data mining engine.

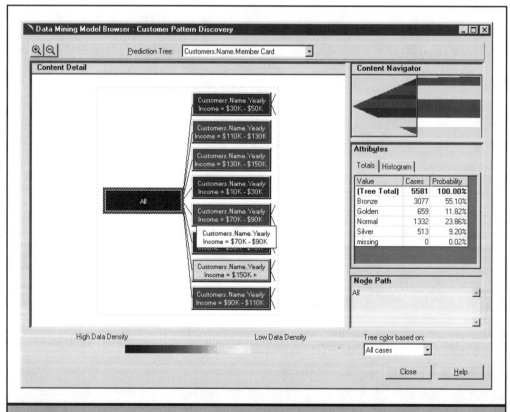

Figure 4-32.   Viewing data mining information in SQL Server 2000 Analysis Manager

English Query

If you're a DBA who does little database development, you've probably wondered why SQL syntax is so cryptic. Actually, compared to other programming languages, the syntax and rules of SQL are quite simple. However, for most people, it's still easier to use a database application designed to develop a "quick report" than it is to design and generate the report manually. Realizing this, Microsoft has included the English Query application, which allows database administrators to create relationships between various types of database information. For example, suppose you program relationships such as "Customers have addresses" or "Orders are shipped to customers." Based on these relationships, English Query can create SQL statements out of phrases such as "How many parts did Store #112 sell in the first quarter of 1999?" If you've ever been on the receiving end of a call from a manager who wants you to design reports, you can see how this feature might be very helpful!

In SQL Server 2000, Microsoft has greatly enhanced the tools used to create English Query information. (See Figure 4-33.) This allows database developers to more easily bring plain-language querying functionality into their applications.

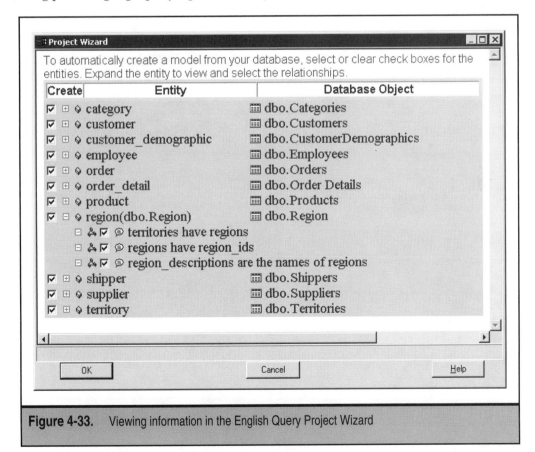

Figure 4-33.   Viewing information in the English Query Project Wizard

SUMMARY

That was a *lot* of information to cover in so few pages! Okay, if you're new to SQL Server, it probably didn't seem like just a "few" pages. Granted, we didn't get into the details of all the features of SQL Server. Instead, we focused on the architecture of SQL Server—how the product works "under the hood." We also focused on two issues that are important in dealing with data protection. The first was security. Unless you're careful to protect your information adequately at the permissions level, it's unlikely that you will be satisfied with your overall data protection strategy. The security architecture of SQL Server 2000 offers many different levels of database security, but you must understand the overall architecture in order to take advantage of them. The second crucial issue is performance. We all try to squeeze the most speed and performance possible out of our given resources. System optimization is important, because it will affect your implementation of data protection solutions. We'll see more examples in upcoming chapters.

With this solid understanding of the inner workings of SQL Server 2000, we can move forward to the task at hand. In Chapter 5, we'll look at the various types of hardware and software available for helping you meet your data protection requirements.

CHAPTER 5

Evaluating Data Protection Solutions

A good data protection plan has several important features. Thus far, we have discussed the importance of planning. Then, we covered information related to working with Windows NT, Windows 2000, and SQL Server 2000. Now, we'll cover the topics of evaluating and choosing backup hardware and software. Choosing a backup solution can be quite confusing, and it's very difficult to make a sound decision without having a technical background on the features to look for.

Understanding the types of backup solutions that are available is a key consideration when determining how you will ultimately implement data protection in your environment. Knowing the speed, capacity, and other features of backup hardware and software will greatly assist you in designing a satisfactory overall solution.

In this chapter, we'll discuss the many considerations you should take into account when shopping for backup products. Keep in mind that these technologies are rapidly evolving to keep pace with increasing business demands. However, the underlying concepts and features remain the same. A good backup solution will meet your organization's requirements for performance, manageability, data storage capacity, and cost. All of the backup products on the market will address some combination of these features. Ultimately, however, you will have to choose the ideal solution based on your business constraints. Therefore, you should use the information in this chapter as a guide to comparing backup hardware and software products.

No book will be able to fully and fairly compare all of the products on the market. Indeed, such a comparison is a moving target because of the many new innovations that are becoming available on the market. Also, as new technologies become available, costs of lower-end solutions decrease. Therefore, wherever possible, I'll provide information about companies that provide data protection solutions, along with links to their web sites so that you can get more information on their products. The goal here is not to provide an exhaustive review of all the available products. Indeed, backup technologies are advancing rapidly, and such coverage would be outdated by the time it made it into your hands.

Instead, we'll focus on the features you should look for in a backup solution that supports Windows NT/2000 and SQL Server 2000. We'll start by making some basic decisions on the type of data protection required. Then, we'll look at considerations you should keep in mind when evaluating server configurations and backup hardware. Of course, no solution will be complete without appropriate software for managing the devices you choose, so we'll also cover issues related to backup software. Finally, we'll discuss ways to ensure that your backup strategy makes good business sense. Let's start by looking at some questions you should answer about your own environment before going shopping.

EVALUATING YOUR ENVIRONMENT

The first step in making any purchasing decision is deciding what you need. Before you can start shopping for hardware and software, you'll need to make sure you understand the needs and constraints of your networking environment. Major areas of consideration include

▼ **Financial constraints**   A simple fact of shopping for almost anything is staying within a budget. Shopping for backup hardware and software is no exception. Understand how much your company is able to reasonably spend. As we discussed in Part I, this decision will largely be based on your business parameters.

■ **Network structure**   Are you working in a distributed environment or on a well-connected LAN?

■ **Applications**   The software programs and applications that are currently in use in your environment will play a large role in your ultimate decision.

▲ **Existing investments**   Most companies already have an existing investment in various data storage and backup hardware and software. You should take into account the details of what you already have when you are deciding what additional resources to purchase.

Clearly, a company that has a well-managed network with no remote backup requirements will choose a very different solution from a company that supports offices located throughout the world. As we've discussed in previous chapters, the individual business environment will play a major role in the overall solution chosen.

Finally, we must consider the inevitable—getting the okay from upper management and executives for that cool new tape drive with the autoloader and all the software necessary to make life easier. In Part I of this book, we talked about evaluating the business issues associated with performing database backups. Here we'll look at how specific technical decisions can be justified from a business standpoint. We'll also examine some ways in which you can best leverage your choices.

Business Issues

As you consider what sort of backup scheme will best support your business, keep the following issues in mind:

▼ **Business requirements**   A common reason for failing to choose appropriate backup technologies is a lack of understanding of the environment. IT staff might see issues from a technical standpoint. For example, if data storage requirements have increased dramatically in past months, a larger and more expensive tape backup system might be chosen. However, in meeting with managers, IT administrators may find that backing up all the information on these servers is unnecessary, because some information can be easily re-created from other sources. Or, perhaps some basic user education about the types of files that should be stored on the network might be in order. Make sure you fully understand the real problems you're trying to solve before you begin your search for new products. Understanding these types of issues is critical to making a sound decision when you're choosing hardware and software.

■ **Costs of administration** Any data protection solution, no matter how automated, will need some level of human involvement. However, the level of effort required from systems administrators can vary widely from product to product. When evaluating the costs of a product, be sure to consider the potential cost of *not* choosing various options. An example that leaps to mind is deciding whether to invest in tape autoloaders (which we'll cover later in this chapter). On one hand, autoloaders can save time and reduce the chances of human error (which, on a manually loaded machine, can include incorrect tape changes or simple forgetfulness). On the other hand, autoloaders can be quite expensive, and in some companies, managers might wonder what systems administrators are being paid for if they don't have time to change the backup media every day.

▲ **Budget** A simple fact of life for most organizations is that money can be scarce. When you're devising a data protection plan, be realistic. Surely, we'd like to ensure that all information is backed up hourly, but this simply isn't financially practical for most businesses. In the best case, you will have sufficient resources for purchasing hardware and software that allow you to save all of your important information regularly. More realistically, however, you'll need to make some trade-offs. It's important that you know what these trade-offs are as you select your backup solution. For example, if only a subset of database information can be protected by the solution you select, you should document this limitation up front. That way, there will be fewer questions if a problem does occur. The question of what to protect, however, can be fraught with political problems—and systems administrators who wish to avoid them should ensure that managers and end users are the ones who make the ultimate decisions. IT should focus instead on ensuring that those decisions are technically feasible and providing any necessary technical advice.

The end of this chapter covers some concepts that you can use to justify an investment in new hardware and software, and describes ways of measuring whether your choices make sense from a business point of view. Now, let's move on to look at some detailed requirements of our solution.

Estimating the Data Volume

Before you can begin to shop around seriously for tape backup hardware, you should have a realistic estimate of the amount of data you will need to protect. Clearly, your approach to backing up 2GB of data would differ greatly from your strategy for backing up a server farm consisting of 2TB. In the following sections, we'll look at ways in which you can determine your current storage requirements and plan for the future. This information will be very important in helping you choose a suitable backup platform.

Measuring Current Storage Requirements

Sometimes, it's easy to estimate data storage requirements. For example, SQL Server 2000 allows you to easily see the size of a database by using Enterprise Manager or Transact-SQL commands. (See Figure 5-1.) On file and print servers, you can quickly find out how much information is currently being stored by viewing disk capacity and the percentage in use. One good way to do this is to use Windows NT Performance Monitor or the Windows 2000 Performance tool. The Physical Disk and Logical Disk objects allow you to view the current usage of your disk resources. Another major advantage of using Performance Monitor for this task is that you can easily find information about remote servers and workstations from the comfort of your own machine.

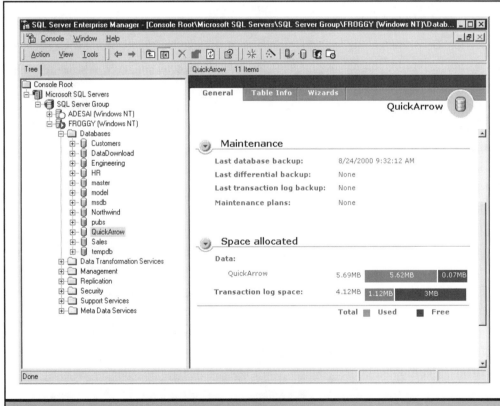

Figure 5-1.   Viewing the size of databases in SQL Server 2000

In Windows 2000, you can also use the Computer Management administrative tool for viewing disk resource information. (See Figure 5-2.) For more information on using Performance Monitor in Windows NT/2000, see Chapter 3. Also, in later chapters, we'll see methods for determining the size of your existing databases and some ways to predict their future size.

Data Compression and Archiving

Note that the data volumes provided by the methods mentioned previously usually reflect the amount of disk space actually being used by databases. When creating database dumps, SQL Server 2000 does not use any native compression. However, the files do compress quite well using other compression software utilities or the native hardware compression techniques that are built into many hardware devices. For some types of data, extremely high compression ratios (above 80 percent) are not uncommon. Storage space is an important consideration, so you will want to factor these compression values

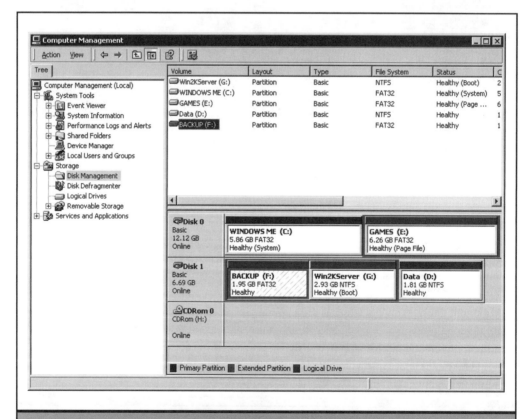

Figure 5-2. Viewing disk usage information using Computer Management in Windows 2000

into your final decision. Also, as we saw in Chapter 3, the Windows NT File System (NTFS) supports the use of compression. (See Figure 5-3.)

Note that there is a trade-off to using disk compression. Although you can significantly reduce the amount of disk space required, the price you pay will be in performance. CPU and memory resources will be used to perform the compression and decompression operations required to access these files. On modern servers, the effects might be negligible in situations with moderate load.

Keep in mind that files are always decompressed when they're read from or written to disk. Therefore, files that are compressed on the hard disk will not be stored in compressed format to tape (unless you also enable compression on your tape device). As you estimate your storage needs, a good practice is to disregard any possible data compression benefits. Even if your data compresses well now, the changing nature of the information might cause it to take up much more space in the future. For example, consider backing up a web site that is currently made up of mostly static HTML files. This text-based data will compress very well. However, suppose that over time your web site grows, becomes graphically intensive, and begins to include large binary files that are

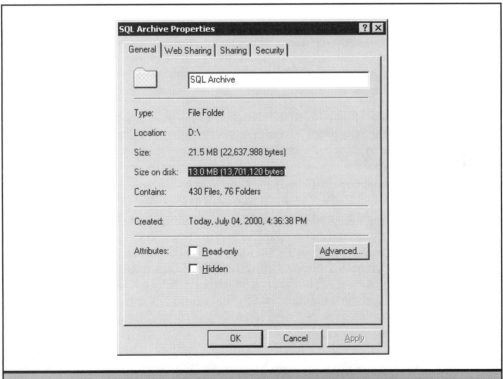

Figure 5-3.   Viewing NTFS compression information in Windows 2000

available for download. These new types of files will not compress as well and may invalidate your compression estimates. Of course, if your data compression system continues to work well for you, you'll have that much more storage room for data growth.

Another popular way of increasing the manageability of company information is to provide for periodic archival of old data. The information might still be valuable, and therefore must be retained, but it may be off-loaded to other types of storage. These alternative storage methods may be cheaper, but are also likely to be less convenient. We'll look at how tape and other hardware backup solutions can help with archiving data. When you are determining your data protection requirements, be sure that you omit any data that will be archived to other types of media.

Planning for the Future

As we have seen, there are several different ways to obtain information about current storage utilization. By using operating systems and database server utilities, you can gain an accurate measurement of exactly how much information you currently support. Things get considerably more complicated, however, when you must predict future requirements. Planning for the future is particularly difficult because business needs often change and data protection technology is continually evolving. For example, even if a database has doubled in size every six months for the last two years, there is no guarantee that it will continue to grow at this rate. Without further information, we might assume that the amount of data will explode as the business quickly grows. However, it's also likely that some of this information will be archived, and techniques such as data warehousing could off-load some of these burdens.

When planning for the future, you should take several factors into account:

▼ **Historical data**   Some say that the best way to predict the future is to learn from the past. If you have historical information on data storage requirements, you'll be better able to make an educated guess. It's likely that you'll have to make inferences, since the amount of data storage three years ago might be a fact that has been lost. One way to find some clues is to look at purchase orders and upgrade logs that show how much storage was available on servers in the past.

■ **Business plans**   A good indicator of the amount of data storage resources that will be required by a company is the future direction of the organization. By working with executives and managers, IT staffers can get a good picture of where the company plans to grow and shrink. For example, if marketing efforts will be increased, it's likely that more employees will be added to that department, and the databases used by that group will increase in size. Similarly, if the organization expects a division to be dissolved, storage resources might be available for other purposes.

▲ **Make your future**   By putting limitations on the amount of information you will back up, you can be sure that certain limits won't be exceeded. Systems administrators may choose to put archive policies in place based on storage used. A typical policy might allow users to store up to 100MB of data on network shares for backup. If this amount is exceeded, certain data can be either archived or removed from the backup schedule. Politically, this can be quite challenging to implement, but it might make sense when data protection costs are significant and increasing faster than budgets.

Based on these guidelines, you'll get a good estimate of the amount of information you want to protect. Keep in mind that the numbers do not have to be exact. As we'll see, backup products come in a variety of capacities. If you're lucky, the choice for your organization, based on data requirements, speed, and budget, will be quite obvious. Otherwise, you can always choose to err on the side of safety by choosing a solution that will scale well in the future.

The "Recovery Window"

As I explained in Chapter 1, it's important to ensure that the data protection solution you choose is capable of restoring your data within an acceptable time frame. The decisions you make regarding your recovery requirements will greatly affect the types of products you select.

Let's look at an example of where this information is useful. Suppose you have a database server that is used heavily during the day, but there is a period of six hours during which backups can be performed. Based on this information alone, you might decide upon a solution that provides for backing up information during this period. A desired data transfer rate is an important consideration when evaluating backup hardware. Rates are usually measured in megabytes per second (MB/sec). In your environment, you can easily calculate such a value by simply dividing the amount of data to be stored or recovered by the maximum amount of acceptable time for that data transfer. For example, if you need to recover approximately 20GB of data in two hours, you'll need a backup solution that can handle a data transfer rate of at least 10GB per hour (or approximately 5.5MB/sec). Be sure to keep in mind the administration time it will take to perform a restore.

If you later learn that managers expect at most one hour of downtime during critical business hours, you probably will not be able to meet these recovery requirements with the given hardware. Various methods for recovering data may be employed to meet these goals. For example, redundant hardware and disaster recovery options (described later in this chapter) can greatly reduce recovery times.

Live vs. Offline Database Backups

Although the underlying concepts are the same, there are several additional concerns that you must be aware of when performing backups of databases. First and foremost, it's important to understand that databases must be backed up in a state that is consistent to a point in time. This is essential to protect the validity of information. In Chapter 4, we covered the fact that SQL Server's data files cannot simply be copied as can other types of data files. This is because the data files themselves may not be consistent to a specific point in time. Let's look at the two main methods of performing database backups—live backups and offline database backups. (We'll look at the technical details of each option in Chapter 6.)

One of the main complications involved in backing up database files is that they are generally in use—or live—at all times. This makes simple file copy operations inconvenient to perform, since the database server must be stopped before the files are accessed. In some situations (for example, in an environment where the server is only needed during normal business hours), this might be acceptable. However, in others, it is not.

Fortunately, there are good solutions for performing backups of databases while they are in use. "Live" backups involve the transfer of information from a currently running database directly to a backup medium (usually another disk partition or to removable media devices such as tape drives). The data is copied using a specialized process that takes a "snapshot" of the data at a particular point in time and stores it to tape. The process is responsible for tracking any changes that occur to the database during the backup operation itself. Figure 5-4 provides an overview of a live database backup process.

The general process of performing offline database backups is to perform an operation that copies information from the data files and stores it to another file. (See Figure 5-5.) This "dump" file contains information that is consistent to a point in time and can be used to restore the database. The dump files themselves are not in use and can therefore be backed up like any other data files that are stored in the file system.

The disadvantage to offline backups is that creating dump files can negatively affect performance—especially that of the disk subsystem—and can require large amounts of disk space that is essentially useless for any purpose other than storing these redundant copies of data. There are, however, other solutions for these types of problems (backing up directly to tape, for example).

There are actually many reasons for performing live backups of your databases. Perhaps the most common is the volume of data. As we'll see later in this chapter, disk resources can be considerably more expensive than tape storage. Large databases consume much disk space that might otherwise be used by clients. Another reason for performing live database backups is performance. Creating dump files can use CPU and memory resources, and thus degrade the overall performance of the server. In situations where database server availability and performance is critical around the clock, live backups may need to be performed whenever possible.

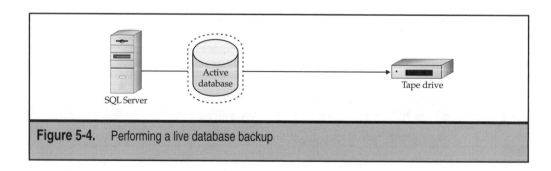

Figure 5-4. Performing a live database backup

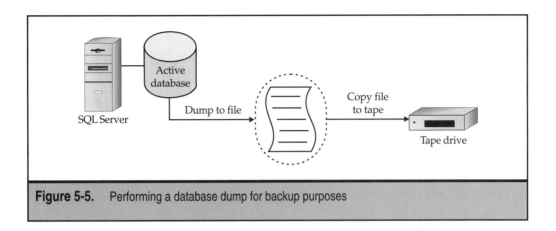

Figure 5-5. Performing a database dump for backup purposes

When shopping for backup hardware, you'll need to make sure that the product you select supports the types of backups you plan to perform. In general, all backup software will allow you to perform offline backups. However, software packages must be specifically designed to allow for hot backups. As we'll see in Chapter 6, SQL Server 2000 can perform both operations. Later in this chapter, we'll look at third-party software packages that can provide similar features.

Leveraging Your Existing Resources

One important factor in determining the type of data protection hardware and software you need is not what you lack, but what you already have. For example, if several of your servers are already performing local backup operations, you will want to determine how best to incorporate the existing tools into your new solution. Perhaps software is available that can manage all of those servers from a single console, thereby allowing centralized administration while maximizing the value of the original investment. Or perhaps your system includes a remote site that is currently performing its own data protection. If the current backup routine is acceptable, you will want to exclude this amount of data when considering new backup hardware and software purchases. Additionally, in an environment where funding is constrained, you might need to look at unconventional backup methods. For example, in a workgroup environment, several client machines may have free hard disk space. Copying information between systems can be used to protect against hard disk failures and can provide for adequate data protection until a server is deployed for centralized storage.

Leveraging the existing infrastructure, however, can sometimes be counterproductive. The cost savings associated with managing older hardware might be offset by increased administration. An obvious example would be a tape backup drive that does not have enough capacity to store all important information on the same media. You'll definitely hear from systems administrators who must constantly swap tapes on these machines. Apart from the tedium of the process, it can be much more error prone. Finding a balance between making the best of existing hardware and completely discarding your existing solutions can be challenging, but it will help you maximize your investments.

Network Topology

In most environments that consist of more than a few client machines, backups are performed over the network. It is this backbone that connects all the computers together and is responsible for all communications. A *local area network (LAN)* is usually defined as a network that is owned and operated by an organization. Generally, this is restricted to machines that are located in the same geographic location and connected by Ethernet cables. In general, the speeds offered on LANs are quite high. As more machines are added to such a network, however, the network can become saturated and cause a bottleneck for various types of applications. The solution is to divide these connected machines logically and thus decrease the sharing of media.

There are several ways that larger networks can be formed from many little ones. It is beyond the scope of this book to discuss the issues associated with network design, but routing and switching technologies can make a big difference in how backups are performed. For example, if all of your company's servers are located on an isolated subnet that is separated from others by a switch or router, performing backups of all servers can be performed without causing excessive traffic for other machines. Figure 5-6 shows an example of a network connected by a router.

Network issues are especially important when *wide area networks (WANs)* are used. In contrast to LANs, WANs are not entirely controlled by an organization; they are at least partially dependent on leased public lines. An example of a WAN would be several remote offices connected by analog, ISDN, frame-relay, or T-1 lines. (These types of lines provide much lower bandwidth than typical LAN connections; consequently, the amount of data that can be transferred over a WAN is severely limited.)

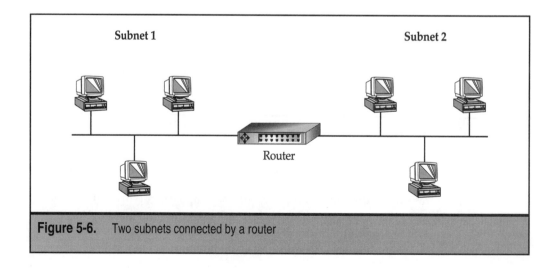

Figure 5-6.   Two subnets connected by a router

NOTE: The Internet is an excellent example of collaboration among many different types of interconnections. The Internet is unique in that it is a global public network. Internet Service Providers (ISPs) and telecommunications companies provide the backbone of this network, but the Internet is available to almost anyone who has the necessary equipment and software. However, issues such as traffic congestion and reliability are very real and must be taken into account.

A good data protection strategy will consider the existing network topology and take full advantage of the resources already in place. In the case of several remote sites that are connected by a slow WAN, a separate tape backup drive attached to a server in each location might be best. If all data is stored on a single LAN, however, a centralized backup solution is worthy of consideration.

CHOOSING SERVER HARDWARE

Before we consider the various choices available for backup hardware and software, it's important to examine your server hardware purchase decisions. Choosing the appropriate server hardware can have many benefits. The first is increased performance—spending your money wisely will pay off in a better end-user experience and a better return on your investment. When it comes to performing backups, if your existing platform has enough power, the impact of performing backups can be minimal on the end-user experience. The major components of a server include the CPU, memory, and disk subsystems; all three will have significant bearing on the overall performance of your information system. Let's look at each of these components in turn.

Processor(s)

If I were to ask you to describe the hardware configuration of a particular server, what information would you provide first? I'd be willing to guess that you'd mention the processor architecture and clock speed. ("Oh, that's a Dual Pentium III 600 MHz machine.") Nowadays, much of the hype about system performance surrounds the CPU. Popular marketing would have you believe that there is a nearly linear relationship between the speed of a CPU and the real-world performance you'll achieve. Companies tout that you'll get everything from faster Internet access to increased productivity once you buy a higher-speed CPU.

In actuality, however, most applications rarely tax the CPU to its fullest extent. On the client side, perhaps some of the most processor-hungry applications are high-end image editing tools and other graphics software packages, as well as newer computer games. Many years ago (in the days when 486 PCs were cool), the CPU did act as a bottleneck for many applications. That is, applications would often be waiting for CPU time in order to complete their tasks. The user, in turn, would also be dependent on the speed of the process to accomplish useful work.

These days, you probably wouldn't notice any benefit in running Microsoft Word, for example, on a computer processing a half billion operations per second. When bottlenecks occur, the culprit is likely to be one or more of the various other subsystems within the client computer. Bus speeds, memory limitations, network throughput, and disk subsystem performance are much more likely to limit your overall experience.

The story can be considerably different on the server side, however. The general rules still remain true—for most common server applications, CPU performance might be the least of several other bottlenecks. Accessing information from a disk subsystem can be several orders of magnitude slower than accessing data from memory. Similarly, the CPU itself is often waiting for data from RAM. For applications such as file and print services, extra memory and improved network connectivity can cause noticeable performance increases.

However, on machines that perform calculation-intensive tasks (such as OLAP servers and other statistical-analysis applications), the CPU speed can be very important. Also as important is the amount of Level 2 (L2) cache available with the CPU and at what speed it runs. The size of L2 cache for modern processors ranges from 128KB to over 2MB, and the speed of the cache can range from 66 MHz to the speed of the processor itself. L2 cache can help reduce bottlenecks caused by the CPU waiting for information from RAM.

Nowadays, there are several CPUs from which to choose. At the time of this writing, the most popular options are from Intel (**www.intel.com**) and AMD (**www.amd.com**). Other Intel-compatible alternatives are also available from VIA (which has purchased CPU-maker Cyrix; **www.via.com**), Transmeta (**www.transmeta.com**), and several others. Note that you should be sure that the processor and computer architecture are on the Microsoft-approved hardware compatibility list and the system is capable of supporting the Windows NT/2000 operating systems.

So what's the bottom line when it comes to choosing a processor architecture? If money will allow, you generally won't go wrong by buying a computer with the fastest CPU available on the market. One of the main reasons is that hardware vendors match the fastest processors with faster technology all around (such as system buses, memory, and disk controllers). The drawback, of course, is that cutting-edge systems are usually very costly.

If you're like most of us, however, you have a limited budget and need to choose your specifications carefully. In general, most applications would probably benefit more from additional RAM than from an extra 100MHz of processor speed. The overall evaluation of the CPU requirements of your application, however, must be determined by your actual needs. Such information can be obtained by using the Processor object in Windows NT/2000 Performance Monitor (as covered in Chapter 3).

Now that we've covered the CPU system, it's time to move on to other potential bottlenecks.

Memory

Memory, or random access memory (RAM), is an extremely important resource for modern computers. In general, increasing the amount of memory in a machine can have a very positive impact on overall performance. RAM comes in various specifications. Usually, RAM "access times" are measured in nanoseconds (billionths of a second).

Modern operating systems, such as Windows NT/2000, store frequently used information in RAM; this process is called *caching.* You can see the effects of caching simply by running a query on a SQL Server 2000 machine and then repeating the same query. The first time the query is executed, it might take SQL several seconds to generate the result. If the same query is then performed again, however, the answer will probably appear more quickly. This is because during the first execution, the records that SQL uses to compute the result are cached temporarily to RAM. When the query is run the second time, the database server can read the data from the cache instead of making costly trips to the hard disk.

As mentioned in Chapter 4, SQL Server 2000 has the ability to use large amounts of memory (up to 64GB). If you're looking for hardware platforms that support large amounts of RAM (more than 2GB), you should consider consulting OEMs that are willing to support those configurations before making an investment. In some cases, specific hardware modifications and tweaks must be made in order to get these configurations working properly, and support from the vendor can be critical in ensuring that the server works as expected.

On the OS level, a good way to measure the utilization of memory is to view various counters of the Memory object in the Windows NT/2000 Performance Monitor application. Parameters to look for include the number of page faults per second. A *page fault* occurs whenever data that is required is not found in memory and must be loaded from disk. This process dramatically decreases performance for the operation. Additional parameters to monitor include the total amount of memory in use (which you can quickly see using Windows NT/2000 Task Manager, as shown in Figure 5-7). Although the specifications and technologies vary, the general rule of thumb is that the more RAM you have in the system, the better.

Disk Subsystems

When it comes time to select disk subsystems, the choices may be obvious. In general, workstations and client computers often use the Integrated Device Electronics (IDE) bus for connecting storage devices. On the server side, however, machines routinely use the Small Computer Standard Interface (SCSI) specification. These technology choices are often taken for granted, and systems administrators rarely take the time to determine the *real* reasons for these choices. Let's begin by looking at each specification and then compare the pros and cons of each.

The IDE specification was originally designed as a standard for allowing storage devices in PCs to interact with the system bus. Currently, there are many different standards for IDE hard disks. Older drives support the Programmed I/O (PIO) Modes that are generally identified by a number (1 through 4). Ultra Direct Memory Access (UDMA) technology has increased the performance of the system bus considerably by allowing disk-based data transfers to occur with little impact to CPU performance. And, dramatically faster interfaces such as ATA/66 and ATA/100 have become readily available in midrange machines.

An IDE *channel* supports up to two devices—one master and one slave. Most modern motherboards include at least two IDE channels, thereby supporting up to four devices.

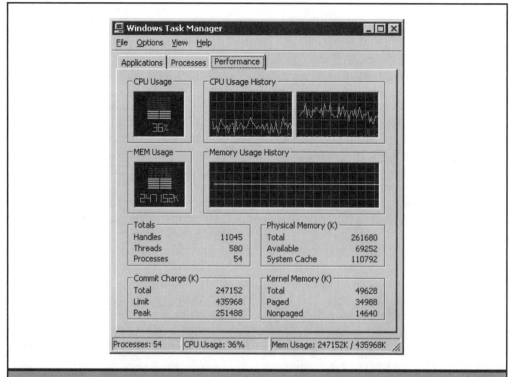

Figure 5-7. Viewing memory information using the Windows 2000 Task Manager

In addition to hard drives, many other devices can take advantage of the IDE bus. Common peripherals include CD-ROM drives and other removable media devices (such as tape or Zip drives). However, the types of devices are restricted to internal hardware only. In general, IDE hardware is cheaper than equivalent SCSI hardware.

SCSI interfaces work similarly to IDE in that they provide a way for the system's buses to interact with the disk subsystem. But the main similarities end there. The SCSI specification allows up to eight devices to be used on a single channel. The adapter itself is one of the devices; therefore, seven other devices (such as hard drives and CD-ROM drives) can be attached to a single-channel adapter. To support more devices, SCSI adapters that allow multiple channels are available. SCSI adapters and devices are more expensive than their IDE counterparts. However, on the server side, most systems administrators are willing to spend the extra money for the performance. As the SCSI controller handles the majority of I/O, less burden is placed on the CPU. Also, data transfers can occur simultaneously—that is, multiple devices can communicate on the same bus at the same time in parallel. This also increases performance. An added benefit of the SCSI specification is that it supports the use of both external and internal devices, which enables you to use many more peripherals than will fit inside a server chassis.

In some implementations, systems administrators may choose to use both the IDE and SCSI subsystems in the same machine. This can provide for low-cost support of peripherals that don't require very high performance while at the same time reducing costs. More important disk subsystems might then be attached to SCSI controllers. Table 5-1 compares the basic features of IDE and SCSI controllers and devices.

Table 5-2 lists the maximum speeds achievable by devices of various SCSI specifications. There are several aspects of these bus speeds to keep in mind when working with SCSI devices in the real world. First, speed estimates are normally based on the maximum throughput capacity of a SCSI *adapter*, not the bandwidth of the devices it connects. Therefore, if you have one hard disk connected to an 80MB/sec controller, it's highly unlikely that you'll see that level of throughput. Second, there can be some confusion over the meanings of various standards, so you should always verify actual performance statistics with your hardware vendor before making a purchasing decision. Finally, many different types of SCSI connectors are used for connecting internal and external SCSI devices. Be sure you know which types of cables and connections you'll need in order to implement your chosen solution.

Attribute	IDE	SCSI
Cost	Lower cost of devices and controllers	Higher cost of devices and controllers
Performance (throughput)	Slower (up to 66MB/sec)	Faster (up to 80MB/sec)
Number of devices	2 per channel	8 per channel (including the controller)
CPU requirements	High in older drives/controllers; low in newer ones with DMA technology	Low (data exchange usually managed by SCSI controller)
Types of devices	Internal only	Internal and/or external
Access times	Typically < 10ms	Faster (typically < 8ms)
Hard disk speeds	5,400 rpm to 7,200 rpm	7,200 rpm to 10,000 rpm

Table 5-1. Comparison of IDE and SCSI Technology

SCSI Standard	Bus Speed
SCSI-2	10MB/sec
SCSI-2 (Fast/Wide)	20MB/sec
UltraSCSI	20MB/sec
UltraSCSI (Ultra Wide)	40MB/sec
Ultra2 SCSI	80MB/sec
Ultra 160/m (proposed)	160MB/sec
Ultra3 SCSI	160MB/sec

Table 5-2.   Comparison of SCSI Bus Speed Specifications

When dealing with SQL Server and other relational databases that manage their own write operations, you must understand the potential effects of write-caching technologies. The basic idea behind write caching is to increase write performance of the disk subsystem. This is achieved by queuing several requests to record information to the disks in RAM or on the hardware controller itself. Programs and the OS "think" that the information has been committed to disk when actually it has not. The beneficial effect is that multiple write operations can be performed at the same time, thus increasing performance. The drawback, however, is that if an unexpected failure or restart of the server occurs (most commonly due to a loss of power or an OS crash), data might be left in an inconsistent state. When dealing with RDBMSs, such as SQL Server 2000, this can leave files in an inconsistent state. To avoid this type of problem, many modern disk controllers contain a battery backup on the controller itself. In the event of a power failure, the battery backup ensures that information that has not yet been committed to disk is retained in memory. When the controller is again powered on, it can then store the information, thus ensuring consistency in the files. Despite these features, it might still be worthwhile to disable write caching, especially on servers whose primary function is running SQL Server 2000.

RAID

In Chapter 3, we covered the basics of RAID technology. If you're not familiar with the concepts behind RAID, now would be a good time to go back and review them. In this section, we'll cover the details of RAID implementations as they affect SQL Server 2000. The three main issues to consider are fault tolerance, performance, and disk space usage. Table 5-3 shows how these parameters are affected at various RAID levels.

RAID Level	Minimum Drives	Read Performance	Write Performance	Fault Tolerant?	Disk Space Lost
RAID 0 (Disk Striping)	2	Increased	Negligible	No	None
RAID 1 (Disk Mirroring)	2	Increased	Increased	Yes	50% of total space
RAID 5 (Disk Striping with Parity)	3	Increased	Decreased	Yes	Size of one disk in the array

Table 5-3.   Effects of RAID on System Performance

Besides the standard levels of RAID, additional levels that involve the combination of multiple methods may be implemented. These are often referred to by means of notation such as RAID 5+0 or RAID 50 (two RAID 5 arrays that are mirrored). These implementations combine various RAID levels in order to increase fault tolerance and/or performance and to decrease lost disk space. Keep in mind, however, that none of these solutions is likely to provide all three benefits, so trade-offs are involved. Determining which trade-offs are appropriate is the job of the systems administrator.

In general, it is recommended that SQL Server use RAID for both fault tolerance and increased performance. These benefits are well worth the cost (loss of usable disk space), because fixed storage costs are rapidly decreasing. Although the Windows NT OS can support software-based RAID implementations, there are several potential drawbacks:

▼   Overall system performance will decrease because the CPU is used to handle all parity calculations.

■   Modifications to the disk configurations might require server reboots, which can cause downtime.

▲   Software-based disk mirroring (RAID 1) can cause downtime if the primary hard disk fails.

On the plus side, software-based RAID can be an inexpensive alternative to hardware-based solutions, especially when disk I/O performance is not critical. For more information on implementing Windows NT/Windows 2000 RAID features, see Chapter 3.

Hardware-based RAID solutions are much more flexible and offer additional advantages:

▼ **Increased performance**   Hardware RAID controllers include their own CPU that is dedicated to managing the calculations necessary for creating parity information. This off-loads much of the duty from the main CPU, which can then work on other tasks, such as processing SQL Server queries.

■ **Support for more storage**   Because hardware RAID controllers are often used in mission-critical environments and for applications that require large amounts of storage, they are designed to support many SCSI devices. Although a single SCSI channel is limited to attaching seven devices (in addition to the controller itself), multiple SCSI channels can be put together to support increasingly large arrays.

■ **Hot-plug capability**   Some RAID controller and chassis configurations allow systems administrators to add and remove drives from a server without first powering it off. This can greatly increase uptime in systems that require the periodic addition of storage space. It also allows for quickly and easily replacing failed disks within an array.

■ **Hot spares**   Sometimes, having a RAID controller automatically use a spare disk is preferable to replacing a disk that has failed. The standby disk is not included as part of an array; it exists solely to take over the functions of a failed one. Such a *hot spare* is good protection against a complete data loss and alleviates any possible need for immediate human intervention.

▲ **Configuration flexibility**   Modern RAID controllers allow users to dynamically reconfigure certain disk configurations without the loss of data. For example, systems administrators can add a drive to a stripe set with parity (RAID 5) without having to back up all the data, reformat the drive array, and then restore the data. Not only is this convenient, but it also prevents potentially costly server downtime.

The potential drawbacks to adopting these solutions are the initial expense and the training that you may need in order to configure them properly. However, most organizations will find that the increased performance and flexibility of hardware RAID are well worth the costs. RAID solutions are available from many hardware vendors.

NOTE: The issues that surround write-caching controllers apply to hardware-based RAID solutions as well. Before implementing a backup scheme that includes database servers or write caching, be sure that you have a firm understanding of the trade-offs involved.

Another useful technique involving the use of RAID controllers is the use of SQL Server 2000's file and filegroup architecture. Although it requires additional administrative effort, the use of multiple data files for a database can help spread data across multiple physical hard disks or logical RAID volumes. Through the use of files and filegroups, systems and database administrators can exert finer control over exactly which data is stored on particular physical disks. When managed properly, this can further increase database server performance. For more information on using files and filegroups, see Chapter 6.

Uninterruptible Power Supplies

An uninterruptible power supply (UPS) protects against lost or corrupt data by giving the system time to save the data properly in the event of a power outage. A UPS can also prevent downtime in areas where power is unreliable—or where downtime is unacceptable. Through the Windows NT/2000 UPS service, a UPS device can be configured to execute an automatic batch file if the power goes out and/or to shut down the system completely.

Table 5-4 is a brief index of vendors who offer power-related products. You can obtain additional information and details about UPS solutions from these vendors.

Which machines in your network should have UPS protection? In some cases, the answer is quite easy: many users rely upon servers, and they store critical data, so they must

Company	Web Site
American Power Conversion (APC)	www.apc.com
CyberPower	www.cyberpower.com
Opti-UPS	www.opti-ups.com
Power & Data Technology	www.powerdatatech.com
Power Protection Unlimited	www.upspower.com
Powerware	www.powerware.com
Systems Enhancement	www.sechq.com
TCS Power Protection	www.smartups.com
TSI Power	www.tsipower.com
Universal Power Systems	www.upsi.com

Table 5-4. Vendors That Offer Power-Related Solutions

be available at all times. In some cases, however, you might also want to protect any workstations that are running critical tasks or performing operations that might result in significant data loss if the machine were to shut down unexpectedly. (Engineering workstations are a good example.) Additionally, if users are expected to have continuous access to system resources, you need to ensure that the necessary network devices—routers, hubs, and so on—remain active.

There are several characteristics of a UPS that you should consider before making a purchase. The most important issue is the amount of power that the battery can provide. This value is often measured in volt-amps; it reflects how much power the unit can put out per unit time. To determine your power requirements, refer to your hardware documentation. (Some UPS vendors provide information on common hardware devices at their web sites.) You'll need to determine how many of your hardware devices, and of which kinds, can be adequately supported on a single UPS. Another consideration is the amount of time (usually measured in nanoseconds) that a UPS will take to react to a power outage. (Most units will kick in almost immediately.) Find out also whether the device you're buying comes with software drivers for supported platforms. These tools and utilities are extremely useful for monitoring and managing power supplies.

Another important benefit of using UPS devices is that they automatically compensate for *brown-outs* (dips in power), *spikes*, and *surges* (short bursts of high energy), which might otherwise cause damage to costly computing equipment. UPS manufacturers can give you information regarding the level of protection that their products provide. Most UPS manufacturers also offer some type of insurance for the devices protected by their products. For example, if you've purchased a UPS to protect a network server, but an electrical spike subsequently damages the server, the UPS vendor may reimburse you for the cost of replacing it. If you're depending on this type of protection, be sure that you understand the "fine print" in any such guarantee.

CAUTION: Take the time to read about which types of devices are (and aren't) supported by the UPS you've chosen. A common way to destroy a smaller UPS, for example, is to plug in a laser printer! Although there is probably little business reason for connecting a laser printer to a UPS, the voltage required by certain types of printing devices during warm-up can far exceed the maximum power output of a typical UPS. Keep this in mind, or you might be left with a very expensive doorstop!

Once you've bought a UPS, be sure to test it before you incorporate it into your system. Most UPS units include buttons that can simulate power loss. (Of course, you could also just unplug the cord on the back of the device!) The battery backup within the UPS unit should come online within a few nanoseconds, thereby preventing the loss of any information or any downtime. And finally, even if you've invested in UPS protection, you should ensure that you also have redundant circuits. In the event that multiple UPS units are plugged into a single electrical wiring loop, any failure in that loop will result in loss of power to all the machines connected to it. As always, it is very important to minimize the risks associated with single points of failure.

EVALUATING BACKUP HARDWARE

When it comes to actually backing up data, the performance and capacity of your backup devices will probably have the single biggest impact on your overall solution. Businesses have placed increased importance on the needs of their data storage devices, and actual data volumes tend to grow dramatically in many businesses. Fortunately, hardware vendors have answered many of the demands associated with backing up large quantities of data. For this reason, the market for backup hardware is constantly changing. What might be considered a high-end device this year will undoubtedly be lowered to midrange status within a few years (or even months). However, the basic concepts related to evaluating and selecting backup hardware remain the same. The main goals are performance, capacity, and manageability. In this section, we'll examine these parameters and provide an overview of the various technologies available today. Rest assured, you'll be able to use the same criteria for evaluating newer technologies as they become available on the market.

Characteristics of Backup Devices

One of the first things you're likely to examine when evaluating a backup product is the set of features offered by the device itself. The effectiveness of your tape backup device will likely be one of your most important considerations. Here are several points that you should keep in mind when shopping for tape backup equipment:

▼ **Upgradability** Can the current hardware be used with other technologies? If not, what is the likelihood that industry vendors will provide backward-compatible storage options in the future? Although vendor promises are not worth much as far as assurance, you should choose products that are widely supported in the industry; you can be reasonably sure that compatible solutions will continue to be developed in the future.

■ **Performance** If you have been surfing vendor sites for information about hardware devices, then you are undoubtedly familiar with performance claims. Usually, these are based on a volume of data backed up per unit time (for example, "500MB/hour"). These values are important, but take care to determine the validity of such claims. Consider the conditions under which the device was tested (and if those details aren't available, don't be shy about requesting them). For example, if text files were used in the test, then much "robust performance" could be attributed to data compression. On the other hand, if the files used were already compressed, then the performance numbers would indicate the true throughput of the device.

▲ **Reliability** A common measurement of reliability is called the mean time between failures (MTBF). Usually stated in hours, the MTBF gives an idea of how long, on average, a device can be expected to survive under constant working conditions. Table 5-5 lists some typical MTBF values.

Device	Mean Time Between Failures (in hours)	Notes
Backup device	100,000 to 500,000	Environmental conditions and amount of use will greatly affect the life of tape backup devices.
CPU fan	20,000 to 40,000	Failed fans can lead to CPU and motherboard damage that results in time-consuming hardware replacements.
IDE controller	~300,000	Many controllers are built into motherboards and may be difficult to replace.
IDE hard disk	~300,000	Failed disks will almost always result in lost data.
SCSI/RAID controller	~300,000 to 1,000,000	Failure of a RAID controller can cause data corruption regardless of the type of RAID employed.
SCSI controller	~300,000	Failure of a SCSI controller can cause many devices to become unavailable.
SCSI hard disk	~500,000	Failed disks will result in loss of data unless redundancy is configured and enabled.
Server power supply	100,000 to 400,000	Look for servers that have redundant power supplies.

Table 5-5.   Mean Time Between Failure (MTBF) Values for Common Computer Components

Average values should serve only as a reference, because claims are often made based on figures attained in a controlled environment. One way to protect yourself against damage caused by the failure of parts is to invest in hardware that can monitor itself. For example, many current motherboards include temperature sensors that monitor heat generated by the CPU. If normal operating temperatures are exceeded (when the machine experiences, for example, a CPU fan failure), an alarm will go off, alerting systems administrators.

Based on these considerations, you will probably be able to find a device that fits your business requirements. Of course, the tape backup device does not work by itself. Thus, we'll next consider the types of data buses available on the market.

Data Buses

In addition to the speed of the tape drive, you'll want to consider the performance of the bus on which the tape drive runs. Earlier in this chapter, we looked at a comparison of IDE versus SCSI buses for running server hard disks. Drives also support a variety of hardware interfaces, with a wide range in performance and usability characteristics. For example, although parallel ports are the slowest method, they enable you to easily move tape drives between systems. The IDE interface supports internal drives only and is the standard in most desktop systems. SCSI devices are the best choice for mainstream servers and support both internal and external devices. Other technologies, such as Fibre Channel buses, are available for even higher throughput requirements. Table 5-6 compares the maximum

Bus Technology	Maximum Speed	Devices per Bus	Notes
Ethernet	10MB/sec	Unlimited	Networks can be divided via switches and routers to allow more devices per subnet.
Fast Ethernet	100MB/sec	Unlimited	Networks can be divided via switches and routers to allow more devices per subnet.
Gigabit Ethernet	1,000MB/sec	Unlimited	Networks can be divided via switches and routers to allow more devices per subnet.
Fibre Channel	100MB/sec	Determined by device capability	Fast throughput bus over large distances (up to 500m).
FireWire (IEEE 1394)	25MB/sec (controller speed; device speeds may vary)	Many (based on the controller)	Serves as a high-speed multipurpose bus for external devices.

Table 5-6. Comparison of the Speeds of Various Bus Types

Bus Technology	Maximum Speed	Devices per Bus	Notes
IDE	66MB/sec	Two per IDE channel. (Most PCs have two built-in channels.)	There are several different specifications for IDE bus throughput.
Parallel port	~600KB/sec	Devices can be daisy-chained.	Widespread support; good choice for portability.
SCSI	80MB/sec	Seven per channel (including the controller). Multiple channels per adapter are available, and multiple adapters can be used on a single system.	There are several SCSI specs. (See Table 5-2.)
Universal serial bus (USB)	12MB/sec (initial specification); 400MB/sec (advanced specifications)	Many devices can be supported through the use of hubs and daisy-chaining.	USB is targeted as a replacement for other device attachment methods, including serial ports, keyboard connectors, MIDI/game ports, and parallel ports; device support is currently available only on Windows 98 and Windows 2000.

Table 5-6. Comparison of the Speeds of Various Bus Types *(continued)*

speeds attainable by a number of these products. Ethernet speeds and characteristics were included for comparison, although no tape backup devices exist that connect directly to Ethernet ports.

Again, as with any technology, you should verify real-world performance with vendors. For example, buses may support extremely high throughput, but other conditions may prevent actually attaining those levels of performance. A good example is Ethernet. For various reasons, it is difficult to achieve speeds close to the full 10MB/sec speed that is claimed. Impacts are at least as great for Fast Ethernet and Gigabit Ethernet technologies. Doing adequate research before you select your data buses will go a long way toward ensuring the success of your backup solution.

Media Options

Most tape drives are described relative to the types of media they support. The type of media has significant impact on the storage capacity and performance of the device. When you're weighing your media options, there are several factors to consider:

▼ **Capacity** Does the media hold a reasonable amount of data? With removable drives, you can always use multiple sets of media, but it is much more convenient and practical to have the majority of information fit on one storage unit.

■ **Durability** If tapes will be handled regularly (for example, by computer operators), it's important to consider their durability. Does the cartridge or media protect against accidental exposure of sensitive components? Is the cartridge suitable for physically sending across the country or internationally (via postal carriers)?

■ **Cost** How expensive is the media? Although the cost of the tapes and other removable cartridges might seem cheap, keep in mind that this will be a recurrent expense for your organization. A good way to evaluate relative expenses is by measuring cost per megabyte. For example, a tape might hold 1.6GB (~1,600MB) of data and cost $30. This would result in a cost per megabyte of approximately 1.8 cents. Keep in mind, however, that the initial price tag is only one consideration among many, and that the cheapest solutions might have very costly drawbacks.

■ **Active life** How often can the media be used before it must be replaced? If you will be regularly reusing tapes, for example, how long can you rely on them before they must be replaced? Usually, active life estimates will be stated based on hours of use.

▲ **Shelf life** It may not be something you look at first, but the shelf life of the media you select is extremely important to consider. In many cases, magnetic media and optical storage are designed to survive for decades. You increase this life span by storing the media in a controlled environment. Also, you shouldn't worry too much about the fact that the media won't last forever; at some point you'll need to upgrade your backup solution, and that will probably involve migrating a lot of your data to new media.

Based on these criteria, there are several different types of media from which you can choose. In the past, a backup device was almost decidedly a "tape drive." Magnetic media is reliable and inexpensive. It also has a longer shelf life than some of the alternatives. However, recent advances in technology have increased the variety of dependable backup equipment. Table 5-7 lists various types of backup drives and their characteristics. (The capacities indicated are for uncompressed data.)

Drive Type	Capacity	Speed	Best Use	Notes
4mm DAT	Up to 4GB	Slow (~800K/sec)	Workstation backups	Intermediate in price and performance
8mm DAT	Up to 7GB	Medium (~1MB/sec)	Server and workstation backups	Intermediate in price and performance
Advanced Intelligent Tape (AIT)	25+GB	Fast (6MB/sec)	Workgroup/ enterprise backups	Good cost and performance; a good solution for large backup environments
CD-ROM writers	650MB	Slow (~900K/sec)	Frequently accessed archives; SW distribution	Media can be written to only once; compatible with most read-only CD-ROM drives
CD-RW (CD-rewritable)	650MB	Slow (~900K/sec)	Frequently accessed archives	Rewritable media; incompatible with older CD-ROM drives
Digital Linear Tape (DLT)	70+GB	Fast (3MB/sec)	Enterprise backups	Good cost and performance characteristics; a good solution for large backup environments
DVD-RAM	5GB to 17GB	At least 500K/sec	PCs and workstations; long-term archiving and data distribution	Technology and standards are still emerging. Cost per megabyte is low.
Jaz drives	1GB to 2GB	Slow to medium (varies based on data bus)	PCs, workstations, or small servers	Although product is readily available in many PCs, cost per megabyte is relatively high.
Quarter-Inch Cartridges (QIC)	Up to 4GB	Medium (~1MB/sec)	Workstation backups	Drives and media are inexpensive.
Zip drives	100MB to 250MB	Slow to medium (varies based on data bus)	PCs or workstations	Although product is readily available in many PCs, cost per megabyte is relatively high.

Table 5-7. Characteristics of Various Backup Device Types

Note that you should always determine whether storage capacities for selected tape devices and media are based on compressed or actual data capacities. Most vendors will advertise devices and media that store 4GB of data as 4GB (uncompressed) / 8GB (compressed). The assumed compression ratio of 2:1 is wishful thinking in many real-world scenarios. When you're deciding upon an appropriate system, consider the type of data you'll be backing up. SQL Server 2000 database dumps often compress exceptionally well. (More than 90 percent compression is possible, based on the algorithm.) Text and data files will generally compress very well, but program files and other binary files will normally not achieve a 2:1 compression ratio.

Advanced Backup Solutions

There are several additional options that might fill some of the gaps left by "standard" backup solutions. Here's a partial list:

▼ **Tape striping**   As with disk striping (RAID), tape striping can greatly increase backup performance by storing data using two or more backup drives. Depending on the backup methodologies used, the tape drives can be used in parallel for both backup and recovery operations, thereby reducing the amount of time used in these operations.

■ **Media changers/autoloaders**   If you've ever felt that switching tapes is a perfect job for robots, you're not alone! Robotic media changers can be used to automatically feed media to drives based on a predefined schedule. They won't complain about the tedious tasks you force them to do, and they can be quite reliable. This can be a great solution if your backups don't fit on a single piece of media. However, autoloaders can be expensive (at least in the short term), and must still be set up and managed carefully to ensure that the proper tapes are being used.

▲ **On-demand recovery**   A common procedure in many businesses is for an employee to call the help desk and initiate a request for file restoration. If such requests are rare, they are easy to manage through a manual process. For larger organizations, however, much time can be spent recovering user files. Some tape backup solutions allow users to automatically request files for restoration. Although the user must still wait while the files are accessed from the appropriate media, the process is automated and does not require the time of the help desk personnel or systems administrators. On-demand recovery options work especially well with media changers.

In evaluating backup hardware, you're likely to find many other features that will be helpful. One example is cleaning indicators on tape drives that periodically remind systems administrators to insert a cleaning tape. (These tapes can clean the physical heads on the device and can prolong the accuracy of read and write operations.) All of these features are likely to be useful, but it is up to you to determine whether they are worth the cost and are relevant to your business environment.

Vendors of Third-Party Hardware

Now that we have a good understanding of the various types of backup hardware available, it's time to examine some real-world solutions. Many companies market tape backup hardware and software. Table 5-8 lists a number of them and describes the types of products offered by each. You should verify this information before making any purchasing decisions, because product specifications and capabilities may change.

Company	Web Site	Products
ADIC, Inc.	www.adic.com	High-end, automated backup devices
ATL Products, Inc.	www.atlp.com	DLT equipment
Benchmark Tape Systems Corp.	www.benchmarktape.com	DLT drives and autoloaders
Castlewood, Inc.	www.castlewood.com	Removable storage devices for PCs
Compaq StorageWorks Solutions	www.compaq.com/products/storageworks	Medium- to high-end storage devices
Exabyte, Inc.	www.exabyte.com	Medium- to high-end storage devices
Hewlett-Packard Storage Solutions	www.hp.com/storage	Medium- to high-end storage devices
IBM Corp.	www.storage.ibm.com/hardsoft/tape/	Medium- to high-end storage devices and accessories
Imation, Inc.	www.imation.com	Storage devices and media
Iomega Corp.	www.iomega.com	Low-end backup devices for PCs
OnStream, Inc.	www.onstream.com	Low- and midrange storage devices for PCs and servers
Overland Data, Inc.	www.overlanddata.com	Mid- to high-end storage devices and accessories

Table 5-8.   Vendors Offering Tape Backup Hardware

Company	Web Site	Products
Procom, Inc.	www.procom.com	Mid- to high-end storage devices and accessories
Quantum, Inc.	www.quantum.com	Disk and tape storage devices for PCs and servers
Seagate Technology, Inc.	www.seagate.com	Medium- to high-end storage devices
Sony Storage Solutions	ccpgprod.sel.sony.com/ ccpg/ccpg_eu_main	Storage solutions for PCs and servers
StorageNow, Inc.	www.storagenow.com	Reconditioned storage devices
SyQuest, Inc.	www.syquest.com	Removable storage devices for PCs
Tandberg Data, Inc.	www.tandberg.com	Medium- to high-end storage devices

Table 5-8.   Vendors Offering Tape Backup Hardware *(continued)*

Most vendor web sites have white papers and technical explanations of the advantages of various solutions. Be sure you understand the technical issues when evaluating their claims. For example, some vendors may claim overall higher capacities or throughput, but make sure that they're using reasonable estimates for data compression and real-world devices. A controller that can handle up to 80MB/sec data throughput will not buy you much if you are connected to a single tape backup device that can sustain only a fraction of that speed. Also, "burst speeds" are often quoted, but in the real world, these values may be of limited relevance. In any case, being an informed buyer will help you to avoid many potential surprises.

EVALUATING BACKUP SOFTWARE

Regardless of the hardware you select, you'll be working most closely with the backup software you choose to implement. Although the built-in utilities provided with Windows NT and Windows 2000 might be enough for smaller organizations, most businesses will probably choose to invest in products that offer more features and management flexibility. From the software console of a backup product, you'll be able to perform the majority of common functions that are required to implement and maintain your data protection plan. In the next few sections, we'll cover some useful features and other considerations you should keep in mind when choosing backup software. Then, we'll look at some specific products that might work well for your business. Let's start with a general list of criteria for considering backup software.

Software Features

There are several major software features that you should consider when evaluating backup-and-recovery software packages. Although most of the major platforms will include the same basic functions, certain features will make some platforms better—or more appropriate for your business needs—than others. When shopping for backup software, be sure to look for the following:

▼ **Centralized administration**　The software package should allow for the administration of multiple backup servers and devices from a single interface. Furthermore, the administration tools should be available from remote workstations. For some environments, the presence of a web-based interface can be a great plus.

■ **Usability**　The application interface should be intuitive and easy to use while providing the power and flexibility required to get the job done. Tools such as a calendar interface for scheduling backup operations and a unified view of media catalogs can be time-savers and can reduce potentially serious organizational problems.

■ **Scalability**　The backup software you choose should support any additional hardware you plan to use in the future and should contain modules that cover most of your backup needs. For example, if you're choosing a software package for local server backups, make sure that it supports the use of autoloaders, in case you need to upgrade in the future.

■ **Hardware support**　Before you choose to implement specific backup software, find out whether the application specifically supports your backup device. Most makers of backup software provide a hardware compatibility list that contains tested devices. Even if the devices you're using are not on the list, they may be supported through various standards. For example, most backup applications are able to access any devices that are supported by the Windows NT/2000 platform. In any case, make sure that the hardware and software you choose are compatible, before you implement any products.

■ **Pricing**　Does the product that you plan to purchase have a reasonable pricing model? For example, if you plan to back up your networked client machines, are separate licenses required for each one, or is a "network server" license available? One of the most common business constraints is budget, so you should do adequate research into pricing models to avoid paying much more money in the future. (We'll discuss licensing in detail later in this section.)

■   **Technical support**   Although you may not expect to need it, technical support for backup software products is an important consideration. Even if you have on-site experts in specific backup software, you should always be able to contact the product manufacturer with technical questions. Ideally, the manufacturer will have a direct high-priority line for situations in which downtime or data loss has occurred. Also, be sure that systems and network administrators are aware of the backup and recovery contacts that are available. The time immediately after a critical server failure is not a good occasion to determine that your disaster recovery software is not the best.

▲   **Disk space requirements**   In order to increase the speed of accessing catalog information from tapes, many backup software packages store catalogs, backup logs, and administrative information on the hard disk of the server computer. The amount of disk space that is used can be quite high (especially when many servers are being backed up or significant data changes occur regularly). When evaluating backup software, be sure to estimate and plan for the amount of disk space that will be required.

Although you can probably think of several other constraints for your own business environment, the preceding list should at least give you some criteria on which you can judge potential backup applications. Remember that the quality of the decision you make here will determine how easily you'll be able to protect information in the future. Now that we have an idea of the basic considerations, let's move on to examine some of these features and options in detail.

Special Modules

Earlier in this chapter, we looked at the issues associated with performing hot and cold database backups. I mentioned that without special software, databases and other types of servers that mark files as "in use" can't be properly backed up. Examples of these types of servers include Microsoft Exchange Server and Microsoft SQL Server. Both platforms must have full access to files while they are running. Furthermore, files must remain consistent to a certain point in time. For these reasons, special backup software is required to perform hot backups of files.

Most major data protection software packages provide optional modules that can be installed for handling these special cases. For example, a SQL Server module might integrate with the Named Pipes backup architecture of SQL Server to store live database information in a consistent format without requiring the server to be stopped or a database dump to be made. Of course, the same features are provided within SQL Server 2000 itself. When evaluating these special options, be sure to consider their cost and the features that are provided. You may find that performance is increased and administration integrates well with the rest of your backup solution. Or, you might decide to invest in a whole new backup solution, using SQL Server's utilities to manage database dumps and tape storage.

In addition to special modules for SQL Server and other databases, many backup software vendors offer other options. For example, if you'll be using a tape autoloader, you'll need management software that can handle tape libraries. Or, if you need to keep data synchronized between multiple servers, file and directory replication tools are available. Each of these special modules will likely cost more in initial software purchases, but they might be worthwhile investments, because they can save time and reduce the chance of errors.

Disaster Recovery Options

One of the main problems with restoring data in the event of a full system crash is the number of steps that might be required before performing a restore operation. Typically, this includes the following process:

1. Replace failed hardware (if any).
2. Reload the operating system along with any necessary updates or patches.
3. Reinstall all required drivers, including those for the backup device.
4. Install the backup software.
5. Begin the restore process.

In Chapter 8, we'll look at these operations in more detail. The overall process need not involve this many time-consuming steps, however. Many backup packages offer disaster recovery options that can be used to boot the system from a minimal set of disks (or other media). These boot disks load a minimal "operating system" that accesses your tape device and directly restores your information. The result is the savings of a great deal of time by avoiding the process of reinstalling the OS and all necessary drivers and software. Apart from the convenience, the investment in disaster recovery options can be priceless when you need to replace a failed mission-critical server, for example, where downtime is very costly. If a disaster recovery option is available with your selected backup software package, you should consider purchasing that option.

Licensing Models

When evaluating backup software, one of the criteria you will need to consider is the cost of the product. Understanding pricing and licensing issues related to data protection software can be difficult. There are several different licensing models that, if you don't understand the terminology, can cause a lot of confusion. Let's look at some of the common licensing models used by third-party backup software vendors:

▼ **Single-server licensing**   Single-server licenses cover backups for information stored on only one server machine. This might include information copied from various clients, but as long as the data being backed up resides on this machine, it is covered by the license. This is a good pricing model for businesses that have only a few servers and do not back up information stored on client workstations.

- **Single-client licensing**   Single-client licensing grants you permission to back up information on only one machine. Usually, this machine will be a desktop client PC. Although this is a good solution for home offices and small-network users, the cost of purchasing multiple "personal editions" of backup software limits the usefulness of single-client licensing in larger business settings.

- **Per-client licensing**   If you will be backing up multiple client machines using a single tape backup application, this model bases your price on the number of clients that will be backed up. For example, if you plan to store data from 100 workstations on your network, you will pay for 100 per-client licenses. This option is convenient if you have a small number of clients currently and plan to grow in the future, or if you only back up some clients on your network.

- ▲ **Site licensing**   In large network environments, it can become very difficult to manage backup server licenses. For example, every time a new server or client machine is installed and brought online, systems administrators may need to keep track of the licenses required for backups. Additionally, the cost for each of these licenses can be very high. To meet these demands, many providers of tape backup software allow for site licenses, which enable a given site to use as many licenses as required. Usually, a *site* is defined as a business unit located in a specific building or city. Therefore, distributed companies might need to purchase multiple site licenses, one for each of the various locations.

Your software vendor will probably offer more than one licensing option. Your choice of licensing methods will determine the overall cost of the product and will help you determine whether it fits within your business constraints. If you are unclear on pricing issues, be sure to seek clarification from the company itself or from a reseller. Understanding pricing and licensing issues up front can save a lot of money and avoid surprises in the future.

Now that we've covered some of the basic issues related to evaluating third-party backup software, let's move on to look at some specific products.

THIRD-PARTY SOFTWARE PRODUCTS

In Chapter 3, we looked at how backup and recovery software included with Windows NT 4 and Windows 2000 can meet the basic needs of protecting information. SQL Server 2000 also includes several options for backing up information, even while the database is in use (a hot backup). For most single-machine procedures and simple backup operations, these utilities will perform the necessary tasks. However, certain features that pertain to networkwide data protection plans require other packages. The preceding section mentioned some of the features to look for. Fortunately, you are not limited to the tools that are built into the Windows NT/2000 OS and Microsoft SQL Server 2000. In this section, we'll examine the features available from third-party backup and data protection software packages available on the market. The information won't be an exhaustive review, nor will features be compared directly. However, I will provide links to web sites that can provide more information.

> **NOTE:** The information in this section is not intended as an endorsement of any specific product. It is presented here only to let you know about the options that are available in the market and to point to sites from which you can receive more information. All information is based on the version of the software mentioned. You should always verify the advertised feature sets and configuration information before investing in any hardware or software.

Vendors of Backup Software

Choosing backup software can be quite confusing. The information covered in the preceding section was intended to help you enumerate the options that you require or want in your own environment. In this section, I've limited the packages evaluated to those that explicitly support backups on Windows NT 4 or Windows 2000. Some products integrate well with SQL Server 2000 (that is, they allow hot backups, as described in Chapter 6), while others only allow for backing up database dumps (cold backups). Table 5-9 lists some of the companies that make backup software and briefly describes the types of products they offer.

Company	Web Site	Products
ADIC Software	www.adic.com	Backup management software for Windows NT, UNIX, and other platforms
Barratt Edwards International (BEI)	www.ultrabac.com	UltraBac for Windows NT and SQL Server 2000
Casahl Technologies	www.casahl.com	Replic-Action, for real-time data transfer between various database platforms, including SQL Server 2000
Computer Associates	www.cai.com/arcserveit	ArcServeIT cross-platform backup application SQL Server Agent module

Table 5-9.   Vendors of Backup Software

Company	Web Site	Products
St. Bernard Software	www.stbernard.com	Open File Manager, which works with all backup software solutions
Storactive	www.storactive.com	LiveBackup, which includes file recovery and disaster recovery options
Veritas	www.veritas.com	Backup Exec, which includes modules for Microsoft BackOffice

Table 5-9.   Vendors of Backup Software *(continued)*

As is the case when shopping for any business product, you should fully understand the level of support available. For example, backup software might claim to "support SQL Server 2000." You might then assume that the software can perform hot backups of SQL Server databases. Depending on how you evaluate that statement, however, it might mean that the package is only capable of backing up offline databases or dump files. Additionally, be sure to understand the licensing models for the software you purchase, because that will probably play a large role in your decision. As with hardware, the more educated you are about the various products and features that are available, the better your decisions will be.

Data Protection Utilities

In addition to backup software packages, there are several tools and utilities that can make managing and administering PC-based networks easier. In the following sections, we'll cover some utilities that protect against viruses, partition hard disks, and duplicate drives. Wherever possible, I will provide links to companies that provide these software packages, so that you can obtain more information. Let's get started by examining the issue of disk duplication.

Disk Duplication

One problem with performing standard backups is that they generally only copy the files that are accessible on your hard drive. Although this will generally include the OS and any user data files, it does not include information stored in the boot sector. If a hard disk should fail completely, you might need to reinstall the OS and the backup software before you can even *begin* the recovery process. This might be acceptable in some cases, but it is clearly quite painful and time consuming. In other cases, you might want to record an "image" of a machine, including *all* of the data on the hard disk, so that you can easily recover it or copy the contents to another machine. Although you can do a reasonable job by copying the contents and restoring the boot sector, the issues become more difficult when you must support multiple operating systems and partition types. That's where disk duplication comes in.

Disk duplication is commonly used in larger organizations to enforce standardization of software configuration for new computers. A common practice is to wipe hard disks clean of all their data as soon as they're received from the manufacturer and then load a corporate "image." These images include the OS and any software required for users to do their jobs. Usually, multiple images are created based on business requirements. For example, there might be a base image that includes the OS and any applications required by all users at the company (Microsoft Office 2000, for example). In addition, there might be different images for members of the engineering department and for people in sales, configured specifically for those users' respective needs. Figure 5-8 illustrates how multiple images might be used.

There are two main methods of performing disk duplication. The first is through the use of dedicated hardware. In this method, hard disks are usually removed from desktop computers and attached to a special controller. This controller attaches to one source hard disk and one or more destination hard disks. When the disk duplication operation is started, the controller copies all the data from the source hard disk to the destination hard disk(s). This ensures that all of the information is copied, bit by bit, from the source to other disks. The end result is several hard disks with identical contents. The drives can then be replaced in their original machines for use. Although hardware disk duplicators can be faster than other methods, they can be quite costly. Also, additional work is involved in removing and replacing hard disks from PCs.

Disk duplication can also be performed using various software tools. These utilities are usually inexpensive and require no special hardware in order to operate. Two examples are Symantec Software's Norton Ghost (**www.symantec.com**) and PowerQuest's

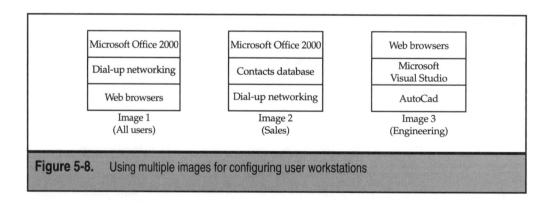

Figure 5-8.   Using multiple images for configuring user workstations

Drive Image (**www.powerquest.com**). Both of these tools allow you to create an image of one or more partitions on your hard disk and store them in a single file. You can then use the file to restore data to the same or other machines. Utilities are also available for performing selective restores of just a few files.

The software utilities can be made extremely useful through the creation of a special network boot floppy—a disk from which a machine can be booted and have access to the network. Whenever a machine fails or becomes unbootable, a system administrator can boot the system with the floppy, connect to a network share, and then run the appropriate utilities to reload a default configuration to the machine. Overall, disk duplication methods can be very useful in systems deployment and in PC backups. If you haven't done so already, consider investing in disk duplication methods.

NOTE: You should be aware of several issues when performing disk duplication in a Windows NT environment. Every Windows NT–based object is given a unique Security Identifier (SID). Objects such as users and files are expected to have unique SIDs in a networked environment. The main problem is that duplicated computers will have the same SIDs as other machines. Although they will operate properly, this duplication can cause various security and usability problems. Fortunately, solutions are available. Most manufacturers of disk duplication hardware and software provide an "SID changer" utility. Windows 2000 machines have similar problems, which can also be resolved using tools available from Microsoft. For further information on SID issues (and for solutions to the problems they cause), contact the manufacturer of your disk duplication product.

Virus Scanners

Computer viruses can cost IT departments and end users a lot of time and frustration. Although the majority of viruses are harmless, some can cause data loss. We covered information about scanning for viruses in Chapter 3. In this section, we'll provide information on some common commercially available virus protection tools. Table 5-10 lists some manufacturers of virus scanning products.

The basic purpose of a virus scanner is to automatically find infected files on the local PC. The program does this by comparing disk contents against library files that indicate the "signatures" of various known viruses. Virus scanners are usually installed on all client machines and are scheduled to run automatically. Figure 5-9 provides an example of a virus-scanning tool's interface. Although this is a good solution for environments with a small number of PCs to manage, there are two main problems with this configuration in large network environments: First, installing antivirus software on client PCs can be time consuming and generally will require visiting each desktop machine. Second, ensuring that virus scanners are kept up-to-date with the latest virus definitions can be a tedious and error-prone process.

Fortunately, many vendors of antivirus software offer products designed specifically for networks. For example, some applications allow you to remotely administer

Company	Web Site	Product
Carmel Software Engineering	www.carmel.co.il	Carmel Anti-Virus
Central Command	www.avp.com	AntiViral ToolKit
Computer Associates	www.cai.com/antivirus	InoculateIT; InocuLan
DataFellows	www.datafellows.com	F-Secure AntiVirus
Network Associates	www.mcafee.com	McAfee VirusScan
Norman Data Defense Systems	www.norman.com	Norman Virus Control (formerly Thunderbyte Anti-Virus)
Panda Software	www.pandasoftware.com	Panda AntiVirus
Symantec	www.symantec.com	Norton AntiVirus

Table 5-10. Vendors of Virus-Scanning Software

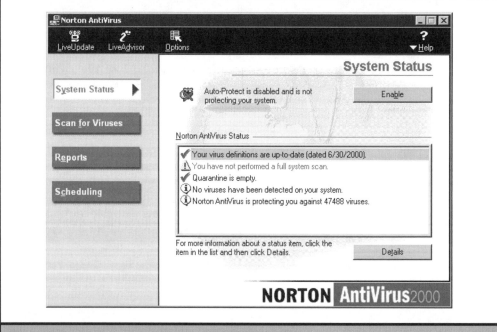

Figure 5-9. Using Norton AntiVirus 2000 to scan for viruses

and update the client-side virus-scanning software from a central location. Others perform virus scans through logon scripts. Regardless of the virus-scanning procedures you choose, do keep in mind that these scans can be quite annoying to users. You will probably save yourself much grief, for instance, if your solution does *not* call for a scan of local hard drives at every login. Such frequent virus scans are rarely necessary and, in fact, will probably hurt productivity more than the overwhelming majority of viruses might. As with any other security or data protection strategy, your virus protection routine should revolve around the needs of the business and cause as little disruption as possible to the users who work there.

Disk-Partitioning Utilities

One of the plagues of working with disk management on Intel-based machines is that we're limited by a partition-based system that was designed for machines over a decade old. Nowadays, there are several different types of file systems that an OS might require. In the Windows world, the list includes FAT, FAT32, and NTFS. Linux and OS/2 systems require their own file systems. One of the challenges of managing various partition types is that you have to plan ahead. Until recently, adding or resizing partitions involved backing up all the data on the disk, reworking the partitions, and then restoring all the data. This can be a time-consuming and error-prone process. Fortunately, new utilities such as Partition Magic, from PowerQuest (**www.powerquest.com**), allow you to dynamically resize your partitions without losing any data. (See Figure 5-10.) Partition Magic supports many different file systems and offers both DOS-based and Windows-based interfaces for maximum flexibility. These types of tools can save a lot of time when you're supporting complex configurations or maximizing the usable space on your system.

Benchmarking Software

When comparing data protection solutions and selected server hardware, your goals will be simple: to find a system that provides high-performance and that fits within your budget. So how do you know just how fast a computer really is? As I mentioned earlier, computer-marketing campaigns often cite the speed of the CPU as the single most important factor. However, in the real world, this may not be a valid measurement of performance. For example, a machine may have a very fast CPU, but a slow disk I/O system. If your applications and database servers depend greatly on disk access, then the processor speed may make little difference.

That still leaves the question of how you would really measure performance. Perhaps the most valid test would be to purchase the system, configure it to your specifications, and measure its performance as you run your own applications on it. Unfortunately, the time and resources required to do this might be prohibitive (and few vendors would give you this option).

Fortunately, there is another way to gauge system performance. There are several different industry-standard benchmarks that can be used for measuring the performance of

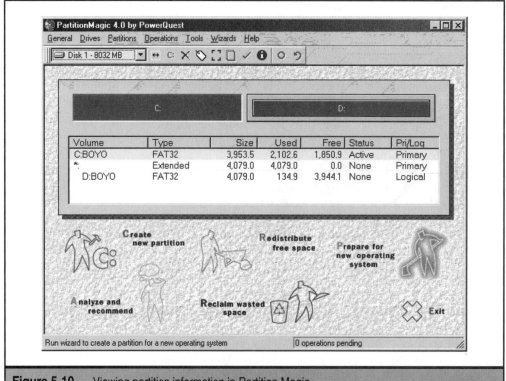

Figure 5-10.   Viewing partition information in Partition Magic

your workstation and server computers. Each performs tests in different ways. Figure 5-11 shows a typical results screen from the WinBench application, and Table 5-11 lists some common benchmarks and what they test.

Although the general idea behind benchmarks—running computers through a set of tests and recording the results—is a good one, the details can get quite complicated. It is important to understand exactly what benchmarks are measuring. Usually, the providers of these benchmarks will make detailed information about their testing methodologies available. Benchmark results can be very useful when comparing multiple machines. However, note that while one machine might "beat" another one in a specific benchmark, the results might be reversed in another benchmark. Also, you can use benchmarks to verify the performance of your hardware configuration against that of others using similar devices. Many online benchmark sites offer a forum for other users to post their own results.

The bottom line is fairly simple: although benchmarks can be helpful in measuring performance, it is up to you—the evaluator—to properly understand and interpret the results.

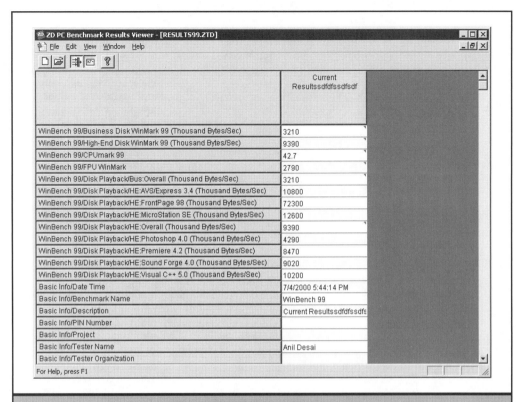

Figure 5-11.   Viewing test results in WinBench 99

Benchmark Name	Company	Web Site	Notes
3D Mark 2000	Mad Onion (formerly FutureMark Corporation)	www.MadOnion.com	Tests overall system and video performance for games; allows comparisons with online databases of system performance statistics gathered from other users
3D WinBench	Ziff-Davis BenchMark Operations	www.zdbop.com	Measures the 3D graphics performance of computers

Table 5-11.   Common Benchmark Applications

Benchmark Name	Company	Web Site	Notes
BenchMark Factory	Quest Software	www.benchmarkfactory.com	A database server performance benchmarking tool that allows the creation and execution of various test suites based on a load designed by the database administrator
Content Creation (CC) WinBench	Ziff-Davis BenchMark Operations	www.zdbop.com	Tests the performance of workstation computers that are used for creating multimedia contents. Similar in design to the WinBench tests, this benchmark uses a suite of commonly used graphical and video design applications.
iBench	Ziff-Davis BenchMark Operations	i-bench.zdnet.com	A cross-platform benchmark that tests the capabilities of popular web browsers on a variety of platforms
NetBench	Ziff-Davis BenchMark Operations	www.zdbop.com	Measures I/O performance for file servers; allows testers to configure a load of a variable number of clients to determine performance limits
ServerBench	Ziff-Davis BenchMark Operations	www.zdbop.com	Measures the performance of client/server application servers using multiple PC as clients
SysDBMark	Business Application Performance Corporation (BAPCo)	www.bapco.com	Measures the performance of various database servers by simulating load and measuring results
SysMark 2000	Business Application Performance Corporation (BAPCo)	www.bapco.com	Provides benchmarks that measure the performance of computers as they perform common tasks (such as working with productivity applications)

Table 5-11. Common Benchmark Applications *(continued)*

Benchmark Name	Company	Web Site	Notes
TPC Benchmark Suites	Transaction Processing Performance Council (TPC)	www.tpc.org	An independent nonprofit agency that has created benchmarks for measuring database performance and scalability under various forms of load. The TPC benchmarks are widely recognized as the industry standard for database performance comparisons.
WebBench	Ziff-Davis BenchMark Operations	www.zdbop.com	Measures web server performance on a variety of platforms
WinBench	Ziff-Davis BenchMark Operations	www.zdbop.com	A suite of tests that measure the performance of various components of a computer system (including CPU, memory, video, hard disks, and other I/O devices)
WinStone	Ziff-Davis BenchMark Operations	www.zdbop.com	A benchmark that runs a suite of common productivity applications to gauge real-world client computer performance

Table 5-11.   Common Benchmark Applications *(continued)*

MAKING SOUND BUSINESS DECISIONS

In this chapter, we've discussed many hardware and software products that can help your company implement and manage a successful data protection plan. Throughout this book, I will continue to emphasize the importance of reaching *business* goals with technology. A good data protection solution will not only meet your technical requirements, but will also fit within your business constraints. One of the limited resources you will have to deal with is your company's budget. In Chapter 2, we talked about various factors to consider when you're determining the cost and value of protecting information. So—how can you make sure that your purchasing decisions make good business sense?

For some purchases, it can be quite easy to determine the true cost of what you are buying. If all other parameters (such as quality) are held constant, a pizza that costs $10 is a better deal than one that costs more. (This is an important consideration for authors of technical books!) When dealing with other "investments," however, the situation gets much more complex. Let's consider the case of backup software. Clearly, a major factor in your decision will be the initial outlay—the costs of the software itself and all necessary licenses. But do these figures really tell us how much the product will *cost*? Factors such as the cost of training network and systems administrators in using the new product are likely to be significant, as will be any downtime required to install the software on production servers. Though they are not quite as easy to measure as the "sticker price" of a product, these other factors are at least as significant. The specifics of how secondary costs affect your business will be one of your main concerns. Unfortunately, there's no way I could write a table of "estimated costs" that would apply to more than a few readers of this book. However, there are some general methodologies used for estimating the costs and overall quality of an investment. In this part of the chapter, we'll look at some issues that you'll want to consider when determining the *real* impact of a data protection solution.

Total Cost of Ownership (TCO)

I've already alluded to the fact that when an item's costs are being measured, the purchase price is only the beginning. Anyone who has ever owned an unreliable car is painfully aware that the initial cost of something is sometimes only a fraction of the total money spent. In business, this larger total is known as the Total Cost of Ownership (TCO). The idea behind TCO is that an organization must measure all the costs in its environment in order to get an accurate picture of the business situation. Cost categories include not only the initial purchase price of an item or service, but also the funds allocated toward implementation, training, support, and so on. The item in question and the environment in which it will be used are factors that determine specific costs. Of course, a complete TCO analysis can itself be costly in terms of money, time, and other business resources. On the whole, however, TCO-based planning can actually save a great deal of money. Companies that can properly identify and reduce their areas of high costs have an edge, in the long run, over their less-efficient competitors.

If you'd like more detailed information on TCO in IT environments, here are some good resources:

▼ **Microsoft TechNet Information** Microsoft has been placing a lot of emphasis on the TCO model. As more and more IT decision makers are looking at overall expenses, Microsoft can provide information about the cost of incorporating various Windows-based solutions into an overall IT strategy. For more information on tools, technologies, and cost studies, go to **www.microsoft.com/technet**.

■ **The Gartner Group** The increasing industrial emphasis on TCO can be largely attributed to the research, studies, and methodologies proffered by the Gartner Group. For more information, visit **www.gartnergroup.com**. This web site (much of which requires a paid subscription) includes information designed to help you analyze TCO in your own environment. Included are tables of cost areas that you should take into consideration when measuring the total cost of your own environment. Using industry-standard benchmarks, you'll be able to see how your organization's business practices and costs compare to the efficiency of others.

▲ *Windows NT Network Management: Reducing Total Cost of Ownership* (New Riders Press, Indianapolis, 1999). This book (written by me) includes a lot of information on measuring and calculating TCO, and describes the various technical tools, utilities, and practices available for controlling costs in a business environment. Technical solutions (virtual private networks, for instance) are discussed not for technology's own sake, but rather with a focus on how they can help you overcome the financial challenges in your own business.

Now that we've completed our *very* brief overview of TCO analysis, let's look at how we can apply this information in conjunction with another common business acronym, ROI.

Return on Investment (ROI)

Often, the results of a TCO analysis will reveal that the true cost of an item or technology is far higher than initially realized. The logical question then becomes "Is it worth it?" This is where the idea of Return on Investment (ROI) comes in. Simply put, ROI is measured to help determine whether the implementation of specific technology is worth the expense. Typically, ROI is calculated in terms of time or money, and is expressed as a ratio. It is a number that measures how quickly you will break even on an investment (and start seeing tangible benefits from it). The more accurate your TCO information, the more accurate will be your ROI.

To calculate ROI, you should start by dividing the expected financial benefit (the "return") by the amount invested. A good investment will have a value above 1 (the higher the value, the better). It may also be meaningful to express ROI in terms of time and/or money. The ROI on a new tape backup device, for example, might be one year. That's the time it will take you to recover the costs of purchasing, installing, and using the unit for one year versus keeping your old device. Again, you should factor in items related to TCO, such as training and implementation. However, be sure that you also emphasize the benefits (reduced administration cost, downtime prevented, and so on).

The information presented here on TCO and ROI can be quite useful in several ways. First, if you're an IT support provider, you'll probably need to get "sign-off" from management and executives before you can implement a company-wide backup strategy. By emphasizing TCO and ROI figures, you'll have a good way to justify your technical solutions. You'll get a lot of mileage out of statements like "We'll start seeing savings on IT support issues three months after we deploy Product X company-wide." Otherwise, if *you* are the decision maker, you'll have a good way to measure the quality of certain business decisions. Either way, continue to keep these ideas in mind as we start looking at backup solutions in more detail.

SUMMARY

In this chapter, we examined some issues that you must resolve before choosing specific data protection products. We began by considering the types of backups to be performed, the recovery requirements of your organization, and other business issues. We then identified some points that you'll want to keep in mind when choosing server hardware. Armed with this information, we began to look at the various tape devices and other data protection equipment available on the market. To complete the picture, we discussed backup software platforms and other utilities that can be used to make life easier for systems administrators. Of course, none of these solutions will be of much use unless they fit within your business constraints—so at this point we took a brief departure from the technical issues to explain the calculation of TCO and ROI—two figures which, when managed wisely, can go a long way toward ensuring the success of your data protection strategy.

And now, with the fundamental information out of the way, it's time to move on to the real technical work—planning and performing database backups on SQL Server 2000. We'll examine these processes closely in Chapter 6.

PART III

Backup Procedures
and Methods

CHAPTER 6

Performing Database Backups

In Parts I and II of this book, we examined the importance of properly planning for backups, emphasizing how you can best evaluate your business requirements and then use that information to form a data protection plan. It is important to keep in mind that protecting the information stored in your SQL Server databases is only part of a much bigger picture. We began by discussing the importance of planning for company-wide data protection decisions. Next, we discussed the importance of protecting your operating systems—Windows NT 4 or Windows 2000—since a database server is only as secure as the network operating system (OS) on which it resides. We then covered the architecture of SQL Server 2000 from several different angles. We focused on security and performance, as these two topics will affect your backup strategy most. Finally, we moved on to evaluating the types of hardware and software available for helping you protect your information. With any luck, you are by now fairly clear on what sorts of hardware and software you need; if you're still deciding, you should at least have a good idea of what's available in the marketplace.

That brings us to the current chapter. If you're technically knowledgeable, you probably jumped to this chapter first. Before going on, however, I should stress how important it is to first review the information on planning and evaluation covered in the earlier chapters of this book. Without adequate foresight, the best technical implementations might be worthless (or worse, even counterproductive). You're likely to find that implementing backups in SQL Server 2000, for the most part, is a very simple process. With just a few mouse clicks, you can implement a suitable data protection plan. That's a mixed blessing, however, as it might make you think you can get by without planning or truly understanding how SQL Server works. Needless to say, that's not a good thing, as it can lead to same poor decisions! With that out of the way, let's learn how to perform database backups.

Now, it's time to look at a task that's just as crucial to effective data protection: implementing the actual backups. Even the best-designed plans are useless if they are not executed properly. In this chapter, we'll focus on the steps required to perform database backups on SQL Server 2000. I'll start with information on how you can best design storage for your SQL Server databases using new features and capabilities in the product. Then, we'll cover different backup operation types, from a technical standpoint, after which we'll be ready to cover the actual steps and commands you can use to perform backups on your SQL Server. If you've worked with other relational database server products in the past, you might think that this is a very complicated process. Fortunately, I think you'll find it quite easy to implement a suitable data protection plan (regardless of your technical background with the product).

Finally, we'll end with three sections that cover some very useful features of SQL Server 2000: the automation of backups and other jobs, the ability to easily import and export data, and methods for optimizing backup performance. That's a tall order, so let's get started!

DESIGNING SQL SERVER STORAGE

Before you jump into deciding how your SQL Server information should be backed up, it's a good idea to examine your current storage configuration. SQL Server 2000 supports many different configuration options for storing data. An important part of any data protection strategy is to plan for the efficient storage of information. For small databases, the best plan might be the simplest one: the use of a single data file. However, for larger databases and more complex disk configurations, more planning is required. In these environments, data might be distributed across multiple physical devices by means of files and filegroups. In this part of the chapter, we'll cover the various issues you should consider when designing the storage configuration for your SQL Server installation. Fortunately, in most cases, if your current configuration is not the ideal one, you can modify the settings before implementing your backup and recovery plan.

It's important to first estimate the amount of data you'll need to back up and how long the backup will take. Other concerns include when the backup will be performed and how users will be impacted by the operation. As mentioned several times throughout the book, the real goal is a balance between security and usability. If your backup procedures prevent your users from doing their jobs efficiently, you should reconsider the methods you are using.

Storage Estimation Tools

The Microsoft BackOffice Resource Kit is a separate set of utilities and documentation designed for use with Microsoft BackOffice applications. It includes several utilities that can be useful for planning data protection. The Resource Kit is available at many bookstores and also directly from Microsoft (go to **mspress.microsoft.com** for details). Also, if you're a Microsoft TechNet subscriber, you will automatically receive the BackOffice Resource Kit on CD-ROM (see **www.microsoft.com/technet** for more information on TechNet). Keep in mind that most of these utilities come without support from Microsoft and can be quite rough around the edges. Be sure to read the Books Online that are installed with the Resource Kit for more information on the utilities. By default, you can access the tools included on the CD-ROM after installing them by clicking Start | Programs | Resource Kit | Tools Management Console (see Figure 6-1). Some useful utilities related to backups and data protection include the following:

▼ **DataSizer** This simple Excel spreadsheet can be used to help you determine the size of the data you're trying to back up. It uses formulas that calculate your storage requirements based on values that you input. To get useful results, you'll need to be able to estimate the typical row size for your database tables and the number of rows you expect to add or modify per day. Additional information about indexes and other objects can also be helpful. Figure 6-2 shows an example of the spreadsheet.

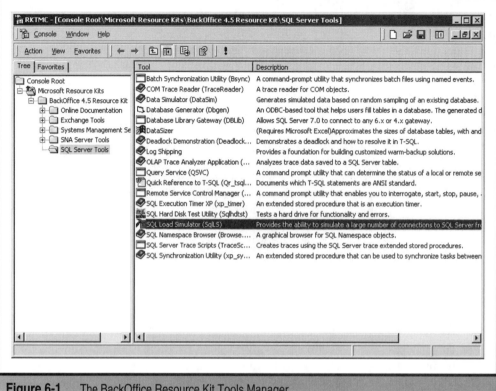

Figure 6-1. The BackOffice Resource Kit Tools Manager

■ **SQL Load Simulator** One of the main challenges with testing backup and other database solutions is the lack of available client connections. On one hand, you want to simulate a lot of clients. On the other, you can't afford to run tests on production databases. If you want to measure the performance of your SQL Server installation, you can use SQL Load Simulator to simulate multiple concurrent connections to the machine from one or more clients. This is particularly useful if you want to measure the effects of performing a backup while queries are being run against a database. Load Simulator accepts one or more SQL query files and prompts you for the number of connections to simulate. It then opens that number of simultaneous connections to the server you specify and runs the scripts repeatedly (see Figure 6-3).

As statistics are recorded during the process, you can analyze the results when you're done, to get an idea of the response times and throughput you could expect in the real world. When testing this way, keep in mind that you might exceed certain parameters. For example, if you attempt to simulate 100 concurrent connections from a single workstation, the network bandwidth or

	A	B	C	D	E
23	Reserved free rows per page	6			
24					
25	Index Row Size Calculation				
26	Index Row Header	1			
27	Null Bitmap	3			
28	Variable Length Columns Total Size	0			
29	Total Index Row Size	18			
30	Index Rows Per Page	405			
31	Data pages	21,202			
32					
33	Clustered index rows per page	404			
34	Clustered index pages (level 0)	53			
35	Clustered index pages (level 1)	1			
36	Clustered index pages (level 2)	1			
37	Total pages (data plus index)	21,257			
38	**Table Size**	**174,137,344**			

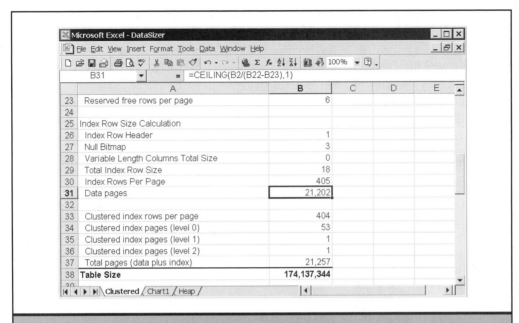

Figure 6-2. Using the DataSizer spreadsheet to view information

Thread	SPID	Status	Iteration	Fields	Bytes ±	Min. Time	Max. Time
1	12	ExecDir	23	4994	31834	78	500
2	10	ExecDir	23	4994	31834	109	516
3	28	ExecDir	4	681	4341	172	172
4	11	ExecDir	23	4994	31834	94	516
5	15	ExecDir	24	5221	33281	62	500
6	14	ExecDir	23	4994	31834	109	516
7	9	ExecDir	23	4994	31834	78	516
8	22	ExecDir	23	4994	31834	109	188
9	20	ExecDir	23	4994	31834	110	203
10	17	ExecDir	23	4994	31834	125	516
11	21	ExecDir	23	4994	31834	110	187
12	23	ExecDir	22	4767	30387	125	188
13	16	ExecDir	24	5221	33281	109	500
14	18	ExecDir	23	4994	31834	93	500
15	27	ExecDir	9	1816	11576	156	203
16	19	ExecDir	23	4994	31834	110	485
17	13	ExecDir	24	5221	33281	109	500
18	24	ExecDir	17	3632	23152	109	188
19	26	ExecDir	9	1816	11576	140	188
20	25	ExecDir	16	3405	21705	140	188

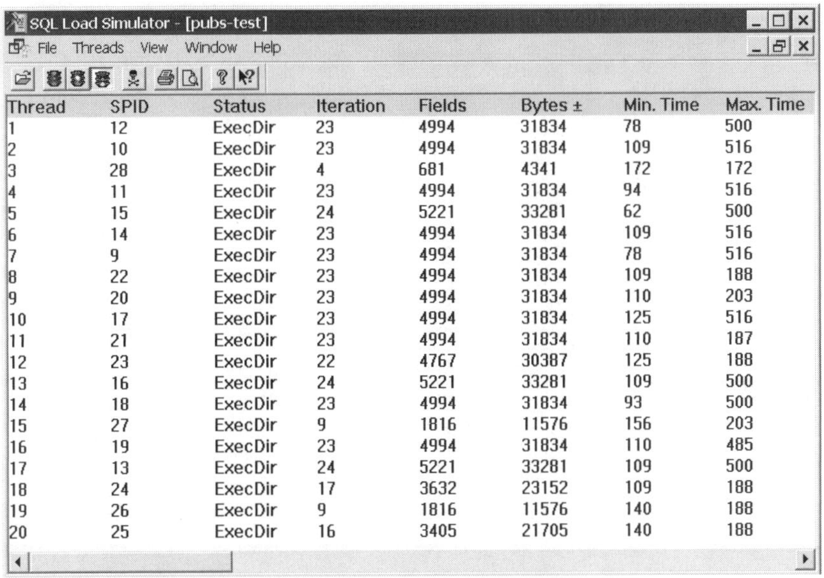

Figure 6-3. Using the SQL Load Simulator to generate work for SQL Server

the processing power of the client might be the bottleneck. Also, be aware that queries will run much faster after they are cached. The results you receive might be quite different when many different types of queries are being run against the database. Nevertheless, SQL Load Simulator can be useful in making best guesses of anticipated server capacities.

■ **Database Generator**   This utility is used for generating data to be loaded into a database. It is a Visual Basic application that provides an interface for generating data. Users can specify the number of data records per day and the types of values to be loaded into the database. Database Generator is a little rough around the edges, but it can be useful. Data Simulator, described next, is another tool that can be used for the same task.

■ **Data Simulation Tool**   Often, the problem for DBAs is that there's just too much data to manage. When planning your backup solution, however, you might have the opposite problem: *not enough* information to adequately test your hardware and software. The Data Simulation Tool is a simple Visual Basic application that can connect to a table within an existing database, analyze the data that is stored there, and then automatically generate random data to increase the size of the database. The tool takes input parameters in the form of a VBScript file and then generates the number of INSERT commands you request (see Figure 6-4). These parameters specify how the data should be generated. You can either save this file for later use or execute it against the current database. Although much of the data will be randomized, this is a good way to artificially grow test databases for testing backup performance.

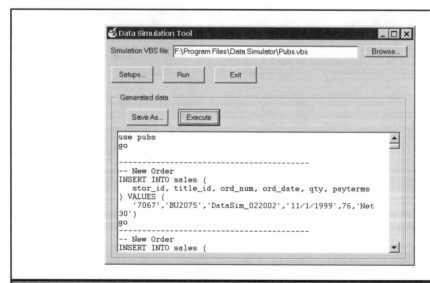

Figure 6-4.   Generating test data with the Data Simulation Tool

▲   **SQL HD Test**   This utility can be used to test the speed of disk I/O on your current system. It can be useful in determining the impact of redundant array of independent disks (RAID) or other hardware-level modifications you might have made to your system. The tool is rough around the edges, so you'll need to make sure you understand the various commands and switches before running the program successfully. The results will be information similar to what you might receive when you run the Windows NT Performance Monitor, but the tests focus more on issues related to database server performance.

This by no means is an exhaustive list of all the tools and utilities included in the BackOffice Resource Kit. In this section, I've listed only those tools and utilities that might be of use to database and systems administrators interested in planning for and testing backup and recovery options. For more information on the Resource Kit, see **www.microsoft.com/backofficeserver**.

RAID

In Chapter 3, we looked at an overview of RAID technology and how it can be implemented on the Windows NT/2000 platform (via the operating system). In Chapter 5, we looked at other implementations of RAID, including the advantages of using hardware-based disk controllers for this purpose. The important benefits of using RAID technology are that it can increase performance, provide for fault tolerance, and simplify administration. In this section, we look at each of these benefits in turn and determine how they pertain to the design of your SQL Server storage configuration.

We've already covered fault tolerance: when redundancy is built into a disk array, the failure of a single disk will not cause a loss of data. Although there may be a decrease in performance and a decrease in usable disk space, certain types of RAID solutions will allow you to quickly and easily replace a failed disk without stopping network service. This increases uptime and, ultimately, ensures that your users can work uninterrupted in the event of a failure.

When data is retrieved from multiple physical disks in a disk subsystem, the results are faster data access and increased throughput—both of which are benefits that can greatly increase database performance. Finally, as we'll see in the next section, configuring files and filegroups to specifically store information across physical devices involves extensive planning and understanding of the underlying data structure. For most environments, however, the cost associated with purchasing RAID solutions for database servers is a good investment.

NOTE: In Chapter 5, we discussed the issues related to using write-caching disk controllers. In some cases, a failure of a RAID controller or an unexpected restart of the server (due to, for example, a loss of power) can cause database files to be left in an inconsistent state. Be sure to review that information before implementing a hardware-based RAID solution.

Files and Filegroups

Although RAID can be simple to implement, there are some situations in which you might want additional flexibility in configuring where specific data resides. Disk striping with parity (RAID Level 5) allows for distributing information across multiple physical devices, but it doesn't allow you to pinpoint a single device for the storage of specific information (such as a large database table or transaction log information). For example, if you know that three tables in your database will be the most heavily used, you might want to place each of them on physically different disks. That way, you can reduce the contention for reading information and reduce the bottlenecks that occur when the busiest databases compete for the same limited I/O resources. Furthermore, you might want to place the transaction logs for these databases on specific devices based on the expected amount of data-modification queries. The use of files and filegroups (which we briefly examined in Chapter 4) allows for this type of flexibility. Let's look at the process of implementing files and filegroups in SQL Server 2000.

Files

SQL Server 2000 databases are made up of at least one file (called the *primary data file,* whose default extension is *.mdf) and at least one transaction log file (whose default extension is *.ldf). A database can use additional data files (called *secondary data files,* whose default extension is *.ndf) or transaction log files for storing database objects. Files have two names: a physical name, such as c:\MSSQL\DataFile2.ndf, and a logical name, such as DatabaseFile2, used for most administrative purposes.

As mentioned in Chapter 4, data files are set by default to grow or shrink automatically as needed. This greatly decreases the need for administration and management of files, because they can change based on the needs of the database and users. Usually, you will specify these options when creating a data file. You can do this in Enterprise Manager by the following process.

STEP-BY-STEP: CREATING AND CONFIGURING DATA FILES

1. Expand the tree for the server on which you want to create the database.

2. Right-click the name of a database server and select New Database. The Database Properties dialog box will appear.

3. Type a name for the new database. This information will be used to generate default data filenames.

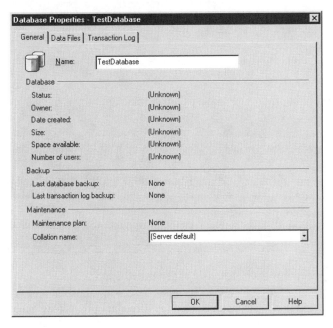

4. Click on the Data Files tab. Note that you will see a default primary data file. The location of this default file will be based on the settings you chose when you installed SQL Server 2000. The default filename will be based on the name of the database that you provided in the previous step.

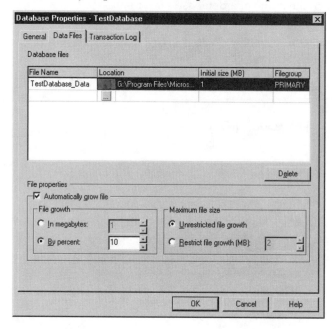

5. In the options for each data file that you add to the database, you can specify several parameters. First, you'll need to decide whether you want the file to grow automatically. If you check the Automatically Grow File check box (which is enabled, by default), you can choose the amount of growth that will occur (In Megabytes or By Percent) each time the file runs out of space. You can also specify a maximum size for this file (Unrestricted File Growth, the default, or Restricted File Growth (MB), for which you can specify a size in megabytes).

6. Select the Transaction Log tab. Note that you can also add files for the transaction log and that the options are similar to those for data files. There is one difference, however: transaction logs cannot use filegroups (which we'll cover in the next section).

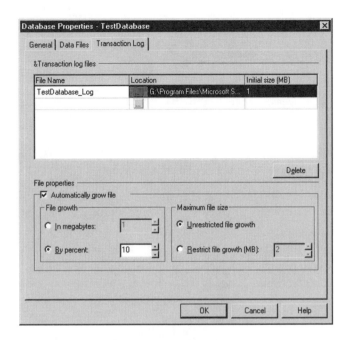

7. Click OK to create the data file(s) and the database.

The process is similar if you want to modify the settings after the database has been created. The physical data file structure can also be specified during the creation of a database using the CREATE DATABASE command. To specify data file options when creating a database, use the following syntax:

```
CREATE DATABASE database_name
[ ON [ PRIMARY ]
        [ < filespec > [ ,...n ] ]
        [ , < filegroup > [ ,...n ] ]
]
[ LOG ON { < filespec > [ ,...n ] } ]
[ COLLATE collation_name ]
[ FOR LOAD | FOR ATTACH ]
```

```
< filespec > ::=

( [ NAME = logical_file_name , ]
    FILENAME = 'os_file_name'
    [ , SIZE = size ]
    [ , MAXSIZE = { max_size | UNLIMITED } ]
    [ , FILEGROWTH = growth_increment ] ) [ ,...n ]

< filegroup > ::=

FILEGROUP filegroup_name < filespec > [ ,...n ]
```

For example, the following command creates a database that resides on a single 10MB data file that is set to automatically grow by 10 percent until it reaches 100MB:

```
CREATE DATABASE TestDB
ON
  ( Name = 'TestFile',
    FileName = 'c:\SQLData\TestFile.mdf',
    Size = 10MB,
    Maxsize = 100MB,
    Filegrowth = 10%)
```

Later in this section, we'll look at how you can alter the settings for your existing data files. Another useful feature is to use the automatic scripting options included in Query Analyzer. By right-clicking on the name of a database, selecting All Tasks, and then clicking on Generate SQL Script, you can automatically generate a script that includes the creation of the physical files and/or filegroups (described in the next section) for your database (see Figure 6-5). This feature is also extremely helpful when you're trying to learn the syntax of the CREATE DATABASE command.

You can also generate automatic database creation scripts using new features in SQL Query Analyzer (which we covered in Chapter 4).

Although dealing with files in this manner works well for smaller databases, it can be quite difficult to administer a large number of files individually. For example, you might need to create dozens of files for a database in order to meet performance requirements. Fortunately, there's a solution to that problem as well.

Filegroups

SQL Server 2000 *filegroups* are collections of data files that are created to ease the administration and use of multiple files. The relationship between files and filegroups is one-to-many. That is, a file can belong to only one filegroup, but a filegroup can consist of more than one file. Logically, filegroups work just like data files. Database objects can be stored on a filegroup, which in turn is made up of several OS files. The three types of filegroups are as follows:

▼ **Primary** Includes the primary data file and any files that are not part of another filegroup. This filegroup always exists for a database, even though it might not be explicitly specified.

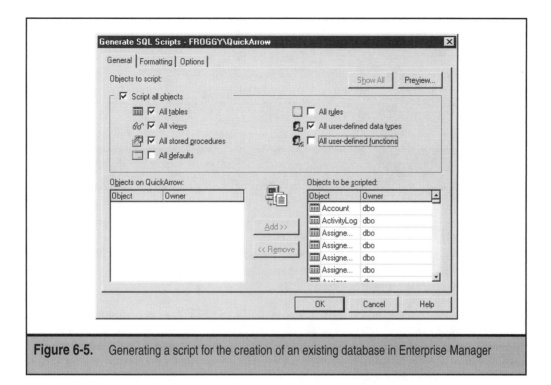

Figure 6-5. Generating a script for the creation of an existing database in Enterprise Manager

- **Default**   The filegroup that is used to contain all database objects for which a filegroup is not specified.

- **User defined**   Filegroups that are created by a DBA using Enterprise Manager or Transact-SQL commands.

Every database has a *primary filegroup* that is created by default when a database is created. All of the system tables that are stored within every database are stored on the primary filegroup. When creating new database objects (such as tables), database administrators and designers can choose a filegroup on which to store the object. Databases have a default filegroup that is used for the storage of new database objects if the user does not provide this information when they are creating the object.

Additionally, database objects can be placed in files within other filegroups, as needed. The types of objects that can be specifically placed in certain filegroups include tables, indexes, and large data types (text, ntext, or image data). The end result is that the storage requirements for these database objects can be distributed evenly among the various physical disks where the different files reside. Figure 6-6 shows the relationships between the various physical and logical files we have discussed thus far.

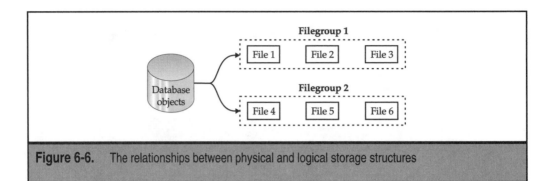

Figure 6-6.   The relationships between physical and logical storage structures

REMEMBER: When planning for the use of filegroups, be aware of the restrictions. First, filegroups can be used only by databases. Transaction logs cannot use filegroups. Second, a filegroup can be used by only one database. It is important to keep these facts in mind, because they may cause problems when you're implementing storage options.

When writing data to objects that reside on filegroups, SQL Server compares the amount of free space available on each of the data files. It then stores information on the various files based on the amount of free space remaining. This method ensures that the available space within a filegroup is used efficiently. Once all the files are "full," SQL Server can then automatically expand files as needed (assuming that automatic file growth is enabled). This method reduces the overhead required to grow data files and ensures that the files within a filegroup are used efficiently.

Another useful feature of filegroups is that they can be designated as read-only (see Figure 6-7). That is, all of the objects that are stored within a specific filegroup cannot be written to. This is useful if you have one or more database tables that are used primarily for reference information (often called *lookup tables*) and you do not want them to be modified by applications or users. Read-only filegroups can be used to increase performance by reducing the overhead generated by maintaining a transaction log and performing checkpoints.

Although the use of files and filegroups provides database administrators with much flexibility in designing storage, most small- to medium-sized databases will work just fine using a single data file and a single log file. Additionally, technologies such as RAID can be used to achieve the same effect—spreading data storage across multiple physical devices—with lower administration overhead. That is, to the database server (and database administrator), it appears that all of the data resides within a single file, whereas the data is

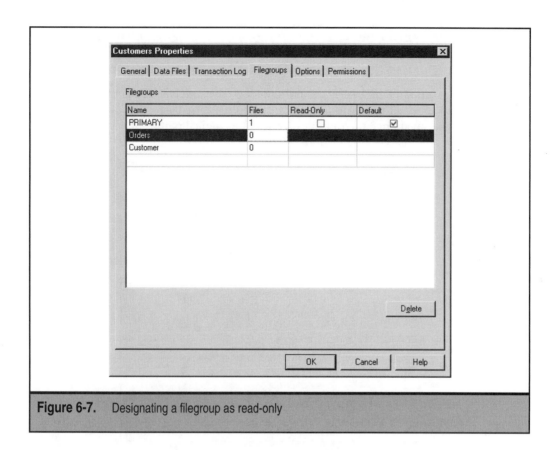

Figure 6-7.   Designating a filegroup as read-only

actually spread across multiple physical disks. For certain types of databases, however, the ability to store indexes and tables on particular files can be worth the extra effort by providing significant improvements in performance by reducing disk I/O contention.

Now that we've covered files and filegroups, let's look at how to create and manage them. In the following sections, I'll provide instructions for performing various tasks with Enterprise Manager and Transact-SQL commands.

Specifying Filegroups for a New Database

To create a SQL Server database that spans more than one filegroup, use the following procedure in SQL Enterprise Manager.

STEP-BY-STEP: SPECIFYING FILEGROUPS FOR A NEW DATABASE

1. Right-click on Databases and select New Database.

2. On the General tab, specify the name of the new database. Select the Data Files tab and specify the files and filegroups you want to use for the database. Note that you can change the default physical and logical names of the data files, as well as automatic sizing options.

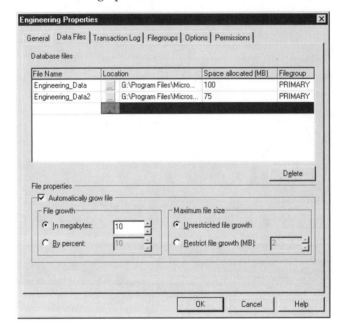

3. Click OK to create the data file(s) and the database.

To create a database using files and filegroups with Transact-SQL, use the following syntax:

```
CREATE DATABASE database_name
[ ON [ PRIMARY ]
        [ < filespec > [ ,...n ] ]
        [ , < filegroup > [ ,...n ] ]
]
[ LOG ON { < filespec > [ ,...n ] } ]
```

```
[ COLLATE collation_name ]
[ FOR LOAD | FOR ATTACH ]

< filespec > ::=

( [ NAME = logical_file_name , ]
    FILENAME = 'os_file_name'
    [ , SIZE = size ]
    [ , MAXSIZE = { max_size | UNLIMITED } ]
    [ , FILEGROWTH = growth_increment ] ) [ ,...n ]

< filegroup > ::=

FILEGROUP filegroup_name < filespec > [ ,...n ]
```

For example, the following command creates a database that spans three filegroups:

```
CREATE DATABASE Sales
ON PRIMARY
   ( NAME='Sales_Primary',
     FILENAME='c:\Data\Sales_Primary.mdf',
     SIZE=4,
     MAXSIZE=10,
     FILEGROWTH=1),
FILEGROUP Sales_FileGroup1
   ( NAME = 'Sales_Group1_File1',
     FILENAME = 'c:\Data\Sales_Group1_File1.ndf',
     SIZE = 1MB,
     MAXSIZE=10,
     FILEGROWTH=1),
   ( NAME = 'Sales_Group1_File2',
     FILENAME = 'c:\Data\Sales_Group1_File2.ndf',
     SIZE = 1MB,
     MAXSIZE=10,
     FILEGROWTH=1)
LOG ON
   ( NAME='Sales_log',
     FILENAME='d:\Logs\Sales_Log.ldf',
     SIZE=1,
     MAXSIZE=10,
     FILEGROWTH=1)
```

Altering Filegroups for an Existing Database

If you have an existing database and want to change its storage parameters, you can use the following procedure in Enterprise Manager.

STEP-BY-STEP: ALTERING FILEGROUP SETTINGS FOR AN EXISTING DATABASE

1. Right-click a database object in Enterprise Manager and select Properties.

2. Select the Data Files tab. Note that you can view and change settings for the data file(s) on which this database resides.

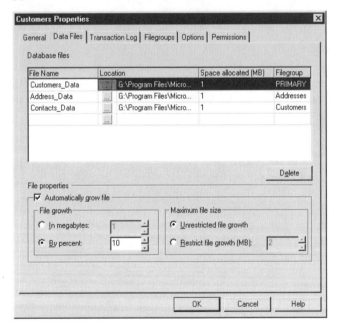

3. Change the file, filename, and filegroup properties to match your storage requirements.

To change filegroup settings for an existing database using Transact-SQL, use the following commands:

```
ALTER DATABASE database
{ ADD FILE < filespec > [ ,...n ] [ TO FILEGROUP filegroup_name ]
| ADD LOG FILE < filespec > [ ,...n ]
| REMOVE FILE logical_file_name [ WITH DELETE ]
| ADD FILEGROUP filegroup_name
| REMOVE FILEGROUP filegroup_name
| MODIFY FILE < filespec >
| MODIFY NAME = new_dbname
| MODIFY FILEGROUP filegroup_name {filegroup_property | NAME = new_filegroup_name }
| COLLATE < collation_name >
}

< filespec > =

( NAME = logical_file_name
[ , NEWNAME = new_logical_name ]
   [ , FILENAME = 'os_file_name' ]
   [ , SIZE = size ]
   [ , MAXSIZE = { max_size | UNLIMITED } ]
   [ , FILEGROWTH = growth_increment ] )
```

Viewing File and Filegroup Information

In many cases, the information you receive through Enterprise Manager will be what you're looking for in regard to storage. However, SQL Server includes built-in stored procedures that can be used for showing information about files and filegroups using Transact-SQL. Table 6-1 provides some commands that can be used to find more information about files and filegroups.

Command	Information Displayed
sp_helpdb	Database size and configuration
sp_helpfile	Data file details
sp_helpfilegroup	Filegroup details
sp_spaceused	Space used by the database and free space remaining

Table 6-1.   Useful Stored Procedures for Viewing File and Filegroup Information

Figure 6-8 shows the results of running a system-stored procedure using SQL Query Analyzer against a sample database that spans multiple filegroups.

Specifying Storage Options for Objects

Now that you know how to create files and filegroups, it's time to take advantage of these storage options. To specify storage options when creating database tables in Enterprise Manager, follow the steps described next.

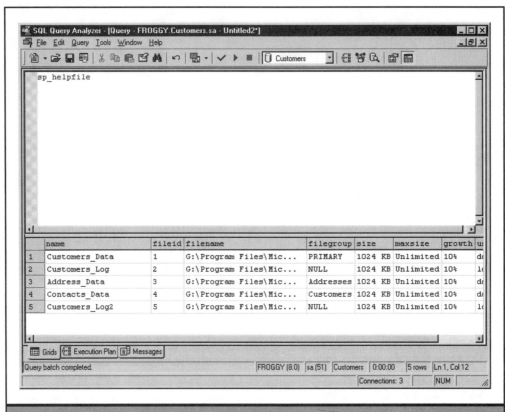

Figure 6-8. Using a stored procedure to view file and filegroup information

STEP-BY-STEP: SPECIFYING STORAGE OPTIONS FOR A NEW TABLE

1. Select and expand the database in which you want to create the table.

2. Right-click Tables and select New Table.

3. When prompted, enter a name for the table.

4. To specify storage options for this object, click the Table and Index Properties button on the toolbar.

5. Specify the settings for the filegroup to be used by your table:

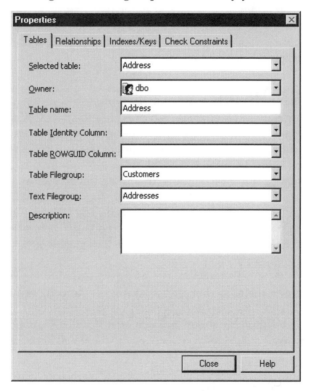

6. Notice that you can specify a different filegroup for any text columns in the table.

You can also use Transact-SQL to specify which file or filegroup the object will physically reside in. For example, you might use the following command to create the Customers table on Filegroup 1:

```
CREATE TABLE Customers (
    CustomerID        int     PRIMARY KEY,
    CustomerName      char(50)

)
ON Sales_FileGroup1
GO
```

Physically, information would be stored in the files that make up this group.

Alternatively, we might specify a file in which the table should be stored, or specify the settings for an index. (For further information on creating database objects, see SQL Server Books Online.)

Optimizing Storage Design

As you can see, using files and filegroups can provide a lot of flexibility in designing your storage options. In many installations, determining the best placement for files in this way might be very difficult. First of all, a good understanding of the usage of the database and its objects is required. To help in finding this information, you can use the various SQL Server performance-monitoring tools (described in Chapter 4). However, these statistics might change over time in accordance with business directions. Usually, a team approach to determining how to best arrange data files is best. Often, database and application developers can provide information about the behavior of an application (and any expected change). With this information, a database or systems administrator can determine how to best handle the data.

If ease of administration and increased performance are both important goals, RAID solutions offer many of the same benefits as using files and filegroups. The drawback, however, is that advanced backup and recovery options related to filegroups cannot be used. The optimal solution in many environments will be to use both RAID and filegroups for very large databases. We'll cover the technical benefits of filegroup backups later in this chapter.

SQL SERVER 2000 BACKUP METHODS

In the preceding discussion, we saw how the use of files and filegroups can help meet the needs of data storage. This same model can be quite helpful in determining database backup methods. Let's start looking at the different types of backups available in SQL Server 2000. You will most likely need to use more than one type in a well-designed backup plan. In this part of the chapter, we'll describe the backup types available and then cover how you can best plan for their use based on your data protection requirements. In all cases, we'll cover at least two ways to get the job done: using the graphical tools that are part of Enterprise Manager, and using Transact-SQL commands.

You may be wondering why you should even bother with the less-intuitive Transact-SQL commands when most operations can be performed within Enterprise Manager. In many cases, Enterprise Manager is the best solution, because it does not require the knowledge of specific syntax. However, when you're creating automated scripts or dealing with very large or complex databases, you might need the additional power afforded by Transact-SQL commands.

NOTE: In version 6.5 and earlier of SQL Server, the term DUMP was used to describe backup operations, and the term LOAD referred to restorations. In addition to the terminology, many differences exist in how these backups are handled. For more information, see the online help files for earlier versions of SQL Server. (The majority of the information in this chapter pertains specifically to SQL Server 2000.)

Offline vs. Online Backups

One of the first decisions you'll need to make about your backups is *how* the data will be stored. Offline, or "cold," backups are performed when the database is shut down and users are not connected. Because the files are not marked as "in-use," the database files can be backed up like any other OS files, with standard backup software (such as the backup utilities included with Windows NT and Windows 2000). Offline backups are useful for environments in which it is possible to shut down the database server for the period of time that is required to back up the database files (including the transaction log). Provided that no changes occur to these files during the backup, all information will be left in a consistent state. After the backup is completed, the database can be restarted.

Offline backups leave much to be desired. First, it is not always feasible to stop database servers every time backups must be performed. Second, starting and stopping database servers can decrease performance as the procedure and data caches are reset. A good alternative is to use online, or "hot," backups. Administrators perform online backups when the database server is online and is being accessed by users. Although it is likely that performance will be decreased during the operation, it is not necessary to stop the database server during the operation. To perform online backups, software that is aware of database issues must be used.

CAUTION: You should never use a tool that claims to back up "open files" to protect SQL Server data. Although the files themselves may be backed up, they will likely be left in an inconsistent and unusable state due to changes that occur during the backup process.

As we saw in Chapter 5, most backup packages allow for saving information to disk, tape, or network devices. Although tools that support this operation can perform online backups, there is another alternative: make regular database dumps to disk devices, and then back up the dump files. The whole operation involves the creation of a database dump (which is, essentially, an export of all the data and objects in a database) to a file system file. This file can then be backed up using normal tape-backup software, since dump files are not marked as "in-use" and are stored as logically consistent at a specific point in time. The main advantages to this method of data protection are that no special database options are required for the backup package, and database and OS backups can be combined in the same backup sets. The drawback of performing database dumps is that they can require excessive disk space (usually equal to the size of the database plus the transaction log at any given time). Figure 6-9 shows the flow of data in a database dump scenario.

NOTE: As we'll see later in this chapter, SQL Server 2000 includes features for performing online and offline database backups, as well as dumps of data to disk files.

Taking Databases Offline

In previous versions of SQL Server, performing certain operations (such as database re- stores) were problematic. The main reason was that these operations required a database administrator to have exclusive access to the database before the operation could be car- ried out. One way to solve this problem was to manually use the sp_who (or sp_who2) stored procedure to determine which users(s) were in a database and then use the KILL command to terminate those connections. This was a rather painstaking process, and it was difficult to ensure that no new connections would be established before the real task—such as a database recovery—was started. The other method for removing data- base connections (and preventing them from being created) was to stop the entire SQL Server Service and then start it in single-user mode. Of course, this had the disadvantage of disconnecting all connections to *all* databases and prevented users from accessing the entire installation. Clearly, a better method was needed.

Fortunately, SQL Server 2000 includes the ability to take a database offline. This can easily be done in Enterprise Manager by right-clicking on a database, selecting All Tasks, and then clicking on Take Offline (see Figure 6-10).

When a database is taken offline, it is made unavailable for use. The database can be taken offline only when no users are currently accessing the database. Once the database is marked as offline, it cannot be accessed by any users. Users attempting to connect to the database will receive the following error message:

```
Database 'Test' cannot be opened because it is offline.
```

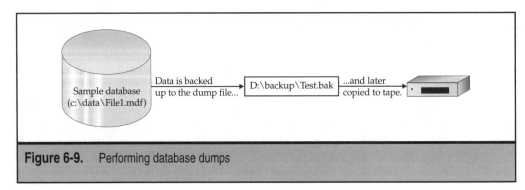

Figure 6-9. Performing database dumps

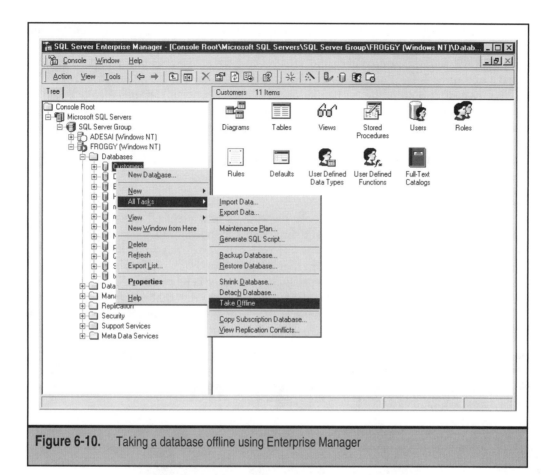

Figure 6-10.   Taking a database offline using Enterprise Manager

However, with the database offline, a database administrator can perform maintenance operations (such as backups and restores). Once the operations are complete, the
database can be brought online (by right-clicking on the database name, selecting All
Tasks, and then clicking on Bring Online), and it will be ready for use.

Attaching and Detaching Databases

Sometimes, it is necessary to move raw data files to different directories on a server or between database servers. However, you cannot simply move the files in the file system
while a database is online because the files themselves will be marked as being "in-use."
You could, however, shut down SQL Server and then move the data files. However,
when SQL Server was restarted, it would not be able to find the files and would mark the
databases as "Suspect." So how *should* you move data files?

In SQL Server, you can attach and detach databases on an installation of SQL Server. This can most easily be done in Enterprise Manager by right-clicking on a database, choosing All Tasks, and then clicking Detach Database. Note that you will have the option of updating the statistics for a database before you detach it (see Figure 6-11).

To reattach a database, you can simply right-click on the Databases folder for the server to which you want to attach the database. Then, select All Tasks and Attach Database. You'll see a dialog box that can be used for finding the appropriate data files (see Figure 6-12).

We'll cover the details of attaching and detaching databases in Chapter 9.

Comparing Backup Schemes

The overall goal of performing database backups is to protect all of your information. Based on time, resource, technical, and financial constraints, however, it might not be possible to back up all of the information as frequently as desired. In many environments, for example, the volume of information that must be stored is simply too large. In others, limitations on the capacity of hardware devices and media have placed restrictions. Fortunately, there are several different ways to perform backups that can work within such constraints. In the next few sections, we'll look at how we can use the types of backup operations that are available for administrators of SQL Server 2000.

NOTE: In Chapter 2, we examined the various types of backups available at a basic level. They included full, incremental, and differential backups. If you're unfamiliar with those types of backup procedures, now would be a good time to review that information.

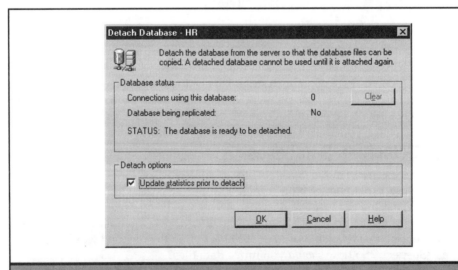

Figure 6-11. Detaching a database in Enterprise Manager

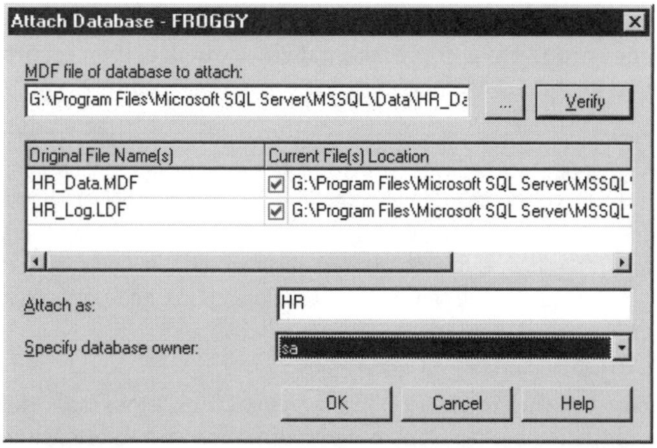

Figure 6-12.   Attaching a database in Enterprise Manager

Full Database Backups

The easiest type of backup to understand is a full database backup. As its name implies, a full backup operation stores all the data and objects that are currently part of a database. This includes the information stored within tables, as well as the definitions of objects, such as triggers, stored procedures, views, and user permissions. Each full backup is consistent up to the time of the *end* of the preceding full backup. Additionally, full backups are the only type of backup that can be performed on the *master* database. A full backup is performed according to the following sequence:

1. The backup operation starts copying data from the beginning of the physical file(s) for a database and makes note of this time.

2. The data and objects stored in the data pages are read from the media serially. At this point the backup process does not track any transactions that may modify the files during the process itself. The pages are written to the backup media, as they are, until all the information has been stored. The result is a fast backup operation, but the pages are consistent to different points in time.

3. After all data pages have been copied, the backed up data must be made consistent to a single point in time (in order to ensure transactional consistency and data integrity). Any changes made to the data since the beginning of the backup operation are now obtained from the transaction log and recorded at the end of the backup file. The result is a database backup file that is consistent up to the time of the *end* of the backup operation.

This process, diagrammed in Figure 6-13, is very efficient, mainly because the backup operation does not wait for transactions and other database modifications to finish. It reads the data pages serially and copies the data in sequence, then records all the changes at the end of the process.

> **REMEMBER:** Although full backups do store information from transaction logs, they do not truncate the log itself at the end of the operation. Therefore, if you are using only full backups in your data protection plan, you must periodically truncate the transaction log as a separate operation. For ease of administration, you can schedule this job to occur automatically. Or if you are sure that other types of backups will not be required, you can set the Truncate Log On Checkpoint option for your database.

Transaction Log Backups

As we saw in Chapter 4, the transaction log is critical for the normal operations of the database. This logical file is used to improve performance and to ensure database integrity by storing a record of all the changes that occur to a database before they are made. In SQL Server 2000, as in most relational databases, you can choose to back up the transaction log only at specific points in time.

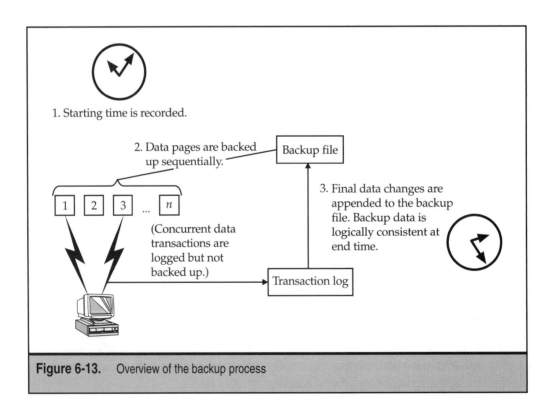

Figure 6-13. Overview of the backup process

Backing up the transaction log provides two main functional advantages:

▼   The amount of information stored in transaction logs will likely be much less than the size of the entire database itself. Because of this, backing up the transaction log can take less time.

▲   The use of transaction log backups can allow for *point-in-time recovery*. This feature allows database administrators to recover databases up to a specific time during the day. If, for example, a user ran a SQL command that deleted all the information in a table at 3:15 P.M., the table could be restored up to its current state at 3:14 P.M.

NOTE: By default, the transaction log is truncated after it is backed up. If you have special requirements (for example, if you're creating multiple backups of the transaction log), you will want to disable
this option.

Typically, database administrators schedule transaction log backups to occur between full backups. For example, if a full backup is performed every night, transaction
log backups might be scheduled to occur every three hours during the day. We'll get into
the details of transaction log files in Chapter 8. For now, it's important to understand that
to recover data for a database using transaction logs, you must have a copy of the last full
backup of the database plus an *unbroken sequence* of transaction log backups since the
backup completed. Figure 6-14 shows the files required for a sample recovery to a specific
point in time.

Differential Backups

In order to provide additional flexibility in backup operations, SQL Server 2000 includes
the ability to perform differential backups. Differential backups work much like transaction log backups in that they record all the changes that occurred in the database since the

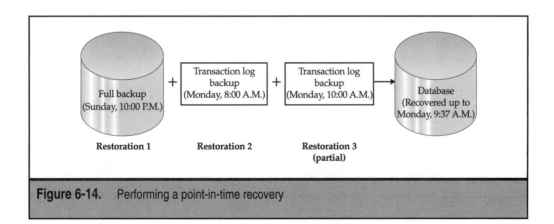

Figure 6-14.   Performing a point-in-time recovery

last full backup. Notice that this is different from transaction log backups, which are used to record transactions (data modifications) that occurred since the last transaction log backup. Differential backups record all the changes that occurred in the database since the last full backup. If the latest differential backup is corrupt or otherwise unavailable, you still have the option of using the prior differential backup. As is the case with a full backup, after recovery, your database will be left in a state that is consistent up to the time that the backup is completed. Figure 6-15 shows how restoring a full backup, then a differential one, can result in a consistent database.

Differential backups are implemented on a schedule that is very similar to that of transaction log backups. That is, they are usually scheduled to occur at predefined times between full backup operations. If you attempt to perform a differential backup and no full backup has been made of the database, you will be warned and will not be allowed to create the backup. This is important since a differential backup must be used in conjunction with a full backup when restoring a database. Later in this chapter, we'll see that SQL Server 2000 also offers significant performance improvements over differential backups performed in SQL Server 7.

File and Filegroup Backups

In some cases, databases are so large that performing a full backup is not feasible at any time. In this case, you might choose to back up only certain files at certain times. In Chapter 4, we mentioned that database objects could be stored on specific files. SQL Server 2000 allows database administrators to back up one or more files from such a database in a single operation. Figure 6-16 depicts the structure of a database that uses multiple files. Notice that the tables are stored in specific filegroups.

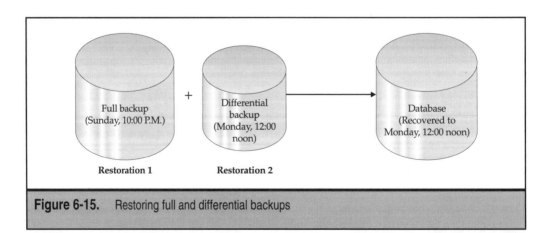

Figure 6-15. Restoring full and differential backups

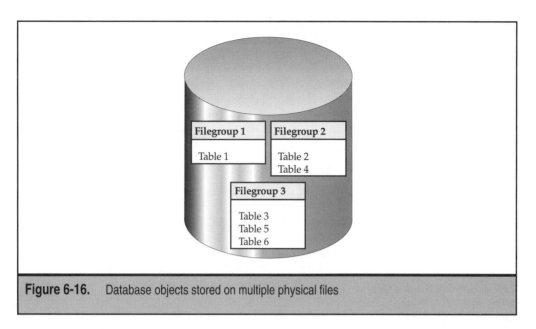

Figure 6-16. Database objects stored on multiple physical files

Table 6-2 shows a sample backup schedule that might be employed for a database that consists of multiple data files. It shows when certain files will be backed up. By using the backup schedule described in Table 6-2, you can reduce the amount of data that is backed up during each operation and still keep tables consistent. However, if you lose the entire database, you will need to restore each file individually. All of the backups must be valid and usable before the database can be brought online again. Overall, however, the ability to perform file and filegroup backups provides the flexibility to manage large databases with limited hardware and other resources.

Backup Filegroup	Contents	Day of the Week (at 1:00 A.M.)
Filegroup 1	Table 1	Friday
Filegroup 2	Table 2 Table 4	Saturday
Filegroup 3	Table 3 Table 5 Table 6	Sunday

Table 6-2. Sample Backup Schedule for Databases That Span Multiple Files

Combining Backup Operations

For larger databases, full, differential, and transaction log backups can be combined. If implemented properly, these operations together can provide a good level of data protection while minimizing the impact on performance. Generally, it is recommended that you perform differential backups between full backup operations and that you perform transaction log backups between differential backups. Although this may seem like a lot of work in setting up your data protection plan, it provides for a high level of data protection, allows for point-in-time recovery, and minimizes the negative performance effects that backups can have on users. We'll revisit this idea in Chapter 7.

Choosing Database Recovery Models

Often, database administrators have to make trade-offs between performance and security of data. For example, if it's critical that information is not lost in your database, you might choose to perform very frequent transaction log backups. However, this would be at the expense of performance, as there will always be some overhead involved in generating the transaction log backups. On the other hand, if performance was the most important factor and data loss was acceptable, you might choose to truncate the transaction log at every checkpoint.

A major architectural change in SQL Server 2000 is the feature of database recovery models. In previous versions of SQL Server, database administrators had little flexibility in controlling the use of transaction logs. There are three main database recovery models supported in SQL Server 2000. Table 6-3 lists the various recovery models that are available and describes their effects on recovery operations.

Recovery Model	Meaning	Backup and Recovery Issues	Notes
Full	All transactions are logged.	All backup and recovery operations can be performed.	Used when data recovery is important, but can result in decreased performance.
Bulk Logged	All transactions except bulk operations are logged.	Can recover to the end of the latest full, differential, or transaction log backup; cannot perform point-in-time recovery.	Good balance of data protection and performance as long as bulk operations can be easily re-performed.

Table 6-3. Comparison of SQL Server 2000 Recovery Models

Recovery Model	Meaning	Backup and Recovery Issues	Notes
Simple	Logging of transactions is disabled (similar to "truncate log on checkpoint" in earlier versions of SQL Server).	Can only use full and differential backups (transaction log backups cannot be used); cannot recover past end of last backup.	Offers highest performance and lowest disk space usage, but lowest amount of data protection. Should only be used if loss of data between backups is acceptable.

Table 6-3.   Comparison of SQL Server 2000 Recovery Models *(continued)*

The Bulk Logged operation reduces the size of the transaction log because it does not log the following operations:

▼ SELECT INTO

■ bcp

■ BULK INSERT

■ CREATE INDEX

■ Creation of indexed views

▲ Manipulation of text and image data types (including WRITETEXT and UPDATETEXT)

In general, the Simple recovery model is most useful for relatively unimportant systems such as testing, staging, or development servers. Since it does not offer a high level of data protection, you should understand the limited backup and recovery options available.

When new databases are created, they will have the same recovery model as the *model* database. With SQL Server 2000, database administrators can easily change the recovery model used for a database, even while the database is operational. This is done by using the ALTER DATABASE command. For example, to set the recovery model for the Northwind sample database, you can use the following statements:

```
-- Set recovery mode to Full
ALTER DATABASE Northwind
SET RECOVERY Full
GO
```

```
-- Set recovery mode to Bulk Logged
ALTER DATABASE Northwind
SET RECOVERY Bulk_Logged
GO

-- Set recovery mode to Simple
ALTER DATABASE Northwind
SET RECOVERY Simple
GO
```

It is important to note that transaction log backups can only be performed if the database recovery model is set to Full or Bulk Logged. We'll cover additional details related to performing recovery based on the database recovery model in Chapter 8.

Establishing a Backup Schedule

In general, you should always perform a full or differential database backup immediately after you perform a nonlogged operation. *Nonlogged operations* are those that either cannot be recorded in the transaction log or are purposely declared as nonlogged to prevent the log from filling up. As mentioned above, examples include performing bulk copy operations (performed with the bcp command or Data Transformation Services, for example), executing SELECT INTO statements, and dealing with text data types (using the WRITETEXT and UPDATETEXT commands). When SQL Server encounters these operations, it records the fact that they were performed (along with any changes to physical data files or pages), but does not record the content of the records that have been added or have changed. Therefore, transaction log backups will be invalid and cannot be applied after they occur.

Performing a full or differential database backup after nonlogged operations will ensure that, in the event that you need to recover information, the last backup will be in a consistent state. Other advantages include a certain level of fault tolerance, because if certain backups end up being corrupt or unavailable, other files can be used to restore to a point after the last full backup was performed.

Accommodating Your Users

The major negative effect of performing backups will be a reduction in overall system performance. Other trade-offs include the following operations, which cannot be performed during a database backup:

▼ Creating indexes

■ Creating or deleting database files

■ Performing nonlogged operations (as described in the preceding section)

▲ Expanding or shrinking the database

The users' needs should be a primary concern during backup operations. If usage is heavy during a certain time of day, you might choose not to back up information during that time, to avoid negative impacts on performance. However, if the data is very valuable, you may need to perform backups during this time; if so, do let your users know of any potential performance lags. Also, keep in mind that usage patterns might be very different from what you expected. Although it is unlikely that users will be modifying information in the middle of the night for a local database, international data repositories might be used heavily around the clock.

Historically, systems and database administrators often spent much time determining an optimal "backup window." In some cases, they even made the system temporarily unavailable to avoid any problems that occurred with the backup. With SQL Server 2000, these efforts may be largely unnecessary. Database administrators should measure the impact of performing backups on their live systems. In many cases, you'll likely find that the impact is minimal and that you may not even need to specifically define a backup window. Of course, you'll still want to schedule the operations to occur at a specific time when loads are below their peak.

Now let's combine the information we've covered so far into a backup schedule.

Sample Backup Schedule

In this example, we'll assume that XYZ Corporation maintains a database of all its sales transactions. Data is collected and input from 300 cashiers in 30 stores. The normal operating hours for the stores are from 7:30 A.M. to 6:00 P.M., Monday through Saturday, with most stores closed on Sundays. Performance at the point of sale is vital, because it affects business. Table 6-4 provides a sample data protection schedule combining the various backup types.

Operation	Day of the Week	Starting Time(s)	Notes
Full backup	Sunday	4:00 P.M.	User activity is minimal on Sunday afternoon.
Differential backup	Monday Tuesday Wednesday Thursday Friday Saturday	8:00 A.M. 12:00 noon 5:00 P.M. 8:00 P.M.	No significant database changes are expected outside the hours of 8:00 A.M. to 8:00 P.M.

Table 6-4.   Sample Data Protection Schedule

Operation	Day of the Week	Starting Time(s)	Notes
Transaction log backup	Monday Tuesday Wednesday Thursday Friday Saturday	9:00 A.M. 10:00 A.M. 11:00 A.M. 1:00 P.M. 2:00 P.M. 3:00 P.M. 4:00 P.M. 6:00 P.M. 7:00 P.M.	A maximum of one hour of data loss is tolerable.

Table 6-4.   Sample Data Protection Schedule *(continued)*

Notice that Table 6-4 makes some critical assumptions. Before such a schedule is mandated, managers and users should be in agreement, for example, that losing up to one hour's worth of data is acceptable in a worst-case scenario. Spreading backup times throughout the day and using differential and transaction log backups minimizes the performance impact that is likely to occur as a result of the backup operations. Hopefully, with this solution, XYZ's customers and employees won't have to wait as long for transactions to complete during busy times.

In Chapter 7, we'll see how these backups can be used, including the details of what you can do if certain backups are corrupt or invalid. And, in Chapter 8, we'll determine additional backup schedules and present scenarios that will provide for more specific requirements.

Additional Backup Solutions

In addition to the types of backups described already, there are several other ways to protect information. In this section, we'll take a brief look at some more advanced data protection options.

▼ **Data Transformation Services (DTS)**   By using DTS to copy data to and from other data repositories, you can protect your organization's most important information. Depending on the type of data, this might be an ideal solution. For example, if daily summaries of sales performance are more important than a list of the actual transactions, you might want to calculate this data periodically and store the results in an Excel spreadsheet.

■ **Replication**   Although the primary purpose of replication is to distribute information, it can serve as a good way to back up information. SQL Server 2000 supports several different types of replication. If you have requirements to distribute information across a WAN or to multiple servers, replication can make sure that the information stays synchronized. When implemented properly, replication can provide for an automatic off-site copy of important information. The trade-off (it's always something!) is the bandwidth that is required for transferring data and a possible loss of some information after a server failure.

■ **Standby servers**   Often referred to as "warm backup" devices, standby servers provide the ability to perform a quick recovery from a failed server situation. The idea is that a second server will always maintain a copy of all the data stored on the production machine. To keep data synchronized, a constant process called *log-shipping* is used. In this process, transaction logs are periodically created on the production server and are then automatically restored to the standby machine. In the event of a failure, the standby server can be reconfigured with the name and network information of the production server, or users can be redirected to the new machine. Note, however, that this change must be handled at the client or application side, since the information about the server will change. Although some downtime will occur, it will be nowhere near the amount of time required to rebuild an entire database or server from scratch.

▲ **Clustering**   A *cluster*, defined simply, is a collection of machines that appear to act as one. There are two main benefits to clustering your servers. The first is fail-over support. In a clustered configuration, if one server becomes unavailable, the other automatically takes its place, thus eliminating downtime. The other benefit is an increase in performance caused by load balancing. In this configuration, multiple disk, memory, processor, and network subsystems can work together to provide information to users as quickly as possible. Clustering technology is complex and expensive because it involves sharing hard disks and providing for redundant network connections. However, it provides for maximum availability and can increase performance. The goal is for failures to be transparent (other than possible loss in performance).

Each of these technologies can be quite complex (although Microsoft has made them easy to work with in SQL Server 2000). Since they're such powerful features, further discussion in a book about backup and recovery is a must! We'll cover these data protection options in detail in Chapter 9.

SQL SERVER 2000 BACKUP AND RECOVERY ARCHITECTURE ENHANCEMENTS

When it comes to dealing with databases of any size, data protection is one of the foremost concerns. (The fact that you're reading this book is good evidence that you already realize this!) Often, many decisions must be made regarding how the data should be protected. We looked at the important issues related to planning for and developing a data protection plan in Part I.

With the release of SQL Server 2000, Microsoft has included many new enhancements related to backup and recovery. One of these is support for restoring backups from a previous version of SQL Server. In SQL Server 2000, database administrators can restore backups that were created on SQL Server 7. Note, however, that the reverse is not true—that is, SQL Server 2000 backups cannot be used by SQL Server 7.

In Chapter 4, I provided an overview of many of the new features and enhancements in SQL Server 2000. And earlier in this chapter, we looked at some specific methods that can be used to enhance backup operations. In this section, we'll look at some of the features that are new (and/or improved) in SQL Server 2000, and we'll discuss how they may affect your backup and recovery plans.

Fast Differential Backup

As I mentioned earlier, the idea behind differential backups is to store only the data that has changed in a database since the last full backup. For many types of databases, this method offers several advantages over the use of transaction logs. First and foremost, in highly active systems, differential backups store only information about the actual data that has changed. When it comes time to perform a recovery, SQL Server does not need to rerun all of the transactions in the log in order to place the database in a consistent state. Instead, it can just reread the modified pages and write them back to the "live" database. The overall result can be a dramatic saving in time. Differential backups also tend to be smaller than transaction log backups, thus saving valuable disk or tape space.

In SQL Server 7, the differential backup process had the advantages that I mentioned previously. However, there was one drawback: differential backups could take quite a while to perform since SQL Server had to scan through all of the pages in the entire database to detect changed data. This has been improved in SQL Server 2000. Now, SQL Server can quickly and easily pinpoint which data pages have been changed without scanning the entire database. The result is that differential backups are performed much more quickly—another advantage of using them.

Snapshot Backups

Although the standard SQL Server 2000 backup and recovery operations will be sufficient for many environments, it is sometimes necessary to be able to produce a quick, exact copy of a database. This may be done for fault-tolerance purposes and to protect against data loss or downtime in the event of a failure of disks. Snapshot backups provide a mechanism for making an immediate copy of a database on another machine. This "snapshot" can then be sent to another machine that may be responsible for performing a backup of it. As the backup operation is running on another system, there will be no performance impact to the original system.

We'll revisit the concept of snapshot backups in Chapter 10. Snapshot backup solutions are available through third-party vendors that support this technology. For more information, see the Microsoft SQL Server web site at **www.microsoft.com/sql**.

Log-Shipping

The idea behind log-shipping is to periodically use transaction log backups to keep two databases synchronized. For example, let's consider the case of two servers—one named Production and another named Standby. There is a database called Sales on each server (assume that they are currently synchronized). A database administrator may design a system that automatically performs a transaction log backup on the Production server, copies it to the Standby server, and then restores the transaction log on the Standby server. As long as the Standby server is left in a read-only state, the data can remain consistent between the two machines. In the event of a failure, the database administrator can instruct users and applications to connect to the Standby server.

Although log-shipping was a supported operation in previous versions of SQL Server, it had to be implemented manually. This was a painstaking process that required database administrators to track and verify the proper shipment and application of log files. Although tools available in the SQL Server Resource Kits could be used, the process was fairly difficult to implement and manage. As shown in Figure 6-17, in SQL Server 2000, log-shipping is now an operation that is supported through the use of the Database Maintenance Plan Wizard.

We'll cover the details of implementing and managing log-shipping in Chapter 9.

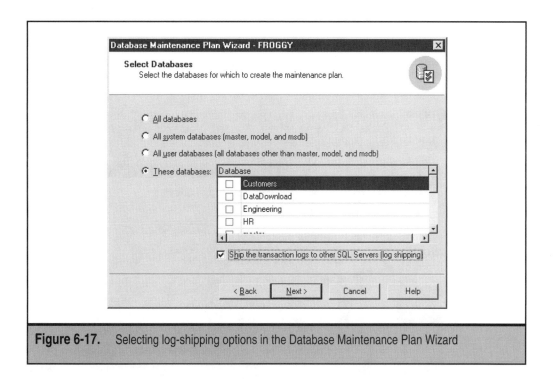

Figure 6-17. Selecting log-shipping options in the Database Maintenance Plan Wizard

Copy Database Wizard

A common operation in many organizations is to copy databases between servers. This is often done, for example, to create another instance of a database for reporting purposes or for testing. In previous versions of SQL Server, the process was reasonably simple through the use of backup and restore operations. However, differences in server configuration (for example, different directory structures) could make the process somewhat tedious.

In SQL Server 2000, the Copy Database Wizard can be used to more easily move or copy databases between installations of SQL Server 2000. Using this process, you can transfer any user database (the master, model, and msdb databases cannot be transferred) and upgrade SQL Server 7.0 databases to SQL Server 2000. The process does not support changing the name of the database, so database administrators must ensure that naming is consistent between machines. A useful feature of the Copy Database Wizard is that a third server can be used to copy information between two other servers. This decreases the amount of processing and data transfer load on each of the machines, while still getting the job done.

NOTE: Copying databases is generally an operation that should be performed for testing and development purposes. It is not designed to be a replacement for regularly scheduled backups!

To copy a database using the Copy Database Wizard, you can utilize the following procedure.

STEP-BY-STEP: USING THE COPY DATABASE WIZARD

1. In Enterprise Manager, right-click on the name of an instance of SQL Server 2000. Select All Tasks | Copy Database Wizard. You will see an overview of the information that the wizard will require:

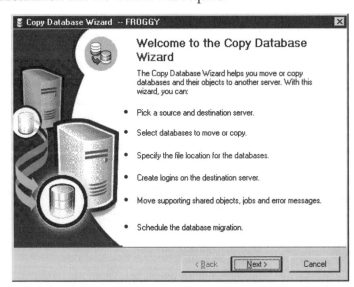

2. To begin the process, click Next. You will be prompted for information about the source server. Click Next to continue.

3. Enter information about the destination server. Click Next to continue. Note that the source and destination servers must be different servers or different instances of SQL Server 2000. Click Next.

4. In the next step, you'll be required to choose which database(s) you want to copy to the destination server. Note that the dialog box shows information about the status of the database on the destination instance. If the status is displayed as "OK," the copy can be performed. Place a check mark in the appropriate box to move or copy the desired database(s). Click Next to continue.

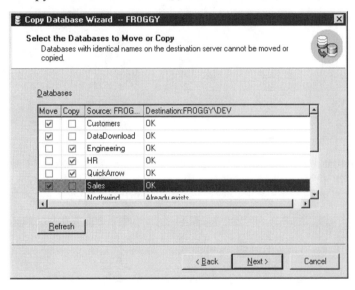

5. In the Database File Location step, the Copy Database Wizard will inform you of any conflicts or problems that may occur during the data transfer:

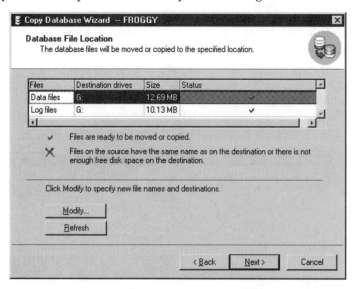

6. To change database file options, click on the Modify button. Here, you'll be given the opportunity to change the location of any of the physical files on the destination server. Click OK to continue, and then click Next.

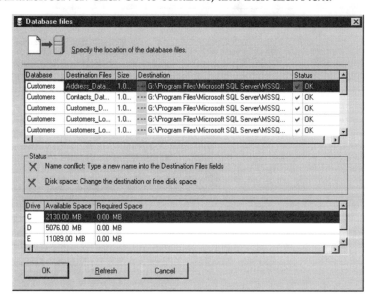

7. You'll be prompted to enter information related to which objects and settings you want to copy to the destination database. Make the appropriate choices, and then click Next.

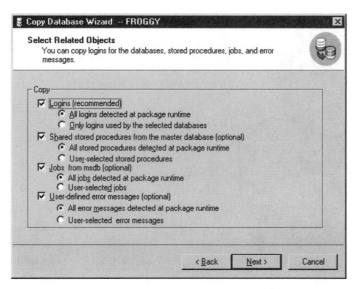

8. In the final step of the Copy Database Wizard, you'll be given the option to define the operation you specified as a Package. The Package can then be run immediately or be scheduled to run at a later time. Make the appropriate choice and click Next to continue.

9. Finally, you'll be provided with a summary of the operations you specified. Note that you can copy this text and place it in your server documentation, if desired. To begin (or schedule) the Copy Database operation, click Finish.

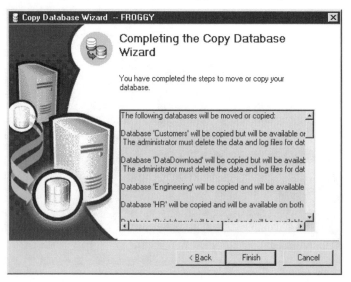

Logical Log Marks

A huge benefit of performing transaction log backups is the ability to perform point-in-time recovery. One of the problems related to working with point-in-time recovery, however, is in determining exactly when the unwanted transaction was performed. For example, suppose a database user knows that he or she accidentally ran a poorly written transaction that deleted much valuable information. However, the user only knows that the transaction ran "sometime just before lunch." In previous versions of SQL Server, you would have to guess the time of the transaction and recover to that point. If you chose a time that was too early, you would not recover as much data as possible. If you chose one that was too late (after the bad transaction was run), you'd still have the data corruption problem and would have to restart the recovery with another guess.

As you can see, the process can be quite tedious and error prone. In SQL Server 2000, Microsoft has included the ability to place logical names for marks in the transaction log by naming transactions. For example, the following transaction syntax can be used:

```
BEGIN TRANSACTION WITH MARK 'Dangerous Transaction'
     DELETE FROM Employee WHERE ID > 1173
COMMIT TRANSACTION
```

The information for the logical log marks is stored in the **logmarkhistory** table. When performing a recovery operation, you can use the WITH STOPATMARK = 'markname' or WITH STOPBEFOREMARK = 'markname' option to restore to a point in time related to the running of the transaction. We'll cover the details of performing this type of recovery in Chapter 8.

IMPLEMENTING SQL SERVER BACKUPS

As I mentioned in the introduction of this book, the steps required to perform backup and recovery operations are actually a very small part of a good data protection plan. However, they are one of the most important; you can plan for months, but if you don't properly execute the designed plan, it will be of little value. In this part of the chapter, we'll look at the various commands and features available in SQL Server 2000 for performing backup operations. The first step will be preparing security and media for backup operations. Then, we'll start with the easiest method: the Database Maintenance Plan Wizard. Using the wizard will provide new users with a good idea of the types of operations that are possible in SQL Server 2000. Next, we'll move on to more detailed methods for situations in which you require additional control of your backups. Finally, we'll look at some other ways of transferring data into and out of your SQL Server installation.

Let's get started by looking at the steps you'll want to take when preparing to perform backups.

Preparing for Backups

Before you implement a data protection solution, it's important to take the time to ensure that you are ready to perform the required operations. Let's look at some of the prerequisites and considerations you should take into account before you perform database backups.

Assigning Permissions

When managing backup security permissions, systems and database administrators normally take the most utilitarian view—that is, giving full permissions to those who need to perform backups. In various database products (including early versions of SQL Server), managing these permissions was quite difficult. In SQL Server 2000, however, Microsoft has included several built-in security roles for easing the administration of security. (We covered these in detail in Chapter 4.)

By default, the systems administrator (the *sa* login) has the permissions to perform any operations on the database. All members of Windows NT/2000 Administrators group are automatically mapped to this login, as well. Although you can assign logins to roles at the server level, it is more likely that you'll want to give specific operators permissions on existing databases. To perform backups of a database, users must be members of the db_owner or db_backupoperator role on the database. Alternatively, you can create additional roles and/or users that have the required permissions to perform backups. Once the appropriate permissions have been assigned, you can move on to the actual steps required for performing backups.

Working with Backup Media

The term *backup media* is used to describe any type of storage on which you can record data. The term refers to physical storage and is limited to disk or tape. A *backup device* resides on the media and is a logical storage structure that stores information in an organized format.

Before you can execute a backup or recovery operation, you must first decide which type of device you want to store your information on. The choices available in SQL Server 2000 include the following:

▼ **Disk devices**   As the name implies, disk storage devices reside on hard disks. A disk device is specified by a full pathname that points to a file within the file system (for example, c:\Backups\Backup.bak). When creating backup files, you should be sure to use an organized naming convention and verify that locations to which backups will be stored have enough space.

When performing backups, you can refer to the backup device using its physical name (the full path and filename of the file) or with a logical name given to this device. The logical name is preferred, because it abstracts the underlying file system path and filenames, it is easier to remember, and reduces the chance that you'll make mistakes when specifying where your backups should dump information. When storing files, you may choose to use remote storage devices. For example, to store information on a remote server, you can use the Universal Naming Convention (UNC) pathname \\Server1\Backups\server1.bak. Of course, the SQL Server service account must have access to this remote share before data can be dumped remotely.

When implementing disk devices and choosing file locations, you should carefully consider the reasons for the backup. In general, it is not advisable to store backups on the same physical disks as the databases themselves, because if the disk itself fails, both the database and the backups will be lost. You can circumvent this sort of loss by using fault-tolerance technology (such as RAID, mentioned earlier), or by providing frequent backups of the database dumps and storing them on a remote machine or on tape. Additionally, if you want to provide only for point-in-time recovery (and not against hardware failures), storing files to the same disk is acceptable.

■ **Tape devices**   If the server on which SQL Server resides contains a tape backup device, you can use it for storing backups. The main advantages of tape media are that storage is less expensive and the media is removable. However, tape storage devices have slower access times and slower throughput. Local tape devices in SQL Server 2000 use a special notation of a double backslash followed by a period (for example, \\.\tape1). SQL Server 2000 does not support the direct use of remote tape storage devices (that is, tape devices that are physically attached to other servers) for backups. However, if you want to back up remotely, you might choose to dump data to a disk device first and then back it up over the network using another utility.

▲ **Named Pipe devices**   Named Pipe devices are not supported directly through the SQL Server 2000 administrative tool, but they can be accessed via the BACKUP command. This method is provided mainly for third-party software products to receive and process information from SQL Server. (We looked at some of these in Chapter 5.) Named Pipes are logical network connections that can be accessed from the same machine or other computers, such as clients or other servers.

To create a disk, tape, or Named Pipe dump device, you can use Enterprise Manager or the sp_addumpdevice stored procedure. For example, the following command creates a disk dump device using Transact-SQL:

```
EXEC sp_addumpdevice 'disk', 'DatabaseDumpDevice',
 'c:\Backups\BackupFile.bak'
```

All backups are stored in Microsoft Tape Format (MTF). The name is somewhat misleading, because, although it was originally created for storing data sequentially on tape devices, the same format is used for disk devices, as well. MTF is used for keeping database files and objects in a consistent format regardless of file locations and device types.

NOTE: Since the Windows NT and Windows 2000 Backup utilities also use the Microsoft Tape Format for recording data, you can store operating system and database server backups on the same media. However, you should ensure that only one operation will occur at a given time to avoid contention for the tape device.

When a backup is performed, a database administrator may choose to perform one of three operations. First, if this media has never been used before, it can be initialized. The initialization process writes the appropriate header information to the backup device and prepares it for storing the first backup set. The other two options are available if the device has already been initialized. To preserve the contents of the device and add the backup set to the end, the APPEND option is specified. To delete all existing contents of the device, the OVERWRITE option is specified. (We'll see how to qualify these operations later, when we discuss the BACKUP command.)

Configuring Media Retention

One of the last things you'll probably want to see when your data is at stake is a systems or database administrator fumbling through a pile of media chanting, "It's *got* to be in here *somewhere!*" Avoid this frightening scenario by making sure that your backup tapes are clearly labeled. Keep in mind that it is very easy to forget to change tapes and thus have a full backup overwritten by the last transaction log backup. Organization is extremely important, because you will likely be managing many different pieces of removable media as well as disk-based backups. Fortunately, SQL Server offers ways to help manage media and devices.

SQL Server 2000 includes a "media retention" value that can be defined as a serverwide setting. This value specifies the default amount of time that must elapse before backups expire and the media can be reused. The purpose is to protect against accidental overwriting of media files. If you attempt to overwrite data before the retention period has passed, SQL Server will give you a warning. This option can, however, be overridden in the event that you are sure the media is no longer needed. The default setting is to retain media for 0 days (thereby effectively disabling the feature). To set the media retention value using Enterprise Manager, use the following procedure.

STEP-BY-STEP: CONFIGURING MEDIA RETENTION VALUES IN ENTERPRISE MANAGER

1. Right-click the name of a server and select Properties.

2. Click the Database Settings tab.

3. For Default Backup Media Retention, select a value for the number of days that the media should be retained. Valid values are from 0 through 365.

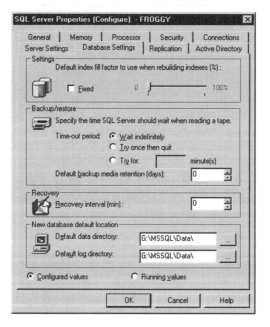

4. Click OK to save the setting.

You can perform the same configuration change from Transact-SQL by using the system-stored sp_configure procedure. (See SQL Server Books Online for details.)

Media Sets and Families

Two other features designed to help organize backups are media sets and media families. When dealing with multiple tape drives and removable storage devices, it can become very difficult to keep track of backups. A *media set* is the group of all media that is used in a database backup. For a simple backup to a single tape, the media set consists of only one tape. In the case of multiple tape devices and media, the situation becomes more complex, as shown in Figure 6-18. Here a single large backup job requires three tape devices, each of which uses three tapes. The total media set consists of nine tapes. This concept is important during recovery, since restoring the database will likely involve all the tapes in the media set.

A *media family* consists of all the tapes or other media that are used for backup by a single device, as shown in Figure 6-19. The first tape (or disk) in each media family is called the *initial media,* and all others are referred to as *continuation media.* SQL Server keeps track of the sequence of these tapes. (As we'll see in Chapter 7, this information is very important when you're trying to restore an entire database.)

When more than one tape backup device is used for backing up a database, multiple media families are combined within a single media set. (Notice that the media set shown in Figure 6-18 contains three media families, each with one initial media tape and two continuation media tapes.)

The RESTORE command can be used to view information about backup devices and their contents. (Again, we'll cover this information in Chapter 7.)

Database Consistency Checker Commands

Although it is no longer a required part of database maintenance, you may want to regularly check your databases for any problems such as data corruption. The Database Consistency Checker (DBCC) commands have been created to do just that.

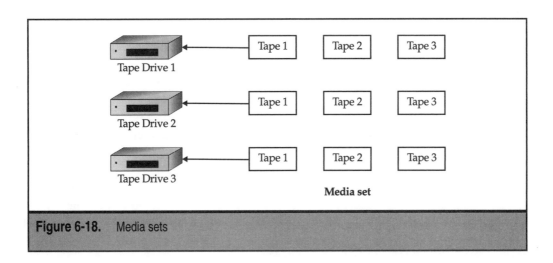

Figure 6-18. Media sets

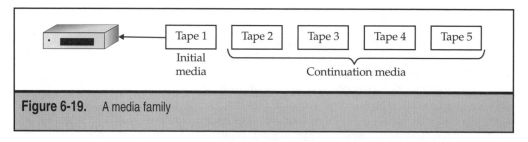

Figure 6-19.   A media family

If you're used to the lethargic performance of DBCC on earlier versions of SQL Server, you'll be pleasantly surprised to find that the checks now run much more quickly and with less impact to overall server performance. Table 6-5 provides a list of DBCC commands that you can use when working with database backups and integrity checks. These commands can be run directly from SQL Query Analyzer or via scheduled jobs.

For a complete list of DBCC commands (along with their syntax), see Appendix A. Now that we have looked at some of the ways to plan for and manage backups, let's move on to actually performing these operations.

Command	Function	Notes
DBCC CheckDB	Verifies internal structure of database objects	Should be run regularly to check for and correct minor database errors
DBCC ShrinkDatabase	Removes unused space to reduce the size of data files	Used to recover disk space
DBCC ShrinkFile	Shrinks a single data file to recover unused space	Used to recover disk space
DBCC Help	Provides syntax for a specific DBCC command	
DBCC CheckAlloc or DBCC NewAlloc	Verifies proper usage of space in database files	Should be run regularly to check for minor problems in data allocation
DBCC CheckFileGroup	Verifies that all filegroups are available	Used when databases are not functioning properly
DBCC CheckTable	Verifies the integrity of all the data for a table within a database	Used if errors are being returned from some queries

Table 6-5.   Partial List of DBCC Commands

The Database Maintenance Plan Wizard

Microsoft has realized that many SQL Server users don't care about the behind-the-scenes work performed by database servers. Users are more interested in making sure that information is backed up regularly; we want solutions that are simple yet powerful. The Database Maintenance Plan Wizard is a valuable tool for meeting these goals. Accessible through Enterprise Manager, it walks you through the types of information you must provide before implementing a good backup solution. The wizard then uses this information to create and schedule the necessary database backup operations.

Although the Database Maintenance Plan Wizard makes it easy to implement backups, you should not let this tool fool you into thinking that these operations will take care of all of your work. Before implementing the basic operations, you should ensure that you have clearly defined your data protection plans before beginning to walk through these steps. With that out of the way, let's start looking at how you access the Database Maintenance Plan Wizard and respond to the various prompts you'll receive.

STEP-BY-STEP: USING THE DATABASE MAINTENANCE PLAN WIZARD

1. In Enterprise Manager, select the server for which you want to create the plan.

2. From the Tools menu, select Database Maintenance Planner. Click Next at the introduction screen to begin the process. The wizard will guide you through a series of pages and selections. Note that you can also launch the Database Maintenance Plan Wizard by right-clicking on the name of a specific database and selecting All Tasks | Maintenance Plan.

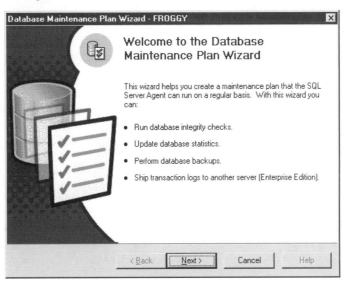

3. **Select Databases**   On the first page of the wizard, you'll be given the option of backing up one or more databases on your server. Subsequent steps will use the database(s) you select in this step.

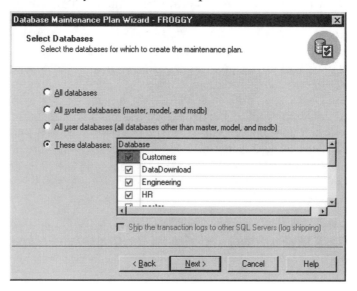

The various options on the Select Databases page include

- **All Databases**   This option is best if you want all the databases on this server to be backed up at the same time. In environments where there is little activity during certain hours of the day, backing up all databases is the easiest method to administer. Also, as new databases are created on the server, they, too, will be backed up with the jobs created.

- **All System Databases (master, model, and msdb)**   This backs up all the system databases that are required for proper functioning of SQL Server 2000. You should back up at least the *master* database after any changes are made to the system tables.

- **All User Databases (all databases other than master, model, and msdb)**   Choose this option when you plan to back up the system databases separately or with a different schedule. It will ensure that any new databases created on the server will also be backed up by the job.

- **These Databases**   If you want to use different backup plans and schedules for different sets of databases, you can use the Database table to choose the databases that will be backed up together. It will be slightly more difficult to manage and keep track of multiple backup jobs and schedules, so it's important that you document which databases are being backed up and when the process occurs. Also, note that if you add new databases to this server, they will *not* automatically be backed up by the jobs you create here.

You'll also see an option that allows you to configure log-shipping. We will cover that topic in Chapter 10, so leave the box unchecked for now. When you have selected the appropriate databases, click Next.

4. **Update Data Optimization Information**   In addition to backing up data, you will probably want to schedule jobs that perform routine maintenance on your databases. The options in the Update Data Optimization Information window will apply to the databases you have selected in the previous step.

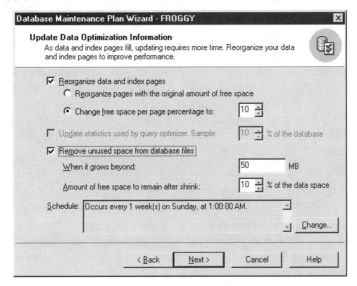

Although these jobs take time to perform, it is a good idea to perform them regularly if your business constraints allow. The choices include

- **Reorganize Data and Index Pages**   As the data contained in database objects changes, pages can become fragmented or full. If a page of data is full, new pages must be created to accommodate the additional information. Choosing this option causes all the indexes for a database to be dropped and re-created. The result will be indexes with optimized data layout, allowing queries that rely on them to be executed more quickly. Free space is normally kept on data pages so that some amount of information can change without requiring additional pages to be created. You can choose either to keep the original amount of free space (which is equal to the value specified as the FILLFACTOR) or to reset the free space on each page to a given percentage that you specify. After reorganizing the changes, data modifications through UPDATE and INSERT queries may be faster.

- **Update Statistics Used by Query Optimizer**   When SQL Server executes a query, it uses information about tables, indexes, and other database objects to find the most efficient way to retrieve and return the data. As data in the database changes, however, the statistics may be out of date. Selecting this option sets the job to sample a portion of the database to update the statistics. For large databases, you'll want to choose a smaller percentage of the database for generating sample statistics, because this will greatly improve performance of the operation. The overall result is a potential increase in the speed of processing SELECT queries.

- **Remove Unused Space from Database Files**   As we mentioned earlier in this chapter, SQL Server 2000 can automatically grow and shrink database files as needed. This results in nearly automated administration of data files. However, in some cases, it can lead to the expansion of data files beyond what is required. During this operation, you can choose to have SQL Server automatically remove any *slack space*—space that is available on the disk for the data files, but that does not contain any useful information. Because removing unused space requires processing and disk I/O time, you can specify how much unused space must be present before the operation occurs and how much unused space should be left in the database after the operation is complete.

- **Schedule**   You can specify when this job will run by clicking the Change button next to the Schedule field. The Edit Recurring Job Schedule dialog box appears.

  Here you can specify when operations will occur. Notice that you can select almost any regularly occurring schedule using this dialog box. We'll see the same interface in subsequent job scheduling steps of the wizard. After you make your selections, click Next.

5. **Database Integrity Check**   On this page, you can choose to create a job for checking the integrity of the database. If you select Check Database Integrity, the DBCC CheckDB command (described in the preceding section) will be run. You can choose whether to run the checks on indexes and whether to automatically repair any minor errors that might be found if you do choose to include indexes. Finally, you can choose to perform tests prior to backups. If this option is checked and inconsistencies are found in the database, the files will not be backed up. This prevents the storing of inconsistent data files (which, depending on your backup settings, might overwrite other database backups or result in unusable database backup files).

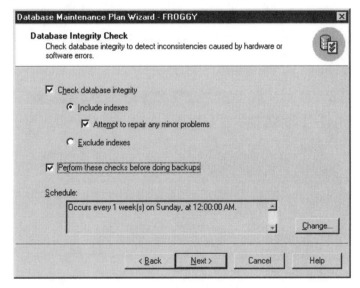

6. **Specify the Database Backup Plan**   Now that we've selected the performance and consistency checks, it's time to determine how we want to back up the data itself. This page of the wizard is shown next. At this point, you can choose to perform all the other operations without backing up the database. Note that if you uncheck this box, no data will be backed up. For backup operations, you can specify whether the backup should be verified. This option instructs the job to compare the data stored on the backup media with the information currently in the database. Note that although this option verifies information, it is not a replacement for performing regular restore tests. Also, in most cases, a backup with verification can take nearly twice as long as a backup only. Next, you can choose whether you want to back up the information to a tape device or to disk, and specify the appropriate media or location. If you choose a tape device, you'll need to choose one of the devices listed in the drop-down list. As in the previous steps, you can schedule the jobs to occur at specific times. For the following steps of this exercise, I'll assume that you chose to perform backups to disk.

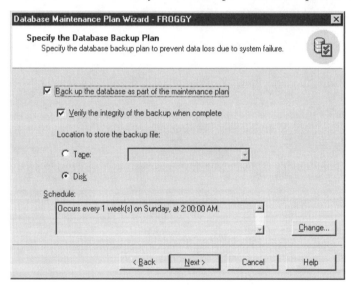

7. **Specify Backup Disk Directory**   This page is displayed only if you chose to back up to disk in the previous step. Here, you can specify the directory into which backups will be stored. By default, all files will be stored in the same directory and will be named based on the name of the database and a date/timestamp. To organize the backups differently, you can choose to create a separate directory for the backup of each database. A very helpful feature is the ability to automatically delete files that are older than a certain date. This allows you to automatically keep a historical set of backups without eventually filling your hard disks completely. The default file extension for the dump files is .bak, but this, too, can be changed if, for example, your backup software normally ignores files with that extension.

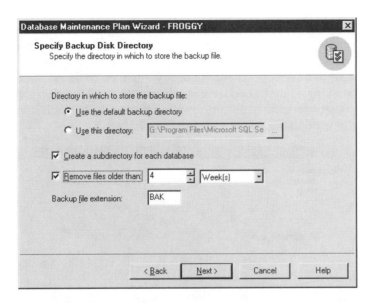

8. **Specify Transaction Log Backup Disk Directory**   I mentioned earlier that the use of transaction logs in backups can be helpful for restoring to a point in time without incurring all the overhead required to perform full database backups. If you choose to back up the transaction log, you may choose whether or not the backup should be verified and whether you want to store the data to disk or tape. In some cases, it might make more sense to back up databases to tape (because they are large) and transaction logs to disk (because they are smaller and can be restored much more quickly from disk). If you chose to save to disk, you will be presented with a dialog box that prompts you for information regarding where the backups should be stored.

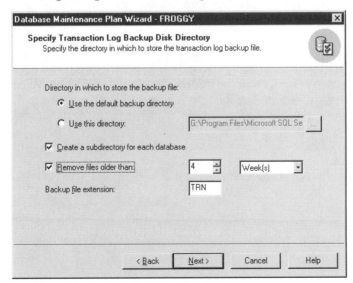

9. **Reports to Generate**   Since backup operations will run behind the scenes, you can choose to log the results of the operations to text files that can later be examined. Better yet, if you have set up e-mail profiles for server operations, you can have these reports automatically e-mailed to them. Some organizations might want to set up a special e-mail distribution list for all of the appropriate administrators and have this information sent to them. We'll cover the details of creating and managing "Operators" in Chapter 8.

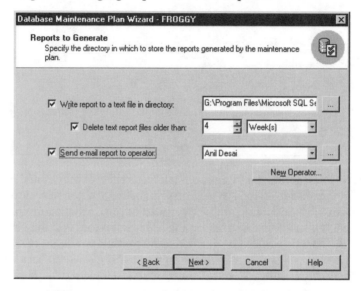

10. **Maintenance Plan History**   Managing backups on multiple servers can be quite a chore. Although you can get the information you want by examining log files or e-mail messages (set up in the preceding step), you will probably also want to store a history of all the operations within the msdb database. In the Maintenance Plan History dialog box, you can choose to record backup operation information and to limit the number of rows used for historical data. If you are managing multiple database servers, a good way to centrally view information is to store all the information in the msdb database on a single SQL Server machine. The Remote Server option allows you to do just this.

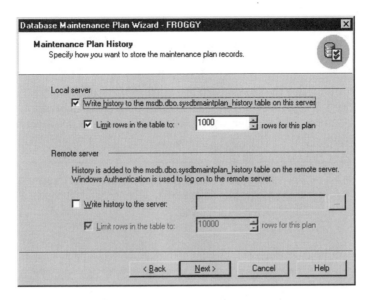

11. **Completing the Database Maintenance Plan Wizard** At long last, we've covered all the available options and are ready to save the plan. The only required item here is to name the plan. This name will be used to identify the various jobs that will be created based on your selections. It might also be helpful to copy the text in the dialog box and store it in a text file, to document your selections. When you click Finish, the jobs will be created and scheduled in SQL Server.

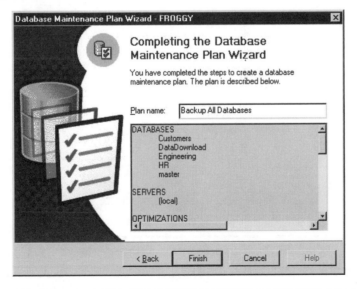

This may have seemed like a lot of steps for a wizard, but the details you've selected will be used to tailor the jobs you've created to meet your business requirements. Once the jobs have been created, you can easily view and modify their properties in Enterprise Manager: expand the Management folder under the server of interest and click Jobs. You'll see a list, much like the one shown in Figure 6-20, of all the actions that are scheduled to be performed on this server. By selecting the properties of an item, you can change various details. Later in this chapter, we'll look at the various details involved in performing SQL Server jobs.

NOTE: For the backup job to run, the SQL Server Agent service must be started. It is highly recommended that you set this service to start automatically when the server is booted and that you periodically check to ensure that the service is running.

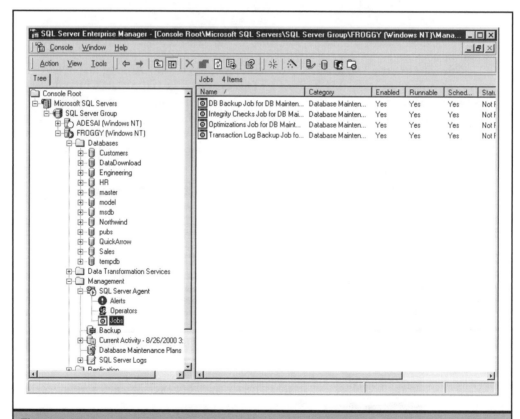

Figure 6-20. Viewing a list of jobs created by the Database Maintenance Plan Wizard

Modifying Database Maintenance Plans

Most technical professionals understand that business needs will change over time. Therefore, the responses you provided to the Database Maintenance Plan Wizard might need to be changed. One way to create a new Database Maintenance Plan is to delete the old plan and then start again. Fortunately, however, there's an easier way. You can simply use Enterprise Manager to view the Properties of an existing plan. You can also use this interface (shown in Figures 6-21 and Figure 6-22) to make changes to existing Database Maintenance Plan settings. Once you make the changes and click OK, the jobs that were created for this plan will automatically be modified to reflect your changes.

In Chapter 7, we'll cover the details of using the sqlmaint.exe command-line utility for running Database Maintenance Plan operations from the command line.

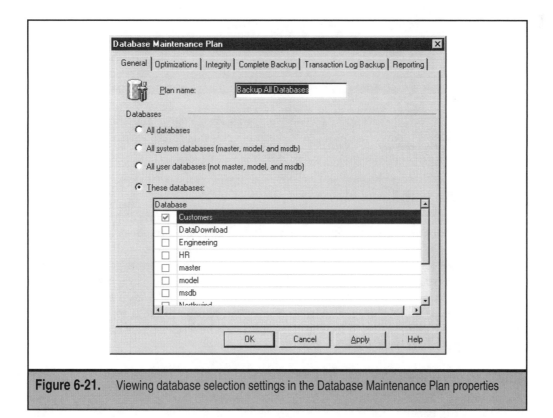

Figure 6-21.   Viewing database selection settings in the Database Maintenance Plan properties

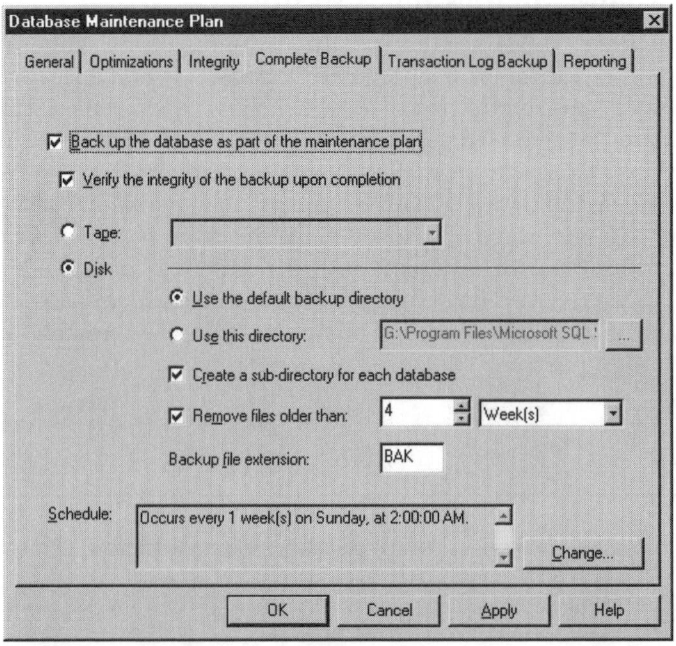

Figure 6-22.   Viewing backup settings in the Database Maintenance Plan properties

Performing Backups

As we saw earlier, the Database Maintenance Plan Wizard is a good solution for covering most of your backup requirements. It can handle issues related to backing up databases, performing consistency checks, and managing the transaction logs. It also allows you to easily schedule jobs to occur. So why use anything else? The main reason to customize backup jobs is for the control and flexibility you will gain. Various scenarios require file and filegroup backups to one or more devices. Additionally, you might want to create scripts that can be used by other administrators or can be scheduled to occur periodically. In the following sections, we'll look at the commands and operations necessary to perform the types of database backups discussed earlier.

Using Enterprise Manager to Perform Backups

As mentioned earlier in this chapter, full database backups are the basis for other types of backups. A full backup stores to the backup device you specify all the information about data and objects in a database. The easiest and most intuitive way to perform backups is to use the graphical tools included with SQL Server 2000. To perform backups using Enterprise Manager, you can use the following procedure.

STEP-BY-STEP: PERFORMING BACKUPS USING ENTERPRISE MANAGER

1. Expand the server on which you want to perform a backup.

2. Right-click the name of the database you want to back up and select All Tasks
   | Backup Database. This opens the SQL Server Backup dialog box:

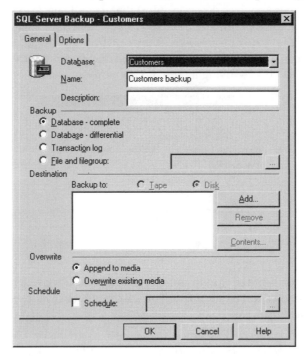

3. Choose the backup type in the Backup area. Depending on the backup history
   for this database, some of the options for this database may be unavailable. For
   example, if you have never performed a full database backup, you will not be
   able to perform a differential or transaction log backup. The various backup
   types available include the following:

   ■ **Database – Complete**   A full backup of all database information.

   ■ **Database – Differential**   A backup of all changes that have occurred on
   this database since the last full backup.

   ■ **Transaction Log**   A backup of all transaction log entries since the last full,
   differential, or transaction log backup.

   ■ **File and Filegroup**   The ability to select specific files and/or filegroups to
   be backed up. By clicking the "…" button in the lower-right corner (above
   the Help button), you will be able to select the items to back up. When this

option is chosen, note that you will only be backing up database objects that reside on these files. To have a complete database backup, you must schedule other operations that back up the remaining files.

4. Select a destination device in the Destination area. Choose whether you want to store the backup information on a disk or tape device. If your database has previously been backed up to one or more devices, those devices will appear in the list by default. The Remove and Contents buttons let you review or change the use of these devices. Keep in mind that a single backup operation must use either all disk or all tape devices. To add new devices, click the Add button (you'll see the dialog box shown in the illustration). If you will be storing to disk, you can choose to specify a filename or a dump device to which data will be written. If you are using a tape device, you can specify options for media.

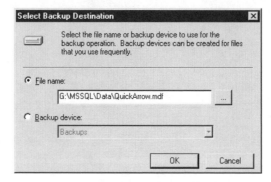

5. Select an overwrite option in the Overwrite area. Choose whether the backup destination should be overwritten or whether data should be appended to the existing file or device.

6. Use the optional Schedule field, if you wish, to define or select a schedule for the current backup job. You can access this field by clicking the ellipsis ("…") button. The options here are

   ■ **Start Automatically When SQL Server Agent Starts** The backup job will be run the next time SQL Server Agent is started. This might be a useful option if you want the job to run immediately after a server is rebooted.

   ■ **Start Whenever the CPU(s) Becomes Idle** The backup job will occur when the server is not busy, according to CPU usage. You can set the CPU threshold value in Enterprise Manager by right-clicking the SQL Server Agent service and selecting Properties. Note that you should not choose this option for jobs that must be run regularly, especially on busy servers.

   ■ **One Time** The backup job will occur once, at the time that you specify. The backup job settings will not be available after the job has executed.

   ■ **Recurring** The backup job will run on a recurring schedule, based on the options you choose.

7. Specify any preferred job options. The Options tab of the SQL Server Backup dialog box allows you to specify details for the job:

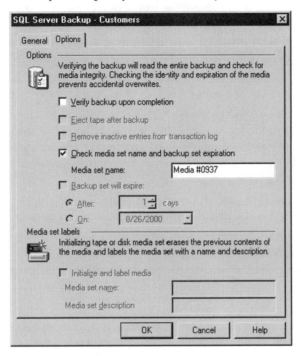

Many of the options will be dependent on the type of backup you chose to perform in the General tab. The options are as follows:

- **Verify Backup Upon Completion**   After the backup process is completed, SQL Server will automatically verify the contents of the backup against the contents of the live database. This ensures that the data was stored in a consistent state and is readable. However, it takes considerable time and server resources to complete.

- **Eject Tape After Backup**   This option is available only when backups are being sent to tape devices. It might be useful to eject tapes after a job is done to alert systems and database administrators that the job is complete and that a tape might need to be changed. If you'll be writing multiple backups to this tape, however, leave the box unchecked.

- **Remove Inactive Entries from Transaction Log**   For transaction log backups, this option truncates the log after the backup is done. This removes all the entries that have been backed up and, depending on settings for the file, releases the disk space back to the file system. In general, you will want to use this option. However, if you have to make multiple copies of the transaction log or if you want the log backups to be cumulative, you can uncheck the option.

- **Check Media Set Name and Backup Set Expiration** As described earlier in this chapter, you can set a default expiration date for all backups stored to this media. To enable this option, you need to specify a media set name. SQL Server will verify that the media set in the device has the same name and will alert you if you are attempting to overwrite unexpired backups.

- **Backup Set Will Expire** If you want to override the default expiration options for the current backup set, you can specify when the backup set can be reused. This option is only available for tape media.

- **Initialize and Label Media** These operations will be available if you are creating new disk or tape devices or want to delete the contents of existing media. When the media is initialized, you can specify a Media Set Name and Media Set Description. This information can be very helpful in organizing your backups.

8. When you are satisfied with the settings for the backup job, click OK to accept the job. If the job is scheduled to run immediately, you will see a progress bar notifying you of the status of the job. Otherwise, it will run based on the schedule you selected.

Using Enterprise Manager provides a good overview of the configuration options available for performing backups. The preceding procedure is probably the quickest and easiest way to back up a single database if you know exactly what you want to do. However, you may want to have greater control over the process. Let's take a step in that direction: using the Create Database Backup Wizard.

Using the Create Database Backup Wizard

SQL Server 2000 includes a Create Database Backup Wizard that can be used to assist novice users in answering questions related to performing backups. To use the Create Database Backup Wizard, you can use the following process.

STEP-BY-STEP: USING THE CREATE DATABASE BACKUP WIZARD

1. In Enterprise Manager, click the name of an existing database.
2. In the Taskpad, choose the Wizards tab. Click on the Backup a Database option within the Manage SQL Server section of the options.

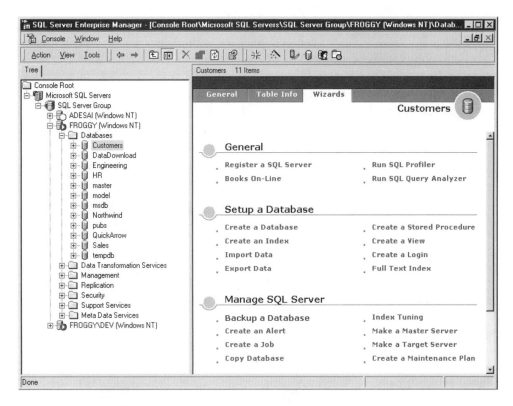

3. You'll see an overview of the steps that you'll perform in the wizard. Click Next to begin the Create Database Backup Wizard.

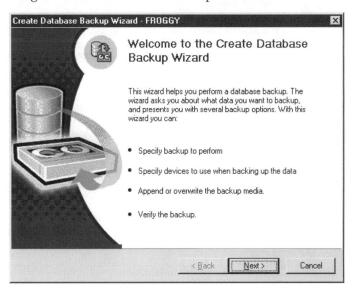

4. **Select Database to Backup** Notice that you can only select one database from the drop-down list. If you need to back up multiple databases, you should use either the Database Maintenance Plan Wizard (covered earlier in this chapter) or Transact-SQL commands (described later). Click Next to continue.

5. **Type Name and Description for Backup** Provide a name for the backup and, optionally, a description. It is always a good idea to include this information, as it can be very helpful when you are searching for specific backups. Click Next.

6. **Select Type of Backup** Choose the type of backup operation you want to perform. The options are to perform a full database backup, a differential backup, or a transaction log backup. Choose Database Backup, and then click Next.

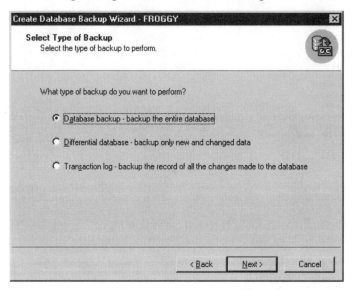

7. **Select Backup Destination and Action** Choose whether you want to back up to tape, to a specific file, or to an existing backup device. Note that there is an option in the Backup Device drop-down list to create a new backup device. Depending on your choice of backup destination, you'll also be able to specify whether you want to append to the device or overwrite its contents. You can also choose to perform a backup verification after the process is complete. Choose the appropriate options and click Next to continue.

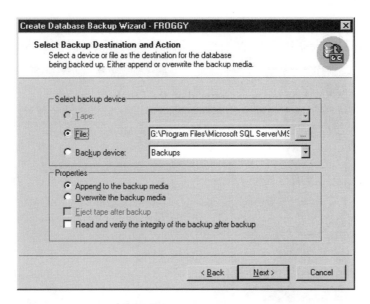

8. **Backup Verification and Scheduling** Here, you'll be able to specify a media set name, set media expiration options, and schedule the backup. Make the appropriate choices and click Next to continue.

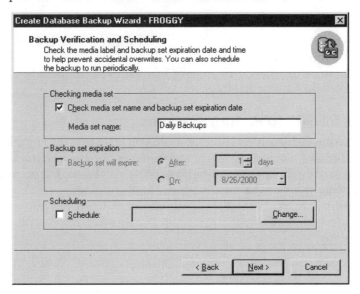

9. Finally, you'll be provided with a summary of the choices you made during the Create Database Backup Wizard. To perform the backup operation, click Finish.

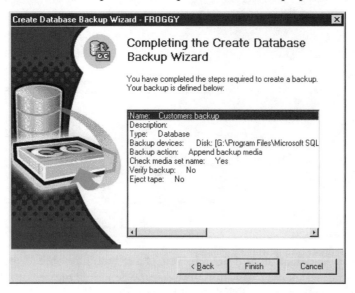

Although you may find the various tools and wizards within Enterprise Manager very easy to use, you may want to generate custom scripts or backup schedules for your databases. You can do this through the use of Transact-SQL commands. Let's look at that topic next.

Using Transact-SQL to Perform Backups

Transact-SQL commands are a good choice when you want to script complex jobs or want more control over available options. The commands can also be easier to use when, for example, you want to run similar operations on multiple databases. The same task can be accomplished with the graphical tools in Enterprise Manager, but if the number of operations is large, this alternative can become quite cumbersome. However, you can build Transact-SQL stored procedures that will run custom jobs by accepting specific arguments.

NOTE: If you're unfamiliar with Transact-SQL scripts, you need to be aware of a few conventions. First, the scripts are not case sensitive. Wherever mixed-case commands are used in this book, they are printed for clarifying the commands. Second, the line formatting for scripts is optional. That is, all scripts are interpreted and run as a single command. Line breaks are generally added for clarity in reading and working with the code.

To back up an entire database using Transact-SQL, you can use the following command syntax:

```
BACKUP DATABASE { database_name | @database_name_var }
TO < backup_device > [ ,...n ]
[ WITH
    [ BLOCKSIZE = { blocksize | @blocksize_variable } ]
    [ [ , ] DESCRIPTION = { 'text' | @text_variable } ]
    [ [ , ] DIFFERENTIAL ]
    [ [ , ] EXPIREDATE = { date | @date_var }
        | RETAINDAYS = { days | @days_var } ]
    [ [ , ] PASSWORD = { password | @password_variable } ]
    [ [ , ] FORMAT | NOFORMAT ]
    [ [ , ] { INIT | NOINIT } ]
    [ [ , ] MEDIADESCRIPTION = { 'text' | @text_variable } ]
    [ [ , ] MEDIANAME = { media_name | @media_name_variable } ]
    [ [ , ] MEDIAPASSWORD = { mediapassword | @mediapassword_variable } ]
    [ [ , ] NAME = { backup_set_name | @backup_set_name_var } ]
    [ [ , ] { NOSKIP | SKIP } ]
    [ [ , ] { NOREWIND | REWIND } ]
    [ [ , ] { NOUNLOAD | UNLOAD } ]
    [ [ , ] RESTART ]
    [ [ , ] STATS [ = percentage ] ]
]

< backup_device > ::=
    {
        { logical_backup_device_name | @logical_backup_device_name_var }
        |
        { DISK | TAPE } =
            { 'physical_backup_device_name' | @physical_backup_device_name_var }
    }
```

Table 6-6 lists the options that can be used with the BACKUP command.

The backup device can be specified either as a predefined logical name for a backup device or as a file system file. SQL Server allows you to specify up to 32 different backup devices for this operation. Here is a simple BACKUP command:

```
BACKUP TestDatabase to BackupDevice1
```

In this example, all of the default settings will be used, along with the contents of the TestDatabase, for copying information to the backup device.

Option	Function	Notes
BLOCKSIZE	Specifies the size of data blocks written to backup media	Default options should be adequate unless otherwise recommended by the tape backup device vendor
DESCRIPTION	Includes up to 255 characters of text describing the backup	Can be viewed when you need to know the contents of a backup device
DIFFERENTIAL	Indicates that a differential backup will be made	A full backup must have been performed prior to the differential backup
EXPIREDATE	Specifies the date on which the backup can be overwritten	If not specified, the server default setting (if any) will be used
FORMAT	Completely overwrites the media header when the backup is performed	Use when you are sure that the information on the tape is no longer needed and you want to begin a new set of backups
INIT	Initializes the backup device	All contents of the backup device will be erased
MEDIADESCRIPTION	Adds a text description to the backup media	Allows system administrators to quickly identify the contents of the media
MEDIANAME	Specifies a name for the backup media	Provides helpful information for cataloging and managing backups
MEDIAPASSWORD	Password-protects SQL Server 2000 database backup files	Database backups that are protected by passwords cannot be restored without the password; therefore, database administrators should ensure that password information is stored safely

Table 6-6. Options for the BACKUP Command

Option	Function	Notes
NOFORMAT	Prevents the backup operation from overwriting the media header	Use when you are sure the media contains a valid header and you do not want to overwrite this information
NOINIT	Prevents initialization of the backup device	Use when you do not want to remove information from an existing backup device
NOREWIND	Does not rewind the tape after the completion of the backup (and, optionally, verification) process. This prevents the tape device from being used by other devices or processes	This option must be supported by the tape device (some devices may automatically rewind in order to store header information)
NOSKIP	Ensures that the media has expired before allowing the backup operation to continue	Best used unless you are sure you want to overwrite backup information
NOUNLOAD	Prevents the tape (or other media) from being ejected at the end of the backup operation	Use when the tape will be reused for other backup operations
PASSWORD	Specifies a password for the backup	Helpful for protecting backups of secure data
RESTART	Restarts a backup operation that has aborted before completion	Append this command to the end of the original command to resume the operation at the point at which it was interrupted
RETAINDAYS	Specifies the number of days before the backup media should be overwritten	If not specified, the server default setting (if any) will be used

Table 6-6.   Options for the BACKUP Command *(continued)*

Option	Function	Notes
REWIND	Rewinds the tape after the completion of the backup (and, optionally, verification) process. This makes the tape device available for use by other devices and processes	
SKIP	Instructs the backup operation to ignore the established backup expiration and media name	Use when you are sure you want to overwrite media that has been formatted but has not yet expired
STATS	Indicates that statistics will be printed during the backup operation; can optionally specify the percentage increment that will be displayed	If no percentage value is specified, the default increment for output is 10 percent
UNLOAD	Instructs the backup operation to eject the tape (or other media) once the backup is complete	Useful for alerting systems administrators when it's time to change tape

Table 6-6. Options for the BACKUP Command *(continued)*

Of course, you can specify much more information when backing up data. For example, the following command will back up all information on the Customers database:

```
BACKUP DATABASE Customers
TO BackupDevice2
WITH
     DESCRIPTION = 'Full backup of Customers database',
     RETAINDAYS = 30,
     FORMAT,
     MEDIADESCRIPTION = 'Media for Customers database backup',
     MEDIANAME = 'CustomersMedia',
```

```
        NAME = 'CustomersFull',
        UNLOAD,
        STATS = 10
```

In this example, we've set a minimum number of days to retain the information on the backup set. We also specified a media description and a media name. Additionally, the media device will be formatted, statistics will be displayed during the operation, and the tape will be ejected from the device when the operation is complete.

File and Filegroup Backups   The BACKUP command can also be used to back up only specific files or filegroups. The command format is similar to that for full backups, but it includes a specifier for files and filegroups:

```
BACKUP DATABASE { database_name | @database_name_var }
    < file_or_filegroup > [ ,...n ]
TO < backup_device > [ ,...n ]
[ WITH
    [ BLOCKSIZE = { blocksize | @blocksize_variable } ]
    [ [ , ] DESCRIPTION = { 'text' | @text_variable } ]
    [ [ , ] EXPIREDATE = { date | @date_var }
        | RETAINDAYS = { days | @days_var } ]
    [ [ , ] PASSWORD = { password | @password_variable } ]
    [ [ , ] FORMAT | NOFORMAT ]
    [ [ , ] { INIT | NOINIT } ]
    [ [ , ] MEDIADESCRIPTION = { 'text' | @text_variable } ]
    [ [ , ] MEDIANAME = { media_name | @media_name_variable } ]
    [ [ , ] MEDIAPASSWORD = { mediapassword | @mediapassword_variable } ]
    [ [ , ] NAME = { backup_set_name | @backup_set_name_var } ]
    [ [ , ] { NOSKIP | SKIP } ]
    [ [ , ] { NOREWIND | REWIND } ]
    [ [ , ] { NOUNLOAD | UNLOAD } ]
    [ [ , ] RESTART ]
    [ [ , ] STATS [ = percentage ] ]
]

< backup_device > ::=
    {
        { logical_backup_device_name | @logical_backup_device_name_var }
        |
        { DISK | TAPE } =
            { 'physical_backup_device_name' | @physical_backup_device_name_var }
    }

< file_or_filegroup > ::=
    {
        FILE = { logical_file_name | @logical_file_name_var }
        |
        FILEGROUP = { logical_filegroup_name | @logical_filegroup_name_var }
    }
```

For example, the following command will perform a backup of specific files only, on a database that uses filegroups:

```
BACKUP DATABASE Customers
FILEGROUP = 'FileGroup2'
TO BackupDevice2
WITH
     DESCRIPTION = 'FileGroup backup of Customers database',
     RETAINDAYS = 30,
     FORMAT,
     MEDIADESCRIPTION = 'Media for Customers database backup',
     MEDIANAME = 'CustomersMedia',
     NAME = 'CustomersFileGroup2',
     UNLOAD,
     STATS = 10
```

This command uses options similar to those used in the previous example, with one exception: only the data and objects that reside on Filegroup 2 will be backed up.

Transaction Log Backups   The BACKUP command can be used to back up only the transaction log of a database, using the following syntax:

```
BACKUP LOG { database_name | @database_name_var }
{
    TO < backup_device > [ ,...n ]
    [ WITH
        [ BLOCKSIZE = { blocksize | @blocksize_variable } ]
        [ [ , ] DESCRIPTION = { 'text' | @text_variable } ]
        [ [ , ] EXPIREDATE = { date | @date_var }
            | RETAINDAYS = { days | @days_var } ]
        [ [ , ] PASSWORD = { password | @password_variable } ]
        [ [ , ] FORMAT | NOFORMAT ]
        [ [ , ] { INIT | NOINIT } ]
        [ [ , ] MEDIADESCRIPTION = { 'text' | @text_variable } ]
        [ [ , ] MEDIANAME = { media_name | @media_name_variable } ]
        [ [ , ] MEDIAPASSWORD = { mediapassword | @mediapassword_variable } ]
        [ [ , ] NAME = { backup_set_name | @backup_set_name_var } ]
        [ [ , ] NO_TRUNCATE ]
        [ [ , ] { NORECOVERY | STANDBY = undo_file_name } ]
        [ [ , ] { NOREWIND | REWIND } ]
        [ [ , ] { NOSKIP | SKIP } ]
        [ [ , ] { NOUNLOAD | UNLOAD } ]
        [ [ , ] RESTART ]
        [ [ , ] STATS [ = percentage ] ]
    ]
}
```

```
< backup_device > ::=
    {
        { logical_backup_device_name | @logical_backup_device_name_var }
        |
        { DISK | TAPE } =
            { 'physical_backup_device_name' | @physical_backup_device_name_var }
    }
```

The following is an example of a simple log backup command:

```
BACKUP LOG Database1 to BackupDevice2
```

We're using a very simple command, but, if necessary, the same options as specified in earlier examples could be used. The difference is that, this time, only the transaction log for the database is backed up. By default, the transaction log will be truncated at the end of the operation.

The following example uses Transact-SQL to create a database, to perform a full and several transaction log backups, and then to restore the backups. Note that you may need to change some of the file locations based on the configuration of your server.

```
-- -------------------------------------------
--  "SQL Server 2000 Backup and Recovery"
--   Sample database backup script
-- -------------------------------------------



--—STEP 1: Create a sample database for the backup using default settings
CREATE DATABASE BackupTest
GO



--—STEP 2: Create a disk-based backup device
EXEC sp_addumpdevice
     @devtype = 'DISK',
     @logicalname = 'Backups',
     @physicalname = 'C:\Temp\Backups.bak'
GO



--—STEP 3: Perform a full backup of the database
BACKUP DATABASE BackupTest TO Backups WITH
     Name = 'Full Backup',
     Description = 'Full Database Backup of BackupTest',
     INIT
GO
```

```
--STEP 4: Perform the first transaction log backup
BACKUP LOG BackupTest TO Backups WITH
       Name = 'Transaction Log Backup 1',
       Description = 'First Transaction log backup of BackupTest database',
       NO INIT
GO




--STEP 5: Perform the second transaction log backup
BACKUP LOG BackupTest TO Backups WITH
       Name = 'Transaction Log Backup 2',
       Description = Second Transaction log backup of BackupTest database',
       NO INIT
GO
-- End Script
```

We'll cover the details of restoring databases in Chapter 7.

Useful Stored Procedures

SQL Server 2000 includes many system-stored procedures for viewing and modifying server settings and database objects. Table 6-7 lists some stored procedures that are helpful for planning and performing backup operations.

Procedure	Function	Syntax

sp_addump device	Adds a dump device for use in backups	`sp_addumpdevice`
		`[@devtype=] 'device_type',`
		`[@logicalname=] 'logical_name',`
		`[@physicalname=] 'physical_name'`
		`[,`
		`[@cntrltype=] 'controller_type'`
		`|`
		`[@devstatus=] 'device_status'`
		`  ]`

sp_configure	Configures serverwide settings	`sp_configure`
		`[[@configname =] 'setting']`
		`[, [@configvalue =] 'value']`

Table 6-7.   Useful SQL Server stored procedures

Procedure	Function	Syntax

sp_db option	Changes database options	`sp_dboption`
		`[[@dbname =] 'database']`
		`[, [@optname =] 'option']`
		`[, [@optvalue =] 'value']`

sp_drop device	Deletes an existing dump device	`sp_dropdevice`
		`[@logicalname=] 'device'`
		`[, [@delfile =] 'delfile']`

sp_help	Displays information about any database object	`sp_help` `[[@objname =] 'object']`
sp_helpdb	Displays information about a database	`sp_helpdb [[@dbname=]` `'database']`
sp_help device	Displays information about an existing dump device	`sp_helpdevice` `[[@devname=] 'device']`
sp_helpfile	Returns information about the files used by a database	`sp_helpfile` `[[@filename =] 'file']`
sp_helpfile group	Returns information about the filegroups used by a database	`sp_helpfilegroup` `[[@filegroupname =] 'filegroup']`
sp_monitor	Displays performance and other statistics about SQL Server	`sp_monitor`

sp_spaceused	Displays information about the disk space used by a database or table	`sp_spaceused`
		`[[@objname =] 'object']`
		`[, [@updateusage =] true | false]`

sp_who	Displays information about users who are connected to the server	`sp_who` `[[@login_name =] 'username']`

Table 6-7. Useful SQL Server stored procedures *(continued)*

Figure 6-23 shows sample results of the stored sp_helpdb procedure. (For a more complete list of stored procedures and further details on the various parameters, see Appendix A.)

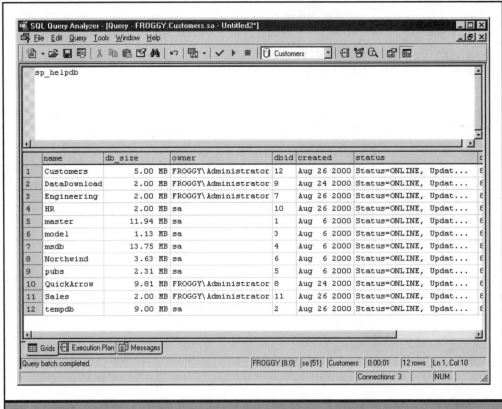

Figure 6-23. Viewing the results of the sp_helpdb stored procedure

When using stored procedures, you can specify arguments in one of two ways. The first is by the sequence of the arguments. If you want to specify each of the parameters in the same order as expected by the stored procedure, you do not need to enter the parameter name. For example, you could enter the following command:

```
sp_addumpdevice 'disk', 'dumpdev1',
'c:\Backups\Device1.bak'
```

However, if you wish to use the parameters out of order, you need to specify the parameters by name. Here is an example:

```
sp_addumpdevice @logicalname = 'dumpdev1',
@devtype = 'disk',
@physicalname = 'c:\Backups\Device1.bak'
```

Details on using each of these stored procedures (including the format requirements for each of the parameters) are available in SQL Server Books Online.

OPTIMIZING BACKUP PERFORMANCE

One of the common questions asked about backups is how much of an impact performing backups has on the usage of a database. That is, will clients still receive satisfactory performance if I run a database backup during busy hours? The short answer is that backup operations will usually cause less than a 10 percent decrease in overall server performance (based on general guidelines provided by Microsoft). However, if you are working in a mission-critical environment, you should test these values before assuming that they're accurate. (Certain other types of operations, such as long-running transactions, can cause similar performance hits.)

The bottom line is that when you're planning backup operations, you should measure performance impacts of these operations and plan accordingly. Fortunately, SQL Server includes many tools for monitoring overall performance. In this part of the chapter, we'll provide details on monitoring backup performance. Then, we'll look at some best practices for optimizing the performance of backup operations.

NOTE: In Chapter 4, we discussed the use of such tools as Performance Monitor, SQL Server Profiler, and SQL Query Analyzer. If you're unfamiliar with these tools, I recommend that you review that chapter now.

The Optimization Process

Before starting to change configuration settings, you should fully understand the process of optimizing performance, which breaks down into the following steps:

1. **Establish a baseline**. Determine how your current system is performing. Do you tend to experience slowdowns when more users are accessing the system, or is performance generally uniform throughout? Using this information, you can tell how the changes you make affect performance.

2. **Identify bottlenecks**. Often, performance problems are elusive. For example, if a user told me that "Web pages load too slowly," I'd be tempted to assume the bottleneck was her modem. However, if she has fast access to the Internet, then it would be much more appropriate to check the hardware configuration. Similarly, be sure you understand the slow steps in your backup process. If backing up data to tape is slow, is the real problem the device or is it a slow SCSI controller that runs on the ISA bus?

3. **Make one change at a time**. Once you've identified the problems, it's time to try solving them. It's important to make only one change at a time. Otherwise, the presence of multiple variables might confuse your conclusions.

4. **Reevaluate the performance**. After changes have been made, you should always retest your environment. First and foremost, make sure that you haven't eliminated any needed services. Backups might run very quickly if no one can connect to your database server, but this clearly isn't an acceptable "performance optimization" technique.

5. **Repeat, as necessary**. Whether or not you have improved performance, you might choose to repeat these steps to isolate and move other bottlenecks. It may sound rather dismal, but performance optimization is usually a constant process.

There are a few misconceptions that can cause problems in the overall methodology. The first step is to realize that the goal is to *move* the bottleneck. If we define a *bottleneck* as the slowest step in a given process, you'll realize that this can never be removed entirely. Second, realize that the goal is usually to reach acceptable performance. Although it would be nice to always squeeze every last piece of computing power out of our machines, time and money constraints often prevent this from happening. Sometimes, we just have to settle for *good enough* instead of perfect. With this is mind, let's look at some ways to monitor performance.

Using Performance Monitor

SQL Server 2000 includes several objects and counters for Performance Monitor that can be used to estimate the throughput of backup and recovery operations. Windows NT/2000 Performance Monitor can be used to monitor the progress of a backup or recovery operation. (For more information on using Performance Monitor, review Chapter 3.) The default Performance Monitor shortcut included in the SQL Server 2000 program group provides a good set of counters for monitoring general database performance. You will probably want to add a few additional counters to the server, as well. The most useful counters for measuring backup performance are the SQLServer:BackupDevice object and the Device Throughput Bytes/sec object. Figure 6-24 shows an example of the information you can view in Performance Monitor.

A Few Final Tips . . .

The information provided by Windows NT/2000 Performance Monitor is probably very helpful in isolating bottlenecks. We've already mentioned that the most important step in increasing throughput of backups is to identify the real performance problem. It's possible that with current backup technologies, your disk subsystems may be slowing down the whole operation. If that's the case, your money might be better spent in upgrading your disk controllers or implementing RAID instead of upgrading the backup devices. When dealing with small databases, you will probably be satisfied by the performance of the default backup operations. However, when performing larger backups, you'll likely want to squeeze every possible bit of performance out of your system. Here are some tricks you can use to maximize performance:

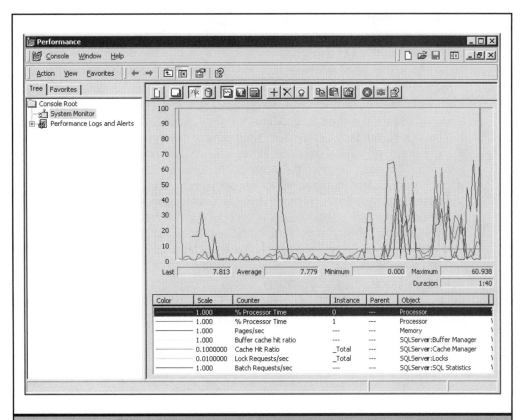

Figure 6-24. Viewing SQL Server 2000 performance statistics in Performance Monitor

▼ **Use parallel backup devices.** One of the bottlenecks in most backup and recovery operations is the destination device. Reading and writing information to and from tape backups and disk devices is usually relatively slow compared to the processing power and memory reserves available in modern servers. A good way to increase performance is to use multiple tape devices in parallel. That is, you should back up data to two or more devices at the same time. You're likely to see the greatest performance gain when dealing with tape drives, as media access and throughput are slower with tape than with disk devices. Once your parallel devices are in place, you can measure your performance gains by using Windows NT Performance Monitor, as described earlier.

■ **Use an efficient data protection strategy.** As discussed earlier in this chapter, there are several different types of backup operations. By strategically using full, differential, and transaction log backups, you can make sure that you're efficiently protecting information in accordance with your business requirements. If data only needs to be backed up daily, it might be counterproductive to "overprotect" information, due to performance hits. Similarly, investing in better backup hardware might make life easier on everyone—from users to database administrators.

- **Compress your backups.** With the speed of modern CPUs, the performance trade-off required to compress data is minimal, whereas the data volume saved can be significant. SQL Server does not perform any compression on database dumps. Since most databases contain mostly text information, these files generally compress very well. Compression ratios of 3:1 are not uncommon. If you have a lack of available space for performing backups or if you want to improve performance, consider using a compression utility to reduce data volumes before they're backed up. Alternatively, most current tape backup devices have the ability to perform compression on the fly—that is, the data to be written is sent to the storage device that compresses the data, before it is written to the media.

▲ **Upgrade your hardware.** Die-hard performance optimizers might consider this cheating, but I'm willing to take that chance! If you have reached what you believe are the limits of your current hardware, it might be time to upgrade. Again, you'll need to determine where the bottlenecks are. Cost-effective upgrades such as faster SCSI controllers, additional network interface cards, and additional memory can make a world of difference. In general, purchasing and installing additional RAM can go a long way toward improving overall SQL Server performance. Some tape backup hardware manufacturers might make it easier to "trade up" to newer backup technologies by offering credits on old hardware. Do your homework and find out how to best stretch your investment dollars with strategic upgrades.

Using these techniques, you'll surely be able to squeeze a little more life out of your existing hardware, software, and network investment.

SUMMARY

In this chapter, we focused on the technical details of backing up SQL Server databases. We started by looking at how you can best design your SQL Server storage options. Technologies such as RAID and the use of filegroups can provide a good solution for almost any environment. We then looked at how the various backup types—full, differential, and transaction logs—can be used to reduce performance impacts of backup operations. When it comes time to perform backups, the Database Maintenance Plan Wizard can take care of a lot of the tedious work. If you need more power and control over these operations, though, there are plenty of tools and commands that can be used. Finally, we covered some ways to monitor and optimize the performance of backup operations.

The good news is that you've now reviewed a lot of information that can be used to protect your data. With this technical information in mind, you should continue to the next chapter, where you'll find several tips for performing backups with SQL Server 2000. Many systems and database administrators might stop here. After all, the data is protected, so what more could anyone want? In Chapter 8, we'll look at how you can use these backups to *recover* the information you're so carefully protecting. We'll see how critical it is not only to be aware of, but also to rehearse, the actual steps that must be taken when data loss occurs.

CHAPTER 7

Restoring Databases

In previous chapters, we discussed the importance of creating a valid data protection plan based on business requirements. We looked at ways to secure information within the operating system and to back up data in SQL Server. The goal in all of those chapters was to find and implement measures that are designed to protect your organization's data.

In this chapter, we'll look at performing a task that is just as important. Although recovering data may not be a regular operation in your own environment, the ability to do so is the very reason to perform backups in the first place. Nevertheless, many environments spend much time in implementing backup processes—that is, essentially, making sure that data is copied off to another location such as tape or network devices. However, they seem to fall short in planning for the recovery of important information. Perhaps that's because recovery operations tend to be much less common. Whereas backups must run regularly to store recent copies of data, restore operations are only performed when problems occur. And, in many IT environments, there's so much work to do that recovery is one of those tasks that's left on the back burner. "I'll figure it out when the need arises" might be a common response. Regardless of the reasons, however, understanding SQL Server 2000's database recovery architecture is an absolutely vital part of data protection.

Much of the information in this chapter is based on topics covered earlier. To make the most of the information in these sections, you should first review the information covered in Chapter 6. You've likely put forth significant effort to make sure that your data is safely stored on another type of media. Recovery can be a perplexing situation if you don't understand how all the pieces of the puzzle fit together. How and what you recover will largely depend on the reasons for recovering your information. In this chapter, we'll look at methods and procedures for recovering data.

PLANNING FOR DATA RECOVERY

A common instinct is to wait until a problem occurs to figure out how best to recover information. Unfortunately, we don't truly appreciate the importance of our critical systems until they become unavailable due to some type of failure. Even a small database may be relied upon by many users who require that information to fulfill their job responsibilities. We've already covered reasons for performing data protection operations in earlier chapters. Here, we'll cover the importance of planning for data recovery. This topic, though often overlooked, is just as important as the steps involved in performing database backups. If incorrectly applied, a database restoration operation can cause more problems than the original hardware, software, or network failure that required it. With that in mind, let's look at some general best practices to keep in mind when planning for data recovery.

Establishing Recovery Procedures

The time following the loss of significant data is not the best time to plan for the operations required. Apart from being a stressful situation, we don't always think as clearly under pressure. For these reasons, it's important that you take the time to create and maintain data recovery procedures *before* they're actually needed. Included in these processes should be the technical steps required to recover information as quickly as possible and best practices for performing the necessary steps. It is just as important to ensure that procedures for notifying users and management are clearly spelled out. This can help tremendously when trying to prioritize what must be done when data loss occurs.

Coming up with a basic data recovery plan is only one step of the process. The second challenge is to effectively communicate this plan to the appropriate individuals. An IT-related company intranet can be very useful to meet this goal and will ensure that all necessary individuals have up-to-date information about current backup processes. Data recovery operations will likely involve everyone in the organization—from end users to IT staff to executive management.

Next, we'll look at ways in which your organization can create and document specific recovery procedures based on your data protection plan.

Performing Test Restorations

When you're under pressure to bring back data that has been lost, it is no time to begin learning about the restoration procedure. Understanding the technical issues related to restoring information is only one step of a much larger process. It's up to systems and database administrators to ensure that they can carry out the procedures required to restore a database with minimal hesitation in a real environment. That's where the idea of performing test restorations comes in.

The most obvious reason to perform test restorations is to validate your backups. Only by actually recovering data can you be sure that the operation will work properly. Performing test restorations not only ensures that your backup procedures work, but also helps you to develop a typical time estimate for how long a restoration will take. It also provides practice for the real thing and can aid in developing a set of procedures that less-experienced database administrators can follow, should the need arise.

You'll also need to determine how frequently you want to perform your test restorations. The most important thing to remember here is not to become complacent because of a few successes. The fact that your last four restoration operations were successful doesn't mean that you can slack off on the next one. That said, performing restoration operations does take time and effort, and these costs should be weighed when making plans. For example, performing a test of every backup might be ideal, but doing the tests weekly or monthly is much more practical from a business standpoint.

Testing Your Backups

Though doing so might sound like common sense, many administrators neglect to test the quality of their backups by actually restoring data. You're sure that something is being written to the tape, but are you sure that it can be retrieved? The backup utilities included with SQL Server and Windows NT/2000 allow you to perform a verification operation that compares the files on your backup media to those currently on your hard drive. Although you can be reasonably sure that this means your backup is usable, the best test is to do a complete restoration on a test machine. It's quite possible that certain database files will be in an inconsistent state, or files that were in use during backups may be missing. Depending on your business requirements, you may choose to get the experience by doing the restoration yourself, or assign the task to a help desk technician.

You will need a mechanism for performing test restore operations. Generally, you will not have the luxury of performing these operations on production servers. Therefore, a second offline server (one that's rarely used or might be used for development and testing) would be very useful. The machine does not have to have the same hardware configuration as the production server (although the closer the configurations are, the better). Additionally, the ability to host multiple instances of SQL Server 2000 on the same machine (which we covered in Chapter 4) can be very helpful. A database administrator can set up a second instance of SQL Server and use it to test backup and restore processes.

A major benefit of performing test restorations is that you can document the exact procedure required and you can time the process. Being comfortable with the entire process of restoring information will serve you well, especially in potentially stressful situations in which data loss has occurred. Some general tips to keep in mind during test restorations include

▼ **Remember your business requirements.**   In Part I of this book, we looked at many criteria you must consider when implementing a data protection plan. One of the major issues is recovery time—how long can your users wait before a server or database is brought back online? When testing and documenting your restoration procedures, be sure that your operations fit within this recommended recovery window. If they do not, now is the time to talk with management about what else might be done. Either the business requirement will have to be modified or additional resources (such as another database administrator or a replacement server) might be required. Knowing these factors up front will help reduce the blame placed on systems administrators for events such as hardware failures.

■ **Document the process.**   If you're a database administrator, you might ensure that you understand the database recovery process. But, what if you're not the one performing the operations? Although, in an ideal situation, no one else would have to perform data recovery, circumstances might require less-experienced individuals to do it. In documenting the steps required to restore information, be sure to provide enough detail so that others can perform these tasks, if necessary. Screenshots and step-by-step procedures are often very helpful. It's also a good idea to have others review and test the instructions before a problem occurs. Documentation is also important for generating an estimate of the time required to perform the process—information that your managers will likely want immediately after data loss or downtime occurs.

■ **Consider data loss scenarios.**   There are many different ways in which data loss can occur. For example, some problems occur due to incorrect user actions, while others occur due to failed hardware. It's important to have adequate procedures for handling these different situations. For example, if some user data is lost, you clearly do not need to restore the *master* database. The best solution might be to restore only a single table that is stored on one of several filegroups. Again, providing documentation for these operations is the best way to help others understand the issues surrounding database backups.

▲ **Keep and use spare servers.**   One of the major challenges of performing data recovery operations is that you generally can't do them on production machines without negatively impacting your users. Although it can be costly, the best way to test your data recovery processes is to use a second server. With another machine, you can test OS restorations and recovery of data from various scenarios. And, systems and database administrators should be able to use these machines for learning how to work with SQL Server 2000. There are, however, a few things you should keep in mind when doing such tests. First, at the network OS level, make sure that your server does not retain the same network configuration as the production server. Having two servers with the same IP address, for example, can cause network problems and prevent the accessibility of both machines. A good way to avoid this is to move the test server to an isolated network (connected only to a small hub, for example). Next, ensure that your data is really consistent on this recovery test server by having test clients connect to it and perform operations. You might find that some applications do not work without first making configuration changes to the server.

Table 7-1 documents the steps involved in a full server recovery.

The estimates in this table might seem very conservative. In some cases, it is much better to make an error in stating that it will take *longer* to recover data than it actually will. This accounts for any potential problems that might occur, without the need to change time estimates. Note that the time spent performing many of these steps could be reduced through different implementations. For example, if a hot standby server (that is, an existing server with a similar configuration) is available, it may not be necessary to repair the hardware fault and reinstall the OS. In the example in Table 7-1, this would save over an hour of time!

Step	Operation	Time Taken (mm:ss)	Running Total
1	Replace failed hardware or entire machine.	25:00	25:00
2	Reinstall Windows NT or Windows 2000 OS.	30:00	55:00
3	Install tape backup drivers and reboot.	10:00	65:00
4	Perform full restoration of failed partition(s).	120:00	185:00
5	Reboot system and verify that it's working.	15:00	200:00
6	Bring system online and notify users.	15:00	215:00

Table 7-1.   Steps Required for Performing a Full Server Recovery

Generating Test Restoration Scripts

It is a good idea to test your system following the completion of any type of data restoration operation. In some cases, it makes sense to write actual SQL scripts for restoring information should a loss occur. As an example, a basic script file might automatically drop a database and re-create information from the backup of another database. Although having such scripts available can save a lot of time and reduce chances for errors, there are drawbacks. First and foremost, the scripts must be kept up-to-date. Whenever a change occurs in the backup process, a corresponding change must occur in the restoration scripts. In some cases, an inaccurate or outdated restoration script can be worse than not having one at all, since inconsistencies or even data loss might occur.

A data restoration process might proceed according to the flowchart in Figure 7-1.

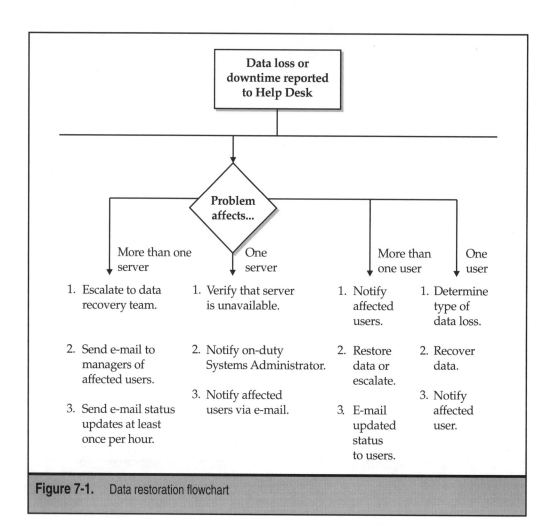

Figure 7-1.   Data restoration flowchart

The term *script* has a dual meaning when we're talking about databases. Another method of planning for data recovery might involve the generation of automatic SQL Server jobs or scripts that perform corrective actions. In Chapter 6, we looked at how SQL Server Agent can be used to schedule tasks to be performed automatically. Although automating database recovery generally isn't an easy task, properly tested scripts can alleviate much of the manual work involved in recovery and can prevent downtime. For example, in the case of the log file partition filling to capacity, a job that automatically deletes old backups and temporary files might keep your server in business while you order that additional hard disk.

In creating your test scripts, you should take into account not only the availability and accessibility of your database server, but also any client or application changes that might be required. For example, if you need to redirect all of your client machines to a standby server, you'll need to know how to reconfigure the applications they're running to access another machine. All of these considerations must be made when generating restoration scripts. The time and effort required to create and maintain them will pay off when data loss or downtime occurs.

Delegating Roles and Responsibilities

Emergency response professionals have learned a lot about human nature when working in extreme situations. Perhaps one of the most important lessons they have learned is that roles and responsibilities should be specifically assigned to individuals involved in the emergency situation. If you've ever seen a situation where emergency assistance is needed, you might have recognized the problem. Usually, someone telephones for help, but often there is a moment of confusion while people are trying to decide whether someone else has already called for help. A much better method is to point to a specific individual to perform the task. If this person is unable to do it, he or she can still call for the assistance of others. In any case, that person *owns* the issue and is responsible for seeing it through to completion.

When planning for recovery, everyone must know his or her roles and responsibilities. In a crisis situation, be sure to do the following:

▼ **Notify IT personnel.**   In many cases, users might be the first to notice (or *cause*) the loss of important information. In such cases, it's important that they immediately notify the appropriate personnel. One of the worst things that can happen is for untrained personnel to attempt to fix the problem themselves. This can lead to even more downtime and permanent data loss. This notification might involve calling a special phone number dedicated to high-priority issues.

■ **Notify affected users.**   One of the biggest problems related to downtime is that affected users rarely know what is going on. If a server is inaccessible, for example, a person might ask a coworker to access the same resource. If he or she is unable to do so, one of them should call the help desk to report the problem. In organizations of any size, however, this can result in a flood of calls to the help desk and to IT staff. One way to avoid the deluge is to immediately provide information regarding the downtime someplace where users can easily find it. A company intranet or the "please hold" message for the help desk's telephone line is ideal. Users should know that they can check these places first for immediate notification of problems.

Unfortunately, in their haste to notify users, IT departments generally tend to send messages that raise more questions instead of providing answers. For example, a simple statement that "Server1 is unavailable due to a disk failure" might be meaningful to IT staffers, but users will have many questions: "Is data loss expected?" "How long will the server be unavailable?" "What exactly is on Server1, and does it affect me?" Therefore, all data- and server-availability messages should include several pieces of information:

- **When the error occurred** Users should be aware of which data might be lost and how they might have been affected. For example, if an e-mail server went down, users would be able to determine which messages should be sent again.

- **Recommendations on user actions** In many cases, users can help alleviate the problem and can plan for its correction. For example, if a file/print server is unavailable, users should not try to reconnect to it until the problem has been resolved. Otherwise, excess network traffic and connection requests might impact other users. Additionally, users should be notified of business processes. In some cases, it might be necessary to record information using old-fashioned pen and paper.

- **Which systems are affected** In most cases, it is a good idea to spare users from technical details. Instead, information on which servers, resources, or services are affected should be sufficient.

- **Expected time of resolution** Users are probably most interested in knowing when they can resume their normal job functions. With this in mind, be sure to include your best guess. It's also important to state that this is only an estimate.

- **Updates** No one wants to listen to a three-day-old message about server downtime that has already been fixed. Be sure to keep downtime notification messages current, and inform end users about when they will receive updated status information.

- **Expected effects** If any data loss is expected, this is the place to mention it. For example, if transaction log backups are performed hourly, users should know that any information that has been entered during the last few hours might need to be reentered.

- **Replace hardware.** If replacement hardware is required, one or more individuals should be designated to perform this task. If spare hardware is kept for this purpose, the task might be very easy. If not, the process may require calling a vendor for replacement parts or attempting to scavenge what's necessary from other machines.

■ **Execute recovery operations.**   Obviously, someone needs to get to work as soon as possible on recovering information. Ideally, this person should be a well-trained IT professional who is familiar with data recovery operations. In some cases, however, such a person may not be available.

■ **Inform management.**   In many organizations, managers and executives want to know what is going on *every minute*. This is clearly unreasonable and counterproductive. A good manager will leave IT professionals to do their jobs and trust in a successful outcome.

▲ **Perform other functions.**   Perhaps one of the most important rules to remember is that not everyone needs to help with the recovery operations. When data loss occurs, it might be much more efficient to allow one or a few individuals to coordinate dealing with the problems.

The tasks listed are not necessarily placed in chronological order. In some environments, for example, it might be important to ensure that all users are aware of the problem, before beginning data recovery. For example, in a shipping and receiving dock, systems and database administrators might advise users to temporarily record information manually while the database is unavailable. They must then later input the information from the manual records.

Again, it's easy to forget to include all of the above information when urgent situations do arise. Therefore, it might be helpful to create a template (as a document or e-mail message) that contains the basic outline of the types of information to be provided. This would ensure that something critical (like the names of the servers that are affected) is not left out.

In a small environment, an individual might assume all of the roles just listed. That may sound like a lot of work, but this should be anticipated, given the importance of maintaining data protection procedures. Finally, when data loss occurs, one of the worst situations to be in is to have, in addition to the stress of finding out what went wrong and how to correct it, a constant stream of managers interrupting the process. When data loss or downtime occurs, the focus of all individuals should be on correcting the situation. Although it might be a human reflex, placing blame and deciding how to prevent the problem in the future are topics that are best left until after a resolution to the immediate concern is found.

Creating Contingency Plans

There is a whole area of IT practices related to *business continuity planning* (BCP). Many businesses have found that their success and viability depend on the availability of their computing resources and information. This is especially true for "e-businesses" and companies that provide services on the Internet. In many of these cases, the services of these computers *are* the product.

The purpose of contingency planning is to provide for the recovery of information and reinstatement of uptime in the event of serious and unexpected failures. Developing a plan and obtaining the necessary hardware, software, network, and personnel resources can be quite costly. However, in some cases, it is absolutely necessary. For example, in the United States, millions of people count on government programs for their livelihood. Any interruption in these services due to technical malfunctions can cause unnecessary hardship.

A common method of contingency planning includes the presence of a backup site. Although it's a dismal thought, in the event of a complete catastrophe (such as a natural disaster), necessary information can be transferred to another area of the world, and a parallel network environment can be established. Creating and maintaining business continuity plans can be a long and difficult process. Usually, organizations will work with outside expert consultants to create, implement, manage, and support a contingency plan. With these plans in place, an organization can protect its operations from all but the largest, most severe catastrophes. It is well beyond the scope of this book to discuss the various issues concerning contingency plans and business continuity. However, you should be aware that creating such plans involves much more than the IT department—the entire organization must be committed to ensuring that such plans are created and executed properly.

DATA LOSS SCENARIOS

Before you can begin to plan for recovering information, you should be able to envision the various scenarios in which data loss might occur. In some cases, you might experience the complete loss of a server due to a serious hardware failure. In others, it might be just a few files or a database table that must be restored from tape. In any case, you'll want to make sure you understand the issues related to restoring information before you are forced to do so under pressure. In the following sections, we'll look at various scenarios in which data loss might occur and provide an overview of some potential solutions.

Hardware Failures

When speaking of data recovery, the scenario that people seem to think of most often is complete data loss or system failure. Although it could happen, such an event is much more rare than accidental data deletion. Nevertheless, it's important to decide what to do in this worst-case scenario before it occurs.

Generally, when a hardware failure occurs, a server or workstation can no longer function as required for daily operations. Hardware failures might involve components, such as power supplies, hard disks, network cards, or motherboards, or they might involve an environmental problem, such as the loss of a router, making one or more servers inaccessible. The same symptoms may have different causes and will require different actions to resolve. Some general best practices related to dealing with hardware failures include the following:

▼ **Provide for redundancy.** In earlier chapters, we talked about ways to protect data through redundancy. For example, RAID technology and multiple power supplies can prevent common failures. When implementing redundant hardware, it's important to keep in mind which failures you will be protected against. If downtime is not an option, you might want to choose a clustering solution.

This will protect against hardware failures of the servers themselves, but if the machines are located on the same network, a router failure may cause both servers to be unavailable. Of course, you can protect against this by providing multiple routes to the servers, but it takes additional planning. Even with that level of protection, a physical disaster will cause downtime.

■ **Keep spares.**   To the extent your business requirements and budget permit, you will probably want to keep spare hardware available. Although redundancy can protect against many problems, some problems might require an entire server replacement. If, for example, a motherboard component fails, you can simply remove the hard disks from the failed machine and place them in another one. Be sure that the hardware is exactly the same, since differences as minor as network card revisions can require driver changes.

▲ **Enter into a maintenance contract.**   Most major manufacturers of hardware provide a service or maintenance contract. In the event of a failure, parts replacements can be made under the contract. Based on the level of support provided, this might involve a technician visiting on-site to repair failed machines or the shipping of a replacement part. It is important to fully understand the terms of a service level agreement when it comes to support and maintenance contracts. There are few things worse than finding out that "24-hour" support only applies on weekdays or that parts are not guaranteed to be in stock.

By implementing these best practices, you can ensure that when hardware failures occur, you'll be able to deal with them appropriately.

Performing a Complete Reinstallation

One problem that may occur due to a hardware or software failure is the inability to boot the server. Troubleshooting the problem can be quite difficult, because you can't even access a console on the local machine. There are, however, several ways to fix your system when such problems occur. The first step in resolving the problem is to determine what has occurred. In some cases, the problem might be the overwriting of the boot sector on the hard drive. In others, however, much more widespread data corruption or hardware failures may have occurred.

The general process to restore a server from backups involves the following steps:

1. Replace the failed hardware (if necessary).

2. Reconfigure disk devices (if necessary). If you're using RAID, multiple partitions, or other disk configurations, you may be required to repartition your disks before reinstalling the operating system.

3. Reinstall the operating system.

4. Reinstall all software and drivers required to access the backup device (usually only necessary for tape backups).

5. Fully restore the operating system and any data that has been lost.

6. Test the restoration. Following a reboot of the operating system, you should test your server to ensure that it is working.

The preceding operations probably seem like a lot of time-consuming work. Make no mistake, they are! However, based on your business requirements, this might be acceptable. Later in this chapter, we'll look at ways in which you can plan for and manage the time required to restore database information.

Disaster Recovery Options

In Chapter 5, we looked at the types of features that are available in many backup software solutions. One feature supported by several of the packages is often called a "disaster recovery" option. This feature allows systems administrators to recover from a total loss of data on a server (or loss of the server itself) without requiring all the steps necessary for a manual reinstallation. Specifically, disaster recovery options usually include a minimal set of drivers that can be used to access the tape backup or other devices without requiring the installation of the entire OS. This reduces the complete recovery process to the following steps:

1. Boot the system from the disaster recovery media. Usually, this will mean booting from one or more floppy disks, but can also include other bootable media, such as CD-ROM drives.

2. Recover information directly from the appropriate backup tapes.

3. Reboot the computer and perform a restore of any additional data (if necessary).

This process can save considerable time and effort in reloading the OS. However, certain tools require the systems administrator to create and maintain specific disaster recovery media. Be sure you understand the procedures for your backup solution before you have to test it under pressure!

Database and Server Corruption

A primary requirement when using RDBMSs is consistency. All information must be current up to a certain point in time. If it is not, incorrect or misleading data may be reported. Due to hardware or software failures, it is possible for databases to become corrupt. If there is an internal inconsistency in one or more of the database files on your server, you can attempt to fix them. SQL Server includes several built-in tools for dealing with lost information and corrupted server installations. Here, we'll look at tools and methods for recovering from these types of failures.

Automatic Recovery

A common problem that occurs in most environments is the improper shutdown of a database server. This might be due to an unexpected loss of power, a hardware failure, or administrator error. If a database server is stopped, the database might contain some transactions that have been written to the transaction log but have not yet been committed to the database itself. This could lead to a database that is inconsistent to a point in time and may result in additional problems (such as further data corruption).

To protect against data corruption, SQL Server 2000 automatically performs a recovery operation when the service is started. This operation commits any transactions that appear in the transaction log but have not yet been committed to the database, and rolls back any transactions that cannot be completed. This ensures that the information is consistent and that the database is ready for use by clients and applications. Best of all, the process is automatic when the SQL Server service is started and requires no additional effort by a systems or network administrator.

Recovering System Databases

In addition to user databases and objects that are stored on an installation of SQL Server, the database server itself depends on various system tables for proper operations. Table 7-2 provides a list of the system databases and their functions.

In general, if a system database is lost or corrupted, it can be recovered the same way as any other database. We'll cover the specific operations required to restore a database later in this chapter. The tempdb database is a structure that does not require any backups

Database	Contents	Notes
Distribution	Information related to replication	This database is present only if the server is configured as a replication "distributor"; replication services must be stopped before the distribution database can be restored.
Master	Systemwide settings and database structure information	Master is required for proper operation of SQL Server.
Model	A template from which all new databases are derived	By default, model includes various system tables and views; database administrators and developers can create objects in model to make them available in all new databases.
Msdb	Scheduling information used by SQL Server	For scheduled jobs (such as backup and recovery operations) to be performed, the msdb database must be intact.
Tempdb	Temporary information about user sessions; cached query information	Tempdb is automatically re-created whenever SQL Server is started and stopped; therefore, it is not necessary to back up or restore tempdb.

Table 7-2.   SQL Server 2000 System Databases

or recovery, because it is automatically re-created whenever the database server is stopped and restarted. If a corruption of the tempdb database occurs, the server should be able to recover automatically (unless, of course, a hardware failure prevents it). Although this covers the loss of most of the system databases, what if the server will not start? For example, if the master database is missing or invalid, SQL Server may be unable to start. Let's look at ways to deal with this issue next.

SQL Server Startup Options

In some cases, data or software corruption might prevent SQL Server from starting. One way to fix corrupt executable files is to restore from a backup. Alternatively, you can reinstall SQL Server 2000 from the installation media. If the SQL Server installation cannot be started, or if you require special startup options, you can start SQL Server with the command-line switches shown in Table 7-3.

Startup Switch	Function	Notes
/T [Number]	Specifies a trace flag for startup options	This should only be used in special cases when trace flags are suggested by SQL Server Product Support.
-B	Specifies a breakpoint on certain errors	This option is used in conjunction with the –y switch for determining when stack dumps will be generated.
-c	Prevents SQL Server from starting as a service	This can decrease the time it takes to start SQL Server, but using it generally isn't a good idea, because it is more difficult to administer and monitor. Additionally, when the user logs off the computer, the SQL Server service will be shut down.
-d [PhysicalFile]	Starts SQL Server in the master database	If this option is not specified, the installation default settings from the Registry are used.
-e [PhysicalFile]	Starts SQL Server in the error log file	If this option is not specified, the installation default settings from the Registry are used.
-f	Starts SQL Server in minimal configuration (fail-safe) mode	This setting uses the minimal options required to start SQL Server; it can be useful when systemwide parameters have been configured incorrectly.

Table 7-3. SQL Server 2000 Command-Line Switches

Startup Switch	Function	Notes
-g [Number]	Amount of stack memory to reserve	This is useful when it is necessary to limit the amount of memory that SQL Server will use.
-l [PhysicalFile]	Starts SQL Server in the transaction log file for the master database	
-m	Starts SQL Server in single-user administration mode	This allows only one user to connect to the SQL Server installation; it is useful for troubleshooting and performing maintenance operations that require databases to be unused. The CHECKPOINT process is suspended in single-user mode, so operations from the transaction log are not committed to disk.
-n	Prevents events from being written to the Windows NT/ 2000 Application Event Log	It is recommended that you specify an error log file (with the –e switch) if this option is enabled.
-O	Prevents support for Distributed Component Object Model (DCOM)	This is useful for troubleshooting issues related to the remote instantiation of components.
-s [InstanceName]	Specifies the name of the SQL Server 2000 instance to start	This command is useful on machines that have multiple instances of SQL Server 2000 configured.
-x	Prevents SQL Server from recording statistics on CPU time cache usage	This option may increase overall system performance, but limits the ability to troubleshoot and measure performance.
-y [Number]	Generates a stack dump based on a specific error number	This is a useful option for troubleshooting kernel-level and memory-related issues.

Table 7-3.   SQL Server 2000 Command-Line Switches *(continued)*

By default, the –d, –e, and –l switches are defined with startup values. Notice that the switches generally do not require spaces or quotation marks for the arguments. Although, for normal operations, you'll be satisfied with the default startup options, each of these switches can be quite helpful in troubleshooting and customization. As SQL Server 2000 supports the use of multiple instances per database server, you'll also need to specify the name of the instance you want to start if you're taking advantage of this option.

There are several ways in which you can specify and use SQL Server 2000's startup switches. The first is to specify the options in the Services Control Panel applet (in Windows NT 4) or the Services Administrative Tools applet (in Windows 2000). Another, easier way is to specify the options by right-clicking the server name in Enterprise Manager and choosing Properties. By clicking the Startup Parameters button on the General tab, you can add and remove various parameters, as shown in Figure 7-2.

A third option is to start SQL Server from the command line. It is important to note that if you start SQL Server from the command line or by running the executable manually, the database server runs under the current user process. When you log off, the SQL Server instance is automatically shut down. Note that you may need to specify the name of the SQL Server 2000 instance to start. This is done by either changing to the specific directory in which the instance of SQL Server 2000 is installed (for example, C:\Program Files\Microsoft SQL Server\MSSQL$InstanceName\Binn\), or by using the –s parameter to specify an instance. For example, the following command can be used to start the default instance of SQL Server 2000 in fail-safe mode:

```
sqlservr -f
```

The result is shown in Figure 7-3.

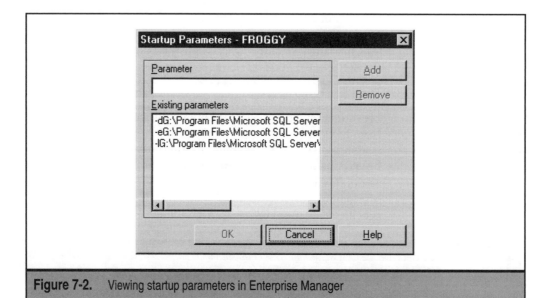

Figure 7-2. Viewing startup parameters in Enterprise Manager

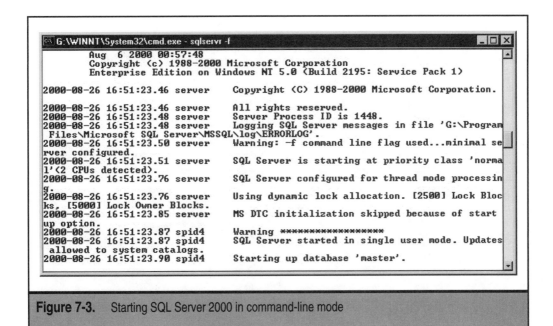

```
 G:\WINNT\System32\cmd.exe - sqlservr -f                              _ □ ×
           Aug  6 2000 00:57:48
           Copyright (c) 1988-2000 Microsoft Corporation
           Enterprise Edition on Windows NT 5.0 (Build 2195: Service Pack 1)

2000-08-26 16:51:23.46 server       Copyright (C) 1988-2000 Microsoft Corporation.

2000-08-26 16:51:23.46 server       All rights reserved.
2000-08-26 16:51:23.48 server       Server Process ID is 1448.
2000-08-26 16:51:23.48 server       Logging SQL Server messages in file 'G:\Program
 Files\Microsoft SQL Server\MSSQL\log\ERRORLOG'.
2000-08-26 16:51:23.50 server       Warning: -f command line flag used...minimal se
rver configured.
2000-08-26 16:51:23.51 server       SQL Server is starting at priority class 'norma
l'(2 CPUs detected).
2000-08-26 16:51:23.76 server       SQL Server configured for thread mode processin
g.
2000-08-26 16:51:23.76 server       Using dynamic lock allocation. [2500] Lock Bloc
ks, [5000] Lock Owner Blocks.
2000-08-26 16:51:23.85 server       MS DTC initialization skipped because of start
up option.
2000-08-26 16:51:23.87 spid4        Warning ********************
2000-08-26 16:51:23.87 spid4        SQL Server started in single user mode. Updates
 allowed to system catalogs.
2000-08-26 16:51:23.90 spid4        Starting up database 'master'.
```

Figure 7-3.   Starting SQL Server 2000 in command-line mode

To shut down this instance of SQL Server, you can simply press CTRL-C. You will be prompted to verify the shutdown of this instance of SQL Server.

Rebuilding Registry Settings

In some cases, the Registry settings that are required for normal operations by SQL Server 2000 may become corrupted. In such a case, you may need to rebuild the appropriate settings before SQL Server will start. This can be done by rerunning the SQL Server 2000 setup process. As shown in Figures 7-4 and 7-5, you can choose Advanced Options and the Registry Rebuild option.

It is important to understand exactly what a Registry Rebuild operation does. First and foremost, this process only rebuilds Registry settings; it does not copy files or re-create any databases. Therefore, you should ensure that the necessary database files are still available. Secondly, you must choose the same SQL Server installation settings (including file directories) that you chose when you originally installed SQL Server. Once you make the appropriate choices, the setup process will rebuild the necessary Registry settings, and (if all goes well) you should be able to restart SQL Server.

Restoring and Rebuilding the Master Database

All information about database objects is stored within the system tables that reside on the master database. This is one reason that a full database backup is recommended after any changes to database structure have occurred. An instance of SQL Server cannot start

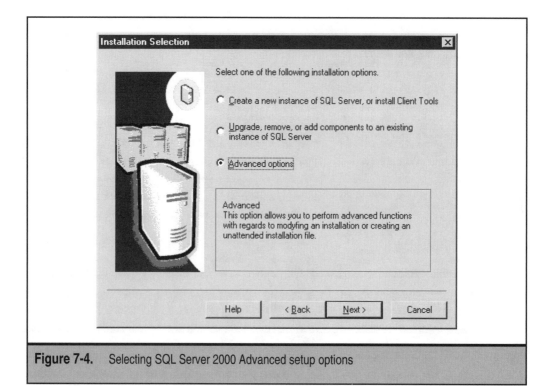

Figure 7-4. Selecting SQL Server 2000 Advanced setup options

if the master database is corrupt, inconsistent, or unavailable. Although the goal of a good data protection plan is to ensure that this does not happen, it is possible for the master database to be lost or become corrupted. The ideal way to fix the problem is to restore the information from a recent backup.

To restore the master database, you'll need to start SQL Server in single-user mode. Then, you can restore it as you would any other database. The specific steps required to recover databases will be covered later in this chapter. Keep in mind that you will need to manually reapply any changes to database objects that have occurred since the last backup of master. The recommended practice is to make a full backup of master after any database structure or object changes. If this hasn't been done or isn't possible, you should make sure that you maintain scripts for all database changes since the last full backup.

But, what can you do if you don't have a valid backup of the master database or if SQL Server will not start? Since it is critical to have a valid copy of this database to start and run SQL Server properly, a command-line utility called Rebuild Master can be used to re-create a default copy of the master database. Once this database has been re-created, you should

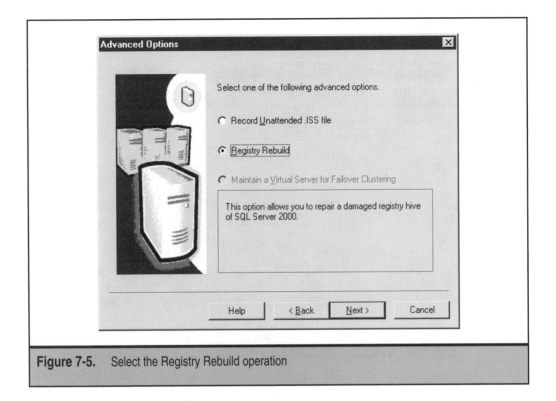

Figure 7-5.   Select the Registry Rebuild operation

be able to restart SQL Server and then restore from a recent backup of the master database. To rebuild the database, you'll need to have access to the rebuildm.exe utility. (By default, this is located in Program Files\Microsoft SQL Server\80\Tools\Binn). The specific procedure required to rebuild the master database is described in the following steps.

STEP-BY-STEP

Rebuilding the Master Database

1. If it's not already shut down, stop the SQL Server service.
2. Run the rebuildm.exe for your SQL Server installation. By default, this file is located in Program Files\Microsoft SQL Server\80\Tools\Binn. The Rebuild

Master application will prompt you for the source directory for the master database files:

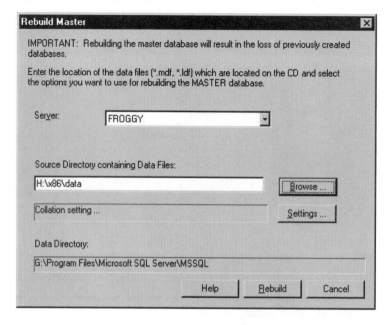

3. Click Browse and find the location of the master database files on the SQL Server 2000 CD-ROM or on a network share that contains these files. The name of the file should be master.mdf.

4. Click Settings and specify the same character set, sort order, and Unicode collation settings you used when you installed SQL Server.

5. When you have made the appropriate settings, click Rebuild to start restoring the master database.

Once you have recovered a valid copy of master, you should be able to start SQL Server in single-user mode and recover from a recent backup. If user database files are still available and valid, you can then reattach them to the server without the need to re-store the files from a backup. We'll cover the commands for attaching databases shortly.

Other Scenarios

In addition to the standard data recovery operations you might need to perform, there are several other operations that might be useful. For example, copying and moving databases between servers can be accomplished using the standard backup and restoration operations. However, this method might be tedious or impractical when moving many or large databases between servers. Fortunately, there are many useful commands in SQL Server 2000 that can be used for managing these tasks. In the next few sections, we'll look at some ways in which you can deal with changing machine names, attaching and reattaching databases, and copying information.

Copying Databases and Data

A common question pertaining to the use of SQL Server 2000 is, What's the best way to copy databases? There are several methods for performing the necessary actions:

▼ **Copy Database Wizard**   New in SQL Server 2000 is the Copy Database Wizard. This tool has been included to greatly simplify the operation of copying databases between instances of SQL Server 2000. It is also useful for upgrading SQL Server 7 databases. We covered the details of using the Copy Database Wizard in Chapter 6. The benefit of this method is that it can copy all necessary database objects, including security information. Furthermore, database administrators can make changes to physical file locations to accommodate different server configurations.

■ **Backup and restoration**   We covered backups in Chapter 6. Later in this chapter, we'll cover methods for restoring information. Using the backup and recovery features built into SQL Server 2000 is a good way to copy all the information in your databases. All database objects, including tables, indexes, and stored procedures, will be properly carried over. The one exception relates to security. As discussed in Chapter 4, the security architecture of SQL Server involves the creation of logins at the server level. These logins are then mapped to database users and roles. If the database logins do not exist on the destination server, you need to either re-create them or remap existing database users to different logins.

■ **Data Transformation Services (DTS)**   DTS is designed not only to move data between compatible data sources, but also to make changes to data during the transfer operation. DTS is an ideal tool for populating data warehouses or for storing information from various data sources in a central location. (We discussed DTS briefly in Chapter 4.) When you want to copy information between databases, DTS's Data Transformation Wizard enables you to quickly copy the data. A major benefit is that you can use many different data sources and destinations for information (including ODBC data sources, text files, other RDBMSs, Microsoft Excel spreadsheets, and Microsoft Access databases). Furthermore, custom "packages" can be created and scheduled to copy data regularly, as needed. During the process, DTS can perform any number of tasks, including sending e-mail to systems and database administrators regarding the success or failure of an operation, or executing a SQL script. When it comes to copying information between installations of SQL Server 2000, the tools and features of DTS might be more than what is needed. If, however, you want to copy data to other data sources or want operations to be regularly scheduled, look into using DTS.

- **SQL Scripts**   Through Enterprise Manager, you can quickly and easily generate scripts for creating database objects. This can easily be done in Enterprise Manager by right-clicking on the name of a database, selecting All Tasks, and then clicking on Generate SQL Scripts. Figures 7-6 and 7-7 show examples of the options that are available. Note that you can choose which objects are scripted and details about the types of statements you want included. The resulting scripts contain only information about the database objects in your database. For example, they include the definition of a table, including data types and any constraints that might be present. The scripts do not, however, contain the INSERT statements required to copy actual data. Overall, generating scripts is a good way to create a "blank" copy of an existing database. The scripts are also quite useful to developers and database administrators.

- **Bulk copy (bcp)**   The bcp utility can be used to copy information to and from SQL Server databases (as well as to and from many other data sources). The

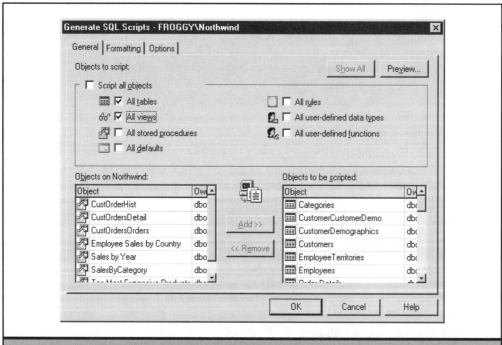

Figure 7-6.   Selecting objects to script in Enterprise Manager

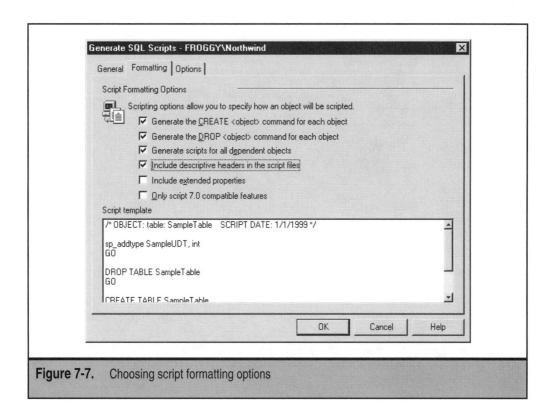

Figure 7-7. Choosing script formatting options

main purpose of bcp is to transfer data in and out of SQL Server 2000. Although the files can be used to transfer information between installations of SQL Server 2000, there are better methods (such as performing a backup and restoration). If you need to move or copy large quantities of data between applications or different types of database servers, however, bcp can help properly format the information for interchange. You can get more information on using this utility in Chapter 8.

▲ **Scripts for server settings** In addition to the database objects you might want to copy, you may want to copy server settings between installations of SQL Server 2000. Fortunately, there's an easy way to script the creation (or re-creation) of Jobs, Alerts, and Operators defined in SQL Server. To do so, right-click the appropriate object(s) in Enterprise Manager and choose All Tasks from the context-sensitive menu. As illustrated in Figure 7-8, you'll have the option of generating scripts for the existing objects. The scripts are useful because they avoid manual data reentry and, in some cases, can be easier to use and maintain than the same options accessed via the GUI of Enterprise Manager.

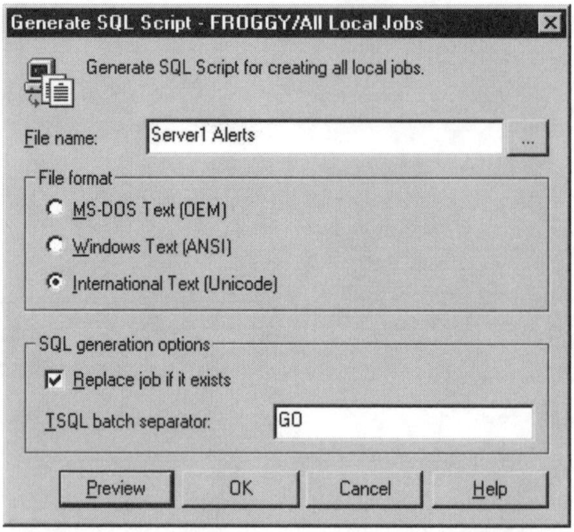

Figure 7-8.   Scripting Alerts in Enterprise Manager

Each of the preceding methods has its strengths and weaknesses, depending on the exact task you're trying to perform. In most cases, you'll have several methods to choose from, and all will perform an adequate job.

Attaching and Detaching Databases

As previously mentioned, there are ways to back up database files while they're offline and not being used. You can detach a database from a server without deleting the actual files on which the database resides. This might be useful, for example, if you simply want to move a data file between servers without performing backup and restoration operations. Let's look at the process in detail.

The first step is to detach a database. In SQL Server 2000, this can easily be done using Enterprise Manager.

STEP-BY-STEP

Attaching and Detaching Databases

1. To detach a database in Enterprise Manager, select the name of the database that you want to detach.

2. Right-click on the name of the database, and select All Tasks | Detach Database. The dialog box will show you two important pieces of information. First, you'll see how many users are currently connected to the database. The database can only be detached if there are no users connected to it. To kill the connections, simply click the Clear button. You will be given the option to notify users that the database is being taken offline.

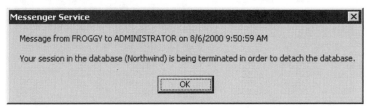

3. Also, if the database is being used in replication, you may not be able to detach it. Note that you have an option to update statistics prior to the detach operation. This is useful for improving performance since the statistics may be out of date when the database is reattached. To detach the database, click OK.

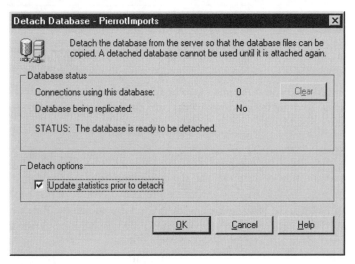

4. Note that after you detach the database, it will no longer be shown in the Databases folder within Enterprise Manager. To reattach the database in Enterprise Manager, right-click on the Databases folder and select All Tasks | Attach Database.

5. You will be prompted to enter information about the physical location of the database files that you want to attach. You should specify the location of an MDF file. If the file is valid, the settings for the attach operation will

automatically be provided. You can choose the name for the attached database and specify the owner. To attach the database, click OK.

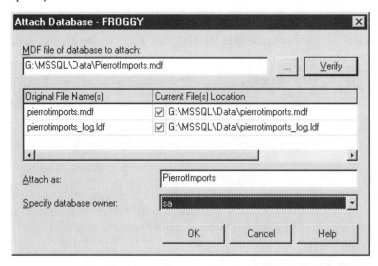

6. The database should now be ready for use and will appear in Enterprise Manager.

Attaching and detaching databases can also be performed through the use of system stored procedures. To detach a database, you can use the sp_detach_db stored procedure, as in the following example:

```
execute sp_detach_db 'Employees'
```

After you execute this command, the database and transaction log file(s) remain intact, but they are inaccessible to the system and to users. You will not see the name of the database within Enterprise Manager or within the system tables. You can now move or rename the data files to another location on the same machine or to another SQL Server 2000 installation.

After you move or rename the files, you can reattach them by using the sp_attach_db command. Information about the data files does not exist on the server, so you must specify the physical location of the files. For example, the following command will automatically reattach the transaction log file(s) associated with the database used in the preceding example:

```
Execute sp_attach_db 'Employees', 'c:\Employees_data.mdf'
```

Procedure	Function	Syntax
sp_attach_db	Attaches the data files of a database to a server; transaction log files are reattached automatically	```sp_attach_db [@dbname =] 'dbname', [@filename1 =] 'filename_n'[,...16]```
sp_detach_db	Detaches database and transaction log data files from SQL Server; the skipchecks option instructs SQL Server not to update the statistics for the database	```sp_detach_db [@dbname =] 'dbname' [, [@skipchecks =] 'skipchecks']```

Table 7-4. Stored Procedures Used for Attaching and Detaching Databases

Note that if a database uses multiple files, you can choose to attach or detach one or more of them within the same command. However, if you remove only some of the data files, you might not be able to access all the objects that are part of the database. Table 7-4 provides a summary of the commands and syntax for attaching and detaching databases.

Changing the Machine Name

An installation of SQL Server 2000 assumes the name of the machine onto which it is installed. For example, if my computer is named WORKSTATION1, the name of the SQL Server installation is also WORKSTATION1. So, what happens when the computer name is changed? SQL Server 2000 does not automatically update its internal settings to reflect the change, and you will receive an error message on startup stating that the SQL Server installation is corrupt. Although the error message might be alarming, you should know that your information is safe. The only problem is that the SQL Server services cannot automatically start. Of course, the easiest way to fix the problem is to change the name of the machine back to its original value.

CAUTION: Changing the name of a SQL Server machine should be done with care, because various tools, scripts, applications, and Enterprise Manager itself might depend on the name of this server to perform specific operations. When the name changes, these settings must be updated as well.

Several steps are required to update SQL Server 2000's settings, as described next.

STEP-BY-STEP

Renaming a SQL Server Machine

1. Rename the machine using the standard network options.

2. Rerun the Setup program, but do not choose any changes in the installed options. Setup will ask you if you want to refresh the current installation. Choosing to perform this action will update the internal references to the machine name.

3. Drop the old server name and add the new one by using the following commands:

```
sp_dropserver <oldmachinename>
GO
sp_addserver <newmachinename>, local
```

This procedure will update the references to the new machine name and should not cause any loss of data. Use this procedure if changes to the machine name are required, but beware of undesired effects on scripts, client applications, and users that use this machine name.

Resetting Corrupted or Suspect Databases

Occasionally, a database might become corrupted due to an improper shutdown or a hardware failure. The symptoms can be somewhat scary: the database may be listed with a gray icon in Enterprise Manager, and logins to the database may not be possible. The easiest method for bringing a database online might be to attempt to reset its status. This can be done using the following stored procedure:

```
sp_ResetStatus 'DatabaseName'
```

This procedure will attempt to roll forward specific database transactions to restore the database to a consistent point in time. If the reset status procedure is unsuccessful, you will probably need to restore the database from the most recent valid backup.

DATA RESTORATION OPTIONS

In this part of the chapter, we'll focus on the ways you can recover from failures in your SQL Server 2000 installation. As we discussed in earlier chapters, many types of data loss can be attributed to user error. A common example is a user executing a DELETE query with an incorrect or missing WHERE clause. In this case, so much data might be lost that a restoration from backup is required.

Remember, however, that recovering a lost or corrupted database might be only part of the solution. In addition to recovering database information, you might need to recover your OS. We covered ways to recover data and programs on installations of SQL Server 2000 in Chapter 3. In that chapter, the basics of fixing situations in which the machine will not boot, reinstalling the OS, and providing for fault tolerance were described. Be sure you understand those processes, because recovering SQL Server 2000 databases is not very useful if your Windows 2000 Server installation is corrupt! Building on the recovery mechanisms covered previously, let's start to look at the actual operations that might be required to recover information stored in SQL Server 2000 databases and objects.

Database Recovery

Although the following terms are often used interchangeably, there is a difference in SQL Server terminology:

▼   **Restoration**   An operation that copies data from a valid backup file to a new or existing database

▲   **Recovery**   The process of bringing a database server back online to a consistent point in time

In general, your restoration operations will likely perform both tasks. In the simplest case, a restoration of a database from a full backup is made. Immediately after the data is restored, a recovery is performed, leaving the database in a usable state and ready to accept client connections.

NOTE: The types of recovery you can perform will largely be based on the recovery model of your databases. If you are unfamiliar with SQL Server 2000's recovery model architecture, review the information in Chapter 6 before you continue.

That covers the basics of using full backups, but what about more complex scenarios involving file, filegroup, and transaction log backups? In these cases, you'll want to perform all of your data restoration operations first. The *last* operation will bring the database back online by performing a recovery. A recovery rolls back any transactions that were not committed in the database at the completion of the backup and rolls back any other operations. The end result is a consistent database that is ready for use. For example, assume that we have a database that was backed up using the following operations:

▼   Full backups every Sunday evening

■   Differential backups completed on weeknights, Monday through Saturday, at 9:00 P.M.

▲   Transaction log backups performed every hour between the hours of 9:00 A.M. and 6:00 P.M.

Assuming a complete loss of the database occurs on Thursday at 11:53 A.M., we'll need to restore from several backups and then recover the database to bring it back online. The exact sequence of steps is as follows:

1. Restore from the full database backup.
2. Restore differential backup from Wednesday.
3. Restore transaction log backups from 9:00 A.M. and 10:00 A.M.
4. Restore the transaction log backup from 11:00 A.M. *with recovery*.

Figure 7-9 illustrates the database restoration and recovery operations required to bring this installation back online to the latest point in time allowable by the backups. When performing a backup, SQL Server also provides the ability to save an "undo log file" to disk. This file is used mainly for the purpose of establishing and maintaining standby servers (a topic we'll cover in Chapter 8).

Fortunately, as we'll see later in this chapter, the tools and utilities included with SQL Server 2000 can make these complex operations much easier to manage. Now that we have an overview of the processes involved, let's move on to look at how we can use the specific backup types.

Using Differential Backups

Differential backups contain only the data that has changed since the time of the last full backup. Therefore, they are generally smaller than full backups and require less time to perform. When recovering data, however, you should keep in mind that you must have a working copy of the most recent full backup before you can begin restoring data. If several differential backups have been performed since the last full backup, you will likely want to use the most recent one. However, any of the backups can be used if, for example, you want to restore to a point before the last differential backup was made or if one or

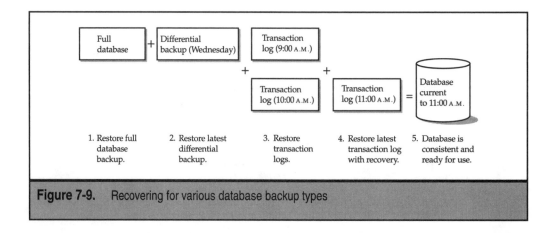

Figure 7-9.   Recovering for various database backup types

more of the backups is corrupt, missing, or otherwise unusable. Differential backups provide a good way to optimize backup plans, but do support some of the functions of transaction log backups (covered next).

Applying Transaction Logs

Transaction log backups are frequently used in circumstances where other backup types are not feasible. The transaction log stores information about the various database transactions that have been performed on the server since the log was last truncated. Generally, backing up the transaction log will take much less time than backing up the entire database, because only information about data that was modified is required. Additionally, less storage space is required to record transaction log backups. In addition to these benefits, transaction log backups provide additional flexibility when performing restoration operations. Specifically, transaction logs can be recovered up to a specific point in time. We'll cover this topic shortly.

When you're recovering data from transaction logs, it is important to remember two points:

▼ **The restoration operation must begin with a valid full or differential backup.**   Transaction log backups can be used only when the last full or differential backup set is available. Restoring from these backups ensures that the database is consistent to a point in time and that all data is present.

▲ **Transaction logs must be applied sequentially.**   When multiple transaction logs are required to bring a database consistent to a time nearest the failure, all of the transaction log backups must be available. Since an unbroken chain of these files is required, you should take great care to ensure that all the files are valid during your backup process. If one of the files is corrupt, missing, or otherwise unusable, you will be able to recover only up to the point where the chain is broken.

These are important concepts when performing recovery because many large database installations rely on the use of transaction logs to minimize data loss in the event of a hardware, software, or user failure.

Recovering Files and Filegroups

A new feature in SQL Server 2000 is the ability to store databases and database objects on specific files or filegroups. In Chapter 6, we noted how database administrators could choose to back up only specific files in a database. This operation can reduce the time required to back up only parts of a database. Although the backup operation isn't complete, it does contain information about specific database objects that are consistent to a point in time. As an example, consider a database with three very large tables. To distribute the activity and administration of these three tables, a database administrator might choose to store each table in a different filegroup on different devices.

The backup scenario may involve backing up each file individually during off-peak hours to minimize the performance impact of the operations. When restoring data, you can specify that only certain files or filegroups should be restored. For example, suppose the Sales and Customers tables are stored on two different filegroups that reside on two different physical disks. If the drive containing the Sales table fails, you could recover only the information from the Sales table without requiring a restore of the Customers table.

Database administrators must be careful to ensure that relational integrity is maintained between these tables. For example, if data in the Sales table is dependent on corresponding information in the Customers table, there might be problems with performing a file or filegroup recovery. Although, as far as SQL Server is concerned, the database is physically consistent, referential integrity may have been broken. For this reason, it is recommended that only logically independent tables be backed up using this method.

Restoring to a Specific Point in Time

One of the most common questions asked about recovering data from databases is what to do first. For example, assume that some type of failure occurs on a busy server, causing the database process to delete or corrupt information that resides within a database. In this case, you might know approximately when the problem occurred and thus want to "roll back" to a time just before it happened. That's where transaction log backups are useful. Assuming that the current transaction log file is available, you'll want to perform the following sequence of steps:

1. Back up the current transaction log. This will ensure that you have a recent backup of transaction information.

2. Restore the database *without recovery*.

3. Apply any required transaction logs.

4. Apply the transaction log backup created in step 1 *with recovery*, stopping at the desired point in time.

The result of this operation is a database that is consistent to a point in time just before the problem transaction or database corruption occurred. Note that you cannot specify which transactions are committed or rolled back, since this could lead to a logically inconsistent database.

RECOVERING SQL SERVER DATABASES

Chapter 6 mentioned the importance of keeping a database consistent to a point in time. If a database server goes down unexpectedly due to a hardware, software, or network failure, the system must be made consistent again before it is usable. By generating database backups, you make sure that you have a copy of your information as it existed at a certain time. You can use these backups to restore data, should the need arise. Based on the types of backups you have performed, you will need to adapt your recovery plan.

In the following sections, we'll discuss the actual commands and operations you can use to restore information using SQL Server. If you haven't done so already, I suggest you read the information covered in Chapter 6. It is important to understand how database devices are created and the various methods for backing up databases. With this background, you should have enough information to start working with the RESTORE command.

Process Overview

Before we dive into the actual commands and operations required to restore databases on SQL Server, you should fully understand some of the concepts related to performing the recovery operations. First, when performing restorations, it is often necessary to use the results of more than one backup operation. For example, we'll see how full, differential, and transaction log backups can be combined to restore database information. By default, after a recovery operation is completed, the database is left in a consistent state and is ready to be operational (that is, ready to accept user connections and data modification commands). This is a good way to restore data when you want to perform recovery from a single full backup file. However, if you plan to apply multiple transaction logs, you'll need to tell SQL Server that the operation is not yet complete and that you plan to perform more recovery operations.

There are two main ways to perform the commands: Enterprise Manager and Transact-SQL commands. The simplest way to perform most common recovery operations is the graphical Enterprise Manager, because it prompts you for the necessary information. If you need more control over the operations, want to script complex recovery options, or have additional requirements, then you will find it worth the added effort of working with the Transact-SQL commands.

Preparing for a Restore

Before you begin a restore of an existing database, you must ensure that no users are currently accessing it. This can be done in SQL Server 2000 by generating a list of the processes that are connected to a database. The Management | Current Activity folder in Enterprise Manager provides a good way to view the relevant information. Note, however, that this display does not update automatically. That is, after you kill a connection, you will need to right-click on the Current Activity icon and choose Refresh in order to update the display.

You can also use the sp_who or sp_who2 stored procedures in Query Analyzer for enumerating the connections to a database. (See Figure 7-10.)

Once you have the process IDs for the necessary connections, you can use the KILL command to terminate the processes. For example, the following command will terminate process ID 132:

```
KILL 132
```

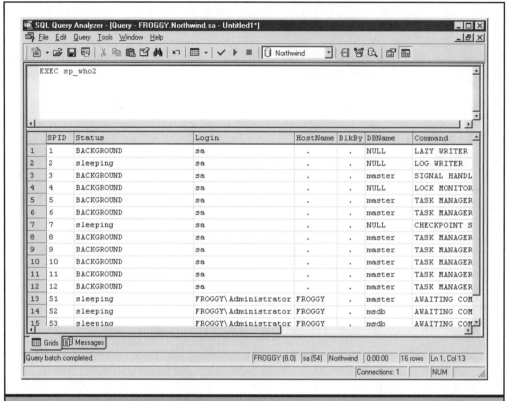

Figure 7-10. Viewing current database connections using the sp_who2 stored procedure

Using Enterprise Manager

As mentioned, using SQL Enterprise Manager is the easiest and least complicated way to perform restorations. Even so, you should fully understand the effects of various recovery scenarios before beginning these operations. The following procedures will show you how to recover databases quickly and easily using Enterprise Manager.

STEP-BY-STEP

Restoring a Database in Enterprise Manager

1. In Enterprise Manager, expand the server on which you want to restore a database.

2. Right-click on the Databases folder and select All Tasks | Restore Database. You will see the Restore Database dialog box.

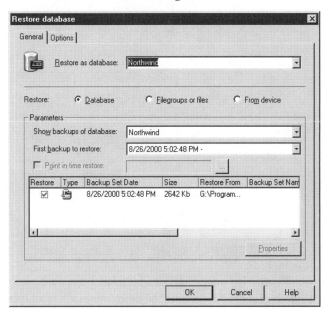

3. Specify the type of restoration operation you want to perform, using the General tab of the Restore Database dialog box. Your options here include the following:

- **Restore as Database**   Specifies the name of the database to which information will be restored. You can choose an existing database or type a name of a new database that you want the operation to create.

- **Restore**   Offers three choices for the type of operation to perform. The default option is to restore the existing database from previous backups. The choices—Database, Filegroups or Files, and From Device—are described next.

  - **Database**   If you have already performed at least one backup of this database, you will be able to choose which backup sets you want to apply. The first option is to select a database name for which to view backups. By default, the option will be the same as the Restore as Database selection, but you can change this option. Using a different option is helpful when you're trying to copy an existing database. Next, you can choose the date and time of the first backup to restore. If transaction log backups have been made, you can also specify a point in time to which to restore. Finally, you can choose which backups to restore. For example, if you have performed one full, one differential, and two transaction log backups, you can place check marks next to the appropriate boxes.

The Properties button gives you more information about the backup, including a description of the operation (if it was specified).

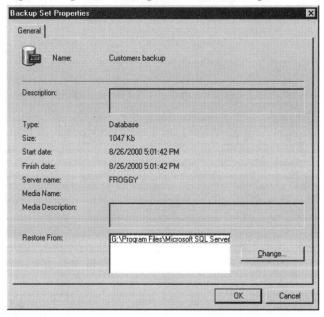

■ **Filegroups or Files** When restoring specific files or filegroups, you must again first choose the database from which you want to select options. Next, you need to select which backups you want to restore:

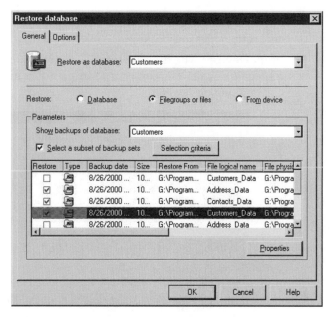

The list of files and filegroups might be quite large, in which case you can click the Selection Criteria button for more options. On the screen that appears, you can choose to display backups only for certain drives or for sets that have been completed after a certain date:

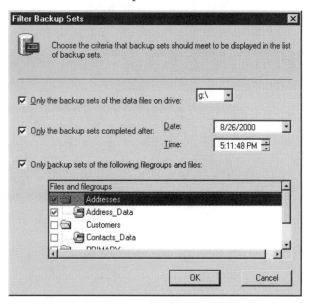

Choosing all files for a drive, for example, can be quite useful when restoring information after replacing failed hardware. Finally, you can

restrict the list to only backups for specific files. Again, this is useful if
only certain files in a backup set have been lost, while the others are intact.

■ **From Device** The third restoration option is to choose a backup from
a specific device. You can choose from one or more backup devices
existing on your system:

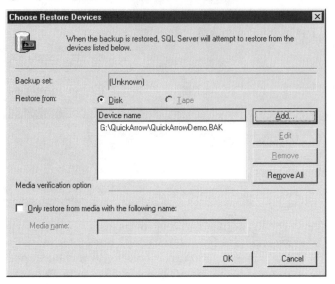

For each device, you can specify the backup number. If you are unsure
of the backup number, the View Contents option will load the header
information from tape. This operation could take a long time for tape
backups, because the entire media might have to be searched to obtain
all the information.

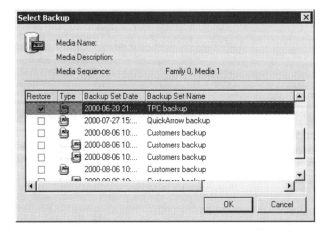

Next, choose the type of backup set you want to restore. The options
include Complete, Differential, Transaction Log, and File or Filegroup. If

you do not actually want to perform the restoration but instead want to mark the selected devices as valid backups of the selected database, you can choose to add the backup information set to the backup history tables. This is useful when you want to use backups from another server and always want the information to be available for quick restorations.

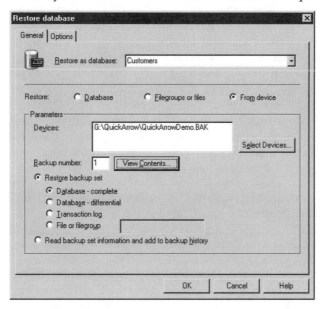

4. Specify options for the restoration process, using the Options tab of the Restore Database dialog box:

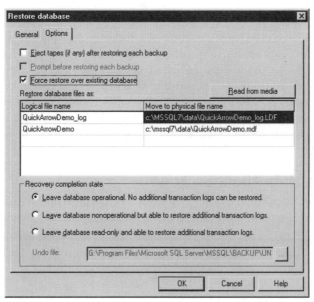

Depending on your choices in step 4, some settings may not be applicable. The first option is to eject tapes after the restoration operation is completed. This can be helpful when you want a reminder to switch tapes. You can also choose to be prompted before restoring each backup. You might choose this option if you want to monitor the process or pause between the operations to give users better performance on a busy server. If a database of the same name already exists, you can choose to force a restoration operation over it. Without checking this option, you will receive an error stating that a database of the same name is already present. Often, you might not want to restore files to their original locations. For example, if a disk has failed or you have reconfigured your partitions, you might want to restore files to a different directory. The Restore Database Files As option enables you to make any necessary changes. Finally, you need to specify the database recovery options. The default is to leave the database in an operational state. If you plan to apply additional transaction logs to the backup, choose one of the other two options—to leave the database offline or to make it read-only. Finally, if the database should be left as read-only, you can specify a location into which the undo file will be saved.

5. When you're ready to start the restoration operation, click the OK button. SQL Server will immediately begin the operation.

Within Enterprise Manager, choosing the types of restoration options you need should be quite simple (as long as you understand the terminology and processes). Now, let's move on and look at how we can create commands to perform the same tasks without the GUI interface.

Using Transact-SQL

Recovery using Transact-SQL commands is similar to the methods used to perform backups. The commands are fairly simple, yet powerful enough to offer a variety of options. Transact-SQL commands can be scheduled to run via SQL Server Agent as Jobs. The commands also are useful for creating scripts that can be run in emergency restoration procedures. Note, however, that recovery scripts should be kept synchronized with backup operations—when one changes, you should always remember to change the other. In the following sections, we'll look at the syntax for the RESTORE command, along with some examples.

Viewing Information About Backups

The RESTORE command can be used to retrieve information about existing backups and files. Table 7-5 lists the commands and their functions; Table 7-6 provides their syntax.

Command	Function	Notes
RESTORE FILELISTONLY	Lists information about the files that reside on a backup device	Includes logical and physical names, file sizes, and filegroup information
RESTORE HEADERONLY	Returns the header information from a backup device	Can take a long time on tape media
RESTORE LABELONLY	Identifies the media in a current device	Can be much quicker than restoring additional information from tape media
RESTORE VERIFYONLY	Verifies that backup sets are present and readable, but does not compare actual data	Use to verify that the proper backup sets have been saved to tape; doesn't replace test restoration processes

Table 7-5.   Transact-SQL RESTORE Commands

Command	Syntax
| RESTORE FILELISTONLY | ```
RESTORE FILELISTONLY
FROM < backup_device >
  [ WITH
    [ FILE = file_number ]
    [ [ , ] PASSWORD = { password | @password_variable } ]
    [ [ , ] MEDIAPASSWORD = { mediapassword | @mediapassword_variable } ]
    [ [ , ] { NOUNLOAD | UNLOAD } ]
  ]
``` |

Table 7-6.   Transact-SQL RESTORE Command Syntax
```

Command	Syntax

RESTORE HEADERONLY	```RESTORE HEADERONLY```
	```FROM < backup_device >```
	``[WITH { NOUNLOAD
		UNLOAD }```
		``` [[,] FILE = file_number]```
		`` [[,] PASSWORD = { password
			@password_variable }]```
			`` [[,] MEDIAPASSWORD = { mediapassword
				``
				```@mediapassword_variable }]```
				```]```

RESTORE LABELONLY	```RESTORE LABELONLY```
	```FROM < backup_device >```
	``[WITH { NOUNLOAD
		UNLOAD }]```
		`` [[,] MEDIAPASSWORD = { mediapassword
			``
			```@mediapassword_variable }]```

RESTORE VERIFYONLY	```RESTORE VERIFYONLY```
	```FROM < backup_device > [,...n]```
	```[WITH```
	``` [FILE = file_number]```
	`` [[,] { NOUNLOAD
		UNLOAD }]```
		``` [[,] LOADHISTORY]```
		`` [[,] PASSWORD = { password
			@password_variable }]```
			``` [[,] MEDIAPASSWORD = { mediapassword |```
			```@mediapassword_variable }]```
			`` [[,] { NOREWIND
				REWIND }]```
				```]```

Table 7-6. Transact-SQL RESTORE Command Syntax *(continued)*

The following syntax is used for specifying a backup device:

```
< backup_device > ::=
    {
        { 'logical_backup_device_name' | @logical_backup_device_name_var }
        | { DISK | TAPE } =
        { 'physical_backup_device_name' | @physical_backup_device_name_var }
    }
```

For example, to see a list of all the files on a specific backup device, use the following:

```
RESTORE HEADERONLY
FROM DISK = 'C:\Backups\Database1.bak'
```

Figure 7-11 shows the results of running a RESTORE command with the HEADERONLY option.

Now that you've seen some useful commands for viewing information about backup devices, let's look at how to perform actual restoration operations.

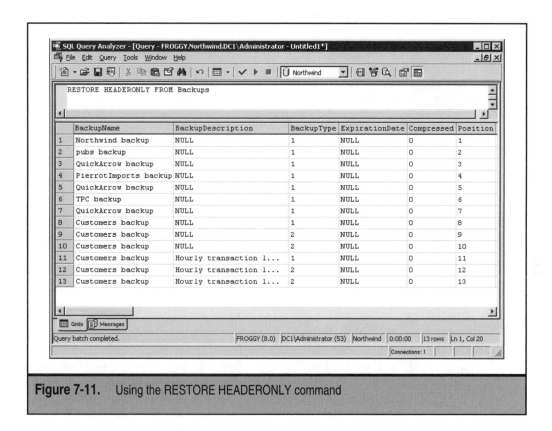

Figure 7-11. Using the RESTORE HEADERONLY command

Restoring from Full or Differential Backups

The RESTORE DATABASE command is used to copy information from full or differential database backups to a new or existing database on the local server. The syntax for the RESTORE DATABASE command is as follows:

```
RESTORE DATABASE { database_name | @database_name_var }
[ FROM < backup_device > [ ,...n ] ]
[ WITH
    [ RESTRICTED_USER ]
    [ [ , ] FILE = file_number ]
    [ [ , ] PASSWORD = { password | @password_variable } ]
    [ [ , ] MEDIANAME = { media_name | @media_name_variable } ]
    [ [ , ] MEDIAPASSWORD = { mediapassword | @mediapassword_variable } ]
    [ [ , ] MOVE 'logical_file_name' TO 'operating_system_file_name' ]
            [ ,...n ]
    [ [ , ] KEEP_REPLICATION ]
    [ [ , ] { NORECOVERY | RECOVERY | STANDBY = undo_file_name } ]
    [ [ , ] { NOREWIND | REWIND } ]
    [ [ , ] { NOUNLOAD | UNLOAD } ]
    [ [ , ] REPLACE ]
    [ [ , ] RESTART ]
    [ [ , ] STATS [ = percentage ] ]
]
< backup_device > ::=
    {
        { 'logical_backup_device_name' | @logical_backup_device_name_var }
        | { DISK | TAPE } =
            { 'physical_backup_device_name' | @physical_backup_device_name_var }
    }
```

Table 7-7 explains each of the parameters for the RESTORE command.

Parameter	Function	Notes
RESTRICTED_USER	Sets the database to allow only members of the db_owner, dbcreator, or sysdmin roles to use the database after the restore operation is completed	Useful when further operations are required after the completion of the restore process. For example, if consistency checks or data modifications must be made, this parameter can prevent users from logging onto the database after the restore operation is complete.

Table 7-7.   Parameters for the RESTORE Command

Parameter	Function	Notes
DBO_ONLY	Replaced by the RESTRICTED_USER option	Provided only for backward compatibility
FILE = *file number*	Specifies which file in a backup set will be restored	Useful when a backup device contains many backup files. Commands such as RESTORE HEADERONLY and RESTORE FILELISTONLY can be used to find file numbers in a backup device.
PASSWORD = *'password'*	Specifies the password for use with the backup set	If the backup device was password protected, this option must be specified before a RESTORE can begin.
MEDIANAME = *'medianame'*	Specifies that a check of the media name should be performed	Restoration operations will only be performed if the media name matches the value of this option. This is useful for ensuring that the correct device is used.
MEDIAPASSWORD = *'password'*	Specifies the password for use with the media set	If the media set was password protected, this option must be specified before a RESTORE can begin.
MOVE *'logical_filename'* TO *'physical_file'*	Specifies that logical files should be moved to another physical location	Useful when restoring from backups made on another server or when data files must be moved due to configuration changes. Multiple MOVE statements can be used to accommodate files and filegroups.
NORECOVERY	Specifies that uncommitted transactions should not be rolled back	Used when additional transaction log restores are expected
RECOVERY	Rolls back uncommitted transactions and leaves the database consistent to a point in time	Used for the final operation in a restore process. The database will be placed online and ready for use at the completion of the operation.

Table 7-7.   Parameters for the RESTORE Command *(continued)*

Parameter	Function	Notes
STANDBY = 'undo_file'	Creates a file that allows recovery operations to be undone	Useful when running standby servers (log-shipping). This topic is covered in Chapter 9.
KEEP_ REPLICATION	Preserves replication settings at the end of the restore operation	Generally used for the implementation of log-shipping (standby servers)
NOUNLOAD	Does not eject tapes at the end of the operation	Useful when subsequent restores from the same media must be performed
NOREWIND	Does not rewind the backup tape at the end of the restore operation	The tape device will be locked for use by SQL Server. This option is useful when additional restore operations must be performed.
REWIND	Rewinds the backup tape at the end of the restore operation	SQL Server will release the device for use by other processes.
REPLACE	Overwrites an existing database with the same name	Useful for restoring over an existing database without first dropping it
RESTART	Restarts a previously incomplete RESTORE operation	To resume an operation, rerun the exact RESTORE command with an additional RESTART parameter.
STATS = [Percentage]	Displays statistics at the percentage interval specified	Useful for monitoring the progress of a RESTORE operation. By default, statistics will be displayed for every 10%.
PARTIAL	Specifies that only specific files and/or filegroups will be restored	Useful when only specific database objects must be restored to an alternate location
UNLOAD	Ejects tapes at the end of the operation	Useful to alert database and systems administrators to switch tapes, if necessary

Table 7-7. Parameters for the RESTORE Command *(continued)*

As a basic example, the following command can be used to perform a restoration from a valid database backup device:

```
RESTORE DATABASE Customers
FROM DumpDevice1
```

The preceding command will begin and complete the recovery operation and leave the database in a consistent and usable state. Additional options can be specified, as in the following command:

```
RESTORE DATABASE Customers
FROM DumpDevice1
WITH
MEDIANAME='CustomersFullBackup',
MOVE 'BackupFile1' TO 'D:\SQL2000\Data\DataFile1.mdf',
MOVE 'BackupFile2' TO 'F:\SQL2000\Data\LogFile2.mdf',
NORECOVERY,
UNLOAD,
REPLACE,
STATS = 25
```

NOTE: An existing database must not be in use if it is to be the target of a restoration operation. If the database is currently in use, you will receive an error message.

Again, the preceding examples are used for restoring data from full or differential backups. If you will be performing additional operations (such as applying transaction logs or restoring individual files and filegroups), you will need a separate command for each. Let's look at these examples next.

Restoring Files and Filegroups

To recover specific files and filegroups using Transact-SQL, you can use the following syntax:

```
RESTORE DATABASE { database_name | @database_name_var }
    < file_or_filegroup > [ ,...n ]
[ FROM < backup_device > [ ,...n ] ]
[ WITH
    [ RESTRICTED_USER ]
    [ [ , ] FILE = file_number ]
    [ [ , ] PASSWORD = { password | @password_variable } ]
    [ [ , ] MEDIANAME = { media_name | @media_name_variable } ]
    [ [ , ] MEDIAPASSWORD = { mediapassword | @mediapassword_variable } ]
    [ [ , ] NORECOVERY ]
    [ [ , ] { NOREWIND | REWIND } ]
    [ [ , ] { NOUNLOAD | UNLOAD } ]
```

```
      [ [ , ] REPLACE ]
      [ [ , ] RESTART ]
      [ [ , ] STATS [ = percentage ] ]
]
< backup_device > ::=
      {
            { 'logical_backup_device_name' | @logical_backup_device_name_var }
            | { DISK | TAPE } =
                  { 'physical_backup_device_name' | @physical_backup_device_name_var }
      }
< file_or_filegroup > ::=
      {
            FILE = { logical_file_name | @logical_file_name_var }
            |
            FILEGROUP = { logical_filegroup_name | @logical_filegroup_name_var }
      }
```

Notice that the major difference between this command and the one used to restore full or differential backups is the specification here of which file and/or filegroup(s) to restore.

Restoring Transaction Logs

To restore from transaction log backups, you can use the following command:

```
RESTORE LOG { database_name | @database_name_var }
[ FROM < backup_device > [ ,...n ] ]
[ WITH
      [ RESTRICTED_USER ]
      [ [ , ] FILE = file_number ]
      [ [ , ] PASSWORD = { password | @password_variable } ]
      [ [ , ] MOVE 'logical_file_name' TO 'operating_system_file_name' ]
            [ ,...n ]
      [ [ , ] MEDIANAME = { media_name | @media_name_variable } ]
      [ [ , ] MEDIAPASSWORD = { mediapassword | @mediapassword_variable } ]
      [ [ , ] KEEP_REPLICATION ]
      [ [ , ] { NORECOVERY | RECOVERY | STANDBY = undo_file_name } ]
      [ [ , ] { NOREWIND | REWIND } ]
      [ [ , ] { NOUNLOAD | UNLOAD } ]
      [ [ , ] RESTART ]
      [ [ , ] STATS [= percentage ] ]
      [ [ , ] STOPAT = { date_time | @date_time_var }
            | [ , ] STOPATMARK = 'mark_name' [ AFTER datetime ]
            | [ , ] STOPBEFOREMARK = 'mark_name' [ AFTER datetime ]
      ]
]
< backup_device > ::=
      {
```

```
            { 'logical_backup_device_name' | @logical_backup_device_name_var }
        | { DISK | TAPE } =
            { 'physical_backup_device_name' | @physical_backup_device_name_var }
    }
< file_or_filegroup > ::=
    {
        FILE = { logical_file_name | @logical_file_name_var }
        |
        FILEGROUP = { logical_filegroup_name | @logical_filegroup_name_var }
    }
```

Earlier, in Table 7-7, we saw a list of the various commands that can be used with RESTORE operations. The RESTORE LOG command includes some additional options. Table 7-8 lists specific options that are unique to the RESTORE LOG command.

Parameter	Function	Notes
STOPAT = *'date/time value'*	Specifies that a point-in-time recovery operation should end at the time specified	Used to roll the database forward to a specific point in time before an unwanted transaction occurred
STOPATMARK = *'mark_name'* [AFTER *'date/time value'*]	Performs the recovery up to the named logical log mark. If AFTER is specified, recovery stops at the first *mark_name* after a specific date/time.	Rolls forward up to and including the named transaction; useful when you want to repeat the specified transaction but not transactions that occurred after it
STOPBEFOREMARK = *'mark_name'* [AFTER *'date/time value'*]	Performs the recovery up to a point in time just before the named logical log mark. If AFTER is specified, recovery stops at the first *mark_name* after a specific date/time.	Rolls forward to a point in time just *before* the named transaction; useful when the named transaction should not be re-performed

Table 7-8. Parameters Specific to the RESTORE LOG Command

The options that are unique to transaction log restorations include the STOPAT statement, which takes a date and time argument. With this statement, transactions will be restored up to this point when performing the recovery. The following command restores all the information from a transaction log backup stored on a backup device, but stops recovering at the time specified:

```
RESTORE LOG Customers
FROM DumpDevice1
WITH
    FILE = 1,
    MEDIANAME = 'TransactionLogs',
    RECOVERY,
    UNLOAD,
    STATS = 10
    STOPAT = 'Mar 22, 2000 3:15 PM'
```

Since the RECOVERY option is specified, the database will be left in a consistent state and will be ready for use by users as soon as the operation completes.

SUMMARY

In this chapter, we looked at various methods for restoring data. Of course, few of these methods would be useful if you have not properly performed your data backups! We started with some general information on planning for data recovery. Then, we moved on to look at the different types of data loss you might experience—in the best case (next to no data loss at all, of course), you would only need to restore a specific table from a database. A much more serious and time-consuming process would be required if you had a hardware failure in your system. After discussing the ways backups can be used to restore information, we moved on to discuss *how* to recover information in SQL Server. There are many ways to effectively use full, differential, and transaction log backups to recover as much lost information as possible. With this information, you should have the details you need to implement and manage a solid data protection plan.

Thus far, we've looked at the technical steps required to back up and restore data. So what's next? Well, if you're like me, you learn better through the use of realistic examples. Now that we have a good understanding of the processes required to back up and recover databases, it's time to move on to some real-world examples of these processes at work. That's the subject of Chapter 8.

CHAPTER 8

Backup and Recovery Scenarios, Tools, and Techniques

So far, we have looked at the technical details related to the backup and recovery operations. For many of you, this technical information will be helpful in designing your own data protection plan. However, the true value of data protection isn't realized until you actually *implement* solutions in your own environment. Often, we spend a lot of time learning technical information but spend little time in actually applying it. That's what this chapter is about. It provides examples of exactly how you should use SQL Server 2000's data protection features given various scenarios. We'll also cover some useful tools and techniques that highlight the features of SQL Server 2000 and help simplify database administration.

In this chapter, we will examine two different backup scenarios. The goal is to illustrate how the many different data protection features of SQL Server 2000 can be effectively used to accommodate various backup requirements. We'll start with a simple case—one that involves a single database that is very small. Then, we'll move up in complexity and data requirements to see how the various backup and restore methods can be combined to find an effective solution based on business requirements. The goal will be to ensure that data is properly backed up and that it is available for restore should the need arise. Then, we will cover the exact steps required to recover data from these backup plans.

Also, in Chapter 9, we'll look at further scenarios and examples related to other data protection methods (such as replication, standby servers (log-shipping), and clustering). In this chapter, I'll only briefly mention these choices wherever they're relevant. For details on these techniques, be sure to read Chapter 9.

OK, we've got a lot of information to cover, so let's get started!

SCENARIO 1: SIMPLE BACKUP FOR A SMALL DATABASE

Although there is often much talk in the industry about high-end storage solutions, high availability, and performance issues, in the real world, there are many databases that have quite simple requirements. Only a few users within a company might use these databases for development purposes. Or, many users may rely upon them, but they are small databases (less than ~250MB) and can be easily managed. In any case, the data is valuable, regardless of the fact that the database might have a simple architecture. Let's start here with a simple backup plan for a typical small database installation.

Requirements and Scenario Overview

A systems administrator, Julian, is responsible for protecting a single SQL Server database that is used by the Sales department to track customers and prospects. The database is approximately 50MB in size, and it is expected to grow to up to 100MB within the next year. The Sales database is normally used during extended business hours, from 6:00 A.M.

to 10:00 P.M. As Julian is a novice when it comes to skills in administering SQL Server 2000, simplicity of backup and recovery are very important goals.

Julian has been active in determining data protection requirements with the vice president of sales. Together, they have determined that up to four hours of data loss are acceptable and that the server may be unavailable for up to six business hours in the event of a serious failure. This decision is not ideal, but it does fit within the budgetary and technical constraints faced by the organization.

The company is operating on a tight budget, and their hardware resources reflect that constraint. The database server is also used as a file server for some users' home directories. The server has a single CPU and a single 9GB hard disk on which all data and the operating system information are stored. The hardware configuration also includes a 4GB DAT tape drive available for system backups.

Analysis

The requirements here are very simple. Julian is responsible for managing the backup of only a single database. Since the database may be taken offline during the night, the systems administrator has a backup window of approximately eight hours. This is more than adequate time to perform a backup of a relatively small database.

Backup Options

It is important to remember (especially for novice database administrators) that simply backing up SQL Server's data files while they are in use is not an acceptable solution. Even though "open file agents" and other such tools can take copies of files that are marked as in use, the data within these files may not be consistent to a point in time, and therefore database recovery using these backups may not work. Therefore, there are three main options regarding the types of backups to perform:

▼ **Hot backups to disk**   For hot backups, Julian would choose to perform a backup of the Sales database to a dump file. Then, the dump file could be backed up to tape using either Windows NT/2000 Backup or any other compatible backup utility.

■ **Hot backups to tape**   Julian could create a SQL Server job that automatically performs a backup of the database to tape during each night. He would probably want to perform the backup at night when load on the system is likely to be lightest.

▲ **Cold backups**   Since the database server is primarily used during business hours, Julian could choose to stop the SQL Server 2000 services during the night and then perform a backup of the data files. Since the database was shut down cleanly, these files could be "reattached" after a restore should the server fail.

In addition to choosing the type of backups to perform, Julian must also determine how often the database should be backed up. As with evaluating any technical requirements, the business concerns (and constraints) are most important. Julian has already taken the most important step—determining business requirements. Based on these details (up to six hours of downtime and four hours of data loss), Julian must determine an acceptable backup solution. He has several choices:

▼ **Full backups**   A full backup will dump all of the contents of the Sales database to a single file at predefined intervals. All backup methods will require the use of full backups to use as a starting point.

■ **Transaction log backups**   The transaction log stores a history of all the transactions that have occurred on the system since the point of the last full backup or the point of the last transaction log backup. To put this in perspective for a systems administrator, transaction log backups are loosely analogous to "incremental" backups in the file system. In order to restore by using transaction log backups, Julian would require the latest full database backup and an unbroken sequence of the subsequent transaction log backups. Transaction log backups provide an added benefit that allows database administrators to perform a point-in-time recovery. Therefore, should some data be accidentally modified or deleted, Julian could restore to the point in time just before the error was made.

▲ **Differential backups**   Differential backups record only the differences in the current database since the last full database backup. To recover in this scenario, the database administrator would need the last full backup and the latest differential backup.

Based on the given business requirements and the available backup choices, let's look at a couple of possible backup solutions for the Sales database.

Solution 1: Full Backups Every Four Hours

In order to implement a simple solution, Julian decides that he would like to perform a full backup of the database every four hours. However, he must decide how he wants to store the database backup files. Since the server has a single hard drive, it is not sufficient to store the backups only within that file system. If the hard disk were to fail, both the data files and the backups would be lost.

Since only four hours of data loss are acceptable, either these backups should be performed directly to tape, or the backup files themselves must be automatically copied to another file server on the network. Julian might choose to perform hot database backups to disk and then schedule a tape backup job to copy this backup to tape using Windows NT/2000 backup or another utility. However, this would generally be inefficient, and the processes must be coordinated and synchronized. That is, the database dump must finish before the tape backup process begins. There will always be some lag time between when the database dump is made and when the file is transferred to a "safe medium."

After considering the options, Julian decides to perform full database backups to tape every four hours. This option is simple, easy to manage, and takes advantage of the available resources. Since other data (mainly, users' home directories) must also be backed up, Julian could choose to store SQL Server and Windows NT/2000 backups on the same media (since both use the Microsoft Tape Format, or MTF).

Enterprise Manager Procedure

Since Julian is not familiar with Transact-SQL, he chooses to implement the backup procedures using Enterprise Manager. Although he could use the Database Maintenance Plan Wizard, the absolute simplest way would be to create a backup of the database and schedule it. The steps he might take are similar to those outlined in the following procedure.

STEP-BY-STEP

Implementing Simple Backups Using Enterprise Manager

1. In Enterprise Manager, expand the local server and the Sales database. (For the sake of the exercise, you may want to choose another database for which you want to schedule backups.)

2. Right-click on the Sales database and choose All Tasks | Backup Database.

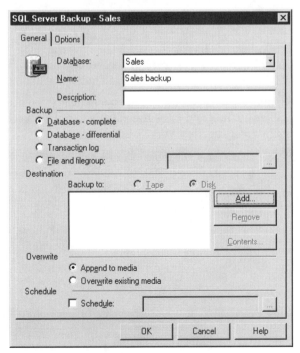

3. The Database drop-down box should show the Sales database as being selected. For the Name field, leave the default setting of "Sales backup." For the description, type **Full backup of Sales database (every four hours)**.

4. For the database backup type, leave the default setting of "Database - complete." This will ensure that a full backup of the database is made.

5. Next, we'll need to specify to where the backup will be saved. In the Destination section, click Add to add a new backup device. To create a new backup, select <New Backup Device> from the Backup device drop-down. For the name of the backup device, type **Sales Backups** and choose the default physical storage location. Click OK to create the backup device and continue.

6. Click OK again to specify that backups should be made to the newly created Sales Backups device.

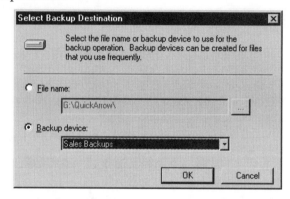

7. As Julian is only interested in storing the latest backup for the database (since backups will be copied to tape), choose the Overwrite Existing Media option.

8. Next, the job must be scheduled to occur periodically. To do this, place a check mark in the Schedule box and click the ellipsis to define a schedule. For the name of the schedule, specify **Every four hours**.

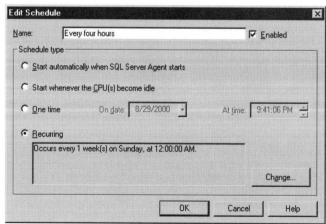

9. Select Recurring under the Schedule Type and click Change. Specify the Daily option and that the operation should run every day. For the Daily Frequency, specify that the job should occur every four hours. And, set the starting and ending times to 6:00 A.M. and 10:00 P.M., respectively.

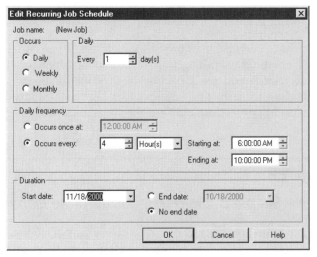

10. Click OK twice to accept the schedule settings.

11. Select the Options tab to specify additional details about the backup job. Several of the options will be grayed out since they apply only to tape backups. Place a check mark next to the Verify Backup Upon Completion option. Click OK to continue.

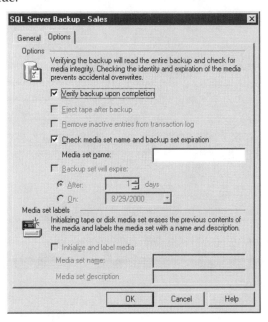

12. Finally, click OK to confirm the backup job settings. SQL Server will automatically create and schedule a job to perform the desired task.

Data Recovery Steps

In the event of the loss or corruption of the Sales database, Julian could perform a simple database recovery from the latest full backup. In Enterprise Manager, he could simply select the database to restore and see a backup history for the database. He could then choose the Sales database from the drop-down list and choose the date and time of the latest backup. The following procedure outlines the steps that Julian might take.

STEP-BY-STEP

Restore from a Simple Backup Using Enterprise Manager

1. In Enterprise Manager, expand the local server and the Sales database. (For the sake of the exercise, you may want to choose another database to restore.) Ensure that there are no users currently connected to this database.

2. Right-click on the Sales database and choose All Tasks | Restore Database.

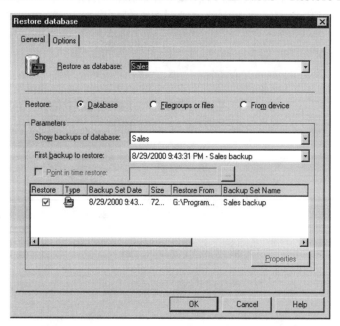

3. By default, the Sales database will be selected, and the dialog box will show the backup history for this database. The latest backup will automatically be selected in the Parameters section. Keep the default settings to restore from the latest backup.

4. Select the Options tab to specify additional restore operation settings. Since we will be restoring over an existing database, we must choose the Force Restore Over Existing Database option. Leave all other settings as their defaults, as the logical and physical filenames will not be changed.

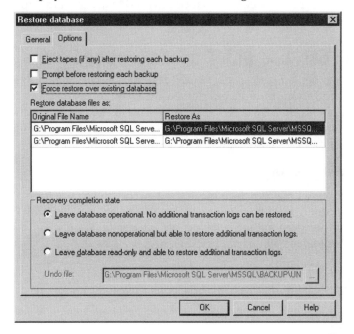

5. To begin the restore operation, click OK. When the process is complete, SQL Server will notify you that the operation completed successfully. Click OK to return to Enterprise Manager.

Evaluation

Based on business requirements and the small size of the database and the large backup window, performing a full database backup several times per day would be acceptable. However, this method might waste a lot of disk space in the long run and may reduce performance when performed during normal working hours.

One potential disadvantage to this solution is that Julian will be unable to perform point-in-time recovery of the database. That is, if an accidental data modification is made, the business may have to lose up to four hours of transactions. Since the business requirements did not specifically mention this requirement, the solution is acceptable.

Another potential concern is that this backup solution did not make any provisions for routine database maintenance (such as the reorganization of data pages and resizing of data files). These steps must be performed manually.

Finally, another flaw is that this solution does not back up other databases, including master, msdb, and model. Since the server is currently only being used for a single database, it might be easier for Julian to reinstall SQL Server or rebuild the master database in the event of a failure. However, this process would take time and effort should a problem occur.

Solution 2: Full Backups with Transaction Log Dumps

As you may have guessed, there are several different ways in which Julian could provide adequate data protection for the Sales database based on the business and technical requirements. Another potential solution is to perform a full backup of the database each night and to perform a transaction log dump every four hours. To simplify the operations, Julian has chosen to write all of the backups directly to tape.

Enterprise Manager Procedure

In Enterprise Manager, the process is quite simple. The best choice for Julian, a novice database administrator, would be to use the Database Maintenance Plan Wizard. He could make the choices shown in Table 8-1. (For more information and step-by-step procedures for using the Database Maintenance Plan Wizard, see Chapter 6.)

Backup Operation	Schedule	Notes
Selected Databases: All Databases	N/A	Although the primary purpose of this procedure is to back up the Sales database, it is also probably a good idea to back up the system databases and any new user databases that might be created on this server.
Database Optimization	Daily at 2:00 A.M.	Based on the size of the database and volume of transactions, this should be an adequate schedule. However, if performance becomes an issue, the frequency of database optimizations should be adjusted.
Full Backups to Tape	Daily at 3:00 A.M.	The primary backup is made during the least busy time of the day to minimize performance impacts.

Table 8-1. Database Maintenance Plan Settings for Full and Transaction Log Backups

Backup Operation	Schedule	Notes
Transaction Log Backups to Tape	Every four hours from 6:00 A.M. to 10:00 P.M.	Transaction log backups should be automatically deleted after one day.
Log Files	N/A	Log files should be stored in a location where they are backed up and should be automatically deleted after four weeks. Also, for ease of recovery, a log of backup operations should be stored in the msdb database.

Table 8-1. Database Maintenance Plan Settings for Full and Transaction Log Backups *(continued)*

Data Recovery Steps

In order to recover from this backup method, the steps are similar to those that we used for restoring from a full backup. The differences are that the Restore dialog box will offer additional settings and options. The first difference is that more than one check box might be enabled by default for the restore operation. The default settings will be to restore the latest full backup and all transaction log backups. (See Figure 8-1.)

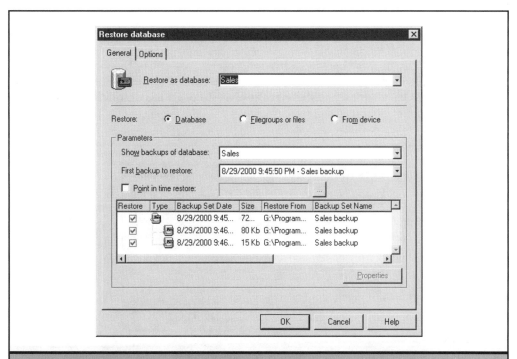

Figure 8-1. Viewing default restore options for full and transaction log backups

The second important difference is that Julian will have the option of selecting to perform a point-in-time restore. This can be done by simply placing a check mark next to the Point in Time Restore option. Julian will be prompted to enter the date and time at which the restoration operation should be performed. (See Figure 8-2.)

To begin the restore operation, Julian would simply click OK, and Enterprise Manager would handle the details of first restoring the latest full backup and then applying the transaction log backups sequentially.

Evaluation

As was the case with Solution 1, the transaction log files would need to be either written directly to tape or copied to another server. In this case, Julian chose to back up directly to tape. This should not be a problem based on the requirements, and the server has the necessary hardware and capacity to store this information. However, Julian should be careful to coordinate his daily file system backups to ensure that there is no contention for the tape drive. Given the relatively large backup window, this should not be difficult to do.

A major benefit of this method is that Julian could perform a point-in-time recovery of this database. In addition to providing for additional flexibility in data recovery, Julian might choose to increase the frequency of the transaction log backups. Simply changing the schedule for the transaction log backups job could do this. The only real concern would be the impact on performance. However, it is likely that he'll find that, for a database this small, the effects will be negligible.

Alternative Solutions

From the simplicity of these backup solutions, you can see one of the many strengths of SQL Server 2000's backup and recover architecture—ease of administration. The requirements here were very simple; so there really was no need to complicate matters with

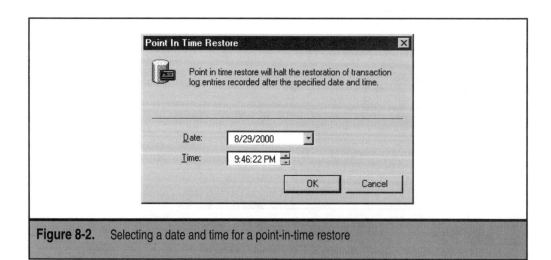

Figure 8-2.   Selecting a date and time for a point-in-time restore

scripts and manual job scheduling. All of the operations were implemented using the GUI of the Enterprise Manager. This is great for Julian, as he is a novice database administrator. The more important decisions, of course, were determining the business requirements (which were handled up front).

Clearly, Julian's company has chosen not to invest a large amount of money in this server. In the future, however, there may be a need to upgrade the server for performance reasons. Additional RAM and a faster CPU could help increase productivity for users of the Sales database. Additionally, Julian might recommend adding hard disks to the server. This would help in improving performance (by placing transaction logs and data files on separate partitions), and in providing for fault tolerance (through RAID technology, discussed in a later scenario in this chapter).

Both of the solutions mentioned above work fairly well given the current business requirements. However, there's a good chance that this database will grow and that simple backups will no longer be practical. As the use of and reliance upon the Sales database increases, the technical solutions must take advantage of additional features of SQL Server 2000. Let's move on to look at a slightly more complicated backup scenario.

SCENARIO 2: BACKUP OPTIONS FOR A LARGE DATABASE

When designing a data protection strategy for large databases, there are many considerations that must be taken into account. For example, it may not be practical to perform a full database backup as frequently as you might like, due to performance impacts. Also, hardware limitations might prevent storing large quantities of redundant data. Regardless of the constraints, the data is still very important, and a suitable data protection plan must still meet business requirements. Fortunately, Microsoft has included many features in SQL Server 2000 that are related to managing such situations.

You may be wondering what is generally considered a "large database." Well, the answer will often depend on your environment and your constraints. For example, if you work in a company with 10 employees, a 2GB database may seem huge. On the other hand, if you're working in a 10,000-employee enterprise environment, managing a 2GB database is just scratching the surface of large data volumes. Although I don't have an exact definition, a valid general guideline for a large database is at least 10GB. For many environments, databases of this size will pose some challenge for data managing and data protection. Of course, changes in technology come with increases in storage capacities and decreases in cost. So, the number is really a moving target. In any case, you should learn some valuable information from this section.

In this scenario, we'll look for some methods for performing backups of large databases. We'll look at how various backup techniques can be used to accommodate backups with a limited set of hardware. Through the use of SQL Server 2000's various backup and restore methods and the efficient usage of storage space, several different ways to store information are possible. Then, we'll see how these backups can be used in various recovery scenarios.

Requirements and Scenario Overview

Sasha, a database and systems administrator, is responsible for all administration of a relatively large SQL Server 2000 database. The database is called Orders and it is used to track all of the organization's sales information as well as some basic inventory data. The current size of the database is 20GB, but it is expected to grow rapidly. All departments within the company use this database, and data modifications (mainly UPDATE queries) are very common. Sasha has taken the time to determine the business requirements for her company. A summary of the relevant requirements is as follows:

▼ Data loss of up to one hour is acceptable.

■ Point-in-time recovery must be possible.

■ Server downtime due to the failure of a single hard disk failure is not acceptable.

■ In the event of data loss or corruption, all data from the database must be restored, and the server must be available for use within four hours.

■ Backup process scheduling is as follows:

An eight-hour backup (12:00 noon to 8:00 P.M.) window is available on Sunday afternoons.

Major backup operations should be scheduled to run between the hours of 1:00 A.M. and 5:00 A.M., if at all possible.

Backups are not required between the hours of 1:00 A.M. and 6:00 A.M.

The data protection plan must minimize performance impacts during the hours of 6:00 A.M. and 1:00 A.M.

The current database server is a dual 500MHz CPU machine with 512MB of RAM and four 9.0GB hard disks configured in a single RAID 5 (Stripe Set with Parity) array. A Digital Linear Tape (DLT) drive with an approximate uncompressed capacity of 20GB is also physically attached to this server.

Due to recent budget constraints within the organization, the purchase of additional hardware for data protection is not possible. Therefore, Sasha has been given a clear assignment: provide the best data protection possible given the existing resources. Perhaps it's not an ideal situation, but it's certainly one that will demonstrate the various methods for backup.

Analysis

The business requirements here are fairly simple, although given the existing resources, they are quite demanding. The current server includes about 27.0GB of usable disk space (as the amount of space equivalent to the size of one of the disks in the array is used for storing redundant information). Therefore, the amount of disk space available for database growth and for temporarily storing backup information is not large. Additional constraints are the business requirements for data backup and data recovery. Given this information, let's look at a potential solution that uses a variety of backup processes to provide for adequate data protection.

Solution: Full, Differential, and Transaction Log Backups

Based on the business requirements provided, it is clear that the simplest backup plan—using only full database backups—is not a viable option. Besides taking a long time for the backups to be performed, the amount of tape and/or disk space required would be prohibitive. Additionally, the performance impacts of performing only full database backups would not meet the requirements for point-in-time recovery and may not fit within the four-hour recovery window. Therefore, a better solution is needed.

Sasha decides to take advantage of SQL Server 2000's three backup methods: full, differential, and transaction log backups. Each of these three operations provides several different benefits:

▼ **Full backups**   A full database backup provides a database dump that is consistent to the point of the end of the backup process. Although, compared to other backup types, they take longer to run, may have a greater impact on performance, and require more storage space, full backups are the basis for all other backup types. Sasha would like to perform full backups as frequently as possible. Based on the data protection scheduling requirements, she can schedule full backup operations to occur every Sunday.

■ **Differential backups**   As differential backups only contain changes to database pages that have occurred since the last full backup, they use considerably less storage space than full backups. Differential backups are generally much faster to perform than full backups. Differential backups can also help reduce the size of transaction log dumps, as they truncate the transaction log upon completion. Sasha decides to periodically use differential backups during the week.

▲ **Transaction log backups**   Transaction log backups generally have a minimal impact on performance and require the least disk storage space, as they contain only a list of modifications that have occurred in the database since the completion of the last full or differential backup operation. Therefore, they can be performed relatively frequently even on busy production servers. Sasha decides to perform transaction log backups hourly during production business hours.

Now that we have a general idea of the types of backup operations that Sasha wants to perform, let's bring them together in a backup schedule.

Backup Schedule

Referring back to the business requirements, Sasha develops a backup schedule that utilizes full, differential, and transaction log backup types. As there is a large enough backup window on Sunday, database optimizations and integrity checks are also scheduled. Sasha chooses to implement and schedule the jobs as shown in Table 8-2. This schedule represents a weekly backup schedule.

Backup Type	Schedule
Full backup	Sunday, 12:00 noon
Differential backup	Monday through Saturday, beginning at 1:00 A.M.
Transaction log backup	Hourly, Monday through Saturday from 6:00 A.M. to 12:00 midnight

Table 8-2.   Weekly Backup Schedule for the Orders Database

Table 8-3 provides another view of the operations that will be performed on each day.

	Sunday	Monday	Tuesday	Wednesday	Thursday	Friday	Saturday
1:00 A.M.	Differential backup	Differential backup	Differential backup	Differential backup	Differential backup	Differential backup	Differential backup
6:00 A.M.	Hourly transaction log backups (6:00 A.M. – 11:00 A.M.)	Hourly transaction log backups begin	Hourly transaction log backups begin	Hourly transaction log backups begin	Hourly transaction log backups begin	Hourly transaction log backups begin	Hourly transaction log backups begin
12:00 noon	Full backup						
6:00 P.M.	Database optimization and integrity checks						
12:00 midnight		Hourly transaction log backups end	Hourly transaction log backups end	Hourly transaction log backups end	Hourly transaction log backups end	Hourly transaction log backups end	Hourly transaction log backups end

Table 8-3.   Daily Backup Schedule for the Orders Database

Implementing Backups

Based on the limited amount of available disk space for backup jobs, Sasha decides to store full database backups directly to tape. She chooses to store differential and transaction log backups to disk, as this method is the quickest. These backup files are reasonably secure against hard disk failures since all of the data and backups are residing on a RAID 5 disk array. Since operating system and file system backups are scheduled to occur nightly on the server, the files are backed up to tape nightly and are moved off-site for safekeeping.

Once the business requirements and technical solutions have been defined, it's time to implement the solution. With her knowledge of SQL Server 2000, Sasha knows that the easiest method for implementing is to use SQL Server Enterprise Manager and the Database Maintenance Plan Wizard. This wizard can create the jobs that are necessary to perform full, differential, and transaction log backups. It can also be used to schedule the jobs to occur according to the provided schedule. The Database Maintenance Plan Wizard does not include functionality for automatically scheduling differential backups. However, these operations can easily be scheduled using the Enterprise Manager interface.

The following process outlines the steps that Sasha might take to implement this backup and recovery plan.

STEP-BY-STEP

Implementing Full, Differential, and Transaction Log Backups Using Enterprise Manager

NOTE: The process described here is based on the business and technical requirements of the scenario presented. It assumes the existence of a database called Orders, but it can easily be modified for use with other databases.

1. Open Enterprise Manager. Expand the Management folder and select Database Maintenance Plans.

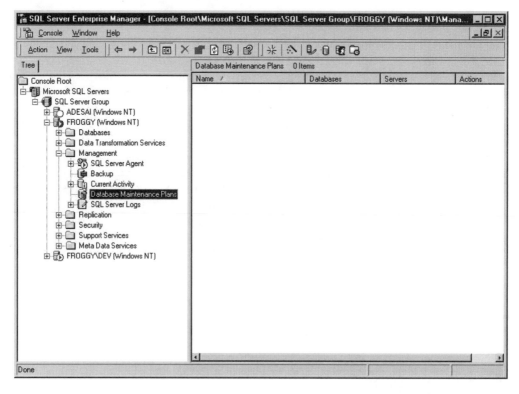

2. Right-click on Database Maintenance Plans and select New Maintenance Plan.

3. Click Next to begin the Database Maintenance Plan Wizard. When prompted to select which databases to back up, choose These Databases and place a check mark next to the Orders database. Click Next to continue.

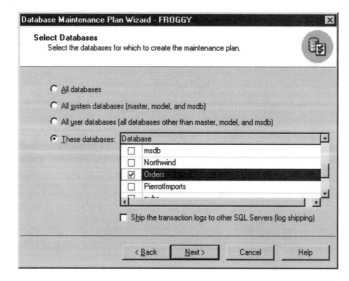

4. Select the following options on the Update Data Optimization Information dialog:

- Reorganize Data and Index Pages

- Change Free Space per Page Percentage to 10% of the Database

- Update Statistics Used by Query Optimizer; Sample 10% of the Database

- Remove Unused Space from Database Files When It Grows Beyond 50MB

- Amount of Free Space to Remain After Shrink: 10% of the Data Space

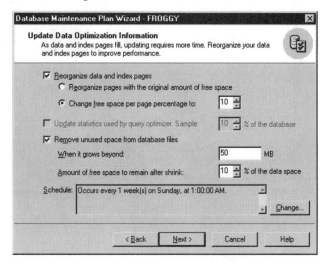

5. To schedule the data optimization jobs, click the Schedule button. Schedule the task to occur every week on Sunday at 6:00 P.M. Click Next to continue.

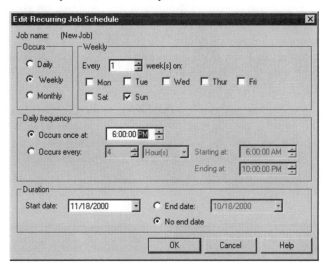

6. For the Database Integrity Check dialog, choose the following options:

   ■ Check Database Integrity

   ■ Include Indexes

   ■ Attempt to Repair Any Minor Problems

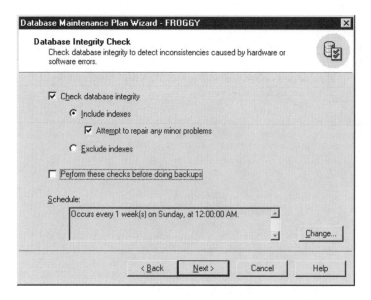

7. To schedule the data integrity checks, click the Schedule button. Schedule the task to occur every week on Sunday at 7:00 P.M. Click Next to continue.

8. Next, it's time to specify the database backup operations. Select the option to back up the database as part of the maintenance plan, and choose to verify the integrity of the backup after it is completed. Choose to store the backup file directly to a tape device. Click the Schedule button to schedule the task to begin at 12:00 noon every Sunday. When prompted, specify information about the tape media set, and click Next.

9. Choose the options to back up the transaction log as part of the maintenance plan and to verify the integrity of the backup when it completes. Choose to store the backups to disk. Click the Schedule button to schedule the job. Specify that the job should occur daily and that the frequency should be every one hour between the hours of 6:00 A.M. and 12:00 A.M. Click OK and then Next to continue.

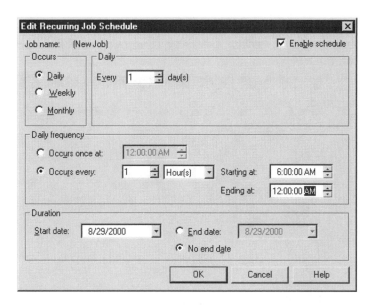

10. Specify that the process should use the default disk directory for the transaction log backups. Choose to remove files older than two weeks. Click Next to continue.

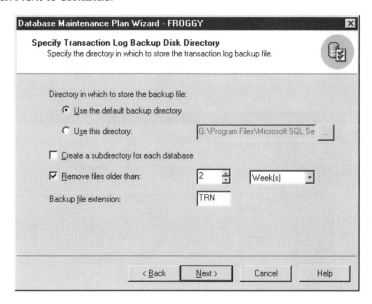

11. Enable the writing of report files to a directory and specify that reports should be deleted after four weeks. Optionally, choose to e-mail the reports to an operator. Click Next.

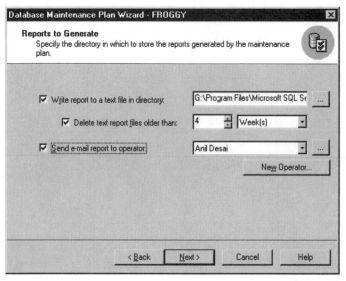

12. Choose to record the backup history on this server and to limit the history rows to 1,000. Click Next.

13. Finally, provide a name for the Database Maintenance Plan. The wizard will summarize the choices you've made. You can copy this text to a text file to document the backup processes. Click Finish to complete the Database Maintenance Plan Wizard and to create and schedule the necessary backup jobs.

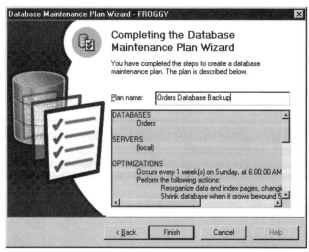

14. Next, we'll need to schedule differential backups. This can be done in Enterprise Manager by expanding the Databases folder, right-clicking on the Orders database, choosing All Tasks, and then clicking on Backup Database.

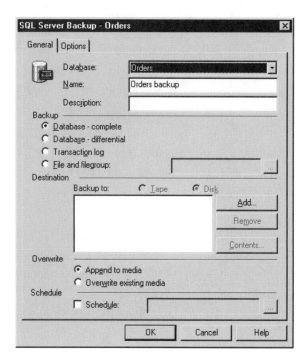

15. Verify that the Orders database is selected in the drop-down list at the top of the dialog box. For the name of the backup, type **Orders differential backup**. For the description, type **Nightly differential backup of Orders database**.

16. For the type of backup, choose Database – Differential. Remove any existing backup devices that may be listed in the Destination section of the dialog box.

17. For the destination, choose Add. Select Backup Device and either choose an existing backup device or create a new one for storing the differential backups. Click OK to accept the selection.

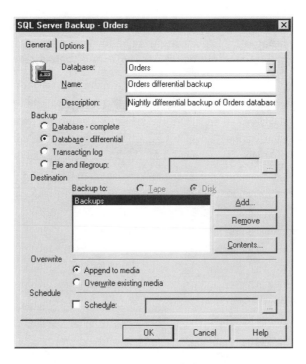

18. Choose to append the backup to the media.

19. To schedule the differential backup job, place a check mark next to Schedule. To modify the schedule, click the ellipsis button. For the name of the schedule, enter **Nightly**.

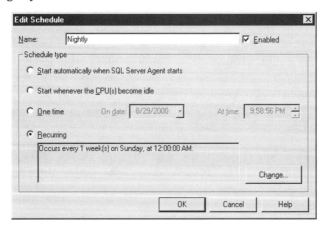

20. Select the Recurring option, and then click Change to specify the schedule. Specify that the job should run daily at 1:00 A.M. every day except Sunday. Click OK twice to accept the schedule settings.

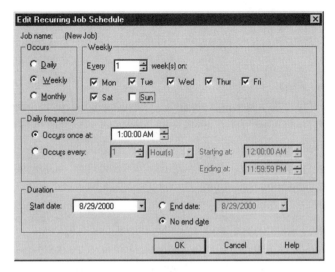

21. Select the Options tab and enable the Verify Backup upon Completion check box. Click OK to schedule the differential backup job.

22. To verify that the proper jobs have been created and scheduled, expand the Management | SQL Server Agent | Jobs icon. You should see five scheduled jobs. For more information about the scheduled jobs, simply right-click on one of the objects and choose Properties.

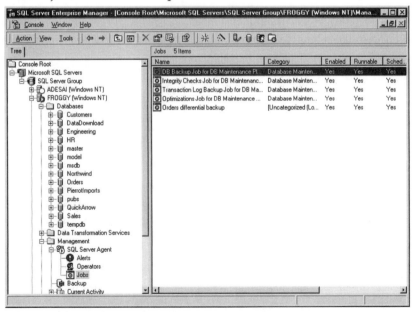

23. When finished, close Enterprise Manager.

Now that we have seen how to implement a data protection plan that uses several different backup types, let's look at the steps that might be required to recover data, should the need arise.

Data Recovery Steps

The combination of full, differential, and transaction log backups can provide a great deal of flexibility when it comes to recovering data. However, understanding the various recovery scenarios is an important prerequisite. The actual steps required to restore the database depend on two factors: the type of data loss that has occurred, and *when* the data loss occurred. Let's look at an overview of how data could be recovered using the above backup types and schedule.

If, for some reason, the entire database is lost, Sasha would first have to fix the failure and rebuild the server. Since the restore window is only four hours, she should ensure that she can perform these tasks quickly or that another server can be used in an emergency. A reinstallation of SQL Server 2000 might also be required (depending on the type of failure). Once this has been done, she could begin the data recovery process. This process would include the following operations:

▼ Restoring from the latest full backup

■ Restoring from the latest differential backup

▲ Applying an unbroken sequence of transaction log backups up to the point of failure

One of the business requirements for this scenario was that point-in-time recovery could be performed. In this case, the sequence of events would be similar to those for a full database restore, except that the final transaction log restore would occur to a specific point in time.

Sasha is an experienced database and systems administrator and understands that the moments following data loss are probably the worst times for developing a restore strategy. Therefore, she takes the time to prepare a data recovery table for failures at various times. A sample of this type of table is shown in Table 8-4.

Evaluation

At first, it may have seemed that performing adequate backups of the Orders database would be quite difficult. After all, the storage resources and backup windows were quite limited. Through the use of full, differential, and transaction log backups, however, Sasha was able to find a suitable solution. The solution meets all of the business requirements, including working within backup time frames, minimizing performance impacts, reducing the chances of data loss, and providing for point-in-time recovery.

The data protection strategy that she devised and implemented works well for the present. Of course, when the budget allows it, she should be ready to add disk space to the configuration, as the database will undoubtedly grow. Although the solution meets all of the current requirements, let's look at some alternatives and other possible solutions that Sasha could have used.

Failure Date/Time	Restore Process
Sunday, 12:00 midnight	Full backup (Sunday)
Monday, 9:37 A.M.	Full backup (Sunday) + differential backup (Monday) + transaction log backups (Monday, 6:00 A.M. – 9:00 A.M.)
Thursday, 3:05 P.M.	Full backup (Sunday) + differential backup (Thursday) + transaction log backups (Monday, 6:00 A.M. – 3:00 P.M.)

Table 8-4. Example Restore Processes for Various Failure Types

Alternative Solutions

From the needs of this backup scenario, you can see one of the many strengths of SQL Server 2000, including a flexible backup and recovery architecture and ease of administration. The requirements here were relatively complicated, but functionality in the database server platform made it simple to implement.

As we mentioned earlier, disk storage resources are fairly limited for this server. Therefore, additional disk space may be required in the near future. If, for some reason, that space is not available, Sasha will have to split the database so that a portion of the data resides on another machine. This could require extensive development effort and would likely prove to be the more costly solution.

There are also other backup and recovery options that might have been considered:

▼ **Network backups**   Although the amount of available disk space on the current production server is limited, there may be available space on other machines in the environment. Since the differential backups and transaction log backups are fairly small, they could have been automatically copied to a secure file server. This would also provide additional data protection, as it prevents against a loss of the backup files if the disk array on the main server should become corrupt.

▲ **Higher-end solutions**   Log-shipping (for maintaining high-availability standby servers), SQL Server fail-over support, and replication might also be data protection possibilities. Although they are more costly (something that the current budget doesn't allow) and require more administration, these methods can provide additional protection of data. We'll cover the details of these methods in Chapter 9.

None of the above options are particularly good choices since, in this scenario, we assumed that the purchase of additional hardware was out of the question. However, Sasha should keep these solutions in mind should business needs and budgets change.

SUMMARY OF SCENARIOS

So far in this chapter, we looked at two different scenarios related to data protection. The first focused on relatively small databases and a simple backup and recovery situation. The second focused on the problem of backing up a large database given only limited resources. Of course, there are many real-world scenarios that fall between the ones I have created. The point, however, is to understand how the various features of SQL Server 2000 can be used to address business and technical challenges. In addition to the scenarios we've examined here, we'll cover some other methods for protecting database information in Chapter 9.

Now that we have looked at some practical applications of SQL Server 2000 data protection methods, let's move on to examining additional information related to backup and recovery. In the following sections, you'll find helpful tips, tools, and techniques related to SQL Server 2000's data storage and management architecture.

AUTOMATING TASKS WITH SQL SERVER AGENT

In many environments, it's often necessary to schedule specific tasks to occur during off-peak hours or at regular intervals. Although some organizations have staff members available for these functions, this generally isn't the best use of resources. Creating scripts related to database backup and management scripts is one task, but having to run them regularly is quite another. That's where SQL Server Agent comes in.

SQL Server 2000 includes the SQL Server Agent service for defining and scheduling jobs. SQL Server Agent can work behind the scenes like an invisible agent who never complains about having to run jobs, regardless of the time of day. In this section, we'll look at how you can use this service to run almost any task on a predefined schedule. Of course, manual intervention will still be required for some tasks, such as configuring databases, changing media, and ensuring that operations occur as scheduled. However, you'll see a great savings in time and headaches if you properly define your jobs. We have also seen how other SQL Server 2000 features—such as the Database Maintenance Plan Wizard—rely on SQL Server Agent. These are all good reasons for taking the time to fully understand and configure this important service.

Let's start by looking at the configuration options for SQL Server Agent and then move on to doing the real work—with jobs, operators, and alerts.

Configuring SQL Server Agent

SQL Server Agent runs as a Windows NT/2000 service. It is designed to run on the system regardless of whether a user is logged in and is responsible for executing scheduled jobs. There are two main options for configuring security for SQL Server Agent. The first is to allow it to run under the "local system account." This account has permissions to run jobs on the local machine only; it cannot access other machines on the network. In a single server environment, this option is the easiest to configure, as it does not require a network username or password. If you want to be able to perform tasks on remote machines, however, you must assign SQL Server Agent a specific Windows NT/2000 user account under which it will log in. You can then assign the appropriate permissions to this account within the domain(s) in your environment.

One method for setting the SQL Server and SQL Server Agent logon account information is through the SQL Server 2000 setup process. As shown in Figure 8-3, you can specify which account(s) should be used for these services.

After installation, you may want to change the account that is used by SQL Server Agent or one of the many other available options related to this service. To set options for the SQL Server Agent service through Enterprise Manager, you can use the following process.

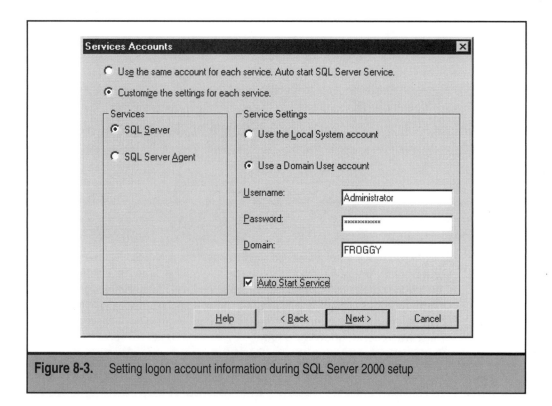

Figure 8-3.   Setting logon account information during SQL Server 2000 setup

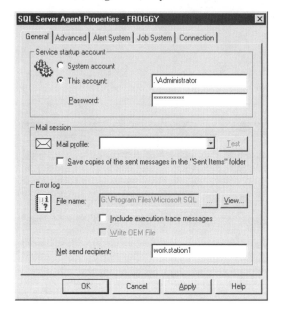

STEP-BY-STEP

Configuring SQL Server Agent

1. Open Enterprise Manager and expand the server object for the SQL Server machine on which SQL Server Agent is running.

2. Expand the Management folder, right-click the SQL Server Agent item, and select Properties. From the SQL Server Agent Properties dialog box, you can configure the various options for the service on the following tabs:

   ■ **General**   In the General tab, you can specify the account that SQL Server Agent will use for running on the system:

   You can either enter a username and password for an existing Windows NT/2000 network account or use the local system account. SQL Server Agent can also be configured to use a specific mail profile for sending e-mail notifications of jobs (described later in this section). If you have already configured a Messaging Application Programming Interface (MAPI) client for this user, you can enter this name in the box. Examples of MAPI clients include Microsoft Outlook and Outlook Express. To keep a record of all outgoing messages within the mailbox for this user, check the appropriate box. Finally, you can choose the name of the file to which SQL Server Agent will log error messages and set related options. You can also specify the name of a server operator who will receive a pop-up message whenever an error occurs.

■ **Advanced** On this tab, you can define the actions SQL Server Agent will take if it crashes:

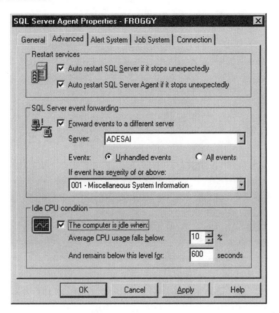

It is recommended that you enable both Auto Restart options so that SQL Server and SQL Server Agent will be restarted in case they stop unexpectedly. When events occur on this SQL Server, you can configure them to be forwarded automatically to another machine. We'll look at multiserver management later in this section. The third set of options is used to define when an "idle time" has occurred. As mentioned earlier, jobs can be scheduled to occur when the SQL Server is idle. Here, you can specify the maximum percentage of CPU utilization and how long the server must remain below that level before a job is fired. Be sure to set reasonable values, because if the settings are too high, your jobs may never run.

■ **Alert System** Whenever a SQL Server alert is fired (described later in this section), SQL Server Agent must know whom to contact and how they should be notified. On this tab, you can specify the format for pager e-mails and define settings for a fail-safe operator. The fail-safe operator is notified if all the other notification events fail. Before you can choose a person for this value, you need to define operators (which we'll cover next).

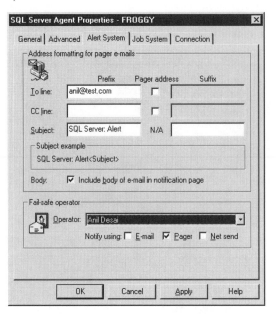

■ **Job System**   In this tab, you can choose to limit the size of the job history log. This prevents the log from growing to unmanageable sizes and using up unnecessary disk space. If you need to keep information for historical reporting, however, you might want to disable this option or increase the number of rows to be saved. You can also specify how long SQL Server Agent will wait for a job to finish if a shutdown request is received. You can view information about the Master server if multiserver administration is configured and this server is configured as a Target server. Finally, you can set security options for the CmdExec and ActiveScripting commands. This is a very important setting, since users with access to CmdExec and ActiveScripting will be able to perform many different functions with Administrator permissions on this server by using operating system commands. By checking the box, you can ensure that only members of the sysadmin role will have this permission. The Reset Proxy Account and

Reset Proxy Password buttons can be used to verify and to reregister the SQL Server Agent account.

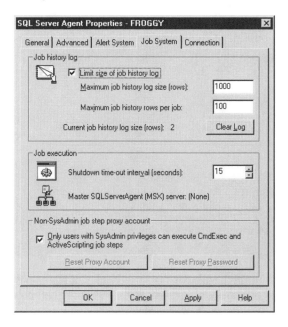

■ **Connection** In this tab, you can specify the login information that SQL Server Agent will use when connecting to SQL Server. You can either use Windows authentication (which works with Windows NT and Windows 2000) or specify a SQL Server login and password. Note that these logins should be given the appropriate permissions for servers on which they need to run jobs. If you'll be using applications or scripts that require connection options, you can specify the name of the server in the Local Host Server setting. Choices for this item can be configured using the SQL Server Client Configuration utility. Note the option for Login Time-Out, as well. This can be useful by dropping connections that have not been used recently. Finally, the SQL Server Alias option allows you to choose from among one or more of the Server connections that you've defined on the local machine.

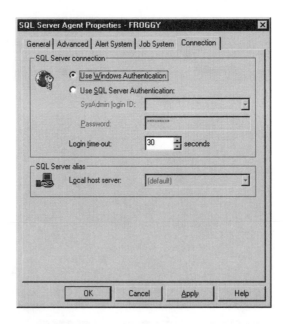

3. When you're satisfied with the options, click OK to save the changes. Note that if you changed the service account, SQL Server Agent may need to be stopped and restarted before the changes take effect.

Once SQL Server Agent is appropriately configured, you can begin to assign it tasks to perform. Let's move on to setting jobs, operators, and alerts.

Defining Operators

In almost all environments, one or more individuals will be responsible for managing and maintaining database servers. Each of these people will have preferred methods of contact. If alerting individuals to specific events were a manual process, computer operators might have a list of individuals who would be contacted for specific errors. Based on the severity of the problem, they might be e-mailed, telephoned, or paged. Furthermore, the contact list will change based on the time of the occurrence. SQL Server 2000 allows systems and database administrators to specify who the server operators are and how they can be contacted should the need arise. To define an operator within Enterprise Manager, use the following process.

STEP-BY-STEP

Defining Operators in Enterprise Manager

1. Within Enterprise Manager, open the Management folder on the SQL Server installation on which the operator will be created.

2. Expand the SQL Server Agent item and right-click Operators. Select New Operator from the list. From the New Operator Properties dialog box that appears, you can configure the various options for the new operator on the following tabs:

   ■ **General**   On this tab, you can specify the contact information and on-duty schedule for server operators:

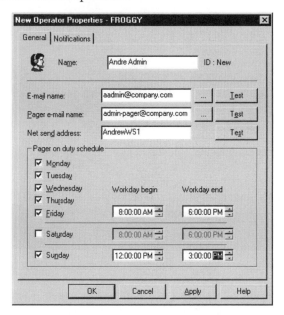

Specifically, addresses for individuals' e-mail and pagers can be entered. Additionally, a Net Send Address can be specified. This item is the name of a workstation or user that is usually available on your network (such as a data center administration console). If the Messenger service is running on the client machine, the user will receive a pop-up box that notifies him or her of the error message. This is useful because it is an immediate notification, ·

but it does not ensure that the user is available to receive it. In general, the Net Send Address should be used only for lower-priority errors or in conjunction with other notification methods. After you enter the settings, you can use the Test button to send a test e-mail, page, or pop-up box. The recipient will be prompted to ignore the message. If pager information has been entered, you'll also be given the opportunity to define an on-duty schedule. These are the days and times that the operator may be notified via pager.

- **Notifications** This tab lets you specify which alerts and/or jobs (if they're configured) the operator should be notified about:

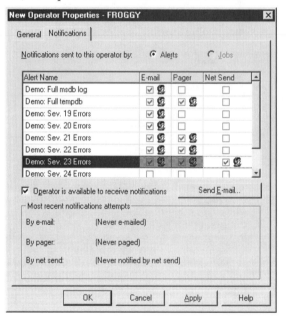

For each item, you can instruct SQL Server Agent to notify the operator by e-mail, pager, or net send. The "master switch" is the check box that sets whether or not this individual is available to receive notifications. This option is very useful if, for example, an individual is on vacation or otherwise unavailable. You also have the option of sending an automatic e-mail message that notifies the operator of his or her on-duty schedule.

3. When you're ready to accept the options you've selected, click OK. The operator will be created and, if configured, will be contacted when alerts are fired.

Using operators to keep track of employee information is a great way to ensure that everyone on the server management team knows his or her responsibilities. There's also a handy option to create a script for all of your defined operators (see Figure 8-4). This SQL file can be used to create some or all of the operator information on other servers. Let's move on to look at the types of jobs and alerts that can be created to notify operators.

Scheduling Jobs

As mentioned earlier, one of the main purposes of SQL Server Agent is to perform jobs automatically. A *job*, defined simply, is a set of actions that can be performed. The job might consist of steps that run SQL Server commands and/or notify individuals. The job can easily be scheduled to occur according to a predefined schedule.

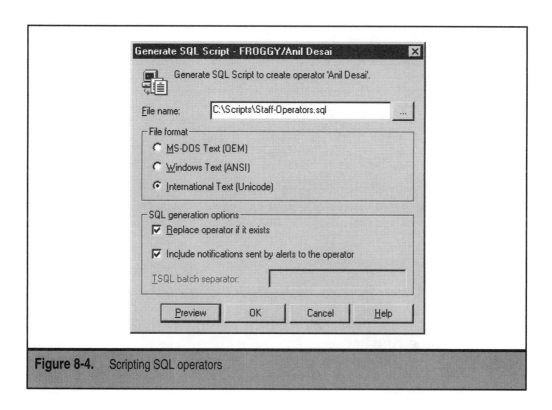

Figure 8-4.   Scripting SQL operators

STEP-BY-STEP

Creating and Scheduling Jobs Using Enterprise Manager

1. In Enterprise Manager, open the Management folder on the SQL Server installation on which the operator will be created.

2. Expand the SQL Server Agent item and right-click Jobs. Click New Job. From the New Job Properties dialog box, you can configure the various options on the following tabs:

   - **General** In this tab, you can specify information about the job itself:

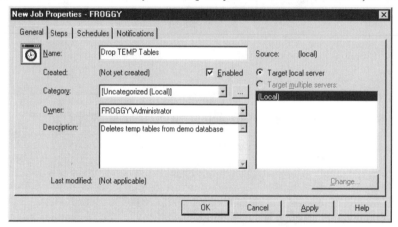

   First, you'll need to name the job. If you were modifying a previously defined current job, you would see when it last ran. You also have options for enabling or disabling the job. SQL Server jobs can belong to a specific category. By default, the list of categories available includes the following:

```
[Uncategorized (Local)]
Database Maintenance
Full-Text
Jobs from MSX (if Master/Target servers are defined)
REPL - Alert Response
REPL - Checkup
REPL - Distribution
REPL - Distribution Cleanup
REPL - History Cleanup
REPL - LogReader
REPL - Merge
REPL - QueueReader
REPL - Snapshot
REPL - Subscription Cleanup
Web Assistant
```

The default selection is Uncategorized, but categories are useful for organizing related jobs. For example, if this job is used to back up databases, you might want to add it to the Database Maintenance category. Next, you can choose a Windows NT or SQL Server user who will be the owner of this job. This user will be able to make modifications to the properties of the job. It is recommended that you enter a description for this job, including any prerequisites and the purpose of the steps. Finally, you can choose to which machines this job applies. As we'll see in the next section, if the server is a Master server, the job might be run on multiple remote machines.

■ **Steps**   The Steps tab is where you actually define *what* actions will be performed by the job.

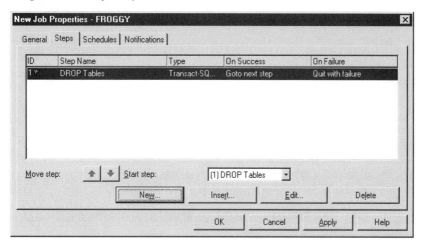

To create a new step for a job, you can simply click New. Jobs have one or more steps that define the actions they can take.

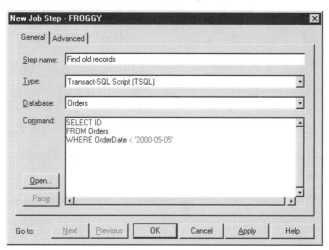

There are several types of actions that can be taken during a step:

Active Script   A command defined in VBScript, JScript, or another supported scripting language.

Operating System Command   A command that is run on the machine from a command prompt. This includes batch files or other OS commands.

Replication Commands   Various steps that interact with the agents used in the replication process can be defined. (For more information on replication, see Chapter 9.)

Transact-SQL Script   Specifies Transact-SQL commands that may be run.

■ **Schedules**   On the Schedules tab, you can specify when the job will occur and when any associated alerts are fired. For more complex scheduling options (such as the second and third Thursday of every month), you can use multiple schedules. In the next section, we'll see how alerts can be used.

■ **Notifications**   On the Notifications tab, you can define several actions to be performed when a job is complete. For each type of notification, the operator can be contacted when the job finishes successfully—or when it fails. Additionally, information can be written to the Windows NT/2000 Event Log. Finally, if you're running this job only once, you can choose to automatically delete the job when it succeeds (or fails).

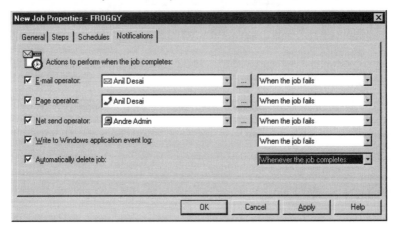

3. When you're satisfied with the options, click OK to save the job.

As you can see, almost any job or function that you can perform on a SQL Server installation can be specified in a job. As is the case with operators, you can also export the actual scripts for any job you have created. These scripts can be used for modifying settings or re-creating the same jobs on other servers. They can also serve as a backup in case information on this server is inadvertently lost. Next, let's look at how you can define alerts.

Defining Alerts

Alerts are events that occur in response to SQL Server messages. When events occur, the SQL Server service writes events to the Windows NT/2000 Application Event Log. You can examine this log manually by using the Event Viewer application in the Administrative Tools program group (for Windows NT and Windows 2000), or via the Computer Management Administrative Tool (in Windows 2000). Although this is a good way to look over the various events that are recorded, receiving notice automatically when an event of interest occurs is really much more convenient. That's where SQL Server alerts come in. Alerts periodically "read" the Application Event Log for specific messages. When an event of interest occurs, SQL Server Agent can take several different actions, described next, to notify the appropriate individual(s).

By default, SQL Server logs errors that are defined to have a severity level of 19 or above. Additionally, you can trigger your applications to write custom errors to the Event Log by including the RAISE ERROR WITH LOG command or by using the extended xp_logevent stored procedure. For more information on using these methods, see SQL Server Books Online.

STEP-BY-STEP
Defining an Alert in Enterprise Manager

1. In Enterprise Manager, expand the server on which you want to define the alert.

2. In the Management folder, expand the SQL Server Agent item. Right-click Alerts and choose New Alert. From the New Alert Properties dialog box, you can configure the various options on the following tabs:

   ■ **General** On the General tab, each alert must be assigned a name, as shown next.

Next, choose the type of alert from the options in the Type drop-down list. There are two major types of alert conditions. The first type is based on specific types of errors that occur on the system (such as a hardware failure). The second type is based on performance conditions. With this selection, you can generate alerts based on limits for any Performance Monitor counters. We'll look at some useful Performance Monitor counters later in this chapter.

You can specify alerts to occur either for errors with a specific error number or for errors of a specific severity level.

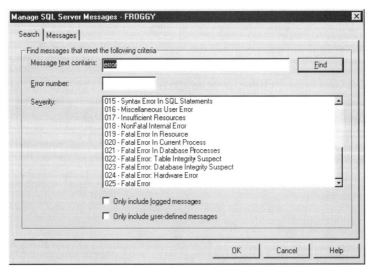

For errors based on severity levels or error numbers, you can use a
Lookup dialog box (accessed using the ellipsis ("...") button) to see
valid options.

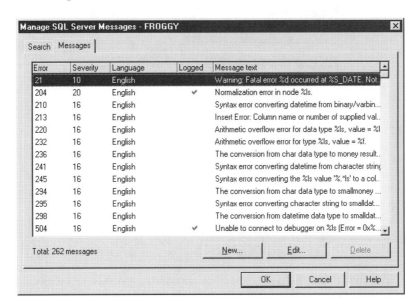

The default option is to fire the alert when the event occurs in any database.
If you have certain databases in your environment that are more important
than others, you can select a specific database from the drop-down list.
Finally, you can specify custom text that will appear in the error message.
Use this to include descriptive text so that you can immediately recognize
the problem when the alert fires. The General tab also shows the history of
the event, indicating when the alert was last fired, when an operator last
responded to the error, and how many times it has occurred.

■ **Response**   So far, we have told SQL Server Agent *when* we want alerts to
fire. The next step is to specify *what* should happen during an alert. On the
Response tab shown next, you can specify various actions.

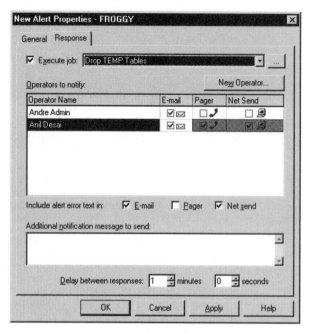

The first choice is to execute a custom job that you have created on this server. This can be very useful for automatic correction of certain problems. For example, if disk space is running low, you can create a job that will automatically delete old backup files. Next, you can specify which operators will be notified and how they will be contacted. The contact options include E-mail, Pager, and a pop-up box using the Net Send command. Additionally, you can add a more descriptive text message. This might be useful for specifying which operators are responsible for responding to the alert and what actions they should take to correct it.

Pay special attention to the Delay Between Responses option. By default, it is set to one minute. Although this might be appropriate for extremely critical errors, it could make you a very unpopular DBA if left as the default for relatively minor issues!

3. Once you are satisfied with the options, click OK to create the alert. Using SQL Server's Enterprise Manager, you can choose to enable or disable your new alert. There is also an option for generating a SQL script file that defines the alert. This can be useful if you want to copy the alert to another SQL Server installation.

Alerts offer many options for conditions and responses. They're extremely useful for ensuring that when operations fail, you're one of the first to know.

Configuring SQL Mail

Users and database administrators alike have come to rely upon communications of all types. One of the most useful (and my personal favorite) is e-mail. E-mail messages are easily accessible, and they can be viewed when systems and database administrators have the time to address issues. Furthermore, they can be easily forwarded or stored for future reference. SQL Server 2000 and the SQL Server Agent services have the ability to send e-mail.

Establishing Mail Profiles

SQL Mail is used to allow SQL Server to send e-mail messages and alerts. It is useful for receiving notifications of completed jobs and—even more important—of failed jobs. Both the MSSQLServer and SQL Server Agent services can use three different types of mail transports:

▼   Microsoft Exchange Server

■   Microsoft Windows NT Mail

▲   Post Office Protocol (POP3) Server

In order to configure SQL Mail, you must first log on to the machine as the user account that is used to run either SQL Server Agent or SQL Server 2000. You must then perform the necessary steps to configure a mail profile for this user. The details of how this can be done are based on the type of e-mail system you are using. For example, Figure 8-5 shows a configuration screen for setting up Internet-based e-mail in Windows 2000.

Once the e-mail settings are configured, SQL Server services will be able to send e-mail messages from the configured e-mail account.

Mail-Related Stored Procedures

It is important to understand how e-mail works with SQL Server 2000 services. SQL Mail can also be used to return the results of a query via e-mail. E-mail is sent using the MSSQLServer service for all stored procedures that are related to mail. Table 8-5 lists some useful stored procedures that are related to sending, receiving, and processing e-mails.

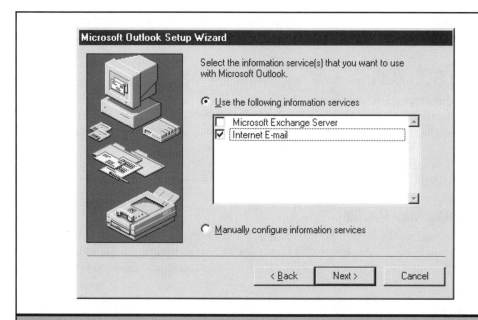

Figure 8-5. Using the Control Panel Mail icon to configure Microsoft Outlook e-mail settings

Stored Procedure	Purpose
sp_processmail	Accesses mail and mail-related extended stored procedures
xp_deletemail	Deletes a mail message
xp_findnextmsg	Sets the current message pointer to the next message in the mailbox (used in loops for processing mail)
xp_readmail	Reads a mail message
xp_sendmail	Sends mail messages (for example, in response to events and alerts)
xp_startmail	Creates a mail client session for use by other SQL Mail stored procedures
xp_stopmail	Ends a SQL Server mail client session

Table 8-5. Useful SQL Mail–Related Stored Procedures

The SQL Server Agent service can be configured independently to send e-mail messages in response to an alert or when a scheduled task generates an event (success or failure). You can configure SQL Server Agent in Enterprise Manager (covered earlier in "Step-by-Step: Configuring SQL Server Agent").

Multiserver Administration

Creating, viewing, and managing jobs in a single-server environment are relatively easy tasks. In general, all you need to do is check the event logs occasionally to make sure that nothing out of the ordinary is happening and that jobs are being performed as scheduled. But what if you're managing many servers? One possible solution is to use SQL Server Enterprise Manager. This tool is designed to manage local and remote installations with the same interface you'd use for a local server. However, having to look through the various messages on each server individually would be quite a chore. And, scheduling jobs to run on multiple machines would be quite tedious and repetitive. Fortunately, there's a solution for those problems.

In SQL Server 2000, you can define one installation as a Master server and specify others as Target servers. The Master server is responsible for receiving alerts and for running jobs on the Target server. It stores information about the various SQL Server jobs that are to be executed. Target servers run these jobs as scheduled and report the success or failure of them back to the Master server. In busy environments, a nonproduction installation of SQL Server can be used for this purpose. To configure this type of centralized management, a database administrator must be a member of the sysadmin role. One or more users can be mapped to the MSXOperator role to receive notifications and be given the ability to create and schedule jobs on remote servers. As mentioned before, the SQL Server Agent service should be assigned to a domain account that has the necessary permissions for accessing other servers to run remote jobs.

NOTE: If you don't have multiple SQL Server 2000 computers available for testing multiserver administration, you can run multiple instances of SQL Server 2000 concurrently to do your testing. Simply use one instance as a Master server and another as a Target server. Although this configuration isn't very useful for standard administration, it's a great way to learn how to use Master and Target servers.

STEP-BY-STEP
Configuring Master and Target Servers Using Enterprise Manager

1. Expand the server you want to define as a Master server.

2. In the Management folder, right-click the SQL Server Agent item. Select Multi-Server Administrator, and then choose Make This a Master. The Make MSX Wizard will appear. Click Next to proceed through its pages.

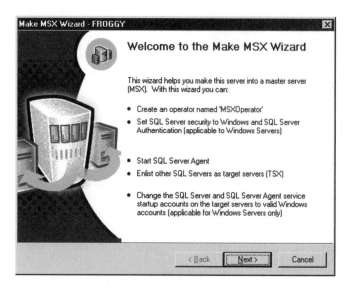

3. **Define the MSXOperator** This operator account will be created on the Master server and each of the Target servers. Multiserver processes will use this account for sending notifications as defined in jobs and alerts. Click Next.

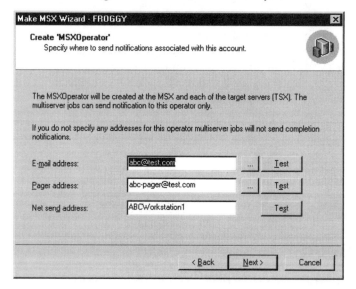

4. **Select target servers** On this page, you choose which servers will be defined as Target (TSX) servers. Each of the servers you add to this list will be available when you perform remote operations. If you haven't already done so, you can register remote servers in Enterprise Manager now by clicking the Register Server button. To register a server, you must have a valid login to that machine. Click Next.

5. **Enter a description for target servers**   Here you are given the opportunity to define additional information for Target servers. This can be useful for keeping track of the purpose and function of each of the machines. Click Next. If SQL Server Agent on one or more Target server(s) is not running under a valid security account, you will be prompted to correct the situation before you can continue. For more information on setting the service account, see "Configuring SQL Server Agent," earlier in the chapter.

6. When you're ready to perform the necessary operations, click Finish to begin running the tasks required for registering the appropriate servers.

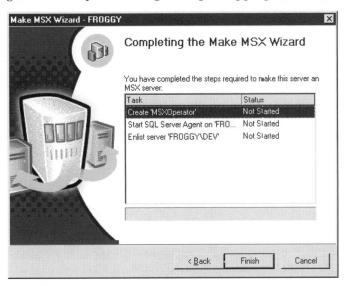

Once you have defined a Master and Target server(s), you will be able to schedule jobs and alerts to work on remote machines. Additionally, all information from these actions can be logged from a central location. In environments that have many jobs and alerts, you might choose to create a SQL Server installation as a Master server for just this purpose. In any case, if you're responsible for managing more than a handful of SQL Server machines, multiserver administration is a valuable asset!

IMPORTING, EXPORTING, AND TRANSFERRING DATA

In addition to the standard backup and recovery operations we've covered throughout this chapter, there are various ways to move data into and out of your SQL Server databases. In this section, we'll look at how you can generate scripts for all of your database objects and how you can perform copies and data transfers between different types of database systems. Using various SQL Server commands and features, you can make these formerly tedious operations a little more bearable.

Generating SQL Scripts

One way to maintain information about your database objects is to generate scripts for creating all the database objects. These scripts can be used by developers to view information about how views, tables, triggers, stored procedures, and other objects are created. Scripts are also useful when you want to create a new blank database that is similar to an existing database. Fortunately, the entire process is done automatically. To generate scripts using Enterprise Manager, use the following process.

STEP-BY-STEP

Generating SQL Scripts in Enterprise Manager

1. In Enterprise Manager, expand the server tree object.

2. Right-click on an existing database that contains database objects and select All Tasks and Generate SQL Script. From the Generate SQL Scripts dialog box, you can configure the various options on the following tabs:

   ■ **General** On this tab, you can choose to script all database objects of a certain type by checking the appropriate Objects to Script box:

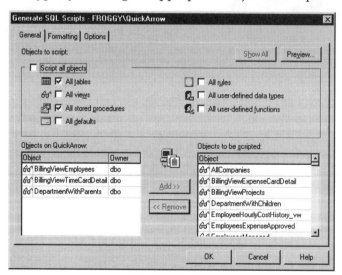

If you want to script only certain objects or object types, simply uncheck the object type, and then use the Add and Remove buttons.

■ **Formatting**   On this tab, you can specify how you want your scripts to be
formatted:

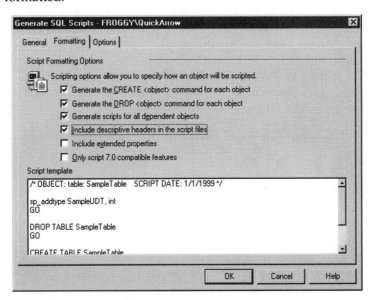

On the lower section of the tab, you can view a preview of the script
output. The Formatting options include the following:

Generate the CREATE <object> Command for Each Object   Specifies
that the script should generate the actual object creation commands for
the objects selected. If this option is not selected, the database objects
won't be created when the script is run—so deselecting it can be useful
if you simply want to drop all existing objects.

Generate the DROP <object> Command for Each Object   Creates
SQL statements that drop existing database objects with names
specified in the General tab. This is a useful option if you're planning
to update existing database objects and do not want to first drop and
re-create the entire database.

Generate Scripts for All Dependent Objects   If you've selected
objects in the General tab but did not specify the objects on which they
depend, you can check this box to script all the dependent objects. For
example, if you select a view but do not select the table on which it is
based, this option will automatically script the creation of both.

Include Descriptive Headers in the Script Files   Adds a line that
describes the name of the object to be created or dropped, along with
a date and timestamp. The headers will not make any difference in
the execution of the code, but they can be helpful in improving the
readability of the code.

■ **Options**   This tab allows you to specify further settings on what types of objects and settings are scripted. The Security Scripting options section allows you to script database users and roles; using these options will prevent you from having to re-create all of the security permissions and assignments after running the script. The Table Scripting options allow you to add items such as the referential integrity statements to the script file. Finally, the File options enable you to specify the file format of the generated script. Note that there is an option to either script one file per object or script all objects into the same file.

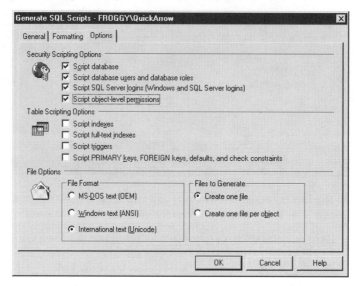

3.   Once you are satisfied with all the settings for the script generation, click OK. Enterprise Manager will prompt you for the location in which the file(s) is to be stored.

You can now open the script file in SQL Query Analyzer or any text editor to view and modify the commands. The consistency of the script output can make life much easier for developers.

Loading Data

Creating a blank schema is useful for several types of testing and for development. However, most databases aren't very useful without data. So far, the backup methods we've discussed have focused on Microsoft SQL Server data sources. The BACKUP commands were designed to dump data from SQL Server databases for possible use in recovering to another installation of SQL Server. In some cases, however, you might want to use a tool to load or transfer data to other data formats. One method that is often used for transferring information is a standard text file delimited by commas (comma-separated values, or CSVs) or tabs (tab-separated values, or TSVs). Many programs that can import and export data use these types of files. For example, Windows NT/2000 Performance Monitor and Internet Information Server can save data in standard text files.

There are several ways to load information into SQL Server. In the following sections, we'll look at how the bcp utility and the BULK INSERT command can be used to quickly load information into an existing database.

NOTE: bcp and BULK INSERT are best used for transferring information between applications or to SQL Server databases when the destination objects already exist.

Using Bulk Copy (bcp)

The bcp utility, outlined here, can be used for exporting or importing large amounts of information to or from SQL Server. The command syntax can be obtained by typing **bcp** from the command line. The results are the following:

```
usage: bcp {dbtable | query} {in | out | queryout | format} datafile
   [-m maxerrors]            [-f formatfile]          [-e errfile]
   [-F firstrow]             [-L lastrow]             [-b batchsize]
   [-n native type]          [-c character type]      [-w wide char type]
   [-N keep non-text native] [-V file format version] [-q quoted identfier]
   [-C code page specifier]  [-t field terminator]    [-r row terminator]
   [-i inputfile]            [-o outfile]             [-a packetsize]
   [-S server name]          [-U username]            [-P password]
   [-T trusted connection]   [-v version]             [-R regional enable]
   [-k keep null values]     [-E keep identity values]
   [-h "load hints"]
```

For data transfers, bcp is based on the ODBC specifications. (Keep in mind that this tool is best used for transferring information when the destination database objects already exist, because commands for creating these objects are not included in the output of the command.) Figure 8-6 displays information about the command-line switches for bcp, and Table 8-6 lists all the bcp parameters.

REMEMBER: The command-line switches used with bcp are case sensitive.

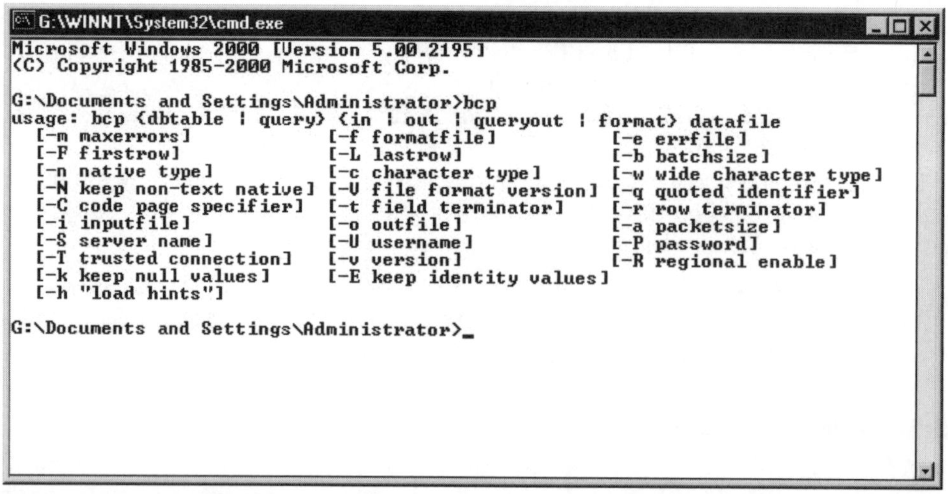

```
G:\WINNT\System32\cmd.exe                                                _ □ ×
Microsoft Windows 2000 [Version 5.00.2195]
(C) Copyright 1985-2000 Microsoft Corp.

G:\Documents and Settings\Administrator>bcp
usage: bcp {dbtable | query} {in | out | queryout | format} datafile
  [-m maxerrors]            [-f formatfile]           [-e errfile]
  [-F firstrow]             [-L lastrow]              [-b batchsize]
  [-n native type]          [-c character type]       [-w wide character type]
  [-N keep non-text native] [-V file format version]  [-q quoted identifier]
  [-C code page specifier]  [-t field terminator]     [-r row terminator]
  [-i inputfile]            [-o outfile]              [-a packetsize]
  [-S server name]          [-U username]             [-P password]
  [-T trusted connection]   [-v version]              [-R regional enable]
  [-k keep null values]     [-E keep identity values]
  [-h "load hints"]

G:\Documents and Settings\Administrator>_
```

Figure 8-6.   Viewing the syntax of the bcp command

Parameter	Value	Notes
database	The database from which information will be imported	Part of a fully qualified database object name
owner	The owner of the table or view from which data will be returned	Part of a fully qualified database object name
table or *view*	The name of the table or view from which data will be returned	Part of a fully qualified database object name
query	A Transact-SQL query that specifies the information to retrieve	Used with the queryout command
in	An import operation	
out	An export operation	

Table 8-6.   Command-Line Options for the bcp Command

Parameter	Value	Notes
queryout	A query that is used for export information	
format	A format file	Requires use of the -f switch
data_file	A file that is used for import/export operations	
-m	*max_errors*	Operation will abort if more than this number of errors occurs
-f	*format_file*	Uses a format file created with the format option; prompts for additional information if not provided in the command
-e	*err_file*	Specifies the path of the error file to which rows that could not be transferred are stored
-F	*first_row*	Indicates the number of the first row to be copied
-L	*last_row*	Indicates the number of the last row to be copied
-b	*batch_size*	Specifies the number of rows per batch copy operation. (A higher number will usually result in better performance.)
-n	native type	Uses native data types for field values. (Without -n, the user is prompted.)
-c	character type	Uses the char data type for copying
-w	wide character type	Uses Unicode characters (nchar) data type for copying

Table 8-6.   Command-Line Options for the bcp Command *(continued)*

Parameter	Value	Notes
-N	keep nontext native	Uses native data types for noncharacter fields and Unicode for characters
-6	6x file format	Uses the SQL Server 6.x data types (does not prompt for information)
-q	quoted identifier	Specifies that quoted identifiers should be used (for example, "data value")
-C	*code_page*	Can use ACP, OEM, RAW, or a number for the code page
-t	*field_terminator*	Used between values (default is \t, the tab character.)
-r	*row_terminator*	Used between rows (default is \r, the new line character.)
-i	*input_file*	Specifies the name of a response file that will answer the prompts
-o	*output_file*	Redirects output from the bcp command to a text file
-a	*packet_size*	Specifies the number of bytes per network packet
-S	*Server*	Specifies the name of the SQL Server installation (default is the local server)
-U	*username*	Specifies the login name used to access the data source
-P	*password*	Specifies the password used to access the data source

Table 8-6.   Command-Line Options for the bcp Command *(continued)*

Parameter	Value	Notes
-T	trusted connection	Indicates Windows NT Trusted authentication (which does not require a username or password)
-v	version	Displays the version of the bcp command being used
-R	regional enable	Uses regional formatting when importing currency, date, and time values
-k	keep null values	Indicates that empty columns will remain null regardless of default values in the destination
-E	keep identity values	Explicitly adds values for identity columns from the data source
-h	*"hint(s)"*	Specifies the sort order and other options for importing data

Table 8-6.   Command-Line Options for the bcp Command *(continued)*

You can obtain a brief listing of the various commands by typing **bcp** at the command line (without any switches). More complete information on the various arguments is presented in SQL Server Books Online. An example of a bcp command is the following:

```
bcp pubs..authors out authors.txt -c -Sdbserver1 -Usa
```

This command exports all the information from the pubs database and outputs it to a text file called authors.txt. Notice that no spaces exist between the switches and the values specified (for example, -Usa specifies the username "*sa*"). The bcp command also has an application programming interface (API) so that it can be called within programs that support ODBC and other data access interfaces. Although the command-line interface is rather cumbersome, you will probably find bcp to be worth the trouble when you're transferring data between different sources.

Using BULK INSERT

The BULK INSERT command is faster than bcp, and it can be used for the same purpose. The primary difference between the two methods is that the BULK INSERT command is run as a Transact-SQL command and is designed only to allow importing of data from a file into a SQL Server table. The syntax for the BULK INSERT command is as follows:

```
BULK INSERT [ [ 'database_name'.] [ 'owner' ].] { 'table_name'
FROM: 'C:\MyData.exp' 'data_file' }
    [ WITH
        (
            [ BATCHSIZE [ = batch_size ] ]
            [ [ , ] CHECK_CONSTRAINTS ]
            [ [ , ] CODEPAGE [ = 'ACP' | 'OEM' | 'RAW' | 'code_page' ] ]
            [ [ , ] DATAFILETYPE [ =
                { 'char' | 'native'| 'widechar' | 'widenative' } ] ]
            [ [ , ] FIELDTERMINATOR [ = 'field_terminator' ] ]
            [ [ , ] FIRSTROW [ = first_row ] ]
            [ [ , ] FIRE_TRIGGERS ]
            [ [ , ] FORMATFILE = 'format_file_path' ]
            [ [ , ] KEEPIDENTITY ]
            [ [ , ] KEEPNULLS ]
            [ [ , ] KILOBYTES_PER_BATCH [ = kilobytes_per_batch ] ]
            [ [ , ] LASTROW [ = last_row ] ]
            [ [ , ] MAXERRORS [ = max_errors ] ]
            [ [ , ] ORDER ( { column [ ASC | DESC ] } [ ,...n ] ) ]
            [ [ , ] ROWS_PER_BATCH [ = rows_per_batch ] ]
            [ [ , ] ROWTERMINATOR [ = 'row_terminator' ] ]
            [ [ , ] TABLOCK ]
        )
    ]
```

The parameters for the BULK INSERT command are very similar to those for the *bcp* command. For more detailed information, see SQL Server Books Online. For example, the following command loads data into a SQL Server table:

```
BULK INSERT MyDatabase..[Sales]
    FROM 'c:.exp'
    WITH
        (
            FIELDTERMINATOR = ',',
            ROWTERMINATOR = '|'
        )
```

Using SELECT INTO

There is another Transact-SQL statement that can be very useful in copying data between database tables. The SELECT INTO command can create a new table based on the result set from an existing query. The following is an example:

```
SELECT    *
INTO      NewAuthorsTable
FROM      Authors
ORDER BY LastName, FirstName
```

Notice that the results of the query will be stored in the new table. However, to use SELECT INTO, the database recovery model must be set to simple or bulk-logged. You can do this by right-clicking on a database in Enterprise Manager, selecting Properties, and then clicking on the Options tab.

Using these various database load commands, you can quickly and easily populate databases and database tables. Although these techniques are not generally used for performing backups, they can be quite handy when you're *testing* them.

The SQLMaint Utility

In Chapter 6, we looked at the ways the Database Maintenance Plan Wizard can be used to automatically create and schedule the operations required to execute the steps in data protection. If you looked at the detailed steps of the actual jobs created by the wizard, you would have noticed the commands are similar to the following:

```
EXECUTE master.dbo.xp_sqlmaint N'-PlanID ECFC3F27-F89A-4849-BEBE-8C2D361DD078
-WriteHistory  -VrfyBackup -BkUpMedia DISK -BkUpDB  -UseDefDir  -BkExt "BAK"'
EXECUTE master.dbo.xp_sqlmaint N'-PlanID ECFC3F27-F89A-4849-BEBE-8C2D361DD078
-WriteHistory  -RebldIdx 10 -RmUnusedSpace 50 10 '
```

When one of these jobs is actually called by the SQL Server Agent job engine, the xp_sqlmaint extended stored procedure is called. The details related to the operations to be performance (as well as a unique identifier for the database maintenance plan) are provided as optional command switches.

The sqlmaint command-line utility can also be used directly to perform the same tasks from a command prompt. This utility is located in the Binn directory of the SQL Server installation directory (for example, in "C:\Program Files\Microsoft SQL Server\MSSQL\Binn"). To obtain a list of command parameters, simply type **sqlmaint** from this directory. The results are as follows:

```
sqlmaint
[-?] |
[
    [-S server_name[\instance_name]]
    [-U login_ID [-P password]]
    {
```

```
        [ -D database_name | -PlanName name | -PlanID guid ]
        [-Rpt text_file]
        [-To operator_name]
        [-HtmlRpt html_file [-DelHtmlRpt <time_period>] ]
        [-RmUnusedSpace threshold_percent free_percent]
        [-CkDB | -CkDBNoIdx]
        [-CkAl | -CkAlNoIdx]
        [-CkCat]
        [-UpdOptiStats sample_percent]
        [-RebldIdx free_space]
        [-WriteHistory]
        [
            {-BkUpDB [backup_path] | -BkUpLog [backup_path] }
            {-BkUpMedia
                {DISK [      [-DelBkUps <time_period>]
                             [-CrBkSubDir ] [ -UseDefDir ]
                    ]
                | TAPE
                }
            }
            [-BkUpOnlyIfClean]
            [-VrfyBackup]
        ]
    }
]
<time_period> ::=
number[minutes | hours | days | weeks | months]
```

Table 8-7 lists the purpose of each of the options for the sqlmaint command.

Parameter	Meaning	Notes
-?	Returns information about the command-line options for the sqlmaint.exe command	If this parameter is used, no other commands or parameters are valid.
-S server_name [\instance_name]	Specifies the instance of SQL Server on which the command will be run (for example, "Server1," or "Server1\Instance2")	If not specified, the command executes against the local server.

Table 8-7.   Parameters for the sqlmaint Command

Parameter	Meaning	Notes
-U login_ID	Specifies the login ID to be used when connecting to the server	If not specified, Windows NT authentication will be attempted.
-P password	Specifies the password for the login	Only valid if a username is specified (see -U login_ID)
-D database_name	The name of the database on which the command should operate	
-PlanName name	Specifies a database maintenance plan name from which a list of databases should be obtained	The sqlmaint command will only obtain a list of databases from the Database Maintenance Plan. (All other options and settings must be specified at the command line.)
-PlanID guid	Specifies the PlanID (in the form of a globally unique identifier)	The sqlmaint command will only obtain a list of databases from the Database Maintenance Plan. (All other options and settings must be specified at the command line.)
-Rpt text_file	Specifies the filename and path for the report file	The sqlmaint command will automatically append a numerical date/timestamp string at the end of the filename (for example, Nwind_maint_199612011023.rpt). A UNC path name can be used for saving reports on a remote server.

Table 8-7.   Parameters for the sqlmaint Command *(continued)*

Parameter	Meaning	Notes
-To operator_name	Specifies an Operator that is to be notified of the completion of the job	In order for the notification to be sent, SQL Mail must be properly configured and the Operator must be defined.
-HtmlRpt html_file	Specifies the location and name of an HTML report to be generated	A date/time string is automatically appended to the end of the filename. A UNC file path can be used to store the report on a remote machine.
-DelHtmlRpt <time_period>	Deletes all HTML reports in the same directory as the current report path that are older than the time period specified	<time_period> is expressed as an integer followed by one of the following: [minutes | hours | days | weeks | months] (for example, "10hours" or "15days").
-DelHtmlRpt	Deletes HTML files that have names similar to the current HTML report setting (minus the date/timestamp)	<time_period> is expressed as an integer followed by one of the following: [minutes | hours | days | weeks | months] (for example, "10hours" or "15days")
-RmUnusedSpace threshold_percent free_percent	Removes unused space from the database(s) accessed by the sqlmaint command	The threshold percent specifies the size the database must reach before the operation is attempted, and free percent refers to the target amount of free space after the operation completes.
-CkDB | -CkDBNoIdx	Specifies that a DBCC CHECKDB command should be run as part of the command	For more information on DBCC commands, see Appendix A.

Table 8-7.   Parameters for the sqlmaint Command *(continued)*

Parameter	Meaning	Notes
-CkAl | -CkAlNoIdx	Specifies that a DBCC NEWALLOC command should be run as part of the command	For more information on DBCC commands, see Appendix A.
-CkCat	Specifies that a DBCC CHECKCATALOG command should be run as part of the command	For more information on DBCC commands, see Appendix A.
-UpdOptiStats sample_percent	Specifies the percentage to be used as a sample size for the UPDATE STATISTICS command	Used with the -UpdSts command to decrease the amount of time it takes to recalculate statistics
-RebldIdx free_space	Rebuilds indexes in the database	The free space parameter specifies by what percentage the free space should be reduced (a value of 100 indicates no reduction).
-WriteHistory	Writes information about the maintenance operation to the msdb database	For further details, see Appendix A.
-BkUpDB [backup_path]	Specifies the backup path for the database dumps	May be used in conjunction with -BkUpLog; a tape device path may be used (for example, \\.\Tape1)
BkUpLog [backup_path]	Specifies the backup path for the transaction log dumps	May be used in conjunction with -BkUpDB; a tape device path may be used (for example, \\.\Tape1)
-BkUpMedia	Specifies the type of media for the backup operation	Options include DISK or TAPE

Table 8-7.   Parameters for the sqlmaint Command *(continued)*

Parameter	Meaning	Notes
-DelBkUps <time_period>	Deletes backup files after a specified time period	<time_period> is expressed as an integer followed by one of the following: [minutes | hours | days | weeks | months] (for example, "10hours" or, "15days").
-CrBkSubDir	Instructs the sqlmaint command to create a separate subdirectory for each of the database(s) that will be backed up	
-UseDefDir	Specifies that the default backup directory should be used	
-BkUpOnlyIfClean	Specifies that backups will occur only if the check database commands exited successfully	When this option is enabled, it prevents backups of corrupt databases; however, database administrators must monitor backups closely to ensure that they are being performed.
-VrfyBackup	Performs a verification after the backup operation is completed	

Table 8-7.   Parameters for the sqlmaint Command *(continued)*

For example, the following command can be run from the command line:

```
sqlmaint -PlanID ED1FC14A-D7F6-4997-8225-A5E684ED7EE5
-To "Anil Desai"
-Rpt "G:\Program Files\Microsoft SQL Server\MSSQL\LOG\
     DB Maintenance Plan10.txt"
-WriteHistory  -RebldIdx 10 -RmUnusedSpace 50 10
```

This command performs the standard database optimization jobs that may be scheduled using the Database Maintenance Plan Wizard. It can be easily run on demand from the command line.

The xp_sqlmaint extended stored procedure can also be used to run the sqlmaint command. The benefit of using this method is that it can be easily executed from a SQL script or can be executed through the use of SQL Query Analyzer. For example, the following command can be used to perform backup operations:

```
EXECUTE master.dbo.xp_sqlmaint
N'-PlanID ED1FC14A-D7F6-4997-8225-A5E684ED7EE5
-To "Anil Desai"
-Rpt "G:\Program Files\Microsoft SQL Server\MSSQL\LOG\
    DB Maintenance Plan14.txt"
-WriteHistory  -VrfyBackup -BkUpOnlyIfClean -CkDB
-BkUpMedia DISK -BkUpDB  -UseDefDir
-DelBkUps 4WEEKS -CrBkSubDir -BkExt "BAK"'
```

As you can see, there are many options for the sqlmaint command. Perhaps the best way to learn the appropriate syntax for an operation is to start with the examples that are generated by the Database Maintenance Plan Wizard. To do this, simply right-click on any of the Jobs created by the wizard and select the Steps tab. By clicking the Edit button, you can see the exact command syntax that was automatically generated. (See Figure 8-7.) You can then modify these commands for your own purposes.

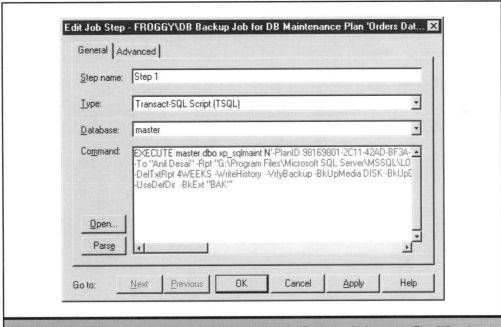

Figure 8-7. Viewing the properties of a job created by the Database Maintenance Plan Wizard

Now that we've looked at some useful SQL Server 2000 features for making database administration tasks easier, let's look at some helpful tools and techniques.

ADDITIONAL SCRIPTING TOOLS AND TECHNIQUES

There are many tools and techniques that experienced database administrators often use to make their jobs (and, in turn, their lives) much easier. In this final part of the chapter, we'll look at a few miscellaneous scripting tools and techniques that can save time and increase functionality.

Resetting "Suspect" Databases

If a database is left in an inconsistent state (for example, due to a system failure), SQL Server might mark the database as "suspect." In Enterprise Manager, the database will be shown with a gray icon. This can be a scary situation for many systems and database administrators since Enterprise Manager won't let you access the database at all, and Query Analyzer won't let you perform a "USE" command on the database. So, what can you do?

Fortunately, this problem can sometimes be solved quite easily. To reset the status of a suspect database, you can use the sp_resetstatus stored procedure. The syntax for this stored procedure is as follows:

```
sp_resetstatus [ @DBName = ] 'database'
```

That's the good news. The bad news is that if this stored procedure does not work, you will have to execute the DROP command on the existing database and then restore it from the most recent backup.

Restarting Interrupted Backup and Restore Operations

If a backup or restore operation is interrupted (for example, if the power fails), you can restart the backup or restore operation from the point it was interrupted. This can be useful if you restore large databases onto other servers as an automated process. If the automated process fails near the end of the restore operation, you can attempt to restart the restore operation from where it left off, rather than restoring the whole database from the beginning. This is done by simply adding the RESTART parameter to the operation. As a sample case, the following backup command,

```
BACKUP DATABASE Customers
TO Disk = 'c:\Data\Backups\CustomersBackup.bak'
WITH FORMAT, STATS = 10
```

could be restarted using the following command:

```
BACKUP DATABASE Customers
TO Disk = 'c:\Data\Backups\CustomersBackup.bak'
WITH FORMAT, STATS = 10, RESTART
```

The same argument can be used in the WITH clause of a RESTORE command to resume a database restore operation.

Managing the Size of the Msdb Database

On database servers that perform many or frequent backup operations, the size of the msdb database can increase greatly over time. This is because rows of historical data are stored for each of the backup and restore operations that are performed on the server. In most cases, the number of rows added within the tables of the msdb database will be negligible. However, if frequent backup or restore operations are being performed (for example, on a database server that contains many small databases), the size of msdb might grow considerably.

The negative effect of having a large msdb database is that certain operations (such as performing a backup or restore) can take considerable time. This is because Enterprise Manager must search through these fairly large tables in order to find the information it needs.

The sp_delete_backuphistory stored procedure resides within the msdb database and can be used to reduce the size of the backup history in the msdb database. The syntax of this stored procedure is as follows:

```
sp_delete_backuphistory [ @oldest_date = ] 'oldest_date'
```

It automatically deletes rows that refer to backups or restore operations that were performed before the date specified.

Creating a Script That Writes Scripts

If you're a database developer or database administrator, there's a good chance that you'll run into some repetitive tasks that could easily be handled through a SQL script. Often, you'll need to perform some type of operation on all of the objects within a database. For example, you may want to grant a specific user role or login permissions on many of the objects within a database. In this case, you can use a SQL script that writes other SQL scripts. For example, the following code can be used to generate SQL statements that carry out a GRANT command:

```
SELECT 'GRANT SELECT, UPDATE ON ' + table_name + ' TO User1'
FROM Information_Schema.Tables
WHERE  table_name like 'cust%' and table_schema = 'dbo'
```

The result might be the following lines:

```
GRANT SELECT, UPDATE ON Customer TO User1
GRANT SELECT, UPDATE ON CustomerData TO User1
GRANT SELECT, UPDATE ON CustomersAddress TO User1
GRANT SELECT, UPDATE ON CustomersOrder TO User1
```

You can simply copy and paste these lines into the Query Analyzer window and run them to execute the actual statements. (See Figure 8-8.) The overall result is a large savings in time (and, possibly, keyboards)!

Centralizing Server Registrations

In some network environments, there are many installations of SQL Server. These servers may be scattered throughout the network. Even in small organizations, it's not uncommon for developers or engineers to have local copies of SQL Server on their workstation machines. Enterprise Manager is a useful tool for managing SQL Server installations, whether they are on the local machine or located across the world. However, the trick is in having a list of SQL Server registrations so that you have connection information for all of these machines.

In Enterprise Manager, you can obtain registration from a centralized server. This is done by highlighting a server in Enterprise Manager and then choosing Tools | Options.

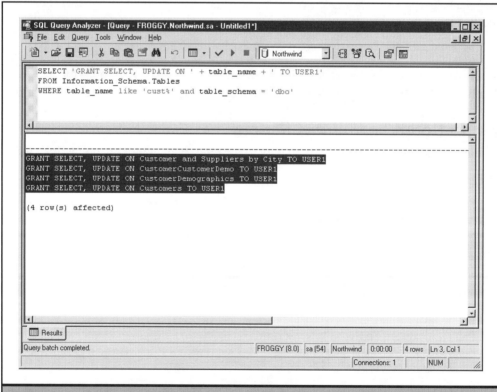

Figure 8-8. Using a SQL script to generate SQL statements

In the Server Registration section of the dialog box, you'll see an option to read this information from a remote machine. Simply specify the remote server name from which to read the information (see Figure 8-9), and you'll be able to access connection information for other known servers. This is a handy technique in environments that have more than a few machines, and it sure beats trying to memorize the names of your important database machines!

Changing the Name of a SQL Server Installation

In many cases, changes to business and technical requirements might warrant a change in the name of a machine that is running SQL Server 2000. Although changing the network identification of the computer is a simple process via the operating system, SQL Server must be reconfigured to use the new name information. If you have already tried this, you are probably familiar with the error message that notifies you that your installation of SQL Server may be corrupt. Although the error message might sound scary, the problem can be fixed quite easily.

After changing the machine name of a computer running SQL Server, you may first need to perform a reinstallation of SQL Server. Then, you can update the settings using two stored procedures: sp_dropserver and sp_addserver. For example, the following set

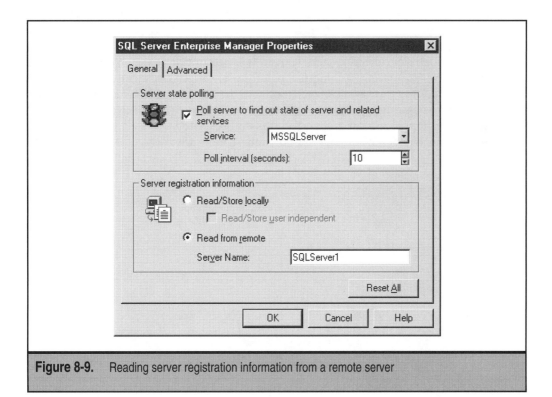

Figure 8-9. Reading server registration information from a remote server

of Transact-SQL commands updates SQL Server's internal references to use the new machine name.

```
EXEC sp_dropserver 'oldmachinename'
GO
EXEC sp_addserver 'newmachinename', local
GO
```

SUMMARY

In this chapter, we looked at some examples of applications for the technical information that we learned in previous chapters. Although it's possible that none of the scenarios described your data protection requirements exactly, there's a good chance that you'll be able to take some of the ideas and incorporate them into your own environment. If you're like me, you probably learn techniques through examples much better than through plain technical information. After all, not many people would remember the syntax of the BACKUP command unless they often used it for their daily job tasks.

So what's next? Clearly, we have covered a lot of information about typical backup and recovery scenarios. However, even a combination of all the tools and techniques presented here may not be enough for enterprise-level data protection. In many companies, the standard backup and recovery options available through SQL Server provide an adequate solution. In other environments, however, you might need even more data protection. In the next chapter, we'll discuss some advanced options available for protecting information. These tools and techniques include replication, clustering, and the use of standby servers. Though the implementations might be quite different, the goal is the same—to provide as much protection of your information as possible. Although these techniques often impose greater cost and administration burdens, they can be used to perform the ultimate in data protection! We'll cover these more advanced topics in Chapter 9.

PART IV

Advanced Data Protection Methods

CHAPTER 9

Advanced Data Protection: Replication, Log-Shipping, and Clustering

So far, we've covered the fundamental steps involved in establishing a data protection strategy: planning for and implementing security, backup processes, and recovery procedures. For many business environments, the proper application of these steps will provide adequate data protection. However, as organizations become increasingly reliant on their information technology resources, greater demands on uptime and performance may be required. For example, e-commerce companies and web-based enterprises place the utmost importance on their computer systems. Almost always, these systems involve the use of a database server.

In mission-critical situations, advanced data protection methods can be invaluable. Often, budgets will allow for the implementation of additional server hardware resources and the implementation of features designed to increase reliability. In this chapter, we'll look at some ways to use advanced features in SQL Server 2000 to protect information. Specifically, you can use replication to distribute data to remote servers, to increase performance, and to provide for high levels of data protection. And, standby servers can be created by implementing log-shipping. These servers allow for the recovery from a failure in a very short amount of time. Finally, clustering technologies can provide the utmost in reliability. Let's get started by looking at an overview of the main goals for mission-critical SQL Server 2000 systems.

OVERVIEW: SCALABILITY, RELIABILITY, PERFORMANCE

There are many goals behind the design of SQL Server 2000. If you've worked with the product (or have at least heard about some of the new features), you may be aware that many of the improvements are in areas that help push SQL Server into situations that involve higher-end mission-critical solutions. There are several key areas in which SQL Server 2000 has been improved:

▼ **Scalability** This refers to the ability of SQL Server to take advantage of bigger and faster machines. For example, if I could perform x number of transactions on a single server, will I be able to perform twice x transactions if I double the number of CPUs? The same is true for memory—can SQL Server 2000 take advantage of large amounts of physical RAM (for example, greater than 4.0GB)?

■ **Reliability** A system is considered reliable when it can be depended upon to consistently carry out the tasks for which it is designed. Reliability is often measured as a percentage of uptime (for example, 99.99 percent), indicating the proportion of time that the server is available for use.

▲ **Performance** One of the most commonly cited features of database servers is their ability to perform a specific number of transactions in a given unit of time. For example, a database server might be able to carry out 500 transactions per second. Database administrators often try to squeeze the maximum number of transactions from their servers. The end result is increased performance (and happier users).

In the following sections, we'll discuss some of the improvements in SQL Server 2000 that are related to larger installations.

Scaling Up vs. Scaling Out

We're fortunate enough to be working in a time when even run-of-the-mill servers will meet the demands of many applications. For example, a 50GB database might run fine on a workgroup server (depending on the user load, of course). Nowadays, current CPU speeds are measured in gigahertz, and most servers ship with a minimum of 256MB of RAM. Nevertheless, many of us have encountered situations in which that's not enough. Applications and users require additional computing resources in order to obtain reasonable response times and throughput. And, e-businesses have bet their entire shops on the capabilities of their database servers. So what can you do to curb the hunger for more power?

When it comes to scalability, there are two main options. The first is to "scale *up*". This method of scaling involves the upgrade of a server to faster hardware. Or, it might involve the migration of databases to a new, larger server that is more efficient or better designed for the load. As we discussed in Chapter 5, the most important factors affecting SQL Server's performance are memory (RAM) and processing time (CPUs). Fortunately, SQL Server 2000 has been designed to scale well by taking full advantage of more system resources. For example, with SQL Server 2000, you can take advantage of up to 64GB of memory using the Advanced Windowing Extensions feature of the underlying operating system. And, with SQL Server 2000, Enterprise Edition, you can take advantage of up to 32 CPUs. Figure 9-1 provides an example of scaling up.

As anyone that's ever upgraded a server can tell you, you can often achieve dramatic performance improvements from relatively simple upgrades. However, there are limits. For example, in the days when 486-based servers were state of the art, system architectures weren't designed to make efficient use of large amounts of memory or multiple

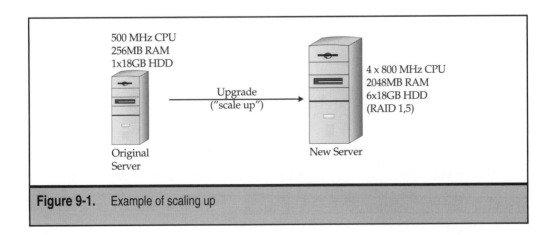

Figure 9-1.   Example of scaling up

CPUs. The same problem can occur today—for some applications and databases, the performance benefits of adding CPUs and memory to a system may begin to provide diminishing returns. For example, moving from a single-CPU architecture to a dual-CPU architecture may provide a substantial performance increase. However, moving from a 16-way server to a 32-way server might provide a marginal improvement in performance (and a considerable increase in cost). So what's a qualified database administrator to do? Fortunately, there's a good solution: scaling *out*.

Scaling out refers to distributing the load for a database or an application to multiple physical machines. This can be done in many different ways. One technology that can be used for this purpose is called clustering. We'll discuss the details of this type of solution later in this chapter. Another method is to change the application architecture. For example, Figure 9-2 shows how application-processing tasks can be distributed among many servers. Another example might occur when you move frequently used databases to other servers.

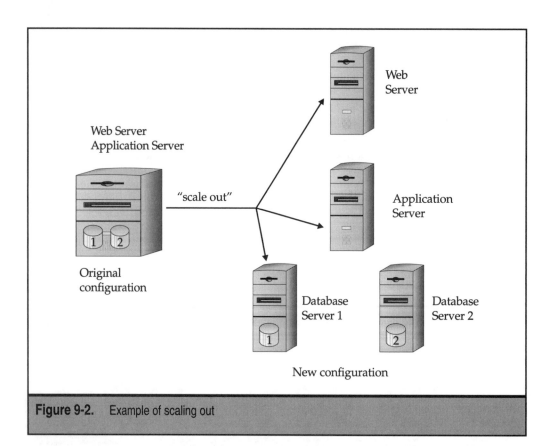

Figure 9-2. Example of scaling out

Performance

Performance is the magical feature that many systems and database administrators allude to when determining the quality of a solution. Performance can be measured in many different ways. For example, you might measure it by determining the amount of time that elapses between when a user submits a transaction to the server and when that transaction is completed. There are several keys to increasing performance.

Regardless of what you might hear from marketing and advertising groups, the single biggest issue is application design. If you create a poorly implemented application, no amount of memory, CPU, or other resources will magically cure the problem. If you take the time to design a well-tuned and efficient application, on the other hand, you may find that you can save your money on server upgrades and still get excellent performance.

In earlier chapters, we looked at several of the new performance-related features of SQL Server 2000. The list of improvements include

▼ Fast differential backups

■ Parallel index creation

■ Parallel DBCC operations

▲ Efficient use of multiple CPUs and large amounts of memory

Reliability

Several new features in SQL Server 2000 increase the platform's reliability. These features are closely related to the core of the product and deal with issues such as memory management, a self-tuning architecture, and the automated handling of important alerts and error conditions. Although they may not be the most visible feature of SQL Server, they are arguably the most important; it doesn't matter what a database platform can do if systems and database administrators can't rely on it to consistently complete the task.

SQL Server 2000's support for multiple server instances increases reliability and provides administrative advantages. As each of the instances can be configured independently, a server can be used for multiple purposes. The use of multiple instances can also prevent ad hoc queries from slowing overall performance and can aid development and testing (as instances can be stopped and restarted independently). The additional flexibility of using multiple instances of SQL Server 2000 offers database and systems administrators a whole new bag of tricks!

So far, we've looked at some very important improvements and features in SQL Server 2000. Now, let's look at the details of some advanced data protection solutions.

SQL SERVER'S REPLICATION MODEL

In an ideal world, none of your employees would ever need to leave the comfort and security of your LAN. Furthermore, all of your network resources would reside within one physical building in which all employees worked. In this case, all of your data would be stored in the same location (the "data center") and made available to those who need it via a reliable high-speed network. There would be no need to store data in various different geographic locations, since all connections would be treated as equal.

In the real world, however, things are quite different. Users require data regardless of their location. Your network connections have different characteristics and bandwidth capabilities. First, network connections across WANs generally are slower and more expensive than networks located within a single building or campus. They may also be less reliable. A typical setup for a medium-sized company, for example, might consist of a large corporate office plus many other remote or branch offices located in various cities throughout the world. Users in every office must have access to information, but it is much too costly to connect them all with the same high-speed access available on a LAN.

To accommodate these scenarios, it is often necessary to distribute data between multiple servers while simultaneously ensuring that all the information remains synchronized. For example, if a salesperson updates customer information in New York, that information should also be updated in the Austin, Texas, database. Furthermore, the changes should be propagated based on business requirements. In some cases, such as financial transactions, it is important that the time between updates on different servers is minimized. In other cases, one day or more of "lag time" is acceptable. Solving problems related to working with distributed information is the job of *replication*—a feature in SQL Server 2000 that facilitates the distribution of data across multiple servers. Figure 9-3 illustrates how replication can reduce networking and resource demands in a distributed environment. Notice that when it comes to data protection, replication automatically provides an off-site copy of

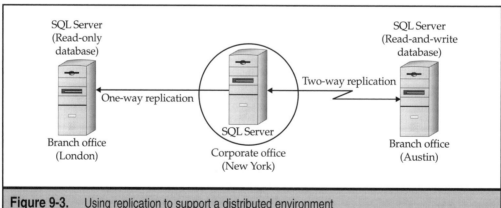

Figure 9-3.   Using replication to support a distributed environment

information. Although, in general, replication is not a good substitute for standard backups, it is a good way to ensure that you have multiple copies of information.

The replication model in SQL Server 2000 provides a powerful but easy way to manage distributed information. In the following sections, we'll look at the architecture of the replication model and explore how it can best be implemented. Let's start with an overview.

Replication Architecture

Microsoft included many features and technologies in SQL Server 2000 to make its replication features powerful yet easy to administer. Basic design goals include the following:

▼ **High performance and scalability**   In order to keep large quantities of data synchronized, you must use efficient methods of transferring information. Common ways to meet this requirement include sending only the changes that occur in a database instead of the database itself.

■ **Reliability**   Businesses rely on replication to ensure that their databases are consistent and up-to-date. The information stored in these repositories is critical for decision support and online transaction processing (OLTP). For this reason, the replication features of SQL Server must be robust and reliable, even when there is a high volume of transactions. One method for ensuring that information is kept consistent is known as *two-phase commit*. This operation ensures that data that must be updated on multiple servers is either all committed or all rolled back, thus preventing inconsistencies.

■ **Simplified administration**   A common problem relative to working with other RDBMSs is that establishing and maintaining replication can be quite complicated. Some of the complexity is due to the nature of the operations involved. Some of it, however, is due to non-user-friendly tools and features. As we'll see in a later section, Microsoft has designed SQL Server 2000 to be easy to administer. Through the use of wizards and the Enterprise Manager console, most common replication scenarios can be quickly set up by systems or database administrators.

▲ **Interoperability**   Although it would be nice if all of your database servers ran on a single platform, the reality in most businesses is that heterogeneous systems are often used to store data. These *"data repositories"* may include standard text files, spreadsheets, relational database servers, and mainframes. Although their functions may at first seem very different, the end goal is the same—to store information and make it available to users. SQL Server 2000 includes many features that support the interchange of information between these various data sources, as well as with other installations of SQL Server. These features make replication readily accessible in SQL Server 2000—and a good solution for distributing information.

Planning for Replication

Before you decide you want to implement replication in your environment, you should define your business requirements. Implementing and maintaining replication will take time, effort, and network resources. Additionally, the overhead associated with replication can reduce overall database server performance. As you're deciding whether to implement replication as part of your data protection strategy, be sure to make the following considerations:

▼ **Evaluate your database needs.**   One of the most common reasons to use replication is to distribute information across slow network connections. If you require that information in multiple locations be kept synchronized, you should determine how much lag time between updates is acceptable. In many environments, data might need to be updated only a few times per day. If real-time concurrency of all servers is truly necessary, you should be prepared for the time and expenses required. In some cases, replication is a good solution for distributing data. In others, however, it might be more practical to use alternate means.

■ **Evaluate your network topology.**   Distributing information between remote servers requires network bandwidth. To keep your servers synchronized, you must have enough data throughput capacity on your slowest network links to support this information. Before you decide to deploy multiple servers with replication, you should estimate the amount of data that will change in each location. Based on these estimates, you can determine an approximate bandwidth requirement. Finally, you must factor in the other uses for these network connections. If, for example, users require a WAN connection for access to the company intranet, all the bandwidth in the connection might not be available for transferring database changes.

■ **Consider all the alternatives.**   If you need to make information available in multiple areas, make sure replication is the appropriate method. For example, a retail establishment might require only daily sales summaries to be transmitted to the corporate office. If this is the case, then simply sending summary database information or even generating regular reports would be more useful. If you're trying to use replication primarily for backup purposes, consider using the standard backup and recovery mechanisms included in SQL Server 2000. Some of these features might result in a less costly and easier-to-administer solution than replication.

▲ **Take stock of available staff.**   Microsoft has created a simple yet powerful administration architecture for replication. However, in order to successfully implement and manage a replication solution, you'll need to allocate individuals with the appropriate skills. Although setting up basic replication settings in SQL Server is quite easy, a good knowledge of network architecture and the replication process will be crucial later on for troubleshooting problems. Be sure you'll have the staff you need well before your databases become unsynchronized due to a configuration problem.

Once you've thought through these issues, you'll probably have a good idea of whether SQL Server's replication features are practical for your environment. Assuming that they are, let's move on to look at how replication actually works in SQL Server 2000.

Creating Publications

To bring some order to the terms and operations required for implementing replication, Microsoft has used a "Publisher-Subscriber" metaphor. This makes the terminology used for managing replication in the SQL Server 2000 world easy to understand. Several major areas must be defined before you can implement your replication. First, you must determine *what* to replicate. In SQL Server terminology, a *publication* is a grouping of data that is to be replicated. It is a collection of one or more articles. An *article* specifies the exact information to be replicated. An article may be a complete database table or only part of one. The following are the different types of articles:

▼ **Full table**   A full table that is used for replication. All rows and columns of the table are made available.

■ **Horizontal partition**   A set of rows that is made available for publication. For example, a database administrator might replicate data for the current year only, although the table itself contains much more information.

■ **Vertical partition**   A subset of the columns of a table that is made available for publication. For example, a database administrator might define that only 3 columns out of a 15-column table are to be made available for replication.

▲ **Results of a stored procedure**   A stored procedure is simply a SQL query that is encapsulated as a database object. For more granular control of the information contained in an article, a database administrator can use the results of a stored procedure for publishing information. This method enables the administrator to select only certain rows and columns, as well as format and transform the data.

All of these methods enable you to specify exactly which information is replicated. In general, it is a good idea to replicate only the needed information, because that will increase performance and decrease network bandwidth requirements. Figure 9-4 illustrates the differences between these types of articles.

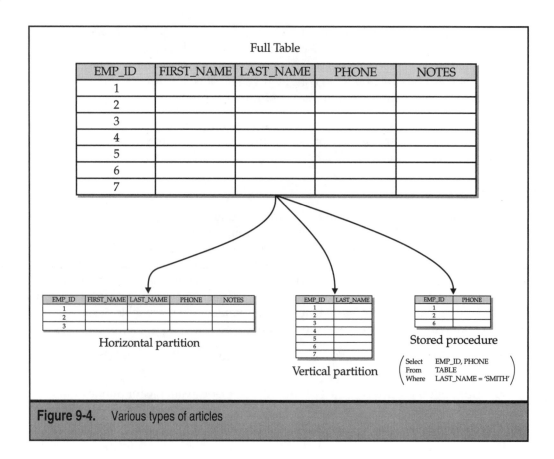

Figure 9-4.   Various types of articles

Replication Server Roles

When dealing with replication, you'll need to define logical roles for each of the servers involved. The roles supported in SQL Server 2000 include the following:

▼   **Publisher**   The source of the information that is replicated. It contains a master copy of the articles that are to be made available to other servers. Each item has only one Publisher, regardless of whether or not Subscribers are also able to update the information.

■   **Distributor**   Responsible for maintaining a record of the changes that are to be sent from the Publisher to one or more Subscribers. Servers that operate as Distributors hold a copy of a special database named *distribution*. The exact method in which this database operates varies based on the type of replication being performed.

▲ **Subscriber**   The logical destination for information made available by Publishers. In some replication configurations, Subscribers can make updates to data and send them back to Publishers.

Figures 9-5 through 9-8 provide examples of some common replication scenarios.

NOTE: These roles are only logical ones. A single SQL Server can have any combination of roles. For example, one server might be configured as a Publisher only, or it may serve as a Publisher for some articles, and as a Distributor and a Subscriber to other articles.

As you can see, there are many different ways in which replication can be implemented. This flexibility allows you to adapt replication solutions to a wide array of business requirements.

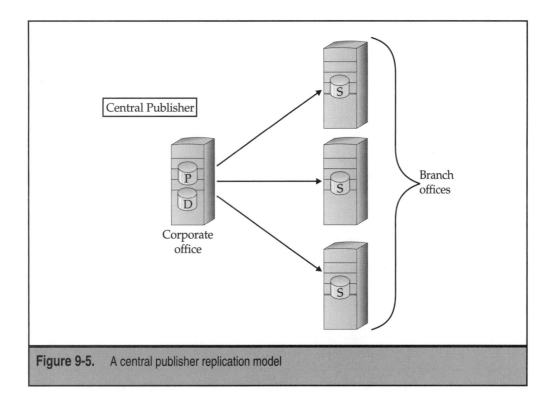

Figure 9-5.   A central publisher replication model

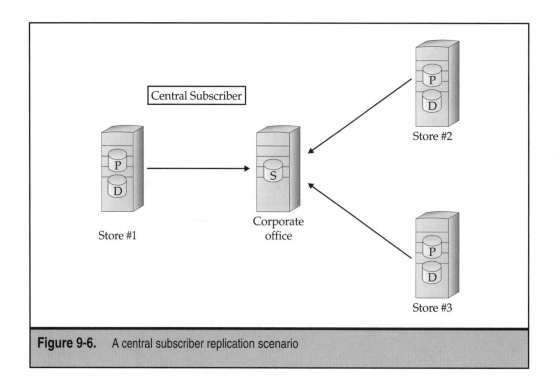

Figure 9-6.   A central subscriber replication scenario

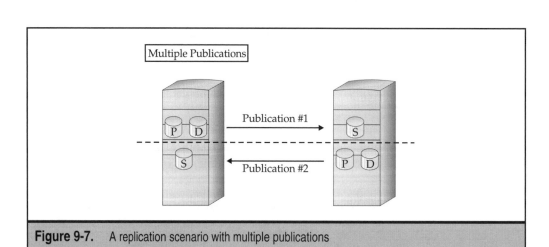

Figure 9-7.   A replication scenario with multiple publications

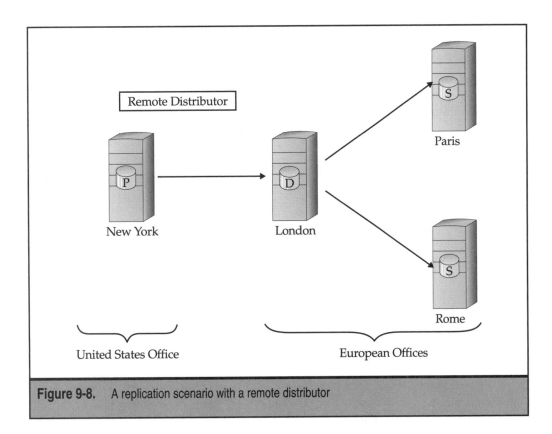

Figure 9-8.   A replication scenario with a remote distributor

Replication Operations

The term *replication* refers to the actual transfer and synchronization of information between various data repositories. In SQL Server 2000, there are two main types of replication operations that can be performed:

▼   **Pull subscription**   The Subscriber initiates a request for information from a Publisher. This is useful in situations involving many Subscribers, because it eases administration. It is also useful for "public" information. For example, a company might make a list of its products and services available to all of its third-party business partners by allowing them to create pull subscriptions. You might also want to implement pull subscriptions when you will be replicating between servers that might not always have persistent network connections. In this case, whenever a connection and sufficient bandwidth is available, administrators at remote Subscribers can initiate a transfer of the information.

▲ **Push subscription**   The Publisher automatically sends data to one or more SQL Servers configured as Subscribers. This is useful if you want to automatically send information when a change occurs or if you want to perform security and administration at a central server. In all types of replication operations, information is transferred between the Publisher and Subscriber, using the Distributor as an intermediate.

Depending on your specific business requirements, you can determine which type of replication best fits your needs. In many cases, the decision will be obvious, but in others both push and pull subscriptions will be viable options.

Replication Methods

After you determine what to replicate and which machines will perform these functions, it's time to define *how* the data should be kept consistent. A fundamental trade-off in designing replication scenarios is between data consistency and performance of replication servers. On one end of the spectrum, information might rarely be synchronized. On the other end, data is never out of sync between the various servers. It is important to realize that greater data consistency can require more server and network resources and can thus reduce performance. Therefore, your business must accurately define data consistency requirements.

SQL Server supports several different replication methods:

▼ **Snapshot replication**   Used to take an image of the database at a certain point in time. This image is then made available to one or more Subscribers, either based on a schedule or on demand. This is a good choice if you are distributing information from a central repository to many read-only servers. A common example is a retail merchant (the Publisher) making product availability and pricing information available to resellers (the Subscribers). An important point to remember with snapshot replication is that *all* information from a publication is sent to the client with each refresh. Although this reduces the processing overhead required, it can place much greater burdens on bandwidth and networking infrastructure. Therefore, snapshot replication is generally recommended only for transfers of relatively small amounts of data.

■ **Transactional replication**   Used to monitor and record all information about INSERT, UPDATE, and DELETE statements, which is useful if strong data consistency between servers is required. Changes to the data contained within databases can be sent to the necessary Subscribers either immediately or at predefined intervals, which ensures that information is kept up-to-date at all Subscribers, but places greater demands on network availability. An important feature of transactional replication is that a given piece of information should have only one Publisher. Therefore, this method is best for databases in which the information is already logically partitioned. For example, for a company with multiple store locations, each of which modifies its own sales data only, information can easily be collected at a corporate office.

■ **Immediate-Updating Subscribers** Allows Subscribers to update information and transfer any changes back to the Publisher immediately. In the simplest configuration of snapshot or transactional replication, the data transfer will be one way. That is, information will be modified at a Publisher, and these changes will then be transferred to Subscribers. However, various business requirements might require Subscribers to be able to update their copies of information. In this case, the Immediate-Updating Subscribers option can be used. You can enable this option when articles are created for replication. Immediate-Updating Subscribers can allow modifications of their local information as long as the Publisher is updated at the same time. All other Subscribers to the publication are then updated with the next scheduled update. This allows for distributed data changes while simultaneously ensuring that information is kept synchronized. However, since Subscribers can update information only when they have access to the Publisher, you must ensure that you are working over a reliable network connection.

■ **Merge replication** Designed for situations in which you must allow multiple databases to be updated independently but still be kept synchronized. This is ideal, for example, if you have unreliable or slow network connections. In this scenario, you want users to be able to update their local copies of databases and then reconcile these updates with other servers. That's exactly the purpose of merge replication. A major challenge in merge replication is determining who "wins" if a conflict arises. For example, consider the situation in which the same database row is updated on two different servers. When this type of conflict occurs, SQL Server automatically resolves it based on a predefined set of rules. Either time-based replication can be used, or certain servers can be given higher priorities than others. In all cases, however, the conflicts are managed and the data is kept consistent on all servers.

▲ **Queued updating** A new feature in SQL Server 2000 replication is queued updating. Queued updating allows changes to be made at Subscriber databases even if they do not have an active connection to the Publisher. The transactions are simply queued at the Subscriber until network connectivity is available. The transactions are then transferred between the replicated databases. Of course, the logical problem is that changes to the same data could have been made at both databases. Fortunately, there are methods for automatically resolving conflicts, as well. Queued updating is a good solution for scenarios in which network connectivity is not always reliable and when data modifications at Subscribers are relatively rare.

Figure 9-9 plots data independence versus data consistency for various types of replication operations. Each of the replication types has different characteristics.

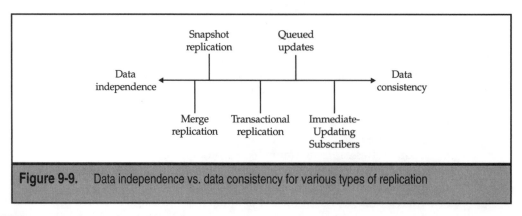

Figure 9-9.   Data independence vs. data consistency for various types of replication

NOTE: In some situations, it is perfectly valid to combine different types of replication. The ultimate decision will be based on your business requirements and your technical and physical constraints.

Now that we've seen the various operations that might be required to set up and carry out replication, let's look at the actual processes that meet these requirements.

Replication Agents

To ensure that all of the necessary replication actions are performed, SQL Server includes the following five Agents, each of which is responsible for a specific action within the replication system:

▼ **Snapshot Agent** Responsible for generating the information specified within the articles of a publication on a Publisher and storing it within the distribution database on the Distributor. This is the information that is potentially sent to Subscribers. Each publication has its own Snapshot Agent, so snapshots can be generated on separate schedules for different types of information.

■ **Log Reader Agent** Responsible for reading information from the transaction log of the necessary databases specified in a publication, if transactional replication is enabled. The Log Reader Agent is actually run on the Distributor, and each of the publications has its own Log Reader Agent.

■ **Distribution Agent** Responsible for applying information stored in the distribution database to Subscribers. Depending on the type of replication chosen, the Distribution Agent may run on the Distributor or the Subscriber. Also, in SQL Server 2000, this process may run on a completely separate server.

■ **Merge Agent** Responsible for determining and recording incremental data changes that occur on databases participating in replication. It does this by comparing the data in the initial snapshot that was created with the information in the database at the time the process runs. Depending on the specifics of the replication configuration, the Merge Agent may run on the Publisher or the Subscriber. The Merge Agent may, for example, run on the Subscriber if two-way replication is enabled. Or, this process may run on a completely separate server.

▲ **Queue Reader Agent**   Responsible for queuing and applying transactions when queued updating is enabled. It is also responsible for resolving any conflicts that might occur.

These processes are executed as required by the replication configuration. The SQL Server Agent runs all the processes and is responsible for ensuring that they are performed as required. If, for some reason, SQL Server replication is not working properly, you should check the status of these Agents to pinpoint the problem.

Enhancements in SQL Server 2000 Replication

As businesses become more distributed and WAN links become cheaper, faster, and more reliable, organizations are increasingly implementing replication solutions. In SQL Server 2000, Microsoft has enhanced the implementation, administration, and trouble-shooting of replication. We have already discussed some of the improvements over past versions of SQL Server in the previous sections. In addition to the features already described, new replication functionality and features in SQL Server 2000 include

▼ **Support for new SQL Server 2000 features**   As mentioned in Chapter 4, there are many new features and functionality in SQL Server 2000. Fortunately, replication supports the use of these new database objects, including materialized views and user-defined functions. Additionally, replication supports the use of multiple SQL Server instances on the same machine. (We'll see in a later section how this can be very useful for developing, testing, and maintaining replication settings.)

■ **Initial snapshot generation**   Generating the initial snapshot of a database can be a time-consuming and resource-intensive operation. In previous versions of SQL Server, the initial snapshot had to be generated at the Publisher and then applied to the Subscriber. When setting up replication for many servers (or on a few busy servers), this can be inefficient. In SQL Server 2000, database administrators can generate initial snapshots for Subscriber computers and then apply them individually through the use of removable media or network connections. Additionally, the snapshot files themselves can be compressed to save disk space and conserve network bandwidth.

■ **Detaching and attaching Subscriber databases**   In past versions of SQL Server, you could not simply "move" a Subscriber database to another server. Rather, the process involved dropping replication on one server and then re-creating all of the replication settings on another server. In SQL Server 2000, database administrators can detach a Subscriber database from one server and then reattach it on another server. All Subscriber configuration information is retained.

■ **Support for schema changes**   Database administrators can now make changes to the structure of database objects and have these changes automatically sent to Subscribers. This eases administration by allowing common tasks such as adding, modifying, or dropping a column in a table.

■ **Support for scripting** In many cases, it might be useful to run SQL scripts before or after the transmission of replication information. SQL Server 2000 allows database administrators to define scripts to run during various events (such as after a snapshot is applied on a Subscriber database). As these scripts run as part of the replication architecture, database administrators no longer have to schedule tasks to run based on predefined schedules. The scripts themselves can support several different options, including the transfer of objects such as indexes and the application of constraints.

■ **Use of "remote agents"** In SQL Server 2000, the Distribution and Merge Agents (both of which can consume significant amounts of resources on busy servers) can be off-loaded to another computer. This other computer (which may be a nonproduction server) can then take the load that would otherwise have been placed on the Distributor and Subscriber machines.

■ **Improved replication administration** In SQL Server 2000, the replication wizards and dialog boxes have been improved to provide a more intuitive setup process for replication options. Additionally, there is more functionality in the Replication Monitor (which serves as a central console for monitoring replication transactions and details). We'll see examples of these improvements in later sections of this chapter.

■ **Programmability and automation enhancements** SQL Server 2000 includes many improvements for developers who create custom replication solutions. Improvements can be seen in the Component Object Model (COM) specifications and functionality, as well is in other scripting and programming tools.

■ **Tighter integration with Data Transformation Services (DTS)** As we saw in previous chapters, DTS can be an extremely useful tool for transferring data between servers and data sources. In SQL Server 2000, DTS and replication can coexist to provide customizability and additional flexibility in replication scenarios.

■ **Queued updating** We described this feature in an earlier section. However, it's worth mentioning again that queued updating allows systems and database administrators to deal with various network constraints in a reliable way.

▲ **Integration with Active Directory** SQL Server 2000 publications can be searched for and accessed via the Active Directory. This makes it easier for potential Subscribers to find exactly the publications they need without first knowing the name and network information for the server on which the publications reside. Figure 9-10 shows the Server Properties dialog box that can be used to enable the listing of publications and other SQL Server information in the Active Directory. This functionality is provided through the Microsoft SQL Server Active Directory Helper Service.

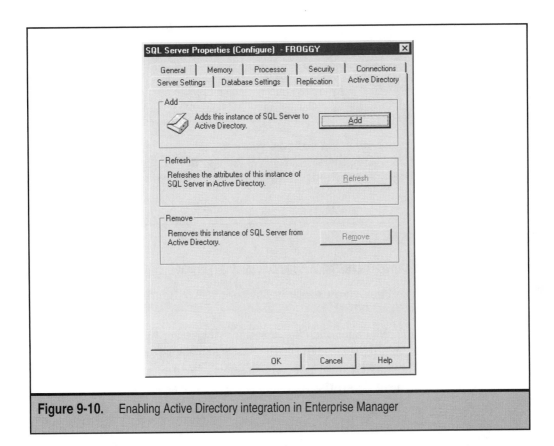

Figure 9-10.   Enabling Active Directory integration in Enterprise Manager

Now that we have a good understanding and overview of how SQL Server 2000 replication works, let's move on to examine methods for actually implementing replication.

IMPLEMENTING SQL SERVER REPLICATION

In previous sections of this chapter, we discussed how to plan for replication and provided a detailed look at the various types of replication supported in SQL Server 2000. Now it's time to apply that information in implementing and configuring replication settings. Before going on, however, be sure you understand which methods are best in your environment. It is usually a good idea to practice setting up replication on nonproduction servers and using test databases, as misconfigurations might cause data loss or inconsistencies. Although the operations themselves are quite complex, SQL Server includes many wizards that can be used for performing common tasks. With that in mind, let's start by describing how to enable replication.

NOTE: The use of multiple instances of SQL Server 2000 on the same machine can be very helpful in testing replication settings with only a single server. You should understand, however, that performing replication between two instances on the same machine does not take into account network connections and reliability issues that you may experience on production servers.

Enabling Replication

Before you can configure replication options, you'll need to enable replication on an installation of SQL Server. Although the SQL Server 2000 setup process, by default, installs all the features you'll need, replication is not enabled until you explicitly perform the following process.

STEP-BY-STEP

Enabling Replication Using Enterprise Manager

The steps in this exercise assume that you have not yet configured replication for this installation of SQL Server 2000.

1. Open Enterprise Manager and click the name of a server for which you want to enable replication. If you do not see the Taskpad view in the right pane, right-click on the server, select View, and then click Taskpad.

2. In the right pane of Enterprise Manager, click the Wizards button.

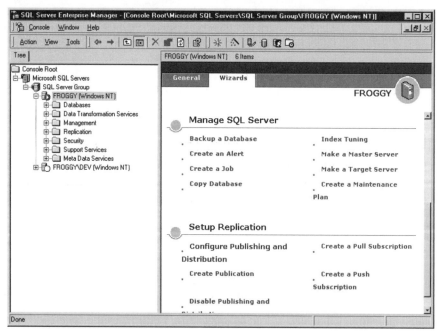

3. Under the Setup Replication section, select Configure Publishing and Distribution. This will start the Configure Publishing and Distribution Wizard. Click Next to begin the wizard.

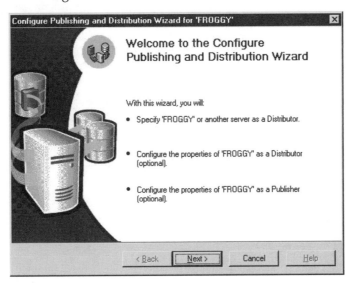

4. **Select Distributor**   Before you can configure replication, you must specify one server as the Distributor. On the Select Distributor page of the wizard, either make the current server a Distributor or connect to another server that already contains a distribution database. Click Next.

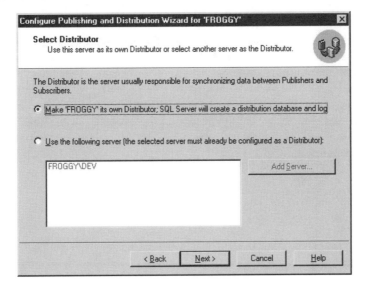

5. **(Optional) Configure SQL Server Agent**   In order for replication to function properly, the SQL Server Agent service must be running. If the service is not properly configured, the wizard will prompt you regarding whether you want the SQL Server Agent to be configured to start automatically. Choose Yes, and then click Next to continue.

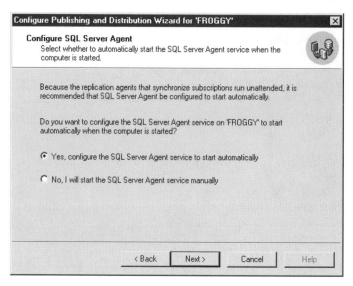

6. **Specify Snapshot Folder**   During the snapshot creation process, Subscribers must be able to access snapshot information over the network. In this step of the wizard, you must specify a shared folder that will be available to the Subscribers via the network. Note that this cannot be a mapped drive path or a local drive letter (for example, "D:\Data"), as Subscribers will not be able to access the folder using that drive letter. Instead, you should use a Universal Naming Convention (UNC) pathname (for example, \\Server1\ReplData\). You will need to separately ensure that the security permissions for this directory allow Subscribers to access it. The default file system location for the snapshot folder is the ReplData folder located under the "Program Files\Microsoft SQL Server\MSSQL" folder. Enter a network path and click Next to continue.

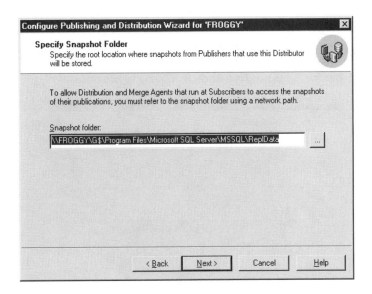

7. You will be reminded that Subscriber SQL Server installations must be running under a network account that has Administrator permissions on this server. If you are sure the configuration is correct, click Yes to continue.

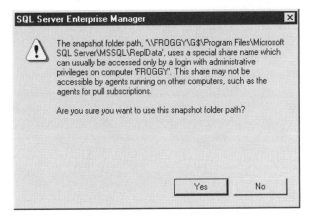

8. **Customize the Configuration** In the next step of the wizard, you will be prompted to specify additional replication configuration options or to choose the default settings. For the sake of this exercise, choose Yes to define custom settings for the configuration and click Next to continue.

9. **Provide Distribution Database Information** In this step, you'll be prompted to provide information about the name and location of the distribution database. By default, the name of the database is "distribution." For administrative simplicity, it is recommended that you retain this name. You can also specify the physical folders in which the distribution database will be created. This can be helpful if you want to move replication-related databases to various physical disk devices on your server for performance reasons. Confirm the settings and click Next to continue.

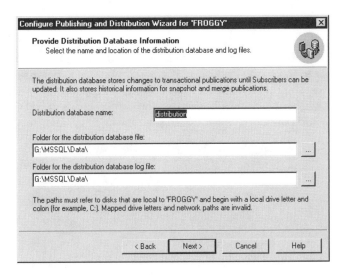

10. **Enable Publishers** After you choose and configure a Distributor, you may designate one or more Publishers that are permitted to use it. Enable a Publisher by placing a check mark next to the name of the server. Note that you can use the New button to create a new SQL Server registration if the instance you want to enable is not already located in the list. Place a check mark next to the SQL Server installations that should be able to use this installation as a publisher.

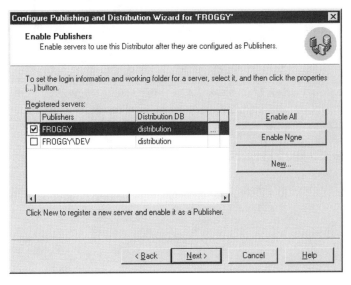

11. To specify additional Publisher properties, click the ellipsis in the rightmost column of the Registered Servers table. This allows you to specify both the folder into which snapshot information is stored and the login that will be used by the Distributor to access the Publisher. If you allow the SQL Server Agent account to be used, you should ensure that this account has appropriate permissions on a remote Publisher machine. Otherwise, you can specify a valid SQL Server username and password. Click OK to save the settings, and then click Next.

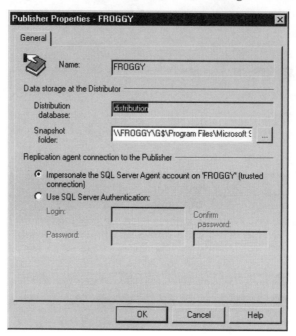

12. **Enable Publication Databases** On this page of the wizard, you can specify one or more databases as being available for replication and choose the types of replication supported. The two main types are transactional (which includes snapshot replication) and merge. Select the databases and types of replication you want to make available, and then click Next.

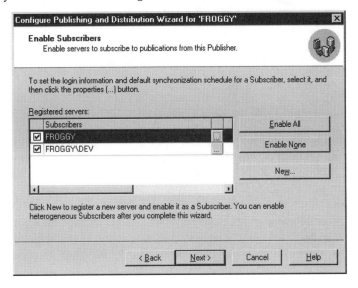

13. **Enable Subscribers**   If you chose databases for publication in the preceding step, you'll need to set the login information for Subscriber servers.

To specify options for the Subscribers, click the ellipsis button. You can also specify the schedules for the data transfers by making the appropriate settings on the Schedules tab. If the server you want to configure as a Subscriber is not in the list, you can add it by using the Register Server button. Once you have chosen to enable the appropriate Subscribers, click Next to continue.

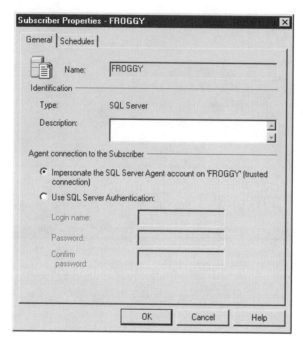

14. You will see the Completing the Configure Publishing and Distribution Wizard page. The text box will display a summary of the replication settings and choices you made. It may be helpful to copy and paste this text into another file for use in documenting your replication configuration. Simply click the Finish button to commit the changes. Enterprise Manager will automatically configure the distribution database (if specified) and enable any Publishers or Subscribers you specified in previous steps. The server is now ready to participate in replication. Click OK when informed that the server is now configured as a Publisher.

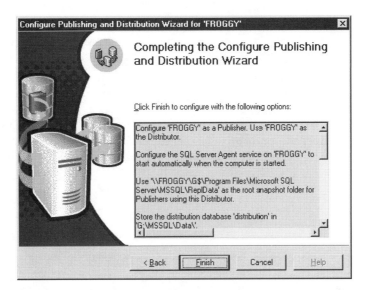

15. Once the replication configuration is complete, you'll be shown a dialog box that provides information about the Replication Monitor feature that has been added to Enterprise Manager. Click Close once you have read the information.

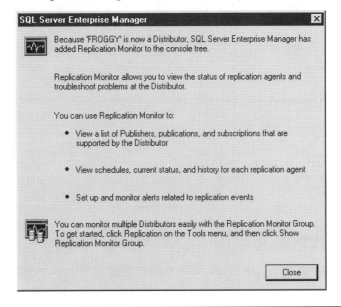

Once replication is configured on your server, you will see some changes in Enterprise Manager. First, any database that is configured as a Publisher will have a small hand displayed under its icon, to indicate its shared status. A new folder entitled Publishers will also be available under the sections for these databases. Additionally, you'll see that Replication Monitor (covered later in this chapter) has been added to the interface. These changes are illustrated in Figure 9-11.

Note that you can easily disable replication by choosing the Disable Publishing and Distribution option in the Enterprise Manager Taskpad view. This process removes any replication settings you have made and can delete the distribution database. (See Figure 9-12.)

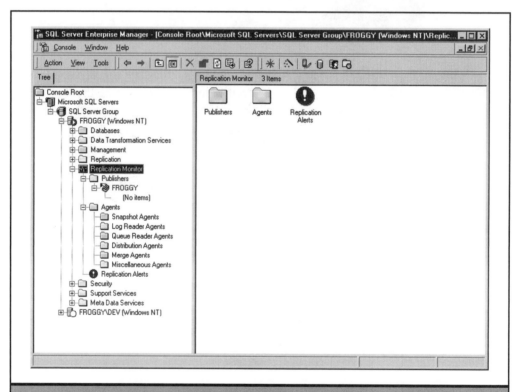

Figure 9-11. Viewing replication information in Enterprise Manager

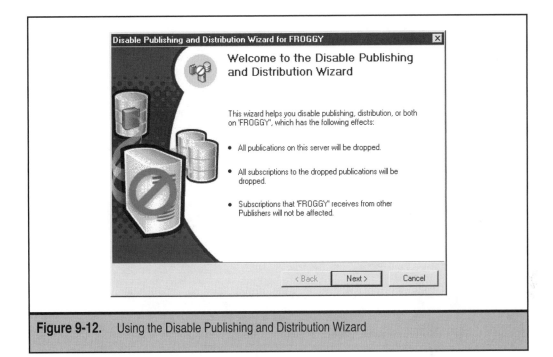

Figure 9-12. Using the Disable Publishing and Distribution Wizard

Creating and Managing Publications

By enabling replication, you have specified a distribution database and may have also configured Publishers and Subscribers. This alone does not set up the specific publications,
however. After you configure replication, it's time to determine exactly which information
will be available to other servers. Again, the easiest way to do this is within Enterprise
Manager, using the included wizards. The steps within the wizard provide you with ample
information about each of the available settings and options. Nevertheless, you should be
familiar with the type of replication you plan to use before beginning these steps. The following procedure walks through the process of managing publications.

NOTE: In order to successfully complete the steps in this procedure, you must first have configured
the server for replication. You must also have a Distributor configured and available for use. (This may
be the same server.) In this exercise, we'll be making certain assumptions about the types of replication to implement. However, your business requirements may differ, and the exact steps in the wizard
will vary based on the details of your replication configuration.

STEP-BY-STEP

Creating a Publication

1. Open Enterprise Manager and click the name of a server for which you want to configure publications. If you do not see the Taskpad view in the right pane, right-click on the server, select View, and then click Taskpad.

2. In the right pane of Enterprise Manager, click the Wizards button.

3. Under the Setup Replication section, select Create Publication. This will open the Create and Manage Publications dialog box.

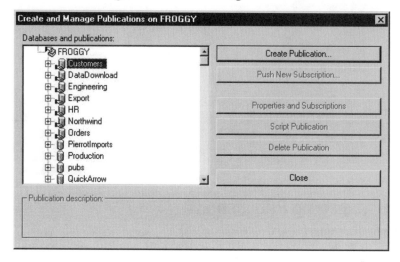

4. In this exercise, we will be creating a new publication for the Northwind database. (If you do not have a copy of the default Northwind database on this server, either restore a copy of the database from the SQL Server 2000 CD-ROM or use another database.) To begin the process, select the Northwind database, and then click Create Publication. This will start the Create Publication Wizard. Note that there is an option to view advanced options. For the sake of this exercise, place a check mark in that box, and then click Next to begin the Wizard.

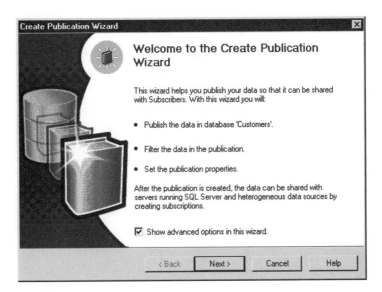

5. **Choose Publication Database**   In the first step of the wizard, you'll be prompted to choose the database for which you want to create a publication. Select Northwind and click Next to continue.

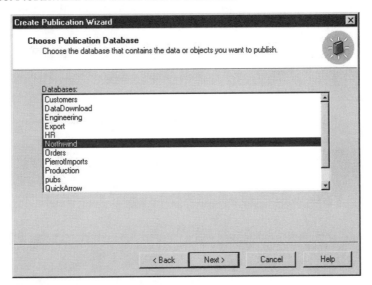

6. **Select Publication Type**   On this screen, specify the type of publication you want to create. For the sake of this exercise, choose Transactional Publication. Note that you may want to change this setting based on your business requirements. Also, the exact steps that show up in the following pages of this wizard will be based upon the selection you make here. Click Next.

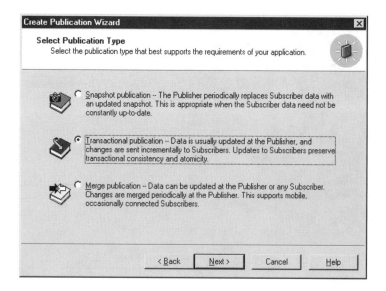

7. **Updatable Subscriptions** Here, you'll need to determine whether Subscriber machines will be allowed to update their copies of data in the publication. There are two main options available to Subscribers: Immediate Updating and Queued Updating. To allow Subscribers to choose either type of updating, place check marks in both boxes. Click Next to continue.

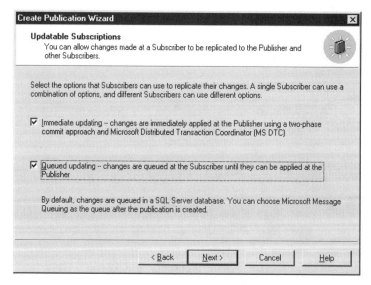

8. **Specify Subscriber Types** Before SQL Server can determine how data should be transferred between servers, you must tell it which types of servers will be participating in the replication. The choices include SQL Server 2000 (the only

selection that is checked by default), SQL Server 7.0, and other "heterogeneous" data sources (such as Oracle or other database types). Leave the default setting of only SQL Server 2000 and click Next to continue.

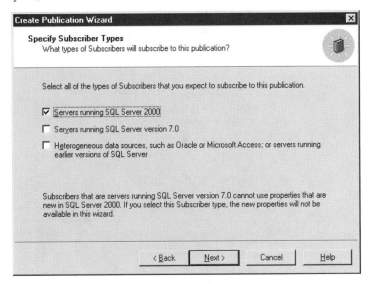

9. **Specify Articles** Now, it's time to specify exactly which database information will be made available as part of the publication. Notice that you have options to include or exclude database objects individually. The types of database objects that can be included in the publication include tables, stored procedures, and views (including materialized views).

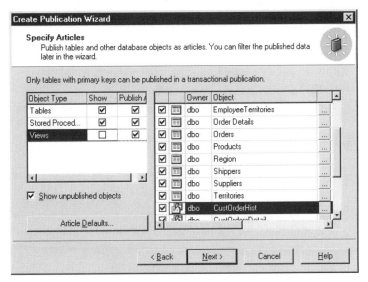

10. In addition to the basic settings already mentioned, you can specify advanced options by clicking the ellipsis button next to each table. For example, for table objects, you can choose Snapshot and Identity column settings. You can also specify the default behavior for articles by clicking the Article Defaults button.

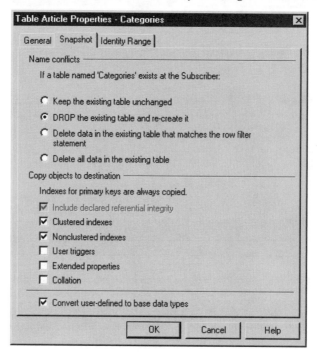

11. Select at least one article to publish as part of the publication, and then click Next to continue.

12. **Article Issues** Based on the replication settings you've chosen thus far, you will see a summary of issues that may exist for published objects. For example, the wizard may notify you that a unique identifier column must be added to specific tables or that specific objects that are referenced by other objects (for example, tables referenced by a view) must be included. For details about each of these issues, see the Description text. Click Next to continue.

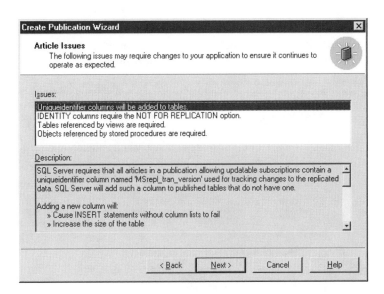

13. **Select Publication Name and Description** In this step, you can provide a name and description for the publication. These values can be very useful, especially if you have specified multiple publications for the same database. Good practices include specifying which tables are published (or the type of information) and the type of replication used. Click Next.

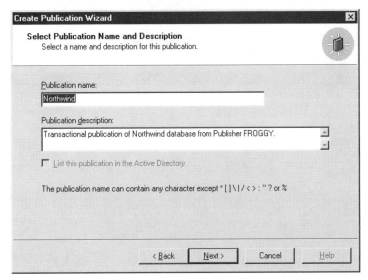

14. **Customize the Properties of the Publication** So far, we've determined what will be published (the articles) and how the data will be kept synchronized with Subscribers (the replication method). Additionally, we can now define

data filters and customize other properties related to the publication itself. For example, one option is to specify only certain table columns for replication. For the sake of this exercise, choose Yes, and then click Next.

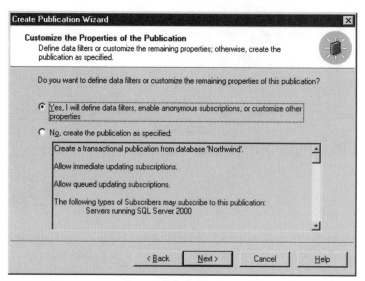

15. **Filter Data** In order to provide the most granular control over which portions of data are replicated, you can implement horizontal and/or vertical partitioning (described earlier in this chapter). To enable these settings, simply place a check mark in either or both of the options. For the sake of this exercise, select vertical partitioning, and then click Next.

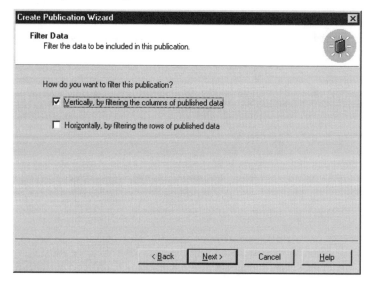

16. **Filter Table Columns**   Since you have selected to enable vertical partitioning, SQL Server must know which columns you want to replicate for this publication. Select at least one column for each of the objects. (The default is to have all columns enabled for replication.) Click Next to continue.

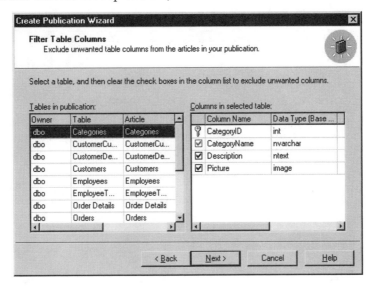

17. **Allow Anonymous Subscriptions**   In this step, you can choose whether you want to allow anonymous subscriptions to this publication. If you choose Yes, all authorized servers will be able to subscribe to this publication. If you select No, you must specify which server(s) will be able to subscribe to it. Select Yes, and then click Next.

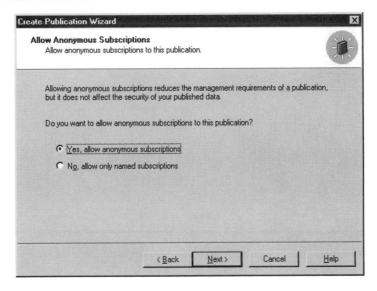

18. **Set Snapshot Agent Schedule**   To determine when the data will be refreshed and stored in the distribution database, you can specify a schedule for the Snapshot Agent. You can also enable the option that specifies that a snapshot will be created immediately as part of the operations for the wizard. Enable this option and click Next.

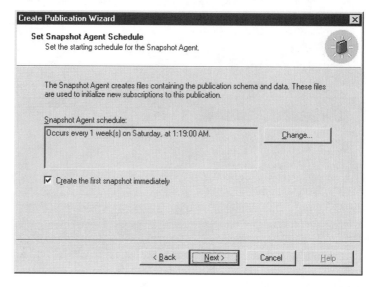

After you make the appropriate selections, the Create and Manage Publications Wizard provides you with a list of the operations you've selected. It might be helpful to copy and paste this information into a text file so that you remember the exact settings.

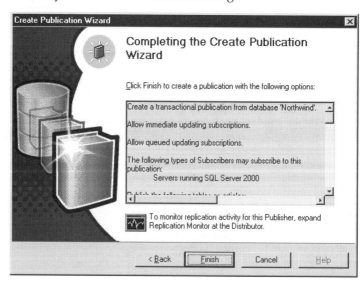

To commit the changes and begin processing, click the Finish button. Once the operation is complete, the publication will be available to Subscribers. Click Close to complete the process.

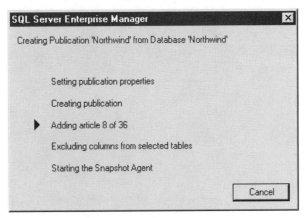

The previous process may seem like a lot of steps just to set up one publication. One reason is that we chose to specify as many details as possible, but there's a good chance that the defaults will be appropriate for many of your own replication requirements. Although a lot of options are available, if you've planned for the type of replication you want to support, the answers to the questions should be obvious. Going through these steps can take as little as a few minutes.

NOTE: You can set up multiple publications for the same database. This is a useful scheme if, for example, you want to make different subsets of data available or if you want to use different replication methods for various Subscribers.

Click the Properties and Subscriptions button in the Create and Manage Publications window to view all the options that are available for each publication. In some cases, you might want to make minor changes to the publication without going through all the steps in the wizard again. (See Figure 9-13.)

Another useful option allows you to generate SQL scripts for creating this publication or setting valid logon information for replication. This is useful if you want to transfer the replication settings to another server or if you want to create a publication creation script for restoring replication settings after a database restore. (See Figure 9-14.)

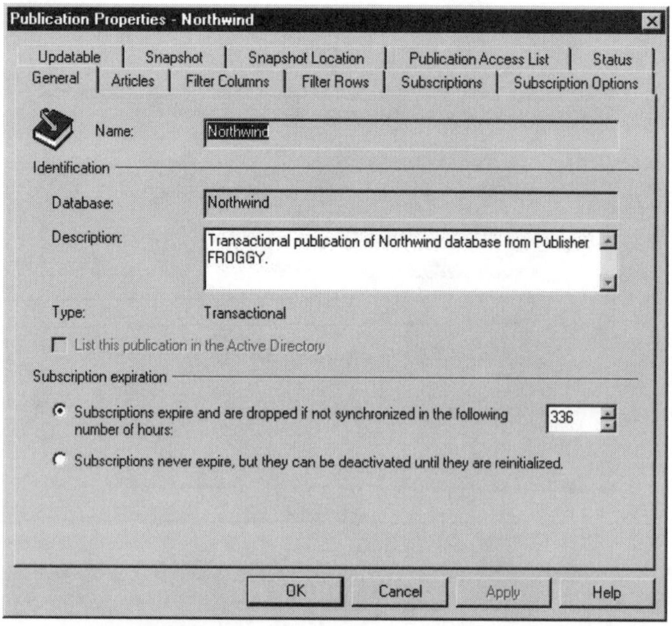

Figure 9-13. Viewing the properties of a publication

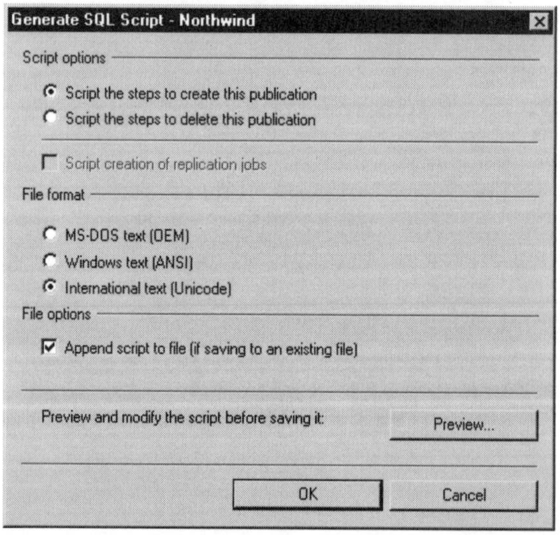

Figure 9-14. Generating a script for a publication

Creating Push and Pull Subscriptions

So far, we have covered two important steps in implementing configuration: First, we configured a machine for replication by establishing a Publisher and a Distributor. Then, we defined a publication for use by Subscribers. Now, it's time to take the final step: implementing the transfer of data to Subscribers.

After you set up the various types of publications you want to make available, it's time to create push and pull subscriptions. Like the other tasks related to replication, this can easily be set up by using wizards. The basic steps involve choosing a source publication and then specifying a destination database. Figure 9-15 shows the beginning screen of the Pull Subscription Wizard.

In most cases, you'll probably want to create a new database to serve as a container for the replicated items. You'll also be able to specify how often subscriptions are refreshed. Options range from continuous refreshing to running them on specific schedules. For example, Figure 9-16 shows the options available when connecting to a transactional replication publication.

For more information on the exact steps required to push or pull subscriptions, use the appropriate wizards or see SQL Server Books Online.

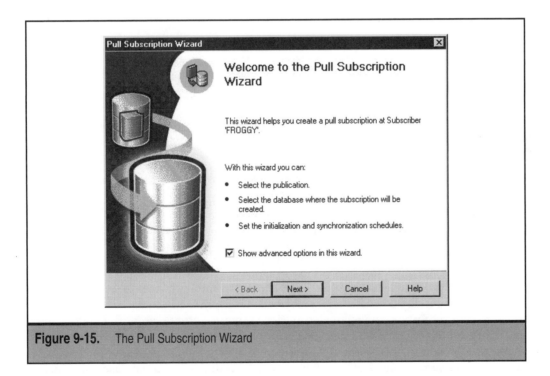

Figure 9-15. The Pull Subscription Wizard

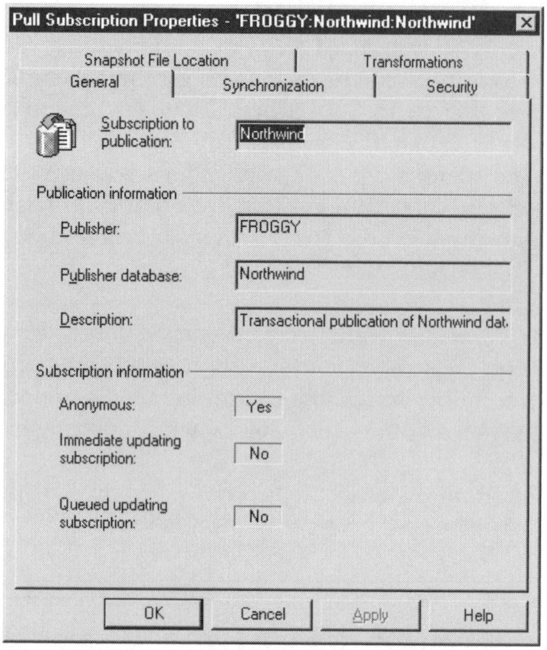

Figure 9-16. Subscribing to a publication using transactional replication

NOTE: You can set up replication between databases on the same server. Although this might cause an unnecessary decrease in performance, it's a great way to test your replication settings before making them available to other machines across the network. The same applies for replicating across multiple instances of SQL Server 2000 on the same machine.

Using Transact-SQL

Although the quickest and easiest way to configure replication is by using the wizards in Enterprise Manager, you might want to use Transact-SQL commands so that you can access the additional features they offer. Transact-SQL commands can also be used to create custom jobs or modify those that were created in Enterprise Manager. For example, if you want to set up complex replication scenarios on many servers, you can create a single script or stored procedure that quickly performs the necessary operations. Furthermore, Transact-SQL commands support more options than are available using the GUI tools. Table 9-1 lists some of the useful system-stored procedures that can be used to configure and manage SQL Server replication.

Procedure	Function
sp_addarticle sp_droparticle	Creates or removes an article and adds it to or removes it from an existing publication
sp_adddistributiondb sp_dropdistributiondb	Creates or drops the distribution database (used for storing replication information on a Distributor)
sp_addmergepublication sp_dropmergepublication	Creates or drops a new merge publication
sp_addmergesubscription	Creates a new push or pull merge subscription
sp_addpublication sp_droppublication	Creates or drops a new publication for use in snapshot or transactional replication. (Articles can be added to the publication with sp_addarticle.)
sp_addpublication_snapshot sp_droppublication_snapshot	Creates or drops a new Snapshot Agent for refreshing snapshot information
sp_addpullsubscription sp_droppullsubscription	Creates or drops a new pull subscription at the Subscriber
sp_addsubscriber sp_dropsubscriber	Adds or removes a replication Subscriber; also supports non-SQL Server Subscriber types
sp_addsubscription sp_dropsubscription	Adds or removes a subscription to/from an existing publication
sp_articlefilter	Allows for horizontally partitioning the data in an article
sp_grant_publication_access sp_revoke_publication_access	Adds or revokes a login to the access list for a publication
sp_helparticle sp_helpmergearticle	Displays information about articles
sp_helpdistributiondb	Displays information about the distribution database on a Distributor
sp_helpdistributor	Displays information about a Distributor and the distribution database
sp_helpsubscription	Displays information about existing subscriptions

Table 9-1. Common Replication-Related Stored Procedures

By using these commands, you can work with replication settings. A good way to learn about how the stored procedures are used to create publications is to generate a script for an existing one. This script can then serve as a template for the proper command syntax. Although the table mentions the most common stored procedures and their functions, the complete list of system-stored procedures used for replication operations is much larger. For a more complete list, stored procedure syntax, and further documentation, see Appendix A.

Network Considerations

Before SQL Server replication will function properly, you'll need to ensure that you have network connectivity to each of your machines. This normally isn't a problem if you're connecting to your servers either on a private network or by using the Internet. However, it is a major concern if SQL Server must communicate with other machines through a firewall. In that case, you need to ensure that the appropriate networking ports are opened on the firewall and that all SQL Server installations are configured to use them. This can be set up using Client Network Utility and SQL Server Network Utility, available in the Microsoft SQL Server 2000 program group. Figure 9-17 shows sample default settings in SQL Server Network Utility.

By default, SQL Server 2000 uses TCP Port 1433 to communicate with other servers using the TCP/IP protocol. Using the SQL Server Network Utility and the Client Net-

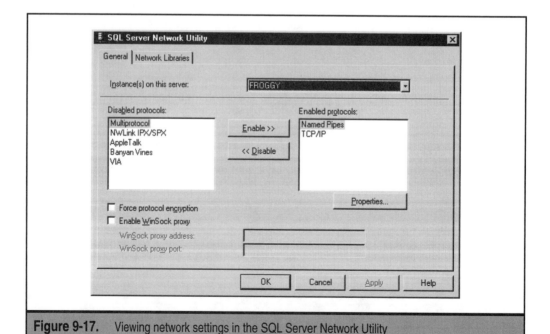

Figure 9-17.   Viewing network settings in the SQL Server Network Utility

work Utility, you can change this port assignment. Only one instance of SQL Server can respond to a specific port. Therefore, if your machine is running multiple instances, you must choose different TCP/IP ports for those instances. If you are unable to communicate with other installations of SQL Server using standard network connections, you'll need to make changes in your network design. Keep this in mind when setting up replication in your environment.

Working in Heterogeneous Environments

SQL Server 2000 has been designed to perform two-way replication with various data sources. These sources may include any type of data repository that is supported through the ODBC or OLEDB database access methods. For example, an Oracle server might function as a Subscriber to a SQL Server database. Bear in mind that with these types of data sources, you will not have access to all the features of SQL Server 2000. Additionally, some custom development may be required to integrate other types of servers or data repositories. Fortunately, the SQL Server architecture has been designed to be flexible, and documentation and programming objects are available for various development languages. For details about the limitations of replication, see SQL Server Books Online.

Monitoring SQL Server Replication

After you have set up replication, you'll need to ensure that it is working properly. There are several parameters that might affect its proper operation. Network connection availability and performance are two of the main considerations. We've already mentioned several ways to ensure that SQL Server replication is working. In this section, we'll look at several ways to view information about replication and monitor-related activities. This is a vital function for businesses that depend on replication services.

Configuring the Replication Monitor

SQL Server Enterprise Manager includes the Replication Monitor tool for quickly and easily viewing status and conflict information related to replication. This tool can give you periodic updates of the status of replication and is useful in ensuring that everything is working properly. Before relying on the information presented in Replication Monitor, you should make sure that you have made appropriate settings to the display. This can be done by right-clicking the Replication Monitor item in Enterprise Manager and selecting Refresh Rate and Settings. You'll see the refresh rate settings in the dialog box shown in Figure 9-18. Here you'll be able to configure the update frequencies and other time intervals for Replication Monitor.

REMEMBER: Although a smaller replication status refresh time will give you more accurate information, it can also increase system resource usage. For example, if you have many Subscribers at remote locations, this can cause a lot of WAN traffic. The Performance Monitor tab in the Refresh Rate and Settings dialog box enables you to specify the path in which the default Performance Monitor chart information is stored.

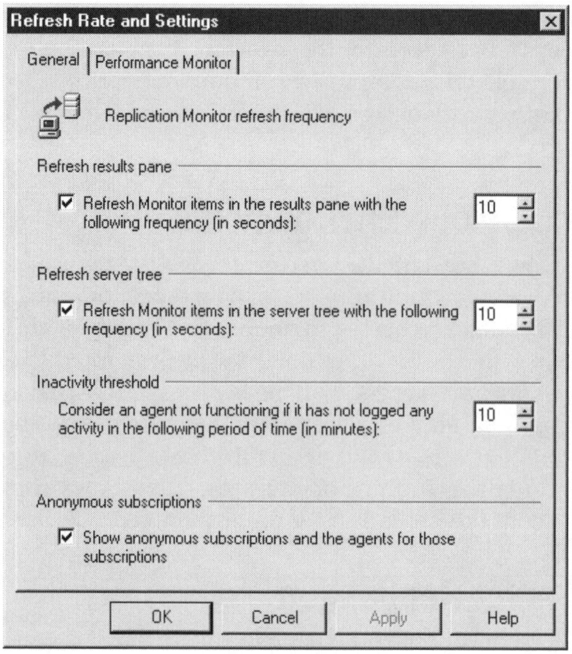

Figure 9-18. Viewing refresh rate settings for the Replication Monitor

Figure 9-19 shows the types of information you can see using Replication Monitor. By right-clicking various items, you can see even more details about replication conflicts and Agent settings.

Setting Replication Alerts

In many organizations, replication is a vital operation that must be carried out properly for business purposes. Therefore, if problems with replication occur, you'll want to

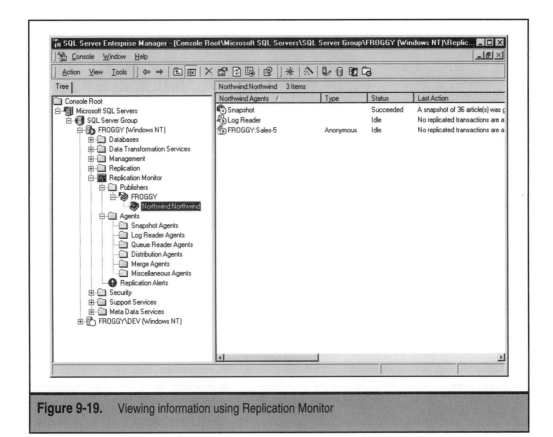

Figure 9-19. Viewing information using Replication Monitor

ensure that you have set up the appropriate alerts. Figure 9-20 shows the default alerts that are included when you enable replication.

NOTE: These items are not enabled by default; you will likely want to configure notifications and operators for each of the items in the list. Additionally, you'll probably want to add more alerts, based on the importance of certain publications and how replication is configured. (For more information on configuring jobs, alerts, and operators, see Chapter 4.)

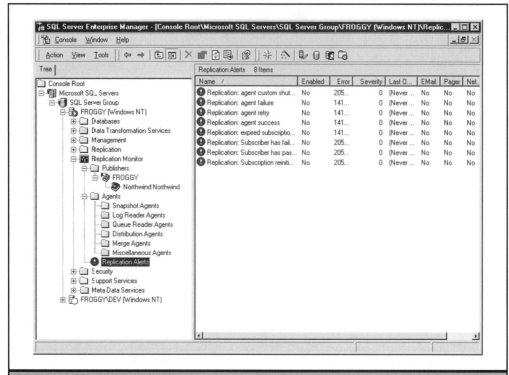

Figure 9-20.   Viewing the default replication alerts

Using Performance Monitor

In addition to the tools available within Enterprise Manager, you can monitor performance using other Windows NT/2000 tools. For more information on using Performance Monitor, see Chapter 3. In this section, we'll look at some specific parameters related to replication performance. When SQL Server is installed, you'll be able to access various Performance Monitor counters related to replication. The easiest way to access a Performance Monitor chart with useful information is to right-click the Replication Monitor item in Enterprise Manager and select Performance Monitor. This automatically opens a chart with useful information pertaining to replication. (See Figure 9-21.) Table 9-2 lists these objects and counters.

You'll probably want to customize the default Performance Monitor options to highlight important information. On busy servers, this is a good way to measure the performance impact of enabling various types of replication and their settings. Also, depending on these settings, you might also want to change the interval used for monitoring replication performance statistics. The default update rate may be too high on servers that expe-

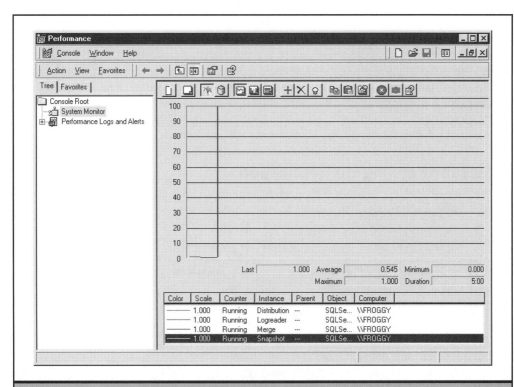

Figure 9-21.   Viewing replication-related statistics in Performance Monitor

Object	Instance	Notes
SQLServer: ReplicationAgents	Distribution	Displays performance statistics related to the SQL Server Distribution Agent process
SQLServer: ReplicationAgents	LogReader	Displays performance statistics related to the SQL Server LogReader Agent process
SQLServer: ReplicationAgents	Merge	Displays performance statistics related to the SQL Server Merge Agent process
SQLServer: ReplicationAgents	Snapshot	Displays performance statistics related to the SQL Server Snapshot Agent process

Table 9-2.   Default Replication Performance Monitor Counters and Objects

rience moderate usage. Finally, it's important to realize that other processes may be competing for resources on the same server. If replication transaction throughput is low, the problem might be related to one of many different parameters. For example, if your network connections are saturated, the servers may not be able to communicate properly. On the other hand, if your server is extremely busy, the problem might be due to database server processes competing for memory and CPU resources in generating and updating replication information. In any case, using Performance Monitor can help to determine the causes and effects of enabling replication on your servers.

Strategies for Backing Up Replication

It is important to understand that replication is generally not a good replacement for adequate backup and recovery processes. Rather, replication should be used in conjunction with a well-designed data protection plan. Depending on the type of replication you choose to implement, there may be some special requirements for your backup and recovery procedures. These will be based on your business requirements and on the type of replication you implement (snapshot, merge, or transactional replication). Also, keep in mind that your backup strategy may change as your replication configuration changes.

In general, you will want to back up the Publisher and Distributor databases for most types of replication. This provides for several levels of protection. First, if either of the databases is lost, you can always restore them from the most recent backup. If the backup is recent enough, this can avoid a complete reconfiguration of the replication topology. Also, you'll be able to perform point-in-time recovery operations (if you're using transaction log backups). This can be useful to recover from accidental data modifications at the Publisher or at any of the updating Subscribers. Finally, in some cases, you may want to back up the Subscriber databases, as well. This can reduce the recovery time should one of the databases be lost and can avoid a slow and costly rebuild of a database snapshot. Fortunately, all of the information regarding backup and recovery processes that we covered earlier (see Chapter 6 and Chapter 7) still applies. That is, replicated databases can be backed up and recovered similarly to other databases. Finally, you'll want to back up the master database, the distribution database, and any published databases whenever you make a change to the information that is being replicated. Of course, database administrators must be aware of the impacts of these processes on the overall replication topology.

SQL SERVER LOG-SHIPPING

In many scenarios, it's important to make sure that your database server is available, even under the worst-imaginable circumstances. In such situations, it might be practical to purchase and maintain a second installation of SQL Server 2000 that is kept up-to-date with production database information. In the event of a failure of the primary database server, you can redirect users to the new machine. This method has several advantages:

▼   If a loss of information does occur, you can easily use a second "live" copy stored on another machine. This second copy can include all user databases *and* the system databases.

▲   Regardless of the type of failure—whether a failed hard disk or the entire server—another replica of the information is available for use immediately.

Backup and recovery can address some of these issues. For example, if I have a completely redundant server and a failure occurs in the production server, I can immediately start restoring information from a recent backup. However, the restore operation will take time that can be quite costly. This is a good situation for the implementation of standby servers.

Log-shipping is supported only on SQL Server 2000, Enterprise Edition. As described in Chapter 4, this version of SQL Server will run on the following operating system platforms:

▼   Windows NT 4.0 Server

■   Windows NT 4.0 Server, Enterprise Edition

■   Windows 2000 Server

■   Windows 2000 Advanced Server

▲   Windows 2000 DataCenter Server

Additionally, Microsoft provides some support for compatibility with SQL Server 7.0 SP2 (or later) and SQL Server 2000 log-shipping. For more information, see the SQL Server Books Online.

Now that we have the basic information out of the way, let's look at the details involved with log-shipping.

Overview of Standby Servers

Standby servers function by keeping data synchronized between multiple SQL Server installations. One SQL Server is used for production purposes. This is the server to which clients normally connect. Another machine—the standby server—contains a replica of all information stored on the production server. Whenever a change is made to a database residing on the production server, it is also made in the databases stored on the standby server. The main goal is to ensure that the databases stay synchronized. If the production server fails, clients can be redirected to use the standby server. Although the process is manual, the impacts of downtime are minimal, and systems administrators will have time to troubleshoot the original problem.

In some ways, replication can be used to keep data consistent between servers. For example, transactional replication will ensure that all the information on remote servers stays consistent with that on the current server. However, this solution requires a lot of server

SQL Server 2000: Backup and Recovery

resources and can significantly decrease performance on busy production machines. A reasonable level of data consistency might be expected from frequent backup and restoration operations, but, again, the disk I/O and CPU resources might make this prohibitive. A standby server works by constantly backing up transaction log information and then automatically restoring that data to a second server. The database on the second server is set to a read-only mode to prevent any modifications to the information. In addition to conserving resources, this process automates the synchronization, thus ensuring that information on the standby machine is synchronized with data on the primary server.

We already mentioned that when a production server fails and a standby server is brought online, clients and applications must manually reconnect to the new production server. When planning for and implementing standby servers, be sure that application developers, managers, and end users are aware of the processes. The afternoon following a critical server failure is not a convenient time to educate users on creating and managing ODBC connections!

Now that we have a good understanding of the goals and functions of standby servers, let's move on to look at how this can be implemented.

Log-Shipping Scenarios

There are several different scenarios in which log-shipping can be implemented. To fully understand exactly how this solution works, let's look at a few common configurations. One configuration (the simplest example) is the case of a production server and a single dedicated standby server. Let's call the first server Production and the second server Standby. The Production server hosts three important databases: Orders, Customers, and Inventory. A database administrator has implemented log-shipping so that these three databases are kept synchronized between the two servers (that is, backups from Production are regularly sent to Standby). In this relatively simple case (illustrated in Figure 9-22), one of the servers will be used only in the case of a failure. Should the Production machine become unavailable for any reason, the database administrator would instruct clients to connect to Standby instead. She could also work with application administrators to reconfigure applications to point to that server.

One of the inherent drawbacks of a simple log-shipping scenario is that the standby server is not being used during normal everyday operations. If things go well and the Production server never fails, this server will *never* be used. Clearly, this can be expensive, and it is not the most efficient use of resources. Therefore, another configuration for log-shipping involves production databases on both servers that are involved in the log-shipping process. Let's rename the machines Production1 and Production2 for this example.

In this case, the catch is that the "live" (or updatable) copy of any given database must be on one server or the other. However, production databases can reside on either machine. As an example, consider the same three databases we discussed earlier (Orders, Customers, and Inventory). In another solution, we might choose to implement a live copy of the Orders and Customers database on Production1 (which is a larger, faster server) and place the live version of the Inventory database on Production2 (a smaller server). Each server would use log-shipping to keep a consistent copy of the data on the other server, as shown in Figure 9-23.

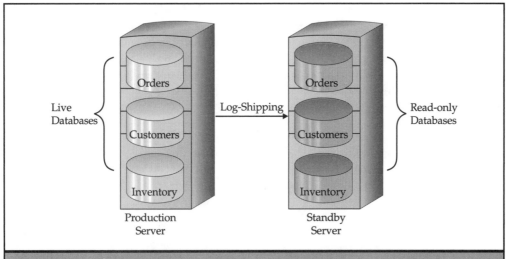

Figure 9-22.   A simple log-shipping scenario

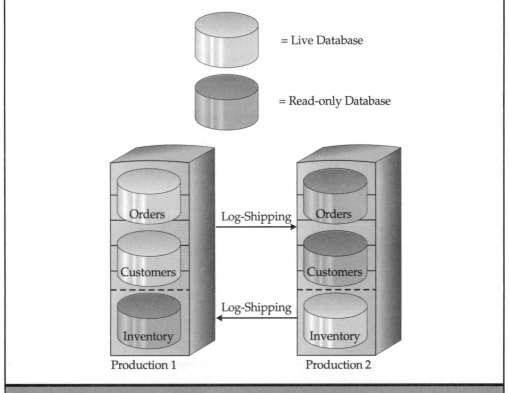

Figure 9-23.   Using two "live" servers in a log-shipping configuration

Other log-shipping scenarios can include a single production server and multiple standby machines. Although this might at first seem like a solution for only the most paranoid database administrators, it has another advantage: since the standby databases are set to read-only, they can be used by users and applications for reporting purposes. Figure 9-24 provides an example of such a scenario. This further maximizes the usage of the resources used in the log-shipping scenario.

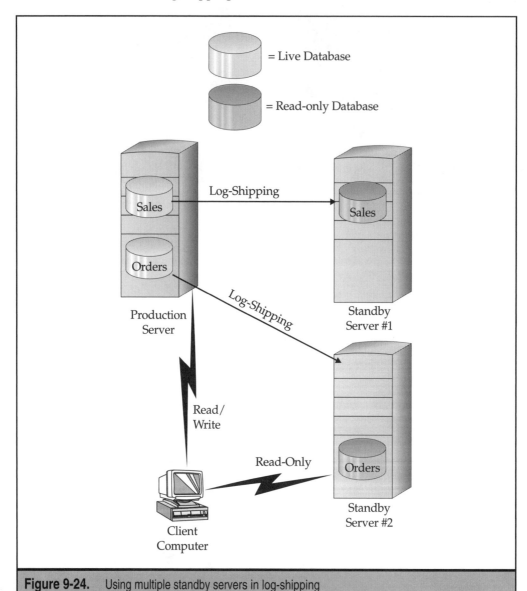

Figure 9-24.   Using multiple standby servers in log-shipping

If you've followed the overview and examples so far, you probably understand the issues related to log-shipping. Now, let's look at the details.

Implementing SQL Server Log-Shipping

Standby servers are set up through the use of normal and transaction log backups. This process is known as *"log-shipping."* In previous versions of SQL Server, log-shipping was an available solution. As it's based on standard backup and recovery methods, there really wasn't much to "supporting" it. However, the catch was that database administrators were responsible for coordinating the many manual operations that were required. This was no small task, even with help from some scripts provided in the SQL Server Resource Kit (part of the Microsoft BackOffice Resource Kit). The result was that log-shipping solutions were available only to knowledgeable DBA's who had the time, skills, and patience to implement the processes. Fortunately, the process has been greatly simplified in SQL Server 2000. In fact, as we'll soon see, it's now integrated as a part of the standard Enterprise Manager operations.

If you're unfamiliar with the standard backup and recovery commands, I recommend you review the information presented in Chapter 6 and Chapter 7 before you continue. In the following sections, we'll look at how backup and recovery commands can be used in the implementation of a standby server.

The Log-Shipping Process

The first task is to set up a standby server. To do this, you'll need to create a second installation of SQL Server 2000. This can be created on a different machine (which you'll probably want to do for data protection reasons). Or, it may be a separate instance of SQL Server 2000 on the same server. The latter method is convenient and useful for testing log-shipping functionality. However, if you choose to use only a single server using multiple instances (as we will in the following step-by-step procedure), you should understand that network connectivity issues may arise when you implement this configuration on two servers. Nevertheless, SQL Server 2000's support for multiple instances is a great feature when learning about implementing log-shipping.

In the following steps, I'll refer to one installation as the *production server* and the other as the *standby server.* Again, note that these two "servers" may be different instances of SQL Server 2000 that are running on the same machine. Let's start by looking at the steps that would be required to set up log-shipping. In the following sections, we'll see how these steps can be implemented through the use of Enterprise Manager or through the use of Transact-SQL commands.

To set up the standby server with an initial copy of the necessary databases on the production server, first back up the databases on the production server. Then, restore these databases to the standby server, but use the STANDBY clause to specify that the database should be placed in standby mode. This will create a baseline copy of the database on the standby server and create an "undo log" file. The undo log file contains a copy of the data pages that were modified by any uncommitted transactions in the transaction log.

After you make a copy of the production database(s) on the standby server, you're ready to start synchronizing information by using transaction logs. This is the technique known as log-shipping. It involves the creation of a database transaction log dump on the production server. This backup includes a list of all the transactions that have been executed on the production server since the last full backup completed. The dump file must then be made accessible to the standby server (either by using an automated copying process or by creating network shares). Finally, the database information is then restored at the standby server, using the STANDBY clause, and ensures data consistency on the standby server. A monitor server is used to coordinate all of these actions. Since the monitor server is critical in ensuring that log-shipping works properly, it is recommended that the monitor server be a machine separate from the source server. That way, in the case of failure of the production server, log-shipping information is not lost.

If you need to bring the standby server online (due to the failure of the production server), the process is as follows:

1. If possible, back up the current transaction log on the production server. If this is not possible (for example, due to a disk failure), then you will not be able to recover data up to the point of failure.

2. If available, restore from all transaction log backups that have not yet been committed. This includes the transaction log backup that you made in step 1 (if it is available). Remember that you must have an unbroken sequence of transaction logs when restoring.

3. Execute the RESTORE command and the WITH RECOVERY option to bring the standby server online. This will ensure that the database is valid and will allow users to connect to it as they did to the old server. Keep in mind that clients may need to reconfigure their settings, because they will now be connecting to a different machine with a different network name and address.

Before you set up log-shipping, you should ensure that your configuration meets several requirements. First, the MSSQLServer and SQL Server Agent services on all of the machines to be used in the log-shipping process must have access to log-shipping plans and to the source and destination servers. Also, you must be a member of the sysadmin server role in order to set up log-shipping. Finally, you will have to create a network share that is accessible to all of the destination servers. This share will contain the transaction logs that will be copied and applied at the standby servers. With all of that out of the way, let's look at how you can implement log-shipping.

Using Enterprise Manager

You can set up a standby server by using the Database Maintenance Plan Wizards and graphical tools included with SQL Server 2000. For details on using these features, see the information in Chapters 6 and 7. Here, we'll look at the details of implementing log-shipping. The key to performing log-shipping properly is to automate the processes and schedule them. To do this, Transact-SQL commands are quite convenient. Let's look at the simplest way to implement log-shipping first.

The following process outlines the steps required to set up log-shipping using Enterprise Manager.

STEP-BY-STEP

Implementing Log-Shipping Using Enterprise Manager

Log-shipping requires the use of at least two separate instances of SQL Server 2000. In order to complete the steps in the following exercise, you must have two instances of SQL Server 2000 running on the same machine. However, if you want to use two instances of SQL Server running on separate machines, the process is very similar. Note that log-shipping is only supported on SQL Server 2000, Enterprise Edition. (Developers can test the same functionality using the Developer Edition of SQL Server 2000.)

1. Before beginning the implementation of log-shipping, you will need to create and share a folder on the production server. This folder will contain the transaction logs that will be copied by standby servers. Therefore, the standby servers must be able to access the shared folder. Make a note of the physical pathname and the share name for this folder, as we'll be using it in the last steps of this exercise. For help in creating a shared folder, see the Windows NT/2000 documentation.

2. Open Enterprise Manager. Expand the instance of SQL Server 2000 that will be used as the primary server. Create a new database on this server and call it Production. Choose all of the default options for the database.

3. Expand the Management folder, right-click on Database Maintenance Plans, and select New Maintenance Plan. This will start the Database Maintenance Plan Wizard.

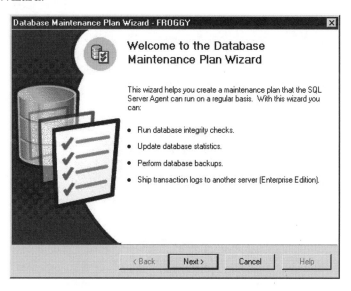

4. To begin the Database Maintenance Plan Wizard, click Next. You will be prompted for information about the server(s) on which the maintenance plan will be created. Place a check mark next to the server that will be used as the primary instance, and then click Next.

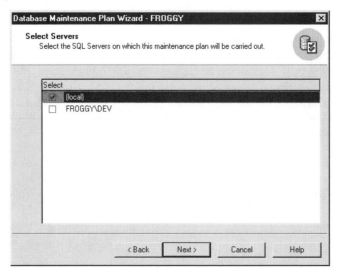

5. **Select Databases** In this dialog box, you will be required to choose the database(s) that will be used in the maintenance plan. Select These Databases, and then place a check mark next to the Production database. Place a check mark next to the Ship the Transaction Logs to Other SQL Servers option. Note that you can only choose a single database if you want to implement log-shipping with the Database Maintenance Plan Wizard.

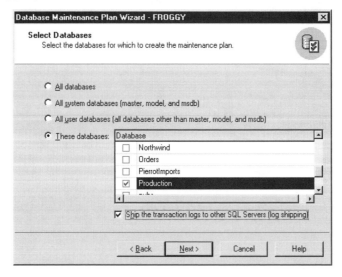

6. **Update Data Optimization Information**   If you're familiar with using the Database Maintenance Plan Wizard, you'll recall that it allows you to define and schedule various operations. In this exercise, we'll implement only the options related to log-shipping. Therefore, you should disable all data optimization options and click Next.

7. **Data Integrity Check**   Leave the default setting (disabled) and click Next.

8. **Specify the Database Backup Plan**   Enable database backups and specify a backup schedule based on your business requirements for this database. Click Next to continue.

9. **Specify Backup Disk Directory**   Specify the storage options for storing database backups. (You do not have to store the backups within the share you created in step 1.) Click Next.

10. **Specify Transaction Log Backup Disk Directory**   Specify the physical backup directory that you created in step 1 of this exercise for the location of the transaction log backups. You may also choose to remove transaction log files after a specified period of time. You should ensure that this time is greater than the interval that you plan to set for log-shipping. Click Next.

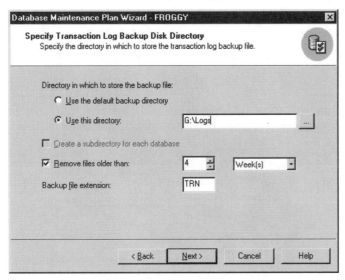

11. **Specify the Transaction Log Share**   In this step, you'll need to specify the path and name of the network share you created in step 1 (for example, \\Primary\Logs). You can click on the ellipsis to browse for the share. Enter the appropriate value, and then click Next.

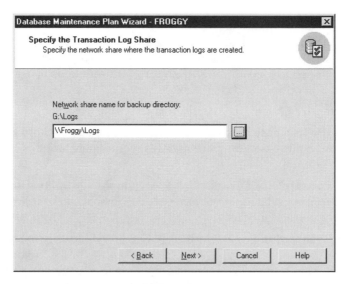

12. **Specify the Log-Shipping Destinations**   To add a destination server for the log-shipping operations, click the Add button.

13. **Add Destination Database**   In this dialog box, you'll be prompted to enter the configuration information for the standby servers you wish to configure.

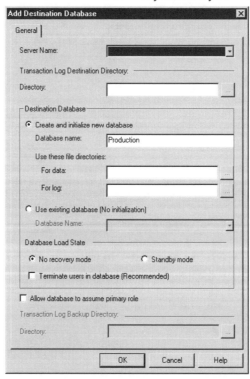

The options are as follows:

- **Server Name** The name of the destination server. This must be a separate instance of SQL Server 2000, Enterprise Edition.

- **Transaction Log Destination Directory** This will be the physical directory on the destination server that will contain copies of the transaction logs shipped from the primary server.

- **Destination Database** You choose either to create and initialize a new destination database on the standby server or to use an existing database. If you choose to use an existing database, you must ensure that you have made a copy of the database to be shipped and that the database was restored with the NORECOVERY or STANDBY options. If you choose to create and initialize a new database, you can specify the physical filenames from the database and log files. (Note that these paths refer to the *destination* server, not the source server.)

- **Database Load State** You can choose to leave the destination server in either no recovery mode or standby mode. If the database is left in no recovery mode, users will not be able to access this database. If the database is left in standby mode, users will be able to access the database, but it will be set to read-only. You can also choose whether you want to terminate all user connections in this database. This is helpful if users might be accessing the destination database during recovery operations, and it is highly recommended that the option be enabled to prevent disruption of log-shipping processes.

- **Allow Database to Assume Primary Role** Enabling this option specifies that this destination server can assume the role as the primary server should the initial production server fail for any reason. If you enable this option, you must specify a transaction log backup directory that can be used for storing logs if this server becomes a primary server. Note that this directory should be accessible to any other machines that may be participating in the same log-shipping configuration. Note that the standby database must have the same name as the production database in order for this option to be enabled.

14. Make the following selections:

    - **Server Name** An instance of SQL Server 2000, Enterprise Edition, other than the primary server.

    - **Transaction Log Destination Directory** Leave the default setting.

    - **Destination Database** Choose to create and initialize a new database and leave the default name ("Production").

    - **Database Load State** Choose Standby Mode and place a check mark in the Terminate Users in Database box.

■ **Allow Database to Assume Primary Role**   Place a check mark in this box. Specify a shared directory on the destination server.

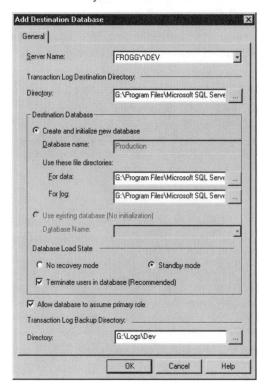

15. Click OK to accept the Destination Server properties, and then click Next to continue.

16. **Initialize the Destination Databases**   In this step, you can choose to perform a full database backup as part of the initialization process. Or, you can choose to use an existing backup file for the database. Note that if you choose the latter option, the wizard will automatically copy this backup file to the log-shipping directory that you specify. Select the option to perform a full database backup now and click Next.

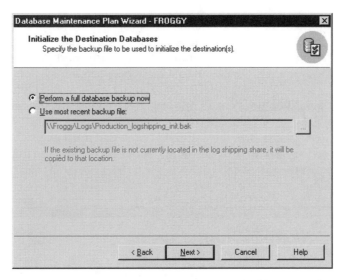

17. **Log-Shipping Schedule** In this step, you'll be able to specify the frequencies for the log-shipping process. This is an important consideration since it determines the maximum amount of acceptable data loss. However, if you set the frequency too high, you may experience a significant impact on performance. The Copy/Load Frequency determines how often log files are shipped from the source server to the destination server(s). The Load Delay sets the minimum age for the transaction log backup before it can be restored. This setting is useful if you want to prevent a transaction log from being restored on the destination server in the case of data corruption on the primary server. Finally, the File Retention Period specifies the amount of time that the transaction log backups will be retained before they are automatically deleted. Choose the defaults for all options, and then click Next.

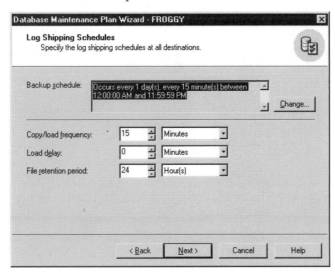

18. **Log-Shipping Thresholds**   Here, you can specify the thresholds that must be exceeded before the log-shipping processes assume that an operation has failed and that an alert should be generated. The Backup Alert Threshold setting defines the amount of time that can elapse between transaction log backups on the source server. In this exercise, for example, we specified that transaction log backups should occur every 15 minutes. If we choose the default setting, then an alert will be generated when three consecutive backups fail. The Out of Sync Alert Threshold specifies the amount of time that must elapse between when a transaction log backup is made on the source server and the log load operation is to be performed on the destination server(s). Choose the default options, and then click Next.

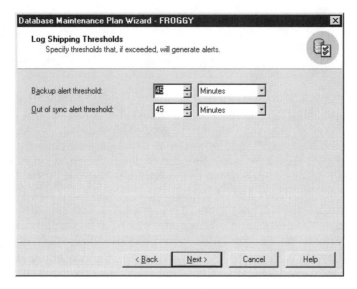

19. **Specify the Log-Shipping Monitor Server Information**   In this step, you can specify the name and login information for the log-shipping monitor server. As mentioned earlier, it is recommended that this server not be either the source or destination server. However, for the sake of this exercise, choose the default option (the source server), and then click Next.

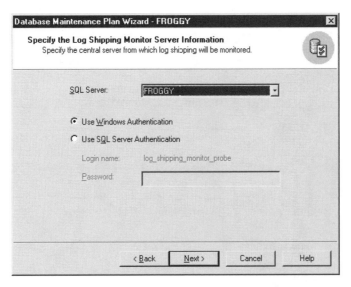

20. **Reports to Generate** Choose the directory and options related to backup and recovery reports and click Next.

21. **Maintenance Plan History** Choose maintenance plan history settings and click Next.

22. **Database Maintenance Plan Wizard Summary** The final step of the Database Maintenance Plan Wizard will provide a brief overview of the options you selected. For the name of the plan, type **Production database log-shipping**. To begin the various jobs that are required to implement log-shipping, click Next and then Finish.

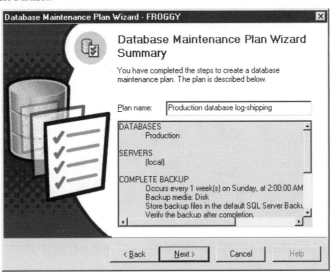

23. If all steps are successful, you will receive a message informing you that the configuration is complete. Click OK to complete the wizard.

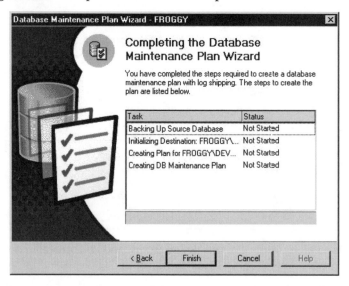

Okay, so I never said that implementing log-shipping was going to be quick! However, with the use of the Database Maintenance Plan Wizard, the process is quite simple. Although many steps are required to set up log-shipping, most of the options are fairly intuitive or clearly defined.

After the initial creation of the log-shipping configuration, you can always modify settings by right-clicking on the name of the Database Maintenance Plan in Enterprise Manager and selecting Properties. Figure 9-25 shows the Log-Shipping tab, which you can use to remove log-shipping or change settings. You can also click the Edit button to make configure changes (see Figure 9-26).

Next, let's see how you can monitor the status of your log-shipping configuration.

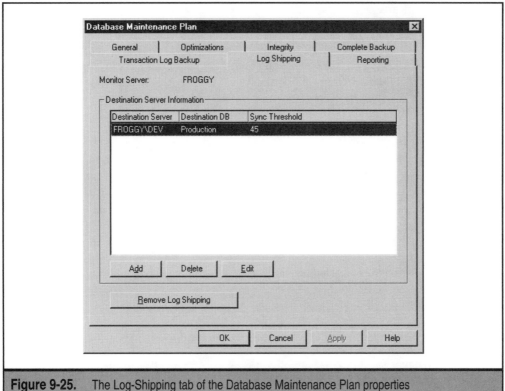

Figure 9-25.   The Log-Shipping tab of the Database Maintenance Plan properties

Monitoring Log-Shipping

After you have installed and configured log-shipping, you will be able to use the Log-Shipping Monitor tool via Enterprise Manager. This tool is located under the Management folder for the server that is configured as the log-shipping monitor. As shown in

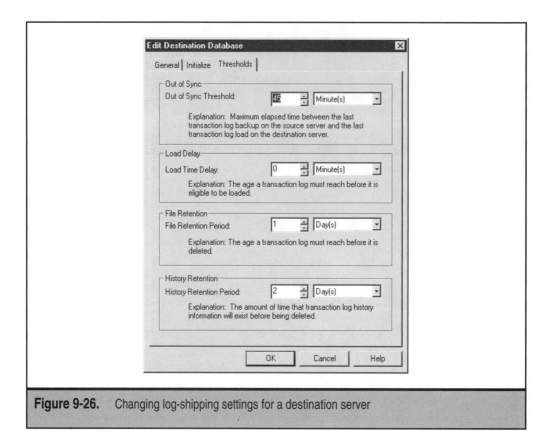

Figure 9-26. Changing log-shipping settings for a destination server

Figure 9-27, the Log-Shipping Monitor provides information about the status of a log-shipping pair of servers. You can also right-click on a server pair in the listing and find additional details about the status. (See Figure 9-28).

Now that we've seen the steps that are required to set up log-shipping in Enterprise Manager, let's look at another way of implementing log-shipping.

Using Transact-SQL Commands

Transact-SQL commands provide a great way to script your backup and recovery processes. They're especially useful for standby servers, because you can place all of these commands in script files or stored procedures and execute them at specific times by using the SQL Agent. However, using Transact-SQL to implement a full log-shipping configu-

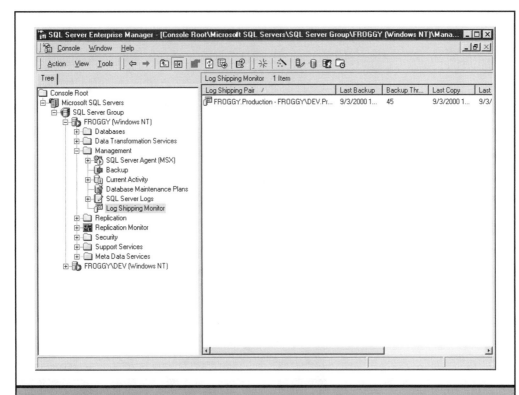

Figure 9-27. Viewing log-shipping status information via the Log Shipping Monitor

ration (including monitoring) can be a challenging task. There are two main reasons that you might want to implement log-shipping via Transact-SQL. The first is that your servers are not running SQL Server 2000, Enterprise Edition. The second is that you require additional control over the log-shipping process.

NOTE: The SQL Server 2000 Resource Kit (part of the Microsoft BackOffice Resource Kit) contains scripts and utilities that can be used for implementing log-shipping. I highly recommend that you refer to these scripts if you plan to implement log-shipping via Transact-SQL.

In this section, we'll look at an overview of the basic process used to implement log-shipping via Transact-SQL. The goal is not to provide a complete script, but rather to

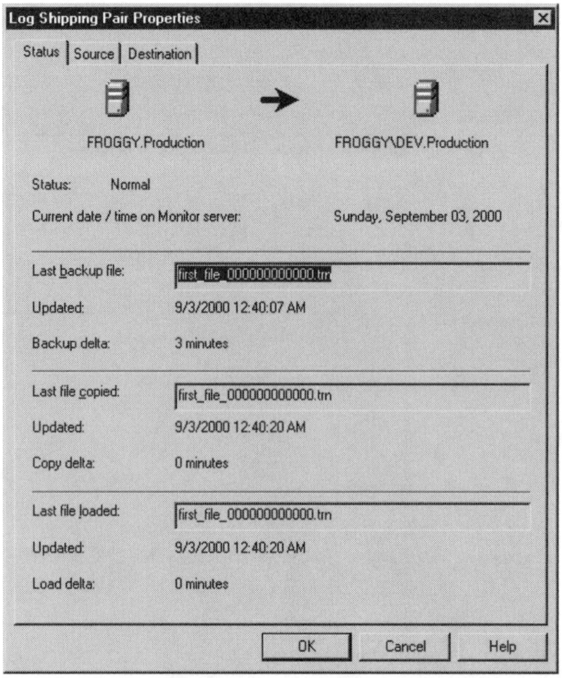

Figure 9-28. Viewing details about the status of a log-shipping item

provide some guidelines for implementing log-shipping. The following Transact-SQL commands will provide a sample of the steps required to implement a standby server for the Customers database.

1. To create a backup of the Customers database, execute the following command on the production server:

```
BACKUP DATABASE Customers TO BackupDevice1
```

2. Then, copy the database dump to the standby server. To restore this database on the standby server, use the following command:

```
RESTORE DATABASE Customers FROM BackupDevice1
    WITH STANDBY = 'C:\Backups\CustomersStandby.ldf'
```

3. Now that you have set up the initial copy of the Customers database on the standby server, you'll need to create a transaction log dump on the production server. Do this with the following command:

```
BACKUP LOG Customers TO BackupDevice2
```

4. Finally, restore this log file to the standby server:

```
RESTORE LOG Customers FROM BackupDevice2
    WITH STANDBY = 'C:\Logs\Log0001.ldf'
```

Backing up and restoring the log file is a process that should be performed at regular intervals. How often this process is performed will be based on your business requirements. On busy servers, you might want to perform the operations every few minutes. On less active servers, it might be acceptable to perform the log-shipping every few hours.

In the event of a database failure, you should try to back up the active transaction log from the production server by using the WITH NO_TRUNCATE option, as in this example:

```
BACKUP LOG Customers
    WITH NO_TRUNCATE
```

If this is not possible, you will still be able to recover, but you will not have the latest information in the database. Next, use the RESTORE LOG command with the STANDBY option to recover any transaction logs that have not yet been restored. After the last transaction log restoration operation, you'll want to use the RECOVERY option, as shown here:

```
RESTORE DATABASE Customers
    WITH RECOVERY
```

This will place the database back online and ready for use.

Log-Shipping Stored Procedures

Table 9-3 provides a list of stored procedures that can be used to monitor and modify the behavior of SQL Server 2000 log-shipping. These procedures are helpful when you need to modify the settings made through the Database Maintenance Plan Wizard or if you want to obtain log-shipping information through Transact-SQL scripts. For more information about using these stored procedures, see the SQL Server Books Online.

Overall, the implementation of standby servers can greatly reduce the amount of time required to reinstate a usable server. Although application and client reconfiguration might be required, recovering the necessary data will take only a fraction of the time. For many organizations, this level of protection is all that is required. For others, however,

Stored Procedure	Function
sp_add_log_shipping_database	Specifies that a database is being used in log-shipping
sp_delete_log_shipping_database	Removes log-shipping from a database
sp_add_log_shipping_plan	Adds a log-shipping database maintenance plan
sp_delete_log_shipping_plan	Deletes a log-shipping database maintenance plan
sp_add_log_shipping_plan_database	Adds a database to a log-shipping database maintenance plan
sp_delete_log_shipping_plan_database	Removes a database from a log-shipping database maintenance plan
sp_add_log_shipping_primary	Adds a primary log-shipping server
sp_delete_log_shipping_primary	Removes a primary log-shipping server
sp_add_log_shipping_secondary	Adds a secondary log-shipping server
sp_delete_log_shipping_secondary	Removes a secondary log-shipping server
sp_get_log_shipping_monitor_info	Returns status information about any two servers used in a log-shipping relationship
sp_can_tlog_be_applied	Verifies that a database is in a state such that a transaction log can be applied to it. This is useful for troubleshooting problems related to log-shipping.
sp_change_monitor_role	Modifies the roles of servers used in log-shipping
sp_remove_log_shipping_monitor	Disables log-shipping monitor functionality on a specific server
sp_change_primary_role	Removes a primary server from a log-shipping role

Table 9-3.   Stored Procedures Related to Log-Shipping

Stored Procedure	Function
sp_resolve_logins	Tests logins on a new primary server based on login information from the old primary server (useful for testing configuration after a failure)
sp_change_secondary_role	Converts a secondary server to the primary server for a database (useful after a failure of the primary server)
sp_update_log_shipping_monitor_info	Updates log-shipping monitoring information for a primary/secondary server pair
sp_create_log_shipping_monitor_account	Creates a SQL Server account for use by a log-shipping monitor process
sp_update_log_shipping_plan	Updates and modifies information related to a log-shipping database maintenance plan
sp_define_log_shipping_monitor	Specifies a server to operate as a log-shipping monitor
sp_update_log_shipping_plan_database	Updates information about a database that is part of a log-shipping plan

Table 9-3.   Stored Procedures Related to Log-Shipping *(continued)*

server failures must be imperceptible to users. We'll cover an appropriate solution for this sort of situation in the following section.

SQL SERVER CLUSTERING

Increasingly, businesses rely on their information systems to be available to provide products, services, and decision support. The costs of downtime can be tremendous, especially for the new breed of Internet-based companies. Think about it: how many times would an e-business have to lose your order or have an unavailable site before you chose never to shop with them again? If you're like me (and millions of other potential web shoppers), the answer is "not many."

In these situations, the hardware costs of having multiple servers and preventing downtime are small in comparison to the importance of server uptime. So far, we've looked at several ways of protecting your information, including backup and recovery, replication, and the use of standby servers. Although these are good ways to ensure that your information is not lost, they fail to provide one feature—the transparent fail-over of an unavailable server to another available one. In this situation, clients should not even notice that a major catastrophe has occurred in the server room or that critical resources were taken down for maintenance.

What might seem like high levels of uptime on paper can translate into frustrating productivity or loss of business for users. Table 9-4 lists various uptime percentages and the actual amount of downtime that will be experienced if each level is met. Just five percent downtime can amount to more than a half month of server unavailability in a year. On the other end of the spectrum, notice that 99.999 percent uptime does not even provide enough time for a full server reboot *once per year!* This is where the idea of clustering comes in.

Simply put, *clustering* allows two or more physical servers to act as one logical server. Clients may see a whole array of servers as a single machine, and applications interact with it as such. The benefits are great—when one server is unavailable, another can automatically take its place. This increases uptime and provides for high availability. Additionally, the servers can work together to balance the load between multiple clients. For example, if three managers decide to run large reports at the same time, each might be redirected to a separate machine for processing. In many cases, downtime might be required for server upgrades and/or maintenance (such as applying Windows NT/2000 Service Packs or application updates). Systems and network administrators should be able to take down a single server within a cluster with minimal impact to client machines. Again, all of these processes should occur behind the scenes and remain transparent to the user. Figure 9-29 provides a logical depiction of how a cluster might operate.

Percentage of Uptime	Downtime per Year (in seconds)	Downtime per Year
95%	1,576,800	18.25 days
97%	946,080	10.95 days
99%	315,360	3.65 days (87.6 hours)
99.9%	31,536	8.76 hours
99.99%	3,153.6	52.56 minutes
99.999%	315.36	5.26 minutes
99.9999%	31.536	31.54 seconds

Table 9-4. Approximate Real-Time Values of Uptime Levels

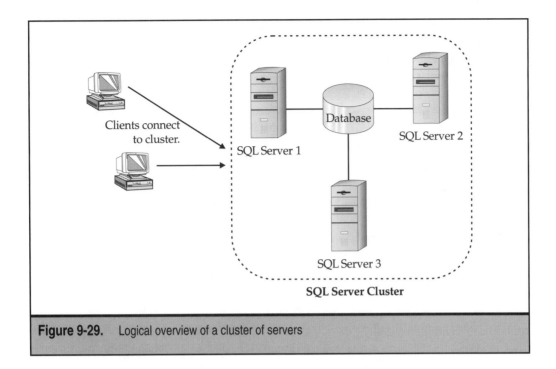

Figure 9-29.   Logical overview of a cluster of servers

The ideas related to clustering probably seem quite logical, and you might think they'd be easy to implement. In the real world, however, clustering on the Windows NT/2000 platform is much more complicated. There are limits to what can currently be done with hardware, software, and networking devices. In this part of the chapter, we'll focus on the concepts, tools, and technologies available for evaluating and implementing clustering architecture. The intricate details of implementing a SQL Server clustering solution are beyond the scope of this book. This is mainly because implementation details will vary greatly based on the specific hardware solution. In general, you will get these details from third-party hardware vendors that provide clustering solutions.

That doesn't mean we won't dive into a lot of technical detail, however. First, we'll look at many of the issues related to planning for and evaluating clustering schemes for your business environment. Based on this information, we'll move on to an overview of how clustering can be implemented on the Windows platform. Let's start by looking at some issues related to planning for clustering.

Planning for Clustering

As with the decision to implement any type of technology, before you choose to implement clustering, you need to properly define the business need. I often hear business leaders (and even some technical ones) equate "important" servers with clustering solutions. However, clustering is simply not always the best solution. There are many other ways to achieve high availability, and implementing a clustering solution can be a huge management burden (especially if your IT staff is untrained or overburdened). We'll see in the next sections that implementing clustering can be time consuming and costly. Therefore, it's very important to fully define the business reasons for choosing a clustering-based solution.

Before you undertake the tasks related to implementing a cluster, you should ensure that clustering is necessary in your business environment. Here is a checklist of considerations that should help you make your decision:

▼ **Determine reasonable uptime requirements.** Ask about network downtime in many companies, and the quick reaction will be "No downtime is acceptable." Although it might seem to make sense that servers always be available, there are several trade-offs involved in a 24×7 network environment:

- The hardware and software required to make this work can be very expensive.

- Much costly planning must go into the systems that provide for complete hardware redundancy.

- Applying upgrades and patches can be an overall benefit, but may require planned downtime.

Based on these concerns, business leaders may find that having certain services—such as a company intranet—unavailable for small periods of time throughout the year is acceptable.

■ **Evaluate costs.** Clustering hardware and software can be quite costly to plan for, purchase, implement, and manage. To determine whether this technology is suitable in your environment, you should first measure the costs related to employing and maintaining a clustering solution. If the costs fit within a reasonable budget, you next need to evaluate the actual costs of downtime in your organization. If, for example, the unavailability of a server for several hours per year is less expensive than the costs associated with protecting the server, then clustering may not make good business sense. Be sure to take into account the Total Cost of Ownership (TCO), including the cost of training IT staff, purchasing software, keeping up with technology, and other factors. You'll likely find that the implementation cost is only a fraction of the overall burden of clustering solutions.

■ **Define "*availability.*"** In your environment, is availability based on whether a server is up and running properly, or is the real test whether or not users can access it? For example, a server might be operating properly, but a network problem may prevent users from accessing it. Depending on how you define the term availability, in this case you may or may not be experiencing downtime. In many cases, accessibility of resources is the true test. The server is useless if no one can access it. However, this might be different for servers that participate on the Internet, for example. Internet outages or traffic congestion might prevent some users from interacting with a web server, while others can get to it just fine. In this case, there is a problem that is beyond the control of the organization itself. Therefore, when you plan for a clustering solution, you should be sure to eliminate other single points of failure (such as electricity, network connections, and so on).

- **Analyze the reasons for downtime.** When downtime occurs on computing resources, it's important to research and note the root cause of the problem. In some types of server crashes, it might be difficult or even impossible to determine the exact cause of the problem. In other types of crashes, the issue might be much more evident—for example, a loss of power or a failed hard disk. We're well past the days when server crashes are seen as an inevitable solution. Often a hardware- or driver-related problem is the culprit. In any case, it's important to analyze the information on failures to determine where improvements might be made. For example, if a primary cause of downtime is from hardware failures, redundancy might be a good solution.

- **Plan for downtime.** Although the focus of this section is ensuring that critical business functions remain available, it is important to create plans for handling situations in which problems do occur. It's far too easy for IT departments to become complacent—"The servers are clustered, so I'm not worried about a single failure." In many cases, alternatives to the use of computing resources might be required. For example, if a sales- and order-tracking database is unavailable, individuals might be required to manually record transaction information using pen and paper. If this might be required, managers and employees must be aware of the types of information they'll need to record and the necessary procedures *before* problems occur.

- **Plan for planning.** Implementing a clustering solution can be quite a challenge for most IT professionals. Regardless of past experience, even "experts" must consider both the nature of the applications that must remain available and all the potential failures that can occur. The planning process is just as important as actually installing your new software and hardware, because it can determine the overall success of your clustered environment. Many companies will want to hire or consult with specialists in data availability solutions to ensure that their plans are viable. As we'll see later in this chapter, many resources for information are also available from third-party hardware manufacturers.

- **Standardize your hardware and software.** Although supporting standard hardware and software platforms is a good idea for all data protection plans, you should especially plan to use supported configurations for clustering. Figure 9-30 shows a dialog box illustrating Microsoft's support policies in the Windows 2000 Cluster Service Configuration Wizard. Clustered servers must have special hardware to communicate with each other in case a network failure occurs and to keep information synchronized. These methods are often

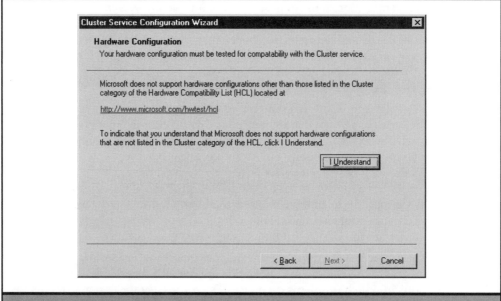

Figure 9-30. Viewing information about supported cluster hardware platforms in the Windows 2000 Cluster Service Configuration Wizard

proprietary and require technical knowledge of the hardware implementation. Consistency in server hardware and software can also reduce operating costs by reducing the specific knowledge required for troubleshooting. Additionally, features such as monitoring and prefailure notifications can reduce the possibility of downtime due to failures.

■ **Test your solution.** Regularly testing backups is a recommended part of any backup strategy. That applies especially to clustering, for two reasons: First, the fact that clustering technologies are being used indicates the importance of the primary servers involved. Because increased uptime is a major goal, taking these servers down for testing usually isn't an option. Second, clustering technologies should be thoroughly verified on a test network so that systems administrators are aware of any issues that might arise when a fail-over occurs. Using the results of these tests, IT staff should be able to understand and verify the complex technical issues related to clustering.

▲ **Do not slack on your backups.** Although clustering mechanisms are designed to protect data and server uptime, they are not a replacement for standard backup practices. Clustering will not protect against the accidental deletion of data from a database or the corruption of system files due to misconfiguration. Also, although it is unlikely, both servers in a cluster could fail due to, for example, a natural disaster or a strong power surge. Indeed, the use of a cluster can help in backing up data since you may choose to perform backup operations on only one server. This will allow the other server to continue to operate at maximum performance, thereby reducing the impact on clients.

Microsoft itself performed many of the preceding planning steps for its own Information Technology Group (ITG). ITG evaluated its current servers and causes for downtime and found that a lot of the downtime was related to a small subset of servers. These machines were often rebooted because of problems in their configurations. Based on these findings, Microsoft decided to standardize on a specific server hardware platform and leave off some potentially troubling applications, such as virus scanners. ITG also developed standards and conventions for server naming and configuration. For more information on the problems and solutions found by ITG, see "High Availability SQL Server Platform Engineering" (**http://www.microsoft.com/technet/showcase/ itops/availsql.asp**).

By now, you should be familiar with some of the issues related to planning for clustering. Of course, you'll be able to determine specifically how this technology will help you meet business goals only after you evaluate your own environment. With these ideas in mind, let's move on to examine the technical details of how clustering technologies work.

Clustering Technology

Clustering offers high availability (greater uptime) through fault tolerance and load balancing (spreading the resource access load across multiple machines). Although the goal—to make multiple servers act as one logical server—is quite simple, the actual process can be quite complex. There are also numerous ways to cluster. With that in mind, let's look at some typical clustering technologies and how they work within a backup and recovery scenario.

Network Load Balancing

One type of clustering setup involves balancing the load between multiple machines at the network level. For example, many large companies employ dynamic routing devices or software to share the load between several web servers. This router automatically ensures that servers are available, before sending clients to them, and also makes decisions based on the workload of each machine. In this case, the servers themselves are unaware that any type of clustering is occurring. Similarly, clients see the cluster as a single machine. This arrangement provides for increased uptime and performance without the reconfiguration of applications. Figure 9-31 shows a sample load-balancing configuration.

Active/Passive vs. Active/Active Nodes

Nodes in a cluster can be arranged in either of two main ways. In the *active/passive* configuration, cluster nodes are configured in such a way that one server is active and the other is passive. If the active server fails, the passive server automatically reconfigures itself to

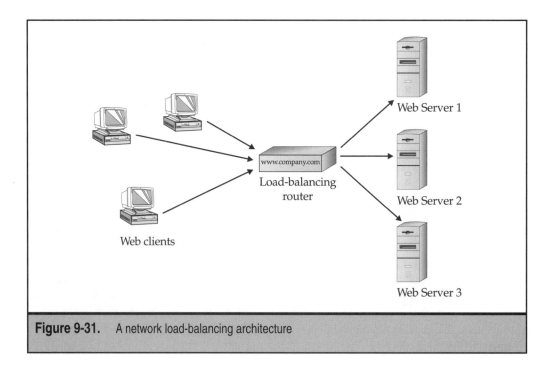

Figure 9-31. A network load-balancing architecture

assume the workload of the failed server. Figure 9-32 shows you what typically occurs in an active/passive fail-over cluster. Originally, Server 1 is active and is providing services to the clients. Meanwhile, Server 2 contains a copy of all data in a shared disk configuration. When Server 1 fails, Server 2 becomes active and immediately assumes the function of Server 1. The clients continue to operate normally.

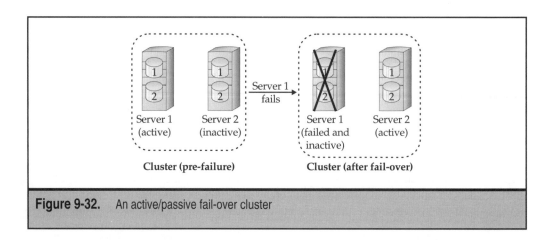

Figure 9-32. An active/passive fail-over cluster

A major difference between using clustering and using standby servers is that this changeover occurs without affecting any end users or requiring client reconfiguration. The fail-over is transparent to users and applications. The problem with the active/ passive fail-over scenario is that one of the machines in the cluster is effectively useless until a failure occurs. This is the problem with redundancy—potential resources cannot be used to increase performance.

But, what if clients could access both machines at the same time? This would prevent wasting server resources and would still allow clients to connect if one of the machines fails (although performance would be decreased by approximately 50 percent). This type of configuration is known as an *active/active* cluster, because both machines are available for general use, but they act as one. Clients may not even be aware that two servers are participating in the cluster, and they may refer to each server by using the same logical name. Figure 9-33 provides an example of an active/active clustering configuration. Notice that the two active nodes are not providing the same resources to clients: Server 1 provides access to Databases 1, 2, and 3, while Server 2 offers access to Databases 4 and 5.

Regardless of whether the configuration of servers is active/passive or active/active, the network will probably need to fail-back when the primary server comes back online. Alternatively, you could have the backup server perform all the necessary functions. However, some organizations choose to reduce costs by lowering the hardware options on the fail-over server.

Now that we have a good idea of how server nodes can participate in a cluster, let's look at how multiple machines can access the same storage devices.

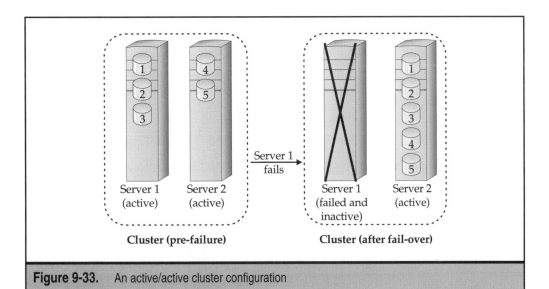

Figure 9-33.   An active/active cluster configuration

Sharing Storage Resources

In the previous section, we considered how active and passive servers can be combined in a cluster. An important requirement in this type of clustering is that information stored on hard disks be available to the machines sharing that information. Generally, the disk array itself is protected by using redundant hardware. But, if the entire server fails, another machine can access the same devices but take over the processing of other types of client interaction. For this to occur, there must be some way for a node in a cluster to assume control over disks formerly controlled by the failed server. Three main ways exist to configure disk sharing at the server level:

▼ **Shared-nothing configuration** Each disk device is accessible to only one server at a time. If a failure of one node in the cluster occurs, the other one takes over these resources. Physically, the hard disks are usually attached via controllers that allow more than one server to access a disk array. Additionally, some disks might be "owned" by each node. Figure 9-34 illustrates an instance of a shared-nothing configuration. For example, consider a scenario that includes six physical disk devices. Server 1 might be responsible for "owning" disks 1, 2, and 4, while Server 2 owns disks 3, 5, and 6. (Recall that clients should see Server 1 and Server 2 as one logical machine.) When resources are requested from the cluster, the request is forwarded to the appropriate node. If Server 1 fails, Server 2 will assume control of all six disks and take on the extra workload necessary for ensuring that users maintain access to all needed resources.

■ **Shared-everything configuration** Each node in the cluster contains a copy of the same data. Physically, this might be implemented either as multiple servers

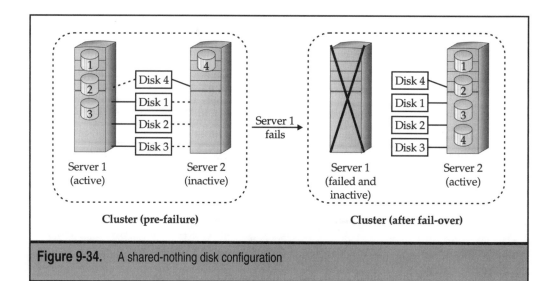

Figure 9-34. A shared-nothing disk configuration

that have access to the same disk devices using a shared controller, or through software methods that can keep data synchronized. We already looked at two ways to do this—standby servers (using log-shipping) and replication.

▲ **Mirrored disk configuration**   Each server controls its own disk devices, as shown in Figure 9-35. Whenever data is written to one disk, it is automatically written to the disks controlled by other nodes in the cluster. The main advantage is that special hardware that allows the same disk devices to be shared between physical servers is not required. However, a limitation of this method is that data will always be unsynchronized (although for a very brief period of time).

As we'll see later, the Enterprise Edition of SQL Server supports the use of shared-nothing disk configurations. The best method to use will be based on your business requirements and a thorough evaluation of the merits of solutions from third-party hardware vendors.

Application Support

To take full advantage of clustering, applications should be "cluster aware." Although the basic clustering processes might be available at the OS level, many other issues must be considered. For example, "active" web sites might store client information in session and application variables. This information must be kept synchronized between multiple servers if a transparent fail-over is expected to occur. If special provisions for this are not made, clients will temporarily lose their connection information. For SQL Server applications, this means that all clients will need to reestablish their database connections before they can continue. A cluster-aware client application might automatically include error code that transparently reattempts to connect to a server before giving the end user an error message. As we'll see later in this section, features in SQL Server 2000, Enterprise Edition, have been designed to address such issues when running on Windows NT 4.0 Server, Enterprise Edition, Windows 2000 Advanced Server, and Windows 2000 DataCenter Server.

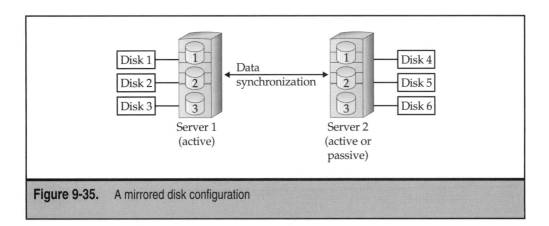

Figure 9-35.   A mirrored disk configuration

Microsoft Clustering Solutions

Clustering technology is relatively new to the PC marketplace. Nevertheless, Microsoft has included several features in high-end versions of its products that can increase both uptime and performance. Specific products and features include the following:

▼ **Windows NT 4 Server, Enterprise Edition**   Offers support for Microsoft Cluster Services, Windows Load Balancing Services (WLBS), Very Large Memory (VLM), and increased symmetric multiprocessing (SMP). WLBS allows clustering to be configured at the network level and is used to distribute resource requests among machines in a cluster. These features allow Windows NT to scale to extremely high-end-server hardware platforms.

■ **Windows 2000 Advanced Server**   Meets the needs of high-end servers by supporting up to eight-way SMP, VLM, and clustering services. These features map closely to the support included in Windows NT 4, Enterprise Edition. This platform supports two-node fail-over configurations and Network Load Balancing (NLB, the replacement for WLBS).

■ **Windows 2000 DataCenter Server**   Designed to support advanced hardware, this product is aimed at high-performance and mission-critical enterprise-level applications. Microsoft has reported that the OS will support up to 32 CPUs and large amounts of physical RAM. Because of its hardware dependencies, DataCenter Server will be available directly from OEM server manufacturers, who will ensure its compatibility with their products. DataCenter Server also includes all the clustering options available in the Advanced Server Edition. Initially, the DataCenter edition supports up to four-node fail-over configurations, but increased server support is planned for future updates.

■ **Microsoft Cluster Services (MSCS)**   Designed to support automatic fail-over at the OS level, this is available as part of Windows NT Server, Enterprise Edition, Windows 2000 Advanced Server, and Windows 2000 DataCenter Server. Additionally, MSCS allows for load-balancing between applications that are designed to work with it.

■ **Windows Load Balancing Services (WLBS)**   Available as a service on machines running Windows NT Server, Enterprise Edition, WLBS provides for dynamic load balancing at the network level. WLBS directs clients to different servers based not only on the servers' current workloads, but also on performance values, which can be tweaked by systems administrators. Each server that participates in a cluster must run WLBS, but the memory requirements are usually very low. Since it is implemented as a software program, however, it does consume other server resources, such as CPU time. Overall, WLBS can provide a convenient solution for balancing the data load among multiple clustered or nonclustered servers (such as machines running Internet Information Server).

▲   **SQL Server 2000, Enterprise Edition**   Designed to work with Windows NT 4
Server (Standard or Enterprise Edition) and the Windows 2000 Server, Advanced
Server, and DataCenter Server Editions, this can take advantage of multiple
CPUs supported by the underlying OS, as well as VLM for additional physical
memory (up to 64GB in Windows 2000 DataCenter Server). It also supports the
use of both active/active and active/passive fail-over configurations for the
purpose of high availability, and it allows the configuration of only two nodes in
a cluster. Note that clustering for performance increases (that is, load balancing)
is not yet supported in the SQL Server product line. Depending on the
configuration, one or both servers can be active. However, if both servers
are designated as active, they must be running separate databases. When a
failure of one node occurs, it automatically and transparently assumes the
machine name and network address of the failed server.

By properly combining these technologies, you'll be able to design a clustering solution that satisfies your organization's high uptime requirements.

Implementing SQL Server Fail-Over Support

Certain clustering features will be restricted to "cluster-aware" applications. All of these
products have different limitations, and setting up a reliable cluster is not something you
should expect to implement and properly test within a few days.

According to Microsoft documentation, a specific installation process for setting up
SQL Server fail-over support must be used. The OS and features must be installed in the
following order:

1. **Implement the hardware solution.**   Purchase and configure a Microsoft-
    supported clustering platform. Details on the implementation will be available
    from the third-party hardware vendor. (I'll provide some references later.)

2. **Install the base operating system with clustering services.**   Options for the
    base operating system include the following:

    ■   Windows NT 4 Server, Standard Edition

    ■   Windows NT 4 Server, Enterprise Edition

    ■   Windows 2000 Server (Standard)

    ■   Windows 2000 Advanced Server

    ■   Windows 2000 DataCenter Server

3. **Configure OS-level clustering services.**   Install and configure shared disk
    resources within the base operating system. For example, on Windows 2000
    machines, the system can be configured by adding the Cluster Service (if it
    was not installed during the operating system installation). This is shown in
    Figure 9-36. The next step is to choose to configure the Cluster Service (shown
    in Figure 9-37) and then to follow the steps in the Cluster Service Configuration
    Wizard. (See Figure 9-38.)

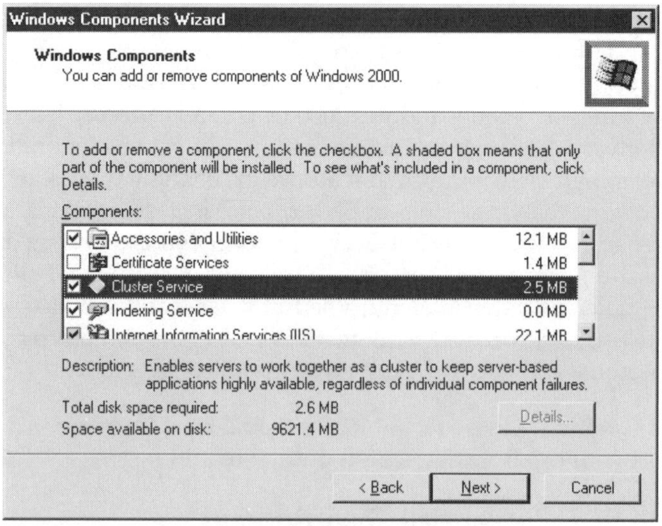

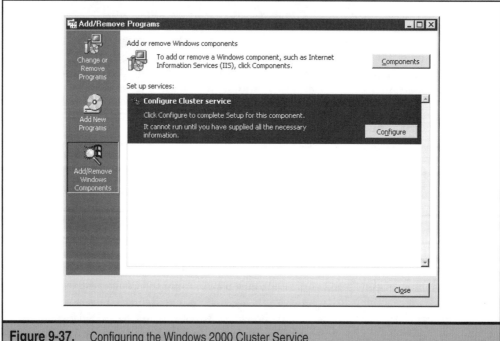

Figure 9-36. Installing the Windows 2000 Cluster Service

Figure 9-37. Configuring the Windows 2000 Cluster Service

Figure 9-38. Using the Windows 2000 Cluster Service Configuration Wizard

4. **Install and configure Microsoft SQL Server 2000, Enterprise Edition.**   During the setup process, you will have the option to install SQL Server as the first node in a new cluster or as an additional node in an existing cluster.

5. **Use the SQL Server Fail-Over Wizard.**   This wizard will walk you through the steps required to define which disks and applications are shared and will show you how nodes within the cluster should be configured. Before doing this, you'll have to perform the preceding installation procedures for at least two servers (one for each node of the cluster). Note that if your installation of SQL Server is currently using replication, you need to drop all replication settings and reconfigure them, because SQL Server uses different methods for naming other servers involved in replication.

The preceding list of steps provides only a brief overview of the actual operations required. To actually configure SQL Server, Enterprise Edition, for fail-over support, you can use the SQL Server Fail-Over Setup Wizard. The basic steps involve specifying which disks will be shared between the nodes and setting fail-over parameters. It is beyond the scope of this discussion to go into the exact steps required because details will vary based on the specific hardware platform you choose. Another reason is that the exact clustering configuration you employ should be based on your specific business needs (as discussed earlier). Additionally, specific hardware and software vendors may require custom settings in order to properly configure MSCS and fail-over operations. Be sure to check with these resources first. After you set up your clustering solution, you can use the Cluster Administrator tool for further configuration and management of cluster nodes. For more information, see the version of Books Online that accompanies the Enterprise Edition of SQL Server 2000 (as shown in Figure 9-39).

Supported Hardware Platforms

SQL Server fail-over support will work with specially designed hardware platforms. It is highly recommended that you choose a hardware solution that is listed as supported in the Microsoft Windows Hardware Compatibility List (HCL). You can get a complete list of available solutions by visiting the Windows Hardware Compatibility List web site (**http://www.microsoft.com/hcl/default.asp**). From this site, shown in Figure 9-40, you'll

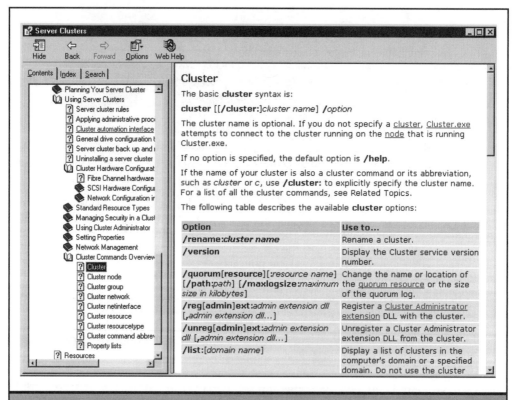

Figure 9-39.   Viewing clustering implementation information in SQL Server Books Online

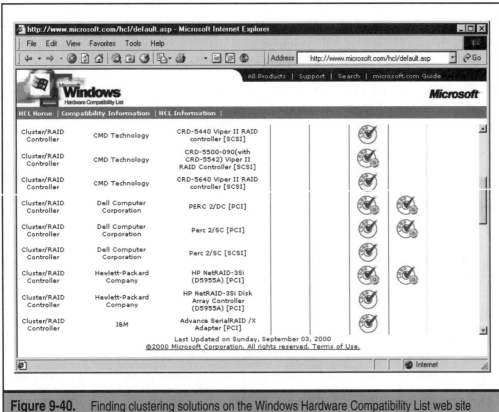

Figure 9-40. Finding clustering solutions on the Windows Hardware Compatibility List web site

be able to see an exhaustive list of vendors that offer clustering-related solutions. At the time of this writing, the relevant categories include

▼ Cluster
■ Cluster/FibreChannel Adapter
■ Cluster/Multi-Cluster Device
■ Cluster/RAID
■ Cluster/RAID Controller
■ Cluster/RAID System
▲ Cluster/SCSI Adapter

In general, you will probably want to purchase two identical servers, for ease of maintenance and configuration. SQL Server fail-over support can be configured with different servers (as long as they are both compatible). However, you cannot mix nodes running SQL Server on Intel platforms and Alpha platforms. Several hardware platforms are supported by Microsoft.

Clustering technology is currently an area of active development, and new products are being announced frequently. More information on hardware, software, and service providers that support solutions based on advanced Windows NT/2000 and SQL Server 2000 is available at "SQL Server Enterprise Edition Hardware and Service Partners" (**www.microsoft.com/SQL/productinfo/vendors.htm**) and "Cluster Hardware FAQ" (**www.microsoft.com/ntserver/ntserverenterprise/exec/moreinfo/ClusterHardware.asp**).

The Future of Clustering Technology

Despite the potential uptime and performance benefits of clustering, the technology has been slow to evolve in Windows-based products. The main reason is the underlying complexity of making applications work on multiple system architectures (many of which carry the burden of support "legacy" technology and standards that are well over a decade old). As you may have noticed, there's still more to be desired in the realm of clustering in Windows NT/2000 environments, including the following:

▼ Support for more nodes in fail-over configurations

■ Support for load balancing at the application level (to decrease the costs associated with implementing clusters and improve overall performance)

■ Clustering support on mid- and low-range servers (allowing many small servers to take the place of a few large ones)

■ Simplified implementation, management, and recovery from failures

▲ Improved reliability

This is a tall order, but with the pace of innovation in data protection technologies, you can expect to see more demand for clustering. With that will come better support, more options, and decreased costs. All of these features will make clustering a more accessible solution for many businesses.

There are also several resources for more information related to high availability and clustering from Microsoft and other third-party hardware and software vendors. Table 9-5 provides several good starting points for web research on clustering and related technologies.

Resource	Web Site	Content
SQL Server web site	www.Microsoft.com/sql	Information on hardware, software, and support for SQL Server
Microsoft TechNet Reliability Resources	www.microsoft.com/technet/reliable	Resources providing information on high-availability solutions for Windows NT/2000
Microsoft Windows web site	www.Microsoft.com/sql	A central site for information about all versions of the Windows-based operating systems
Microsoft Seminar Online	www.Microsoft.com/seminar	Audio and video presentations related to Microsoft products

Table 9-5. Resources for More Information on High-Availability Technology

SUMMARY

In this chapter, we looked at some advanced features and methods for protecting information and increasing server uptime. We began by covering SQL Server 2000's replication architecture. If you plan to use replication in your environment, it's important to plan for it and to understand the various methods by which it can be implemented. Next, we looked at the actual steps required to set up replication. Although the ideas behind these steps are fairly complex, the numerous wizards and features in SQL Server 2000 Enterprise Manager make setting up replication a simple task. By properly creating publications and configuring Publishers, Distributors, and Subscribers, replication is an excellent way to distribute information throughout your organization while simultaneously ensuring that information is kept synchronized.

Next, we looked at the use of standby servers. Microsoft has dramatically simplified the creation and management of standby servers in SQL Server 2000. Standby servers provide a way to ensure that you have a "warm" backup of your server in case anything goes wrong. Of course, there are limitations to the scenarios that you're protected against. If uptime is a critical requirement in your business, then SQL Server's fail-over support is likely to be worth the cost and effort. With this safeguard in place, another server can automatically take over the functions of a failed or otherwise unavailable machine without severely impacting clients.

Although these solutions are not appropriate for every business, they do represent excellent options where uptime and performance requirements outweigh the costs. Be sure to evaluate the use of advanced data protection techniques when employing a data protection plan in your own environment.

CHAPTER 10

Case Studies: Solving Business Challenges

W e've covered a lot of technical information in previous chapters. Topics have ranged from creating a plan for protecting your information to the technical details of choosing and implementing a backup and recovery solution. Along the way, we've focused on critical business and technical details. So, what's left? The real challenge is to apply all of this information to fit the needs and requirements of your own organization. For technical staff and management, working within financial and other resource constraints to find the best data protection solution can be quite a challenge. Unfortunately, no reasonably sized book would be able to cover even a fraction of the types of real-world challenges most of us face in our own companies. Still, IT professionals often hear about the importance of understanding business requirements and getting the "big picture."

Many of us prefer to learn by example. It's one thing to talk about the high-level issues associated with evaluating business requirements and developing a data protection plan. It's quite another thing to apply this to the real world. Actually doing this in an organization can be much more complicated than a few hundred pages of text might suggest. In this chapter, I will present several mock case studies. The names of the organizations and individuals are fictitious, but in most cases, they reflect real-world scenarios. One problem with case studies is that they tend to be overly specific. For example, I might describe how Company XYZ solved a very specific backup challenge for its medium-sized data center. Although some lessons learned from the process might be useful to others, the details will differ from those affecting your own company. The other potential problem with case studies is that they can be quite boring to read! Too many facts and statistics can make for dull reading.

To avoid these problems, I've tried a different approach in this chapter. During the process of writing this book, I often conferred with peers about their own data protection experiences. I would sometimes hear some pretty good stories. They would all end with something interesting like, "…but it was the wrong tape!" It's great to be able to learn good technical information in the context of entertaining accounts. I probably can't beat many of those stories with straight technical information. So, I decided that instead of trying to beat them, I'd try to *join* them! To present the actual case studies, I'll be using narrated fictional accounts of the tools and techniques employed. Similar to most case studies, each of the organizations we'll examine has many challenges. In some cases, technology has helped the company, whereas in others, the poor implementation of solutions has hurt it. As with any real-world scenario, there are numerous constraints—including financial and human resources. The actual details of each scenario are less important than the ideas upon which they're based. For example, learning how one company evaluated the type of data protection it required is much more important than seeing that it chose to implement a DLT autoloader.

OK, enough of the introduction—let's cut to the chase!

CASE STUDY 1: MOM & POP'S BLOOMIN' GARDEN SHOP

In the first case study, we'll examine the data protection needs of a small business. As we'll see, this small company has many constraints that make adequate planning for a maintainable solution extremely important.

Introduction

Mom & Pop's Bloomin' Garden Shop (often referred to as "Mom & Pop's") is a small business that specializes in selling lawn care products. The company has three store locations, each of which sells goods and services and provides advice to customers regarding lawn care. Although the main business focus of the company has little to do with technology, the owners—Iris and Bud Thorne—have decided that they can use computing technology to their benefit. Employees of all three locations are considered experts in lawn care, so each is responsible for giving advice to other employees as well as to customers. Employees have different areas of expertise, however. To maximize the benefit to the customer, employees will be asked to enter common questions and answers into their local database. Additionally, they plan to track sales information and allow store managers to create their own word processing documents and spreadsheets.

Following is some basic information regarding Mom & Pop's Bloomin' Garden Shop:

Name of company	Mom & Pop's Bloomin' Garden Shop
Business profile	A small company that sells plants and offers advice to gardeners
Number of employees	12
Number of sites	Three stores in the same city
Major business challenge	Synchronizing and protecting knowledge base and POS data among stores
Future business plans	Negligible growth over the next year; the eventual addition of one more store is in the foreseeable future

The Players

These are the key people involved in planning data protection for Mom & Pop's Bloomin' Garden Shop:

▼ **Iris Thorne ("Mom")**   Mom is skeptical of technology and her main goal is to keep the focus of the business on what they do best—growing and selling plants.

- **Bud Thorne ("Pop")**   Pop has recently been talking to a friend of his who "does stuff with computers." The friend has mentioned several ways in which technology could help ease their business problems. Though he's not technical by any stretch of the imagination, Pop doesn't mind occasionally dabbling in basic PC maintenance tasks.

▲ **Lily**   Bud and Iris's daughter. She has worked with computers as an end user and, as a business major at the local college, understands the benefits that computers can bring to the workplace.

Company Overview

To meet its information-management goals, Mom & Pop's Bloomin' Garden Shop clearly needs a better way to track information than a traditional paper-based one. On the advice of their daughter Lily, Mom and Pop have decided to place a basic computer that will run Microsoft Windows 98 in each of their three store locations. These machines are used for three separate applications:

▼ **Point-of-Sale (POS)**   An application that stores and processes sales transactions

- **Gardening Knowledge Base**   A small database containing common questions and answers from customers regarding lawn care issues

▲ **General Business Tools**   An application that creates signs and performs calculations on a basic spreadsheet application

The computer in each store has Microsoft Office installed. Both the POS application and Gardening Knowledge Base are simple front-end programs that store information in a Microsoft Access database. The stores all have access to the Internet through analog modems and can also connect directly to each other, if necessary. With this technology, however, Mom and Pop had to think of data protection. Let's see how they did it.

The Story

Pop had always had an interest in working with computers, but not much technical background. Lately, he has found himself coming into the shop earlier each day just to work with the POS and Gardening Knowledge Base applications he purchased at the local computer store. "I can't believe how long we've been able to get by without this technology," he said to Mom. "With these computers in each store, we won't have to wonder about sales during the week. Plus, we can keep track of all of those questions customers have. I'd even like to put together a newsletter for our best customers—you know, such as Martha, who buys a lot of stuff each month."

Mom knew much less about computers, but she trusted in Pop's decision. After all, it would be nice to be able to manage these types of information and store them accordingly. Within the next few weeks, Pop, with the help of Lily, had set up a computer in each of the three store locations. He personally trained the store managers on using the applications, and they, in turn, trained their employees. Overall, the employees of Mom & Pop's were excited at the opportunity to use newer tools.

The basic "network" setup for the company was quite simple. Stores could use their dial-up accounts to connect to the Internet, if necessary. Additionally, they could connect to each other directly using modem connections. With the help of an outside consultant, Pop was able to set up an automated process that copied files from the two other stores to Store 1. However, the consultant brought up several interesting points. First and foremost, the data had to be backed up. "Well, I already have copies of the POS and Knowledge Base databases at each of the three stores—isn't that enough?" The consultant informed Pop of the inherent fallibility of computer hardware and software and the very real threat of user interactions corrupting data. Pop was very receptive to the advice. Since he couldn't afford much more of the consultant's time, he decided to implement a solution himself.

Based on their current setup, a preliminary list of business requirements was defined, as follows:

Technical Process	Business Requirement
Archival	Data archival is unnecessary, because the total volume of data is small.
Client workstations	Backups are not required, because all important information is stored on the server at each store.
Data retention	All data should be retained in a separate database on the server in Store 1.
Downtime	The business can afford up to two days without the use of computers.
Knowledge Base	Data must be synchronized nightly, and all information should be backed up on the computer in Store 1.
Off-site storage	Tapes are taken to the bank once a week, along with weekly cash deposits.
POS database	Daily sales information should be backed up during the day to protect against data loss due to database corruption or failure.

The basic goal was to copy all relevant information from the store locations to the server in Store 1. All data on the main computer in Store 1 would be backed up using a Zip drive—a device that met the budget and data capacity requirements. After he installed the unit himself, Pop was ready to handle the details. "This computer stuff isn't so difficult to understand," he explained to Lily. "It's a lot like protecting our paper records in a safe."

Based on that analogy (and Lily's technical input), Pop's solution involves implementing the following processes:

1. POS transactions will be copied to a floppy disk by a scheduled process several times during the day at each store. The daily sales information will easily fit on this media, and the backup can be used in case an error occurs in the database, causing a loss or corruption of data.

2. An automated dial-up process will use FTP to transfer the daily sales information from each store to the main server in Store 1.

3. A Microsoft Access macro then will import all the daily sales information from each store into a central database. If data is missing, the macro will notify Pop that something has failed. In this case, he can call the appropriate store manager(s) and ask them to manually resend the files.

4. To back up the data at Store 1, Pop configured an automated process that will copy the main Microsoft Access database to a Zip drive nightly. Each week, he will take these Zip disks off-site to the bank, along with the weekly deposits.

"That ought to cover all the bases," Pop said, as he admired his handiwork. Mom and Lily agreed that it looked like a good system. Other than the costs for the consultant, they were all quite pleased with how things turned out.

Analysis

For the most part, Mom, Pop, and Lily were right—the solution chosen is adequate for now, and should provide for the types of data protection required. At first, it might not seem like a very technical solution. Notice that Pop never purchased any specific backup software, and chose a very affordable removable storage device for backup. And, his "home-grown" data protection methods are manually implemented and are dependent on several automated processes working properly. Notice, however, that Pop's methods result in what can be seen as *replication over a wide area network (WAN)*. It might take some imagination to see at first, but in some ways, he has reinvented the wheel. The difference is that Pop's wheel is much cheaper.

The total amount of data that must be backed up daily for each store is less than 8MB, and this amount is not expected to increase much in the future, because few transactions actually occur in the database each day. The only function on the computer that might be considered of high importance is the POS feature. However, the stores can do without even this in the event of a system failure, by temporarily recording sales information using pen and paper and then later manually entering the information into the systems. The use of backups to a floppy disk can help in recovering information, should the need arise.

For a small shop like Mom & Pop's, this solution is adequate. It provides for the minimum level of data protection while meeting the financial and technical constraints. The main goals of this solution are for it to be easy to maintain and for the solution to be inexpensive. Note that other than the casual advice provided by their daughter Lily, Mom and Pop have no information technology department or access to knowledgeable technical staff. Therefore, the solution must be easy to implement. The key to the solution was the realization that the data needed to be protected. Consequently, a list of requirements for data protection was developed. With that out of the way, the only task left was to implement the solution.

With any luck, Mom & Pop's will grow in the near future. With increases in revenue, Mom and Pop will be able to spend some money on making their process more efficient and robust. For example, instead of using several Microsoft Access databases, they could "upsize" to SQL Server 7 and use replication features to transfer data between stores. And, a more reliable and higher-capacity tape backup solution might be implemented at Store 1. Of course, this would require some technical input from a consultant who understands the real issues.

Overall, Pop's efforts seem to have paid off. He now has access to important information from his stores and has provided for its protection. That's not bad for a small "Mom & Pop" shop!

CASE STUDY 2: ALIEN MINDS, INC.

Mom & Pop's situation may seem quite trivial to experienced network and systems administrators who deal with these types of issues every day. One of the luxuries of planning for Mom & Pop's business is that it didn't expect to change much in the near future. That allowed time and implementation resources to play less of a role in the overall solution. As we're about to see, these luxuries aren't often part of a quickly growing high-tech startup company.

Introduction

The overwhelming success of Alien Minds' entertaining software title "Space Syndicate" surprised even their optimistic founders. No one thought that a computer game completely devoid of violence would ever sell this well. Almost instantly, Fox and Dana, the owners of Alien Minds, found themselves with more potential investors than they had ever dreamed, and the growth of the company has been explosive. In the last three months, Alien Minds has gone from a company of only 3 individuals to one with more than 30. And there's no sign of that slowing down in coming months, as demand for more of its games is incredible. With this growth, however, came many of the sloppy practices that may have seemed inevitable.

Following is some basic information about Alien Minds, Inc.:

Name of company	Alien Minds, Inc.
Business profile	A software company that specializes in the development of cutting-edge computer games
Number of employees	35
Number of sites	One building
Major business challenge	Organizing data protection while accommodating rapid growth
Future business plans	To grow to over 100 employees within the next 11 months

The Players

These are the key people involved in planning data protection for Alien Minds, Inc.:

▼ **Fox** CEO and cofounder of Alien Minds, Inc.

■ **Dana** President and cofounder of Alien Minds, Inc.

■ **Jude** Director of Sales and Marketing

■ **Ivan** A member of the IT team responsible for systems administration

▲ **Maya** Lead Help Desk technician, responsible for managing internal and external technical support operations

Business Challenges

At Alien Minds, Inc., rapid staffing plans have produced a group of highly qualified individuals, but also a lack of organization. For example, the company has chosen to standardize primarily on Microsoft SQL Server 7 as a database platform. This decision was made for several reasons, including cost, ease of administration, and performance. However, no single individual is assigned to the role of database administrator. And, although a formal IT department exists, developers and other employees often install and configure their own software. Consistency between installations is rare, and servers seem to spring up daily on the network. Data protection for critical servers and information is largely overlooked.

In addition to maintaining its current IT infrastructure, Alien Minds has several other technical challenges. Struggling with an almost constant lack of office space, many users have chosen the option to work from home. In this case, they've decided to utilize new technologies, such as cable modems and Digital Subscriber Loop (DSL) devices (in addition to the standard dial-up modems) to provide remote connections. To further support this scenario, almost all employees have been given laptop computers.

As we're about to see, all of these issues can lead to problems when you're implementing your data protection plan.

The Story

"So, I asked Ivan to come up with a data protection plan…" The words seemed harmless enough just a few short weeks prior to the meeting, but Fox would end up regretting saying them. It was 4:00 P.M. on a Thursday afternoon when Fox uttered these words, in the presence of four department managers and miscellaneous personnel huddled around a computer monitor. Ivan's excitement clearly was enough to make up for the lack of interest from the others. The subject was data protection—something that the organization realized it was lacking when an "Investor Presentation" stored on a file server was accidentally overwritten. No known backup of the information existed, and the meeting had to be postponed. In reaction to the embarrassing data loss, Fox commissioned Ivan to come up with a data protection plan.

"The first thing we need is a DLT drive with an autoloader," Ivan began, before everyone had a chance to sit down. "We can get a good deal on one from AllStorage, Inc. Of course, we'll also need software. It looks like SuperStor.com has a solution that can back up all of our SQL Server machines and the Exchange Server." So far, Ivan had managed not to lose everyone with his usually bewildering "techiness." The silence that filled the room was rare at the startup company. Somehow, everyone expected more from the presentation. But Ivan just waited for praise of his idea. Jude finally broke the silence, "Uhhh… How much will all of this cost?" she asked as politely as possible. "It costs $16,000 for the hardware and about $4,000 for the software," Ivan replied. Resisting the urge to pull up the Windows calculator, he provided an executive summary: "$20,000 altogether."

It was time to push for some more details; $20,000 wasn't unreasonable, although some thought it too high and others thought Ivan was being far too conservative. "So, Ivan, have you found a good way to back up the production database servers? If I remember correctly, the problem was that they had to be backed up frequently to avoid any data loss, but they run almost 24 hours a day." Not wanting to admit that this "little detail" had slipped his mind, Ivan replied, "I think we can take care of it between 3:00 A.M. and 4:00 A.M. by stopping the server for an hour while the backup runs." Anticipating the next question, he continued, "But, I'm not sure how much data we'll need to back up, and I haven't yet looked at the performance benchmarks for the DLT drive." It was a minor loss, but not enough to discourage the hard-core techie from fielding more questions.

Maya, lead tech on the Help Desk, had a few questions of her own. "Ivan, several of my users seem to be quite confused about backups. They don't understand why they should bother storing data on their H drive if 'everything' is being backed up nightly. Furthermore, I've had two users complain that IT wasn't able to restore files that they had requested." Seeing some serious challenges to his technical authority, Ivan responded quickly. "The two restoration issues were isolated incidents. It turns out that one of the full backup tapes was accidentally mislabeled and reused for the following night's differential backup. Regarding the H-drive thing, users should know that we're not backing up the data on their laptops." Maya looked enlightened, though not much happier. "Even *I* didn't know that. Would it be possible for us to work together to create some documentation and procedures on backup policies?" Ivan reluctantly nodded. He enjoyed writing documentation slightly more than physically moving PCs throughout the building.

Next, it was Dana's turn. The questions she posed were direct and relevant. "Ivan, before you purchase and implement anything, we need to make sure it fits the current infrastructure and plans." This was greeted with a quick reply, "I'm sure we'll be able to back up all of our information on a DLT drive, and the software is pretty easy to set up." Dana wasn't satisfied. Having many highly technical users was both a benefit and a liability, because employees would regularly "take care of things" for themselves. Dana continued, "At last count, I noticed more than 20 separate instances of SQL Server running on everything from laptops to the four-way server in Room 207. Even though I've been trying my hardest, I still don't have a complete list of all the administrator passwords for those boxes. What am I supposed to do when new servers have to be rolled out with only a few days' notice? And, we'll need to designate someone to make sure that all of these machines are configured properly in the backup software. That way, we won't have to start sweating when users ask IT to restore some files." Ivan had run low on responses and, in his own peculiar way, agreed to discuss the issue further with Jude after the meeting.

And so it continued. As more questions were asked, it became clearer that either Ivan didn't do his homework or the department heads didn't provide him with the information he needed. Finally, Fox brought the talks to a conclusion, "Well, I think we all have a lot of work to do to find a good backup solution. Ivan—it looks like you'll need to talk to the department heads to come up with a clearer idea of what we all need. Everyone else, be sure you put together a list of backup and recovery requirements. Next Thursday, after our lunch meeting, I'd like us all to get together and discuss the results so we can implement a solution as soon as possible. Oh, and thanks to everyone for taking part in this exercise!"

The resolution seemed to make sense—everyone would get together with Ivan individually to talk about their data protection requirements. Based on this information, Ivan would put together a list of business requirements and run it by everyone, including Dana. This probably wouldn't be the end of the story, though. Ivan's challenges may just be beginning. The data protection "requirements" that departments will have will probably far exceed their budgets. The real challenge will be in finding the right solution at an acceptable cost. Clearly, there was still some lack of communication. Ivan made sure of that by ending the meeting with a confirmation: "So, does this mean I should hold off on ordering the DLT drive?"

Analysis

The lack of a data protection plan can be a scary thing. Alien Minds has already suffered from data loss, although it was relatively minor. As you can see, its data protection "plan" relies heavily on faith (a topic that's better covered in other, much larger books!). Fortunately, the key players understand that this has to change. The employees have decided that it's best to confront the problem of managing and maintaining data head-on instead of resorting to the much more common practice of waiting until more data loss occurs. After hearing Ivan's recommendations, they were made painfully aware of the fact that the real solution involves a lot more than purchasing and implementing technology. You really can't blame Alien Minds, Inc., for its situation, since it has focused on other, equally important issues, such as growing the business and keeping up with customer demands.

Having overcome the problem of ignoring data protection altogether, the real challenge here is to come up with some overlying strategies that apply to the organization as a whole. We can expect each of the department representatives to take a long look at how they use their current servers and workstations. Based on this, they'll be able to develop a first draft of their data protection requirements. Ivan will probably bring in his expertise on pricing the software and hardware to meet these challenges. If this undertaking is managed properly, the end result will be a usable data protection plan that will let everyone rest easier knowing that critical information is protected.

CASE STUDY 3: JAVA THE HUTT, INC.

In the preceding case study, Alien Minds, Inc., is a small but quickly growing business. The players worked well as a team in coming up with some good solutions for their growing pains. In this case study, we'll move up to a company of larger size and one that is more distributed. Java the Hutt has a popular chain of coffee shops located throughout the United States. The company is just a few years old, so sustaining its high rate of growth has required many budget constraints. Therefore, it probably isn't a big surprise that this company's data protection plan is less than perfect.

Introduction

A major concern for Java the Hutt, Inc., is containing costs. Because the company has a widely distributed network consisting of stores throughout the country, the amount of money being poured into IT seems staggering to its owners. Still, the company relies heavily on its IT resources to remain competitive.

Following is an overview of Java the Hutt, Inc.:

Name of company	Java the Hutt, Inc.
Business profile	A successful chain of retail coffee shops and bakeries located in the United States
Number of employees	~1,500
Number of sites	200 stores located throughout the country
Major business challenge	Managing costs of protecting data
Future business plans	To sustain growth of 10 new stores per quarter

The Players

These are the key people involved in planning data protection for Java the Hutt, Inc.:

▼ **Monica** Founder and majority owner of Java the Hutt, Inc., Monica plays a very active role in overseeing the operations of the company.

■ **Neil** As Director of Field Operations, Neil must account for both daily business operations at the store level and the profitability of the business as a whole.

■ **Gordon** The IT manager for Java the Hutt, Inc., he is responsible for managing all technical aspects at the corporate office and at store locations.

▲ **Terry** She is General Manager for Store 188, one of Java the Hutt's busiest and most profitable locations.

Business Challenges

The main issues faced by Java the Hutt are related to its distributed store model. Tracking sales information is important—and is one of the reasons for the company's recent success. To meet this need, each Java the Hutt store has a single server that runs a proprietary database application. Store employees depend on this system as a "cash register," and workers at the corporate office depend on this data for real-time performance analysis. Generally, it's a well-oiled machine, but one area that has been neglected is data protection. Although data is replicated from the stores to the corporate office, data loss at the store level is not uncommon. Java the Hutt has a formal IT department that is responsible for these types of issues, but a lack of funding for this department has led to less-than-optimal data protection decisions.

The Story

Monica brought the noisy bunch of Java the Hutters to order by clearing her throat. It was time for the weekly operations meeting, and all of the "bigwigs" were there. The atmosphere seemed somewhat tense, and for good reason. "I guess we all have an idea of what happened at Store 188," she began. "It seems that a failed server prevented employees at that location from entering new sales. It took over *four hours* to get a replacement machine to the store. Then, it took another two hours to get the machine back up and running." Most of the faces looked pretty grim as people stared into their gourmet-coffee cups. Neil ran some numbers in his head estimating the amount of revenue from loss of business. But there was more. "The worst part, however, was that we lost a lot of important sales information for the past two days. From what I know, the backups and data replication processes failed, and no one was notified."

It wasn't a pretty picture. Apart from the cost of lost business, there was a lot of finger-pointing going on behind the scenes. "Whose fault was it?" was the question on everyone's mind. Anticipating the obvious, Monica began with, "Whose fault was it?"

followed by a long pause. "Although the goal of this meeting is not to lay blame, we're going to find out how to make sure this doesn't happen again. Terry, why don't you start by telling us what happened?"

Terry wanted nothing more than to yell at everyone else for the problem, but she managed to restrain herself. "Yesterday morning, we started business as usual and were having an average morning rush. About halfway through it, though, our terminals stopped responding. I walked into the back office and heard the server making a lot of loud noises. I immediately called the Help Desk, and after nearly 15 minutes, I got to report the problem." She no longer sounded as constrained. "For a few minutes, I told my cashiers to keep records on paper, but the line was going out the door. I had the pleasure of walking out to the line and telling them we had an emergency and had to close. To those who had already been waiting for a while, we gave away the coffee. Monica told you the rest—we were closed for pretty much the whole day. I couldn't even get a decent estimate on when we could reopen for business, so I kept all 15 employees on the clock. In short, it was a nightmare!" Nothing more had to be said—the effects of the downtime were obvious, and the impact to Java the Hutt's business (and image) was not good.

It was Monica's turn to step in. "Terry, did you notice that the backups hadn't been functioning properly?" Trying not to be defensive, Terry explained that she has hundreds of responsibilities to keep the store running and that looking on a computer screen every morning is not at the top of the list. "Besides," she said, "there's not a whole lot I can do if the backups failed, anyway."

"Neil, what do you expect the downtime cost us?" Monica asked. It was pretty easy to estimate. He was the resident [coffee] bean counter and would have an estimate before his name was uttered. Neil began, "Based on lost revenues alone, I would estimate that we lost at least $15,000. But that's just the tip of the iceberg. We're also going to have a heck of a time working through this in Accounting, and we happened to make the front section of the local newspaper this morning. Did anyone notice that?"

"Any more of these icebergs, and we'll all have a lot of stock in the Titanic of coffee shops!" Monica tried to smile at the tension-relieving joke, but it wasn't enough. Everyone wanted answers, and would settle for nothing less. It was time to stick it to the "IT Guy." "Gordon, you understand the technical issues better than any of us. What's your take on this situation?"

"It was inevitable," Gordon said. His statement was blunt, to the point, and frustrated almost everyone. "Sooner or later, a server failure was going to cause a problem. For over three years, I've been asking each of you to place more money into performing data protection. But, no one seemed to get it! After all, why put money into something when you don't get a good return on investment. Based on last year's budget, we were lucky to deploy the servers for Region 7 on time, let alone perform adequate backups for dozens of stores!" Gordon was right, and Monica knew it. He had tried hard to make everyone understand the importance of proper backup and recovery procedures. But everyone was at fault. Gordon's data protection cost estimates were astronomical. No one wanted to begin to volunteer funds to cover the costs. Monica knew she was guilty, as well. "I should have paid more attention to this issue, and for that I apologize. I understand that it was a tough sell for you, Gordon. I don't think any of us hold you or the IT organization solely responsible for what happened."

Gordon was visibly relieved. It was the first good news he'd heard in the last 24 hours (most of which he spent awake trying to troubleshoot the server with his technicians). "What should we do to avoid this in the future, Gordon?" Monica asked. It was about time somebody paid some real attention to IT's advice, he thought. "There's so much, I don't even know where to start!" he said in a single, loud breath. "Here's what I'd like to do…" he began. Gordon suggested many resolutions:

▼ Create a "high-priority" line at the Help Desk. That way, Terry wouldn't have had to wait to report the problem.

■ Install a backup system that allows for centralized administration. That way, the IT department wouldn't have to depend on store managers to monitor the backup processes.

■ Purchase backup servers for each region. In the event of a failure, a store manager or Help Desk technician would physically drive the machine down to the site of failure. If the failure was not due to the disk subsystem, the drives could be easily pulled out of one machine and inserted into another. If a disk had failed, replacement drives would be available.

■ Implement fault tolerance for the store servers. The standard configuration for each of the stores was a RAID-capable server, but only one drive was included. For the price of purchasing two more hard disks, each store would be well protected against disk failures.

▲ Establish written policies for data protection so that all departments would be aware of the amount of data protection they had "bought."

Gordon took care to mention that the costs for almost all of these "upgrades" would be less than that for a few hours of downtime or the loss of sales data. He mentioned his attempts at implementing these changes, but described in detail how the lack of funding made it impossible. It was a rare occurrence, but it seemed that everyone at the meeting listened attentively, and most were even taking notes!

"What would it take to deliver all of this, Gordon?" Monica asked. Gordon, back to his normally humorous self, exclaimed, "Show me the money!" The first real laughter of the meeting ensued and then died down. But, a lot of the tension had been alleviated, and the mood had become quite constructive. It was Monica's turn to offer a resolution.

"I know several people in this room understand that a good portion of our expenditures are toward technical resources. Some of you have referred to the IT group as a 'black hole for profits.' But, our spending may not be enough. I've been reading about a lot of companies that are implementing chargebacks for IT and other internal services. The idea is that every department and store would pay for the IT services that it uses.

That way, we'd see Gordon's group as less of a 'money-pit' and more of a service that we depend on and pay for. I realize that there would be some challenges in implementing this idea, but at least they'd be decisions we would all be responsible for making." Gordon looked quite happy at the idea, one that he had proposed a few quarters ago when the company hadn't been doing so well. From the looks on the other faces, it seemed that others were willing to give the idea a shot. That's good, because with Monica's backing, they'd have little choice in considering the idea. "We'll all meet tomorrow morning in this office to discuss the idea. If any of you are unable to make it, let me know and send a delegate from your department. And, I'd like to hear from some cashiers and clerks at the store level, as well. Terry, see who's interested in coming. And, thanks to all of you for remaining level-headed in this unfortunate time."

It was a strange situation. The company had just had a terrible disaster at one of its busiest stores. A lot of money was lost and resolution seemed to be a distant hope. In fact, by the end of the meeting, nothing was really resolved. Nevertheless, everyone seemed to leave happy and hopeful that data loss problems would soon be less of a concern.

Analysis

The catalyst for this conversation is a common one—because of human nature, we usually wait until accidents occur before we understand their true possibility. Then comes the blame game, hopefully followed by some constructive ways to avoid such problems in the future. Java the Hutt's main problem is not a lack of money. Clearly, the company is very successful and is planning for rapid growth. Arguably, the main issue is awareness of data protection. In that respect, it seems that Gordon had a lot of good ideas, but they were largely ignored due to a focus on other business issues.

Monica's solution sounds like a good one. It places the burden of paying for IT on those who use the department's services. In short, this translates to everyone in the company. It also places a heavy but healthy burden on the IT group: they'll be constantly forced to deliver better service at better prices. In some ways, the challenges for Java the Hutt's relationship with IT is just beginning. In other ways, however, the biggest hurdle has already been cleared!

CASE STUDY 4: XENICO PHARMACEUTICALS

Java the Hutt's business challenges are real issues that are often faced by many companies each day. Handling the various requirements for data protection while staying within a reasonable budget can be challenging, at best. Java the Hutt is a medium-sized company that was able to meet some of these challenges through an eye-opening experience. Data protection issues become even more complicated as companies grow and more people, hardware, and software are required to meet business requirements. In our final case study, we'll look at how a representative enterprise addresses data protection issues.

Introduction

Xenico Pharmaceuticals is an industry-leading designer and manufacturer of prescription and over-the-counter drugs. The company has state-of-the-art laboratories and research departments that operate in a largely independent manner from each other. This business setup was due to deliberate plans for small but efficient workgroups and was also the side effect of the takeover of several smaller startup biomedical companies. The company is currently widely distributed, and offices range in size from 20 employees up to several thousand.

Name of company	Xenico Pharmaceuticals
Business profile	A drug research and development firm that markets and sells its own pharmaceuticals
Number of employees	32,500
Number of sites	Offices in 40 cities worldwide
Major business challenge	Meeting the needs for data protection and security in a highly distributed environment
Future business plans	Currently, growth is not very rapid. However, the company must be able to react quickly to the success of a new product.

The Players

These are the key people involved in planning data protection for Xenico Pharmaceuticals:

▼ **Carlos**   Carlos is Chief Executive Officer (CEO).

■ **Uma**   As Chief Information Officer (CIO), Uma is ultimately responsible for the IT infrastructure of the company and for determining future strategic directions for the company.

■ **Trentina**   Trentina is Vice President of Sales & Marketing.

▲ **Isaac**   A consultant who has been working with Xenico for over a year, Isaac's responsibilities include evaluating and auditing the current IT infrastructure, including policies, procedures, and implementation.

Business Challenges

The IT department at Xenico is under a lot of pressure. Being a technology-focused company, the network infrastructure is extremely important. Put bluntly, the main problem is that everyone has his or her own idea of how it should be done, but no one wants to pay for it. Lately, several problems have brought the issues of security and data protection to light. First, there have been rumors regarding the leakage of information from within the company to some smaller competitors. The fact that several of Xenico's highest-paid researchers have been hired away by these companies doesn't help reduce suspicions.

Protecting information has always been an important concern for Xenico, but it seems that policies have become lax and are not being enforced. Additionally, most departments are not satisfied with the current data protection policy. Restoring files is as much fun as pulling teeth, and few people have much confidence in the backups themselves.

The Story

The lights went down in the room and the tired, prepackaged PowerPoint slide began. "Managing Data Protection at Xenico Pharmaceuticals" was the title. Despite the donuts and various sources of caffeine found in the room, everyone looked tired. Not surprisingly, the slide's title didn't help. "We're here to determine the data protection plan for fiscal year 2001," began Carlos. "I've been hearing a lot of concerns from all areas, and I think that this is an important enough topic for us to focus on it now."

"A few years ago, we all doubted the value of IT," he continued. "But, we all know that Xenico.com is probably one of the best decisions we made this year." Faces brightened up as thoughts of last year's bonus checks entered their minds. These were followed by images of the company's new web site that provided information on its products for consumers and business partners. Xenico had received several industry awards for its thorough and useful web site. Xenico.com was the brain-child of Uma, now the CIO of the company. Carlos concluded, "Today, we're going to talk about securing and protecting our internal information. Uma?"

As Carlos yielded the stage to Uma, the small crowd grew more attentive. "I can't quite express how happy I am that our current Internet strategy is working well. The several million dollars we made would not have been possible without all of us working together. However, this year, we need to look toward revamping our data protection plan." She could have sworn that she heard sarcastic mumbling to the effect of "What data protection plan?" Never one to be ostracized by the audience, she rose to the challenge. "Yes, we do have one!" Most of the audience at least chuckled. Somehow, they were all playing on the same side again.

Uma continued, "Some of you may know Isaac. He's been consulting with us for quite a while and has been working behind the scenes to make sure our IT department is up to the task and that it remains efficient. Lately, we have noticed that several areas of our network have poorly implemented security measures and that backups for many of our servers are intermittent, at best." It was an accurate assessment and one with which the audience almost unilaterally agreed. "To solve this problem, we'll be taking several additional measures. I'll spare you all the technical details for now, but I want to get agreement on one point before I move on." She sounded sincerely authoritative and had everyone's attention. "We must agree that data protection is not a task that is the responsibility of just the IT department. We're *all* responsible for ensuring that Xenico and its assets remain protected." She continued to give some examples of how managers and end users should be aware of password policies, acceptable usage terms, and backup and recovery policies. Uma lived up to her promise and spared them the technical details. She did, however, promise to make the policies and procedures more easily accessible via the company intranet.

A few weeks passed since the board meeting, and it was time to take action. With the help of Isaac, Uma developed a data protection policy that was found acceptable by all of Xenico's senior management team. Now, it was time to implement the plan by getting into the details. She delegated these tasks to the various sections of the IT department.

Although you would never have guessed it from the board meeting, the data protection scenario was quite grim. That's the real reason a consultant was brought in to analyze the situation. The two main challenges were in maintaining security and data protection and in minimizing the performance impact of backup and recovery. A lot of effort was required to meet these goals, since backup and recovery of data were issues that occupied a large portion of the Help Desk's time. This became very evident when Uma interviewed various department heads at a special meeting the previous week.

There was always a delegate from the Sales & Marketing department to throw a wrench in the works. It wasn't the department's fault, of course. Sales and marketing efforts were crucial to the success of the company, and everyone realized that all of their paychecks depended on its efficiency. Trentina, never one to be at a loss for words, chimed in. "We could really use the ability to access our old sales proposals. I know it sounds wacky, but some of those things from five years ago can be quite useful. The only problem is that they've been archived, and we don't know how to access the 'archive drives.'" Another challenge and another attempted resolution: "Actually, the archived tapes are taken to our bank vault and stored there in a special climate-controlled room. It would be pretty difficult to get the data back. If you need something every once in a while, I could perform a restoration of it." That's not what Trentina wanted at all, but she let it slide for now. Besides, others had already motioned that they were next in the long line of questions.

Clearly, the idea of refreshing the current data protection policy and making it accessible to employees was part of the battle. With that came a better understanding of everyone's responsibility in the matter. For example, Uma was pleasantly surprised that Trentina's department had no problem with paying for a "recovery on demand" option for its current backup solution and for the purchase of additional hard disks for its file server. "All you had to do was ask!" she said.

Many technical changes had to be made to ensure that security was maintained. Xenico had recently begun to experience intermittent server failures and loss of data. The exact cause for each of these incidents was unknown, but one of the current employees was under suspicion. The current server configuration consisted of a single Administrator account. The password for this account was known by five IT staff members, each of whom required use of the account to perform his or her job function.

To solve some of the obvious configuration problems, IT managers were told to set up separate accounts for each of the users with Administrator access. Each of these users would have a regular account and an Administrator account. They would be instructed to use the Administrator account only when necessary. The password of the original Administrator account was changed and was given only to the IT manager. Additionally, server auditing was set up to track any systemwide changes. Uma also instructed systems administrators to review the audit log regularly. Since IT staff work in shifts, logon hour restrictions were set for specific users. Workstation logon restrictions were enforced so that only workstations in the IT department could access servers. Password policies were revised and account lockouts due to bad passwords were enabled. Finally, remote administration software was configured to restrict the IP addresses from which Administrators may log on.

All of these changes resulted in a better-enforced security and data protection plan for a large enterprise. Based on the new policy and communications with department heads and users, Xenico Pharmaceuticals has an excellent opportunity to regain trust in its information systems.

Analysis

The key to protecting information for such a large enterprise environment is communications. All users should be aware of the data protection policies and should have some say in their design. The other portion of the solution—the technical one—was accomplished by means of some relatively minor changes to the server configurations. By utilizing the new setup, it will be possible to track when users log on as Administrators, and to know which individual performed this action. If the problems truly were simple mistakes or coincidental, the server logs would show when changes were made and, in most cases, the effects of these changes. If the problems were caused by malicious intent, on the other hand, management would have a way of uniquely identifying those responsible. It was important that all of those affected were notified of changes during the implementation of these security features, and the reasons for each were well explained.

This solution is fine for the present moment and meets many of the challenges the organization faces. In the future, however, the company will need to address other business problems. The data protection policy itself should be treated as a "living document." As business needs change, so, too, should the policies. Constant input from users is also a must. Remember, a good data protection plan will involve a good balance between security and usability. So far, Xenico Pharmaceuticals is well on its way to setting up an optimal environment, thanks to Uma and the cooperation of other employees.

SUMMARY

Although I've tried to cover several different types of companies, it's unlikely that your organization matches any of these case studies exactly. (If it does, I assure you that it is a strange coincidence!) Although the situations in these case studies may seem to belong in arbitrary categories, you should have been able to gain some insight into how your business could better plan for data protection. For example, you might have enterprise-level requirements for some areas of your company, while other requirements might be more like the Mom & Pop scenario. Such a mix would be the case if your company focused on the shipping industry but also had a few small databases that were used for such things as the company contacts list.

In any case, make no mistake—developing and maintaining a good data protection plan can be quite a challenge! With the information provided in this book and your own technical expertise, however, that challenge should be one that you will be able to overcome. Good luck!

APPENDIX A

SQL Server 2000 Backup and Recovery Reference

SQL Server 2000 includes many tools, utilities, and commands that can make the administration of your database server easy and efficient. Throughout the technical chapters of this book, we have looked at many methods for performing tasks related to backup and recovery. In most cases, we looked at the practical and most common operations you're likely to perform in real-world environments. I suspect that for the majority of readers, this will meet their needs.

However, there's much more under the covers of SQL Server 2000! There are hundreds of stored procedures, Transact-SQL commands, and views that can be used for obtaining specific information about your database server and the database objects it hosts. This appendix is designed as a supplement to the technical information presented in earlier chapters. The content is intended to serve as a useful and practical reference for technical details related to data protection in SQL Server 2000. If you haven't done so already, I highly recommend reading at least Chapter 4, Chapter 6, and Chapter 7 before you continue. The technical information in these chapters will help you understand the relevance of the details provided in this appendix.

NOTE: SQL Server 2000 contains a large number of commands and extensive functionality. There is simply not enough room to discuss all of the stored procedures and commands that are available within the product. In this appendix, I focus on the items that I feel are most relevant to the processes of backup and recovery. If you are looking for a complete list of commands, consult SQL Server 2000 Books Online.

With that out of the way, let's take a look at the underlying structure and commands available for working with SQL Server 2000.

SYSTEM STORED PROCEDURES

A stored procedure is simply a Transact-SQL command that can be called by users and other procedures. SQL Server 2000 includes many built-in stored procedures for performing common tasks. Throughout this book, I have described relevant stored procedures wherever related technical processes were mentioned. For example, in Chapter 6, we discussed the stored procedures that could be used to manage files and filegroups. In the following sections, I'll provide lists of useful stored procedures.

Useful Stored Procedures

I mentioned earlier that there are hundreds of stored procedures available by default with SQL Server 2000. In order to help bring organization to these various commands, Microsoft has provided categories for stored procedures. Table A-1 lists these categories and their purposes.

Category	Purpose/Function	Example
Catalog procedures	Used to obtain information about SQL Server database objects. Users and developers are advised to use Catalog procedures to obtain information since they abstract the complexity (and potential changes) to the underlying system tables.	sp_help
Cursor procedures	Used with cursors	sp_describe_cursor
Distributed Queries procedures	Used to implement and manage Distributed Queries	sp_addlinkedserver
SQL Server Agent procedures	Used for monitoring and scheduling activities for use by SQL Server Agent	sp_add_job (creates a new SQL Server Job)
Replication procedures	Used for configuring and managing replication settings	sp_helparticle (returns information about a replicated article)
Security procedures	Used for managing permissions and other security settings on database objects	sp_addlogin (adds a new SQL Server login)
System procedures	Used for general operations related to the configuration of SQL Server 2000	sp_configure (shows configuration options for the server)
Web Assistant procedures	Used by the Web Assistant for automatically generating web-based information from database information	sp_runwebtask (executes an existing Web Assistant task)
General Extended procedures	Used to allow SQL Server users access to external programs	xp_cmdshell (executes an operating system command and returns the output to the user)
SQL Mail Extended procedures	Used to provide e-mail functionality (send and receive) through the use of SQL Mail	xp_sendmail (sends an e-mail message using SQL Mail)
OLE Automation procedures	Used to access OLE and COM objects through the use of Transact-SQL	sp_OAGetProperty (returns property information from a component)

Table A-1.   Categories of SQL Server's Stored Procedures

You can run stored procedures in a multitude of ways. For example, application developers can make calls to stored procedures from their applications using any of the supported programming interfaces included with SQL Server 2000. Database developers and database administrators can also use the SQL Query Analyzer tool to run ad hoc stored procedures. Figure A-1 provides an example of the results you can obtain by using the following Transact-SQL command:

```
sp_spaceused
```

Note that the results include information about all of the databases on the current server and the amount of disk space they use. Some stored procedures are designed for providing information to end users and database administrators. For example, Catalog stored procedures return details about database objects. Others are used primarily by SQL Server itself. Good examples are the Replication stored procedures. Although they can be used for manually scripting the creation of replication, the preferred method is to use the replication tools and wizards in Enterprise Manager. (See Chapter 10.)

Table A-2 lists stored procedures that are useful when designing, implementing, and monitoring data protection solutions.

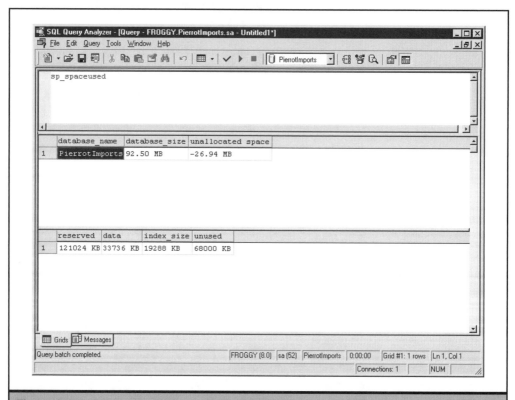

Figure A-1.   Viewing the results of a stored procedure in SQL Query Analyzer

Category	Stored Procedure	Purpose/Common Use
Catalog	sp_columns	Provides a list of columns for the specified database object
Catalog	sp_databases	Provides a list of databases and their sizes
Catalog	sp_server_info	Returns information about the configuration of SQL Server
Catalog	sp_statistics	Returns information about statistics for a table or an indexed view
Catalog	sp_stored_procedures	Returns a list of stored procedures in the current database
Catalog	sp_table_privileges	Returns information about security settings for specific database objects
Cursor	sp_cursor_list	Returns information about the status and properties of open cursors
Cursor	sp_describe_cursor	Provides detailed information about a specific cursor or cursors
Distributed Queries	sp_addlinkedserver	Adds a new linked server to the current SQL Server configuration
Distributed Queries	sp_catalogs	Returns a list of databases or schemas from a linked server
Replication	sp_addarticle	Adds a new article to a publication
Replication	sp_addmergepublication	Creates a new merge publication
Replication	sp_addsubscriber	Add a new subscriber for an existing publication
Replication	sp_droparticle	Deletes an article from a publication
Replication	sp_helparticle	Returns information about an article
Replication	sp_helpsubscriberinfo	Returns information about the subscriber(s) for various publications
Replication	sp_replcounters	Returns performance and synchronization statistics related to replication

Table A-2. Partial List of Useful Stored Procedures

Category	Stored Procedure	Purpose/Common Use
Replication	sp_repltrans	Returns a list of current transactions that are marked for replication but have not yet been transmitted to subscribers
Security	sp_addlogin	Creates a new SQL Server login (also, sp_droplogin)
Security	sp_adduser	Creates a new database user (also, sp_dropuser)
Security	sp_changedbowner	Changes the owner of a database
Security	sp_denylogin	Disallows a login from being used without deleting the login
Security	sp_helplogins	Returns information about SQL Server logins
Security	sp_helprole	Returns information about SQL Server roles in a database
Security	sp_password	Lets you change passwords for SQL Server logins
SQL Server Agent	sp_add_alert	Creates a new SQL Server Agent Alert
SQL Server Agent	sp_add_job	Adds a new SQL Server Agent Job
SQL Server Agent	sp_add_operator	Adds a new SQL Server Operator
SQL Server Agent	sp_help_job	Returns information about a SQL Server Agent Job
SQL Server Agent	sp_help_jobschedule	Returns scheduling information about a SQL Server Agent Job
SQL Server Agent	sp_start_job	Immediately starts a SQL Server Job
SQL Server Agent	sp_update_jobschedule	Updates the schedule settings for a SQL Server Agent Job
System	sp_adddumpdevice	Creates a new database dump device for use in backup and restore processes (also, sp_dropdevice)
System	sp_attach_db	Attaches a database to the instance of SQL Server (also, sp_detach_db)
System	sp_configure	Configures various parameters and settings for the instance of SQL Server
System	sp_dboption	Sets database options

Table A-2.   Partial List of Useful Stored Procedures *(continued)*

Category	Stored Procedure	Purpose/Common Use
System	sp_executesql	Executes a Transact-SQL command that has been generated in a string
System	sp_help	Returns information about database objects (can be used without any parameters to return a list of objects in the current database)
System	sp_helpdb	Provides a list of databases on the current server
System	sp_monitor	Displays performance statistics related to the current instance of SQL Server
System	sp_refreshview	Refreshes the definition of a SQL view (used when the structure of underlying tables changes)
System	sp_rename	Renames database objects
System	sp_renamedb	Renames a database
System	sp_resetstatus	Resets the status of a database that is marked "suspect" due to data file corruption or a system failure
System	sp_spaceused	Lets you view the size of a database; used for estimating the size of a full backup
System	sp_who	Returns a list of current processes that are currently connected to SQL Server (also, sp_who2)
Web Assistant	sp_dropwebtask	Deletes a Web Assistant task
Web Assistant	sp_makewebtask	Creates a new Web Assistant task
Web Assistant	sp_runwebtask	Runs a Web Assistant task

Table A-2.   Partial List of Useful Stored Procedures *(continued)*

Useful Extended Stored Procedures

In addition to the standard stored procedures that are available in SQL Server, several extended stored procedures can be used. Extended stored procedures can be executed using the same syntax as stored procedures. However, they generally access data, commands, or functions that are not part of SQL Server 2000. They are useful when users or applications need to access information or run commands on the server. For example, the xp_cmdshell command can be used to execute an operating system command (provided that the calling user or application has the necessary permissions). Figure A-2 shows the results of the following extended stored procedure command:

```
EXEC master..xp_cmdshell 'dir G:\'
```

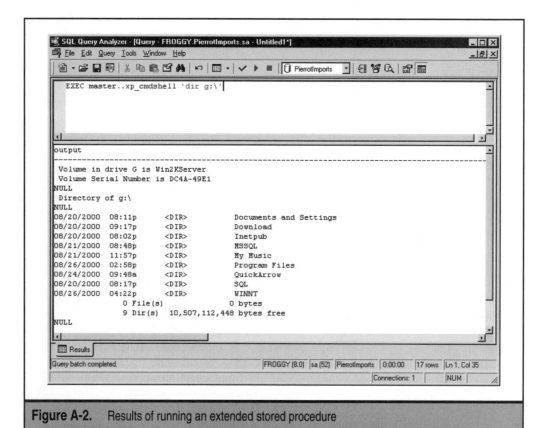

Figure A-2.   Results of running an extended stored procedure

Table A-3 provides a list of commonly used extended stored procedures.

Extended Stored Procedure	Common Use	Notes
xp_cmdshell	Executes an operating system command and returns the results to the calling application	Security must be managed when using this extended procedure since commands run under the context of the MSSQLServer process.

Table A-3.   Partial List of Useful Extended Stored Procedures

Extended Stored Procedure	Common Use	Notes
xp_sendmail	Sends e-mail messages	Useful for generating notices within Transact-SQL scripts; requires proper configuration of e-mail settings; requires SQL Mail to be configured and running
xp_sqlmaint	Executes the sqlmaint.exe command line	Switches for the sqlmaint utility can be specified as the argument of this stored procedure. (For more information, see Chapter 8.)
xp_msver	Displays information about the version of SQL Server	Useful for determining details about a server configuration, including build numbers
xp_logininfo	Displays information about specific SQL Server logins	Useful for viewing security permission information
xp_sqlinventory	Captures various statistics and information about the SQL Server installation and stores this data in a table	
xp_loginconfig	Displays information about the login security configuration for the server	
xp_sqltrace	Allows database administrators and developers to monitor the performance of specific procedures and transactions	Traces can be defined within applications and within Transact-SQL scripts. Alternatively, you can use SQL Profiler to trace specific transactions using a GUI interface.
xp_startmail	Starts the SQL Mail process	SQL Mail must be running in order for SQL Server to be able to send and receive e-mail messages; can also use xp_stopmail.
xp_readmail	Receives e-mail messages	Requires SQL Mail to be configured and running

Table A-3.   Partial List of Useful Extended Stored Procedures *(continued)*

Extended Stored Procedure	Common Use	Notes
sp_OACreate	Creates a new automation component for use with SQL Server. The component can then be accessed through Transact-SQL.	Developers can write their own automation components for use with SQL Server 2000.
sp_OADestroy	Destroys an instance of an OLE automation component	Components should be destroyed after they are used in order to free up memory resources.
sp_OASetProperty	Sets properties for automation components	A component reference must be created before this procedure can be used (see sp_OACreate).
sp_OAGetProperty	Retrieves property information from automation components	A component reference must be created before this procedure can be used (see sp_OACreate).

Table A-3.   Partial List of Useful Extended Stored Procedures *(continued)*

DBCC COMMANDS

The amount of routine manual maintenance that must be performed has been greatly reduced in SQL Server 2000. This is done mainly by automated and scheduled processes
that verify the integrity of databases and ensure that data and other information are kept
consistent. In some cases, however, you may want to manually run (or schedule) commands that can return information about database objects. That's the purpose of the
Database Consistency Checker (DBCC) commands.

Note also that many DBCC commands can produce output in tabular form (using the WITH TABLERESULTS option). These results can then be used to populate tables and provide information for other procedures, processes, or applications. For more information on using this syntax, see SQL Server Books Online.

As with stored procedures, Microsoft has organized the various DBCC commands into categories. In the next sections, we'll look at the various DBCC commands and their purposes.

Validation Commands

Validation DBCC commands are designed primarily for performing routine checks of database integrity and to prevent or fix database corruption issues. For example, Figure A-3 provides the results of running the following DBCC command:

```
DBCC CHECKDB
```

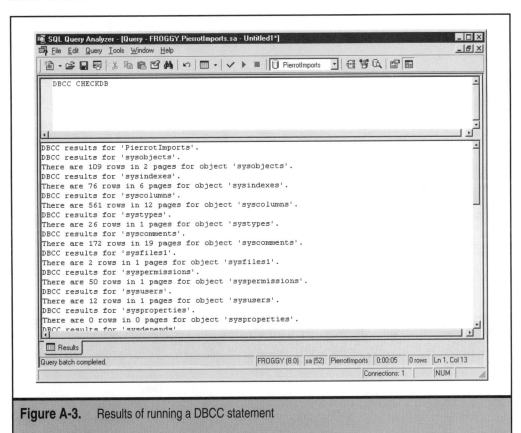

Figure A-3.   Results of running a DBCC statement

Table A-4 provides a list of validation DBCC commands and their functions.

DBCC Command	Common Use	Syntax
DBCC CHECKDB	Verifies the consistency of a database and fixes minor errors that may be present	DBCC CHECKDB ('database_name' [, NOINDEX | { REPAIR_ALLOW_DATA_LOSS | REPAIR_FAST | REPAIR_REBUILD }]) [WITH { [ALL_ERRORMSGS] [, [NO_INFOMSGS]] [, [TABLOCK]] [, [ESTIMATEONLY]] [, [PHYSICAL_ONLY]] }]
DBCC CHECKALLOC	Verifies the disk storage consistency for a database	DBCC CHECKALLOC ('database_name' [, NOINDEX | { REPAIR_ALLOW_DATA_LOSS | REPAIR_FAST | REPAIR_REBUILD }]) [WITH { [ALL_ERRORMSGS | NO_INFOMSGS] [, [TABLOCK]] [, [ESTIMATEONLY]] }]

Table A-4.   DBCC Validation Statements

DBCC Command	Common Use	Syntax
DBCC NEWALLOC	Identical to DBCC CHECKALLOC	Supported for backward compatibility only
DBCC CHECKTABLE	Verifies the integrity of database tables	DBCC CHECKTABLE ('table_name' | 'view_name' [, NOINDEX | index_id | { REPAIR_ALLOW_DATA_LOSS | REPAIR_FAST | REPAIR_REBUILD }]) [WITH { [ALL_ERRORMSGS | NO_INFOMSGS] [, [TABLOCK]] [, [ESTIMATEONLY]] [, [PHYSICAL_ONLY]] }]
DBCC CHECKIDENT	Verifies the Identity values in a specific table and, optionally, changes the seed value	DBCC CHECKIDENT ('table_name' [, { NORESEED | { RESEED [, new_reseed_value] } }])
DBCC CHECKFILEGROUP	Verifies the structure of all objects stored within a specified filegroup	DBCC CHECKFILEGROUP ([{ 'filegroup' | filegroup_id }] [, NOINDEX]) [WITH { [ALL_ERRORMSGS | NO_INFOMSGS] [, [TABLOCK]] [, [ESTIMATEONLY]] }]

Table A-4. DBCC Validation Statements *(continued)*

DBCC Command	Common Use	Syntax
DBCC CHECKCONSTRAINTS	Verifies that data adheres to table constraints	```DBCC CHECKCONSTRAINTS [('table_name' | 'constraint_name')] [WITH { ALL_ERRORMSGS	ALL_CONSTRAINTS }]```
DBCC CHECKCATALOG	Verifies that information in actual database objects is consistent with the information stored within the master database	```DBCC CHECKCATALOG ('database_name') [WITH NO_INFOMSGS]```

Table A-4.   DBCC Validation Statements *(continued)*

Maintenance Commands

DBCC Maintenance commands are intended for periodic maintenance of databases. They can be used to verify database structure and ensure that performance is optimized. Table A-5 provides a list of these commands and their syntax.

DBCC Command	Purpose	Syntax
DBCC DBREINDEX	Rebuilds indexes for the specified tables or materialized views	```DBCC DBREINDEX (['database.owner.table_name' [, index_name [, fillfactor]]]) [WITH NO_INFOMSGS]```

Table A-5.   DBCC Maintenance Commands

DBCC Command	Purpose	Syntax
DBCC DBREPAIR	Drops a damaged database; primarily supported for backward compatibility. (DROP DATABASE is recommended.)	

DBCC INDEXDEFRAG	Defragments clustered indexes by physically reordering data pages	`DBCC INDEXDEFRAG`
		`( { database_name |`
		`database_id | 0 }`
		`, { table_name |`
		`table_id |`
		`'view_name' | view_id`
		`}`
		`, { index_name |`
		`index_id }`
		`)   [ WITH NO_INFOMSGS`
		`]`

DBCC SHRINKDATABASE	Reduces the size of data files in a database by removing inactive pages	`DBCC SHRINKDATABASE`
		`( database_name [ ,`
		`target_percent ]`
		`[ , { NOTRUNCATE |`
		`TRUNCATEONLY } ]`
		`)`

DBCC UPDATE USAGE	Detects and fixes errors in the system tables related to the size of database objects	`DBCC UPDATEUSAGE`
		`(  { 'database_name' |`
		`0 }`
		`[ , { 'table_name' |`
		`'view_name' }`
		`[ , { index_id |`
		`'index_name' } ] ]`
		`)`
		`[ WITH  [ COUNT_ROWS ]`
		`[ , NO_INFOMSGS ]`
		`]`

DBCC SHRINKFILE	Reduces the size of a particular data file by removing inactive pages	`DBCC SHRINKFILE`
		`( { file_name | file_id`
		`}`
		`{ [ , target_size ]`
		`| [ , { EMPTYFILE |`
		`NOTRUNCATE |`
		`TRUNCATEONLY } ]`
		`}`
		`)`

Table A-5.   DBCC Maintenance Commands *(continued)*

Status Commands

In performing routine database maintenance and administration, you may want to obtain additional information about SQL Server and database objects. The DBCC Status commands (listed in Table A-6) can be used for this purpose.

Miscellaneous Commands

In addition to the DBCC Validation, Maintenance, and Status commands (which are often used as part of a data protection plan), there are several other DBCC statements that can be used. Table A-7 provides a list of useful DBCC commands that fall under the Miscellaneous category.

DATABASE OPTIONS

There are several options that administrators can set for SQL Server 2000 databases. These options affect the behavior and properties for an entire database. They can be set in Enterprise Manager by right-clicking on a database and selecting Properties. The settings are visible in the Options tab. (See Figure A-4.)

DBCC Command	Purpose
DBCC INPUTBUFFER	Displays the last command executed by a specific process ID. (A list of process IDs can be obtained with the sp_who command.)
DBCC OPENTRAN	Provides a list of the oldest active transaction in the current database
DBCC OUTPUTBUFFER	Displays the latest results sent to a specific process ID in hexadecimal and ASCII format
DBCC PROCCACHE	Displays information about the SQL Server procedure cache
DBCC SHOWCONTIG	Displays information about the fragmentation of physical files for database objects
DBCC SHOW_STATISTICS	Displays distribution statistics for a specified database table (useful for performance tuning)
DBCC SQLPERF	Returns information about the amount of space used by the transaction log for all databases on the current server
DBCC TRACESTATUS	Returns status information for enabled trace flags
DBCC USEROPTIONS	Displays the settings of the SET parameters for the current user session

Table A-6.   DBCC Commands Used for Gathering Status Information

DBCC Command	Purpose
DBCC dllname (FREE)	Unloads an extended stored procedure DLL from memory
DBCC HELP	Returns syntax information for a DBCC command
DBCC PINTABLE	Instructs SQL Server to retain the pages for a specific table in memory
DBCC ROWLOCK	Enables locking levels for SQL Server 6.5 databases
DBCC TRACEOFF	Disables the tracing of a specified flag
DBCC TRACEON	Enables the tracing of a specified flag for performance monitoring and debugging
DBCC UNPINTABLE	Removes the pages for a specific table from memory

Table A-7.   Miscellaneous DBCC Commands

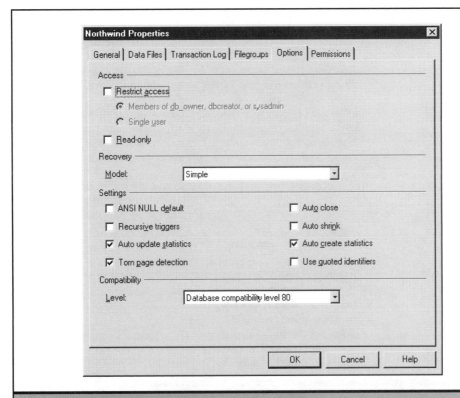

Figure A-4.   Viewing database options in Enterprise Manager

Database options can also be changed using the ALTER TABLE command. (See SQL Server Books Online for further syntax information.) Table A-8 provides a list of the various database options that are available for SQL Server 2000 databases.

Option	Meaning	Notes
Restrict Access	Restricts the users who can access a database; can restrict access to members of db_owner, dbcreator, or sysadmin roles, or to a single user only	Useful when performing database restore or recovery operations or other operations that require exclusive access to the database
Read-Only	Sets the database in read-only mode. In this mode, the database cannot be modified via standard SQL queries or DML commands.	Used when database information should not be changed (for example, in the use of standby servers or in certain types of replication)
ANSI NULL Default	Sets the default setting for columns in database tables; when enabled, new columns are set to NULL, by default.	
Recursive Triggers	Enables triggers to cause the firing of other triggers. When disabled, the actions of a particular trigger will not cause another trigger to fire, but the transaction will be completed.	Generally, recursive triggers are allowed to preserve data integrity. It is the responsibility of database application developers to ensure that circular references are not created. Disabling recursive triggers might be useful in troubleshooting data modification problems or for improving performance.
Select Into/Bulk Copy	Allows nonlogged transactions to be performed on the database. Common nonlogged operations include the SELECT INTO command (which creates a new table from the results of a SQL query) or the Bulk Copy (bcp) command that can be used for the bulk import of data.	Enabling this option can increase the performance of certain operations and can decrease the size of the transaction log.

Table A-8.   SQL Server 2000 Database Options

Option	Meaning	Notes
Truncate Log on Checkpoint	Specifies that the transaction log will be truncated whenever a checkpoint occurs for this database	Enabling this option reduces the size of the transaction logs, but prevents the use of transaction log backups.
Torn Page Detection	Allows SQL Server to automatically detect incomplete ("torn") database pages that might occur due to a power loss or failure of a server	Enabling this option ensures data integrity by marking a database as suspect in the event that only a portion of a page was written to disk.
Auto Close	Specifies that a database should be automatically closed when all of the active users close their sessions	Useful when maintenance is required on a database, but you do not want to terminate current user connections.
Auto Shrink	Allows SQL Server to automatically shrink the size of data files by removing unused space	Shrinking of data files can increase usable disk space, but the operations required to shrink and expand files can decrease performance.
Auto Create Statistics	Specifies that SQL Server should automatically create statistics on database objects whenever they do not exist	Query performance can be dramatically increased when statistics are created. The statistics are used by the query optimizer to determine the best method for retrieving and modifying data.
Auto Update Statistics	Specifies that SQL Server should automatically update the statistics on objects in this database	Automatically updating statistics ensures that the statistics are kept up-to-date as data changes. The overall benefit is increased performance due to more efficient decisions by the query optimizer.
Use Quoted Identifiers	Specifies that a double-quote character (") can be used to identify database objects. When this option is disabled, only the single quote (') character can be used as a string identifier.	

Table A-8.   SQL Server 2000 Database Options *(continued)*

Option	Meaning	Notes
Compatibility Level	Specifies the version of SQL Server compatibility for the database. Available options are level 60 (SQL Server 6.0), 65 (SQL Server 6.5), 70 (SQL Server 7.0) and 80 (SQL Server 2000).	Compatibility levels can affect the output of queries and are often used when migrating applications and servers to newer versions.

Table A-8. SQL Server 2000 Database Options *(continued)*

INFORMATION SCHEMA VIEWS

A common task for systems and database administrators is to obtain information about various database objects. For example, a developer might want to quickly obtain a list of all of the tables within a specific database. Or, a user might want to search through all of the tables for a specific column name. Although a user might query system tables directly for information, this presents several problems. First, the user must have access to these tables. Second, querying system tables can be a tedious, cumbersome, and error-prone process. You would be required to understand the relationships between system tables and create your own joins just to get basic information. Finally, the structure of the system tables may change between versions of SQL Server, thereby requiring retraining (for users), or rewriting of scripts. Microsoft makes no guarantees that system table changes will provide for backward compatibility with scripts that query these tables directly.

Fortunately, there's a better way. The information schema views were designed for quickly viewing information about specific database objects. Figure A-5 shows the results of running the following query:

```
SELECT *
FROM Information_Schema.Tables
WHERE Table_Name LIKE 'Cust%'
```

Table A-9 lists each of the available information schema views and their purpose. These views can be very helpful when trying to extract information from SQL Server 2000 objects.

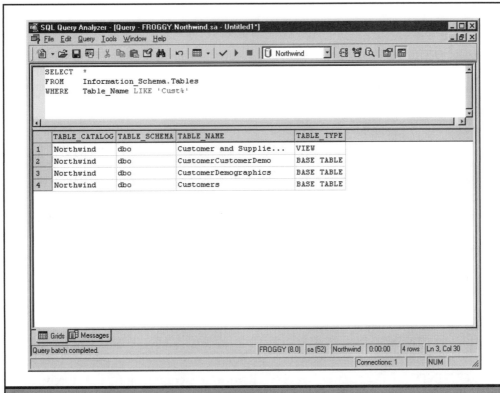

Figure A-5.   Viewing the results of an information schema query

View	Purpose
CHECK_CONSTRAINTS	Returns information about CHECK constraints
COLUMN_DOMAIN_USAGE	Returns a list of columns that use user-defined data types
COLUMN_PRIVILEGES	Returns security privileges on columns
COLUMNS	Returns a list of all columns in all tables and views

Table A-9.   Information Schema Views and Their Purpose

View	Purpose
CONSTRAINT_COLUMN_USAGE	Returns a list of columns that have constraints
CONSTRAINT_TABLE_USAGE	Returns a list of tables that have constraints
DOMAIN_CONSTRAINTS	Returns a list of user-defined data types that have rules bound to them and are accessible to the current user
DOMAINS	Returns a list of user-defined data types that are accessible to the current user
KEY_COLUMN_USAGE	Returns a list of columns that are used as primary and/or foreign keys
PARAMETERS	Returns a list of user-defined functions or stored procedures that are accessible to the current user
REFERENTIAL_CONSTRAINTS	Returns a list of foreign key constraints in the current database
ROUTINE_COLUMNS	Returns information about all of the columns accessible to the current user
ROUTINES	Returns a list of functions and stored procedures accessible to the current user
SCHEMATA	Returns a list of databases to which the current user has access
TABLE_CONSTRAINTS	Returns a list of constraints in the current database
TABLE_PRIVILEGES	Returns a list of columns and security privileges for the current user
TABLES	Returns a list of tables and views in the current database
VIEW_COLUMN_USAGE	Returns a list of all columns in a database that are referenced by views
VIEW_TABLE_USAGE	Returns a list of all tables in a database that are referenced by views
VIEWS	Returns information and the definition for all views in the current database

Table A-9. Information Schema Views and Their Purpose *(continued)*

SQL SERVER CONFIGURATION OPTIONS

One of the major advantages of the SQL Server 2000 database server platform is that it is largely self-tuning. That is, through the use of various algorithms and monitored statistics, the server is designed to adapt to various situations. However, no system is perfect, and sometimes knowledgeable database administrators and application developers will be able to better predict the behavior of their database servers than will the database server itself. That's where the configuration options for SQL Server enter the picture.

Although they're not commonly modified in many installations, there are several SQL Server configuration options that can be set. The easiest and safest way to make changes is to use Enterprise Manager. This is done by simply right-clicking on the name of a database and selecting Properties. You'll see many choices on the various tabs that are available. (See Figure A-6.)

Although it's a convenient method for making changes to server configuration, only some of the settings can be set through Enterprise Manager. For all of the rest, you'll be required to use Transact-SQL to make the necessary changes. Or, you can make the changes

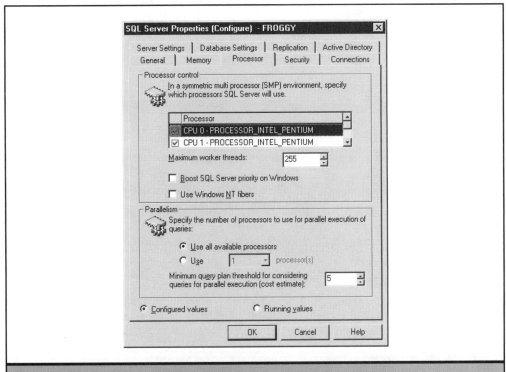

Figure A-6.   Viewing SQL Server configuration options in Enterprise Manager

using the sp_configure stored procedure. This stored procedure uses the following syntax:

```
EXEC sp_configure 'Setting name', 'Value'
```

To get a list of the available options and their settings, simply run the sp_configure stored procedure without any parameters. (See Figure A-7.)

The stored procedure will return information about the various settings, the minimum and maximum values, and the configured and run values. Note that some settings may not take effect immediately. Rather, they will require a restart of the server. Therefore, the configured values (the ones that you have currently set) may not match the run values (the ones that are currently running). After changing one of the options, you must then run the RECONFIGURE command for this setting to take effect (if the setting does not require a restart of the server). Also, some options are listed as "Advanced options." In order for these settings to be changed, you must first set the Show Advanced Options setting to 1.

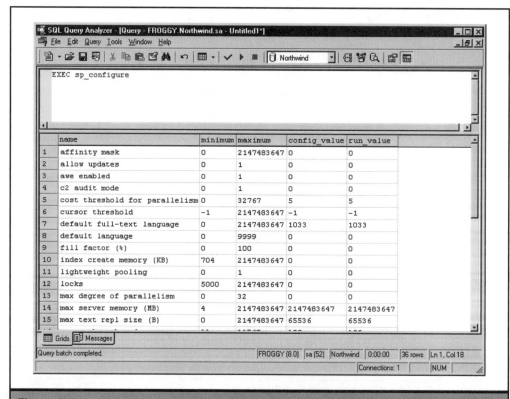

Figure A-7.   Viewing SQL Server configuration options in Query Analyzer

Table A-10 provides a list of the various SQL Server configuration parameters and their effects.

Option	Effect
affinity mask	In multiprocessor systems, this setting reflects the tendency of threads to work across processors.
allow updates	Specifies whether direct updates of system tables can be made
awe enabled	Enables Address Windowing Extensions (AWE) for supporting up to 64GB of memory
c2 audit mode	Sets auditing settings in accordance with C2 recommendations
cost threshold for parallelism	Specifies the minimum query cost for the query to be distributed across multiple processors
cursor threshold	Specifies the number of rows that are generated for certain types of cursors
default full-text language	Sets the default language for full-text indexes
default language	Sets the default SQL Server language
fill factor	Sets the default fill factor used when indexes are created
index create memory	Controls the amount of memory used during index creation processes
lightweight pooling	Improves performance on multiprocessor systems by reducing context switching
locks	Sets the maximum number of locks for the server
max degree of parallelism	Limits the number of processors that can be used for a single query
max server memory	Sets the maximum amount of memory that can be used by SQL Server
max text repl size	Specifies maximum size of text and image data types that can be used for replication

Table A-10.   SQL Server Configuration Options and Their Effects

Option	Effect
max worker threads	Sets the maximum number of threads that are available to the SQL Server process. Changes to this setting may improve performance.
media retention	Specifies the default number of days for media retention settings. (See Chapter 6.)
min memory per query	Sets the minimum amount of RAM that will be used to process a query
min server memory	Sets the minimum amount of memory that can be used by SQL Server
nested triggers	Specifies whether or not triggers can cause the firing of other triggers
network packet size	Sets the default size of network packets sent by SQL Server
open objects	Sets the maximum number of database objects that can be open at a specific time
priority boost	Specifies that SQL Server should run at an elevated priority. This option may be used when the primary purpose of a machine is to run SQL Server.
query governor cost limit	Sets the query cost limit. If queries exceed this cost, they will not be executed.
query wait	Sets the amount of time that queries will wait if sufficient memory for processing the query is unavailable
recovery interval	Sets a limit on the amount of time that SQL Server should use to perform automatic database recovery. (This process occurs after an improper shutdown of SQL Server.)
remote access	Controls support for logins from remote servers
remote login timeout	Sets the timeout for remote logins
remote proc trans	Specifies settings for distributed transactions

Table A-10. SQL Server Configuration Options and Their Effects *(continued)*

Option	Effect
remote query timeout	Specifies the amount of time that must elapse before a remote query is considered to have timed out
scan for startup procs	Allows SQL Server to automatically run certain stored procedures when the SQL Server services are started
set working set size	Specifies an exact value for the amount of memory SQL Server should use. This option overrides dynamic memory allocation settings.
show advanced options	Allows users to change advanced SQL Server configuration options
two digit year cutoff	The cutoff year for two-digit years (used for Year 2000 compliance). If values are less than this number, the date is considered to be in the 1900s; if values are greater, they are considered to be in the 2000s.
user connections	Sets the maximum number of user connections allowed for the server
user options	Specifies global default user session options

Table A-10.   SQL Server Configuration Options and Their Effects *(continued)*

Table A-11 provides detailed information about the various configuration values that are available for SQL Server configuration options. Note that the table includes information about whether the setting requires a restart of SQL Server and whether it is an advanced option.

BACKUP AND RECOVERY SYSTEM TABLES

SQL Server stores information internally about databases and objects within databases. In earlier chapters, we discussed the importance of the master database and of various system tables within each of the databases. Understanding the structure of these various tables can be helpful when you're looking for specific information. In general, the information in each of these tables is intuitive enough for experienced database developers and administrators to use.

It's important to note that direct modifications to system tables are highly discouraged. A few mistakes in configuration settings can cause databases to be reported as

Option	Requires Restart?	Advanced?	Self-Configuring?	Minimum	Maximum	Default
affinity mask	✓	✓		0	2147483647	0
allow updates				0	1	0
awe enabled	✓	✓		0	1	0
c2 audit mode	✓	✓		0	1	0
cost threshold for parallelism		✓		0	32767	5
cursor threshold		✓		–1	2147483647	–1
default full-text language		✓		0	1	1033
default language				0	9999	0
fill factor	✓	✓		0	100	0
index create memory		✓	✓	704	1600000	0
lightweight pooling	✓	✓		0	1	0
locks	✓	✓	✓	5000	2147483647	0
max degree of parallelism		✓		0	32	0
max server memory		✓	✓	4	2147483647	2147483647
max text repl size				0	2147483647	65536
max worker threads	✓	✓		10	1024	255
media retention	✓	✓		0	365	0
min memory per query		✓		512	2147483647	1024
min server memory		✓	✓	0	2147483647	0
nested triggers				0	1	1

Table A-11.   Details About Server Configuration Options

Option	Requires Restart?	Advanced?	Self-Configuring?	Minimum	Maximum	Default
network packet size		✓		512	65536	4096
open objects	✓	✓	✓	0	2147483647	0
priority boost	✓	✓		0	1	0
query governor cost limit		✓		0	2147483647	0
query wait		✓		-1	2147483647	-1
recovery interval		✓	✓	0	32767	0
remote access (RR)	✓			0	1	1
remote login timeout				0	2147483647	20
remote proc trans				0	1	0
remote query timeout				0	2147483647	0
scan for startup procs	✓	✓		0	1	0
set working set size	✓	✓		0	1	0
show advanced options				0	1	0
two digit year cutoff				1753	9999	2049
user connections	✓	✓	✓	0	32767	0
user options				0	16383	0

Table A-11.   Details About Server Configuration Options (*continued*)

corrupt or can prevent certain operations from working properly. These are serious problems that can cause a loss of data or require the reinstallation of SQL Server. With that in mind, querying system tables is generally a fairly safe operation and is one that can often provide you with insight into the details of how the SQL Server data storage, backup, and recovery engines function.

In the following sections, we'll take a look at the various tables that are present in user databases, the master database, and the msdb database.

System Tables in Master Database

Table A-12 lists the tables in the master database and describes their functions. For more information about the columns in the various tables, use the sp_help stored procedure. Detailed notes are also available in SQL Server 2000 Books Online.

CAUTION: Modifying the system tables directly is not recommended.

System Table	Purpose
sysaltfiles	Records information about the files that make up a database
syslockinfo	Contains information about database locks
syscacheobjects	Records details about how the database cache is being used
syslogins	Lists logins for the server
syscharsets	Contains information about character sets supported by SQL Server
sysmessages	Contains a list of SQL Server error messages and descriptions
sysconfigures	Lists configuration options for SQL Server and their settings
sysoledbusers	Lists login mappings used for linked servers
syscurconfigs	Shows current configuration options for SQL Server
sysperfinfo	Provides information about SQL Server performance statistics
sysdatabases	Provides information about all of the databases hosted on the server
sysprocesses	Provides information about client and system processes running on the SQL Server
sysdevices	Lists all backup devices available on the server (including disk, tape, and network backup devices)
sysremotelogins	Lists logins that can be used to execute remote stored procedures

Table A-12.   System Tables Contained Within the Master Database

System Table	Purpose
syslanguages	Lists languages supported by SQL Server
sysservers	Lists servers that this installation of SQL Server can access via OLEDB

Table A-12.   System Tables Contained Within the Master Database *(continued)*

System Tables in All User Databases

Table A-13 lists the tables that are present in every database and describes their functions. For more information about the columns in the various tables, use the sp_help stored procedure. Detailed notes are also available in SQL Server 2000 Books Online.

System Table	Purpose
sysallocations	Contains information about allocation units for indexes
sysindexes	Provides information about indexes
syscolumns	Provides information about the columns within all tables
sysindexkeys	Provides data about the keys used by indexes
syscomments	Lists SQL statements that define database objects such as views, triggers, and stored procedures
sysmembers	Displays information about user/role membership
sysconstraints	Contains information related to database constraints
sysobjects	Lists all database objects
sysdepends	Provides dependency information for database objects (for example, dependencies between views and the tables they reference)
syspermissions	Gives information about security permissions
sysfilegroups	Stores information about database filegroups
sysprotects	Provides information about security permissions set with GRANT and DENY commands
sysfiles	Stores information about database files

Table A-13.   System Tables That Are Found in All User Databases

System Table	Purpose
sysreferences	Provides information about primary key/foreign key relationships within the database
sysforeignkeys	Provides information about foreign key constraints
systypes	Provides information about user-defined data types
sysfulltextcatalogs	Lists full-text catalogs within the database
sysusers	Lists valid database users

Table A-13.   System Tables That Are Found in All User Databases *(continued)*

Backup Tables in Msdb Database

SQL Server 2000 relies heavily on the tables and data stored in the msdb database in order to complete its functions. These tables are particularly important for systems and database administrators who are implementing data protection solutions. For more information on the various terms and features mentioned in these descriptions, see Chapter 6.

backupfile

This table contains information about each database or log file that has been backed up:

Column Name	Data Type	Nullable?	Length
backup_set_id	int	No	4
first_family_number	tinyint	No	1
first_media_number	smallint	No	2
filegroup_name	nvarchar	No	256
page_size	int	No	4
file_number	numeric	No	9
backed_up_page_count	numeric	No	9
file_type	char	No	1
source_file_block_size	numeric	No	9
file_size	numeric	No	13

Column Name	Data Type	Nullable?	Length
logical_name	nvarchar	No	256
physical_drive	varchar	No	260
physical_name	varchar	No	260

backupmediafamily

This table contains information about backup media families (groupings of media that are used for backups):

Column Name	Data Type	Nullable?	Length
media_set_id	int	No	4
family_sequence_number	tinyint	No	1
media_family_id	uniqueidentifier	No	16
media_count	int	No	4
logical_device_name	nvarchar	No	256
physical_device_name	nvarchar	No	520
device_type	tinyint	No	1
physical_block_size	int	No	4

backupmediaset

This table contains information about backup media sets (groupings of media that are used for backups):

Column Name	Data Type	Nullable?	Length
media_set_id	int	No	4
media_uuid	uniqueidentifier	No	16
media_family_count	tinyint	No	1
name	nvarchar	No	256
description	nvarchar	No	510
software_name	nvarchar	No	256
software_vendor_id	int	No	4
mtf_major_version	tinyint	No	1

backupset

This table contains information about backup sets:

Column Name	Data Type	Nullable?	Length
backup_set_id	int	No	4
backup_set_uuid	uniqueidentifier	No	16
media_set_id	int	No	4
first_family_number	tinyint	No	1
first_media_number	smallint	No	2
last_family_number	tinyint	No	1
last_media_number	smallint	No	2
catalog_family_number	tinyint	No	1
catalog_media_number	smallint	No	2
position	int	No	4
expiration_date	datetime	No	8
software_vendor_id	int	No	4
name	nvarchar	No	256
description	nvarchar	No	510
user_name	nvarchar	No	256
software_major_version	tinyint	No	1
software_minor_version	tinyint	No	1
software_build_version	smallint	No	2
time_zone	smallint	No	2
mtf_minor_version	tinyint	No	1
first_lsn	numeric	No	13
last_lsn	numeric	No	13
checkpoint_lsn	numeric	No	13
database_backup_lsn	numeric	No	13

Column Name	Data Type	Nullable?	Length
database_creation_date	datetime	No	8
backup_start_date	datetime	No	8
backup_finish_date	datetime	No	8
type	char	No	1
sort_order	smallint	No	2
code_page	smallint	No	2
compatibility_level	tinyint	No	1
database_version	int	No	4
backup_size	numeric	No	13
database_name	nvarchar	No	256
server_name	nvarchar	No	256
machine_name	nvarchar	No	256
flags	int	No	4
unicode_locale	int	No	4
unicode_compare_style	int	No	4
collation_name	nvarchar	No	256

Restore Tables in Msdb Database

The tables shown next are related to restore devices and operations.

restorefile

This table contains information about files that have been restored:

Column Name	Data Type	Nullable?	Length
restore_history_id	int	No	4
file_number	numeric	No	9
destination_phys_drive	varchar	No	260
destination_phys_name	varchar	No	260

restorefilegroup

This table contains information about filegroups that have been restored:

Column Name	Data Type	Nullable?	Length
restore_history_id	int	No	4
filegroup_name	nvarchar	No	256

restorehistory

This table contains information about all of the restore operations that have been performed on the server:

Column Name	Data Type	Nullable?	Length
restore_history_id	int	No	4
restore_date	datetime	No	8
destination_database_name	nvarchar	No	256
user_name	nvarchar	No	256
backup_set_id	int	No	4
restore_type	char	No	1
replace	bit	No	1
recovery	bit	No	1
restart	bit	No	1
stop_at	datetime	No	8
device_count	tinyint	No	1
stop_at_mark_name	nvarchar	No	256
stop_before	bit	No	1

Database Maintenance Plan Tables in Msdb Database

For most installations of SQL Server 2000, database administrators rely upon Database Maintenance Plans for carrying out backup and recovery processes. Here, we'll look at the msdb tables that are used by the Database Maintenance Plan Wizard and the SQL Agent job scheduling processes.

sysdbmaintplan_databases

This table contains a list of the Database Maintenance Plans present on the server:

Column Name	Data Type	Nullable?	Length
plan_id	uniqueidentifier	No	16
database_name	sysname	No	256

sysdbmaintplan_history

This table contains a history of actions performed by a Database Maintenance Plan:

Column Name	Data Type	Nullable?	Length
sequence_id	int	No	4
plan_id	uniqueidentifier	No	16
plan_name	sysname	No	256
database_name	sysname	No	256
server_name	sysname	No	256
activity	nvarchar	No	256
succeeded	bit	No	1
end_time	datetime	No	8
duration	int	No	4
start_time	datetime	Yes	8
error_number	int	No	4
message	nvarchar	No	1024

sysdbmaintplan_jobs

This table contains information about jobs that are attached to Database Maintenance Plans:

Column Name	Data Type	Nullable?	Length
plan_id	uniqueidentifier	No	16
job_id	uniqueidentifier	No	16

sysdbmaintplans

This table contains details about Database Maintenance Plans defined on the local server:

Column Name	Data Type	Nullable?	Length
plan_id	uniqueidentifier	No	16
plan_name	sysname	No	256
date_created	datetime	No	8

Column Name	Data Type	Nullable?	Length
owner	sysname	No	256
max_history_rows	int	No	4
remote_history_server	sysname	No	256
max_remote_history_rows	int	No	4
user_defined_1	int	No	4
user_defined_2	nvarchar	No	200
user_defined_3	datetime	No	8
user_defined_4	uniqueidentifier	No	16
log_shipping	bit	No	1

Log-Shipping Tables in Msdb Database

The msdb database contains special tables that are used for tracking the details associated with log-shipping. For more information about log-shipping, see Chapter 10.

log_shipping_databases

This table contains a list of databases on which log-shipping is enabled:

Column Name	Data Type	Nullable?	Length
database_name	sysname	No	256
maintenance_plan_id	uniqueidentifier	No	16

log_shipping_monitor

This table contains statistics and status information related to log-shipping:

Column Name	Data Type	Nullable?	Length
monitor_server_name	sysname	No	256
logon_type	int	No	4
logon_data	varbinary	No	256

log_shipping_plan_databases

This table contains log-shipping settings for databases on which this feature is enabled:

Column Name	Data Type	Nullable?	Length
plan_id	uniqueidentifier	No	16
source_database	sysname	No	256

Column Name	Data Type	Nullable?	Length
destination_database	sysname	No	256
load_delay	int	No	4
load_all	bit	No	1
last_file_copied	nvarchar	No	1000
date_last_copied	datetime	No	8
last_file_loaded	nvarchar	No	1000
date_last_loaded	datetime	No	8
copy_enabled	bit	No	1
load_enabled	bit	No	1
recover_db	bit	No	1
terminate_users	bit	No	1

log_shipping_plan_history

This table contains a history of actions performed based on log-shipping settings:

Column Name	Data Type	Nullable?	Length
sequence_id	int	No	4
plan_id	uniqueidentifier	No	16
source_database	sysname	No	256
destination_database	sysname	No	256
activity	bit	No	1
succeeded	bit	No	1
num_files	int	No	4
last_file	nvarchar	No	512
end_time	datetime	No	8
duration	int	No	4
error_number	int	No	4
message	nvarchar	No	1000

log_shipping_plans

This table contains details about log-shipping plan parameters and configuration options:

Column Name	Data Type	Nullable?	Length
plan_id	uniqueidentifier	No	16
plan_name	sysname	No	256

Column Name	Data Type	Nullable?	Length
description	nvarchar	No	1000
source_server	sysname	No	256
source_dir	nvarchar	No	1000
destination_dir	nvarchar	No	1000
copy_job_id	uniqueidentifier	No	16
load_job_id	uniqueidentifier	No	16
history_retention_period	int	No	4
file_retention_period	int	No	4
maintenance_plan_id	uniqueidentifier	No	16
backup_job_id	uniqueidentifier	No	16
share_name	nvarchar	No	1000

log_shipping_primaries

This table contains information about log-shipping primary servers:

Column Name	Data Type	Nullable?	Length
primary_id	int	No	4
primary_server_name	sysname	No	256
primary_database_name	sysname	No	256
maintenance_plan_id	uniqueidentifier	No	16
backup_threshold	int	No	4
threshold_alert	int	No	4
threshold_alert_enabled	bit	No	1
last_backup_filename	nvarchar	No	1000
last_updated	datetime	No	8
planned_outage_start_time	int	No	4
planned_outage_end_time	int	No	4
planned_outage_weekday_mask	int	No	4
source_directory	nvarchar	No	1000

log_shipping_secondaries

This table contains information about log-shipping secondary servers:

Column Name	Data Type	Nullable?	Length
primary_id	int	No	4
secondary_server_name	sysname	No	256
secondary_database_name	sysname	No	256
last_copied_filename	nvarchar	No	1000
last_loaded_filename	nvarchar	No	1000
last_copied_last_updated	datetime	No	8
last_loaded_last_updated	datetime	No	8
secondary_plan_id	uniqueidentifier	No	16
copy_enabled	bit	No	1
load_enabled	bit	No	1
out_of_sync_threshold	int	No	4
threshold_alert	int	No	4
threshold_alert_enabled	bit	No	1
planned_outage_start_time	int	No	4
planned_outage_end_time	int	No	4
planned_outage_weekday_mask	int	No	4
allow_role_change	bit	No	1

Job Tables in Msdb Database

SQL Server jobs are actual processes that carry out the tasks required for backup, recovery, and other maintenance operations. In these final sections, we'll look at the tables that store information about jobs.

sysjobhistory

This table contains information about the history of jobs that have been performed on the server:

Column Name	Data Type	Nullable?	Length
instance_id	int	No	4
job_id	uniqueidentifier	No	16
step_id	int	No	4
step_name	sysname	No	256
sql_message_id	int	No	4

Column Name	Data Type	Nullable?	Length
sql_severity	int	No	4
message	nvarchar	No	2048
run_status	int	No	4
run_date	int	No	4
run_time	int	No	4
run_duration	int	No	4
operator_id_emailed	int	No	4
operator_id_netsent	int	No	4
operator_id_paged	int	No	4
retries_attempted	int	No	4
server	nvarchar	No	60

sysjobs

This table contains information about the various jobs that are defined on the server:

Column Name	Data Type	Nullable?	Length
job_id	uniqueidentifier	No	16
originating_server	nvarchar	No	60
name	sysname	No	256
enabled	tinyint	No	1
description	nvarchar	No	1024
start_step_id	int	No	4
category_id	int	No	4
owner_sid	varbinary	No	85
notify_level_eventlog	int	No	4
notify_level_email	int	No	4
notify_level_netsend	int	No	4
notify_level_page	int	No	4
notify_email_operator_id	int	No	4
notify_netsend_operator_id	int	No	4
notify_page_operator_id	int	No	4
delete_level	int	No	4
date_created	datetime	No	8
date_modified	datetime	No	8
version_number	int	No	4

sysjobs_view

This view contains information about the jobs that are scheduled on the server. It presents information that is easier to read when compared to querying the system tables directly.

Column Name	Data Type	Nullable?	Length
job_id	uniqueidentifier	No	16
originating_server	nvarchar	No	60
name	sysname	No	256
enabled	tinyint	No	1
description	nvarchar	No	1024
start_step_id	int	No	4
category_id	int	No	4
owner_sid	varbinary	No	85
notify_level_eventlog	int	No	4
notify_level_email	int	No	4
notify_level_netsend	int	No	4
notify_level_page	int	No	4
notify_email_operator_id	int	No	4
notify_netsend_operator_id	int	No	4
notify_page_operator_id	int	No	4
delete_level	int	No	4
date_created	datetime	No	8
date_modified	datetime	No	8
version_number	int	No	4

sysjobschedules

This table contains information about the schedules defined for the various jobs on the server:

Column Name	Data Type	Nullable?	Length
schedule_id	int	No	4
job_id	uniqueidentifier	No	16
name	sysname	No	256
enabled	int	No	4
freq_type	int	No	4
freq_interval	int	No	4

Column Name	Data Type	Nullable?	Length
freq_subday_type	int	No	4
freq_subday_interval	int	No	4
freq_relative_interval	int	No	4
freq_recurrence_factor	int	No	4
active_start_date	int	No	4
active_end_date	int	No	4
active_start_time	int	No	4
active_end_time	int	No	4
next_run_date	int	No	4
next_run_time	int	No	4
date_created	datetime	No	8

sysjobservers

This table contains data about the history of job executions and the results of the processes:

Column Name	Data Type	Nullable?	Length
job_id	uniqueidentifier	No	16
server_id	int	No	4
last_run_outcome	tinyint	No	1
last_outcome_message	nvarchar	No	2048
last_run_date	int	No	4
last_run_time	int	No	4
last_run_duration	int	No	4

sysjobsteps

This table stores information related to the steps that make up parts of SQL Server jobs, along with the commands and settings for each of these steps:

Column Name	Data Type	Nullable?	Length
job_id	uniqueidentifier	No	16
step_id	int	No	4
step_name	sysname	No	256

Column Name	Data Type	Nullable?	Length
subsystem	nvarchar	No	80
command	nvarchar	No	6400
flags	int	No	4
additional_parameters	ntext	No	16
cmdexec_success_code	int	No	4
on_success_action	tinyint	No	1
on_success_step_id	int	No	4
on_fail_action	tinyint	No	1
on_fail_step_id	int	No	4
server	sysname	No	256
database_name	sysname	No	256
database_user_name	sysname	No	256
retry_attempts	int	No	4
retry_interval	int	No	4
os_run_priority	int	No	4
output_file_name	nvarchar	No	400
last_run_outcome	int	No	4
last_run_duration	int	No	4
last_run_retries	int	No	4
last_run_date	int	No	4
last_run_time	int	No	4

SUMMARY

Whew! That was a lot of information. You shouldn't feel bad if you weren't able to memorize all of the material in this appendix—it happens to even the best SQL Server DBAs. In this appendix, we looked at a great deal of technical information related to how SQL Server works "under the hood." This appendix should serve as a useful reference when you need to pinpoint a problem or want to completely understand how certain processes and settings are implemented. Although there are far too many commands, tools, and operations to memorize, sometimes just knowing that these commands exist can save you hours of troubleshooting.

APPENDIX B

Resources for More Information

In this book, we've taken a look at the concepts related to developing a data protection strategy, both for evaluating potential solutions and for implementing the solutions you choose. My goal in writing this book has been to answer the majority of readers' questions related to planning for and implementing data protection technologies. However, there's so much information available that no single resource can cover it all. For example, in Chapter 5, there are several lists of hardware and software vendors who develop backup products for Windows NT/2000 and SQL Server. It is impossible to cover all of the solutions in depth within these pages (and to keep this information current by the time you read this). However, all of the vendors have expertise in their respective fields and provide information via their web sites.

Although I'd love to claim that I know it all when it comes to performing backup and recovery operations for SQL Server databases, I've actually relied upon several resources for information. In this appendix, I'll provide some reliable resources for more information related to working with Windows NT/2000 and SQL Server 2000. Whether you're troubleshooting or you just want to know more about a specific application, tool, or feature, these resources are great places to start.

MICROSOFT RESOURCES

Microsoft provides many different types of support and methods for obtaining information related to its products. Options include the Internet, paid telephone-based support, and authorized technical training classes. A major challenge for a company as large as Microsoft is supporting its products. The best software in the world may not be worth much if there aren't enough people who know how to use it effectively. In the following sections, we'll look at some resources for more information from Microsoft.

TechNet

Microsoft's TechNet provides a wealth of information on implementing, supporting, managing, and troubleshooting Microsoft's operating system and BackOffice products. TechNet is a subscription-based program, although much of the useful content from the library is freely available on the Internet. Subscribers receive TechNet "issues" monthly on CD-ROM or DVD-ROM media. TechNet is an invaluable resource for IT professionals who work with Microsoft products. If you need assistance with a specific error message or software bug, TechNet is the first place to look.

The TechNet library includes the following:

▼ Microsoft *Technical Information* and *Knowledge Base*, including all support articles (updated each month)

■ Feature technical articles regarding the use of Microsoft products

■ Service Packs and updates for Microsoft products

■ Microsoft Resource Kits and additional utilities

■ Microsoft BackOffice evaluation products

▲ Microsoft Seminar Online content (described later)

The main interface of the Microsoft TechNet CD-ROM allows you to search quickly and efficiently through thousands of technical articles related to any keywords. Some of the same content is also available at no cost via **www.microsoft.com/technet**. (See Figure B-1.)

Microsoft Developer Network (MSDN)

Developers who write applications on and for Microsoft operating systems have special needs. First, they require licenses and media for all major Microsoft products. Next, they need documentation of the various application programming interfaces (APIs) and sample code for implementing these solutions. Finally, all of this information and content must be updated frequently to keep pace with Microsoft's product updates and new technology.

MSDN was designed to meet these goals. Like Microsoft TechNet, MSDN is a subscription-based product that distributes information on CD-ROM or DVD-ROM media. Subscribers receive copies of all major Microsoft products (including international

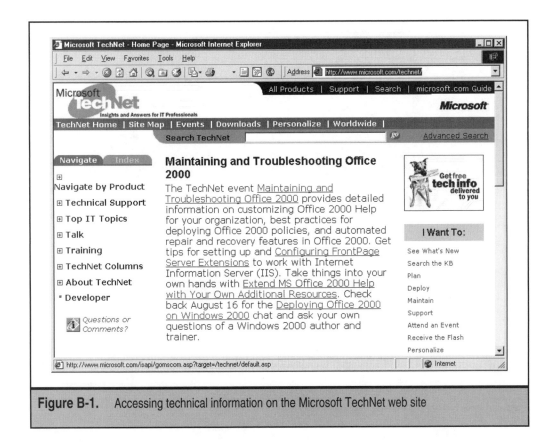

Figure B-1.   Accessing technical information on the Microsoft TechNet web site

versions) and up-to-date documentation for Microsoft Visual Studio and other development tools and APIs.

The MSDN Library is also available on the Internet for easy reference by developers and those who require specific technical information. Figure B-2 shows the types of information that are available using the MSDN Online web site (**http://msdn.microsoft.com**).

Knowledge Base

The Microsoft Knowledge Base consists of product support bulletins, bug reports, and troubleshooting information for working with Microsoft products. Microsoft uses the letter Q followed by six digits that uniquely identify each of the documents available (for example, Q123456). Information in the Knowledge Base is available from Microsoft's TechNet and through Internet resources.

Microsoft has made its extensive Knowledge Base available online via the Internet. To access the Product Support Services site, point your browser to **support.microsoft.com**. Using this site, you'll be able to search for information on any Microsoft product by entering text search strings. Figure B-3 shows the Microsoft Product Support web site (**support.microsoft.com**).

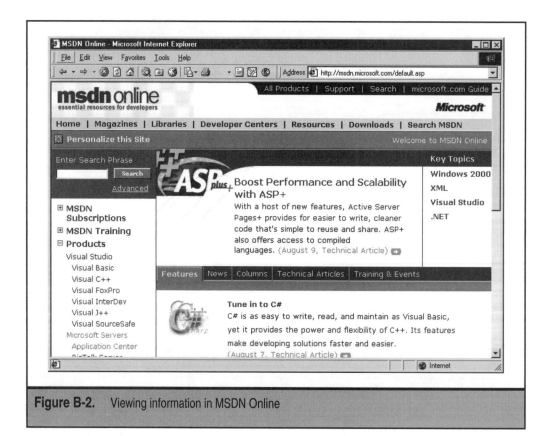

Figure B-2. Viewing information in MSDN Online

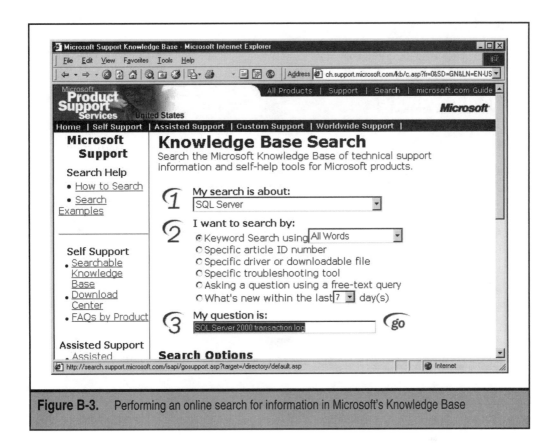

Figure B-3. Performing an online search for information in Microsoft's Knowledge Base

Seminar Online

Many of us have attended conferences to obtain valuable technical information and solutions for our real-world problems. Although the interaction at conferences is rewarding, it's often difficult to take the time away from the office to keep up on new technology.

Fortunately, web-based product and technology information is available free from Microsoft via the Seminar Online web site at **www.microsoft.com/seminar**. (See Figure B-4.) By utilizing web-based audio and video streaming technologies, visitors to this web site can receive online technical content similar to that received at "live" conferences. The format includes descriptive "slides" along with voice narration. It's available on demand, and it works well even in low-bandwidth situations.

Phone-Based Technical Support

For technical and usage support on Microsoft products, users can call Microsoft's phone-based support. Pricing structures and levels of support vary based on the product, purchased support options, and special arrangements with companies. Although it's not

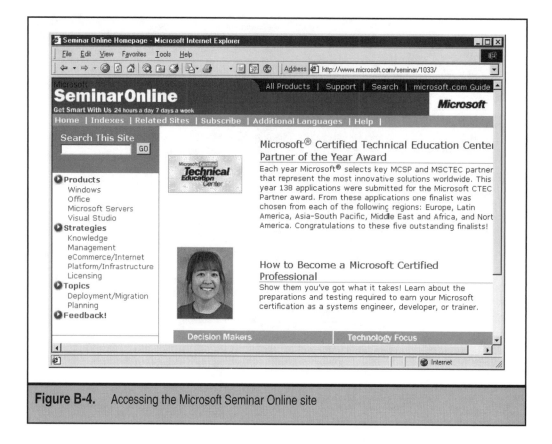

Figure B-4.   Accessing the Microsoft Seminar Online site

the cheapest alternative, direct support from Microsoft engineers can be useful for solving specific problems when you've exhausted other alternatives. For more information on contacting Microsoft Technical Support, see **support.microsoft.com**.

Training and Certification

If you want to learn the ins and outs of specific Microsoft products or technologies in an instructor-led classroom setting, Microsoft Authorized Technical Education courses may be for you. Classes range from half-day sessions to two-week, in-depth training. For a complete list of classes and authorized training centers, go to **www.microsoft. com/train_cert**. (See Figure B-5.) This site also provides a wealth of information for those who are seeking Microsoft certifications. Table B-1 lists the major certifications available from Microsoft. For more information on the requirements for each of these certifications, see the Microsoft Training and Certification home page.

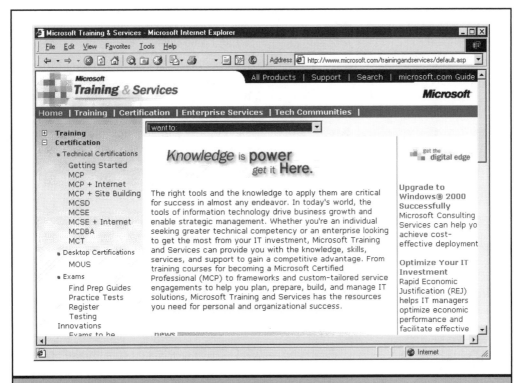

Figure B-5.   The Microsoft Training and Certification web site

Certification	Target Professionals
Microsoft Certified Professional (MCP)	IT professionals with expertise in at least one Microsoft product
Microsoft Certified Professional + Internet (MCP + Internet)	MCPs who have additional experience in implementing Microsoft's Internet technologies
Microsoft Certified Professional + Site Building (MCP + Site Building)	MCPs who are responsible for building and administering web sites
Microsoft Certified Systems Engineer (MCSE)	IT professionals who plan for, implement, and manage Windows NT/2000 and BackOffice products

Table B-1.   Various Microsoft Certifications

Certification	Target Professionals
Microsoft Certified Systems Engineer + Internet (MCSE + I)	IT professionals who have passed the requirements for the MCSE exam and have additional experience working with Internet technologies
Microsoft Certified Database Administrator (MCDBA)	Developers and administrators of SQL Server
Microsoft Certified Solutions Developer (MCSD)	Software developers who use Microsoft products for planning and implementing business solutions
Microsoft Certified Trainers (MCT)	Professionals with expertise in Microsoft products who want to teach Microsoft Official Curriculum courses

Table B-1.   Various Microsoft Certifications *(continued)*

IT RESOURCES

We've already looked at some of the information available from Microsoft on the Internet. In addition to those sites, a wealth of information is available on the Internet. In this section, I'll point you to some useful web sites and other online resources.

Web Sites

In addition to the Microsoft resources covered earlier, several excellent web sites are available for finding Windows NT/2000, SQL Server 2000, and database-related information. Web sites can provide the most up-to-date information on news and are easily accessible. However, you should always consider the source of technical information and try to verify information before you depend on it. Table B-2 lists some of these resources, and Figure B-6 shows a useful SQL Server 2000 web site.

Magazines

When it comes to keeping up with new technologies and learning tips and tricks for working with specific products, magazines can be an excellent resource. Table B-3 lists several magazines that are dedicated to keeping readers up-to-date on the latest features of the products they cover. By no means is this an exhaustive list, but it offers you some good starting points for keeping current on SQL Server and Windows NT/2000 technology.

Resource	Web Site	Content
Beverly Hills Software	www.bhs.com	Reviews and downloads of Windows NT/2000–related applications and utilities
CNet's News.Com	www.news.com	IT industry news and information, updated daily
Hardware Central	www.hardwarecentral.com	Hardware product reviews and technical discussions
Microsoft Security web site	www.microsoft.com/security	Up-to-date information about the most recent security issues discovered on the Windows platform
Microsoft SQL Server web site	www.microsoft.com/sql	White papers, case studies, evaluation information, and downloads related to SQL Server
NT Security.Net	www.ntsecurity.net	Up-to-date information about Windows NT security issues
SQL Index	www.sqlindex.com	Links to information regarding development, and administration resources for SQL Server and other RDBMSs
SWYNK.com	www.swynk.com	News and technical information related to SQL Server, including useful scripts
The Ultimate Collection of Windows Shareware (TUCOWS)	www.tucows.com	A large repository of shareware programs, with special focus on Internet applications

Table B-2.   Useful Web Sites

Resource	Web Site	Content
Windows NT Systems	www.ntsystems.com	Tools and utilities for working with Windows NT
Winfiles.com	www.winfiles.com	Windows-related shareware programs
Ziff-Davis Anchordesk	www.anchordesk.com	Daily information about IT products, events, and news

Table B-2.   Useful Web Sites *(continued)*

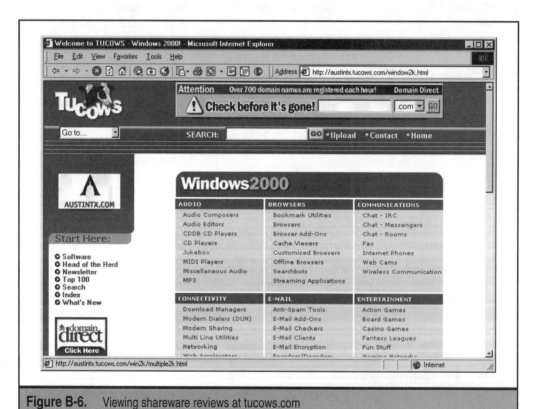

Figure B-6.   Viewing shareware reviews at tucows.com

Magazine	Web Site	Notes
Windows 2000 Magazine (formerly *Windows NT Magazine*)	www.winntmag.com or www.win2000mag.com	Provides detailed tips, techniques, and tools for working with Windows NT/2000
SQL Server Magazine	www.sqlmag.com	An excellent resource for developers and administrators of SQL Server
Microsoft Certified Professional Magazine	www.mcpmag.com	Includes in-depth technical articles for Windows NT/2000 professionals, as well as information on Microsoft certifications
EWeek (formerly *PCWeek*)	www.zdnet.com/eweek/	A weekly magazine that covers the latest news from the industry and reviews hardware, software, and networking products

Table B-3.   Useful Computing Industry Magazines

USENET Newsgroups

As remarked by Abbott Joseph Liebling in *The New Yorker*, "Freedom of the press is guaranteed only to those who own one." The Internet has allowed many more people to freely express thoughts and ideas. Though they rarely receive the same level of attention as the web, USENET newsgroups are an excellent forum for discussing issues and obtaining information. All users of these newsgroups can post information. Of course, these unmoderated forums can be both good and bad. The majority of the information resources I've presented thus far have been mainly one-way communications. What if you want to ask a specific question or participate in interactive discussions on the Internet with peers? The best place to do this is USENET, the Internet's public news network. USENET uses a TCP/IP-based protocol called the Network News Transfer Protocol (NNTP) to share discussion group information worldwide. Almost all Internet service providers offer access to news servers, and there are hundreds of thousands of regional and global newsgroups on the Internet. For example, Microsoft's public news server is available at **msnews.microsoft.com**.

Popular newsgroup clients can be downloaded from the Internet. Figure B-7 shows how Microsoft's Outlook Express might be used to access a public Microsoft discussion group.

If you'll be working with news servers often, client software is the way to go. For specific news searches, however, it may be easier to use a web-based interface. Deja (**www.deja.com**) provides exactly that—a web-based engine for searching through millions of messages posted worldwide. (See Figure B-8.) If you're searching for obscure information, this is the place to go! Deja.com also offers many other resources in the form of online "communities." In these forums, users can discuss products and topics of interest.

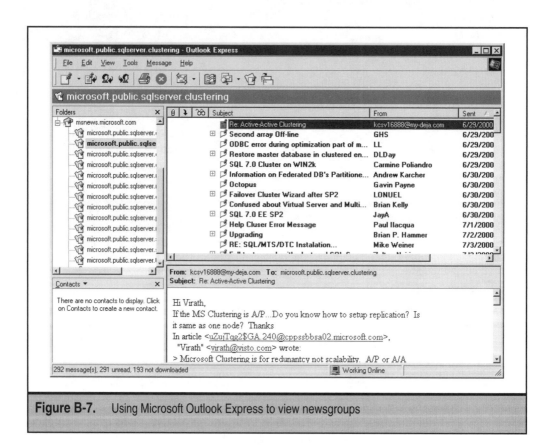

Figure B-7. Using Microsoft Outlook Express to view newsgroups

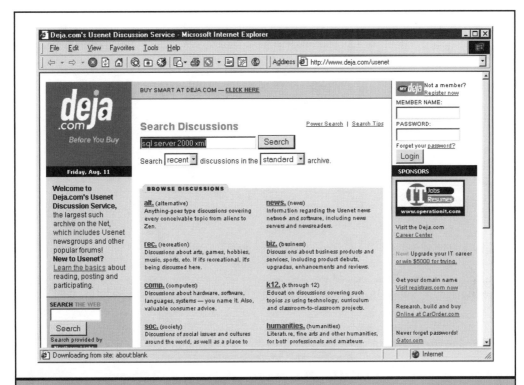

Figure B-8.   Searching newsgroups using Deja.com

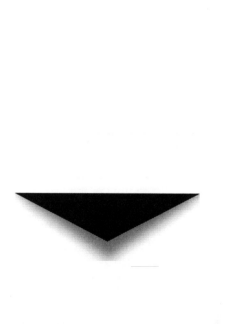

Index

A

T

 U